Edmund J. James and the Making of the Modern University of Illinois, 1904–1920

Edmund Janes James, President, University of Illinois, 1904–1920. Courtesy of the University of Illinois Archives.

Edmund J. James and the Making of the Modern University of Illinois, 1904–1920

WINTON U. SOLBERG
AND J. DAVID HOEVELER

UNIVERSITY OF
ILLINOIS PRESS
Urbana, Chicago, and Springfield

© 2024 by the Board of Trustees
of the University of Illinois
All rights reserved
Manufactured in the United States of America
C 5 4 3 2 1
∞ This book is printed on acid-free paper.

Library of Congress Cataloging-in-Publication Data

Names: Solberg, Winton U., 1922–2019, author. | Hoeveler, J.
David, 1943–, author.
Title: Edmund J. James and the making of the modern University
of Illinois, 1904-1920 / Winton U. Solberg and J. David
Hoeveler.
Description: Urbana : University of Illinois Press, 2024. | Includes
bibliographical references and index.
Identifiers: LCCN 2024009255 (print) | LCCN 2024009256
(ebook) | ISBN 9780252046131 (cloth) | ISBN
9780252047367 (ebook)
Subjects: LCSH: James, Edmund J. (Edmund Janes), 1855–1925.
| University of Illinois at Urbana-Champaign—History. |
University of Illinois at Urbana-Champaign—Presidents—
Biography. | College presidents—Illinois—Biography.
Classification: LCC LD2375.J36 S65 2024 (print) | LCC
LD2375.J36 (ebook) | DDC 378.0092 [B—dc23/
eng/20240418
LC record available at https://lccn.loc.gov/2024009255
LC ebook record available at https://lccn.loc.gov/2024009256

For Nora, May, Eli, Vincent, Grayson, and Charlie

Contents

Preface **ix**

Abbreviations and Acronyms **xiii**

PART I: THE LARGER UNIVERSITY

CHAPTER 1. A New Leader at Illinois **3**

CHAPTER 2. Money and Politics **13**

CHAPTER 3. The Graduate School **25**

CHAPTER 4. Infrastructure for a Research University **41**

CHAPTER 5. The Intellectual World of Edmund J. James **57**

CHAPTER 6. A University at War **85**

PART II: ACADEMICS

CHAPTER 7. The Physical Sciences **123**

CHAPTER 8. The Life Sciences **145**

CHAPTER 9. The Social Sciences **163**

CHAPTER 10. The Humanities **180**

PART III: EDUCATING FOR THE PROFESSIONS

CHAPTER 11. The School of Education **213**

CHAPTER 12. Engineering (with Physics and Mathematics) **219**

CHAPTER 13. The Law School **231**

CHAPTER 14. Agriculture (and Home Economics) **251**

PART IV: STUDENTS

CHAPTER 15. The Collegiate Revolution   **265**

CHAPTER 16. Women   **299**

Afterword: An Illinois Promise   **325**

Notes   **341**

Index   **397**

Preface

J. DAVID HOEVELER

IN AN OUTSTANDING CAREER of academic scholarship Winton U. Solberg wrote two books on the early history of the University of Illinois, and another on the University of Illinois College of Medicine in Chicago. Other works appeared along the way. Completion of his book on the Arctic expedition in search of Crocker Island left one work in progress, the third volume of the history of the University. But at the amazing age of ninety-six, Wint announced that he could go no further with the work. At this point I received an invitation from Wint's daughter Gail to undertake the project of doing whatever proved necessary to shape the manuscript into publishable form. I very happily accepted the challenge.

In March 2019 I had a meeting in Urbana with Wint, Gail, Laurie Matheson, director of the University of Illinois Press, and John Paul Goguen, University IT Specialist. A second meeting later on included University Archivist Bill Maher. We discussed many aspects of the book and I felt much encouraged by the enthusiasm of the group for the project. Sadly, though, Wint died in July of that year. While I felt the loss of a dear friend, I also had to face the reality that I was quite alone in carrying out the work of completion. I had hoped to have conversations with Wint as I worked on the book, getting his advice and opinions about matters with which I was dealing. But my new situation made me the more resolved to have a book that would do justice to his years of labor on this project. And I feel like I have become a partner with Wint in a joint endeavor that's a privilege, too.

This book has a special meaning for me. I met Winton Solberg during my semester break, senior year, at Lehigh University in January 1965. Anticipating graduation that spring, and graduate school in the fall, I had arranged to visit some universities and meet with professors in my field. At Urbana Wint took me on a tour of the University Archives to show me where he was doing his current research on a history of the University. Later in the summer, when I was readying for a long drive from Connecticut to start school at Illinois, I received an invitation from Wint to work as his research assistant. So began my academic career, spending many hours in the University Archives, pursuing material relevant to the institution's first decades. Here also emerged the great zeal I then discovered for studying American higher education. And now I am ending that career where I began it.

All of us agreed on the major work to be done. Wint had worked tirelessly on archival materials and the early manuscript had immense detail. So, I had directions from the Press to reduce its size, considerably. I concurred with that imperative. At the same time, we knew that I needed to fortify the manuscript with historiography, to provide more of recent scholarship in the many aspects of the study. I edited and rewrote all of the chapters, effecting, I hope, something of a uniform style. What really has excited me in this adventure, however, is discovering other aspects of the history. This new material has led me to write several new chapters. I have added more on Edmund J. James and introduced chapters on student culture and on women, among others. Wint had always said that President James was the most commanding figure among the University's presidents, and was badly understudied. I hope I have made a correction. But, as Wint wrote in an essay on James, no monument on the Illinois campus today honors the work of this important intellectual, academic reformer, and university leader.

One thing helped me in focusing this book. Upon his retirement from the Illinois presidency Edmund James prepared a book he titled *Sixteen Years at the University of Illinois: A Statistical Study of the Administration of President Edmund J. James*. It is a vast accumulation of data, covering subjects like land and buildings, money, faculty hires, libraries and museums, student organizations, colleges and schools. And it's loaded with stats; in fact, one could consider it a quick-reference handbook. With this information available I felt free to concentrate on intellectual content and to make the book less encyclopedic and more selective, emphasizing the University's areas of strength and academic significance, and giving expanded attention to President James's intellectual life and academic leadership.

To this end I also had in mind Wint's first volume, which he subtitled "An Intellectual and Cultural History." I put that emphasis on this volume, too. The university is, after all, a place of intellect, art, discovery, and creativity. Wint wrote several chapter portraits of individual faculty. I have added more individuals and placed all these "Faculty Portraits" within chapters appropriate to these scholars' respective academic disciplines. To this extent also the book inquires into the place the University had within the larger intellectual currents of the United States and the world, and how its scholars helped define their own academic disciplines in an era of great transformations. And finally,

x   Preface

I have sought to bring some connection and continuity to this large record of variety and change, in an Afterword I have titled "An Illinois Promise."

We have not included a formal bibliography. One can find listings of the published writings of Edmund J. James at these locations:

The Online Books Page: Online Books by Edmund J. James
(James, Edmund J. (Edmund Janes), 1855–1925)
http://onlinebooks.library.upenn.edu/webbin/book/lookupname?key=James%2C%20Edmund%20J%2E%20%28Edmund%20Janes%29%2C%201855%2D1925

A Bibliography of the Published Writings of Edmund Janes James.@ https://core.ac.uk/download/pdf/29153782.pdf

Wint dedicated his book on the University of Illinois College of Medicine to his grandchildren, in 2009. I am pleased to follow suit with this book.

In addition to those mentioned above I would like to express my appreciation to others in the University of Illinois Archives and at the Press who gave valuable assistance to me in advancing this project: Gary Smith, Sammi Merritt, Katie Nichols, Will Doty, Linda Stepp, Marcella Lees, Joanna Kaczmarek, Jameatris Yvette Rinkus, Jennifer Argo, Kevin Cunningham, Jim Proefrock, Roberta Sparenberg, and Renee Cote, my always helpful copy editor.

David Hoeveler and Wint Solberg, March 2019, Urbana (courtesy of Gail Solberg).

Abbreviations and Acronyms

AAAS	American Association for the Advancement of Science
AAAS	American Academy of Arts and Sciences
AALS	Association of American Law Schools
AAPSS	American Academy of Political and Social Science
AAU	Association of American Universities
AAUP	American Association of University Professors
ABA	American Bar Association
AEA	American Economic Association
AHA	American Historical Association
ALA	American Library Association
AME	African Methodist Episcopal
AMS	American Mathematical Society
ANB	American National Biography
AQ	Alumni Quarterly
AQFN	Alumni Quarterly and Fortnightly Notes
BT	Report of the Board of Trustees of the University of Illinois (with volume number and dates)
CESL	College Equal Suffrage League
CPI	Committee on Public Information (Creel Committee)
DI	*Daily Illini*
GD	Graduate Dean
GSF	Graduate School Faculty
IOBB	Independent Order of B'nai B'rith
ISDC	Illinois State Council of Defense

James, *Sixteen Years*	Edmund J. James, *Sixteen Years at the University of Illinois: A Statistical Study of the Administration of Edmund J. James*. Urbana: University of Illinois Press, 1920
JEGP	Journal of English and Germanic Philology
MIT	Massachusetts Institute of Technology
NACWC	National Association of Colored Women's Clubs
NBHS	National Board for Historical Service
NLIL	National Liberal Immigration League
PASP	Publications of the Astronomical Society of the Pacific
SATC	Students' Army Training Corps
SDC	[Illinois] State Council of Defense
Solberg 1	Winton U. Solberg, *The University of Illinois 1867–1894: An Intellectual and Cultural History*. Urbana: University of Illinois Press, 1968
Solberg 2	Winton U. Solberg, *The University of Illinois 1894–1904: The Shaping of the University*. Urbana: University of Illinois Press, 2000
USDA	United States Department of Agriculture
WESA	Women's Equal Suffrage Association

PART I

The Larger University

CHAPTER 1

A New Leader at Illinois

IN OCTOBER OF 1905 the University of Illinois staged a big event. Edmund James loved this kind of affair. There gathered at the campus at Champaign and Urbana a large group of invitees. College and university presidents arrived from around the country (Charles R. Van Hise of Wisconsin, James B. Angell of Michigan, soon to be president of Harvard Abbott Lawrence Lowell) and indeed from around the world (Oxford and Cambridge sent delegates). Prominent scholars represented different academic fields. A national meeting of boards of trustees took place there, too. A variety of conferences addressed matters important to American higher education: the place of religion, the role of the state, institutional governance, education for the business world. Men of the clergy offered sermons and prayers as local churches also held special services. Students performed a play. A military group, the student University Brigade, had reviews by Illinois Governor Charles Deneen and others. From all over the state came dozens of civic clubs (e.g., the Chicago Women's Club) and professional organizations (e.g., the American Philosophical Society). The University presented twenty-five honorary degrees and also used the occasion to dedicate the long-awaited Woman's Building. All these events over the course of six days had a subsidiary role in the main drama of the affair: the installation of Edmund Janes James as the new president of the University of Illinois.[1]

• • •

The four decades after about 1870 had witnessed profound changes in American higher education. Many formerly liberal arts colleges became universities. Venerable Harvard, Yale, Princeton, Columbia, and Pennsylvania added graduate schools to their offerings, and new universities, notably Johns Hopkins, Chicago, Stanford, and Clark, emerged. Meanwhile, the Morrill Act (1862) had changed the landscape of higher education. It offered federal land holdings to states that they would sell for money to provide instruction in agriculture and the mechanical arts (engineering) without excluding the liberal arts. States took advantage of this federal bounty to reinforce existing state schools or to establish new ones.

Illinois stood in this second category. The state used the Morrill income to found a university in 1867. Named Illinois Industrial University, it assumed the motto "Learning and Labor." And it proclaimed as its mantra "Labor vincit omnia" ("Work conquers all"). But in time the name changed to the University of Illinois and the institution moved, as did other universities, into a more expansive instructional program and into advanced scholarship by its leading faculty. James entered his new office as Illinois's fourth president, preceded by John Milton Gregory (Regent, 1867–1880), Selim H. Peabody (second Regent, 1880–1891), and Andrew S. Draper (1894–1904).

Born in Jacksonville, Illinois, on May 21, 1855, James was the first of the six children of Colin Dew James and his second wife, Amanda K. Casad. Some years later, in 1917, three years before he retired from the Illinois presidency, James paused to prepare a reminiscence about his father and the experiences of growing up with this committed man of the ministry. He tells us that Colin James was born in Randolph County, Virginia in 1808. The paternal line in America goes back to James's great-grandfather's arrival in Virginia from Wales in 1750. William B. James, the grandfather, was born and grew up in West Virginia. Colin James had ten siblings. Several points stood out in Edmund's recollections of his father. He recalled vividly the life of a Methodist circuit-rider: Colin James not only had to make regional visitations; he also moved the family constantly. Edmund remembered that his father was compelled to move twenty times between 1834 and 1863. One of those places, Jacksonville, Illinois, as noted, became Edmund's birthplace. The boy long recollected sitting on top of a wagon and seeing the country from that vantage. He also grew, however, to a later appreciation of life in its variety and judged this "constant removal" to be a source of intellectual stimulation. And, to be sure, the family had a wide circle of personal friends and acquaintances. A friend especially dear to the Jameses was one Edmund Janes, a Methodist bishop. The parents named their son in his honor.[2]

So, Edmund James grew up a Methodist. His father imbibed the denomination's enumerated moral taboos. They included horse racing, card playing, dancing, and reading novels. The minister led revivals and camp meetings, having been converted at one himself, and gave four years to mission work. Colin James had little schooling, but he cultivated an intellectual life. He took theology seriously and had a household library of religious literature. He thereby sharpened his arguments for the critique of Calvinism, as the Methodists since the founding by John Wesley had always embraced Arminianism—free will and free grace—in opposition to Reformed (Calvinist) theology. And he represented a wing of American Methodism that sought to move beyond its frontier beginnings and advance intellectually, as in the founding of collegiate institutions like Wesleyan in Connecticut, Northwestern in Illinois, and Boston University. Colin James strove to create an interest in reading and circulated books along the routes of his itineraries. He also served on the boards of several colleges.[3]

Religious politics constitutes another influence on Edmund. Methodist morality readily wielded its judgments in affairs of political party and state. Edmund's grandfather had left Virginia because of his pronounced opposition to slavery. Colin James had like feelings, and Edmund remembered his father as "an old-line Whig" and then later a Republican. He was "a very strong Union man" and ardent supporter of President Lincoln. He fully sanctioned the prohibitionist movement, but not to the point that he would bolt the Republican Party in presidential elections.[4]

A maternal influence also figures prominently in the James biography. Colin James had married Eliza Ann Plaster in 1839. She died ten years later and in 1850 he married Amanda K. Casad, Edmund's mother. Born in Illinois, she was the daughter of a traveling minister, Anthony Wayne Casad, who later became a well-known physician. The couple had to move out of town as Amanda's father and brother did not take kindly to her marriage to a Methodist minister. Amanda surpassed her husband in love of culture and intellect. She essentially home schooled her children and awed Edmund not just with her love of Shakespeare but with her mastery of his plays: "She knew Shakespeare by heart," her son remembered. Whatever moral taboos Colin placed on novels mother Amanda seems to have countered by striving to instill in her children a love of English literature.[5]

For his formal education, James attended Illinois State Normal School where he studied Greek, Latin, and history, and then went to Northwestern University, where for one year he pursued the classical curriculum. The following November James matriculated at Harvard. An opportunity soon took him to Germany, where universities gave priority to scientific research, graduate study, and service to the state.[6] At the University of Halle, where he enrolled in October 1875, he studied political economy under Johannes Conrad, who, like the German university professors in general, emphasized the role of the state in economic and social affairs. Conrad and other historical economists taught students how to formulate and administer policy. They founded the *Verein für Socialpolitik*, which investigated social issues and agitated for reform. James wrote his dissertation on the American tariff system. He graduated with a PhD in August 1877. While in Germany, James also attended lectures in Berlin and Leipzig, and although invited to remain in Halle, he nonetheless decided to return home. But he left with a profound reverence for German institutions and for German thinking. Now he and other young reformers would pose against laissez-faire economics, with its current intellectual underpinnings in John Stuart Mill, the models of the positive state, with its intellectual props in the jural, political, and philosophical sciences derived from German historical thought.[7]

James could find no university position when he came home to America, so he served as principal of the Evanston, Illinois, high school for a year, then assumed the same position at the Model High School of Illinois State Normal University. Meanwhile, he started to publish papers. He wrote many articles, but never published a book.[8]

James and colleague Charles De Garmo became the proprietors of the *Illinois School Journal: A Monthly Magazine for Teachers and School Officers*, which they transformed into a crusading periodical. James wrote editorials and articles on federal aid to education, German and American universities, the history of pedagogy, and other topics. He also contributed to John J. Lalor's *Cyclopaedia of Political Science, Political Economy, and the Political History of the United States*, in its three volumes (Chicago, 1881–1884). His article on the history of political economy in volume three helped bring the German school of economic thinking to the attention of American readers.

James's contributions to Lalor's *Cyclopaedia* won him an audience and led to his appointment to the Wharton School of Finance and Economy of the University of Pennsylvania.[9] Joseph Wharton, a Philadelphia ironmaster who had made a fortune in various enterprises, thought that the nation's colleges were failing to educate businessmen. To counteract that situation, Wharton provided the University of Pennsylvania with the needed funds for a business program. Then William Pepper, who became the University provost in 1881, backed Wharton's proposal. In September the Wharton School of Finance and Economy opened in the University's College Department. But the Penn faculty had no enthusiasm for a business program. For two years the school consisted of only two faculty members who taught a dozen juniors and seniors. The school had a poor reputation.[10]

Pepper decided that the business program had to advance. In 1883 he instructed faculty member Albert S. Bolles to recruit additional faculty. Both men thought that the Wharton School had to become part of the dynamic new education for which German universities provided the model. The school would furnish a higher liberal and practical training for the business classes. Bolles knew of James through his writings, and on July 3, 1883, he appointed him professor of public finance and administration in the Wharton School, and professor of political and social science in the Department of Philosophy, as its graduate work was named. Pepper and Bolles wanted James at Penn as agent of a new German model for the University.[11] James, age twenty-eight, with a German PhD and a German wife (he had married in 1879), began laying the new foundations of the Wharton School.

James could now pursue his ideal of combining scholarship and practicality. He attracted students to his classes, faculty to his programs, and business and civic leaders to his causes. In September 1885, emulating the German model, he introduced the first research seminar at Penn: Seminar for Political and Economic Science. Along with Provost Pepper James had a central role in organizing a research-oriented graduate school. He also joined a set of young American economists who rebelled against laissez-faire thought, at a time when that ideology had the status of orthodoxy in American colleges and universities. James taught a course in public finance and administration that explored federal, state, and local revenue systems along with the taxation and expenditure theories of German authorities and British economists. Eager to apply research to economic, social, and political problems, James became an active reformer, as a later chapter will describe.

Meanwhile, in 1886 James demonstrated the range of his interests and his remarkable productivity. He triumphed with a long disquisition on "The Relation of the Modern Municipality to the Gas Supply." In it he described how various American municipalities supplied gas to residents, comparing their practices with those in the United Kingdom, Germany, and France. According to James, the "Gas Ring," a venal group of politically well-connected managers, operated the Philadelphia gas supply for their own enrichment, passing on to customers the cost of employing thousands of hangers-on. A supply of rich and pure gas at low cost was a necessity in a modern city, James observed, but the manufacture and distribution of gas made the business a practical monopoly. People had to choose then between a monopoly managed by the public in the interest of the public and a monopoly in private hands. This essay enhanced James's reputation locally and nationally. In his classic study of American economic thought in this era, historian Sidney Fine called James's essay the most comprehensive analysis by a new-school economist of the supposed advantages of public ownership of natural monopolies over private ownership.[12]

In 1887 Bolles resigned and Provost Pepper made James chairman of the economics department and placed the Wharton School in his hands. Along with his duties at Wharton, James contributed to the debate on public issues. He continued to publish articles, including "Socialists and Anarchists in the United States," "Economic Effects of the Saloon," "Pedagogy in American Colleges," "The Degree of Ph.D. in Germany," and "Manual Training in the Public Schools in Its Economic Aspect." James especially promoted higher commercial education in America. The training of businessmen was essential in the struggle for national supremacy, he believed, and to check the materialism bred by commercial life, the nation needed businessmen who had a university education.

In September 1890 the American Bankers Association invited James to present a paper at Saratoga Springs, New York, on the establishment of schools similar to the Wharton School within the nation's existing universities and colleges. At present, James explained, an American youth who had completed grammar school and envisioned a business career faced a problem. Should he seek a situation in a business house, ending his school education and trusting to the friction of active life for further education, or should he go to some other school and trust to the benefits of the training to make up for the practical knowledge that he might get in a factory or a bank? What paths were open to the youth who wanted more education before going into business? The student might take a medical or a theological course, a law course, a civil or mining engineering course, or one in architecture, in each of which he would find something of value. But few students would take these courses unless they intended to enter the corresponding profession. There remained, then, the commercial, or business, college and the literary college. The former had done great work and was doing great work, James said, but one could scarcely call that training a higher education. The knowledge there imparted did not suffice to fit a young man for commercial life, wise management of a private estate, or efficient public service. Literary colleges, on the other hand, could not answer the modern demand for the higher training of the businessman. A vigorous discipline in the classics and higher mathematics undoubtedly sharpened a young man's intellectual faculties, James stated, but it tended to draw him away from a life in business. Very few successful businessmen had college degrees, James observed, noting that if we find it desirable for our businessmen to have a higher training, we must offer some curriculum that would appeal to them.[13]

The Bankers Association arranged for the publication of James's address. It is indeed an important document, marking the development of James's thinking about higher education and its purposes and thus anticipating his educational leadership at Illinois. But it also places James within the intellectual direction of the Progressive movement in the United States. All in that movement recognized the immense problems posed by the new industrial and commercial order in America. But they brought to their judgments less a disdain or contempt for business than a fear of its power. Its autonomy, its unregulated activity, had corrupting effects, they believed. Its operations worked to bring all the other components of society into its orb. Hence, in James's view, all the greater was the imperative that the business classes have a large, liberal education, marked by an expansive, inclusive vision of the world and the forces that moved it. He especially emphasized here not so much the traditional classics but instead the new social sciences—history, economics,

8   PART I. THE LARGER UNIVERSITY

and political science above all. The business classes, he believed, needed to see their work in terms of a large cooperative commonwealth, an organic whole. This education, he avowed, "is an education that will broaden and liberalize them, quicken their sympathies, beget and increase a public spirit which shall find its greatest happiness in seeking and utilizing means of promoting the common welfare." Society as a whole, James could then say, would gain from the new business education, linking the practical with the social and cultural.[14]

But the businessman himself also gains, James told the bankers. Courses in history, the U.S. Constitution, political institutions, foreign politics and national histories (especially close-up study of one nation), and the long history of business's relation to government (banking regulations, poor laws, taxation, labor laws, paper money, bimetallism), as well as the rival philosophies and ideologies that seek to influence policy—these courses "will contribute to making [the business student] an educated man, knowing something more about his business than the ordinary hand-to-mouth practical man, having a wide view of the relations of his business to other lines of business and to society as a whole." Here, for James, the two ideals linked and they yielded in the end an education for citizenship—progressive and enlightened, the best training "the world has yet seen." In a sense, James was trying to make America safe for business and business safe for America.[15]

James's address and the movement to establish similar schools excited many individuals. The Bankers Association in turn directed its executive council to devise an arrangement by which their association might promote the founding of schools of finance and economy for the business training of their children.[16] Convening at New Orleans in November 1892, the bankers printed excerpts from letters endorsing the proposal. The bankers' Committee on Schools of Finance and Economy suggested that the association send "some eminent man of learning" to Europe to examine such schools there and report back.[17] Accordingly, the bankers invited James to accept this assignment, which he did. His extended European tour took him to Vienna, Prague, Paris, Germany, Antwerp, Venice, Turin, Florence, Genoa, Naples, Belgium, and Rome.[18]

James continued to make public addresses and publish papers. These activities, along with his efforts to reform Philadelphia, however, aroused faculty conservatives and trustees. On April 23, 1894, Provost Pepper resigned, and on May 15 Charles C. Harrison replaced him. A wealthy man with two Pennsylvania degrees (BA, 1862; MA, 1865), Harrison had served as a university trustee since 1876. He strongly disliked James, resented his independent authority and large salary, and disparaged the Wharton School. On January 1, 1895, his first day as provost, Harrison informed James that he did not consider him a suitable person to occupy a university chair. He had shamefully neglected his work and had produced nothing of scholarly worth, Harrison charged. James had written prolifically on matters of great public concern, but he had not published a book. Nevertheless, James, forty years old, resigned effective October 1.[19]

According to historian Steven Sass, when James left Philadelphia, "he had largely completed his self-appointed task. He had decisively taken Joseph Wharton's school out of the ranks of the American college and had redesigned it along modern university lines. In so doing he had given the institution a position of leadership in American higher education and in the administration of public affairs. His vision of the practical university would remain the foundation of the Wharton School program."[20]

• • •

James went from the Wharton School to the recently established University of Chicago, to serve as professor of public administration from 1895 to 1901. There he also became director of University Extension, an autonomous enterprise designed to supply beyond the campus the course offerings of the various academic departments. President William Rainey Harper approved of James's program, but it gave rise to faculty discontent. Harper greatly admired James. "Believe me," he wrote to James in 1904 before undergoing surgery, "when I say that among all the men who have worked with me within twenty years, there is no man whom I have esteemed more, and with whom I have worked more affectionately than yourself." In 1905, knowing that his end was near, Harper wrote to James. He wanted him to be an honorary pallbearer at his funeral.[21]

James began a new phase in his career in January 1902 when he was elected president of Northwestern University. He went to Evanston as to a dream fulfilled. He was a Methodist, and Northwestern was Methodist. Henry Wade Rogers, president from 1890 to 1900, had done much to move the college into the modern age, but the University lacked financial resources for the purpose. On June 10, 1900, aware of growing opposition among the Board of Trustees, Rogers suddenly resigned.

James entered his new office in March. A man of vision, he proposed several long-range objectives: expansion of the academic offerings in engineering, business, and education; more physical facilities; hiring of clerical help to free the faculty for scholarly work. But after two years, James felt discouraged. His appeals to trustees and wealthy persons for financial support met polite refusal. The Methodist church encouraged him rhetorically but not financially. He feared spending most of his time on administrative details rather than on building a "new Northwestern." A colleague predicted that James would not long remain "where misunderstandings, misrepresentations, extraordinary cares and worries are the meat and drink upon which ambitious leaders must renew their strength." Offered the University of Illinois presidency in 1904, James accepted with alacrity. He stated his main reason for leaving Northwestern: "with each passing year the opportunity of my doing large things was diminishing."[22]

10   PART I. THE LARGER UNIVERSITY

What, then, led to this next step for James? On March 9, 1904, Andrew S. Draper unexpectedly resigned as president of the University of Illinois, prompting the trustees to appoint a committee to find a replacement. The president of the board wrote to Dean David Kinley inquiring about faculty ideas on a new president. So far as Kinley knew, the faculty had more interest in the type of man appointed than in whether or not he came from the faculty. "I am glad that the eyes of the Board are open at last to the situation here," Kinley added, "and that you intend to see things well-adjusted before we start in on a new administration."[23] The University, Kinley later observed, needed a president "whose sympathies and policy will be towards the development of scholarly research in all lines."[24]

The deans met with the members of the search committee to discuss the situation.[25] Meanwhile, other parties recommended candidates. President Nicholas Murray Butler of Columbia suggested Andrew F. West, a professor of Latin and dean of the Princeton graduate school. An uncompromising classicist who opposed the elective system and granting academic credit in utilitarian subjects, West seemed an unlikely fit for a public university, Draper believed.[26] By mid-July people learned that President James of Northwestern and President Joseph Swain of Swarthmore College had gained much favor in the search, with James having the wider appeal.[27] James may have been preferred over Stephen Forbes and Eugene Davenport, Illinois deans also suggested as possibilities, because James was a humanist. On August 3, Trustee Frederic Hatch informed James that the search committee had chosen him as president; he asked James not to mention the matter. On August 16, the board's search committee reported. The secretary's tally indicated that Alfred Bayliss, the superintendent of public instruction and ex officio trustee, had voted for Stephen A. Forbes, dean of the College of Science. Five trustees had voted for James, while trustees Carrie T. Alexander, Alice Asbury Abbott, and Leonidas H. Kerrick had not voted.[28] James was informed of his election.

On August 16, James A. Patten, a Northwestern trustee, wrote James urging him to stay at Northwestern. It would embarrass Northwestern if James left so soon after his predecessor had departed, he said. On August 23, N. W. Harris, a Chicago banker, asked James to confer with the Northwestern trustees before deciding about Illinois.[29]

On the same day, the Illinois presidential selection committee announced the criteria it had applied in its search. "The presidency should be filled by a man who had attained eminence in general educational supervision." He should have had "a large experience in the operation and management of a university consisting of a number of diverse departments." The president should be a man who had "largely grown up with and was in warm sympathy with the plan and aim of higher education by the state: who was, if possible, a native of Illinois, at least who was for years a citizen of our state and familiar with our constitution, our laws, our free school system, the temperament,

1. A New Leader at Illinois   **11**

character, and resources of our people and the history, traditions, scope, and possibilities of this great University." In addition, he should be "a man of good personal presence, affable, gentle, courageous, and of irreproachable character, and of strong moral influence." The committee had secured such a man—Edmund Janes James—and recommended him as president. This statement seems certain to have materialized *after* James's selection.[30]

• • •

The high point of the week of James's installation came in his address on "The Function of the State University." He began by describing the development of the University to 1904, noting that it had grown to be the largest of the institutions owing their origins to the Morrill Land Grant Act.[31] The institution would become in an ever truer sense a university, James avowed, a university being "that institution of the community which affords the ultimate institutional training of the youth of the country for all the various callings for which an extensive scientific training, based upon adequate liberal preparation, is valuable and necessary." Such training, James attested, prepared one to be an independent investigator in a professional domain. James paid homage to the German university. German universities, he stated, excelled in creating a thirst for scholarship and learning, and if this spirit became general in America it would give the nation an immense scientific and industrial advance. James insisted that the University of Illinois become, in all departments of professional life, "a great center of scientific research and investigation."[32] He further elaborated his vision: The University would include within itself not merely the old professions. It would also undertake scientific preparation for any department of community life that required an extensive scientific training.[33]

James's address reflected Progressive-Era values. The state university, he said, should become a great civil service academy, preparing young men and women of the state for the civil service of state and local governments. The business of government was becoming more complex, James pointed out; it required scientifically trained experts. Also, the state university should become the scientific arm and head of the state administration, expanding upon the work being done in such agencies as the Water Survey and the Natural History Survey. Further, the state university in combination with the normal schools should become for many concrete purposes the state department of education. In short, James, employing a favorite model of his progressive sociology, wanted the University to have an "organic" relation with the whole state structure.[34]

On November 17, *Science* magazine published the entire text of James's inaugural address, making it available to a national audience.[35] Now, with the academic rituals and the addresses over, it was time to renew the grand design of building the modern University of Illinois.

12   PART I. THE LARGER UNIVERSITY

CHAPTER 2

Money and Politics

COLLEGES AND UNIVERSITIES never enjoy full autonomy. From the time of their beginning at Bologna in the late thirteenth century and thereafter at the University of Paris and the universities of Oxford and Cambridge, local and national authorities devised methods for university governance. With the American colonial colleges, often quasi-public institutions, public powers always had some measure of control. And even in the great era of university-making, the late nineteenth and early twentieth centuries, the powerful university presidents—"captains of erudition" as Thorstein Veblen liked to call them—gave much of their time and attention to dealing with forces that controlled their universities' fates. This chapter takes up the presidency of Edmund J. James under these considerations. It looks at the legislature of the state of Illinois, located at Springfield, and at governors, and it looks at the University Board of Trustees. They're all a matter of money and politics.[1]

Many of the older universities along the Atlantic seaboard relied on substantial endowments as well as students' tuition to meet their expenses, but President James had no such luxury. A bold beggar with a grand vision, he bore the brunt of securing operating funds for the University. He lobbied his cause in Springfield and mobilized alumni to do likewise.

In 1904 Illinois ranked third among the states in population. However, this very industrialized state had an obsolete tax system, based very heavily on property. The valuation of real and personal property for taxation derived from laws that provided for assessment at a fraction of the fair cash value. The legislature did not tax the interests that grew out of commercial and industrial development. The rapid increase in state expenditures after 1894 led to a high tax rate on property, an inequitable burden of taxation, and a lack of public revenue that contributed to the deficiency in Illinois public services compared to other states. In 1909 the per capita revenue for state purposes was $6.20 in

Minnesota, $4.12 in Massachusetts, $3.64 in Wisconsin, $3.50 in New York, $2.35 in Pennsylvania, and $1.50 in Illinois.[2]

James operated within this system. Springfield provided the University $1,152,400 in the appropriation for 1903–1905, by far the largest sum to date. James and the board asked for $1,554,500 for 1905–1907. The request included funds for salaries, operating expenses, and enumerated items. This part of the request came to $1,185,000. The University also asked for $50,000 per annum for the Graduate School and $25,000 per annum for the library. The board also requested $369,500 for new buildings, including a physics laboratory and an auditorium. The request met some resistance in Springfield. Both chambers made minor cuts and then a conference committee reconciled the results. The bill enacted largely mirrored the request. It provided $150,000 for a physics building and $100,000 for an auditorium, but nothing for the Graduate School. Governor Charles S. Deneen trimmed the appropriation with item vetoes, but in the years that followed, Deneen gave much support to the University.[3]

Deneen came from southern Illinois, and, like James, had a family history full of Methodism, with reform interests that included anti-slavery. However, he made his name in Cook County, where, as a state's attorney, he won some headline prosecutions of prominent figures guilty of corruption. It took Deneen fifty-eight ballots to win the Republican nomination for governor in 1904, but he went on to an easy victory as the popular Teddy Roosevelt carried the state in the presidential election. Deneen's governorship saw great expansion of the civil service, electoral reform (the direct primary), road paving, and the "mother's aid" law to provide funds for dependent and neglected children. His reforms, by one account, outdid even those of the renowned Peter Altgeld, "in number and importance."[4]

Conditions had changed somewhat by the time appropriations came up again before the legislature two years later. The University was proving its worth, the farmers were backing it, and most legislators wanted recognition as friends of the University. Nonetheless, in 1909 the University's appropriation prompted heated discussion in the General Assembly, partly because the University asked for a larger sum than it had previously and partly because officials felt no urge to raise taxes. But other state institutions also competed for the available funds, creating more opposition to the University. Some criticized its work and others challenged individual items in the appropriations bills, thus creating an atmosphere unfavorable to larger appropriations. However, increased university enrollment and the University's growth in stature led James and the trustees to plead for generous state aid. On January 15, 1909, the board adopted the report of its Committee on Legislative Askings. The general funds bill sought $2,163,400 for the biennium, a little more than a million a year. This part of the request included $550,000 per annum for salaries and ordinary operating expenses, $75,000 per annum for the Graduate School, $75,000 per annum for maintenance of the veterinary college and research laboratory, and $25,000 per annum for increase of salaries for important individuals.[5]

Explaining why the University needed $3,250,000 for buildings and equipment, the board requested $1,000,000 for physical facilities for the biennium. It also asked for $747,300 for agriculture and the Agricultural Experiment Station.[6] Addressing the General Assembly on January 18, 1909, Governor Deneen acknowledged the University's needs and added that many of its branches did work of practical importance to the people of Illinois. In early February, Senator Henry M. Dunlap of Savoy introduced in the Senate a resolution declaring it the sense of the General Assembly that the trustees should adopt a salary policy designed to attract and retain the best academic talent in the United States and in other countries. On March 31 the House concurred. The University was gaining friends in Springfield.[7]

And James was gaining in esteem on campus and beyond. But he never had clear sailing, and opposition from certain board members plagued his early years in the presidency. Thus, in April President James appealed to the alumni to support the University's appropriations bills. He viewed the general bill as more important than the buildings bill and described the University's most pressing needs as more library facilities and an increase in faculty salaries. The average salary of a full professor was $2,851 compared to $4,500 at Harvard, he pointed out.[8] On April 28, however, Trustee Carrie T. Alexander-Bahrenberg attacked the appropriations request when it came before a House committee. She had been and would remain a constant source of irritation to James. Born in Bellevue, Illinois in 1865, she had married Daniel Alexander, a railroad man, and upon his death in 1887 she took over the business, the St. Louis, Bellevue & Suburban Railway. She always boasted about how she managed every detail of it, so who was anybody to challenge her opinion on matters of university operations? Alexander then married William Bahrenberg. Carrie Alexander-Bahrenberg had strong commitments to women's rights and actively served in the state's Equal Suffrage Society. Elected to the board in 1900, a product of Governor John R. Tanner's (1897–1901) political machine, she had opposed the selection of James as president. Now she charged that James was "money mad and drunk with power."[9]

Alexander-Bahrenberg particularly faulted the money proposed for a veterinary college. The funds appropriated for the college two years ago had not been spent for that purpose, she charged, because such a college did not exist. The money had gone to pay the expenses of a trip to Europe that James took to investigate veterinary colleges, she charged. And even now, she added, the veterinary college still did not exist. Alexander-Bahrenberg also attacked the request for $25,000 per annum for special salary increases,

2. Money and Politics   **15**

citing her comparison of university salaries with those in other institutions, which led her to conclude that Illinois was not so badly off. She claimed that President James and the trustees had obtained funds for fictitious purposes and had deceived the legislature. Many legislators were said to agree with her. However, at a special meeting the next day the board endorsed its appropriations bill and condemned the attempt of one of its members "to discredit the unanimously expressed judgment of the entire board and to harass it in its efforts to maintain and build up a university worthy of the state." On the same day the executive committee of the Chicago Illini Club, chaired by William L. Abbott, the president of the Board of Trustees, issued a statement that attributed "traitorous action" and "unworthy and selfish motives" to Alexander-Bahrenberg.[10]

Newspapers throughout the state featured the conflict. Alexander-Bahrenberg, one paper wrote, had fanned into flame the board's smoldering discontent with James and his autocratic regime. Some trustees reportedly said that Alexander-Bahrenberg wanted to become the state superintendent of public instruction and was acting out of personal animosity to James. On May 4, 1909, when the House committee resumed hearings on the appropriations bill, Alexander rebutted her critics. "Since I am accused of being a traitor," she said, "I am going to tell a few things out of school." She reiterated her earlier charges, adding that when the board had considered the bill on January 15, she was the only member who commented on any item; the others had sat there "like bumps on a log." She had opposed only two items in the University's request, she emphasized: $75,000 for the nonexistent veterinary school and $25,000 for salaries for important positions. When informed that President James had said that "politics do not enter into the university," she retorted, "that is all you know about it."[11]

President James followed Alexander-Bahrenberg in testifying before the legislative committee. He vigorously defended the University's proposals. David E. Shanahan, chairman of the committee, grilled James on two matters. Shanahan thought the University was not specific enough in saying what certain requests were for. James replied that the University could itemize the requests for salaries, equipment, and ordinary operating expenses, but separate appropriations for each would reduce the efficiency of the University. Shanahan also objected to the request of $25,000 per annum for special salary increases. That objection gave James the opportunity to make a bold statement. This request, he replied, represented a new salary policy: it gave notice that the University was going to keep its best faculty if it wanted them, not lose them to outside offers. Shortly after James testified, hundreds of telegrams supporting the University flooded Shanahan's office. A day after Alexander-Bahrenberg gave her "sensational testimony," Senator W. O. Potter, a Marion Republican, secured passage of a resolution that called on the Senate to appoint a committee of three to inquire into the truth or falsity of her charges. The resolution was referred to the Committee on Appropriations. No more was heard of it. Nonetheless, in late May Trustee Alexander-Bahrenberg returned to Springfield trying to get the General Assembly to look into the abuses that she claimed threatened to destroy the influence of the University. She accused it of operating like a political machine.[12] On June 14 the University's appropriations bill for 1909–1911 became law. It provided $1,642,500, including $525,000 per annum for salaries and ordinary operating expenses, but nothing for the veterinary college or for salary increases. The trustees had asked for funds for new buildings but had to settle for $250,000 for a university hall.[13]

Although the appropriations fell below his expectations, James labeled the results as on the whole gratifying. But Alexander-Bahrenberg had dealt a serious blow. For a trustee to publicly attack the board's request after she had endorsed it was unprecedented and costly. Although her charges had no foundation—faculty salaries were low—and the General Assembly did provide funds for a mining engineering department yet to be established, she appealed to a growing sentiment that James acted too aggressively in lobbying for the University. Alexander-Bahrenberg had never been James's partisan. Fortunately, he had the ability to ignore personal attacks.

• • •

James and the University of Illinois, as Roger Geiger informs us, were addressing new realities. And one sure sign of American colleges' entry into the new university model did concern money. Budgets increased dramatically—for new buildings, new equipment (especially in the sciences), expanded libraries, and faculty salaries. We enter the "big state" era. Competition became fierce for professors of visible accomplishments in their fields, that is, for their records in scholarship.[14]

James had done well with the legislature since 1905, but in 1911 he surpassed his earlier successes with the University's appropriation. On January 4, in his biennial message to the General Assembly, Governor Deneen presented the needs of the University, calling special attention to those units whose work had a visible practical influence on the lives of the people, specifically in agriculture, engineering, commerce, medicine, the Graduate College, and the state scientific agencies. He broke new ground in recommending establishment of a department of sociological research, a legislative reference bureau, and a municipal reference bureau.[15] The legislative reference bureau may have followed the example of the University of Wisconsin, which made research of its faculty available to state legislators, providing them with bodies of information that could assist in writing effective legislation. Charles McCarthy for many years made the Legislative Reference Library a hallmark of the "Wisconsin Idea" and its formidable role in that state's progressivism.[16]

2. Money and Politics   **17**

• • •

At about this time President James published a letter asking the alumni to support the appropriations bill. In it he declared his intention to create a world-class institution, to make the University of Illinois not "a whit behind the greatest and most important of the historic universities of this or the old world." To reach this goal, the University needed more money by far than did Harvard, Yale, Columbia, Princeton, or Chicago because Illinois was a comprehensive university. It included expensive branches of instruction that the others lacked. And compared to other institutions, the University had to overcome several defects. One was the University library. Illinois also lacked the buildings needed to do its work, James asserted. As of 1908, in the cost of buildings erected in nineteen leading private and state universities, Illinois ranked eighteenth. For the past six years the legislature had given the University an average of $150,000 a year for buildings; at that rate it would take about sixty-six years to realize the University's building needs. An expenditure of about a million dollars a year for ten years would enable Illinois to catch up with other great American universities, James explained.[17]

The president had done his homework; he offered plentiful evidence to illustrate the Illinois situation. In 1909 the University ranked lowest among six state universities in the ratio of the institution's total income to the total population of the state. California led with $1.10 per capita while Illinois had 29 cents per capita. A comparison of the ratio of the income (as of 1904) of nine state universities to the total property in the various states showed Michigan at the top with a ratio of $.00060 and Illinois at the bottom with a ratio of $.00018. In sum, the University needed large additional funding to increase the size and quality of its teaching staff and to erect, furnish, and equip buildings.[18]

It's noted that James placed this information, and this plea, in the *Alumni Quarterly* magazine. Here, as Jerome Rodnitzky has illustrated, James utilized one of the many outreaches he employed to maximize the money situation. At the time of his coming to Illinois, fourteen alumni groups already had emerged in several places. Now James set to work to expand the number, and by 1916 some thirty UofI alumni clubs existed, located in New York, Pittsburgh, St. Louis, and especially important, Chicago. You could even find them in Japan, India, and Brazil. Some of them took up their own fund-raising for the University. James created the *Alumni Quarterly* in 1907 and it immediately had an audience of thousands. Next came a University of Illinois *Alumni Directory*. James urged members to write to their representatives in Springfield, and even to appeal for support on specific university budget items, having read from James what they were and why they were needed. Write to the governor,

18   PART I. THE LARGER UNIVERSITY

too, he urged. Reportedly, on one issue, Governor Frank Lowden in 1917 had received more than a thousand letters, from every state in the Union and from abroad, too. James wanted both students and alumni to guard the University's good name and reputation. Whenever they saw it maligned in the press, they should get the letters going again. The ever-cautious and ever-vigilant James kept a personal card file with one card for every legislator at the Capitol and, with a picture of each, some points about their backgrounds and notes about their attitudes toward the University.[19]

James looked for help wherever he thought he might find it. Often the staff of the *Daily Illini* student newspaper would take up a matter and give it a pitch. When he wanted support for one of his major ambitions, a graduate school, he wrote to high school teachers around the state; they knew what to do. Special needs called for special groups and James strove to have them on board. At one time or another they included professional and occupational associations like the Illinois Bankers' Associations (for certain business programs), the Clay Workers' Association, the Illinois Society of Engineers, and the Live Stock Breeders' Association (for a veterinary college). But the legislature was the place where James committed most of his time and energy, and he excelled at cultivating people. Sometimes, to be sure, this pressure could rub some individuals the wrong way. A Chicago Democrat called James an empire builder, driven by vanity. He did not totally miss the mark.[20] On the other hand, one needs no reminder that James had made his early scholarly mark as a student of government, at all its levels of operation.

But on this matter of state financing, James had decided that he had to take it to a whole new level. Because dependence upon the legislative appropriation for operating funds caused uncertainty, James now called for a state tax that would assure a steady income for the support and maintenance of the University. Beginning in 1905 bills providing for the levy and collection of four-fifths of one mill (a mill being one-tenth of a cent) for each dollar of assessed valuation of taxable property in the state to be set aside and earmarked for the University came before the House. Then, on June 10, 1911, a bill providing for a one mill tax became law. The money collected would remain in a separate fund in the state treasury until appropriated to the University by the General Assembly. The fund could go to current expenses, construction and repair of buildings, and enlargement of the grounds. James anticipated that the mill tax would bring in not less than four and one half and possibly five million dollars per biennium. He prayed for wisdom in handling the funds, and he was ready for a reaction against the continuous increase of appropriations for state universities. It had been a constant in Illinois politics for the last fifteen or twenty years.[21] The mill tax marked a major achievement for President James. By relentless effort James had pleaded for the General Assembly to provide the

2. Money and Politics   19

financial resources needed to operate the University and to enable it to become a great American university. His efforts now began to produce results.

• • •

When the University of Illinois was founded, a board of trustees elected by Illinois voters legally governed the University. Members of the board served six-year terms after winning state-wide elections. The board selected the president, who served the board. The Alumni Association customarily proposed three candidates to the state central committee of the political parties for these elections. The party conventions slated the nominees, who usually gained office when their party won the general election.

From 1904 to 1913 all of the trustees, including Governor Deneen, an ex officio board member, were Republicans. The 1904 elections had brought new members to the board, among them William L. Abbott. An engineering student (Class of 1884), he had not completed the requirements for a degree but had become a successful engineer. In 1885 he organized an electric company that Commonwealth Edison later absorbed. In 1899 Abbott became the chief operating engineer of this company, the world's largest producer and distributor of electrical energy. Abbott had made such outstanding achievements in engineering that the faculty and dean at the University agreed to give him a doctoral degree, despite his not having graduated. Abbott served the board for many years.[22]

Mary Bowen Busey became a board member in 1905. Born in 1854 in Delphi, Indiana, a graduate of Vassar College, she married Samuel T. Busey in 1877 and moved to Urbana. He had been the colonel of an Illinois Volunteer Infantry regiment during the Civil War. Afterwards he engaged in banking, served as mayor of Urbana, and in 1890 won election to Congress (as a Democrat). In 1909 he died in a drowning accident in Minnesota and she became the manager of large farm interests. Mary Busey had long dedicated herself to educational, civic, political, and social affairs, involving herself in some twenty organizations and municipal projects. In 1888 she had joined the First Presbyterian Church in Urbana and in 1906 gave it the money to build a new church. In 1910 she won more votes for trustee than either of the two male candidates. Her social position, political outlook, and long service (until her death in 1930) made her an influential if not always constructive trustee.[23]

When death opened two vacancies, Governor Deneen proposed A. P. Grout of Winchester and Arthur Meeker of Chicago for the places. Grout had been president of the Illinois Livestock Breeders Association. Meeker, a graduate of Yale's Sheffield Scientific School, had served as vice president of Armor and Company, Chicago meat packers. "Armor & Swift agreed to support Meeker. [Rival meat packer] Morris & Co. object," wrote Dean Kinley, who saw a disturbing sign. He wrote to James, saying, "I am sorry that the time

20   PART I. THE LARGER UNIVERSITY

has come when 'interests' must be represented" on the Board of Trustees.[24] The governor appointed both nominees. In 1908 each won election to regular terms. Meeker polled the largest vote of the Republican candidates.

In 1912 a progressive impulse split the Republican Party, whereupon Democrat Woodrow Wilson defeated Teddy Roosevelt and incumbent Howard Taft to become president. Edward F. Dunne, a Democrat, won the gubernatorial election in Illinois. Dunne, "a personable and idealistic Irishman," only the second Democratic governor of Illinois since the Civil War, and only the second Catholic governor in the state's history, won his election with only 38 percent of the vote. He had come from Connecticut and moved with his family to Peoria. He studied at Trinity College, Dublin for three years and earned his law degree from Union College of Law in Chicago. As governor he championed restructuring of the state offices. He formed an eight-member Efficiency and Economy Committee and appointed U of I professor John A. Fairlie to head it. He strongly supported women's suffrage, and under Dunne Illinois became the first state east of the Mississippi River to grant women the right to vote in presidential elections. In the 1912 election, Republican schism also yielded victory for the Democratic slate of nominees for university trustees.[25]

The newly elected Democratic trustees formed a diverse group. Ellen M. Henrotin, born Ellen Martin in Portland, Maine, came from a well-to-do family that had lived on the Isle of Wight from 1860 to 1868. She attended schools in London, Paris, and Dresden. Returning to America, her family settled in Chicago. In 1869 she married Charles Henrotin, who became president of the Chicago Stock Exchange. The couple enjoyed a leading position in Chicago society. Active in women's clubs, Henrotin first won public recognition in 1893 through association with the World's Columbian Exposition, to which she brought a strong feminist emphasis. Her administrative ability led to her election in 1894 as president of the General Federation of Women's Clubs. In 1904 she assumed leadership in the effort to improve the condition of working women. Then in 1910 she turned her attention to the problem of prostitution in Chicago and became an advocate of sex hygiene training in the public schools. With the death of her husband in 1914 she gradually reduced her public activities.[26]

John R. Trevett had attended the University from 1868 to 1870 and then worked at A. C. Burnham, a bank company. When Burnham died, he and Ross R. Mattis reorganized the bank, first chartered as a state bank (later, the Bank of Illinois) in 1903. Trevett served as a captain in the Illinois National Guard and participated in local lodges and municipal affairs. Governor Dunne had once stayed in Trevett's home.[27] In Trevett, James would have a major enemy.

Florence E. Watson was born in Iola, near Effingham, Illinois. She attended the Iola and Flora public schools and Huddleson Academy in Sailor Springs. Her father, a Democratic Party leader, placed her name on the ballot in an

UNIVERSITY OF ILLINOIS
BOARD OF REGENTS

Hon. A. P. Grout

Mrs. Laura B. Evans

Hon. Fred L. Hatch

Hon. William L. Abbott

Mrs. Mary E. Busey

Hon. Allen F. Moore

Hon. Arthur Meeker

Mrs. Carrie A. Bahrenberg

Hon. Otis W. Hoit

President James and several women members of the trustees had an adversarial relationship, especially in the early years of his administration. Courtesy of the University of Illinois Archives.

election the Republicans were expected to win. Only twenty-four years old, Watson won over her favored rivals.[28]

All twelve trustees attended the annual board meeting on March 11, 1913. The board included ex officio members: Francis G. Blair, the state superintendent of public instruction, a Republican and a holdover; Edward F. Dunne; and John T. Montgomery, a Republican and president of the Illinois State Board of Agriculture. The board contained six Republican holdovers who completed its membership: Laura Evans, Arthur Meeker, Allen Moore, William Abbott, Mary Busey, and Otis Hoit.

Relations between the president and the trustees were a problem. In 1898 the board had dealt with the subject by declaring that the functions of the trustees were legislative, not executive, the president being the chief executive and the agent of the trustees. The board strongly disapproved of any disposition to turn university appointments into patronage, and now possibly feared that James had such an intention. Every appointment was to be made upon the basis of merit.[29]

With an eye on the 1914 general elections, each of five political parties nominated three candidates as university trustees. Two of the nine nominees of the Democratic, Republican, and Progressive Parties were female, compared to five of the six nominees of the Socialist and Prohibition Parties. Chicago supplied five of the fifteen candidates. Arthur Meeker of that city had asked James if he would like to have him renominated. The state of Illinois was going to have "one of the great historic institutions of the world," James replied, and everyone connected with it would be glad to have helped build it. Meeker agreed to have his name put on the Republican ticket, but the party did not slate him.

The Democratic Party again won the election. Normally, Democrats would have won all trustee positions. But Laura B. Evans, a Republican, had 457,521 votes and returned to office. Two of the three Democratic candidates gained a seat on the board—Robert Carr (UofI Class of 1893), a Chicago business executive, and Robert B. Ward, a Benton attorney and banker.[30] All the trustees came to the annual board meeting on March 9. With the Democrats now in the majority, Abbott, Carr, and Hoit won election to the executive committee. They named James as president for the ensuing biennium.[31]

By this time James enjoyed wide popularity in the state, had made valuable network connections, including in the legislature, and enjoyed the confidence of the board pretty much across the whole membership, and certainly that of students and faculty. His national reputation had grown. Some even wanted James, a loyal Republican, to be the party's nominee for the U.S. presidency in 1916.[32] Above all, James and the University had gained the support of the populace, a great portion of which seemed to want their state to have a great

2. Money and Politics   **23**

university with a great reputation. The legislature read the popular will and reenforced it in its budgetary beneficence. James would end his career at Illinois on a very high note. But by 1919 health, and the burdens of the presidency, finally prompted him to offer his resignation. The board refused and gave James a leave. He returned but only briefly and left the office in 1920, an honored and respected individual. Shortly thereafter he moved to California and died on June 17, 1925 in Covina.

CHAPTER 3

The Graduate School

GRADUATE EDUCATION ROSE to significance in American higher education during the late nineteenth century.[1] German universities, which emphasized advanced study, seminars, research, and publications for the doctor's degree, provided the model. The opening of Johns Hopkins in 1876 signaled the rise of the university as the paradigmatic form of American higher education. President Daniel Coit Gilman sought to create an institution that emphasized advanced study, research, and publication. In 1880 Columbia established a School of Political and Social Sciences. In 1889 the Catholic University of America introduced advanced work in its School of Sacred Sciences. Clark University opened as a graduate school. In the 1890s Harvard, Yale, Chicago, Wisconsin, Nebraska, and Kansas created graduate schools.

Historian Roger Geiger indicates an important parallel between the changes in American higher education and the transformations occurring in American business in the proximate half-century between 1870 and 1920. The latter situation saw the rise to dominance of very large corporations and trusts. But likewise, "the major research universities had become the corporations of the education industry—organized to gather the lion's share of social resources available to higher education, and committed to produce the most valued educational products for the most important national markets."[2]

At Illinois, graduate work arose partly from the needs of high school, normal, and college teachers for better knowledge and better pay.[3] Illinois offered a graduate program for two types of students. Resident students were college graduates who pursued additional studies on campus. From 1880 to 1891 the University awarded master's degrees to eleven of these resident graduate students. Nonresident students were University graduates who completed in absentia, after no less than three years of professional activity, a course of study equivalent in grade and amount to that required of students in residence.

Students in both categories completed an acceptable thesis. Most nonresidents did their work in engineering or architecture.[4]

In 1891 Professor Thomas Burrill established the Graduate School when he became acting regent. Facilities for advanced study and research became available to college graduates without fees except for laboratory expenses. The diploma of any college or university in good standing assured admission. The University offered four fellowships valued at $400 each. The holders gave five to ten hours of instruction per week in an assigned class during the year. Burrill also exercised control over admissions, approval of programs, and the granting of degrees. A committee consisting of the regents and the college deans oversaw this process, beginning in 1892. Thus, the Graduate School had an identity.

When President Draper arrived, he transferred this role to the Council of Administration, which he headed. At that time most faculty members did not have the qualifications to pursue or direct research, the library lacked sufficient resources for advanced work, and officials viewed the University's mission as undergraduate instruction. Around the country in 1900, fourteen universities formed the Association of American Universities (AAU) to work for greater uniformity in PhD requirements among member institutions. They sought also to promote graduate education and demonstrate that America no longer depended on Germany for advanced study. As Geiger writes: "The creation of the AAU was a declaration by the leading American universities of independence and equality with regard to European universities as well as an endeavor to guarantee the value of their product against 'cheap' foreign and domestic competition." Illinois was not a charter member.[5] Nevertheless, the Graduate School inched forward. In 1898–1899 Illinois had 31 graduate students; Kansas, 42; Indiana, 73; Michigan, 77; and Minnesota, 132. From 1896 to 1903 the University awarded an average of thirteen master's degrees a year. In 1903 the University conferred its first doctorates, one in mathematics and one in chemistry. The Faculty Senate repeatedly declared the importance of extending the graduate work and of emphasizing research. It asked to have its views transmitted to the Board of Trustees.[6] President James wholly concurred.

In December 1904, in addition to its regular appropriation for the 1905–1907 biennium, the board requested $100,000 to enlarge and equip the Graduate School. James informed Governor Deneen that more than 1,500 students left the state every year for other universities because facilities for their work in Urbana simply did not meet their needs. Convinced that legislators did not understand the value of a graduate school, James nonetheless initiated a campaign for a special grant.[7] He identified Illinois teachers as the best group to enlist in this effort. On December 29 the Illinois State Teachers Association passed a resolution to this effect.[8] James urged two thousand superintendents,

26   PART I. THE LARGER UNIVERSITY

principals, and school teachers to convince their legislators that a graduate school could secure the University its proper standing among the nation's higher educational institutions. He also appealed to Chicago newspapers—the *Evening Post*, the *Tribune*, the *Record Herald*, and the *Chronicle*—to endorse the proposition, and they did.[9]

James took the "low" rather than the "high" road in his campaign. Publicly he argued that a graduate school was needed to train school teachers, but in his inaugural address he had declared that a university had a prime duty to promote science and discover new knowledge. In all likelihood his strategy was pragmatic. James needed to win over legislators, so he enlisted a pressure group to convince them that people demanded a graduate school to train teachers.[10] Appearing before the House appropriations committee in Springfield, James urged $50,000 per annum for the Graduate School. The committee reduced the sum to $25,000 for the first year of the biennium and $50,000 for the second year. James arranged to have every legislator receive a letter asking about his support of the Graduate School.[11]

Then in June 1905 James began to reorganize the Graduate School. Burrill agreed to resign as dean at once.[12] James wanted David Kinley, dean of Literature and Science, for the office but was not ready to make promises to him.[13] Kinley hesitated to give up his present positions. If, however, Literature and Arts and Science were all combined and he headed the new unit, he observed, he would have charge of a large undergraduate body with a large faculty whose work would provide the foundation of graduate studies. As dean of the Graduate School, by contrast, he would head a unit without separate funds, without a distinct faculty, without a constituency, and with a certain sentiment in the state against the new arrangement.[14] Kinley consulted Richard T. Ely, his University of Wisconsin mentor, about his options. Ely said he would be inclined to choose the graduate school deanship if he thought it had possibilities, but, he told Kinley, "it is going to be a struggle to put your Graduate School on its feet." It would be impossible to develop it unless the dean of the liberal arts college heartily sympathized with him. Yet Ely had "a good deal of faith in the possibilities at Champaign."[15]

In December 1905 the University Senate adopted a resolution to form a Graduate School faculty and have it replace the Council of Administration as the school's governing body. Kinley endorsed the resolution, which went to the trustees.[16] Thus armed, Kinley defined the terms on which he would accept the deanship. He wanted control of the school placed in the dean, and he wanted a Graduate School faculty. He himself would select the first half dozen members of this faculty and have them manage the school. The new dean must be consulted on appointments of faculty designated for graduate training. He wanted also to reduce the course load of instructors who directed graduate instruction. He desired to improve the library and increase the number

3. The Graduate School   **27**

of fellowships, and to transfer management of the journal *University Studies*, sponsored by UofI, to the Graduate School. He wished furthermore to develop some new field in which the University could make a name for itself rather than build up its advanced work indiscriminately. He insisted on time for writing, and he insisted that the trustees provide for the Graduate School if the legislature did not do so. Finally, if he were to become the dean, Kinley added, he would be leaving what would soon be the most important subordinate educational position in the University. He would feel aggrieved if the liberal arts college dean should have a salary higher than his. His present salary, $3,500, should increase to at least $4,000, he urged. If becoming dean of the Graduate School and director of the School of Commerce were regarded as a promotion, his new position ought to provide $4,500 or $5,000 in salary. If he had to sacrifice the prospects for financial advancement that he had in his present position, then he was not willing to take on the new charge.[17]

In early January 1906 Kinley still stood indecisive because James seemed to want the Graduate School to cover many subjects whereas Kinley thought it better to develop particular fields.[18] On January 20 Kinley rejected the deanship. "The President in his conversations," he told Ely, "says more than he is willing to put in writing." Kinley understood the tactic, but he had passed the point where he was "willing to put myself in the hands of any university president." Kinley's requests seemed reasonable, Ely replied, but whereas "our friend James" had given Kinley positive oral assurances, Ely suggested that Kinley ask James to sound out the trustees as to their views on his salary before committing himself. All things considered, Ely thought $4,000 would be a fair salary.[19]

"Notwithstanding the haziness of the situation," Kinley concluded that he could render more service in developing the graduate work than he could in his present position. In January 1906 he stated his willingness to accept the job. On January 30 the trustees agreed that a special Graduate School faculty be constituted to have charge of the school. They named Kinley as dean of the school and director of the commerce courses at a salary of $4,000, starting on February 1.[20]

• • •

On May 4, 1906, the Graduate School became a separate unit with an executive faculty and a teaching faculty. Kinley nominated the fourteen members of the former for appointment by the president. He chose scholars from departments ready to offer advanced work.[21] For months Kinley and the executive faculty discussed how to implement the advanced work. Because other graduate schools were young and the conditions in each unique, each state institution had to find its own way. Questions persisted: What is the essence of graduate work? What is research?[22] The universities were trying to adapt the German

28   PART I. THE LARGER UNIVERSITY

university model to an American university tradition and to superimpose the graduate program on an undergraduate program. The deliberations resembled those taking place in the Association of American Universities.[23]

In the spring Kinley visited private colleges to enlist their aid in behalf of the Graduate School's appropriations request. Eureka, Knox, and Illinois were friendly, as was Carthage, although not actively so. Lombard was neutral, Monmouth distinctly unfriendly. Some colleges feared competition.[24]

For the 1907–1909 biennium the trustees requested $100,000 for the Graduate School. Governor Deneen endorsed the asking. In his message to the General Assembly, he emphasized the importance of the Graduate School.[25] James appealed to the presidents of the private colleges to lobby the legislature for the appropriation. Though appreciating the work of the Christian colleges, he wanted a university that would cover the entire range of human knowledge, science especially. The University would emphasize graduate and professional studies, leaving to the colleges as far as possible the elementary work of college grade while maintaining a college of literature, arts, and sciences. Most presidents cooperated, but Charles A. Blanchard of Wheaton, M. H. Chamberlain of McKendree, and J. A. Leavitt of Ewing dissented. They could support the Graduate School, they said, if the University would agree to concentrate on the advanced work, "leaving," as Blanchard wrote, "the arts schools to furnish the Christian training which every nation must have or rot down." According to Blanchard, the University furnished an education in essentials inferior to that provided by the private colleges. It did not seem "economically wise," wrote Leavitt, "for all the Christian people of this State to be taxing themselves to build up an institution to rival those of their own."[26]

When the General Assembly provided the requested funds, Kinley boasted that for the first time in history a state legislature had made an appropriation for graduate work. He praised the act for "committing a democratic people to the maintenance and development of education and research on the highest plane."[27] And, once Kinley committed to the Graduate School, he moved energetically. On June 1, 1907, he outlined what the Graduate School needed to advance itself. He named sixteen departments as prepared to offer studies leading to the doctorate; he called for a fund that could aid faculty with their research; and he outlined his plan to offer scholarships and fellowships as a means of recruiting graduate students. Kinley urged James to write the presidents of the private colleges and invite them to nominate candidates for the scholarship offered annually to each college.[28] Although Kinley and James largely agreed on Graduate School matters, James wanted rapid efforts made to offer degrees in as many departments as possible, whereas Kinley still wanted more selectivity. He hoped to gain recognition for the University by bringing in one or two world-renowned scholars who would come to the campus for a year and devote themselves to research and strengthen their fields of study.

3. The Graduate School   **29**

The trustees supported James. On June 10 they recognized twelve subjects as majors for the doctorate—agriculture, botany, chemistry, economics, engineering, English, modern languages, ancient languages, history, mathematics, physics, and zoology. They also identified eight subjects as minors for the PhD and majors for the master's degree—astronomy, geology, philosophy, physiology, household science, education, politics, and psychology. They authorized $20,000 of the 1907–1908 Graduate School appropriation for fellowships and scholarships.[29] A month later the trustees granted assistants and instructors employed at the University and registered in the Graduate School exemption from tuition charges and laboratory fees.[30]

Having launched the Graduate School, Kinley had good qualifications for leading it. He kept abreast of the main currents in American higher education and had a clear vision of what he hoped to accomplish. He defined the main objectives of the Graduate School as the advancement of knowledge by research and publications and the training of a younger generation of scholars and teachers. However, Kinley's temperament was a mixed blessing. Forceful and aggressive, he could be austere, harsh, and taciturn, "a red-haired Scot with a sharp temper," as his secretary recalled, but capable of kindness, too. Jealous of his personal and professional prerogatives, Kinley habitually sought James's advice but did not hesitate to challenge him. In addition to his deanship, Kinley had other roles: professor of economics, head of the commerce courses, president of the American Economic Association in 1913, and vice president of the University starting in 1914.

• • •

University authorities planned the formal opening of the Graduate School to coincide with a conference of Illinois college presidents in 1907. They could not organize the conference in time, but in September the Graduate School opened with 168 students—134 in residence and 34 in absentia. By the end of the year enrollment rose to 211. The official opening was rescheduled for February 1908. The University had hoped to have its efforts to create a strong graduate school rewarded by admission to the Association of American Universities. But the AAU had become elitist since its 1900 formation; it had little desire to expand. The University had twice applied for and twice failed to gain admission because of the adverse votes of Columbia and Chicago. Exclusion had not become a serious handicap until 1904, when Dutch and German universities refused to recognize graduate work done at any American university not a member of the AAU. At that point President Eliot of Harvard prompted the AAU to consider enlarging itself. Illinois won election to membership on January 9, 1908. The news arrived on the eve of the inauguration of the Graduate School,[31] and very good news it was. The University of Minnesota and the University of Missouri joined at the same time as Illinois.

30   PART I. THE LARGER UNIVERSITY

The formal opening of the School occurred on February 4–5 along with the installation of William F. M. Goss as dean of the College of Engineering.[32] The event displayed the kind of academic pomp and circumstance that James loved. On the first day President G. Stanley Hall of Clark University, Dean Andrew F. West of Princeton, President Charles M. Rammelkamp of Illinois College, and President Thomas McClelland of Knox College spoke on graduate study. William A. Noyes of chemistry, Chester N. Greenough of English, and David Kinley participated. Kinley made an excellent statement on the relation of the land-grant college ideal to the promise of American life. (See end of this chapter.) The college presidents' conference took place on April 30, 1908. James and Kinley eagerly wished to cultivate good relations with the state's private colleges. "The friendly attitude that you have taken toward the independent colleges is very different from the former attitude at the University," Joseph R. Harker, the president of Illinois Woman's College, wrote James on April 18, 1908. Harker believed that it would "redound much more to the advantage of the University than the former narrow and half hostile attitude."[33]

With these formalities over, the University asked the legislature for $100,000 for the Graduate School for the 1909–1911 biennium. In his address to the General Assembly on January 18, 1909, Governor Deneen said that the Graduate School promoted original research and investigation of all subjects of interest to people of the state, and that it had raised the University to the plane occupied by the great universities of this and other countries.[34]

James urged the Illinois college presidents to support the request. Blanchard of Wheaton replied that the graduate work ought to be strengthened and he would be pleased if funds to do so were taken from the undergraduate work. The legislature granted $100,000 for the biennium.[35] In 1910, at the Republican Party convention, Governor Deneen praised the University, and the platform makers put in a good word for the University departments that studied the state's agriculture, mining, and other productive industries. "We favor the strengthening of the graduate school of the University of Illinois as the sound, scientific basis of all these and other departments to the end that the University may become still more fully the scientific arm of the State government," the platform declared. "Illinois has taken an advanced position in this movement and should maintain its leadership in this regard." As Professor Burrill exclaimed, "What party platform ever before said anything about a graduate school?"[36]

Kinley and the executive faculty controlled the quality of the Graduate School by approving both the courses offered for graduate credit and the teaching faculty in that school. To take charge of major work for an advanced degree, a faculty member had to have an advanced degree or have shown his qualifications by publications. Some faculty members, especially in technical

3. The Graduate School   31

departments, did not really understand graduate work. Kinley tried to weed these people out of the teaching staff, but some of those deficient faculty had professorial rank.[37]

The new dean moved cautiously in deciding which departments qualified to conduct the advanced work. In 1915 he found the educational status of several departments "still somewhat unsettled" or weak. This group included ceramics, electrical engineering, geology, physiology, psychology, and sociology. Kinley felt uncertain about work in household science and its inclusion in the Graduate School.[38] But Kinley faced pressure to enlarge the circle of departments permitted to offer advanced degrees. In 1914 some geology graduate students and faculty members requested approval for their department to offer the doctorate in certain fields of geology. A committee studied the matter but divided over its report, so geology could offer work only up to the master's degree.[39]

Kinley gave careful consideration to the question of what constituted graduate study. He reported being "nonplussed" as to the character of work for the doctorate in agriculture and engineering. He considered use of the PhD in these lines inappropriate, yet no one had suggested an alternative. So, Kinley made his own specifications. The degree made sense, Kinley conceded, when the candidate studied the fundamental sciences underlying engineering or agriculture, but in that case the student should get his degree in one of the basic sciences. Admittedly, Kinley conceded, one could not easily draw a line separating the scientific and the practical. Perhaps the greatest difficulty for Kinley arose from the pressure from students and faculty in different departments to confine their work to too narrow a field and a tendency to regard the working out of a "problem" as sufficient ground for conferring the master's degree. But the fault applied not only to the technical lines.[40] Kinley feared that graduate students increasingly cultivated small areas of study very intensively but failed to see the relation between their specialty and the larger world. The "foundations of things" must be reconsidered, he urged. And on this point Kinley and James wholly agreed. Kinley named another committee to study the standards of graduate work at Illinois and elsewhere and to consider the relationship of study in engineering and agriculture to the doctorate. Was it sound policy to award the PhD in such subjects as animal husbandry or civil engineering, or should the students earn their degrees in chemistry and mathematics? In 1906 the Graduate School answered the question when it favored conferring the PhD in agriculture and engineering, provided the work done showed high quality.[41]

The admission of qualified students under the standards announced in 1907 led to problems. In 1912, after a faculty committee visited and reported on conditions at Illinois State Normal, the Graduate School ruled that it would admit only holders of the Bachelor of Education degree from ISN to do graduate

32   PART I. THE LARGER UNIVERSITY

work in education. A year later the Graduate School refused admission to a graduate of Kansas State Manual Training Normal School on the ground that it had already refused admission to graduates of Illinois normal schools.[42] Then in 1913 and 1914 the Graduate College attempted to determine which colleges and universities could effectively prepare students for graduate work at Illinois. A committee set forth minimum standards for these institutions to meet. Significantly, the first requirement cited an institution's number of departments in the liberal arts and sciences, and the quality of the faculty. It also included the amount of money available for instructional purposes, the ability of the library and laboratory equipment to meet course needs, and the general standing of the School. As a result, the Graduate School had revised the admissions requirement. Under the new rule adopted on January 20, 1915, and introduced in September, the School allowed admission to graduates of institutions whose requirements for the bachelor's degree substantially approximated those of the University of Illinois and to applicants from other institutions approved by the executive faculty. Admission to the Graduate School in itself did not imply admission to candidacy for advanced degrees.[43]

When several Illinois colleges asked for reconsideration of their ratings, a faculty committee moved Rockford College from Class (or Group) B to Class A. It confirmed the ratings of Carthage, Eureka, James Millikin, Shurtleff, and Wheaton colleges in Class B and one other in Class C, and, following an on-site visit, ordered Illinois Wesleyan's rating of Class B to stand.[44]

To attract students, the Graduate School offered financial aid. Scholars usually received a stipend of $250 and fellows one of $300. In 1908–1909 fifty-four awards went to recipients ranging from nineteen to thirty-six years of age in sixteen departments. The chemistry, mathematics, and zoology departments each received seven awards, the highest of all departments.[45] In 1915–1916 sixty-nine scholarships and fellowships were awarded to departments, with zoology, history, and chemistry all receiving seven, the highest among twenty-one other programs. Practically all first-year students had no resources other than their scholarships. Also, the University inaugurated the college scholarship plan in 1908 to promote good relations with smaller colleges and to recruit good students. Each college could nominate one student a year for a scholarship. In 1909–1910 graduates of twelve colleges received scholarships in eight departments. For several years thereafter from eight to twelve colleges nominated candidates for these awards each year. Apart from mathematics, most of these students were majoring in the humanities or social sciences. Although some of the recipients had poor preparation for graduate work, most of them performed well.[46]

Most graduate students had defined goals. Despite few common interests they organized for academic and social purposes. In 1908 the Graduate Club attracted about 150 members.[47] The Illinois faculty also showed interest in

3. The Graduate School   33

the well-being of this new group in the University. In 1913 the executive faculty appointed a committee to consider ways and means to create "a true community life among graduate students." In January 1915 the committee encouraged the Graduate Club further to acquaint the graduate students with faculty members and to provide graduate students opportunities to meet socially. The committee also recommended building graduate halls for men and for women, segregating graduate from undergraduate students in separate buildings, and reserving library rooms for the use of graduate students and faculty members.[48] And in May 1911 the Graduate College appointed a committee to assist students in finding teaching positions. The committee helped secure high school appointments for graduates, but placement in colleges and universities came mostly by the initiative of professors who corresponded with colleagues in other institutions.[49]

• • •

David Kinley battled vigorously to defend his authority as dean. In 1912, having previously protested the violation of his agreement with James, Kinley complained of appointments made without his knowledge or approval. Because of his obligation to maintain the standard of graduate work, he wanted the privilege to comment on all cases regarding graduate students. Otherwise, he threatened, he did not wish to continue as dean.[50] In one instance, Kinley refused to approve an appointment of a graduate student to a fellowship for study abroad because German professor Julius F. Goebel had gained President James's approval for the student without discussing the matter with him. Moreover, he said, Goebel's proposition could not be considered by itself because other students of equal ability deserved consideration. Kinley also had reservations about Goebel's judgment ("all his geese are swans"). But Kinley finally approved the appointment—the first fellowship for travel awarded by the Graduate School.[51]

Kinley carefully oversaw the Graduate School's financial resources. A small portion went to the dean's office, $20,000 a year or more went to scholarships and fellowships, and as much as possible went to research and publications. He reserved part of the budget to aid faculty members who needed research materials. Usually, he assigned $4,000 or more a year to improve research-related library collections and cataloging. In 1909, with accumulated funds, he channeled $44,000 to the library.[52]

Kinley also insisted that the University provide a medium for publishing research results of scholarly and scientific value. He had played a key role in establishing *University Studies* to give humanities and social sciences faculty an outlet for their work; in 1906 the Graduate School assumed responsibility for its publication. Two years later the Graduate School became the sponsor of the *Journal of English and Germanic Philology*. Kinley provided funds for publication and distribution of the journal, which commanded wide respect. In 1910 he replaced *University Studies* with a new series, the *University of Illinois Studies in the Social Sciences*, a quarterly. *Studies in Language and Literature* and *Illinois Biological Monographs* appeared in 1914. These publications brought the research achievements of the University before a wide academic audience. This arrangement typified one of the key new hallmarks of the research university in the United States—its sponsorship of scholarly journals in the various academic disciplines. Johns Hopkins University had initiated the practice in 1878 with the *American Journal of Mathematics*. In 1906 the powerhouse University of Chicago had no less than twelve such affiliations; Harvard had eight; Columbia six; Johns Hopkins six; Cornell five; the University of Wisconsin three.[53]

President James, eager to expand into areas that might win the University a reputation for research, now financed such ventures through the Graduate School. In 1910 he persuaded the Illinois Historical Survey to gather source materials on the early history of the Mississippi Valley and to collaborate with other state agencies in writing a history of the state of Illinois. He named Clarence W. Alvord of the history department director of the Survey. In appealing to the General Assembly for a separate appropriation for the Graduate School, James assured legislators that the School would provide funds for a centennial history of the state. Although Alvord received his salary from the history department, the Graduate School financed the staff and operating expenses of the Survey, usually $4,000 a year. By 1913, however, Dean Kinley had largely lost interest in the work because Alvord apparently could not form and adhere to a plan. He had extravagant ideas as to how much support he should receive from the Graduate School, Kinley believed, and did not keep Kinley informed about his operations. Nevertheless, Kinley continued to support the Survey.[54]

In 1913 James called upon the Graduate School to provide $10,000 over three years to support the Crocker Land Expedition in collaboration with the American Museum of Natural History and the American Geographical Society. The executive faculty of the Graduate School recommended that the University participate. Two Illinois men, Elmer Ekblaw and Maurice Tanquary, joined the staff of the project.[55] The venture discovered that Crocker Land, an expansive island thought to have been cited by the explorer Robert Perry in 1906, does not exist. But it went on to yield valuable results about the physical character of the Arctic. Returning to the University in 1917, Ekblaw was named a Staff Fellow of the AGS in order to work up a large quantity of Arctic plant material he had collected. In 1924 he obtained a PhD in geography at Clark University. His publications, scientific papers on the Arctic, and popular accounts of adventures in the Polar North left a valuable record.

In 1916 the Graduate School funded an expedition led by Thomas E. Savage and Francis M. Van Tuyl of the geology department. They received $2,000 to make a detailed study of the sedimentary rocks of Hudson Bay and to secure a collection of fossils as a means of understanding the connections of the ancient seas where the early sediments of the Mississippi Valley had settled, and in a general way to increase knowledge of North America's geological history.[56]

Additional research projects supported by the Graduate School included publication of a valuable Irish document, support of the William G. Irwin expedition, and projects carried on by agriculturists and engineers in the University. Kinley thought it desirable to have some kind of organization that would coordinate all of the campus research activities. Accordingly, in November 1916 he proposed the formation of a University of Illinois Institute of Research. Kinley sought by this means to thwart a concentration of the University's forces in industrial research, the problem-solving priority favored by public opinion. He wished to encourage pure research that would illustrate how fundamental science applied to agriculture and engineering. So, the dean drafted a constitution for the proposed institute. James, the University Senate, and every agency on the campus that engaged in research endorsed the idea. On July 31, 1917, James told the trustees that he hoped to submit a formal recommendation as to the constitution of such an institute at the next board meeting. But the war came and no more was heard of the matter. Kinley's proposal, nevertheless, may be seen as the genesis of an idea that eventually evolved into the University of Illinois Research Park.[57]

Despite the problems of development, from 1906 to 1918 enrollment in the Graduate School steadily increased. While total attendance grew, the number "in absentia" or "absent under leave" decreased. Most of the former consisted of individuals working for professional engineering degrees; the latter were candidates for master's degrees who had fulfilled residence requirements and were now completing theses away from the campus. In 1911 the executive faculty abolished the rule that awarded a master's degree after three years of professional practice, all but ending work in absentia. It replaced the absentia classification with a leave-of-absence policy that allowed students who had completed course requirements to take time off to complete their theses or dissertations. This group consisted mostly of teachers. Women constituted a growing number but a fairly constant proportion (18.3 percent) of all the students from 1906 to 1918. Altogether graduate enrollment expanded from 118 in 1904 to 380 in 1920.[58]

Enrollment figures in the Graduate School exposed interesting demographic patterns. Most of the students came from the state of Illinois, but the proportion gradually decreased. In 1907–1908, for example, 146 of 211 students (69 percent) were living within the state, in 1912–1913 192 of 351 (54.6 percent), and in 1917–1918 241 of 451 (53 percent). The 1907–1908 data showed students from 24 other states, with the largest number from neighboring states. Indiana and Kansas each contributed 6. Five years later students from 38 other states

36   PART I. THE LARGER UNIVERSITY

plus the District of Columbia had enrolled in the Graduate School, with 19 from Indiana, 13 from Ohio, 12 from Missouri, and 11 from Wisconsin. The 1917–1918 figures listed 180 students from 41 other states and the District of Columbia, with Indiana represented by 15, both Ohio and Pennsylvania by 13, Iowa, Michigan, and New York by 12 each, and Missouri by 10.

A trickle of foreign students steadily expanded. In 1907–1908 the Graduate School had one student from Japan. Five years later seven foreign countries made the tally. China and Japan each sent five students. The School in 1914–1915 had 27 graduate students from 12 foreign countries, including the Philippine Islands. In 1917–1918, with the world at war, the list included 23 students from 6 foreign countries. China sent 12 and Japan 6. Classification by institutions reveals that most of the graduate students had received their bachelor's degrees from the University of Illinois. In 1909–1910 the first degree of 135 of the 282 students (47.8 percent) was conferred by Illinois, while the first degrees of the other students came from 74 other colleges and universities. In 1917–1918 those with their first degree from Illinois numbered 182 of 451 (40 percent). The first degrees of the others were granted by 126 other American and 9 foreign colleges and universities.

By 1917–1918 the arts and sciences dominated the Graduate School. Of the 420 graduate students in residence that year, 79.5 percent had enrolled in the arts and sciences, 15 percent in agriculture, and 5.3 percent in engineering. The arts and sciences departments with the largest enrollments ranked as follows: chemistry (74), English (32), education (22), history (18), botany (16), zoology (16), mathematics (13), Romance languages (12), economics (11), and physics (11). Agriculture had its largest enrollments in animal husbandry (19) and agronomy (12). In engineering, civil engineering led with 5, while both mechanical engineering and theoretical and applied mechanics had 4. With the reorganization of the Graduate School in 1907–1908 and growing enrollments, the number of advanced degrees given by the University rose dramatically, from 21 in 1906 to 197 in 1917.[59] From 1912 to 1918 by far the largest number of doctorates (53) awarded by any department came from chemistry. These data indicate that the University of Illinois Graduate School now stood as one of the top twenty in the nation in the number of doctorates granted, but the statistics alone, of course, carry no assurances about the quality of the programs.

• • •

President James viewed the advanced work of the University as its primary work. He skillfully orchestrated a campaign to obtain legislative support for a Graduate School and aggressively promoted its development. David Kinley defined in advance the terms on which he would accept the graduate deanship, and after taking office he resented interference in his control of the advanced work. His penchant for autonomy may have proved limiting on occasion. Kinley had good reason to complain about James's incursions, but despite tensions between these two strong-willed individuals, the president and the dean worked together effectively. They cultivated good relations with the state's private colleges while preserving and developing the undergraduate program at the University. In shifting the emphasis within the University from undergraduate to graduate studies, they played a decisive role in distinguishing the publicly supported state university from the private, church-related colleges of Illinois. Kinley labored hard to create a program of graduate study and research and to correlate it with the undergraduate studies. The Graduate School was the leaven in the lump. It trained young people for careers as teachers and investigators while sponsoring and funding research and publications in the physical and natural sciences, the social sciences, and the humanities. Through the advances in knowledge it fostered, the Graduate School gained recognition for the University as one of the world's major centers for the study of science. That recognition had arrived early under James when Edwin E. Slosson included the University of Illinois in his classic study of 1910, *Great American Universities*. Slosson studied fourteen universities and provided expansive reviews of each. He had come to recognize the rise to prominence of several state institutions, including in California, Michigan, Wisconsin, and Minnesota, in addition to Illinois.

• • •

The events that marked the UofI Graduate School opening included, as mentioned, an address by Dean David Kinley. It's a document worth attention. Kinley meant to make a statement on behalf of the highest form of learning, advanced scholarship, and in no narrow perspective. He wanted to show that what graduate education does promotes the highest interests a nation like the United States might expect from it. That is, it enhances our democratic project. However high and remote from the democratic mass that work may appear, this learning in fact sustains and perfects the democratic ideal, Kinley avowed. The address appeared, slightly expanded possibly, in *Science* magazine, and thus reached a large audience. Its theme recurred often in other documents issued by Illinois academics in the James years.

Kinley knew the objections often made to democracy: it signifies the decay of refinement and taste; it erodes intellectual and spiritual activity; it replaces high culture in all its forms with a low utilitarianism and a vulgar materialism. It demands immediate results and thus conspires against "the prolonged meditation" needed for creativity. Art and poetry and philosophy, these critics said, can rest secure only under the protective care of the rich and well born, an aristocracy that can alone keep alive "the pure love of learning." Kinley considered these views "preposterous" and "ridiculous." And one need only

Cars and people flood the campus for the Commencement exercises of 1915. Courtesy of the University of Illinois Archives.

look at the true habit of the aristocracy—self-indulgence—or the behavior of the wealthy in the financial markets—reckless—to mark the abuses of this class.[60]

Although some democratic enthusiasts, Kinley noted, would reduce our higher education to "bread and butter courses" like those in engineering or agriculture, in fact, it is abstract learning, "pure scholarship," that really does promote the democratic cause. For this form of society—democratic—the dean emphasized, does yield to materialism and marks the measure of success in terms of individual acquisition and private possessions. Culturally, that materialism has a philosophical kinship with positivism and all its arrogant claims to limit true knowledge to observable fact, that is, to material reality alone. That standard disparages the life of imagination, the recourse to abstract ideals, spiritual truth, the reality of a public good, a commonweal, Kinley asserted. He intended to attack these notions head on: "The continued success of a democracy," he urged, "not only permits but requires devotion to the pursuit of the most abstract sciences and the loftiest flights of the imagination as well as to those more concrete subjects whose advance ministers to the immediate prosperity of an individual, a class or a community."[61]

These conditions, Kinley asserted, bear directly on the work of the state universities, our public institutions. The Illinois dean reported reading that an eastern university president had judged these schools, our schools, with their utilitarian ethos, as antagonistic to culture, but useful in giving instruction in practical subjects. But for those studies that involve theoretical work, that deal with "things of the spirit," that encourage intellectual independence from the tyranny of a democratic majority, trust to those universities who grow from the beneficence of private wealth, this critic urged. Kinley would have none of that nonsense. He prescribed for Illinois and all her companion "democratic" public universities a commitment to scholarship "in abstract and purely theoretical" subjects. "Their strongest defense," he said, "lies in the fact that a democracy needs to develop scholarship pure and simple, in the abstract—philology, art, philosophy, history, literature—in order to subserve wants that cannot be satisfied by any other kind of knowledge." They provide the antidote to the trends in democracy that otherwise lead to its "decay."[62]

And why is this so? Because no democracy can endure that rests content with material prosperity. "It must have its ideals, intelligence, honesty, honor," to make safe its "public life," Kinley avowed. And we know from whence these ideals come. "It is to the philosopher, the student of literature, the student of the social sciences, aye, to the poet and the artist as well as to the man with a sense of practical administration, to whom we must turn for proper ideals and correct principles." And these entities must have reinforcement and renewed application from new knowledge, from that kind of scholarship that marks the purposes, the very essence of the modern university. He would go further, for this kind of study especially equips us to deal with our most pressing social challenges. Kinley named them: poverty, corruption in city government, immigration, race, money, and taxation. All require scientific education and moral imagination.[63]

And finally, Kinley concluded, were any proof needed concerning the wonderful comparability of democracy with the highest academic scholarship, note that the people of Illinois, through their elected legislators, had voted to establish the means, a graduate school, for conducting that work.[64]

• • •

This chapter has documented the goals and ambitions of those individuals at Illinois who led in creating the Graduate School and who gave it its structure and regulations. Of course, a university's record in advanced scholarship lies in the research of its faculty. Part II of this book will look at some of that record in its several "Faculty Portraits."

CHAPTER 4

Infrastructure for a Research University

HOW DOES ONE BUILD a research university? Along with great scholars, it needs a support system. It needs buildings and classrooms, laboratories, equipment and supplies of all kinds, and auxiliaries, like museums, concert halls, and art galleries. These items constitute what one might call the infrastructure, the availability and arrangement of all the facilities that help to advance a large academic enterprise. Major earmarks of its development at Illinois will appear in the ensuing narrative. But in this period of American higher education's history, when Edmund James endeavored to lead the University of Illinois into a new era, two institutions were emerging into great significance: the university library and the university press. Both constitute not merely physical props but are properly intellectual in nature. When William Rainey Harper took leadership of the new University of Chicago, his plan for this academic leviathan specified five divisions: the University Proper; University Extension; University Press; University Libraries, Laboratories, and Museums; and University Affiliations.[1] Each campus has its own story to tell, and Illinois has a particularly interesting one because it had a very ambitious president who took a very keen interest in these two hallmarks of the modern university.[2]

* * *

As a young man Edmund James took a doctorate in Germany and spent time there. That experience led him to appreciate the role of universities and libraries in advancing knowledge and public welfare. When he arrived in Urbana he quickly judged the university library inadequate.[3] He made it his mission to create a great university library, and the library's marked growth began soon after James became president. From 1895 to 1905 it had received a total of $85,000 from the legislative appropriation, and under James that number rose significantly. A committee including the president, the librarian, and the deans distributed the funds. The library grew mainly by purchase, with high priority given to sets and continuations. James often suggested items to buy, and he approved the faculty requests for books and journals.[4]

Katharine L. Sharp, a graduate of Melvil Dewey's New York State Library School and a devoted Dewey disciple, became head librarian, professor of library science, and director of the Library School in 1897.[5] Aided by a staff of fifteen, she ran an efficient operation.[6] Sharp had a keen eye for valuable titles. In 1905 she bought part of the library of Karl Dziatzko, the Göttingen University librarian, from a German bookseller for $300. The bibliographical segment, some two hundred and fifty volumes and three hundred pamphlets, contained materials on library science, paleography, history of printing, the book trade, and related materials. By about 1906 nine different buildings housed sixteen separate departmental libraries. But the dedicated Sharp worked beyond the limits of her natural strength, for which she paid the price of nervous exhaustion. She needed a period of complete rest. James approved a leave of absence for her in the summer of 1905 and another in 1906. Then on April 1, 1907, Sharp announced her desire to resign, effective September 1. By that time the library then ranked sixth in size among state university libraries.[7]

On June 10, 1907, Francis K. W. Drury, the former order librarian, became acting head librarian and assistant professor of library science. The son of a Reformed Church minister, Drury had earned Phi Beta Kappa honors as a graduate of the Rutgers classical course. He read Latin, Greek, French, and German; had served as assistant librarian in the Theological Seminary of the Reformed Church at New Brunswick, New Jersey; and had studied one summer in the New York State Library School. In 1905 he received an AM from Rutgers and a BLS from Illinois.[8] Drury published books and articles on library administration and other topics, worked with a staff of over twenty, and had a penchant for order along with a sense of humor. He had joined a group called the Bibliosmiles, who had the motto "Homo sum and then some." Members took seriously everything except themselves.[9] Drury kept meticulous records and submitted detailed reports. He and his staff prepared reference lists for various groups. He himself designed a vertical file that could hold over six thousand maps.[10]

Drury had an annual appropriation of $25,000 for the library, but in 1907–1908 the total expenditure for library purposes rose to $34,714 and a year later to $75,259. In May 1908 Drury reported that the library owned 108,383 bound volumes and 13,079 pamphlets. The following year it gained 18,723 volumes. In addition to these acquisitions, Drury also gathered newspapers. He bought the *London Times* from 1830 to 1903 for $900. When a nearly complete index to it from 1817 to 1903 became available at $350, James vetoed the purchase because even a single missing part, he believed, destroyed

42   PART I. THE LARGER UNIVERSITY

its value—a curious opinion.[11] By late 1907 the library nonetheless owned four or five hundred volumes of newspapers. Then in 1907 the University bought the library of Karl Friedrich Wilhelm Dittenberger, late professor of classical philology at Halle. It covered that subject and contained works in several categories of the Indo-European languages, comparative literature, ancient history, archaeology, history of art and literature, geography, chronology, and works of Greek and Latin poets and authors. Two deans and two classics professors favored the purchase, saying that it would lay the foundation for advanced work in the classics. The trustees authorized up to $2,500 for the purpose.[12] The arrival of the Dittenberger Library marked a high point in collection development. The boxes held about seven thousand titles, which would require a full-time specialist a year and a half to catalog.[13] The University then hired Herbert W. Denio for that purpose. Denio had degrees from Middlebury College and the New York State Library School and considerable library experience as well. He proceeded to catalog in Latin, Greek, French, German, Spanish, and Dutch.[14]

In 1909 the University purchased the library of Moritz Heyne, late professor of German philology at Göttingen. His collection of about 5,200 volumes, strong in philology and comparative literature, contained documents from all periods of German literature as well as German dictionaries from the earliest times. The library was "one of the richest and best collections of its kind brought to this country," according to Illinois professor Julius Goebel. Its acquisition had importance for building a strong graduate Germanics department, a matter of great personal importance to James.[15]

The library could house ninety thousand volumes, but as such could not accommodate a growing institution. So, James and the trustees asked the legislature for $100,000 for additions to the building.[16] The library system included a general library and departmental libraries. In 1908 fourteen departmental libraries held a total of thirteen thousand volumes. Only Architecture and Law had attendants for their departmental libraries. A library staff member visited the others to care for them. Drury in turn urged decentralization of the acquisition process as a means of promoting efficiency. He wanted a librarian of each subject collection who would keep up with the literature and recommend books for purchase. By this means each seminar and departmental library would be a working library under a trained bibliographer. This process would lift from the faculty's shoulders the ordering and care of books, and also assure progress in building collections. Drury used comparative data to plead the case for improvement. In 1909, of the twenty-one college and university libraries in the nation with more than a hundred thousand volumes, he noted, Illinois, though fifth in size of the student body, ranked only nineteenth in holdings. Among state universities, Illinois stood second in number of students but fifth in number of volumes.[17]

4. Infrastructure for a Research University   43

For inexplicable reasons James did not make Drury head librarian. In early 1908 he made a thorough effort to evaluate Phineas L. Windsor for the position. Windsor, born in Chenoa, Illinois, the son of a Methodist minister, had earned a PhB at Northwestern in 1895. There he became a library assistant during his senior year. Windsor graduated from the New York State Library School in 1899 and then attended the Albany Law School while working in the New York State Library. He served as an assistant in the Copyright Office in the Library of Congress from 1900 to 1903, and then relocated to the University of Texas. Letters described Windsor as a first-class librarian, a man of eminently good sense and all-around ability, and a great help to faculty and students.[18]

Windsor visited the University in October 1908. On January 13, 1909, James asked if he would consider an appointment as University librarian and director of the Library School at a salary of $3,000. He would rank as a full professor, hold membership in the University Senate, and guide the Library Committee. Windsor accepted and the board's executive committee authorized the appointment.[19] In his new role, Windsor served two masters. President James was the important one, and he was difficult. The two men differed in temperament and style. James acted aggressively and decisively; Windsor was retiring and lackadaisical. James wrote frequently to Windsor with admonishment when he did not file his reports on time or showed indifference respecting other protocols. Further, a large "misunderstanding" emerged over Windsor's title. He wanted James to honor what he understood as James's promise that Windsor have "full professor status." But James did not recommend Windsor to the board for promotion to that status. James told Windsor that he enjoyed all the privileges of professorial "rank" but not that title. The president acted disingenuously here. Nonetheless, he and Windsor did work well together, and James did appoint him to important University committees. Windsor gained distinction among American librarians, winning election to the American Library Association Council in 1913. He became president of the Illinois Library Association and a fellow of the American Library Institute.[20]

Windsor's other master was the Senate Library Committee. As secretary of this committee and the Committee on Apportionment of Library Funds, Windsor had a large voice in the distribution of the library's money. In these positions he earned the confidence of the faculty. Windsor was master in his own domain. When he arrived, the library contained 127,106 volumes and was growing at the rate of nearly 30,000 volumes a year. It had a staff of two dozen plus several student assistants and departments titled Order, Catalog, Reference, Loan, and Binding. Windsor's own principality included both the general library and the departmental libraries. But the loan practice tended to make them circulating libraries. Faculty members checked out books and did

44   PART I. THE LARGER UNIVERSITY

not hasten to return them. Some questioned whether having the same books in two places made sense.[21]

The civil service system complicated Windsor's task. Apart from heads of library departments and student assistants, staff members gained appointment under rules of the State Civil Service Commission. The library drew up a requisition describing the qualifications for the available position. Applicants took an examination prepared and graded by the Library School; the names of those who passed went on the commission's eligibility list. James feared that the list included many "ignoramuses" and that Windsor could do no more than select the best of the lot. Windsor found it especially difficult to employ catalogers, who needed a working knowledge of Greek and Latin or of one or two modern foreign languages, plus a general education at least equal to that of a college graduate. Knowing that he could not likely get a suitable cataloger via the civil service system, Windsor once appointed two students instead. Moreover, civil service rules made it difficult to reward good work or penalize poor work.[22] The civil service system certified fitness at the time of appointment and protection of the employee after appointment. Certification assured competency for certain grades of service but provided no protection of the employee. But it did protect libraries against the unfit, Windsor asserted.[23]

Low salaries posed an obstacle to staff recruitment and retention. In 1913 Windsor reported on an analysis of the income and expenditures of ten women staff members who averaged twenty-eight years old. Nine had bachelor's degrees, all had at least one year of training in library school and many had more, and their library experience ranged from one to five years. Their average annual income came to only $744, while their average annual living expenses came to $770. The women had to rely on others for financial aid or leave for better-paying jobs, Windsor testified.[24] These details illustrated some unintended consequences of Melvil Dewey's feminization of the library profession. Educated women became librarians because they had access to few other jobs. The problem did not pertain to Illinois alone.

Providing library service posed a continuing challenge. In 1912, for example, faculty in the science departments urged that the Natural History Library remain open evenings. Henry B. Ward, head of the zoology department, thought that faculty and graduate students would be likely to use it then, but he opposed opening it to undergraduates in the evening, fearing that they "might interfere with the more necessary use of the books for research work." Windsor, for his part, had no doubt that this library should stay open evenings. James, realizing "the scientific value" of the proposition, said he would try to find the necessary funding.[25] That same year David Kinley complained that it had taken three people about three hours to find current data on the rate of taxation; the task should have taken one person half an hour. The library

4. Infrastructure for a Research University   45

did not keep its public documents up to date, Kinley complained. Cataloging had delays, and researchers could not readily access the material. Perhaps the library lacked sufficient money or staff and the causes may lie beyond the control of any individual, Kinley ventured. Nevertheless, the experience occurred too often. "In fact, I have personally long ago given up expecting to get much help from the library," he lamented. But he was not criticizing Windsor, who was doing as well, with the means at his disposal, as anyone could, Kinley believed.[26]

The library's collections grew by gift, by exchange, and by purchase. Windsor presided over routine collection development, while James devoted himself to special acquisitions. In practice the lines intermixed. Although gifts were a matter of circumstance, the library acquired much material without cost or in exchange. Windsor made systematic efforts to secure more or less ephemeral literature likely to be more important for research than books published for sale.[27] He sent form letters requesting material related to churches and missionary societies, commerce and transportation, economics, education, labor conditions, money and banking, politics and government, social betterment, taxation and public finance, and trade unions.[28] James urged Windsor to acquire official documents at no cost and told Windsor how to get free material.[29]

Windsor was willing to purchase telephone directories of cities of Illinois and elsewhere if he thought patrons would use them. He paid close attention to newspapers, especially Illinois papers, and to American newspapers published in foreign languages. Around 1912 he purchased Ohio newspapers of the 1830s to the 1850s, and in 1915 he acquired twelve boxes of Cincinnati newspapers that the Cincinnati Public Library wished to dispose of.[30]

Often with faculty prompting, the head of the Exchange Division sent form letters to chambers of commerce, charitable institutions, colleges and normal schools, counties with large cities, directors of May Festivals, horticultural societies, hospitals, museums, newspapers, American cities over twenty thousand in population, English, Scottish, and Welsh cities over fifty thousand, YWCAs, and miscellaneous organizations asking for their material.[31] In this way Windsor and his staff assembled a collection of municipal documents. By 1915 the library had 6,416 volumes and 10,340 pamphlets of this material.[32] The library used about a dozen University publications for exchange purposes. They included the annual catalog, bulletins issued by academic units, doctoral dissertations, reports of the Board of Trustees, *University Studies*, and the *Journal of English and German Philology*. The library tried to secure a near equivalent in return for most exchanges. These exchanges, and the gifts, enlarged the collection. From 1909–1910 to 1919–1920 the library acquired 169,322 continuations and separates by gift and exchange, an annual average of 15,393 items. During this period, it also arranged 1,490 new exchanges,

46   PART I. THE LARGER UNIVERSITY

an average of 135 a year. It received 30,780 gift and exchange periodicals, an annual average of 2,798.[33]

According to Windsor, the library had no systematic plan for acquiring books as they came on the market. Instead, it made most purchases with a view to the needs of some academic course or research project. When a faculty member needed books for research, the Library Committee sent the applicant to the Graduate School for financial aid. If it validated the project's worth, the library bought the desired books. In helping those doing research, Windsor explained, the library incidentally built up a great research collection. Some faculty members and departments got the books they wanted, said Windsor, while others objected to the practice.[34]

In 1911 James took a new tack and began to enlist ethnic and religious groups to contribute material relating to their history and culture. This effort may have had its origins in October, when Isaac Kuhn of Champaign, the city's largest clothing retailer, sent the University $25 on behalf of District Grand Lodge No. 6 of the Independent Order of B'nai B'rith and asked that David S. Blondheim of the Romance languages department use the money to purchase books of Jewish interest for the library. He intended the check as an earnest of things to come, he said. James thanked the donors and added that he hoped to get a large number of Jewish people interested in developing a library of Jewish history and civilization at the University, contending that because of the debt that European civilization and religion owed to its Jewish counterparts, nothing of interest to the Jew could fail to have interest to the Christian. Thus, in building up such a center at the University, James asserted, the Jews would not only be magnifying their own calling but contributing to a greater appreciation of the part they had played in world history. In May 1912 Kuhn sent James a check for $500 on behalf of the IOBB. With it Blondheim would buy books for the B'nai B'rith Library of Jewish Literature.[35]

In July the board authorized James to appoint a commission on Jewish-American history and culture with the purpose of devising ways and means of increasing the University collections bearing on the subject of Jewish-American history and culture and to promote the interest of the University and the public in the subject. The board also authorized a commission on German-American history and culture, whereupon James announced his intention to appoint commissions on Dutch, French, Hungarian, Irish, Polish, Scandinavian, and Slavic elements in America.[36] James intended these commissions to stimulate interest in the study of the various ethnic and national groups in the schools and in the public, to collect materials bearing on these groups in the University library, to assist in the scientific investigation of these materials, and to publish and diffuse the results of the research among members of educational institutions and the public.[37] In all these actions James gave another revealing illustration of what he meant by the scientific culture of the modern university—eclectic, diverse, and expansive in its intellectual outreach.

James wanted as commission members individuals prominently identified with their ethnic groups in the nation's leading cities. Thus, with careful calculations he invited Charles J. Hexamer of Philadelphia, president of the National German American Alliance of the United States, to help select the American members of this commission. Working through intermediaries, he tried to secure Kaiser Wilhelm II, no less, as a member of the German-American commission.[38] James also invited Andrew Carnegie to serve on the Scottish-American commission; Carnegie's secretary declined on his behalf. The president also tried to interest Julius Rosenwald and Julian Mack to take a place on the Jewish-American commission. He did persuade Governor Edward Dunne to become chairman of the Irish-American commission.[39]

Along with his domestic efforts, James began buying foreign libraries. In 1912, while in Germany, he acquired the Gröber collection in Romance philology. Gustav Gröber, professor of Romance philology at the University of Strasbourg, ranked as one of the leading Romance scholars in the world. Widely known as editor of the *Zeitschrift für romanische Philologie* and of the *Grundriss der romanischen Philologie*, commonly referred to as Gröber's *Grundriss*, he had won renown for the encyclopedic breadth of his interests. Gröber died in late 1911. His widow offered his library of 6,367 volumes and pamphlets, one particularly valuable for Provencal and Italian linguistics, to Illinois. Jean Baptiste Beck of the Romance languages department at Illinois had been one of Gröber's favorite students, and the widow preferred to entrust the collection to him rather than to a book seller. James purchased the library while in Germany, apparently for 10,000 marks ($2,500).[40]

Also, while in Berlin that year, James had made a careful study of the library of the University of Berlin, which he called the greatest university in the world. The Royal Library and the University of Berlin library together (essentially one) had more than 1.5 million books, he wrote, augmented by twelve departmental and special libraries connected to the university. In addition, government departments located in Berlin had their special collections. As a result, within twenty-five miles of the city hall, scholars had access to five million volumes.[41]

This experience appears to have shaped James's notion as to what he must do to build a great library at Illinois. On June 7, 1912, he laid his views before the trustees. They deserve close attention. No part of a university had greater fundamental necessity than the university library, James began. A great library would under favorable conditions become a great university. But the Illinois library lacked what it needed for its purposes. Comparative data showed its great inferiority to libraries of universities located near other substantial library collections, including those in Berlin and other European cities. Illinois trailed

48   PART I. THE LARGER UNIVERSITY

not only Harvard, Yale, Columbia, and Chicago, but also Cornell, Michigan, Wisconsin, Pennsylvania, Princeton, California, and Brown. The University could not hope to take its place among the great institutions of the world, James insisted, until it had much larger library facilities. The University should look forward to the accumulation of at least a million books as rapidly as possible. Furthermore, the housing of such a collection would require a new building.

James went on. More prospective faculty members at Illinois, he said, had turned down job offers for lack of library facilities than for any other reason. He had asked Windsor and the Library Committee to prepare a statement showing how much money they could wisely devote each year to buying and cataloging books. Then James wanted the trustees to accept this sum as that which the University ought to specify in its budget until the collection numbered at least a million volumes. Library facilities reflected a fundamental distinction between American and European universities, James concluded. One reason why American scholarship had limped along so far behind European scholarship lay in the lack of inspiration and assistance that was afforded by great book collections.[42] Finally, after speaking to the board, James asked the Faculty Senate to create a special committee to study the problems involved in library development. Windsor chaired the committee.[43]

In January 1913 Governor Dunne, in addressing the General Assembly, reiterated James's views, and his language. Although the library had grown rapidly in recent years, Dunne said, compared with the libraries of other great universities it wholly lacked for its purposes. To become a true center of higher educational interests, the library needed to accumulate a million volumes as a basis for future development. The present building should be replaced with a fire-proof one that would reflect the dignity and wealth of Illinois and furnish a model to sister states.[44]

On October 30, 1914, James addressed an overflow student audience in the Auditorium. His remarks on "The Present and Future of the University of Illinois" demonstrated his passion about the potential greatness of the University. The library contained sixty thousand volumes ten years ago, James said, and three hundred thousand as he spoke. But this growth marked only a beginning. "We must have a library to begin with of at least a million, and when we have a library of two million it will only be a fair beginning, and when it is four or five million, as it must be if it is going to serve our purposes, it will have become one of the great libraries of the world."[45]

From 1912–1913 to 1918–1919, the leading American libraries, in number of volumes held, were Harvard, Yale, Columbia, Cornell, Chicago, Pennsylvania, Princeton, and Michigan. Illinois was in tenth place in 1912–1913 and 1913–1914; in ninth place in 1915–1916; and then in eighth place for three years. The expenditure for books at Illinois during these years averaged $58,626 a year, making Illinois second only to Harvard. The staff at Illinois in this period averaged just over fifty persons a year, making it about the third largest of all the university library staffs.[46]

Individual donors also added immeasurably to the library collections. In 1915, for example, historian Evarts B. Greene presented 219 volumes of books and newspapers from the library of his father, Daniel C. Greene, a missionary in Japan from 1869 to 1913. Of the 219 volumes, 46 constituted a file of the *Japan Weekly Mail* of Yokohama from July 1890 to 1913. Most of the books in the collection were in the Japanese language and old and rare.[47]

In 1915 President James gave the library 1,030 bound volumes and 1,145 pamphlets relating to statistics and similar subjects. He named the gift the Carl Martin James Collection in honor of his son (1881–1885).[48] He also donated an illuminated parchment manuscript containing sixty-six folios. Arthur S. Pease of the classics department described it as Latin translations by Aretino of several works of Aristotle on ethics. For these extremely rare books, beautifully printed in Bologna between 1474 and 1476, Pease suggested the title *Aristotelis Ethica Aliaque*. James had the incunabulum bound in dark blue morocco.[49] The next year President James presented to the University 1,732 more bound volumes and a large quantity of pamphlets relating to history, economics, politics, and education in memory of his mother, to whose inspiration he professed to owe whatever interest he had in these subjects. He designated the gift as the Amanda K. Casad Collection.[50] Also in 1916 the Committee on Apportionment asked the trustees to authorize placing an order for about 12,500 pages of manuscripts being held by a Leipzig dealer for Professor Albert H. Lybyer. The manuscripts, dealing with the period 1570–1770, illustrated the relation of Venice and the Ottoman Empire, and Venice and her Levantine possessions with descriptions of life in the Levant. The price was likely to be $2,255, the bill to be paid from the library appropriation for 1916–1917. The purchase was made. "Venetian Manuscript Documents: Originals and Transcripts of the 16th, 17th, and 18th Centuries" now occupy over six feet of shelf space in the Rare Book and Special Collections Library.

In 1916 James sent Windsor a catalog of books relating to Ireland, suggesting that they could use part of the money that the Fellowship Foundation gave the University to enlarge the Irish collection. The catalog may have described the library of James Collins, a Dubliner with an intimate knowledge of Irish history. A book lover, Collins had collected about 7,000 volumes on Irish history, topography, biography, and antiquities, including 127 volumes of newspaper cuttings dealing mainly with the nineteenth century, 139 volumes of bound and 2,590 unbound pamphlets relating to Irish affairs, about 90 Irish maps and plans, and 3,700 selections from Irish magazines. The collection had particular strength in nineteenth-century political and religious history, especially the history of Presbyterianism and Methodism and some rare

50   PART I. THE LARGER UNIVERSITY

Catholic biographical literature. The University bought the Collins Collection in 1917, apparently for $4,289.[51] Gertrude Schoepperle of the English department was then the sole faculty member identified with Celtic and Irish studies at Illinois. New accessions prompted James to advise Windsor to follow the example of the University of Wisconsin and get out a booklet describing the various valuable collections at the University of Illinois.[52] Windsor apparently did not heed the advice.

American entry into the world war in 1917 challenged the library. Knowing that the delivery of periodicals from Europe would face interruptions by the hostilities and wanting to ensure that the library would have complete sets of them, Windsor received permission to pay the book agent Stechert in advance for German and Austrian serials to be delivered after the war so long as the agent was under bond to do so.[53] But the library did make efforts also to address the demands of the war at home. It arranged for some two hundred books dealing with the war and its peripheral issues to be available, by display on special tables, to faculty and students, and to the numerous servicemen in the area.[54]

In August 1918 the University purchased the library of Julius Doerner, an eccentric book collector and antiquarian who had assembled in his Library Clearing House at 633 Wells Street, in an area called the Bowery of Chicago, a collection of books, pamphlets, early newspapers and periodicals, and art works. When he died in 1916 the administrator of his estate apparently sold a large mass of unbound materials as scrap paper, putting the remainder, over fifty thousand books and considerable art work, on sale. The catalog classified over thirty subjects, including newspapers, periodicals relating to American history, and nearly six hundred rare books and pamphlets. James authorized $5,000 for everything listed in the catalog. Uncrating and cataloging the material in more than three hundred cases took several years.[55]

To conclude, Katharine Sharp and Francis Drury placed the library on solid foundations, directing it in an orderly and efficient manner while making some important acquisitions. Their efforts did not suffice for President James, who was determined to create a great library as part of a great university. He made Phineas Windsor his collaborator in that venture. James mounted a campaign to gather materials for the collection while negotiating with foreigners to buy entire libraries. Windsor's great contribution lay in his ability to bring the administration, faculty, and staff together to help realize the goal James envisioned.[56]

In 1919 James went on leave of absence owing to ill health. A year later he resigned as president. At that time the Illinois library held 440,372 volumes, the ninth largest university library in the country. Only Harvard, Yale, Columbia, Cornell, Chicago, Pennsylvania, Princeton, and Michigan outranked it.[57] It contained such treasures as the libraries of Johannes Vahlen, a classical philologist at the University of Berlin, and that of Dittenberger, also in that field, at Halle. James also added the Rudolph Aron library in pedagogy, supplementing the Heyne Collection in German philology and literature, the Gröber Collection in Romance philology, the Collins Collection in Irish studies, the Venetian Manuscript Documents, the Ratterman and Doerner collections in American-related materials, and the Cavagna-Sangiuliani Library. This achievement represented one part of James's overall determination to transform the University of Illinois into a great American university. Indeed, his unrelenting quest and hard negotiations for big-ticket acquisitions mark a distinguishing feature of James's presidency at Illinois. It makes him a standout as well among his presidential peers in the early twentieth century.[58]

• • •

The University of Illinois Press became a vital institutional force slowly and gradually. Early in its history the University published titles related to the functioning of the educational enterprise, for example, the college newspaper and the *Weekly Calendar*. The University could greatly benefit itself, President James said in 1905, by publishing a record of alumni. The board authorized $1,500 toward this expense.[59] The *Alumni Record*, published the next year, 710 pages long with inserts on miscellaneous aspects of the University, also had a directory of alumni associations.[60] Fifteen hundred copies of the book appeared. Because this work proved successful, on July 15, 1912, the trustees appropriated $5,000 to print and publish a new edition.[61]

While the authorities produced this work, David Kinley, dean of the Graduate School, wished to do more. The University, he believed, should publish the results of faculty research. In 1906, at his urging, the trustees appropriated $1,200 per annum to cover the cost of producing *University Studies*. The board authorized inclusion of a bulletin by Professor Harry S. Grindley on the methods of roasting meat. *University Studies* met a need. It later appeared in three series—Social Sciences, Biological Monographs, and Studies in Language and Literature. In 1908, on Kinley's recommendation, the University bought and took over publication of the *Journal of English and Germanic Philology*. In 1915 Dean Kinley recommended that the University issue an edition of 150 copies of *Speculum Regale* at an estimated cost of $2,200. Laurence M. Larson of the history faculty had translated one of the main works of Norwegian medieval literature, titling it *The King's Mirror*. An educational text from around 1250, it dealt with politics and morality and was intended for the king's education. It had much interest for linguistics, but the facsimile manuscript also had importance historically. "It would seem likely to add to the scientific reputation of the University," James observed. The board approved the appropriation of $2,200 from Graduate School Funds for printing *Speculum Regale*.[62]

52   PART I. THE LARGER UNIVERSITY

President James made expansion of the library a high priority in bringing about the modern University of Illinois and enjoyed much success in the effort. Illinoisans will recognize this building today as Altgeld Hall, so renamed in 1941. Courtesy of the University of Illinois Archives.

Dean Kinley advocated strongly for research and publication, many faculty members yearned to publish, and President James favored learned publications and a university press. Accordingly, in 1910 he brought Harrison E. Cunningham to the University. Born in Hoosick Falls, New York, in 1877, Cunningham graduated from the University of Vermont in 1904. In 1906, he became an instructor in French and German and editor of the college catalog and monthly alumni publications at the University of Vermont. At Illinois, he served as assistant registrar and editor of the college catalog and the biennial reports of the Board of Trustees, and he indexed the minutes of the board. Cunningham had mainly editing assignments but he chaired the committees charged with discussing a university press.

On July 2, 1913, the trustees authorized James to submit a plan for a University of Illinois Press, which should take over as rapidly as possible the printing and publishing of University documents. In October James received an appropriation of $15,000 for a "printing outfit." However, a university press held only secondary priority in his mind at this time. For years, though, several academic departments had urged establishing such an enterprise. Belatedly heeding this advice, James appointed a Committee on University Press chaired by Cunningham and including Frank Scott, C. Stanley Sale, W. B. Castenholz, and H. F. Harrington. Scott was a prominent faculty member and former student editor of the *Daily Illini*. Sale was an instructor in civil engineering, Castenholz an instructor in accounting and the University Comptroller, Harrington an assistant professor of journalism. The latter three had lately come to the University. No doubt James counted on Cunningham and Scott to deliver the results he desired. Reporting on May 6, 1916, the committee recommended that the University Press fulfill a three-fold function: to provide a laboratory for the training and instruction of students in the Curriculum in Journalism; to handle all university printing; and to establish a publishing department for issuing and distributing on a commercial basis various scientific publications containing information of interest and value to the public.[63] The committee also considered expenses. A building adequate to accommodate all of the functions of a printing establishment, it calculated, would cost about $75,000, the equipment about $25,000, and furniture and fixtures $10,000. The total cost: about $110,000.[64]

With the prospect now of available funds, the committee recommended purchasing the lot facing Sixth Street immediately behind Dean Davenport's residence on Wright Street, for $6,500 as the site for a University Press building. The lot measured 84.5 feet wide and 174.25 feet deep. The building would house all or part of the courses in journalism, the print shop, University publications, and the University Press. The Comptroller had authority to purchase the lot for the purposes recommended. The trustees approved the recommendation.[65] In early January 1917 Cunningham and James discussed

54   **PART I. THE LARGER UNIVERSITY**

the so-called printing establishment. Kinley apparently offered objections that are not a matter of record.

In connection with University publications, Kinley, as a member of the Council of Administration, asserted that he would not bear responsibility for the present organization and administration of the Illini Publication Company, designed to assume ownership of all University publications, including student journalism. The whole tendency of that organization and its administration, he charged, was to take out of the hands of the council any control over the *Daily Illini*, the campus newspaper. Kinley did not believe that it lay within the authority of the council to surrender this control. The Board of Control had not succeeded in securing an editorial management loyal to the University.[66] These objections were vintage Kinley.

In 1918, with matters falling into place, President James requested authority to organize a University of Illinois Press as soon as circumstances made it convenient. For several years, he explained, the parties involved had been discussing the organization of a University Press to take over gradually the entire work of printing and publishing done by the University through its various departments. He now forecast important savings and a more efficient organization of the publishing work of the University. There had been two or three committees at different times reporting on this subject, James added, and in general the project had had the approval of the trustees. When he finished his statement, the trustees authorized him to organize the University of Illinois Press with a director and the requisite staff.[67] Thus, at last, after faltering movements in this direction, the University of Illinois Press became a reality.

The *Annual Register* for 1919–1920 listed a number of University publications available for sale or free distribution. The document named eight departments or units and the number of items totaled twenty-four. In addition, the press had published twelve named books.[68] The Press's first book had the title *Sixteen Years at the University of Illinois: A Statistical Study of the Administration of President Edmund J. James*. Published in 1920, the book identified itself as the inaugural Press publication. Its preface, by James, had the date of April 2, 1920. The book described various University activities and contained eighteen illustrations and vast statistical compilations. The frontispiece featured a portrait of President James in academic robe, from a painting by Ralph Clarkson. James had suggested that Cunningham might include it. The president had never lacked a sense of self-worth.

By the time this book appeared, James's health had collapsed. He had received the leave of absence from which he did not return. He had counted on holding out over one more session of the legislature when he could see the University Press fairly launched, he wrote to Cunningham. He had faith in the University of Illinois, and wished his ally "the utmost success in your present function. The University of Illinois Press is destined to be one of the

4. Infrastructure for a Research University **55**

greatest Presses in the country [and] if you measure up to the full stature of a Director of such an enterprise—as I believe you will—you will rank among the great printers of the country. Put the imprint 'University of Illinois Press' in every worthy publication including all that is printed outside and you will be surprised at the way in which it mounts up. I shall follow your career with much interest. I shall be glad to receive a copy of everything you publish."[69]

James and Cunningham are closely identified with the creation of the University of Illinois Press. In addition to his quarter-century as secretary of the Board of Trustees, Cunningham had served as editor and business manager of University publications. In 1918 he became the director of the University of Illinois Press. In June 1920 he received an inquiry from William F. M. Goss, president of the Railway Car Manufacturers' Association in New York, about a position there.[70] He declined the opportunity. Cunningham remained active at Illinois for many more years.[71]

• • •

University presses enable scholars to publish the results of their research, and one might ask where Illinois stood in the establishment of university presses. Johns Hopkins (1878) led, followed by Pennsylvania (1890), Chicago (1891), Columbia (1893), Princeton (1905), Yale (1908), and Harvard (1913). Illinois followed in 1918. Illinois thus pioneered among the state-supported universities. Other midwestern universities stood in the following order: Minnesota (1925), Michigan (1930), Wisconsin (1936), Indiana (1950), Ohio State (1957), Purdue (1960), and Iowa (1969). Northwestern, a private university, established a press in 1959.

CHAPTER 5

The Intellectual World
of Edmund J. James

THE PREVIOUS CHAPTERS have documented the presidential leadership of Edmund James in key aspects of the University of Illinois's history. Part II of this book will focus on particular departments and programs. This chapter is a good place to look at James and the larger intellectual world that influenced him and which he engaged in advancing his academic and administrative career. James embraced no one doctrine or orthodoxy. Instead, he drew upon a number of intellectual currents and forged from them a vision that helps us to understand what he was doing at Illinois. It informs us of attitudes and perspectives that governed the way he developed the various academic units and also of how he saw the UofI and the American state universities in general—their place within the democratic ideals of the nation and the social and economic reforms that he ardently championed, and the model of citizenship that he wanted them to encourage. Altogether they describe a leader who merits larger attention in our histories of American higher education.

The earliest influence, of course, came from his Methodist minister father, Colin James. Chapter 1 observed the moral and theological commitments of an energetic circuit-rider and evangelical. But Methodism found a place within a larger religious movement, pietism. It had its explosive beginnings in Germany and grew into other outlets—the Wesleyan revival in England and Methodism in America, as mentioned; Moravianism; and the Great Awakening in the American colonies. Its ur-document came from Philipp Jakob Spener, his *Pia Desideria*, in 1675. Pietism reacted against cold rationalism, Lutheran scholasticism, and church formalism, and it emphasized a turn inward, to feelings and private devotion. It effected, as Claude Welch puts it, "an internalization of truth." Nonetheless, pietism in Germany claimed an important academic outpost. Frederick III in Brandenburg embraced pietism and helped make the University of Halle, with the work of August Hermann

Francke, a theological center of the movement.[1] To this university, many years later, came the young Edmund James.

At Francke's time Halle constituted but one of a sizeable number of German universities. Leipzig, Wittenberg, Tübingen, Heidelberg, Frankfort, Marburg, Königsberg, and Jena numbered among them. They all had state support and all promoted the orthodox Lutheranism of Philip Melanchthon. Halle opened in 1694 and Göttingen in 1737. These latter bore the hopes of many Germans who judged the generality of the universities static if not moribund. The school attracted intellectual progressives who disdained rigid confessionalism and, in addition, Halle gave considerable autonomy to professors. The ruling Hohenzollerns had modernizing ambitions and Halle's offerings now extended to subjects like statecraft, economics, and public administration.[2] Also at Halle, Francke introduced the seminar, a major step in the long path toward the modern research university, in which the Germans led. The seminar reflected the new post-Enlightenment spirit of *Wissenschaft*. The German states, like the rest of Europe, had inherited a methodology for the discovery of truth, in any area of learning, perpetuated from Scholastic-Aristotelian logic, the "clear ordering of arguments." But in the seminar, with fewer people than in the lecture halls, "criticism was encouraged, knowledge was regarded as mutable, less fixed, and new knowledge was there to be discovered." *Wissenschaft* often suggested the character of knowledge as evolving, growing, or emerging, not permanent or static.[3]

Halle had always held an important place in the history of the German universities. From its evangelical beginning it had moved into the era of rational Enlightenment, led by Christian Wolff, who propounded an influential natural theology. His *Reasonable Thoughts* received wide study in all the Protestant universities. Wolff taught at Halle from 1707 to 1728, when the emperor dismissed him. But he returned at the call of Frederick the Great in 1740. Wolff's rationalism, by the end of the century, yielded to philosophical idealism, flourishing at Jena mostly, and Halle, but relocating with its major thinkers to Berlin, as Halle closed during the French occupation. In his noted early study of the German universities Friedrich Paulsen wrote: "To Halle belongs the glory of being the first really modern university, for it was here that the *libertas philosophandi* on which the modern university rests, the principle of untrammeled investigation and untrammeled teaching, first took firm root." But for James Halle had another significance. Here as a student, he could observe how this old city was making the adjustments to the new industrial age in which it now found itself. Germany, time and time again hereafter, provided James the comparative basis for his studies of American cities and their municipal governments.[4]

But more than structural changes and more than subject expansion explain the exciting rise to prominence of the German universities, and their appeal to young Americans like James. The institutional histories all took place within a large intellectual context—German romanticism and its flourishing in the very late eighteenth and early nineteenth centuries. Hence, according to Peter Watson, the significance of the "theoretical innovations, the philosophical and spiritual rejuvenation" at these places. The German faculty sought a new creative dimension for their work and derived the inspiration for that quest from leading philosophers, soon to appear here. "Knowledge" took on a new meaning, seen not as mere facts, but, as Wilhelm von Humboldt put it, "drawn forth from the depths of the mind. Everything must be developed toward an ideal." "Science," *Wissenschaft*, and *Naturphilosophie* ("the scientific branch of [philosophical] idealism") signified an expansive, often intuitive grasp of the whole, the accumulation of individual facts building toward a comprehensive cognizance of being in its holistic dimensions. German thinkers wanted to overcome the limitations, as they saw them, of British empiricism, including Scottish realism, and the pretensions of Continental rationalism.[5]

Immanuel Kant effected the Copernican revolution that so profoundly influenced the ideologies of the German universities. His *Critique of Pure Reason* (1781) and *Critique of Practical Reason* (1788) constituted two of the formative works that his German successors pondered and contested for years afterwards. In taking on the great epistemological questions of what can the mind know and what may we say is "real," Kant sought to reconcile empiricism and rationalism. His conclusion, as summarized by A. C. Grayling: our minds receive the data of experience, external sensation, and impose on them an organizing structure that makes the world appear to us as it does. In this process, the organizing structure utilizes an apparatus of *a priori* concepts (or "forms of intuition") that Kant described, and in a manner that gives us our "experience." (Space, time, and causality play the most critical roles among the twelve forms of intuition.) This organizing process is the work of what's called the Understanding. Kant thus gave a vast and critical power to the mind in making the world in which it functioned. At the same time, however, Kant restricted our knowledge to sense-data; we have no access to any *possible* realm of existence transcendent to the empirical world. Kant laid the basis for the likely existence of such a reality—the sphere of God, morality, freedom (or non-causality)—but did not legitimate any of the claims of theology or the dictates of independent and absolute moral truth. But we have an access through Reason (intuition). Thus lay Kant's modest philosophical idealism, the idea that reality is mental. But his successors wanted to go where Kant would not.[6]

The Kantian system soon dominated the German universities. Students from the principalities and from abroad came to study Kant. And Kant inspired in another manner, through his 1798 publication, *Streit der Fakultätaten*. He offered here a brief for the privileges of the faculty, including complete

5. The Intellectual World of Edmund J. James   59

academic freedom. While much of the faculty served the state and thus had a practical function, philosophy had no utilitarian role, Kant explained. It existed only to pursue knowledge everywhere, and the philosophical faculty (which included the sciences and humanities generally) existed only to protect "the interests of science," that is, science as embracing "all parts of knowledge" with no domain off limits to the philosophy faculty. The philosophers proper should keep watch over the rest of the faculty, upholding the standards of Reason.[7]

Kant's successors in philosophical idealism gave even more thought than he did to the purposes of the university. When Louis Menand and his colleagues sought to identify and anthologize the key documents that mark the beginnings of the research university idea and its later history, they began in Germany. And they looked to the philosophers—Schleiermacher, Fichte, and Schelling.[8]

Friedrich Schleiermacher, a profoundly influential theologian in nineteenth-century Europe, had academic appointments at Halle and Berlin. And he held emphatic views of the university ideal and its particular German idiom. Schleiermacher wrestled with the Kantian system and molded it for his purposes into a theology of subjectivity based on empirical realities.[9] Schleiermacher spoke forcefully for the organic character of all knowledge, a principle shared by all the idealist philosophers, and applied idealistic philosophy to make that idea the essential goal of the modern university. In the realm of knowledge, he wrote, everything is "interdependent and interconnected." The work of scholars, however, necessarily means isolation and detachment from others. These latter have a passion for a part of knowledge and talents for pursuing it. But "only someone who sees the bigger picture" can bring together "all that seems to be divided." The scholar, Schleiermacher urged, must move beyond "the mere accumulation of knowledge." That effort entails the application of "a systematical philosophical spirit," and herein operates "the highest consciousness of Reason." Schleiermacher insisted on speculation as critical to true philosophical, or "scientific" thinking. He idealized the instruction in philosophy as providing the intellectual temperament and habits of thinking for all the rest of the university. "Philosophical instruction is the basis for everything that takes place in the university," he urged. Schleiermacher wanted religion also to embrace this thinking and become "scientific."[10] He thus influenced a movement away from creeds and toward the more open standards of the liberal Protestantism that would have its golden age later in the century.[11]

Johann Gottlieb Fichte also gave philosophical grounding to the new model German university. One of the most important of the post-Kantians,[12] Fichte became the first rector of the University of Berlin, albeit with but a brief tenure there. He, like the other idealist thinkers, saw the university as in need of

60 PART I. THE LARGER UNIVERSITY

intellectual and spiritual rejuvenation. Too much mechanical instruction and rote learning plagued the institutions, he asserted. Professors now needed to take on the task of improving the existing knowledge in their fields. An education "truly scholarly and scientific" was needed. And once again the latter adjective referenced anything but a narrow empiricism. Fichte urged cultivation of a "consciousness" for academic study by the students and teachers, and he celebrated "scholarly reason." He described that habit as denoted by a progression, by which learning, factual at first, moves to a large, holistic awareness of life. The learner will gain a vision, an intuitive power, and thus "a view of reality that can see beyond mere reality." Nobody could script philosophical idealism (to the disdain of many critics) more unabashedly than Fichte (and colleague Schelling). Fichte writes: "But let us carry on, each striving bravely toward his own goal: someday we will come together and each enter fully into the other's domain, for every part, true only in itself, is part of a great, eternal whole, which is revealed only with the fusing together of the individual parts." Further, "[the scholar] will someday live a life rooted solely in the ideal; he will view, shape, and organize reality solely from that standpoint." Fortified by legions of others with lives so transformed, the intellectual awakening will defeat the "almost universal commercialism" that imperils us now, Fichte asserted. Idealism, indeed![13]

But from another source idealism emerges as a virtual program for the entire university enterprise. Friedrich Schelling, "one of the three towering figures of German idealism," published his *The Method of University Study* in 1803. He had secured his first professorship at Jena, already "a hotbed of post-Kantian philosophy and dissent from Enlightenment rationalism."[14] Schelling began on now familiar ground, citing "the organic whole of all sciences," wherein, for educational purposes, mastery in one discipline requires moving into "the harmonious structure of the whole." This "dissolution of the particular into the universal," this *Wissenschaftlehre* in Fichte's famous coinage, Schelling added, moves us to pure knowledge, or knowledge of the Absolute. And hereby we attain the highest reality: "there is no other reality beyond it," for the Absolute constitutes "the highest premise of knowledge; it is primarily knowledge itself," and pure Reason. This is all heady stuff, but one can detect in it the disdain Schelling and the other German thinkers had for mere factual knowledge and the rival claims of practical education. Philosophy had his highest recommendation because "it was not good . . . for practical purposes." But it is "good for waging war against shallow minds and the apostles of utility in science."[15]

Schelling's idealism, like that of the others, had clear religious meaning. "All knowledge is a striving toward communion with the divine being," he wrote. But Schelling wanted religion itself to act like a "science"—expansive in its outreach, flourishing in "rational thinking," and using the tools of a "vital inner intuition." Herein as well lies the function of the university. Its instruction will serve only insofar as it sees the human mind in terms of this expansive quality. But too often, as in Scottish philosophy and other Enlightenment models, Schelling wrote, we conceive the mind as a mechanism of faculties: sensation, understanding, will, and imagination—conscience. But "nothing is more soulless, more soul-killing," than such a presentation. To be sure, the demands of bourgeois society conspire against the true high ideals of the university. Our modern world "pursues empirical ends to the detriment of the absolute." In truth, however, Schelling insisted, universities have "only an absolute purpose."[16] These romantic notions of an "organic knowledge" of all reality made a remarkable extension into the thinking of some later American educational leaders. Illinois's history will provide a vital example, as the ensuing narrative will show. True learning, the philosophers believed, promised much. It constituted not merely a special kind of enlightenment, but spiritual and moral growth of the individual as well. The term *Bildung* came into wide use. It connoted development and advancement in one's higher, interior sensibilities. It promised a better citizenry and a wise and visionary statecraft to serve the nation. *Bildung* had a direct connection to *Wissenschaft*, both drawn from idealist philosophy, because, to use idealism's terms, it connected the subjective development of the individual with the objective forms of knowledge, both indicating evolution and dynamic growth. "Under this system," writes Watson, "discovery—research—was a moral act as much as anything."[17] That ideal had an important reinforcement in the next stage of the German universities' history.

The University of Berlin began in 1808 and Wilhelm von Humboldt answered the call to head the faculty. The University owed its creation to a political crisis. The Napoleonic wars brought the French invasion and occupation that closed down the universities, including especially Halle, which had maintained high status amid decline elsewhere. Prussians felt humiliated; they lapsed into a mood of self-criticism, vexed by their own cultural and moral failings. With the full commitment of Emperor Friedrich Wilhelm III, however, they resolved to start a new university, modern in every sense. Many professors displaced at Halle moved over to Berlin. Many other prominent scholars came from elsewhere. Major names in German philosophy quickly made Berlin the center of post-Kantian idealism. Humboldt now had the opportunity to outline a scheme for a uniquely German university, and he did so in a way that made an enduring influence, an inspiration lasting into the decades ahead.

Humboldt effectively synthesized major ideas from the philosophical idealists. (He worked closely with Schleiermacher.) He envisioned the new university as an integrating force for all higher education in Germany, all its institutions joined in common ideals. "But if one central principle—the pursuit of knowledge for its own sake—finally gains the upper hand in our higher academic institutions, there will be no need to worry about any particular details. Such institutions will be both unified and complete. This is in fact the secret of scientific and scholarly method," he avowed. Humboldt furthermore prescribed the extension of those scholarly standards to "other branches of knowledge and types of inquiry." He promoted *Bildung* as the highest ethical good. "If scholars succeed," he wrote, "they produce young men who can be physically, morally, and intellectually entrusted with freedom and autonomy," and they will not rest content with "a merely practical" life. As for Humboldt himself, he gave much attention to world history and its purposes.[18] And there would soon follow an explosion of studies, and new methodologies in another area of learning—the social sciences.

• • •

Philosophical idealism had faded from dominant influence in Germany by mid-century. It was receiving a strong challenge from positivism and the great popularity of Auguste Comte, and from empiricism, particularly as advanced by John Stuart Mill. *Wissenschaft* lost its expansive reach, and moved into narrower avenues of exploration. New academic disciplines became particularized; each, though, asserting the standards of "scientific" research for its respective field. *Wissenschaft* had "an awesome, almost religious status." The academic journal, publishing new knowledge in the new specialized fields, became a hallmark of the German universities. But it signified also the residue of the earlier, expansive epistemology of the idealist thinkers, and bequeathed to their successors "a self-justifying, open-ended quest for intellectual discovery, radical innovation, and the perpetual expansion of knowledge." That discovery would proceed by careful scrutiny of sources, skeptical approaches to inherited dogmas, and the highlighting of "*Kritik*" as the norm of scholarly inquiry. The German universities in this way gained in academic prestige and won world-wide attention. Now the young Americans, a small stream before the Civil War, flocked in large numbers to Germany, with the University of Berlin the brightest attraction for this group of intellectually starved young men.[19]

What the new generation of German social scientists did would change American intellectual history. It did so especially in economics. Some themes stand out. First, the German thinkers rejected the notion of immutable, natural laws as the governing determinant of economic life. They looked now to the natural sciences and their inductive standards for modes of explanation and the measure of truth. Also, they moved away from a primary focus on the individual, the fantasy of "economic man," and invoked the organic metaphor of society to study collective behavior, and state and public activity. They emphasized that these entities had their own life, and provided a new database for the social sciences. They were avowedly anti-laissez-faire. And as

5. The Intellectual World of Edmund J. James   63

the Germans turned away from abstract laws they focused on historical data. History provided the material of the new economics, political economy, and sociology, disciplines that were now emerging in Germany and soon in the United States as vital categories of the modern university. The social thinkers embraced the large goal of expanding their domains of investigation, to view matters holistically. Now *Wissenschaft* relocated from metaphysics to social science. Historian Jurgen Herbst, then, could appropriately describe this new intelligentsia as the "empirical idealists." The American economist Francis A. Walker spoke for many in his set of young social scientists when he explained how German scholars propelled them toward "a wider and ever widening view" of their subject. The Germans furnished names that American students abroad would soon know well—Wilhelm Roscher, Gustav Schmoller, Adolph Wagner, Karl Knies, Johannes Conrad.[20]

The Germans had a reform program as well, another attraction for the young Americans. They considered political economy a moral disciple and strove to show that ethical norms had a scientific basis. This point captured the imagination of the young American reformers, James's group. Albion Small provides an example. Like James and others, he grew up in a religious family, his father a Baptist minister in Maine. Upon graduating from Colby College, he followed his interest in German thought to study at Berlin and Leipzig. He returned to the United States and received his PhD degree from Johns Hopkins in 1889. Small became president of Colby College and then removed to the University of Chicago in 1892, the first professor in sociology at the new institution. He emerged as a major leader in that field, helping to form the American Sociological Society and creating the *American Journal of Sociology* in 1895. He served as the fourth president of the organization in 1912 and 1913. Small and James had faculty appointments together at Chicago in the late 1890s.[21]

Small acknowledged a great personal debt to the German thinkers and offered his own account, in 1924, of the turn to an ethical economics. He highlighted an address by Adolph Wagner, professor at Berlin, to the Evangelical Church of Prussia in 1871. Wagner issued an indictment of the classical political economy and its primacy of self-interest as a natural and benevolent force in the economic world. As such, Wagner urged, classical thinking "shut[s] out ethical factors from influence upon economic action." It can make no assessments of employer/employee relations; it can make no judgments about immense wealth and luxury and the contrasting less prosperous populations; it cannot speak to the matter of monopoly of landed property; and above all it ignores the critical subject of the state's responsibilities for all these injustices. Small admired especially the rhetorical force and passion in Wagner's speech. He quoted him: "A solution, in the strict sense is impossible. Always, poverty and misery, harm and suffering, welfare and riches, will exist side by side in

64   PART I. THE LARGER UNIVERSITY

This nice composite shows James as a boy, as a student at the University of Halle, and in his ensuing academic and administrative career. Courtesy of the University of Illinois Archives.

this world. It is our business, however, so far as possible, to diminish the evils that grow out of this fact, and to keep the existing inequalities from increasing. We have the means of doing this in progressive measure. If we use these means, we may have then performed our duties." Wagner's speech inspired the founding of the *Verein für Sozialpolitik* the next year, after a major conference held at the University of Halle in July 1872, although movement toward this event had been growing with the advocacies of Schmoller and Knies earlier.[22]

Edmund James had arrived at Halle three years later in 1875 and there he had met Richard T. Ely. James also had brief stays at Berlin and Leipzig. Ely did most of his work with Knies at Heidelberg. Both he and James came under the influence of Conrad, whose seminar at Halle became a gathering point for them and several other Americans. Conrad, raised in Danzig (East Prussia), came from a landlord family, did his doctoral work at Jena, and became full professor there in 1870. Two years later he succeeded the illustrious Schmoller at Halle and remained there for the rest of his career. He also became editor of the influential publication *Jährbucher für Nationalökonomie und Statistik*.

The German-educated students returned to their country to urge German-style reforms. They had the inspiration of seeing realization of reform thinking in the pioneering programs of Prussian Chancellor Otto von Bismarck and in the intellectual model of the Verein. It had formed to counteract another organization, the Congress of National Economy and its laissez-faire ideology. The Verein in turn intended to promote the case for state action, mostly on behalf of the lower classes. "We are convinced," said the *Jährbucher* in 1873, "that the unrestricted play of contrary and unequally strong private interests does not guarantee the common welfare, that the demands of the common interest and of humanity must be safeguarded in economic affairs, and that the well-considered interference of the state has to be called upon early in order to protect the legitimate interests of all." The Verein's leaders, who included Conrad, Knies, and Wagner as co-founders, believed they were advancing a thoroughly "scientific" alternative to the abstract dogma of their rivals' orthodoxy.[23]

So did the Americans, who took the lead from their German mentors. They put in place new academic organizations, and they introduced the "New Economics" to colleges and universities. As an observer commented in 1925, "It would be hard to find anywhere in the history of scholarship a higher average of success and achievement than this little band of pioneers attained."[24] Edmund James was in the thick of this crusade from the beginning. Here we meet another of his early companions who also invites some comparisons to James in James's pre-presidential period. Simon Patten, like James, came from Illinois, born in 1852 into a family of Presbyterians in Sandwich. His father William, described as an "ambitious farmer," pursued interests in religion and politics. He embraced the temperance movement and gave it support as

66   PART I. THE LARGER UNIVERSITY

a state legislator, and also expanded his moralistic politics into the assistance he gave to the Underground Railroad station in his area. Simon had his early schooling in Aurora and then in 1874 took up collegiate studies at Northwestern University in Evanston, where he met James. Then James suggested to Patten that he, too, should come to Halle. Patten, eager for a new intellectual departure, took the invitation and found himself, with James and Ely, in the seminars of Johannes Conrad.[25]

Like the others, Patten reacted enthusiastically to the ideas and operations of the Verein. He came back to America, eager, as he said, to "help in the transformation of American civilization from an English to a German basis."[26] James later recalled hearing Conrad urge the young Americans in one of his seminars:

> I remember very distinctly Conrad's speaking to us Americans who were in his seminary one evening, urging us to organize a similar association in the United States upon our return, emphasizing the fact that times were changing. The old order was passing away, and if economic students were to have any influence whatever upon the course of practical politics, it would be necessary to take a new attitude toward the whole subject of social legislation, and if the United States were to have any particular influence in the great social legislation and the great readjustment of society on its legal side which seemed to be coming, association of this sort would have very real value. I decided then that, as soon as I could, I would begin the agitation for such an association.[27]

So, in 1883 Simon and James drafted a constitution for their proposal: a Society for the Study of National Economy. It self-consciously emulated the principles of the Verein. It dismissed out of hand the notion that "our economic programs will solve themselves" and that individual action will always outproduce collective work. James and Patten also invoked the state and ascribed to it an expansive role in the economy and in promotion of the public good as a high priority. That good embraced a clean environment and safe conditions for workers. Their ideas also reflected the *Bildung* ethos, and they looked to a social renewal denoted by leisure hours for workers, an arrangement that could promote moral and mental growth. And they wanted more: national planning for conservation and the ultimate utilization of the nation's resources. These ideas had some appeal, but struck others as overly ambitious on the side of the public sector.[28]

Richard T. Ely had joined James and Patten in promoting the Society, but then backed off and gave his effort to starting another organization—the American Economic Association. Of James's early colleagues in reform Ely shows the most parallels to him. Born in Lyme, Connecticut in 1854, Ely descended from the early American Puritans. His father practiced a severe Calvinism, but

5. The Intellectual World of Edmund J. James   **67**

Ely remembered him also for his charitable actions. Ely attended Dartmouth College for a while and then went on to Columbia University. His enthusiasm for philosophy, and for German idealism in particular, led him to Germany. He quickly discovered a greater interest in economics, and he spoke for other young Americans in testifying to the intellectual excitement and academic spirit of the German universities, so refreshing a change from the stodgy and cramped character of America's colleges.[29] Ely studied with Karl Knies at Heidelberg and took up from him the cause of an ethical economics, which Ely brought back to the United States. But like the other Americans Ely attended classes at other universities. With James and Patten, as noted, he studied with Conrad at Halle and forged new personal ties with these American scholars abroad. Ely became a major voice of the Social Gospel and gave much attention in his own work to labor history. He taught at Johns Hopkins and then in 1892 left for the University of Wisconsin to head its new, ambitious creation, the School of Economics, Political Science and History.[30]

• • •

Edmund James, after receiving his degrees at Halle, came home to America. He set for himself a three-part agenda. First, he wanted to reconfigure the entire academic discipline of economics ("political economy" as still called here). He wanted to expand the domain of its investigations, and he wanted to break it from the discredited ideology ("laissez-faire") that held it in stranglehold. Second, he wanted to help reshape American higher education. He wished to explain the German system to his fellow countrymen to make them aware of the many alternatives available to them for their universities. And third, he wanted to promote reforms—tangible, state-directed, practical reforms—ones needed for an advanced industrial society and for a modern democracy, in short, for the United States in the late nineteenth century and beyond.

At that time, laissez-faire thinking had manifold locations and yielded a prolific literature. Thus, it was a formidable challenge the New Economics took on in its efforts to discredit the ideology. It had long dominated in academic thought. Free-market individualism had supplied the guidelines for economics in the moral philosophy textbooks of the American colleges. President Francis Wayland of Brown typified that connection in his popular college textbook *Elements of Political Economy*. Williams College professor Arthur Latham Perry gave hundreds of lectures to advance the model. Evolutionary thinking gave renewed power to the competitive market place. The English philosopher Herbert Spencer had a virtual cult following in America, with help from his major champion in the business community, the millionaire Andrew Carnegie. The United States had few pure "Social Darwinists," but William Graham Sumner of Yale merged evolution with classical economics and assured that an initially harsh but ultimately benevolent social order would

68   PART I. THE LARGER UNIVERSITY

arise as the unhindered system worked its ways. In politics, laissez-faire, and its thematic cousin anti-statism, held quasi-official status in the Democratic Party, from Thomas Jefferson and Andrew Jackson to its anti-tariff and states' rights partisans in both the North and South. The public press broadcast laissez-faire as well. E. L. Godkin, editor of *The Nation*, the most influential of American journals, championed the doctrine. As Daniel T. Rodgers has explained, defenders of laissez-faire thinking held their ground on the same models the reformers did. They defended the system as the "natural" one, its "laws" written into nature itself and hence to that extent also "scientific." They also appealed to morality. After all, what could have higher claim to moral truth than the priority of the "free individual"?[31] In his classic intellectual history of this era, Sidney Fine wrote: "In the period between Appomattox and the ascension of Theodore Roosevelt to the presidency in 1901, laissez faire was championed in America as it never was before and has never been since."[32]

Much discussion and debate now flourished as Ely tried to establish a new organization for economics. James entered in late 1885 when he took on Simon Newcomb in the pages of the journal *Science*, the periodical voice of the American Association for the Advancement of Science. Newcomb, an astronomer at Johns Hopkins and a dogged champion of classical economic orthodoxy, had just published his *Principles of Political Economy*. James showed how much he, and others, wanted to redefine a new economics by breaking the subject away from old principles. He right away dismissed Newcomb as a polemicist, wholly out of his league, an astronomer clueless about all the intellectual changes in economic thinking taking place around him. He "sounds like a voice from the dead," ignorant of the new "science" of economics, James proclaimed. The greater offense, however, James believed, lay in the fact that Newcomb had written his book "from the stand-point of extreme individualism," whereas the new science describes "a social and economic organism." And look at the toll this extreme individualism has taken, James urged. Look at the devastation of our forests by private owners. Here and elsewhere, see how "the interest of the individual diverges at a thousand points from that of the whole." Newcomb, James allowed, did acknowledge this problem sometimes and showed a fair-mindedness not always present among other champions of orthodoxy. But altogether, James warned, Newcomb and these others who defend the "existing order" only prepare the way for the communist alterative.[33]

James's piece brought reviews and rejoinders and propelled those with like minds to his to organize the American Economic Association.[34] James later served as its president. As Ely intended, the initial AEA emulated the German Verein. It introduced itself as a "scientific" organization, rejecting inherited and rigid principles, like free trade, that fall outside the standards of empirical investigation and historical grounding. It proclaimed its commitment to the positive state, "an educational and ethical agency whose positive aid is an indispensable condition of human progress." The AEA would have among its purposes the study of "the vast number of social problems" that beset contemporary life, and it would promote new course offerings in the universities to study these problems closely. In its first formulation, then, the AEA registered the triumph of the "ethical economists," the reform-minded and German-educated young Americans now assuming positions of influence in the universities. But within two years the AEA abandoned the statement of principles and no longer featured social reform as its high priority. "Scientific" now no longer signified an expansive, open-ended quest for moral truths; now it meant "scholarship strictly and more narrowly defined."[35] James had another opportunity to advance the reformers' case when the editors of *Science* asked Ely to put together some essays by his group, papers from a recent conference, in an effort to clarify the "New Economics." Contributors would also include major critics of the New Economics. Ely gave a brief "Introduction" and included two of his own essays: "Ethics and Economics" and "The Economic Discussion in Science." Offerings came from Edwin R. A. Seligman, James, and Henry Carter Adams. Richmond Mayo-Smith and Simon Patten also wrote for the reformers. Dissenters Simon Newcomb and Arthur T. Hadley of Yale gave oppositional views. James titled his essay "The State as an Economic Factor," with a dissent from Frank W. Taussig of Harvard.[36]

"There is no more significant difference between what, for lack of better terms, we may call the old and the new schools of political economy than their respective attitudes toward the state." Thus did James begin his essay. The old school, he elaborated, goes back to Adam Smith, who begins the tradition of "orthodox economics." It views matters from the perspective of the individual. Individual action prompts all that leads the world into progress, it believes. So, it follows that we secure progress in proportion to our removing the trammels of government from individual activity. But the new school, fortunately, in James's notions, has taken recourse to historical study of economics and demonstrated the long and important role of the state as a contributor to wealth—as important, in fact, as capital and labor. That's because the creation of wealth comes from "social organization." And the state, "as the representative of society, is the 'great silent partner' in every business event." From education, to law, to protection of natural resources, to its cooperative role in building railroads, the state preserves space for individual activity that individual activity, unchecked, would eviscerate. It is this kind of social capital that makes the individual wealth of Cornelius Vanderbilt possible, James insisted. He also believed that as societies grow in population, as the interconnection of individuals becomes consequentially more complex, the "social" factor rises in importance and mandates the larger coordinating role of government. James intended to offer no blank check for state intervention. The key, he insisted, was "balance."[37]

As the AEA lost its reform focus James took the initiative to establish a new body—the American Academy of Political and Social Science. He wanted as much as ever to make economic study a wide-open enterprise that drew from history, sociology, law, ethics, and all the inclusiveness that constituted, in his mind, "science." A meeting in 1889 led to the first publication from the AAPSS the next year, *Annals*. Its opening salvo included the statement that emerged from the proceedings of the 1890 session. The word "science" appears seven times in the document. And it celebrated the gains of "scientific progress" in other disciplines. Economics and the social sciences will progress by opening up to them, as had already happened in several universities.[38] The organization already had seven hundred members. James became the first president of the AAPSS, an office he held for eleven years. Succeeding issues of the *Annals* show the Society's interest in big policy issues, denoted by its recurring "Symposium" section, modeled after the Verein's journal, and its large participation by social scientists. Contributors to the journal, up to the time James went to Illinois in 1904, included John R. Commons, Thorstein Veblen, Woodrow Wilson, Edward A. Ross, Charles Cooley, Simon Patten, John Bates Clark, Charles M. Andrews, Franklin Giddings, Albert Bushnell Hart, David Kinley, James Harvey Robinson, Lester F. Ward, John A. Hobson, Georg Simmel, W. E. B. DuBois, Walter Weyl, Florence Kelley, Samuel Gompers, Jane Addams, and Morris Cohen.[39]

• • •

James returned from Germany in 1877, MA and PhD degrees in hand. He had school appointments in Evanston and then Normal, Illinois before he gained his ultimate goal, a university position. But even before he became professor of public finance and administration in the Wharton School, he took up another cause. In addition to his publications on behalf of social reform, he wanted to make the case for German higher education as viable for reform of the American universities. This effort he took up in 1881 with three pieces for the *Illinois School Journal*. He titled the first "What is a German University?" and opened with a clear, simple statement: "A German university is a corporation whose objects are the increase and spread of knowledge."[40] And that's the way it should be with our American institutions. James, of course, was entering into a debate, not starting one. The matter of research, and what place it should have in academic life, had been flourishing for two decades or more in the United States. Many American schools had already made the commitment to research. Johns Hopkins University, established five years before James's article, signified the success of the German model in gaining a major foothold in this country. But, to redirect American universities toward the priority of research would require rethinking the work of professors. James stated what anyone reading his piece would probably know: "A college professor," he said, "is an

5. The Intellectual World of Edmund J. James   71

entirely different person in Germany, from what he is here." There's more than a little note of anguish in James's description of the American professor:

> We confine our teachers to the mere routine work of putting into the minds of their students a certain number of text-books. We overload [the professors] with work so that they have no chance to develop. We require them to teach, so many different subjects that they can never acquire more than a text-book knowledge of them. We impose so many hours' work and so much outside responsibility upon them that they are thoroughly wearied, when they get a few moments or hours leisure, and need all the time to recuperate their health. This complaint comes from nearly every college in the country. We impress upon our professors the fact they are first, last and all the time, primarily teachers. They are not expected to make new discoveries. We do not care to have them add to the sum total of our knowledge. All that we desire is that they shall teach our boys what is known.[41]

Further, if American professors were ever to break from this "wooden and mechanical" mode of instruction, more reforms must follow, especially in the classroom. In these post-Germany essays, James made a plea for the lecture system and the seminar as the best way for universities to convey to their students the knowledge that marked their expertise, assuming of course that they had opportunities to acquire expertise. "If a college professor is a student, whose business it is to present the result of his studies in an impressive and attractive form to a crowd of enthusiastic and earnest learners, then the lecture system is the only valuable and practicable method of realizing this idea." But, alas, we have again a situation rare to America. "Of the possibilities of the [lecture] system we know almost nothing in this country," and our college classrooms are full of "know-nothing" students, James lamented.[42]

Then he turned to the seminars. Like so many young Americans in Germany, James considered the seminars "the most important element in many respects of the German university." (James, as noted earlier, became the first professor at Penn to organize a seminar.) Often student clubs formed around these events, providing social life and intellectual stimulus. Professors usually held them at their homes. James reported on one of his seminary experiences, that with Professor Rudolph Haym, "one of the most popular men at Halle," who gave lectures on the history of philosophy. Haym had studied at Halle and Berlin. James recalled the intense study the seminar gave to the philosopher Baruch Spinoza. Haym, in fact, had immersed his scholarship in the German romantic movement, so critical, as earlier observed, to the whole early tradition of the new German university. He wrote biographies of Wilhelm von Humboldt, Hegel, Schopenhauer, and Herder. In all cases, James emphasized, "the object of the [student club] is really to promote original work." "All possible assistance is given to those [students] who aim to do original work."[43]

72   PART I. THE LARGER UNIVERSITY

James's studies in philosophy, it will become apparent later, significantly affected his presidency at Illinois. So did the nature of the PhD program at Halle and the other German universities. James contributed his longest essay in the German series to that subject in 1888. Here he cast a large net. If nothing else the piece shows the extent of his familiarity, by this time, with the whole system in the German states. Illustrations and examples of his points came from the universities at Munich, Königsberg, Jena, Heidelberg, Freiburg, Giessen, Tübingen, Leipzig, Erlangen, and others. But, formidable sounding as it seemed, James observed, the doctoral degree at these schools could be gotten on rather easy terms, at least by today's measure—a year or two of study. One could pursue an assortment of general studies but had to show depth in one academic discipline. James also carefully pointed out that a student pursued his special field with much attention to its historical and intellectual evolution. Thus, in his own field of economics, "the student is expected to know the opinions of all prominent economists in reference to the subject" of his dissertation. What most impressed James, however, and what point he carried into his own academic leadership, was the requirement that all doctoral students enroll in courses taught by the "philosophy faculty." That term designated what we would now signify as the liberal arts, that is, the humanities and the sciences. These specifications exemplified for James the healthy endeavor of the German universities to avoid narrow, arcane, and strictly technical work.[44]

But what about American conditions? How should leaders in this country learn from the Germans and render their achievements appropriate to the United States? James had the opportunity to speak to these questions, and others, in an address he gave in 1897, seven years before he assumed the presidency at Illinois. It was his most important essay to date. James spoke in his role as president of the AAPSS and asked his listeners, at the beginning of his talk, why should the subject of education have a central place in the academic discipline of economics? James, of course, was illustrating for the Academy a point important to all its members: the wide field of investigation and peripheral concerns of the reformer economists, most of them of the German-educated generation. Consider, he said, the new age into which we are entering. Education is no longer mainly the charge of the church. It is the business of government, and to that extent, pertinent to the several branches of public administration. It falls within "the general field of the political social sciences." An organization such as ours, then, James added, must "give a somewhat special attention to this particular subject."[45]

James wanted to paint a larger picture for the Academy. He spoke enthusiastically about how the social sciences had evolved to the point where they fully deserved categorization as "scientific" disciplines. He observed as well that they had grown in numbers and popularity in American universities. "These

5. The Intellectual World of Edmund J. James   73

subjects are real sciences," he avowed, and they demand large space in any program of modern education. Many do not accept this notion, he acknowledged, and a struggle lies ahead for the social sciences and their effort to secure their proper place in higher education. But the modern natural sciences, as they had become distinctly differentiated, had to win a similar battle. They won their place as people more and more recognized their large necessity as vehicles of human progress. Today, James proclaimed, the public increasingly sees the indispensable status of the social sciences in the same large cause. Here is the situation: "the number of people who are interested in these subjects to-day is so enormously greater than ever before, the belief of modern society in the possibility of self-improvement and ultimate perfectibility is so much more vivid than at any preceding period in the life of humanity, that we may fairly say we have entered upon a new era in this respect."[46]

The gift did not stop giving here. James believed that the social sciences could fortify American democracy at a critical point in its progress. Note, he urged, that our advanced industrial and technological society has raised professionalism and specialization into high importance. One receives a prescribed program to study law and become an attorney; likewise with becoming a doctor or a theologian. But, observed James, "in strange contrast to all this," the business of politics, the business of governing and ruling the state, with power to control and direct the state and to determine the lines along which a society advances—we make this "the business of everybody." We entrust it all "to the common man." This is the great American experiment. For still today most countries around the world, James pointed out, have a certain class of people, usually those of wealth or high social station, who dominate the offices of government. But democracy, more than other political systems, requires training of a special kind—a training for citizenship. And here the social sciences become imperative for this work. For how else can we form, among democracy's legions, individuals who are "expert in the business of governing"? The social sciences must therefore command the curriculum all the way down to the primary levels of schooling. We must endeavor to excite American youth about politics and secure their vigilance and attention to the conduct of government, James said. Education thus prepares the way. We have to "lift the individual man and woman out of the narrow round of the routine duties characteristic of the ordinary life up into the larger sphere of communion with the great thoughts that have made our world for us, and with those larger thoughts which have made the universe in which we live." Here James spoke in proximate ways like the philosophical idealists who gave the modern university its original grounding.[47]

This point James wished especially to emphasize as he also brought this subject into the vibrant and often contentious discussion, long active, concerning the college curriculum. James insisted that to realize this large vision, "those

74   PART I. THE LARGER UNIVERSITY

larger thoughts which have made the universe in which we live," we cannot rely on the old model of liberal education. "The old idea that a liberal education can only be obtained from an extensive study of the classics, that strength of mind and purpose can only be derived from a detailed study of mathematics has disappeared along with many another equally defective notion as to the pedagogical nature of various disciplines and branches of knowledge." Those approaches are simply too confining. "Human science," James postulated, becomes ever larger in scope, such that no college program will suffice for mastery. Nevertheless, we need not forsake the still valid objective of collegiate education—intellectual development and mental discipline. Here James wanted to meet traditional critics of the new university model on their own ground. For the modern, the social sciences have the full ability to achieve that very objective, mental discipline, along with the venerable humanistic and scientific disciplines. Thus, for example, political economy, "as it is set forth in the great treatises on this subject," cannot fail to enhance mental development just as surely and as truly as does the mastery of propositions in geometry. And that study has the further benefit of bringing student minds to the live issues of their world and the challenging conditions brought by the dramatic changes therein. The social sciences contribute, in short, to the training of "an intelligent and useful citizenship." James thus could assert confidently that the social sciences are a liberal education in the traditional and best meaning of that term. They, too, fully constitute "the study of man."[48]

All who heard James's address knew its large context. Because amid compelling changes in the American university—research, science, creation of new academic fields, and expansion of the curriculum—there yet were heard the voices of mental discipline and liberal culture. From the famous "Yale Report" of 1828, with its eloquent plea for "the discipline and furniture of the mind" as the primary ingredient of a collegiate education, to the late contemporary spokesmen for the ancient classics as the essence of humanistic learning, the conservative suasion remained quick and pointed in the discussions and persisted into the years of James's presidency at Illinois. Names abound: Charles Eliot Norton at Harvard and later Irving Babbitt at the same institution; Barrett Wendell and George E. Woodbury at Columbia; Alexander Meiklejohn at Amherst; Andrew F. West at Princeton; George T. Ladd and William Lyon Phelps at Yale, and others. Some would make liberal culture an affiliate of religion and spirituality; others proffered their defense without alliances with theology. Some scorned the social sciences and lamented their growth at the expense of Latin, Greek, and moral philosophy. Most of these defenders judged the humanities as indispensable to the growth and nurture of high character and moral living.[49] Many of the smaller liberal arts colleges did valuable work to perpetuate the core goals of humanistic learning amid the ascending credos of positivism and empirical standards of scholarship.[50]

Recent efforts to place these matters into a larger intellectual context also shed some light on James. Julie Reuben's book of 1996, *The Making of the Modern University: Intellectual Transformation and the Marginalization of Morality*, finds that the great leap from the college to the university era had more points of continuity than heretofore noticed. That is to say, leaders of the academic revolution sought to perpetuate, by way of modifying and protecting, the moral and even the religious aspects of the old-time college. Thus, like James and Ely, those who made the case for "ethical economics" and the moral content of the new social sciences may have moved beyond the long-dominant Scottish philosophy and its Baconian defense of fixed moral ideas. But, they argued that their new views made a better case for educated support of an ethical life for individuals and moral social reform for the collective good. These partisans of the new, often following the German lead, would call for a "scientific" understanding of religion, helping further to integrate science into modern intellectual life and meet the rival champions of "science" who would disqualify religion for lack of empirical content. Others maintained that the strict discipline of scientific inquiry fostered habits of self-control and expanded moral awareness. James's writings would seem to fortify that thesis.[51]

But this accommodation could not last. More skeptical thinkers wanted to detach academic study entirely from religion and morality, to make it thoroughly empirical, and to render it consistently "neutral" with respect to moral judgment. These protagonists maintained that they were offering a more authentic appropriation of "science" and upholding its special standards. As Reuben shows, this challenge generated a lively discussion about the real meaning of science, with individuals like James contending for an expansive and inclusive embrace of the largest reality and scope of investigation. The stricter interpreters, however, wanted to curb what they considered speculative excess, in the way that earlier American disciples of Thomas Reid and other Scottish thinkers warned against the expansive intuitive overreaches of Berkeley, Hume, and later the German idealists.[52] Others in the new camp believed that scientific standards, confined to experience, would arrive at a more solid basis for ethics than any nonempirical approach. In all cases, they otherwise argued, the modern university would approach knowledge from a narrow basis, on solid data, discouraging claims for a vast edifice of truth, *a priori* moral certainties, and speculative notions of the absolute. This new cohort, Reuben writes, "began to see the interests of their disciplines in a model of science that stressed the importance of factual description and that associated objectivity with the rejection of moral values." They made specialization the mark of academic excellence. They championed a philosophy of experience.[53]

Also, in generalizing about the German "impress" in American higher education, James Axtell concludes that American scholars could take from

76   PART I. THE LARGER UNIVERSITY

the German *Wissenschaft*, as examined earlier here, and leave out the "animating spirit," or *Geist*, and the associated honoring of *Bildung*, deriving from the German substance then only a more narrowly empirical and utilitarian residue, "practical" research. Here they followed the model of the German intellectuals of the later nineteenth century instead of their philosophical forebears in the first half.[54] Laurence Veysey has a similar conclusion: while there lingered in German scientists the residue of philosophical idealism, one that gave a contemplative quality to their investigations and framed it within "an underlying spiritual unity," most American scientists, by contrast, held to a strict empiricism. But in this country, too, pockets of resistance held out. The University of Illinois, as will be seen, was one of them.[55]

Another effort to give the modern American university its right intellectual framework came from Andrew Jewett in his book *Science, Democracy and the American University: From the Civil War to the Cold War.* He properly turned attention to the subject of "science" in the late nineteenth and early twentieth centuries to recover its meaning to those who promoted it in higher education. We have misled ourselves in reading back from a later model of science as value neutral, detached from political and social priorities, Jewett believed. But "science," to the generation of Edmund James, had a public purpose, a mission. It aspired to influence a better citizenship and furnish the basis of thought and the ethical principles that underscored democracy. It would inspire people to shift from narrow partisanship and focus more on the common good. Science would find its role in tempering passionate and prejudicial polemics and fostering instead a rational public discourse and "a morally vigorous" public culture. This group of thinkers, prominent in the social sciences of the new university, Jewett labels "scientific democrats" and their program "scientific democracy." The author also reinforces Reuben in deflating the science/religion dichotomy in the curricular discussions by enlarging the reach of Protestant liberalism as an accommodating category. Jewett also brings the major intellectual of this period, John Dewey, into its orbit. Both the secularist Dewey and the religious liberals drew upon evolutionary theory and, applying it to society and politics, took recourse to the organic model of the state. That model emphasized inclusion, discredited the ideal of the autonomous individual, and argued for the "social self" in moving away from the model of the competitive market place to that of the active, progressive state as the vehicle of human improvement. Jewett makes the American university the key institutional location of American political culture in this era.[56] Edmund James fits well this interpretive outline also.

• • •

The other point of James's three-part program had his attention focused on politics. In this effort James participated actively in the early phase of the

Progressive movement in American history as it began in the late nineteenth century and emerged confidently in the early twentieth. Progressivism found its intellectual roots in many sources. James stands with those thinkers more comfortable in the realm of secular thought than did other reformers who translated their religious backgrounds into a social gospel movement. But he shared with that group a commitment to moral substance as the measure of political action and policy making. He believed that the organic model of society, which commanded attention to all its components, or constituents, also commanded an ethical measure of those relationships and recourse to social justice as the pathway of politics. Wholly sympathetic to Christian values in assisting these efforts, James nonetheless did not invoke religious principles as such. Human experience supplied him the needed moral standards. And the organic model of society, forged from the new academic social sciences, forces us, James insisted, to shift our focus, and our moral priorities, from the individual to the public interest. Because the social sciences, properly understood and properly taught in our universities, compel that shift, they give us the direction we need in political reform.

James's intellectual interests in this area reached far and wide. He wrote on topics like conservation, taxation and tariff reform, voting and political participation, the city, and especially city government. This chapter will sample three subjects that figured large in the political agitation of the late nineteenth and early twentieth centuries: farmers and their grievances; the railroads and their regulation; and workers and the union movement. For the spokespersons of the Progressive Era, James clearly among them, reform always signified an enlarged and active role for the state. For the generation of James's German-educated social scientists, such a viewpoint emerged easily. From their teachers, introduced above, came an understanding of the state as rooted in history, organic in nature, and committed to the moral as well as the material perfection of society. Here again the transition to social thinking from philosophical thinking registers. Kant, Herder, Fichte, and Hegel raised the state to metaphysical significance. German students, and some of the Americans, too, knew the names of Friedrich J. Stahl, Johann K. Bluntschli, Georg Waitz, Johann Gustav Droysen, and others, whose social ideas were "permeated with those philosophical characteristics which we have come to associate with German Romanticism." However various in detail, all these intellectuals repudiated eighteenth-century individualism.[57] And yet, this thinking also challenged the Americans. They wanted to make it a tool of reform, a priority for public values alongside with, and not in elimination of, traditional American ideas about the free individual. They wanted to influence an improved democracy in the United States, not a retreat into authoritarianism in thought or practice. James certainly had that intention.

78   PART I. THE LARGER UNIVERSITY

James and his colleagues in the New Economics revered the state. Ely equated it to God. James came close to doing so. He rejected notions that government was a necessary evil, that it coexisted with a fallen human nature and man's proclivity for doing bad things. "The capacity for government," James wrote, "is one of the divinest gifts of God to man," a scheme to effect the happiness of his creatures. It is by state interference, too, that "a society is helped out of barbarism" (and, to be sure, by which it can fall back into barbarism). Government is, or ought to be, about promoting better health, better education, and better morals. This progress, James conceded, does involve a reduction of individual liberties, as in the restrictions on drinking and gambling, the mandating of vaccinations and attendance at school, dictating the numbers of wives a man may have, or in setting qualifications for who may practice medicine or engage in other professions. Some say, James observed, that government will erode and fade away as the human race advances. On the contrary, he replied, we should look in that advance for creative opportunities to unite all society, government leading the way. He envisioned a cooperative commonwealth with the state in partnerships with private enterprise to extend ever wider the benefits of modern civilization.[58]

Here James sought to dissolve, to some degree, the rigid notion of "public" and "private" in the common understanding of Americans. Of course, one can see how he was drawing on his German education and the doctrines of the historical school of social thought. James continued to follow the German scene after his return to America, always hoping to fortify the progressive case made by the New Economics in its continuing warfare with its orthodox opponents. Thus, for example, James welcomed an opportunity to review for the *Political Science Quarterly*, a conservative outlet, a book by the Austrian economist Emil Sax, in 1890. It dealt with the subject of taxation, but James appreciated it most for its underlying social model. Sax argued that the state's identity embraces the individual's identity; it does not radically differentiate them. Speaking for Sax, James wrote that "private activity and public activity are both one and the same process." "Every person has individual wants and collective wants." The latter require organizations to help one realize them—social institutions of all kinds, but government especially. On this understanding, Sax and James discredited free market advocates like Adam Smith, Frédéric Bastiat, David Ricardo, and Friedrich List.[59]

The plight of rural America and the struggles of American farmers concerned James. In the 1870s and 1880s, these matters had gained national attention. Institutions like the Grange, the Farmers' Alliances, and then the creation of the Populist (People's) Party moved them into the political arena. Farmers complained of exploitation and discriminatory practices by the railroads and the big eastern banks. They called for nationalization of railroads,

5. The Intellectual World of Edmund J. James 79

telegraph companies, and utilities. They demanded an overhaul of the political structure in the name of greater democracy: the initiative, the referendum, and the recall would create greater accountability to the electors and greater control by them. The Populist Party formed in 1891 and ran its own candidate (James B. Weaver) for the presidency in the election the next year. Edmund James addressed the farmers' situation with two essays in *Science* in 1891.

James believed that historical change underscored the rural crisis and, in German fashion, began with some considerations that framed the crisis. First, he said, our tax system is antiquated. It derives from a time when land constituted the chief wealth of individuals and when a majority of the people lived in the country. But now wealth lies increasingly in the cities; it has been flowing away from farmers. The farmers, as they all know, work in a national, in fact, an international market. Competition comes today from Russia, Europe, Africa, and other places. Local taxation will not suffice. "We cannot hope to get money where it is not," James urged. So, our whole tax system "must be radically changed," as it has become "grossly unjust." We must move away from property as the dominant base of our taxation. James considered this question a moral matter, too. Our system, he said, hurts the modest farmer "who has accumulated from his savings a small farm in proportion to his thrift and savings" while it allows "the extravagant lawyer or physician who makes thousands of dollars every year and lives it all up, to go scot-free of all taxation." This invidious system also favors large holders of capital and injures the small holders. James built into his published piece a barrage of statistics to illustrate his points.[60]

Thus did James diagnose the rural problem. He also wanted to help solve it. The matter involved more than simply tax remedies. Country towns, he said, have deteriorating schools, with many of these communities completely lacking high schools. The railroads have drastically moved people and markets around. Dislocation and disruption have also created income inequalities. Given the new market structure, he stated, farmers need access to distant markets. They need roads. Here James imposed the kind of economic nationalism that was emerging in his thinking. Addressing the issues, he emphasized, must take us beyond local remedies and invoke the state and national governments. We should exempt farmers from state taxation, and shift to other sources for government revenue, he specified; and the state must assist with schools, courts, and aid to the poor, the insane, and the blind. Better, much more taxation should have a federal base and tap the wealth of corporate giants like Standard Oil. Also, we must not think of the national and local economies as separate, integral entities. James employed the organic metaphor to demonstrate that better transportation has immense value for the cities as well as the farms. Thus, we must look at each component of our system "as a part of one and the same system of government, to be used by the people in

80   PART I. THE LARGER UNIVERSITY

the manner and to the extent to which its interest may dictate." Economic nationalism reinforces our proper sense of a collective democracy.[61]

Not farmers alone but in fact the entire American public knew the problem of the railroads. James had addressed the subject four years earlier. The AEA had assigned itself the task of looking into the railroad situation, and James addressed it at the 1887 annual meeting. His talk coincided with the legislation known as the Interstate Commerce Act, congressional action that James welcomed. Because to him nothing in the modern national economy more clearly demonstrated the sacrifice of the public interest to private business than the example of the railroads. The emergence of the railroad to dominance in transportation had changed everything, James believed. Everywhere it created local monopolies (and often chaotic competition). James enumerated the abuses that any alert citizen in the United States at the time knew well. The immense demand for the roads had led many states into making their own contracts with the roads. To entice them, the states allowed any small group, even with little capital, to contract for the construction. These states, James elaborated, then "allowed these parties all sorts of opportunity to enlist the speculative and gambling spirit in the community in their aid," and to "sell out the public and manipulate the stock market." They gave the railroads rights of eminent domain and power "to fix rates at pleasure." The roads formed their own construction companies, with their own personnel as directors; manipulated their bonds; and gave them their business, even as the roads went bankrupt themselves, cheating both the public and the stockholders. The railroads, James elaborated, also built branch lines, driving up both real estate values, by placing stations along their routes, as well as stock values. After stocking and bonding the branch line the parent railroad bought it at a high valuation. Corruption reigned all over.[62]

This subject of American society and its disorders also led James to address the most important, or at least the most worrisome issue of the day, the "social question." It concerned the real fear of class warfare. No other era of American history recorded more labor agitation and labor violence—strikes, work stoppages, bombs. For all the glittering effects of this "Gilded Age" of American history, a fear of social upheaval gripped the American conscience.[63] The literature of social reform in these years comes out of this backdrop, and that literature has many inspirations—Christian social gospel, secular socialism, single tax policy and other monetary changes, and rural discontent, as noted. All set themselves against the laissez-faire ideology. Reinforcing these expressions was the judgment of many more individuals that the American social situation exhibited profound moral wrongs and demanded a committed humanitarian intervention. James added his voice to the chorus.

Part of his effort came in his work to establish a new publication, another organization project of his in the late 1880s. It had the title *Our Day: A Record and Review of Current Reform.* Under the leadership of Joseph Cook, a popular Boston lecturer and social gospeler, *Our Day* had several topical departments. James headed the one called "Labor Reform," Frances Willard that labeled "Temperance," and Professor L. T. Townsend "Education." Another department, "Prevention of Vice" became the preserve of none other than Anthony Comstock! The publication avowed its independence of any political creed or religious denomination but embraced "distinctly evangelical views" and set its goal to unite "Evangelical Christianity with Practical Reform." Participation seemed to require no theological commitment, however, and in fact, *Our Day* promised to welcome both "secular and religious contributors," even as it embraced a religious moralism as the banner of reform programs. James could rest comfortably in that arrangement.[64]

For his essay in this short-lived publication James addressed American fears and considered the prospects of socialism and anarchism. But he flagged these subjects within a larger purpose of looking at American society and offering his sense of the social question. Since 1877, the year of "the Great Strike," he observed, the United States has undergone a constant round of labor discontent, "one strike after another." The labor movement has gained more force, James observed, and has entered into the political arena with aggressive programs to address the ills of the working classes. James read the minds of many Americans when he asked why there was such anger and resentment in this land of opportunity, of high wages, and of unbiased laws, where the son of an illiterate father may become a justice in our courts. In short, why do these workers consider themselves oppressed and down-trodden?[65]

James wanted to lay some groundwork for discussion of this subject; he considered such queries naive and ill-informed. Some would say that only workers can address their grievances and find the means of solving these problems. James replied that it will take much more than that. It will require a lot of insight and a wide and long perspective, the contribution of individuals "thoroughly acquainted with labor history" and having a "grasp of economic principles" and "economic reasoning." He called for people with deep insights into human nature and into "the particular human nature which prevails in this country." Those insights can come only from an abundance of scholarship, wide-ranging in its outreach and inclusive in its gathering of the needed data. For as labor alone cannot give us solutions neither can the equally "obstinate" dogma of employers. In fact, James urged, we should attend much more to the needs of a forgotten "third party," the public. It is the public "which must finally settle the matter." It was an immense challenge, James acknowledged, the more so as both labor and corporations sit large in the public's domain.[66]

Nonetheless, James did concede that labor had the higher ground here, that it faced a dire situation in "the sorrowful fact of widespread suffering in large classes of our population" that the American public must make an effort to

82 PART I. THE LARGER UNIVERSITY

understand. The naive questions Americans ask about the working classes, he said, wholly miss the point. Because it is not simply objective circumstances that define the unhappiness and bitterness of these individuals. It is a subjective matter. And here history becomes crucial for our understanding, James insisted. We know that disparities of wealth and poverty have always described human societies, but something different agitates the contemporary situation. Today the struggling worker sees displays of wealth everywhere. He lives in proximity to them. He sees them in the new journalism that investigates all and reveals all. An acute "feeling of contrast," wrote James, dominates the new subjectivity. The worker sees "luxury which flaunts itself in his face," and this opulence, these squandering habits of the vulgar affluent, register "deep-seated feelings of bitterness and discontent." History and the conditions of modernity have created a profound disparity between the situation of the worker and his wants, the material comfort and abundance that lie daily within his view and, he knows, beyond his reach. No, it's not just a matter of wages. This festering element, this alienated class, rips apart the organic society. We must find the means of restoration. We need a new sentiment, James urged, one rooted in education, "moral, intellectual, and religious."[67]

Discussion of the social classes led almost always to the labor movement itself. In James it had a sympathetic voice. He had a strong interest in the history of the movement, believing that its modern complexities had to be understood from that vantage. Occasionally he took the opportunity to address matters that came right off the newspapers' front pages. Such was the case in 1889. The year before, in Illinois, a violent strike of coal miners, called by one historian "one of the most horrendous episodes in the labor history of the 1880s," occurred, at Spring Valley in the northern part of the state. It involved a reaction against wage cuts and then a lockout. To the reformer Henry Demarest Lloyd this incident, and the reaction of the mine owners, demonstrated just about everything one needed to know about the power of capital in the United States and the attendant plight of the workers who suffered under it. He responded with his short book, *A Strike of Millionaires Against Miners*, in 1890. Lloyd, a New Englander originally, had come out to Chicago and entered journalism. He grew increasingly disaffected with the American economic situation, spoke out strongly against monopoly, and rendered strong attacks on laissez-faire ideology. He made his greatest contribution to the Progressive movement a few years later with his classic polemic against the Standard Oil Company, his book *Wealth Against Commonwealth*.[68]

James reviewed Lloyd's piece on the miners' strike and gave it his full endorsement. He credited the author for avoiding any simple or one-sided appraisal of the issue, though both he and Lloyd here clearly sympathized with the miners. The story began with a group of men entering northern Illinois at Spring Valley and inducing local people and workers to join in their mining

5. The Intellectual World of Edmund J. James　　83

project there. They offered high wages. But some bad business decisions soured the project and the original owners, who had turned the project over to some others, left and took large profits with them. The workers struck, but "a horrible amount of suffering" befell helpless men, women, and children. James felt their pain, and he registered his own anger, too. "Mr. Lloyd's account," he wrote, "makes one's blood boil." It shows "the cruel things" a corporation can do and exposed the myth of capital's benevolence. Lloyd, and James in presenting his account, cited the abuses of the company store, another item of managerial control over workers. The railroads in turn compounded the pattern of exploitation. For his part, though, James emphasized in this incident what it illustrated about workers and what recourse they have. "This account," he wrote, "proves also how quickly the great public forgets, and how deaf is the public ear to the cry of suffering and wrong; and emphasizes, therefore, the necessity of introducing such restrictions on our so-called system of free competition as shall prevent the possibility of such experiments as that in Spring Valley." He added: "Our way out of such difficulties lies not in preaching righteousness . . . but in trying to shape law and industry so that such cases shall not arise."[69]

James also participated in an important effort on behalf of the Knights of Labor this same year, a book titled *The Labor Movement: The Problem of To-Day*. Organized by George E. McNeil, this large collection of essays sought to help bring a "peaceful solution to the Labor problem." Its offerings gave some space to the trade unions but ultimately sought to promote the Knights, which McNeil dubbed "the most wonderful organization of modern times." Knights Grand Master Terrence V. Powderly contributed a statement on behalf of that organization. James had more space than any other in this anthology, leading with three substantial essays: Chapter I, The Rise of the Modern Laborer; Chapter II, History of Mechanical Labor; and Chapter III, Recent Labor Legislation, all three chapters packed with information. James began the first chapter in manner true to his education in the German historical school: "If we would comprehend our present labor problems we must study carefully the conditions out of which they have grown. The modern laborer is a historical product."[70]

Thus, in these ways Edmund James viewed a nation that he judged threatened by rising disorder and confusion, and beset by problems that could often seem intractable. But in all the sectors that challenged politics he found nothing that could not yield at least tentative and proximate resolutions by application of wide knowledge, intelligence, and experimentation. All along, though, James and his fellow intellectuals had their eyes on another domain— the world at large. In the 1890s it was moving relentlessly on a tragic course—a road to war. The next chapter follows President James and the University of Illinois into the years of the great conflict of 1914.

84   PART I. THE LARGER UNIVERSITY

CHAPTER 6

A University at War

AS EDMUND JAMES EMBRACED and sought to advance the cause of Progressivism, he and his fellow intellectuals had their eyes fixed on the scene at home but also on the world at large. The nation took a critical new turn in 1898 when an agonizing President William McKinley made the decision for war in the Philippines and propelled the country onto the path of imperialism. In 1917 President Woodrow Wilson, also a reluctant warrior, asked the United States Senate for a declaration of war against Germany. Every American college and university then had to decide how it would respond to the world situation and how it would make itself useful to the patriotic cause. President James led the University of Illinois in the greatest transformation it had ever made in its history to date. All along, the world was coming to the United States. The last decade of the nineteenth century and the first decade of the twentieth saw record levels of immigration. America was changing. How to respond? This chapter continues the previous one in exploring the intellectual world of Edmund James.

All these developments opened up large arenas for the activities of American intellectuals. This review will focus mostly on that cohort of social thinkers, so many educated in Germany, that, as described earlier, came into prominence in the last two decades of the century—James's network of historians, economists, and sociologists. They entered with confidence into plotting and planning America's entry onto the world stage. Economist Arthur T. Hadley, soon to be Yale's president, claimed that only the academic expert could devise an effective colonial system. Roland P. Falkner, the former colleague of James at Penn, insisted that social scientists can best judge the national interest. And all of the academic social science associations gave overwhelming endorsement to the idea that the national interest called for an imperial policy. Thus, at meetings of the American Historical Association, which had formed a committee on the history of colonies, John Bach McMaster, also of Penn and "a historian of extreme nationalism," called for American possession of new territories and promised beneficial consequences for all parties. The AHA had a large portion of Anglophiles—Charles M. Andrews, Albert Bushnell Hart, Herbert Levi Osgood—who wanted the United States to follow or otherwise succeed Great Britain in a foreign policy that would assure the advance of "empire and liberty." Likewise in the American Economic Association, which also formed a committee on colonies, Richard T. Ely urged retention of the Philippines. John Bates Clark endorsed imperialism as a positive economic benefit to the nation. Only John R. Commons of Wisconsin, who considered colonial ownerships a blessing only to big business, registered anything like a dissent from the course in which McKinley was taking the nation.[1] Of course, many American thinkers and writers opposed imperialism: Mark Twain, Andrew Carnegie, William James, E. L. Godkin, David Starr Jordan, William Dean Howells, Samuel Gompers, William Graham Sumner.

Edmund James wished also to have his academic association take up the subject of American foreign policy. The American Academy of Political and Social Science did so at an 1899 meeting, President James presiding. More than a dozen participants gave their thoughts on the changing world scene. James offered only introductory remarks but he wholly revealed his great interest in the subject and his enthusiasm for discussions of it. We are living, he said, "in one of the most interesting periods . . . of the last five hundred years." All the news of the day reminds us that the world has moved into a wonderful integration, he affirmed. This age of the steam engine and the telegraph demonstrates clearly the oneness of the human race and helps us feel "the solidarity of the whole human kind." James seemingly registered here the intellectual culture he had acquired in Germany, with its expansive approach to all reality and quest for an interrelated unity. Whereas so many of his colleagues in the social sciences feared the changes they observed in the new international dynamics of race and nation, James conveyed a feeling of wonder and possibility. In nothing from our prior history, he attested, do we see "a more important significant prophetic element than in the awakening of Japan and China and of the ever-hastening process of union between the East and the West."[2]

But as Americans pondered how to make adjustments to their foreign policy, they had also to weigh the tremendous impact of a foreign population arriving on their shores in greater numbers than ever before. A commission appointed by President Theodore Roosevelt in 1902 observed what every informed American knew: the pattern of immigration had changed significantly. Now, the commission stated, we see far less a proportion of arrivals coming from England, Scotland, Wales, Germany, and Scandinavia—that is, northern Europe. This "old immigration" was yielding to an influx from

86　　PART I. THE LARGER UNIVERSITY

eastern and southern Europe: Italy, Poland (Russian-ruled), Russia, Lithuania, Estonia, and the Ottoman Empire. Places and nationalities unfamiliar to Americans—Magyars, Serbians, Armenians, Herzegovinians—also swelled the tide. Hence the "new immigration." It also brought a preponderance of Roman Catholics and Jews into a still heavily Protestant United States. In James's first full year in office at Illinois, immigrant numbers passed one million, the largest in the nation's history. Five years later the United States had over twenty-two million foreign-born people in the nation of about seventy million. Add to this cultural mix the flourishing genre of the foreign-language newspaper: 100 Italian; 59 Swedish; 57 Polish; 42 Bohemian; 34 Yiddish; 10 Syrian; and a few others of smaller number.[3]

These changes challenged Americans. Some might see in them the making of a new, large, and powerful nation, an industrial leviathan ready to expand its presence on the world. But probably most reacted with misgivings. When linked to the "social question" and labor violence, immigration raised fears. The matter seemed to focus American attention mostly on race, religion, and ethnicity. One reaction took the form of a new, or revived, cult of Anglo-Saxonism. Popularizers, like philosopher John Fiske, gave facile interpretations of world history and the role assigned to this race in its progress. Writing in 1885, Fiske forecast that "every land on the earth's surface that is not already the seat of an old civilization shall become English in its language, in its religion, in its political habits and traditions, and to a prominent extent in the blood of its people." Josiah Strong, in turn, wrote a very popular book titled *Our Country: Its Possible Future and Its Present Crisis* (1885). Strong, an active promoter of the Congregational Home Missionary Society, recoiled from the dangerous shifts he saw in the United States—the expansion of Catholicism, the rapid growth of cities with their bulging foreign populations. But Strong did not despair. In his chapter "The Anglo-Saxon and the World's Future," Strong affirmed that the Anglo-Saxon race represented two great ideals—civil liberty and a "pure spiritual Christianity." As he read the tea leaves, Strong asked, "[D]oes it not look as if God were not only preparing in our Anglo-Saxon civilization the die with which to stamp the peoples of the earth, but as if he were amassing behind that die the mighty power with which to press it?" He dubbed the United States the "great home of the Anglo-Saxon," this nation now on its providential course of world domination.[4]

American intellectuals, and especially Edmund James's circle of social scientists highlighted in this book, had much to say about race. They presented more sophisticated outlines than the popularizers but, not infrequently, resorted to harsh racial casting and prejudicial renderings of the changes that the new immigration was effecting in American society. Often this group invoked the "Teutonic" theory of American democracy, tracing its roots back to the forests of early Germany and then to England and America. These thinkers had important posts in the new academe of the United States. Herbert Baxter Adams, for example, the "foremost exponent of the Teutonist theory in the United States," had an early appointment at the new Johns Hopkins University, where his students included Richard T. Ely and Woodrow Wilson. Adams, an "old-stock New Englander," had graduated from Amherst College in 1872 and two years later took up studies at Heidelberg. He also enrolled in a history program at Berlin, studying with Johann Droysen and Heinrich von Treitschke. But Adams found his most profound influence in Johann Bluntschli of Heidelberg, in whose seminars on political science and international law he enrolled. Bluntschli celebrated the Aryans and Teutons. He told his students that "the white races are pre-eminently the nations which determine the history of the world." That view became the basis of Adams's teaching.[5]

John W. Burgess, another student product of Germany, also partook of Droysen's seminar and, like Adams, drew on Bluntschli. Burgess, who later had a long, influential role at Columbia, offered his highly important work in 1890, the two-volume *Political Science and Comparative Constitutional Law*. The lasting controversy surrounding this work comes mostly from the views on race that Burgess advanced in it. Burgess embraced the large state views of the German historians and in his case tied that ideal to the political genius of the Teutons, creators of "the political nations *par excellence*." That peculiarity, Burgess believed, gave this race legitimate license to assume leadership in the world economy, establishing and administering national governments. And he saw the American experience, rooted in the primal wilderness, as giving renewal to these critical habits. Burgess depicted an emerging war of the modernizing and civilizing force of Teutonic statecraft against all the forces of "barbarism" that would resist it. He in turn, and to this extent, spoke in favor of restricted immigration into the United States. "We must preserve our Aryan nationality in the state," he wrote, "and admit to its membership only such non-Aryan race-elements as shall have become Aryanized in spirit and in genius by contact with it." Regarding the generality of the "new immigration," Burgess believed that "Uncle Sam does not want such rabble for citizens." Furthermore, by way of contrast to James at Illinois, Burgess built his department at Columbia on the narrowest of bases. Essentially, he considered the university a place for men only—white men. He spoke strongly against the admission of women students and Jewish students. Columbia's historian judges Burgess quite frankly "a confirmed white supremacist."[6]

James reviewed Burgess's book in the first issue of the *Annals*. He summarized its principal ideas, both on race and on the state, observing that Burgess discounted natural rights theories that ascribed personal rights to individuals. Burgess would make the state both the source of all rights and the protector of them. James easily saw how contentious and controversial were the ideas in this book. But he considered it very important, "however much one may disagree with it." And did James so disagree? He did not really say. He promised only to take up the controversies in a succeeding review, one that he never wrote.[7]

Another strain prominent among the American progressive thinkers concerned race, not as an incident of culture, but of blood. As Thomas C. Leonard has explained, the liberal intelligentsia had invoked the organic metaphor to advance their notions of the positive state and their programs for inclusiveness. In doing so, they also opened up to analogies of infection, disease, biological imperfections, and genetic defects. Eugenics followed in the wake. Leonard's book is as informative as it is alarming. Academics, indeed some of the best-known progressive thinkers, have a large place in this study. Thus, the University of Wisconsin, the most important university in the Progressive movement, contributed significantly to racial marking, always under the standard of "scientific" legitimization. So, in John R. Commons's book *Race and Immigrants* (1906) one reads that Black Americans did not qualify for the suffrage because of their "thousand years of savagery." He also judged the new immigrants inferior to previous ones, and a threat to native American workers. Sociologist Edward A. Ross confirmed: "One man, one vote, does not make Sambo equal to Socrates." But an ancient American prejudice now expanded to include people of the new immigration, Slavs particularly.[8]

Much of this thinking marked the extensions of Darwinism into American culture, and it had the significant shift of making these questions about race matters of biological determinism. That emphasis made race identity an intractable fact. Political reform, even education, could have little effect. Thus, Commons wrote that immigration policy, the vital question of who should come into the United States, came down to "race differences." These distinguishing marks, he said, "are established in the very blood and physical constitution" of human beings. Thus entrenched, they pose severe challenges to assimilation.[9] But if science dictates the situation, some believed, then science, too, might prepare a solution. The vogue of eugenics, that is, the "scientific" breeding of human beings, gathered wide public interest in the Progressive Era and a surprising amount of allegiance from intellectuals, and "progressive" ones, too. Ely saw potential for good in eugenics because he considered that it built on what we now know as true: there are "certain human beings who are absolutely unfit, and should be prevented from a continuation of their kind." Commons also embraced the promise of eugenics. Wisconsin, as did other states, passed a forcible sterilization law in 1913, endorsed by Ross and University of Wisconsin president Charles R. Van Hise.[10]

Despite Edmund James's great interest in these subjects, he wrote very little on them. His wide attention to a host of social and political issues simply did not bring race or nationality into his descriptions and prescriptions. Generally, he seemed rather standoffish. The race question appeared an open question to him and as such he did not want it to figure in policy making. But he did

6. A University at War   89

not give credence to absolutists who would maintain that race accounted for nothing at all in human affairs. Thus, in 1896, he wrote a response to a book by William Dalton Babington titled *Fallacies of Race Theories*. The book, a collection of posthumous essays by Babington, insisted that race differences and heredity had no influence on human behavior. Environment shapes just about everything, he insisted. Thus, the author discounted theories of Anglo-Saxonism advanced by Adams, Burgess, and others. And Babington blamed political philosophy and culture, not racial characteristics, for the retarded progress of countries like China. Perhaps so, James replied, but we would still need to understand why those aspects of Chinese life assumed ascendancy whereas other influences had greater importance, as among the Teutons. James found Babington's notions too simplistic, but wanted more investigation of this subject. He concluded as follows: it would not be easy to "demonstrate that racial characteristics had no place in fixing the relative position of the black and white races in the history of civilization." But do we really think that living in Africa would render the white race black, or living in America make it red, "with all which that implies"?[11]

So, James, though shunning biological determinism, was nonetheless no egalitarian when he considered the nations of the world. He made that point clear when he participated in a forum organized by the *Independent* in 1912. Theodore Marburg, a jurist about to become American ambassador to Belgium, had published a piece titled "The Backward Nation." He argued that nations so identified constituted a world threat to life, property, and progress. That situation challenged the other nations to sow "the seed of progress and civilization" in these places, and indeed throughout the world. "It was a racial thing," he said. Because with respect to civilization, Marburg believed, "races differ in their capacity to carry it forward." So, the world has a stake in "the spread of the right blood" and must put in place "the liberal practices" that will secure justice. If we look at the long historical record, Marburg believed, we can affirm that "Anglo-Saxon assertiveness has justified itself." For what makes for backward countries? Marburg asked. "The character of the people governed," he answered. So, he called for "joint action" by the "civilized world" to suppress lawlessness and "save the national life" of backward countries. He envisioned a transformation that would come ultimately from "ideas and ideals" and the fortifying institutions and policies that come in their wake.[12]

The editors of the *Independent* thought Marburg's piece worthy of a large discussion. They invited about a dozen respondents, who gave brief evaluations. James had the first entry and the largest space. He gave clear endorsement to Marburg's argument, with one major exception: he did not credit the race factor that held so much significance to Marburg. But James had no shyness in approaching the subject in terms of superior and inferior nations, though he did so without embracing Anglo-Saxonism. He employed the

90   PART I. THE LARGER UNIVERSITY

analogy of eminent domain in domestic law and applied it to international arrangements. We do not allow one person, James said, to stand in the path of progress when the larger needs of the community are at stake. We need something like the principle of eminent domain that would allow "the interest of the civilized world" to prevail and make way for the progress of the larger human race.[13]

• • •

James took a particular interest in two groups of immigrant people. As noted, the "new immigration" induced a dramatic demographic shift in the American population. Jews numbered heavily in it. Whereas Germany and central Europe had supplied most of the Jews in the United States until the late nineteenth century, eastern Europe and Russia sent millions more out of their homes and villages, the shtetls. Jewish numbers in America, about fifty thousand in 1850, rose to two hundred and thirty thousand in 1880 and to close to a million by the end of the century. (The Pale of Settlement included also part of the former Poland.) The heaviest immigration then followed, with the total reaching almost three million when the war in Europe broke out in 1914. Victims of pogroms perpetrated by the Russian czars, 90 percent of these exiles found their way to the United States and 90 percent of that group located in New York City. Some Americans reacted with fear at the influx and some with hostility. Economic issues prevailed in the debates and discussions, but ethnic-religious ones figured also. The American Federation of Labor, at its 1906 convention, labeled the new immigrants (Jews and others) unassimilable and registered the union's fear of cheap labor. The Immigration Restriction League had organized in Boston in 1894 and sought congressional legislation to abate the influx.[14]

The National Liberal Immigration League followed in reaction to the restriction movement in 1906. Formed from various Jewish groups, it nonetheless spoke for all immigrants as its leaders wished not to have the immigration controversy perceived as only a Jewish matter. The League had an eclectic membership that included Charles W. Eliot of Harvard and Woodrow Wilson of Princeton, and members of Congress, too. When an immigration bill came before the House in 1906 it included a literacy test. The NLIL organized protests around the country and sent delegates to the capital to raise opposition to the legislation. Congress formed an immigration commission to review the matter.[15]

The NLIL pursued other activities and in 1906 arranged for the publication of a large book that would make the case for the Jewish immigrant in America. Edmund James, still new to the presidency of the University of Illinois, agreed to be editor of the anthology. The book consisted of twelve chapters, written by unnamed contributors. They took up subjects like "Philanthropy,"

"Economic and Industrial Conditions," "Religious Activity," "Educational Influences," and "The Jew in Politics." Each of these chapters looked at the Jewish populations in New York, Philadelphia, and Chicago. As editor, James wrote a "preface," one that seemed to address specifically the various fears and suspicions typically found in the American populace. He described Jews as a very durable people, referencing their mobility and constant relocations (so reminiscent of James's own early life). Their long history of persecutions, James said, had tested them as a people but also strengthened those who had come through; a kind of "survival of the fittest," he asserted, that had fortified the whole race. Jews, James pointed out, are a positive presence. They do not bring in contagious diseases. They live untainted by alcohol (always a high recommendation for James) and "foul blood diseases." So, Jews do not become burdens to the social support system of the community. They take care of their own and you hardly ever see Jewish "street beggars." James wished also to highlight the Jewish achievement in education and commitment to it. He finished his preface on that subject: Jewish parents spare "no privation to secure the education and advance of their children. In our schools, the Jewish scholars are, as a rule, bright, attentive, and studious. They excel in mathematics, English, and history. They show special aptitude for studies appealing to the imagination, and the enthusiasm of even the littlest children for the free flag that covers them is a sight to stir the heart of the most heedless scoffer of the immigrant."[16]

James did not so easily make an accommodation to another ethnic group. For decades the Chinese, arriving in huge numbers during the gold fever of 1849 and afterward, had provoked American animosity. The Chinese made up a quarter of the work force in California, where violence against them occurred frequently. (But one need only look at Jacob Riis's classic book of 1890, *How the Other Half Lives*, to measure the negative feelings against this group on the other coast.) The Chinese came in another wave to work on the western railroads, hired in large numbers to build the first transcontinental and other lines. The Chinese American population was overwhelmingly male and unmarried. The Chinese lived by themselves; they hoarded money; they smoked opium. They struck many Americans as a living defiance of free labor and its republican ideals of citizenship. "They were as much threats to free labor and white manhood as chattel slaves had been before the Civil War," as historian Richard White puts it. Of course, the Chinese were the first group targeted by national immigration legislation, in the exclusion act of 1882.[17]

James entered the discussion at this point, early in his career. He wrote a letter to the *Nation* and stated at the outset: "For the first time since I began to read the *Nation* I find myself out of sympathy with its views." His pique centered on the magazine's defense of Chinese labor, made within its general sympathy for free-market policies. That standard had no weight with James.

92   PART I. THE LARGER UNIVERSITY

He instead looked to social-cultural considerations. The Chinese, he said, do not integrate with us. "They are of a civilization so different from ours, and of political, religious, and ethical traditions so different from ours." Ultimately, then, the Chinese represented to James an insurmountable challenge to his ideals of the organic society. Harmonious integration hit a brick wall when it came to this group. Furthermore, James said, our governments do not have the means to protect the Chinese from the manifold attacks on them wherever they settle.[18]

James knew the arguments against his position and the restriction legislation. It violates our tradition, some insisted. James made the claim for national power and control of trade and immigration by citing the restrictions made earlier in the century against the international slave trade. Anti-Chinese feeling, others believed, displayed a racism alien to American ideals and was all too like the Southerner's contempt for Black people. Although James did refer to "a race entirely different from us," one that displayed "a tenacious persistence of type," he had cultural matters in mind and not a biological determinism. In that regard, James added, he would not have allowed either the African slaves or the Chinese laborers to have come to America in the first place. But, James added, if the Chinese were here in great numbers, "I would give them all the rights that any of us have." The *Nation*, probably editor E. L. Godkin, attached a commentary to James's letter and cited the added, useful competition in the labor market provided by the Chinese workers and thus its boost of the national economy. James warned that we should not make "material development" the highest consideration in a matter so complex as this one.[19]

Years later, as president at Illinois, James approached the China question in a different way. By then, the United States had experienced the Boxer Rebellion (1900–1901) as an angry Chinese population fought back against the imperial designs of the western powers. These actions had completely violated Chinese sovereignty in an effort to carve up the country and allot to each nation a section of it for its own economic exploitation. The United States had resisted these actions with Secretary of State John Hay's "Open Door" policy, stated in 1899. It would assure that all of China would lay open for American opportunity in a free competitive arena. James now saw in China a rising star in the East and a great opportunity for the United States. We should work to gain influence in China by an "intellectual and spiritual" outreach that would secure our advantages over the European nations and over Japan, too. Writing in 1907, James proposed an "educational commission," consisting of teachers, engineers, and others, to go out into all the provinces of China, thereby extending an American presence of far lasting appeal and usefulness to both countries. James wanted no program of imperialism, European or American, and believed that the "moral" effects of this educational outreach would have much more beneficial results. In response to a favorite maxim of the imperialists, "trade follows the flag," James replied, "trade follows moral and spiritual domination far more inevitably than it follows the flag."[20]

The next year James saw another opportunity and made a special contribution to American-Chinese relations. The United States, with the European countries, had exacted an indemnity on China to make it pay for damage done during the Boxer Rebellion on their property in China. Executing this act of hubris revealed that China had actually paid too much, and the United States had some seventeen million dollars on its hands. What to do with it? James proposed that the American government establish a scholarship program to bring to America Chinese students who would enroll in American colleges and universities. James sought to bring a new vision to American-Chinese relations.[21]

He wrote up a proposal to this effect and submitted it to President Theodore Roosevelt. The letter reproduced much of the piece he had published the year before, and it had the same design. James could think of no better way for the United States to expand its influence in China. Roosevelt found the idea very appealing and in the message that he drafted to Congress replicated precisely James's arguments. He described the program as "an act of friendship," but also a cultural investment, one that would counter European and Japanese influence in China as well. The American president saw great opportunity in Chinese graduates of the American universities returning to their home country and taking the lead in creating a new China through "American-directed reform." Congress passed the legislation in 1909 and set up a preparatory school in China to help launch the scholarships. That school later became Tsinghu University. Between 1909 and 1929 some 1,300 Chinese students came to the United States in a very successful and highly competitive program. Other nations followed in similar efforts. Over the years the University of Illinois, as one might have expected, educated about a third of the Chinese students who had come here for higher education.[22]

The Boxer indemnity program did not immediately yield the influx of students from China that James expected. They were choosing older universities in the East. But he stood committed to the program and moved to assure its success. He communicated widely with the American missionary teams in China, ones he knew well through his own Methodist connections. On the campus he sponsored the third annual meeting of the Chinese Student Alliance, a national organization of all Chinese college students in the United States, in 1913. He invited the Qing minister to the country, Wu Tingfang, to give a commencement address, in 1908. Above all, James did something to address the well-being of all foreign students at the University. He created the Office of Advisor to Foreign Students, in 1913. To it he appointed a faculty member, English professor James Seymour, and gave him a substantial salary. Seymour proceeded to set up new programs for this part of the student body:

94   PART I. THE LARGER UNIVERSITY

The Chinese Student Club. President James made great efforts to open up connections between China and the University. Courtesy of the University of Illinois Archives.

language enrichment classes, private language tutors, and a host-family program to address the severe difficulty of students from abroad finding housing in Champaign and Urbana. Seymour's initiatives became widely known and widely emulated on other American campuses.[23]

By the time of the war, Chinese students had become the largest of the foreign groups on campus, with thirty-seven, which equaled about one-third of the Chinese students at American universities. Students from Japan numbered twenty-one and from Brazil nineteen. India and Canada, with ten and eleven, followed among the total of thirty-one nations represented. The seven students from the Philippines led among the insular possessions of the United States (with Puerto Rico, Hawaii, and the Canal Zone).[24]

So, on the eve of World War I Edmund James looked out at a United States brimming with reform and full of democratic potential. Of course, he joined many other American intellectuals in making assessments. Some of these others, as noted, took a racial measure, asserting that certain groups had forged the lead in advancing democracy and playing that critical role in the world's progress. Usually, they cited one group—the Anglo-Saxon, with its Teutonic origins. They also dismissed other groups as incapable of making such a contribution and thus even constituting a threat to that progress. James did not take that course. He allowed that race might be a factor, but thought that history superseded it. Not blood but culture, as shaped by long experience over time, played the greater role, he believed. For his part, he looked at one place as having special value and significance to him: Germany, from the formation of its great universities in the time before nationhood,

6. A University at War   95

and in the progress of its governments, from city to state, in the aftermath of its nationhood in 1871. For James, Germany showed what really mattered. It would not be wrong to call Edmund James a thoroughgoing Germanophile.

Germany, James believed, provided the United States valuable models, but it had made a direct, positive contribution as well. "The German element in this nation," he wrote, "has been one of the most advantageous of all those which have flowed into our body politic." He honored particularly the "48ers," the defeated revolutionists of that momentous year in European history, 1848, because they had fought for reforms in their own countries and in America as well. Shortly into his presidency at Illinois, in 1906, James had the opportunity to expound on this history, speaking at the memorial services for Carl Schurz, one of the prominent 48ers in the United States, in Chicago. In their home country, James said, this group prepared the way for the end of absolutism and the advent of constitutionalism. When they went into exile after the revolution many came to the United States and here they became "a blessing out of all proportion to their numbers." They fought against slavery and rallied to the Union cause in the Civil War. Their German experience enabled them to lead in crucial reforms in their new country—civil service, education, public administration. James called them "men of intelligence and culture, men of activity, men of ideals." He had discovered those qualities in Schurz for himself at a very young age, in 1870 precisely, James recalled, when he came across some of Schurz's speeches in his school, and then five years later when he heard Schurz give a public address. "I received an outlook, an enlightenment, if you please, and a moral uplift of such a distinct character that I have always looked back to that dingy hall in Cambridgeport as one of the most important and sacred places on the face of the earth."[25]

And finally, this love affair that James had with Germany had reinforcement from an intimate source, his remarkable wife Anna Margaret Lange James. The two met while he was studying at Halle, in the area where she had grown up, the daughter of a Lutheran minister. She had an early education with the children of the lord of the manor, Herr von Alvensleben, from one of the oldest noble families in Prussia, and her early life reflected the privileged ties the family enjoyed. Her maternal grandfather, William Gerlach, taught philosophy at Halle and had an invitation to succeed Hegel, no less, at Heidelberg in 1820, but he chose to remain at Halle. The line of professors in her family, in fact, went back to a great-great-grandfather who taught the classics at Leipzig. Anna Margaret James loved languages. She mastered both French and Latin and learned to speak a fluent and expressive English. She and Edmund married after he came back to the United States to earn some money at Normal. She was remembered as "an enthusiastic, patriotic Prussian and German." She decorated the James home in Urbana every year on the emperor's birthday. But she embraced the United States, too. The children's

96   **PART I. THE LARGER UNIVERSITY**

Anna Margaret Lange James. Courtesy of the University of Illinois Archives.

rooms had pictures of Washington and Lincoln, whom she wanted the boys to emulate. She made their home into a place of welcome, especially to the new professors and their wives. Edmund and Anna Margaret at that time had three living children: Anthony John, who became a lieutenant in the American navy; Harman Gerlach, professor of politics and government at the University of Texas; and Helen Dixon, a musician and singer. Anna Margaret died in November 1914, her husband and her daughter at her bedside. James immediately established a scholarship program in her memory.[26]

In May 1906 James wrote a letter to Harvard philosophy professor Hugo Münsterberg, informing him that James's son Harman, who had graduated Harvard the previous year, had now entered the law school. James said he wanted his son "to keep in touch with German life and German science." He told Münsterberg that he greatly appreciated his having done so much to promote international good will. In a follow-up response to the philosopher's reply James wrote, "I am doing everything I can to promote in the American people an understanding and recognition of German culture." That was in 1906. Eleven years later the United States declared war on Germany. How might James respond?[27]

• • •

Well before American entry into the Great War began James had made himself a spokesman for preparedness. That policy had a special place in his ideas about the American college and university and about military service and American citizenship. In November 1915 he made a three-week tour to the East Coast, spoke with Secretary of War Lindley Garrison and Major-General Leonard Wood, and testified before Congress. James spoke to the national need for a larger corps of officers for the armed services. The universities should do that training, he urged, stating that they could offer courses for it that students would combine with their main academic programs. They would graduate with double degrees, in electrical engineering and military engineering, for example. Land-grant colleges had a special responsibility to supply this corps of leaders. The government, James specified, should pay each enrolled student $250 a year. The Secretary of War seemed especially favorable to the idea. The next year James went to New York and received good newspaper coverage in that city. Much discussion now centered on James's proposal. Finally, three months before American entry into the conflict the War Department designated the University of Illinois as one of six institutions to initiate an infantry unit of the Reserve Officers Training Corps.[28]

James emphasized in his pushing for these programs that the officer-graduates "must have both a liberal and military education." That feature distinguished them from a West Point training, which he judged "too exclusively military." And he thought that the university programs had another recommendation:

98   PART I. THE LARGER UNIVERSITY

their democratic character. They would draw from all regions of the country. They should also include women. They would have a prominent place at the land-grant schools, which "are peculiarly democratic in their nature," and have always offered military instruction, per the Morrill Act. As these universities are already "strong centers of intellectual life," their programs will forge important links "in the great chain of national defense." James evoked old ideas of republicanism. The student training programs in American colleges and universities would prepare both soldiers and citizens, he emphasized. "A body of officers would have received their training in institutions dominated by *civilian* ideas and ideals." Each goal supplements the other. James also saw military drill as an antidote to the soft living prevalent among too many American youth and to the "greed of Mammon" so embedded in American public life.[29]

American entry into the war lay just around the corner. A desperate Germany, committed to an all-out victory, and soon, announced that it would resume submarine attacks on February 1, 1917. When it did so, President Wilson could no longer keep the nation aloof from combat. On April 2 Congress in Washington assembled to hear his war message and again two days later to follow the American leader into a declaration of war against Germany—a tense and dramatic moment for all assembled there. But Wilson, this man of peace, now felt that he must raise the conflict into high moral ground and idealistic purpose. "The world must be made safe for democracy," he said. The United States must fight so that a new world order can emerge "from the wreckage of Europe torn asunder by the evil spirit of imperial plunder and dynastic rivalries." And we must make this conflict one that preserves and extends the rights that have always defined America, to be embraced "by the hearts of men and women around the globe."

This turn of events gave President James a painful moment. Admitting "how great my admiration is for Germany and things that are German," James wrote a German friend, "I have always been in disfavor with my own people for my views in favor of Germany, and I think that in many lines today Germany stands at the very head of modern nations, and is giving a wonderful example to the world of the essential virile and vital forces which determine the rise and fall of nations."[30] But not for a moment did James allow his personal history to obstruct what now became for him a raging passion—seeing the United States to a complete defeat of Germany. In Chicago when the declaration of war came, James, the very next day, took up the question of loyalty, addressing a "mass meeting" in that city. He appealed to Americans of foreign birth to prove their loyalty to their adopted land in its struggle for democratization of the world. Hours before this talk James had wired President Wilson: "I hereby volunteer for any service whereby I may be of use. In this situation there can only be patriots and traitors."[31]

6. A University at War   **99**

What followed immediately was a campus transformed. Students and professors alike became wholly consumed by the war. It dominated classroom discussions. And, as much as their president, students wanted to be of service to the cause. Many asked for more hours of drill. Hundreds left the campus to join the army or navy or to enroll in the ambulance corps. By mid-May some 1,200 had departed for these purposes. Four hundred more students withdrew before the new semester began in January 1918. The dean of the College of Engineering reported that he had received calls, on four different occasions, from the Ordnance Office of the U.S. Army for some one hundred engineers. Six hundred students enrolled in additional courses about the war established for juniors and seniors. Women students formed groups of knitters with the main purpose of making war clothing for American troops. At the end of April all the classes flocked to a rally, relocated from the Auditorium to the larger gymnasium annex, at which the president addressed them. His remarks, as reported, "vibrated with unusual power and fitness of expression." As the *Daily Illini* observed: "Alternately sitting and standing, singing and applauding, the gathering of students was the largest and the most unusual ever seen at Illinois." President James explained that he did not intend to hold a patriotic really; rather, he wanted questions asked and reactions discussed. In short, he hoped for intelligent discussion, and the event seems to have conformed to that expectation.[32]

James also announced to the War Department that he would make available for its use any of the University's facilities, its scientific and technical labs especially. The first realization of that offer came in the establishment of a training program in aviation, Illinois being one of six schools so designated by the federal government. It quickly enrolled fifty students, with more coming in rapidly. Long discussions with the War Department also led to establishment of an air force base at Rantoul, several miles north of the University. The campus itself looked like an armed camp. "Tents have been pitched east of the armory, giving a touch of the real thing to the south campus," as David Kinley remembered it. The aviators had a dominant visibility. And by October: "The Y. M. C. A, is filled from garret to cellar with military aviators in training, the gym-annex and various classrooms are occupied by the school of aeronautics, the regular military department finds plenty of use for the campus also, the coeds carry their war knitting around with them . . . and war planes from Rantoul are heard overhead."[33]

Women students took on patriotism's work in various ways. The reference above to the knitters documents one of these pursuits. By 1918 one could find every day some two hundred university women, at the University center of the Red Cross in the Woman's Building, making everything from socks to pajamas, surgical shirts to towels, even helmets. Also, female students, 155 in number, enrolled in a course in preparation for hospital service. The Women's League

CLASS IN RED CROSS WORK

Women students take courses for credit, working with the Red Cross in the campus-wide effort to support the American cause in the war. Courtesy of the University of Illinois Archives.

helped to finance the program. Red Cross certification was the goal. Like the men in their military classes, these women students, with the dean's approval, could substitute this course for any other in their regular programs.[34] Finally, to match the sacrificing spirit of the male student enlistees, many of the women imposed disciplinary regimes on themselves. Some foreswore earthly pleasures like candy and between-meal snacks, going to the movies, buying new dresses (fixing up old ones instead), attending dances, and heading off to Chicago on weekends. Others devised a plan for women students to raise $30,000 on their own for the war cause. Professor Evarts B. Green of the history department headed the committee, which raised $14,000 from contributions by students and faculty. Other fund-raising causes included Syrian-Armenian relief, the Red Cross, the University Ambulance unit, the American University Union in Europe, and, of course, the sale of Liberty bonds. At the behest of President James, selected faculty formed the University War Committee. It would serve to coordinate campus causes in support of the war, help students find useful outlets for government service, supply information to media throughout the state, and publish material on topics relating to the war and illustrating the vital role the University was playing in that larger cause.[35]

Illinoisans, like all the nation, had followed the events in Europe with great concern. Throughout the conflict, the *Daily Illini* reported on the battles and the diplomatic activities of the belligerents as the paper had enlisted in the wire services program of the Associated Press. From the very beginning, attention focused on Belgium and the atrocities of the German army as it advanced through that neutral country. On the campus, almost immediately, a drive for "Belgian relief" formed and gained the support of nearly everyone—students, faculty, and administration. By the time of the American intervention the separate drives of these groups had raised $14,000. The Union sponsored relief dances. The YMCA and the YWCA held a joint "Masquerade Party" for Belgian relief.[36] Then another campaign formed—to raise support for the war in general by way of subscriptions. The YMCA involved itself actively and Vice President Kinley took the main leadership. This campus-wide project also proved successful, exceeding quotas set for it.[37]

Throughout the war years all members of the UofI community experienced huge patriotic rallies. President James arranged them and participated in them. He wanted the University to give its blessing to the Allied cause—heart, mind, and soul. He thought no greater cause ever existed. (James himself often paraded around the campus dressed in a military suit of olive drab cloth with leather crosses.) The rallies took place in the Auditorium or in the Armory and thousands gathered for them, the largest ever held on campus. They sang songs. They listened to speeches. The campus musical groups performed. Students helped organize these events and the war had near unanimity of support among them. Some did not always show enthusiasm, but none became outspoken against the war. James, however, showed no tolerance for even the indifferent, denouncing them as "slackers."[38]

James had plenty of assistance in keeping the campus war fervor alive. Faculty did more than contribute to the Belgian relief and the War Fund. They gave addresses at many places beyond the campus. Many went to Washington. And they talked about the war to individual student groups. Sororities and fraternities, other student units like the Cosmopolitan Club and Triangle, and professional groups like Farm House and Pi Phi Rho (forensics) entertained these speakers.[39] David Kinley was especially active. He headed the War Fund Committee and gave three public lectures on the subject "What We are Fighting For," sponsored by the YWCA. On the front page of the *Daily Illini* Kinley made "An Appeal." In predictable fashion Kinley proclaimed that "the world war is a war against war. We are in it to save ideals and institutions whose essence is the spirit of Christianity." "Freedom," "home," and "brotherly love" define our ends in this war. "And we should sacrifice, financially, as much as we can to support the War Fund. Our fighting soldiers deserve no less," Kinley urged.[40] Also, noted visitors came to the University for this same purpose. Probably most important to James was the visit of Albion Small, now dean of the Graduate School of Arts and Letters at Chicago, and James's intellectual partner in the early cause to promote the academic social sciences. He, too, faced the personal dilemma of rejecting the country that had inspired his career. James introduced him as "one of the world's great sociologists." Small titled his address in December 1917, "German Autocracy Must Be Crushed."[41]

Faculty also participated in the war effort by way of offering new courses and reconfiguring old ones. Across the spectrum of American higher education these courses came under the category of "War Aims" or "War Issues" courses. Academic departments all over the country challenged themselves to offer a relevant, creative curriculum. Thus, the History program at Illinois designed History 41 History of War Causes. (The department also put together a campus lecture series to address current aspects of the war, held in the large Commerce Lecture Hall.) Electrical Engineering formed EE 94, an eight-hour course in radio telegraphy, and Geology fashioned a course titled "Topography of the War Zone." There seemed no end in this quest for relevance and academic patriotism. The Department of Romance Languages put together a course that used the textbook *Military French*, for students before they left for the war overseas. These courses were popular among the students. The French course had two sections, with thirty and fifty students in them.[42]

As for the students, they marched in lock step with the campus leadership. They flagged their patriotism and showed no tolerance for skepticism about the war or dissent from the national cause. Two pieces from the *Illinois Magazine* illustrate this point. This publication, a literary outlet for student essays and stories, seldom addressed issues of domestic or foreign politics. But an editorial, "The Ultimate Philosophy," celebrated the lively and various competing systems of thinking on the contemporary scene. However, it said, we will return to these thoughts at a later time because now, in the midst of war, the "only one tenable political philosophy, [is] a philosophy of pure and obedient patriotism." The editorial actually appeared a month before the United States declared war.[43] When war came the next month the magazine summoned submission on the part of all to the federal government. "It is of little moment now whether we as individuals approve of this war." Once we have declared for war, that question, once vital, ceases to have importance, the editorial proclaimed. Sacrifice all for nationalism. "Nothing is important save loyalty to our country." Question nothing and be prepared to sacrifice all to preserve our national ideals.[44] The staff of the *Daily Illini* called for full campus commitment to the war. It wanted all students to have military drilling, with a greater share of the week given to it. This training it judged "an absolute necessity." It called for all women to take "compulsory" courses with the Red Cross.[45]

• • •

Individual faculty made innumerable efforts in using their expertise and the facilities of their academic departments to aid the war effort. This extraordinarily wide array would require much space even in a partial accounting. In one critical area, to cite an example, the American government turned to the University's chemistry department early on. The United States was importing vital materials from Germany before the war and now had to find other sources for them. Commercial companies, such as airplane makers working with the government, also appealed to the University. One firm in Dayton, Ohio needed dimethylgyloxime and was shutting down for lack of it until the UofI professors found a way to produce the substance. For some eighteen months the University furnished almost all the dimethylgyloxime used in the United States. This "Illium," actually developed before the war as a platinum substitute and so named for the UofI, facilitated the making of scientific instruments. Much of the work had classified status and included production of "war gasses," though not including mustard gas.[46] Altogether, the University made over a hundred different compounds and complex organic chemical reagents needed by universities and commercial businesses. From this work the University derived a small profit while producing at cost for the other universities. The president of the American Chemical Society selected five American universities—Johns Hopkins, Chicago, Michigan, Columbia, and Illinois—to help coordinate all these efforts across the nation.[47]

In other activities history professor Evarts Greene again chaired the National Board for Historical Service, a war propaganda agency (see below). The history department also organized a program of lectures, offered by its members, relevant to the war. For example, Professor Laurence M. Larson of the department spoke in May 1918 on "The Sins of German Imperialism." Other faculty worked with other units of the federal government on matters of food preservation, ship construction, and aeronautics.[48] The School of Agriculture and the Department of Household Science made extensive efforts that thoroughly reoriented their standing programs.

James and Library Director Phineas L. Windsor saw another opportunity for University service to the war. Wanting to collect books for army training camps, Windsor asked James to get the approval of the Council of Administration to implement his plan.[49] When the ALA appealed to librarians to serve as volunteer organizers in army camp libraries, a number of Illinois librarians responded. In late 1917 Windsor received a paid leave of absence for two months to serve as assistant director of the ALA's Library War Service in Washington, D.C. Three others—a library clerk, the classics librarian, and Francis Drury—served for brief periods in camp libraries.[50] In August 1918 the chairman of the Library Service Committee of the ALA appointed Windsor state director for Illinois in a campaign to raise three million dollars.[51] During the war James urged Windsor to build up a good collection in military and naval art, science, and history.[52]

Then, in October 1918, amid celebration and fanfare, the Students' Army Training Corps (SATC) made its debut on the Illinois campus. Created by the

104   **PART I. THE LARGER UNIVERSITY**

The Students' Army Training Corps. President James had long spoken for the ideas that underscored this national institution, formed in 1918. Courtesy of the University of Illinois Archives.

War Department and approved by the General Staff under authority granted to the president by the Selective Security Act, it fell under the direct control of the federal Committee on Education and Special Training. The program invited the participation of all American colleges. Once put in place, one commanding officer, appointed by the War Department, would arrive to organize operations at the institutions involved. They in turn accepted the obligation to revise their courses in accordance with dictates from the War Department. The University Board of Trustees authorized President James to prepare the campus for participation. He needed no urging. Additional military personnel would provide instruction for the appropriate courses. Volunteering students then became part of the U.S. armed services and on call for enlistment as needed. They would go directly into the service as officers, an arrangement designed also to fill these ranks in greater numbers than the ROTC program could do.[53]

The program had an immediate impact at the UofI. It greatly restored the student population that had declined at the war's beginning. Enrollment now stood at just under 7,000. Some 2,600 students enrolled in the Army section, 400 in the Navy section, and nearly that many at the University of Illinois College of Medicine in Chicago. The Armory building underwent changes to accommodate the large number of student-soldiers, and houses around the campus were secured for them, including all fraternity houses now leased by the University. SATC students chose new courses appropriate for their intended type of service. War Issues, Military Law and Practice, Hygiene and Sanitation, Surveying, and Map Making might supply the program for infantry and artillery officers, for example. Lieutenant Colonel William R. Abercrombie served as commanding officer. Uniformed students drilled constantly throughout the week, and, as Benjamin Shearer observed, "the presence was everywhere."[54]

The SATC program launched across the country on the specified date of October 1, 1918, called a national day of induction. At Illinois faculty and guests sat on the Auditorium steps, a military band played, and a long line of soldiers extended back almost to University Hall. President James gave a thoughtful speech about the program and the situation in world affairs that it had to address. A splendid affair indeed, but the new arrangement quickly showed severe fault lines and soon complaints issued from every quarter.

The matter came down to the uneasy situation of two campuses—the military and the formal academic—and their basic incompatibilities. The War Department had specified that "academic authorities are alone responsible for the academic instruction"; military authorities had "sole jurisdiction for the drill and the strictly military studies."[55] But the military personnel felt differently and acted in a manner that raised complaints from Vice President David Kinley down to the faculty. The military people wanted to dictate the whole teaching program, or so it appeared to professors who complained that their own research programs and teaching schedules had to yield to these other priorities. They protested also that the SATC students showed little respect for the courses outside the military concentration and posted a record of very poor attendance in their regular academic classes. Within a month of the SATC's operation Kinley said that he had more than a hundred letters from disaffected faculty. The military staff under Abercrombie's command presumed to dictate the entire University instructional program, and "military arrogance" gnawed at the faculty, frustrated at the assumed higher priority the officers gave to their program. Worse, perhaps, the military personnel gave a bad presentation of themselves. "Drinking, profanity, and roughness in the treatment of students," complained Kinley, "were common." Altogether, it looked like a military takeover. "It was not long," Kinley remembered, "before we were not sure whether we were a University or a training camp." And not long before the program closed, the University did take its complaints to the War Department, which obliged by making personnel changes at the campus. But the war ended the next month. The campus welcomed victory, and a return to normalcy.[56]

When war did come to an end, November 11, 1918, the news came to the Illinois campus by way of the Associated Press wire service now used by the *Daily Illini*, at 2 a.m. the next morning. "Within a few minutes the old convocation bell and the siren fire whistle had roused everybody. A big procession including all the campus soldiers was formed, with a band and a color guard bearing 35 flags of the allied nations and war work organizations in the lead." Students aroused Vice President Kinley, in charge of the campus while President James was visiting in Washington, D.C. Townspeople swelled the

106   PART I. THE LARGER UNIVERSITY

President James liked military dress and ceremony. Courtesy of the University of Illinois Archives.

procession as it marched through the streets of Champaign and Urbana. The gathering filled the quadrangle north of the Auditorium. Kinley addressed it, as did a student from the debate team. More talks ensued, followed by raising of the flags of Great Britain, France, and the United States as the band played the national anthem of each nation. It was a time for celebrating and also remembering the many Illini still overseas and the seventy-five Illini who had given their lives for the nation. Kinley said to the assembled throng: "I saw the troops of France depart for the front in 1914. I watched the English boys prepare to cross the channel to France, and I have seen thousands of our American boys departing for the same place. I thank God that the causes for which they have so gallantly struggled have been gained." Before he had left town President James had ordered a suspension of classes on whatever day the war should end.[57]

• • •

Joy reigned on the campus, to be sure, but yet another matter had made its presence and added to the situation of a university in turmoil. It was called the "Spanish flu," a pandemic, it was believed at the time, that had begun in northern Europe and made its way with severe effect in Spain. It first appeared in the United States among military personnel in the spring of 1918. It would take a devastating toll: some five hundred million people, a third of the world's population, had the infection. An estimated fifty million died. The crisis covered the United States and called on resources of governments and health institutions everywhere. About 675,000 deaths occurred, with some 566 in Illinois. With no vaccines for protection, the "Panic" deserved its name from the fear it created amid the rising death toll.

The flu appeared on the Illinois campus in early October 1918. Quickly it registered 130 cases, but with only one judged "serious." Officials urged people to avoid crowds and take normal precautions. But rising numbers created a call for voluntary nurses. Two deaths were reported at Canute Air Force base and then the first death among students on October 10. Now more tangible reactions addressed the advancing threat. Theaters in the Twin Cities closed. The Council of Administration suspended all social events, but kept classes going. And again, the campus changed. Beginning with Beta Theta Pi, fraternities and sororities were reconfigured as infirmaries. The top floor of College Hall was similarly transformed, and Isabel Bevier took charge of an emergency hospital in the gymnasium of the new Women's Dormitory. Infections rose to around three hundred, overwhelmingly affecting male students. The flu was on the wane by the end of the month.[58]

• • •

World War I constituted for Edmund James another chapter in his intellectual career. To move, as he did, from a love for Germany, rooted mostly in his own educational experience, to a position of avowed determination for the United States and its allies to destroy it, required rethinking. And as president of a major university and its leading spokesman James had much explaining to do. How to justify the American cause, to whose purposes he now dedicated a campus transformed? How now might he explain the history that had created such a situation? How to understand the power dynamics of the international scene and the war that, for all its destruction, might yet lead us to a world renewed? In short, how to make sense of it all? When James urged professors and students alike at his university to dedicate themselves to securing American victory, his entreating applied as much to himself as to them.

James's pronouncements may strike one as extreme. They were, but they took place within a wide and sustained dialogue within the American intellectual community, and to take the measure of James, one should consider him in this framework. Carol Gruber's invaluable book, *Mars and Minerva: World War I and the Uses of the Higher Learning in America*, helps considerably in this effort and this section of the chapter draws on it liberally. One point stands out in her study: the American intellectual community, heavily

108   PART I. THE LARGER UNIVERSITY

in numbers and forcefully in rhetoric, supported the American part in this war. It did not do so reluctantly, as if as thinkers they stood innately averse to violence as a means of adjudicating human affairs. No, they did so with zeal; they often reverted to propaganda; and they imposed on dissenters an intolerance for which many would later have severe regrets. If we can understand this behavior, we will also better understand why some have called the Great War "a thinking man's war" and, with respect to James, arrive at a reasonable assessment of him.[59]

Begin with the matter of Germany. A whole generation of American thinkers, pioneers in the new academic disciplines of the university era in the United States, had launched their careers from a basis of scholarly study in the various German universities. German intellectuals knew of that debt, and in an open letter of October 1914, two months into the conflict, appealed to American opinion. Its writers had formed the German University League with an outreach to those "who have enjoyed the privilege of a German university education." They wanted thereby "to strengthen the regard for the Germans and for their aims and ideals, and to secure for them . . . fair play and proper appreciation." This clumsy effort even sought to justify the horrific invasion of neutral Belgium in August 1914. And it included among the signatories Gustav Schmoller and Johannes Conrad, James's German mentor.[60]

But German influence in the American intellectual community had been waning for some time. After about 1900 fewer Americans were going to Germany for extended education. They didn't need to, as American universities had created first-rate graduate programs in all the modern fields. American scholars became increasingly enamored of England now and fit comfortably into the Anglo-Saxon cult so widespread in the late nineteenth and early twentieth centuries. Among the subset of thinkers whom we have compared to James, one can see the shifts and follow them directly into the anti-German, pro-Allies position of their war allegiances. Arthur T. Hadley of Yale had studied with Treitschke in Germany and acknowledged "a great debt of gratitude to him," but later remarked, "perhaps I should be ashamed to confess it now." Hadley's Yale colleague Henry W. Farnam, who had received a doctorate in Germany and who had been a great admirer of things German, now cited "the difficulty if not the impossibility of ever again having that same feeling of interest and sympathy in German life and history which I have cherished since my boyhood." Albion Small also changed his affections. He, like James, cited German militarism as the prime factor in bringing war to Europe: "Germany has done more than all the rest of the world put together in the way of elaborating and publishing this militaristic ideal," Small wrote. Simon N. Patten had a more complicated transition. His German education had persuaded him to notions of the organic society, which had underscored principles of his social reform thinking. At the war's outbreak Patten placed most blame on

6. A University at War   109

Russia and stayed aloof from the anti-German emotionalism of the day. But increasingly he saw that the new order the world needed required the defeat of Germany and the "Hun brutality" that marked its conduct of the war. Germany's domestic politics also warmed Patten to a greater appreciation of the Anglo-American priority of the individual against the autocratic state. By the end of 1916 Patten was endorsing the preparedness campaign. However, the University of Pennsylvania Trustees resented what they had judged to be Patten's unpatriotic notions and moved to terminate his service the next year.[61] The same shifts occurred among historians. Peter Novick writes: "With the American declaration of war on Germany, doubts about the righteousness of the Allied cause all but disappeared within the [historical] profession. Virtually all shared the patriotic enthusiasm which, overnight, became de rigueur." That feeling applied to American social scientists across the board.[62]

When the United States followed President Wilson into war in April 1917, James gave all his immediate attention to winning the war. The only question for him was how the University of Illinois could contribute to that end. The answer came in all the campus transformations heretofore noted. If James had lingering affections for Germany he simply put them on hold, prepared perhaps to abandon them forever. On matters that interested other intellectuals—history, politics, culture—James said hardly a word. He had a singular focus on strategy at home and the institutional arrangements he could make for the national purpose. Not until the next year did James address larger issues pertaining to the war. Then he wanted to make clear to his community why America had entered the conflict and why its soldiers overseas had committed to a thoroughly justifiable cause. He did so at public meetings where the opportunity to speak to local issues also called for attention to transcendent principles.

The University was celebrating Abraham Lincoln's birthday in February 1918 and also entertaining a prominent visitor from France. This visitor of course represented the nation with whom, along with Great Britain, the United States had its major alliance in the war. After some commentary on Lincoln and on the great cultural achievements of France, its momentous revolution, and its contribution to democracy ("You made a turning point in human history"), James turned his attention to the war. He wanted to emphasize the latter point about democracy because, after the Russian revolution of 1917 and then the withdrawal of that nation from the war, the conflict had more the appearance of an ideological one: Democratic America, Great Britain, and France against autocratic Germany, Austria-Hungary, and the Ottomans. James celebrated France as the bright star of human "culture and refinement." Turning to face his guest, he stated, "Such an occasion [as this], Sir, brings with peculiar vividness to the mind of every student of human history, the preeminent services of the French nation to that common civilization, which is the most precious

110   PART I. THE LARGER UNIVERSITY

heritage of us all." Culture and democracy were what the war was about. The resourceful James did not miss the occasion to join the work of universities to promote these ideals and thus to enhance their importance to the war. In their devotion to science and philosophy these institutions strengthen our common humanity, he said. James once again wanted to move beyond race, national prejudices, and historic rivalries. Science and philosophy erode these evil forces, he asserted. "Our only ambition should be to aid the race." France, with its eminent services to our "common civilization," James concluded, can lead us all "in an ever-increasing appreciation and emphasis of the things which bind us together." And, he asserted, the war has already contributed to that important end.[63]

Thus, like many others, James tried to see the war in its largest extensions, consequences, and aftermath. He took another angle on that prospect when he gave an address at a convocation held on the campus to denote the first anniversary of America's entry into the conflict. We're here, he said, "to dedicate ourselves anew to the great enterprise that we have undertaken." He described the war as "a turning point in the history of the world" because it marks a "great issue in the progress of human freedom." He likened it again to the French Revolution in its epoch-making impact. James knew that many people saw the war more cynically and more realistically than he did, as one rooted in secret histories and designs for imperial gains by the participants, or by the victors more precisely. But like others of his thinking, from President Wilson on down, James wanted to justify the war by its potential peripheral effects. As it reignited the ideals of freedom in Americans, James hoped, that new moral energy would turn attention also to our advancement at home. He made a powerful statement:

> We Americans can not in good conscience and with self-respect line up for freedom and fair treatment for the Pole and Serbian without forming a new and more potent resolution that the negro, the Puerto Rican, the Filipino shall have no reasonable cause of complaint under our government. We can not insist that the German Government shall secure political rights to the common man without resolving anew that the ordinary civil rights shall be secured to all our citizens alike, no matter what their color or race or previous condition of servitude; without determining that mobs and lynching parties shall have an end throughout the broad territory subject to the jurisdiction of the Republic.[64]

This country's founding generation, James added, gave us the Declaration of Independence, but nonetheless suffered from a moral blindness regarding slavery. It took a war to end that evil and thus give the Declaration a fuller meaning, "although it is far from being realized fully yet." James's address went on to mention that this war should therefore renew American efforts in

6. A University at War   **111**

yet other ways. "Thus, the time shall be hastened when no man who is able and willing to labor shall suffer for lack of work; when to every one willing to do his share the means for living a decent human life shall be secured; when economic and industrial liberty, shall be recognized as essential elements in that civil liberty chiefly contemplated in the Declaration. Toward all this a decisive and early victory over Germany and her allies will be greatly conducive."[65] Thus did the UofI's president conjoin the large ends of the war to those of moral and political progress at home.[66] How many university presidents in this Progressive Era so deliberately linked the moral issues of the war to the moral issues of race in their own country?

The Illinois president went public again a few months later at the commencement exercises in July of 1918. Here he had a large audience before whom he could set forth several thoughts about the war, the University, and the national interest. He began by talking about science. This war has demonstrated, he said, what we should have known all along: that science has been critical to our military successes to date and that we must have national independence in making those products needed for our defense. But we entered the war in a state of dependency with respect to some critical commodities, optical glass, for example, that we had to obtain from "enemy" territory. James did not specifically mention how the University of Illinois had responded with its physical and chemical laboratories to address the problem. In fact, though, the University was making the optical glass needed on field guns, range finders, periscopes, and other items. But he did emphasize that "only the Universities" can answer this need. "And so university men are in a certain sense coming into their own, because the glare of bursting shells reveals everywhere the scientific foundation of the successful waging of a great war." James wanted most to honor the ideal of what he called "service science." "Nothing but a great universal and pressing war could have brought home to the American people what a service science, properly developed, could render the nation in a time of peace."[67]

Here James highlighted a matter still very heavy on the minds of American college and university leaders—the question of relevance, usefulness, and practicality as the very reasons for higher education. The matter stood in high visibility at the beginning of the university era and assumed more critical importance especially as state universities, needing justification in the eyes of their publics, gave much emphasis to these concerns. Laurence Veysey, in his landmark book, used the term "utility," which formed part of the trinity of standards, along with "research" and "liberal culture," of the new model American university.[68] Gruber prefers the term "service." But private universities celebrated service, too, as witness Charles W. Eliot at Harvard. And Woodrow Wilson himself, speaking as Princeton's president, had given his

112 PART I. THE LARGER UNIVERSITY

famous address, "Princeton in the Nation's Service," in 1902. That quest for academia's relevance has never flagged.[69]

James, in this commencement address in 1918, turned to the war itself and spoke with greater specificity than heretofore. He called it "the greatest war in the history of the human race." And it had its destiny written in the stars. This war would, finally, he believed, secure the achievement of democracy; indeed, the Allied victory would mean a world-wide triumph of American values. "The vast majority of nations are now marching together shoulder to shoulder committed to the principles of our Declaration of Independence." "All monarchical or aristocratic remnants of previous stages of evolution are destined, in my opinion, to disappear," James avowed. Thus, he believed, Germany and Austria represented the major obstacles to this great realization. And here James showed his complete severance from his previous sympathy for Germany. "Germany began this war." It invaded a foreign country (Belgium) and broke its resistance by "a policy of terrorism" and by behavior practiced there and thereafter that he labeled "unspeakable." Germany threatened now to take French lands, seize the coal fields there, and expel the French population. "Has there ever been a more cruel or cold-blooded proposition than this in the history of Christian nations?" James asked. As for himself, he looked to the day when "our victorious boys come marching home again with the Kaiser's scalp dangling at the army's belt."[70]

James may have thought this address his last at the University because he offered his resignation from the presidency just a few months later. Probably the signs of his growing health issues had emerged. At any rate, his commencement speech showed a degree of emotion untypical of Edmund James. As he spoke with increasing idealism about the war, he turned the subject to himself. "I never wished to be older for but the one reason that I might have carried a musket in our Great Civil War; and I have never wished to be younger but for that one reason that I might now be serving a machine gun in the blood-stained fields of France." He mentioned that his elder son had entered the navy and his younger son was about to enlist in the army. Then, addressing the male students: "Oh, my young brothers, I envy you your chance to get personally into this great world conflict on the side of right and justice and mercy."[71] Unusual passion from a scholar, a man of "science"? Not in this war. Richard Ely at Wisconsin recalled how "painful" it was to him that he had not had a greater part "in this greatest war in the world's history." At James's university, Clarence Alvord in the history department felt the vexations of "my own helplessness" at not being more directly involved in the war.[72] Yes, American intellectuals did love this war!

James did speak once more during the war. He gave the address to the large audience gathered at the inauguration of the SATC on October 1, 1918. By this time the war's end and Allied victory lay in view. But now more than ever James wanted a total victory. Peace efforts had been at work throughout the war, mostly calling on each of the belligerents to disclose its war aims, a request the Wilson administration had made through diplomatic channels. In May of that year James had attended a meeting of the "Win the War for Permanent Peace" group in Philadelphia. It objected to any "premature" settlement and urged that the fight continue "until Prussian militarism is defeated."[73] At the SATC festivity James proclaimed the purity of American intentions in the conflict. The war had the singular goal to extend freedom "to the remotest parts of the world," he asserted. The SATC signified to James another key component of the service role of the university. Such an institution as the SATC could occur only in a democratic country, he said. He cited the "war issues" courses that constituted a major part of the SATC's educational program. Such an ideal, "this close union of scholarship and patriotism," played the heartstrings of this university president.[74]

• • •

The zeal for service and the pressure to show loyalty could also turn ugly. Across the nation, and from the presidency on down, America fell into a vigilance that moved against dissenters who spoke out against the war, and rooted out others suspected of disloyalty. "Force, Force to the utmost," said Wilson in a Flag Day address. "Force without stint or limit" against the enemies of the United States, both abroad and at home. The disloyal and unpatriotic must be thrown down "into the dust." Congress went along, passing the Espionage Law that would lead to major U.S. Supreme Court cases after the war, the *Schenck* and *Abrams* cases. The notorious Creel Commission had collateral support from citizens' groups like the American Defense Society and the National Security League that pursued cultural purity and sought to purge the country of all things German—from language to food—and sounded the alarm about the foreign threat carried like a virus among recent immigrants and their radical, un-American politics.[75]

The service ideal and the ethic of total commitment to military victory yielded noble efforts but dangerous deprivation of academic freedom, too. Loyalty to the national cause meant more than turning campuses into military camps and reconfiguring academic programs. Many professors left their institutions temporarily to work in various government outposts in Washington D.C., or elsewhere around the country, and even overseas. Several from the U of I did so. But, as noted, other opportunities existed. The historical profession provides the best example. J. Franklin Jameson, managing editor of the *American Historical Review*, gathered some colleagues from different universities in April 1917. He wanted them to consider what they might do for the country in this time of war. Their meeting resulted in establishment of the National Board for Historical Service. Frederick Jackson Turner, now at Harvard, and Evarts B. Greene of Illinois held original membership. One project of the NBHS had it working with the Department of Education to change high school curriculums so as to teach history in relation to the war. Historians from across the United States responded that they would take up this work, even travel distances to do so. Carl Becker of Cornell was one of them. The NBHS even did research for the national Committee on Public Information. Some wrote pamphlets, including Charles Beard, John R. Commons, Edward S. Corwin, Andrew McLaughlin, and Carl Russell Fish, all prominent scholars. From Illinois also, Stuart P. Sherman of the English department wrote a motivating piece, *An Appeal to Those Who are Neither Hot Nor Cold*. "Grossly simplified arguments" came from all these efforts, Gruber finds, amounting to a kind of "propaganda" that gave a sad measure to this large quest by American higher education for relevance and public sanction for its work.[76]

All the states had their own manifestations of this heady patriotism, and each had its own special targets. University presidents felt themselves under the heavy pressure of public scrutiny. They had to demonstrate their institutions' full dedication to the war, private universities and public even more so. But the pressure did not always come from outside. Almost every university had its own zealots who demanded full conformity of their colleagues and proved eager to move against them if not satisfied with their feelings about the war. At the University of Minnesota, where history professor Guy Stanton Ford, formerly of Illinois, had a major role with the Committee on Public Information and had his name on the federal payroll, academic freedom took a hit. The case of William A. Schaper, political scientist at this university, got national attention, as did that of James McKeen Cattell at Columbia.[77] At the University of Michigan the whole German department, typically under suspicion of disloyalty, saw two of its members come before the Board of Regents for interrogation. One was fired.[78] Richard T. Ely at Wisconsin spoke for many others when he said that "we are fighting for civilization . . . and the struggle is a life and death one." Therefore, with respect to academic freedom, "we cannot take the same position in time of war as we take in time of peace."[79]

The state of Illinois had stark divisions respecting war preparation and war engagement. President James knew this fact only too well. Illinois, for one, had more Germans and Austria-Hungarians than any state in the Union, and Chicago ranked as the world's sixth largest German city, with a mayor who wanted no American boy sent overseas to fight. But there were plenty of superpatriots around to move the state the other way. Governor Frank O. Lowden, a Republican with many progressive credentials, reflected the dialectical thinking exhibited by so many of them. "There is only one test of patriotism in a war like this," he said. "Either we are for the government or we are against it." The Illinois State Council of Defense, headed by tycoon Samuel Insul, had local branches and some hundred and forty thousand volunteers. It flooded the state with propaganda. The ISCD did not like the teaching of German in the public schools and enrollment in these courses dwindled out of social pressure against them. Governor Lowden again found the right words to wring public sentiments on the matter. "You do not get the true American spirit if you are educated in a foreign tongue," he affirmed. He reinforced the point: "The English tongue is the language of liberty. . . . " From the national level the CPI, the Creel Committee, reached down to the state. It even made movies available to the public, ones bearing titles like *The Beast of Berlin* and *To Hell with the Kaiser*. Although the vast majority of German Americans supported the American cause, local officials in Illinois did what they could to diminish the German presence. They changed street names that might honor a German or forbade playing of music by the great German composers. The German Shepherd breed of dog was now the Alsatian and Chicago's German Club now the Lincoln Club.[80]

When the nation went to war, the University of Illinois became a participant.[81] Many celebrated the virtues of patriotism while the campus witnessed a campaign to support the Red Cross and buy Liberty bonds. But in October a professor of Romance languages visited the office of Queen Lois Shepherd, a philosophy instructor with a doctorate from the Uof I, to sell Liberty bonds. He got a surprise. "If I had ten million dollars," Shepherd declared, "I would not give a cent." "Miss Shepherd," the solicitor replied, "I would not make that remark aloud." "Well," Shepherd replied, "that is my answer." The solicitor then visited Arthur C. Cole, a history professor. He too was unwilling to purchase bonds.[82] Students had reported that Cole had told his classes that England engaged in this war only for the purpose of gaining colonies, just as it has always done.[83]

The Liberty Loan campaign had begun only three weeks after the United States entered the war. To finance the war the head of the Federal Reserve, William G. McAdoo, with whom James had met earlier, devised a program of three parts: one, educating the people on the cause and purposes of the war; two, appealing to the patriotism of all Americans, no matter rich or poor, and flooding the country with propaganda posters with this message; and three, using volunteer labor, rather than government workers, to sell the bonds. Three Liberty Loan drives occurred during the war, with another following the Armistice. The Illinois campus met the goals of all these campaigns successfully. James took great pride in the institution's performance. He wrote the Secretary of the Treasury asking him to advise if there were any university in the country "that approaches this record."[84]

116   PART I. THE LARGER UNIVERSITY

On October 31, 1917, William H. Kerrick, a Department of Justice official in Bloomington, came over to Champaign to investigate rumors about faculty resistance to the Liberty Loan drive. In an office that held the pledge cards he singled out those of Shepherd, Cole, and Camillo Weiss, an instructor of civil engineering. He connected the cards of Shepherd and Cole with that of Carl H. Haessler, who had been offered but then denied an appointment in the philosophy department due to his opposition to the war. A member of the Socialist Party, Haessler had organized students to resist conscription. When drafted he refused to serve. Shepherd, Cole, and Haessler associated with like-minded faculty members: James G. Stuart, Sociology; William C. Oldfather, Classics; Richard C. Tolman, Physical Chemistry; and Weiss. Kerrick arranged to meet with the suspects and others at the Urbana city hall. He asked Charles M. Webber, the Urbana postmaster, and Mary E. Busey, a university trustee, to attend as witnesses.[85]

At city hall Kerrick met Shepherd, Cole, and Tolman. Tolman had decided to accompany his friend Cole. When Kerrick indicated that he would like to interview each person privately, Tolman declared that there would be no private interviews; everyone would be present or all would go home. Shepherd followed Kerrick upstairs to the council chambers where Busey and Webber awaited them. She proved difficult. Asked if she had purchased any Liberty bonds, she replied that that was her business. Asked if she was a Socialist, she demanded a definition of Socialist. Urged to be more cooperative lest Kerrick report negatively about her, she said she did not care what he reported. Frustrated, Kerrick declared, "You're a damned, rotten, vile, socialist, anarchist." Shepherd refused to answer questions and was dismissed from the room.[86]

Going downstairs, Kerrick met Oldfather, Shepherd's friend, and Tolman. When Kerrick sought to identify Tolman, Tolman refused to speak to him because they had not been introduced. The group then went up to the council chambers. Here confusion reigned. Busey demanded to know why Oldfather was there. He had come to defend Shepherd, he replied. Was she in trouble? Would he have come to defend Dean Kinley or President James? Kerrick asked. Tolman did not appreciate the way Kerrick had interviewed Shepherd, and added that Kerrick used bad grammar. Fed up with the attitude of "my" faculty, Busey said that if they were in Germany and those questioned had treated Kerrick as they had, they would have been shot. The assembly adjourned at 11:15 that night.[87]

Reports of the meeting emerged the next day in local newspapers. Some of the people questioned, wrote the *Champaign Daily News*, were liberal Socialists, and others were of German descent. They stood "for nothing and against everything." Generally, the local papers conveyed hostility toward the

University, believing that disloyalty flourished there and that the whole matter needed investigation. Within days national newspapers carried stories about the local turmoil.[88]

At about the same time Cole, Shepherd, Oldfather, Tolman, and Frank Lincoln Stevens prepared this statement, addressed to President James:

> We, the undersigned members of the Faculty of the University of Illinois, have been cruelly and unjustly brought into nation-wide notoriety by unfounded and irresponsible charges of disloyalty to the government of the United States.
>
> We declare most positively that we are, and always have been loyal and law-abiding citizens of the United States and have never been guilty of disloyalty to the government in thought, word or deed.[89]

The University community, of course, felt the sting of bad and often malicious accusations. Secretary of the University Frank W. Scott wanted to rally and encourage the alumni. He penned "A Letter on Loyalty" to members of the University of Illinois Alumni Association: "Do not allow to go unchallenged any statement that there is disloyalty at the University of Illinois. No disloyal word has been heard or deed committed at the University or by anyone connected to the University, so far as anyone in a position to know has been able to ascertain. Reports of disloyalty at the University are lies."[90] Dean Kinley blamed the matter on "overzealous locals."[91]

Near the end of the first year of America's involvement in the war, James dedicated the University again to the single-minded focus on victory. Now is not the time, he urged, for debate and discussion about that purpose. Now is the time for action, and that alone. "The only subject we can properly discuss at the present time," he said, "is how to make this campaign speedy and successful, and any discussion of general subjects which delays that efficient and unified action necessary to success is full of danger and full of folly." "The Government," James believed, had the right and necessity to guard against talk that "interferes with action."[92] At one of his patriotic meetings on campus shortly before, James had made these same points. So long as the fight continues, the motto was "Keep Your Mouth Shut."[93]

The disloyalty proceedings continued. A special committee met in Urbana on November 27. It consisted of Cairo A. Trimble, a Princeton, Illinois, lawyer, Robert F. Carr, a Chicago businessman, and Laura B. Evans of Taylorville. James advised the faculty members called before the committee to simply declare their loyalty and not draw distinctions about degrees of loyalty that might be difficult to understand. The meeting began at 8:45 a.m. and lasted until midnight. Trimble directed the proceedings and did most of the questioning. Kerrick participated. Dean David Kinley took the place of President James, who was out of town at the time.[94]

118   PART I. THE LARGER UNIVERSITY

When all relevant witnesses had testified, Trimble adjourned the meeting with the statement that he had no toleration for disloyalty in the University at this time. He would now present the evidence against the accused faculty to the Board of Trustees. The board met on December 11 to consider the special committee's report. We find no disloyalty at the University, it stated. But, it asserted, faculty members were obliged to be "even above the suspicion of disloyalty." The board's statement, in Bruce Tap's judgment, amounted to a disappointing, very compromised position on academic freedom. It read: "It therefore behooves the Faculty to so conduct its deeds and speech that the world may know they are affirmatively loyal. Their academic freedom of speech and idealism in government affairs is now limited by this war to such as may by no means be construed as unsympathetic, either with the fact that we are at war, or with the principles involved therein."[95]

President James expressed satisfaction with the report, but it was a compromise of academic freedom. It did suggest that restrictions on such freedom were temporary. But these restrictions shaped the climate of the postwar University. By 1920 every professor involved in "disloyalty," except Oldfather, had been forced out of the University. Queen L. Shepherd was not rehired for the academic year 1918–1919. Carl Haessler entered federal prison. In 1919, Richard Tolman, who had gone to Washington to work for the Ordnance Department, wanted to return to Illinois, but acting President Kinley prevented it. Kinley had been skeptical of Tolman ever since 1917 when he discovered that Tolman had joined the Anti-Militarism League. Kinley judged Tolman a bad influence on the University. There could be no suppression of reasonable opinion, said Kinley, but he would not tolerate any professor who called into question existing economic, social, or political standards in the presence of undergraduates. Tolman worked in Washington for a few more years. In 1922 he joined the faculty of the California Institute of Technology.[96]

But again, the national situation adds perspective. The American Association of University Professors formed in 1915. It had the purpose of defending academic freedom, but it too succumbed to war-time pressure. In a key statement the AAUP defended universities that dismissed professors whom they judged guilty of "*tending* to cause others to resist or evade the compulsory service law." As Roger L. Geiger observes, "the AAUP wartime policy allowed professors less freedom than even the draconian Espionage and Sedition Acts."[97]

• • •

In many ways the University responded to the war admirably, but it did not escape the conflict over academic freedom without serious consequences. President James skillfully negotiated the perils he confronted. He, like all academic leaders, faced enormous pressures and demands for conformity and displays of patriotism. But enormous pressures are why academic freedom

6. A University at War   119

exists. And to explore different avenues to truth are why universities exist. In war times it's too easy to equate dissent with disloyalty, as the Great War era displays abundantly. Altogether, Edmund James handled matters reasonably well, but did not leave a record of unwavering commitment to the high ideal of academic freedom. The case would differ with Dean David Kinley, who championed a narrower sense of the conduct permissible to professors. Kinley followed James as president of the University, and his experience with what he viewed as radical professors during the war shaped his outlook in the 1920s.

PART II

Academics

CHAPTER 7

The Physical Sciences

PART II OF THIS BOOK moves from a macro history of large events and campus-wide developments to a micro examination. The new American university found its essence in the proliferation of knowledge on which professors drew and to which they contributed. Specialization, of course, became the norm, and it had its structural manifestation in the different colleges, schools, and academic departments that reflected the diversity of modern knowledge. The University of Illinois participated widely in the new excitements that attended intellectual discovery. And a walk around the campus at any time in the James years would reveal buildings and laboratories whose names gave spectral testimony to that fact. Any review in a book of this length must impose selectivity. This section looks at the highlights, but it attempts to give some sense of the intellectual life in this prairie institution, in an "up close and personal" manner. Hence the several "Faculty Portraits" included along the way.

The College of Science

The study of science found its place in the University belatedly. Stephen A. Forbes, professor of entomology and zoology and head of both departments, served as dean of the College of Science from 1888 to 1905. He then devoted a quarter of his time to his departments and the rest to the State Laboratory of Natural History. When Forbes stepped down as dean, Edgar J. Townsend became acting dean of the College of Science while remaining head of the mathematics department. He advanced to full professor in 1905. As of September 1904, the College embraced the following eight departments with faculties of varying size: Botany (4), Chemistry (16), Geology (3), Household Science (3), Physics (6), Physiology (2), Mathematics (9), and Zoology and Entomology (6). Household Science and Mathematics did not have full professors as their heads.[1] In Part II we examine developments in these departments in the Physical Sciences and the Life Sciences chapters (with mathematics and physics reviewed in their connection to engineering).

Edgar J. Townsend, a shy youth who overcame many disadvantages to support himself and earn a college education, had joined the University of Illinois faculty intending not to stay. But he gradually changed his mind. He had suffered a nervous breakdown in 1896 from overwork. With rest he recovered, and in 1898 he took an unpaid sabbatical to go to Göttingen, where he earned a PhD in 1900 with mathematics his major subject and theoretical physics and astronomy his minors. He passed his examination *summa cum laude*. Returning to Urbana, Townsend became the head of the mathematics department and also served as secretary of the Council of Administration.

Townsend's zeal to join the pursuit of science to human welfare seemed boundless. An address he gave in 1910, one published for national attention in *Science* magazine, represents a major document to issue from the University of Illinois in the era covered here. Indeed, Townsend's vigorous educational program reflected ideals that marked the reformist mentality of the Progressive Era and the uses of the university as a prime mover of its agenda. This address merits a close look.

Everyone now agreed, Townsend declared, that the study of the natural sciences afforded a training and discipline as important in awarding the bachelor's degree as that afforded by literature, philosophy, and mathematics. A liberal education required knowledge of the fundamental principles of the biological and physical sciences, he insisted. Literary studies represented only one side of a liberal education. (President James had made this point in his inaugural address.) Townsend now proclaimed that in fact scientific studies embraced the most important element in the great shifts that higher education, in the United States and elsewhere, was now experiencing. He made his appeal to science in terms of three large categories. First, Townsend had great respect and gave much value to the traditional humanistic content—"literary" he called it—of the old curriculum. But, he wrote, "[N]o one can any longer claim to a liberal education who has not by formal and serious study made himself familiar in a broad and comprehensive way with the fundamental principles of the biological and physical sciences."[2]

Also like James, Townsend celebrated the scientific method as the triumph of an intellectual change, long underway, that now justifiably supplanted other ways of thinking—abstract, supernatural, deductive. Thus, he wrote, "The most potent influence in recent educational movements, the dominant factor which more than any other has led us to modify both the content of our college curricula and our methods of instruction, has been the growing importance of the sciences and the development of the scientific spirit." The laboratory and laboratory methods introduced a new method of investigating problems, of any and all kinds, Townsend added. Scientific study stood as an essential element of our new social and economic improvement. Scientific research, with its high empirical standards and practical applications, develops our natural resources and governs the expansion of our industrial and commercial enterprises.[3]

Second, Townsend insisted that, for all the ways one can document the critical and essential role of the sciences in developing the natural resources of the nation for the commercial and industrial conquest of its vast domain, we must give our highest educational commitment to *pure* science. This is because all of the above are grounded therein. "We are too apt to forget," he said, "the contribution that research in pure science has made to the progress of the industries and of the scientific professions." He cited by way of illustration the research in England into coal-tar products by Sir William Henry Perkin and how it had led, unanticipated and surprisingly, to the vast uses of dyestuffs. Thus, this offensive and unwelcome by-product in the manufacture of coke and gas, ignored at first, came to give us all kinds of good things— from food preservation, to medicine, to photography, even to bright colors in our clothing and flavors in our food. We see happenstance results, Townsend exclaimed, that are "startling and wonderful."[4]

On this matter, as Daniel J. Kevles explains, Illinois scientists joined in an expansive conversation. In a noted address in 1883, Henry Rowland, vice president of the AAAS, made a plea for "pure science." He spoke against science for invention or profit, to which too many Americans, he feared, were given, and for "abstract research." In turn Rowland, and other like-minded purists, met the criticism of Alexander Graham Bell and others, who defended both practicality and profit. They charged that the anti-pragmatists displayed an "arrogance of genius," and saw themselves as an exclusive scientific aristocracy.[5]

Townsend had a particular passion for his third category. America had long neglected important areas of activity in which research had much to offer, he believed. Townsend cited as an example sanitation and public health. Until recently, the United States had not a single institute for medical research, although France, Germany, and Japan all did. Townsend referenced the Pasteur Institute in Paris, essentially a school of bacteriology, which opened in 1888. Famous men had worked there. The Berlin Institute of Hygiene had its founding in 1893 for similar purposes.[6] Within the last ten years America had made substantial progress in scientific research, to be sure, and it had a direct bearing on medical practice. As examples, Townsend cited the Rockefeller Institute for Medical Research in New York, which had an endowment of $3 million, the Laboratory for the Investigation of Cancer at Buffalo, the Phipps Institute for the Study of Tuberculosis at Philadelphia, and the Institute for the

Investigation of Infectious Diseases at Chicago. In addition, legislative bodies provided means for the study and control of preventable diseases. Illinois gave about 40 percent of its revenues to these purposes.[7]

Nonetheless, Townsend emphasized, "we are not doing for the public and private health of our people anything like what we are doing for the development of our commercial and industrial interests." Again, Townsend hastened to say that this matter did not reduce simply to problem-based research. The conquest of malaria, a massive benefit to the white race, he illustrated, came from researchers simply curious about the mosquito. Townsend summoned studies to show how one human life saved from death had immense value in dollars to the larger society. Reducing the terrible toll of infectious diseases constituted not merely a benefit to the individuals afflicted, it effected an immense benefit to the larger public. And to this extent, Townsend, reflecting the recourse to government by American progressives everywhere, called upon "states and municipal boards of health" to take more action. In the manner of agricultural and engineering experiment stations he urged public initiative, especially in the universities, in creating experiment stations to study means of enhancing the public health. He looked for laboratories of physiological chemistry, bacteriology, and prevention of diseases. The new knowledge would come from these centers, and governments must take on the responsibility of delivering it to the public and enforcing it by law across the whole spectrum of the population.[8]

Townsend had other roles. He served as the general editor of the American Mathematical Series published by Henry Holt and Co. and received $100 for each volume published. He wrote some of the books in the series. Townsend published a translation of David Hilbert's *Foundations of Geometry* (Chicago: Open Court, 1902). He also wrote two books on calculus with G. A. Goodenough: *The First Course in Calculus* (1908) and *Essentials of Calculus* (1910). He wrote the text and Goodenough listed examples. Townsend also wanted to make available books well suited to the training of engineers. His *Complex Variables* (1915) became a widely used text for graduate students. Townsend viewed his *Functions of Real Variables* (1928) as his most scholarly product. His achievement in mathematics won him a place in *American Men of Science*.

Chemistry

In the early twentieth century, the Illinois chemistry department enjoyed a wide reputation for excellence. Arthur W. Palmer, an Illinois graduate (1883) who had a doctorate from Harvard (1886) and had studied in both Berlin and Göttingen, headed the department. Palmer taught Chemistry 1, the large introductory course, and organic chemistry. He had two tenured colleagues. Samuel W. Parr, a full professor, specialized in applied chemistry. He had an

126 PART II. ACADEMICS

Illinois BS (1884), a Cornell MA (1885), and had studied for a year at the University of Berlin and the Zurich Polytechnic. Harry S. Grindley, an associate professor, an Illinois graduate (BS, 1888) had a Harvard doctorate (1894). He taught general chemistry. The department had eleven faculty members in lower ranks, including four with doctorates, and one woman.

Palmer's sudden death on February 3, 1904, at age forty-three dashed the department's bright prospects. The task of filling the vacancy fell largely to Dean Forbes. As Palmer had done his work in organic chemistry and as the department had men in general chemistry, physical chemistry, and applied chemistry, Forbes wanted someone in organic chemistry with executive ability and the personal traits to represent the University before the public.[9] But the search met many frustrations, leading Forbes to make changes within. He reorganized the department and made an appointment in organic chemistry. With the concurrence of those involved, he abolished the distinction between chemistry and applied chemistry and formed one department.[10] He ratified Parr's title as professor of applied chemistry, promoted Grindley to full professor of general chemistry, and divided the headship of the department. Parr had charge of matters relating to instruction and instructors. Grindley would direct the laboratory and have charge of business and material affairs. Forbes may have gotten the idea of a division from Charles L. Jackson, who said that the plan had worked at Harvard. According to Forbes, however, local conditions virtually compelled the division between Parr and Grindley. In any case, it was ill advised.[11]

Stephen Forbes, as noted, resigned as dean of the College of Science effective June 30, 1905, and Edgar J. Townsend replaced him as acting dean. At the suggestion of Parr, Grindley, and Edward Bartow of the Illinois chemistry faculty, Townsend made a list of six men who would make a suitable department head and then obtained information about them by correspondence. The Illinois chemistry faculty ranked William Albert Noyes of the Bureau of Standards as their first choice.[12] President James asked Noyes if he would accept a position as professor of chemistry and director of the Chemical Laboratory at $3,500, while continuing to serve as editor and secretary of the American Chemical Society. The University wanted to develop the graduate side of the work, with considerable emphasis on research, he told him. James offered Noyes a salary larger than that paid to other faculty members, but he did not think the difference would cause unpleasant feeling.[13] The parties had to overcome some complications before Noyes finally accepted.

What manner of man had cast his lot with the aspiring university? Born on a farm near Independence, Iowa, Noyes represented the seventh generation of the Noyes family in America. He traced his American ancestry to Nicholas Noyes, who had emigrated from England to Massachusetts in 1633. Succeeding generations of the family lived in Massachusetts until William's father migrated to Iowa in 1855. Noyes attended country schools before entering Iowa College (later Grinnell). In 1879 he graduated in both the classical course (AB) and the scientific course (BS). He taught Greek and chemistry in the Grinnell academy for a year, earned a Grinnell MA (1880), and then studied chemistry under Ira Remsen at Johns Hopkins, receiving a PhD in 1882. Noyes had the rank of instructor at the University of Minnesota (1882–1883), then professor at the University of Tennessee (1883–1886), and professor at Rose Polytechnic Institute in Terre Haute, Indiana (1886–1903). In 1889, while on leave, he studied organic chemistry with Adolf von Baeyer at the University of Munich. In 1900 he became the chief chemist of the newly established National Bureau of Standards in Washington, D.C. Here he gained an international reputation. His research enabled him to determine the atomic weight of oxygen, hydrogen, and chlorine. Noyes studied the structure of camphor, and beginning in 1894 he published papers on organic and inorganic chemistry. He also wrote many widely used texts, including *Elements of Qualitative Analysis* (1887), *Organic Chemistry for the Laboratory* (1897), and *A Textbook of Organic Chemistry* (1903). In 1901 Noyes became the editor of the *Journal of the American Chemical Society*, which he made very influential. In 1907 Noyes founded another journal, *Chemical Abstracts*, and took the first editorship. He also had an active membership in the Congregational church.[14]

In September 1907 Noyes took up his new duties. The next month the University formally inaugurated him as head of the chemistry department and director of the chemical laboratory, and did so with much fanfare. Several addresses marked the occasion. H. A. Weber, professor of agricultural chemistry at Ohio State University, spoke on the relation of chemistry to agriculture; William McMurtrie, consulting chemist of the Royal Baking Power Company, spoke on the relation of chemistry to industries; Julius Stieglitz of the University of Chicago addressed the subject of chemical research in American industries; George B. Frankforter, dean of the School of Chemistry at the University of Minnesota, explored the teaching of chemistry in state universities; and Noyes spoke on the contribution of chemistry to modern life. The speakers celebrated not only the centrality of chemistry in agriculture, industry, and other areas of human activity, but also the way in which chemical research in German universities had raised that nation to industrial supremacy and the need for American universities to provide the means and opportunity for chemists to conduct research and train a new generation of chemical researchers. In selecting Noyes to develop the work in chemistry, Stieglitz asserted, Illinois had joined the ranks of those universities committed to giving the highest type of instruction in chemistry. The journal *Science* published the addresses, and the University issued them as a pamphlet.[15] President James loved this kind of academic fanfare.

Noyes strengthened the faculty in his early years as department head. He made several appointments, including Edward W. Washburn, Philip B. Hawk, Azariah T. Lincoln, and Helen Isham. In 1909 Noyes recommended Isham for promotion to associate, describing her as "one of our most valuable instructors in general chemistry," the director of the thesis of a senior, and a researcher who had published an article during the past year.[16] In 1909 the department had two women instructors, and "a great many girls" were taking chemistry. Dean Townsend thought of appointing another female but did not, because "we should not have more than two women instructors in that department, and in this Professor Noyes concurs."[17]

Graduate students had a wide selection of courses: the history and theories of chemistry; inorganic, organic, and physical chemistry; physiological chemistry; the chemistry of flesh; the calorimetry of fuels; and water supplies. Some faculty members taught courses related to their research, including studies relevant to the Illinois economy. Parr published valuable articles on the calorimetry of Illinois coals, for example, and Grindley studied the chemical and nutritive value of meats. Altogether, the chemistry department was well established and would contribute to making Illinois one of the nation's premier universities. As observed in the previous chapter, the chemistry department played the most important role of all university departments during World War I.

Faculty Portrait #1: Harry S. Grindley, Chemistry

When Harry S. Grindley of the University of Illinois made nutrition studies in the early twentieth century, the scientific study of nutrition, or physiological chemistry, was only slowly making its way in American higher education. The first laboratory of that discipline in America began its work in 1874 in the Sheffield Scientific School at Yale. In 1880 the *American Chemical Journal* commenced a series of reports on progress in physiological chemistry, and in 1887 the American Physiological Society came into being in New York. The *American Journal of Physiology* appeared in 1898 and the *Journal of Biological Chemistry* in 1905. The American Society of Biological Chemists formed a year later. Physiological chemistry found its base primarily in the universities in the late nineteenth century. (In 1880 Yale awarded the first PhD in the subject.) Many public and private institutions fostered research. Studies in nutrition figured prominently in the gradual evolution of physiological chemistry in America. In 1887 the Hatch Act authorized federal funds for an agricultural experiment station in each state.

Harry S. Grindley, a nutrition researcher, appeared on the scene at this time. Graduating from Illinois in 1888 with a BS in agriculture, he served as

7. The Physical Sciences   **129**

Grindley did pioneering work in physical chemistry, with studies in diet and nutrition that gained national attention. This picture shows Grindley after he left Illinois. Courtesy of the University of Illinois Archives.

an assistant in chemistry and in the Agricultural Experiment Station at Illinois from 1888 to 1892. A somewhat raw prairie product, from near Mahomet, Illinois, he studied chemistry at Harvard, receiving an ScD degree in 1894. Returning to Urbana, he rose through the ranks, becoming a professor and director of the chemistry laboratory in 1904. Early in his career Grindley authored or coauthored five papers on chemistry.[18] In 1896 he joined other investigators in agricultural experiment stations carrying out studies designed to obtain information on the food habits and food consumption of people in different regions of the country. In 1897 the USDA granted Grindley $250, and in March, with this grant, he began a dietary study on his wife and himself. On June 12 he initiated a similar study on a boarding club of sixteen railroad mechanics. For fourteen days he analyzed samples of everything used on the table with a view to determining the cost and fuel values of the food eaten. The USDA published the results of his research.[19]

In 1898 Grindley cooperated with Jane Addams in Chicago to determine the cost and quality of milk furnished to consumers in and around Hull House.

The results so startled those in charge that they thought it best to reexamine the work done. So, Addams sent to Urbana one hundred samples representing the milk supplied to residents in this area, and Grindley analyzed them. The two published their findings: the milk supply of the areas studied had a very low quality. Probably the milk supply of the entire city was no better. In many cases the milk was adulterated either by the addition of water or by the removal of cream or by both. "The evidence is overwhelming," Addams and Grindley wrote, "in proof that the milk supply of Chicago is remarkably poor." They urged immediate remedial action.[20]

In December 1898 the University provided Grindley $300 to aid his work in cooperation with the USDA.[21] With that support, he began an extended study of the cooking and nutritional value of meats, a study that lasted six years. His motives for this undertaking no doubt varied. We can reconstruct them from both his own statements and the circumstances of the case.

First, meats played an important role in the country's commercial and domestic economy. Statistics showed that the American people consumed more of this food than the people of any other nation—an annual average of about 120 pounds per capita. Illinois ranked high among the states in the production of meat. Nutrition investigations had a critical relation to agricultural production, as their object was to study the nutritive value of the products as they came from the farm. Thus, nutrition studies directly extended the kind of work the experiment stations were doing for agricultural production.[22] Second, Grindley believed that his nutrition studies had scientific and practical value. When he began his work, he noted, scientists could say little regarding the changes produced by the cooking of meat. We had only incomplete knowledge of the chemical and physical transformations that meat undergoes during cooking, he pointed out. Although the cooking of food for the table was one of the oldest arts, it did not constitute a science, he said. Grindley proposed to focus on some key matters: the effects of cooking meats on their digestibility; the nutritive value of cooked meats; the character of the chemical and physical changes that occur when we cook meats by such common methods as boiling, roasting, frying, and broiling; and the influence of cooking on the flavor and palatability of meats. Third, Grindley contended that his studies would promote the reputation of both the Illinois chemistry department and the University. They would put the department "plainly in the lead and at the head of all investigations" on the subject and would let people know what the University was doing. Accordingly, he wanted the bulletins reporting his research, published by the USDA, to be mailed from the *University*, not from Washington, D.C.[23]

With the board's endorsement, Grindley began to prepare his saltpeter (potassium nitrate) study. The significance of this undertaking stands out in historical context. The practice of curing and preserving meats began in

7. The Physical Sciences   131

antiquity in deserts where salts containing nitrate and borax abounded. The Romans added salts containing saltpeter or "nitre" to obtain the desired red color and more than likely the distinctive flavor of meat. Over time, the use of nitrate became common, and in the late nineteenth century scientists began to show interest in the salt-curing method. Research revealed that the color associated with salting was incidental to the preserving effect.[24]

In any case, additives made food adulteration a problem. In 1883 Harvey W. Wiley, a chemist with a medical degree from Indiana Medical College, became chief of the Bureau of Chemistry in the USDA. He assumed leadership in a pure food campaign, calling for scientific study to expose the use of adulterants and arousing public support to enact protective laws. In 1899 Wiley recommended that Congress appropriate funds to investigate the use of preservatives, and in 1902 it approved his proposal. Wiley promptly began tests with human volunteers to determine the safety of chemical preservatives. He established a kitchen and dining room in the Bureau of Chemistry building in Washington, D.C. and recruited twelve young men to participate in his study. The men selected promised to eat all of their meals at the "hygienic table" that Wiley set up, and to consume no other foods or beverages, except water. In return for free meals, the men pledged to serve at least six months, to continue in their usual daily vocations, and to certify at the end of the test period that they had adhered to all the rules. They signed releases agreeing not to hold the bureau responsible for any illness or accident connected with the experiment.

In Wiley's study, all food consumed by and all excretions of each squad member were measured and recorded during the test period. Wiley published a detailed report on each of the additives investigated. The reports showed that certain preservatives posed health hazards. Wiley orchestrated a lobby to eliminate their use, and the public concern he aroused had dramatic reinforcement by publication early in 1906 of *The Jungle*, Upton Sinclair's exposé of conditions in the Chicago meatpacking houses. These events played a major part that year in passage by Congress of the Pure Food and Drugs Act.[25]

The "hygienic table" and "poison squad" developed by Wiley served as a model for Grindley's saltpeter investigation. Even before the trustees approved the plan for a Laboratory of Physiological Chemistry, Grindley began to act. He had persuaded President James to appoint men prominent in physiology, medicine, and human nutrition to a national panel. It would have the purpose of devising and approving the methods to be used in an inquiry to determine the influence on the human body of the saltpeter used in curing meats. On December 1, 1906, James invited several authorities to become members of the Commission for the Study of Problems Relating to Human Nutrition.[26]

On March 30, 1907, the commission held its first meeting at the Fifth Avenue Hotel in New York City. Then on April 25 Grindley gave an account

132   PART II. ACADEMICS

of the nutrition work to the Illinois trustees. He also informed the commission members that the University had received $5,000 from the American Meat Packers Association toward the expenses of the nutrition investigation. The trustees asked the association to assume all responsibility for possible damage suits arising from supposed injuries in connection with "the feeding experiment."[27] In the autumn of 1906 James had begun to deal with Edward Tilden of Chicago and other agents of the anonymous Chicago meatpackers who offered to provide another $50,000 and a site in the Union Stockyards if the University would establish a college and research laboratory of veterinary medicine in Chicago.[28] Tilden, a director of Drover's National Bank associated with Swift and Company, had played the major role in raising the money given by the American Meat Packers Association for the nutrition study.[29]

Grindley had asked "the best practical authorities of the country on the subject" to approve the plans for the "squad experiments."[30] With plans laid and funds in hand, Grindley began his saltpeter study. In August and September 1907 medical doctors gave a fairly rigid physical examination to forty-three of the eighty-five male students who applied to participate in the experiment. Grindley and others selected twenty-four men of average health and development as members of the Nutrition Club. The researchers provided them lodging at 1106 and 1108 Illinois Street. Here a matron took charge of the houses and a chef operated the kitchen. Club members received free room and board in return for participating in the study. They had to sign a pledge in which they agreed to follow the same rules and regulations as Wiley had imposed earlier. Groups A, B, C, and D formed, each with its own dietary prescriptions to follow. An unusually large and costly undertaking, the investigation differed in important ways from all similar studies.[31]

The experiment proper lasted a total of 303 days. When it ended, Grindley began to prepare the data to present to the commission. Arranging it required an enormous amount of labor. All of the original data had gone over to the commission by January 30, 1909. As the work proceeded, Grindley used superlatives in describing to the University trustees the scientific importance of the study and the forthcoming publication. Two volumes appeared in 1911. Barring unforeseen difficulties, Grindley reported on June 28, 1910, volumes 3, 4, and 5 would go to the publisher within six weeks.[32]

The nutrition commission met again in New York City on November 4–5, 1910. The panel approved the title for the publication, authorized Grindley to proceed with publication of volumes 3, 4, and 5, and approved the mathematical and statistical methods that two experts called upon by Grindley had devised to interpret the results of the research. The application of statistical methods to metabolism experiments was entirely new, Grindley said, and would be of untold value in deriving correct conclusions to the study. Commission members also read some chapters to be included in volumes 1 and 2 and accepted

7. The Physical Sciences   **133**

with only minor changes the methods of presenting the results. One could now confidently judge the saltpeter investigation a success, Grindley declared. He proclaimed that with publication of the results the University of Illinois had "fathered and fostered to maturity the most extensive and the most thorough and complete nutrition investigation ever made in this or any other country."

Publication of the massive report, Harry S. Grindley and Ward J. MacNeal, *Studies in Nutrition: An Investigation of the Influence of Saltpeter on the Nutrition and Health of Man with Reference to Its Occurrence in Cured Meats*, began in 1911 and ended in 1929. The books, printed by R. R. Donnelly & Sons, carried the imprint "From the Laboratory of Physiological Chemistry, Department of Animal Husbandry, University of Illinois." Each volume contained the general title page and the names of the members of the nutrition commission, followed by a title page for each individual volume. Harry S. Grindley, *The Experimental Data of the Bio-Chemical Investigations*, volume 3 and volume 4, appeared in 1911 and 1912. Grindley had the assistance of Frederic W. Gill and Harold H. Mitchell on volume 3, and of Gill and others on volume 4. Ward J. MacNeal, *The Data of the Physical, Physiological, and Bacteriological Observations*, volume 5, appeared in 1912. So, Grindley deserves recognition for his nutrition studies and as the pioneer in a tradition of nutrition research at the University of Illinois.

Alas, these weighty volumes seem to have fallen still-born from the press. The reasons for the silence that enveloped them seem readily apparent. The investigation had proved to be much bigger than anticipated. A conflict over authorship and the interpretation of data slowed progress, as did the publication costs. The complete set was unavailable until 1929, by which time physiological chemistry and nutrition studies had advanced considerably since Grindley began his study. Nevertheless, *Studies in Nutrition* marked a major achievement. It had made an important finding in showing that the human body possesses a mechanism for the metabolism of nitrates. It received reference citations from scientists for decades thereafter.

Geology and Ceramics

In 1904 Charles W. Rolfe headed the geology department. He had joined the faculty in 1881. In 1886 he became professor of geology. Rolfe had a master's degree, at a time when the PhD was becoming the badge of faculty members. In 1893 his topographic survey of Illinois had attracted attention at the Columbian Exposition in Chicago. But President Draper treated him disdainfully.[33]

In 1904, with the support of President James, Rolfe did his best to improve his department. The work in geology served students who studied geology as an aspect of modern science, those interested in technical applications, and

134   PART II. ACADEMICS

those who wished to become geologists. To meet the needs of these groups, Rolfe wanted a faculty of five.[34] From 1904 to 1906 the faculty included Rolfe, an instructor, and one assistant. Rolfe published little.[35] He had grown with an institution that changed more rapidly than he did, but he fully cooperated with efforts to strengthen the department.

In 1906 Rolfe and Dean Townsend laid plans to recruit two men who would give part of their time to the geology department and to either the U.S. Geological Survey or the Illinois State Geological Survey. They wanted a specialist in mineralogy and petrography and an expert in the physiographic side of geology who could prepare public school teachers.[36] The plan bore fruit with the appointments of William S. Bayley and Thomas E. Savage as assistant professors. Bayley had both an AB (1883) and a PhD (1888) in chemistry and geology from Johns Hopkins. He had been at Colby College from 1888 to 1904 and at Lehigh from 1904 to 1906. He specialized in petrography and pre-Cambrian geology. He had been business manager of the journal *Economic Geology* since 1905. James promised to recommend him for promotion to associate professor the following year if he made good during his first year.[37] Bayley became an associate professor in 1909 and a full professor in 1914. Savage had degrees from Iowa Wesleyan and the University of Iowa; he had taught geology and biology in Western College in Toledo, Iowa. In 1903 he became assistant state geologist in Iowa. A specialist in structural geology, in 1909 he received a Yale PhD.[38] Rufus M. Bagg, an Amherst College AB (1891) and a Johns Hopkins PhD (1895), joined the faculty in 1907 as an instructor. An expert paleontologist, he had been a professor of geology at Colorado College and the New Mexico School of Mines and a consulting mining geologist. A number of assistants rounded out the staff.[39]

The faculty's size and interests shaped instruction in geology. From 1904 to 1906 the department offered eight core courses: dynamic and historical geology; economic geology; mineralogy, crystallography, and petrography; advanced crystallography; optical mineralogy; physical geography; advanced paleontology; and an advanced course in any of these selections. Students divided their time about equally between the classroom and one of the department's five laboratories. Graduate students could choose from some undergraduate courses and three advanced offerings.

In 1910 Dean Townsend reported that a lack of confidence had developed between Rolfe, the head of the geology department, and certain members of the instructional staff. No doubt the problem arose partly or largely from the disparity between Rolfe and faculty members with doctorates and orientations toward research and publications. "It is perhaps a natural consequence of the situation," Townsend added. "I still think it can be overcome by tact and careful consideration of the rights of those concerned."[40]

7. The Physical Sciences   **135**

• • •

The ceramics department emerged from within the geology department. Rolfe had long wanted to develop the mineral resources of the state. In 1894 he had urged President Draper to ask the General Assembly to provide funds for a laboratory of economic geology. The state had vast and varied sources of mineral wealth; it should support a laboratory where geological materials could be tested with a view to their commercial potential. Rolfe had a special interest in clay, which lent itself to a greater variety of uses than almost any other material resource; and Illinois had an inexhaustible supply.[41] Nothing came of his initial proposal. Nor did President Draper see the great opportunity for the state and the University that lay in developing a ceramics industry in Illinois. President James did.

In the fall of 1904 Thomas C. Chamberlin, a geologist at the University of Chicago, urged Charles S. Deneen, candidate for governor, to establish a geological survey if elected. The Illinois Clay Manufacturers' Association supported a legislative appropriation for an economic survey to be executed by the University. The Board of Trustees agreed to undertake the work and it authorized James to pursue the matter.[42]

Deneen did win the election, and in his 1905 inaugural address he urged the General Assembly to appropriate funds for an efficient state geological survey. Illinois had extensive mineral resources, especially in coal and clay, he stated, but no other interior state that approached Illinois in population and resources had done so little work to exploit these resources. On January 19 Chester W. Church introduced in the House a bill to establish a State Geological Survey.[43]

The Church bill provoked a controversy over the control and location of the survey. The bill proposed to put it under a commission and locate it in Springfield. The commission would be composed of the governor, the secretary of state, the president of the University, and two persons nominated by the governor. Some people said that the governor favored the Church bill. As James understood, the bill was drafted by Rollin D. Salisbury, a University of Chicago geologist. The Church committee heard representatives of Chicago, Northwestern, and the U.S. Geological Survey, but it postponed hearings with UofI representatives.[44]

James strongly opposed the Church bill. He mounted a campaign to amend it in line with another bill that proposed to make the survey a bureau of the University. Governor Deneen maintained a neutral position on the two bills. James wrote him and members of both houses stating his position, and he urged influential trustees, newspaper editors, and prominent alumni to leave no stone unturned in bringing pressure to bear on the governor and members of the General Assembly to locate the survey at the University. He offered

136   PART II. ACADEMICS

powerful arguments: the University is the scientific branch of the state government; the University could give the state an efficient and superior geological survey, as it had done with the agricultural and engineering experiment stations; and the survey would bestow great benefit on the University, constituting "practically an endowment of the Department of Geology." A commission in Springfield, James added, would establish a center of antagonism and rivalry to the University. James went on to explain his case. He dismissed the commission idea as an attempt on the part of the U.S. Geological Survey and professors at Chicago who constituted the geology department to get control of the Illinois State Geological Survey. These men had worked as geologists for pay for the U.S. Geological Survey. Although Governor Deneen wanted the most economical and most efficient survey, as James saw it, not all of the men behind the commission movement had "such an absolutely pure and unselfish motive."[45]

James was a masterly lobbyist. On May 2 a bill to establish the survey at the University passed in the House in a unanimous vote. The Senate concurred, and on July 1 the law became effective. The survey, now a bureau located at the University, came under the direction of a commission composed of the governor, the president of the University, and a person appointed by the governor. The law also charged the University with giving instruction in the geology of clay working materials and their behavior during the process of manufacture. It appropriated $5,000 annually to carry out the work.[46] James had nicely expanded the university infrastructure.

On June 2, 1905, the trustees approved the establishment of a course in ceramics. The board urged that an advisory committee, to which the Illinois Clay Manufacturers' Association might elect members, assist in organizing the course. One scholarship for each county in the state should be granted in ceramics. The University would assign it, on nomination by the Clay Manufacturers' Association, to applicants sufficiently prepared to enter the College of Science and intending to pursue a regular ceramics course. The scholarships would cover four years of study.[47]

The University located the Course in Ceramics, which James appointed Rolfe to head, in two rooms of the Natural History Building loaned by the geology department. Laboratories newly furnished with the necessary machinery and furnaces carried out the technical work. A brick kiln house about twenty feet square, containing two kilns, was built at some distance from the Natural History Building.

The Geological Survey began to map the vast natural resources of Illinois. It disclosed that oil, coal, and clay constituted the most valuable mineral products of the state. In April 1906 James asked Henry Foster Bain to submit a report on the survey's work, especially respecting clays and coals, and have it printed in time for the next legislature. That fall the catalog listed Bain as a lecturer in economic geology at the University, but circumstances prevented him from teaching.[48]

In October James announced the appointment of the Advisory Committee on the School of Ceramics. Its members included Frank W. Butterworth of Danville, home of both the Danville and the Western brick companies; A. W. Gates of Monmouth, general manager of the Monmouth Mining and Manufacturing Company; William D. Gates of Chicago, president of the American Terra Cotta and Ceramic Company; Dilwyn V. Purington of Chicago, president of the Purington Paving Brick Company; and John W. Stipes of Champaign, owner of tile and brick factories.[49] This arrangement reflected as much as any other President James's passion for connections and for critical links that would advance the University of Illinois in public recognition and usefulness.

Ceramics as a science was comparatively new. In addition to offering instruction, the ceramicists investigated problems related to the pyro-chemical behavior of clays. To strengthen the artistic side of the work, Townsend sought information from two men connected with Tulane University, and he tried to obtain some Korean pottery for the University.[50]

Albert V. Bleininger, who came to Illinois from Ohio State in 1907, had two colleagues and the ceramics department reported an enrollment of twenty-six students. The department cooperated with the State Geological Survey in investigating Illinois ceramic materials—paving brick, clays, and raw materials for Portland cement—and the survey published the results.[51] In addition, faculty members conducted research on such problems in ceramics as the viscosity of molten glass and methods for determining the porosity of burned clay wares. They presented their findings at meetings of the American Ceramic Society, whose *Transactions* published many of their papers. Between 1907 and 1914 the *University of Illinois Bulletin* made available twenty-two of these studies on such topics as the efflorescence of brick, fritted glazes, crystalline glazes, and enamel for stoneware. Rolfe had once proposed that a course be offered conjointly by ceramics and the Department of Art and Design, but nothing came of it. The ceramicists were preoccupied with silicate technology, the basis of ornamental and aesthetic ceramics.[52] In 1912 Bleininger resigned from the University to become chief of the division of ceramics of the Bureau of Standards.

The number of students registered for degrees together with special students in ceramics rose steadily over the years as follows: from two in 1905–1906 to seventy-four in 1912–1913. But the number of graduates remained low: only a total of eleven in 1912. But because jobs in clay working plants were plentiful, students often went to work rather than completing their degrees. As enrollments rose, the faculty had less time for research. But they continued to publish, and their publications received wide recognition in the field.[53]

138   PART II. ACADEMICS

•••

The department also offered short courses for clay workers. The state of Illinois had nearly five hundred clay working plants employing approximately twelve thousand individuals who lacked technical ceramic training. For a time, the department held an Annual Clay Workers Institute open to all persons engaged in factory operations and lasting three days. In 1908 twenty-five clay manufacturers took part. In another outreach in 1912 the department introduced a Short Course in Ceramics of two weeks' duration.[54]

From 1904 to 1913 the geology department inched forward in an effort to achieve a level with the other large and vigorous scientific departments. Rolfe pleaded the case for a laboratory of economic geology that would explore the mineral resources of the state, especially clays, and he saw his efforts rewarded. He made his most lasting achievement in the establishment of the ceramics department at the University. The Illinois Clay Manufacturers' Association helped achieve the result. Bleininger raised the work in ceramics to distinction, but his departure dealt a crippling blow.

Finally, the search for a geologist of high scientific standing culminated in December 1915. The board authorized James to make Eliot Blackwelder an offer at $4,000. After some negotiating, Blackwelder accepted the appointment in January 1916, and on September 1 he took up his duties.[55]

Astronomy

At the dawn of the twentieth century astronomy had devoted American followers, the subject was taught in colleges and universities, and traditional methods were used to scan the heavens. But vast changes were impending. At Illinois, work in astronomy arose within the mathematics department. In 1894 three mathematicians drew up a plan for a course of study in astronomy, and George W. Myers went to Germany to earn a doctorate in the subject. In 1896 he returned with his degree and the University began construction of an observatory. Completed a year later, the new facility had modern equipment important for instruction and for the practice of spherical and positional astronomy. Myers analyzed the light curve of the eclipsing binary Beta Lyrae, a remarkable achievement at the time, and he enjoyed popularity as a teacher besides. In 1896–1897 only four of thirty-five leading colleges and universities had more undergraduates in required astronomy courses than Illinois, though Illinois lagged in elective and advanced work. In 1900 Myers resigned and left the University.[56] But to Joel Stebbins belongs the story of astronomy at Illinois in the James era.

7. The Physical Sciences   139

Faculty Portrait #2: Joel Stebbins, Astronomy

Joel Stebbins, Myers's replacement, had developed an intense interest in astronomy at the age of twelve when a teacher introduced him to study of the sun, moon, and stars. He earned a BSc (1899) at the University of Nebraska, remained there for a year of graduate work, and then went to Wisconsin to study under George C. Comstock at the Washburn Observatory. Comstock encouraged him to go to an observatory that emphasized "the new astronomy," that is, astrophysics, the study of the physical and chemical natures of the heavenly bodies and their origin and evolution. Stebbins continued his graduate work at Berkeley, California, where he studied celestial mechanics under A. O. Leuschner, a master of orbit theory. As a fellow at Lick Observatory near San Jose, Stebbins came under the influence of William W. Campbell, a pioneer in stellar spectroscopy and a powerful figure in American astronomy. Stebbins's doctoral dissertation, an investigation of the spectrum of the red giant star Mira Ceti, long remained the principal source of information concerning the spectra of long-period variable stars. Stebbins published a few short papers and could have remained at the Lick or Berkeley, but he had greater ambition. "I landed on my own," he later said, "the position of instructor in astronomy in charge of the observatory at the University of Illinois." On March 10, 1903, the Board of Trustees appointed Stebbins as an instructor in astronomy and director of the Observatory at $1,200 a year.[57]

Stebbins vitalized the work in astronomy at the University. On arriving in Urbana, he found the prospects promising. He had a moderate teaching load and the University supported his research. For two years Stebbins was the only astronomer in the University, and with a colleague he remained the mainstay of the astronomy faculty. Stebbins found his principal research interest in photometry of stars.[58] Observational astronomy had traditionally operated by visual methods, and at first Stebbins proceeded with the eye at the telescope, comparing the brightness of one star with that of another. But the accuracy attained by this method was, as he said, "much the same as though instead of using a balance we should weigh objects by lifting them in our hands."[59]

So, within two or three months Stebbins got the idea of the electrical measurement of starlight from Fay C. Brown, a graduate student. In 1906, at a physics department exhibit, Brown demonstrated a selenium cell. A bell would ring when he turned on a lamp to illuminate the cell and would stop when he turned off the lamp. "Right then and there I got the idea that if an ordinary light will ring a bell why would not the light from a star at the focus of a telescope produce a measurable electric current?"[60]

Their first trial was disappointing. On repeated attempts the photometer proved not sensitive enough to respond to the light of the bright planet Jupiter.

140 PART II. ACADEMICS

But when Stebbins took the photometer off the telescope and pointed it at the moon, "the galvanometer deflection was measurable with plenty to spare."[61] They thought they were on to something. "If our method, or a similar one is ever perfected," Stebbins told Dean Townsend, "it will revolutionize some branches of astronomy."[62]

During the 1907 summer, with the aid of a selenium cell, Stebbins and Brown determined the central phase of a lunar eclipse within one minute of the predicted time, and with more experiments they measured how the moon's brightness varies with phase—its "light curve." They also discovered that the color-sensibility curves of the selenium cells differed, and they succeeded in getting deflections of a few millimeters from a first-magnitude star, Aldebaran.[63]

Selenium behaved irregularly and had an especial susceptibility to temperature changes, so the sensitivity of an apparatus using it could not be increased without limit. On a bitter cold night Stebbins discovered by chance that selenium became more sensitive and extraordinarily more regular with decrease of temperature. Conditions would probably prove best when a cell could be maintained at a uniform temperature of about –4 degrees Fahrenheit, Stebbins believed.[64] An accident led to a further discovery. As Stebbins described it:

> After an exhibit at a meeting I wrapped a cell in a handkerchief for safety and put it in my pocket. Later I forgot about the cell, pulled out the handkerchief, and dropped the cell on a hard floor. It had been a good cell, but now I had two cells each twice as good as the original. Since the extra area of two square inches had only produced irregularities, a smaller cell was all to the good. With this much to go on, I got up my nerve, placed our best cell in a vise, and with a hammer and a chisel gave it a whack to break off about a quarter of it to make a really good cell.

Next, Stebbins and Brown installed this fragment, properly insulated, in an icepack on the twelve-inch refractor. They found that they could measure second-magnitude stars with some accuracy.[65]

Stebbins depended a good deal on the physics department staff to make his apparatus, and he reported on the progress of his investigations at scholarly meetings. He also received research support from the American Academy of Arts and Sciences. In February the AAAS awarded Stebbins $100 for research on the use of selenium in photometry. In June it granted another $100 for his work.[66] As sole author or with coauthor Brown, Stebbins published the results of his studies.[67] During the past year, he proudly announced in May 1908, "there have been more results published from the Observatory than in all the time since it was built."

7. The Physical Sciences   141

By 1910 Stebbins had greatly improved the precision of the selenium photometer. He used his instrument to measure the brightness of Halley's comet, and he demonstrated the precision of the new method by observing the light curve of Algol (Beta Persei). For centuries Algol, the "demon star," had aroused more interest among astronomers than had any other star. Although the principal eclipse of the main body by a large and relatively faint companion had been known and studied, Stebbins showed for the first time the shallow secondary eclipse that visual observers had missed. "Our work superseded and scrapped four previous doctors' theses," Stebbins boasted, "and selenium became rather famous for a time."[68] On December 8, 1909, the Rumford Committee of the AAAS granted Stebbins $300 in aid of his research, it being understood that another grant would follow if results justified the money given.[69]

By 1910 Stebbins had amply demonstrated his worth as a teacher and research scientist. In 1911 he published three more articles in the *Astrophysical Journal*, followed in 1912 by another in the *Astronomische Nachtrichten*. Astronomers in America and in Germany regarded him highly. But Stebbins's status at Illinois needed clarification. Instead of its location as a part of mathematics, Stebbins wanted a separate department for astronomy, and so urged. Illinois was the only state university that had two men with doctor's degrees in astronomy, he noted, and it had more students in astronomy than most of its neighbors. Other universities with less equipment than Illinois had separate departments of astronomy. They included Yale, Columbia, Minnesota, Ohio, Missouri, and Nebraska, not to mention a score of smaller institutions. According to Stebbins, Illinois was the only place that had astronomy connected to a mathematics department. A potential graduate student, he said, would not think of choosing a place for advanced study or of taking a doctorate in a department not strong enough to stand by itself.[70]

In September 1910 Edward C. Pickering, the Harvard astronomer, offered Stebbins a large telescopic mirror. President of the American Astronomical Society since 1905, Pickering had heard Stebbins give a paper on the selenium photometer at the Society's August meeting, and the idea had occurred to him to make every effort to secure for Stebbins a more powerful instrument. "The accuracy with which you determined the changes in light of the variable star Beta Persei has never yet been equalled," Pickering wrote. "If this degree of accuracy could be obtained for the fainter stars, a most important field of work would be opened in astronomy." Three mirrors of sixty inches in diameter then existed, two at Harvard and one at Mount Wilson in California. Pickering offered to loan one of Harvard's mirrors for five years, with an option of another five years, provided Stebbins did good work. To take advantage of the offer the University had to provide a suitable telescope mounting and house.[71]

A year later officials turned their attention to the purchase of a thirty-inch reflector. A suitable one could be had for $2,500. Its purchase, however, was complicated by the fact that Stebbins was applying for a leave of absence for the following year. David Kinley, dean of the Graduate School, recommended that the University buy the telescope and that $2,500 come from the Graduate School fund for the purpose, provided that Stebbins did not "have it in mind to leave us immediately." George C. Comstock, the Wisconsin astronomer, had told Kinley that Stebbins had made himself "perhaps the leading authority on the light measurement of stars." "How much this means, of course," Kinley added, "I cannot judge."[72]

In December, writing from Munich, Germany, Stebbins declared that in view of the acquisition of the thirty-inch reflector "now stored" at the University, the matter of the Harvard mirror would have to wait for some time. Nevertheless, he recommended that the administration go to the legislature to ask for $10,000 to mount the large mirror.[73]

In the fall of 1911, while Stebbins was still experimenting with the selenium photometer, Jakob Kunz of the physics faculty suggested that a rubidium photoelectric cell might perhaps be used instead of a selenium cell in stellar photometry. When Stebbins returned to Urbana, he resumed his collaboration with Kunz.[74] In the physics laboratory Kunz made cells with each of the alkali metals—potassium, sodium, caesium, and rubidium. Stebbins tested the cells, and in 1915 the two men "managed to produce a cell which is twice as sensitive as anything we had before, and this amounts to the same thing as though some good fairy had suddenly doubled the light gathering power of our telescope."[75]

In the summer of 1915 Stebbins took his photometer to the Lick refractor, in the first of what became regular seasonal observational trips to California. He measured variable stars with much greater accuracy than visual or photographic methods could achieve and at a fainter level of brightness than the selenium cell could reach. With the new photometer he obtained a light curve of the variable star Beta Lyrae and new physical information on eclipsing double stars and on intrinsic, regularly pulsating, variable single stars like Delta Cephei.[76]

Stebbins spent many hours in the University Observatory, but for a glimpse of the man at work and in relaxed moments, we must rely on those who knew him from settings other than the University of Illinois. He had a "friendly, outgoing manner and a keen, dry sense of humor," writes a biographer, Donald E. Osterbrock.[77] But according to Gerald E. Kron, a former student and assistant, "young persons all held Stebbins in considerable awe," regarding him as "rather unapproachable." Although on occasion he could be "stern and forbidding," Kron added, he was "a man of great kindness and understanding."[78] Coworkers emphasized "the skill and great patience he had for precision photometric measurements," the importance he gave to "maintaining a detached and philosophical attitude," and his "even-tempered way." They carefully calibrated his little signs. As a colleague wrote:

7. The Physical Sciences   143

When the work was going smoothly and the data book was filling up with good observations he was very apt to begin whistling "La Golondrina." There was another sign reserved for the very finest nights when the apparatus was performing particularly well, or when an especially desired or difficult observation was proceeding according to plan; then the quiet of the dark and lonely dome would be broken by Dr. Stebbins' bursting out with the song "Ah, Sweet Mystery of Life, At Last I've Found Thee."[79]

Stebbins won a reputation for his stories.[80]

Joel Stebbins served as member and officer in many astronomical societies. His peers recognized him for distinguished scientific work. On May 14, 1913, the American Academy of Arts and Sciences voted to award the Rumford Premium to Stebbins for development of the selenium photometer and its application to astronomical problems.[81] This prize, a gold or silver medal valued at $300, had great prestige, one of the most significant awards given in physics in the United States. Stebbins gained this honor at only age thirty-five. Additional honors followed. On April 29, 1915, Stebbins presented an illustrated talk on "The Electrical Photometry of Stars" at the annual meeting of the National Academy of Sciences in Washington, D.C. At its annual dinner the academy awarded Stebbins the Henry Draper gold medal in recognition of his work on application of the selenium cell to stellar photometry.[82]

But, though honored wherever individuals pursued astronomy, Stebbins had trouble in gaining recognition on his own campus. On June 2, 1920, when James retired, the trustees elected David Kinley president of the University. Kinley, as noted, could not understand the significance of Stebbins's work. On October 26, 1921, Stebbins submitted his resignation as professor of astronomy to take effect September 1, 1922. He was leaving to become Comstock's successor as director of the Washburn Observatory at Wisconsin. His letter to Kinley was polite and unrevealing as to the reasons for his departure. "In thus closing my term of nearly twenty years at Illinois I can only express my appreciation of the splendid opportunities I have had here, and it is with great regret that I shall sever the many personal relations in Urbana."[83]

If Stebbins felt pushed from Illinois, he may also have felt pulled toward Madison. During his year there before going to California he had formed an attachment to the area. And no doubt he felt honored to succeed George C. Comstock.

In 1948, at the age of seventy, Stebbins retired from the University of Wisconsin. He then spent ten years as a research associate at the Lick Observatory before retiring again. During these years he continued his studies, publishing his last coauthored paper in 1964 at the age of eighty-six.[84]

144   PART II. ACADEMICS

CHAPTER 8

The Life Sciences

WITH EQUAL AMBITION and hopes President James and his colleagues at Illinois sought to achieve new strengths in another area of science—the life sciences. Their efforts yielded more uneven results than occurred in the physical sciences. But an informative history emerges in a review of physiology, botany and bacteriology, and zoology and entomology.

Physiology

The physiology department had as its head a well-qualified scientist, but one, however, who made himself a source of continuing trouble to President James. We should explore their conflict in some detail.

George Theophilus Kemp, a physiologist, born in Baltimore in 1861, joined the faculty in 1897. He had earned a BA (1883) and a PhD (1886) from Johns Hopkins University. Kemp's early years on the faculty went fairly well. President Draper spoke highly of him[1] but Kemp had difficulty getting funds to equip his laboratory, and he got in trouble by ignoring some red tape.[2] The physiology department programmed its courses for prospective students of medicine, biology, and hygiene. The premedical course formed the core of the curriculum, while the hygiene courses attracted the largest enrollment.

The relation of the study of physiology and medicine at the University to the study of medicine at the College of Physicians and Surgeons in Chicago had complications.[3] In 1904 the authorities entertained the idea of establishing a two-year medical course in Urbana. To do so would require offering courses in human anatomy and Kemp wanted to undertake that work. The lack of them, he explained, meant that some students left the University earlier than they desired, and when they entered the junior year in medical school, they had to go back to freshman courses to get anatomy. So, President James sent

Professor Stephen Forbes to visit Wisconsin and Kansas State to learn how they provided for the subject. In submitting his report, Forbes emphasized the expense of such an undertaking.[4]

Meanwhile, another question about medical education became more pressing. It concerned the status of students at Urbana and the courses needed to make them acceptable at Chicago, upon their graduating. Agitated discussions went on for months. Finally, President James and Dean Townsend, in collaboration with medical school officials, offered a new proposal. They emphasized the fact that physiology at Urbana formed part of the University's medical program. The premedical course at Urbana ought not be called a Course Preliminary to Medicine. It constituted, rather, a combined and continuous medical course and should have a title so indicating: the program in general science and medicine or the six-years' course in medicine. Students at Urbana registering for the combined course were taking medical studies and studying in the medical school just as truly as those in the medical school in Chicago, James and Forbes urged. So, they proposed that students would spend their first three years in Urbana, the last three in the medical school. The course would lead to a BA after four years' work and to an MD at the end of the six-years' course. This plan became effective in 1906. Kemp and his assistant were then listed as members of the College of Medicine faculty.[5]

For a decade the curriculum in physiology proved remarkably stable. In 1904–1905 the department offered six numbered and curiously labeled courses. Number 1, major course, studied the structure of the tissues and the structure and function of the organs. Number 2, advanced course, dealt with the same topics in more detail. Number 3, minor course, practical hygiene, helped students teach physiology in high schools. Number 4, special physiology, included laboratory work: the physiology of foods; the blood, circulation, and respiration; the excretions, especially urine analysis; general physiology of nerve and muscle; advanced vertebrate histology; and special work to train prospective high school teachers in methods of demonstration. Number 5, investigation and thesis, gave seniors an opportunity for research. Number 6, hygiene, dealt with the problems of everyday life. Kemp and Jeanette Carpenter Lincoln, an instructor in physical training, taught this course, one required for women taking physical training for credit.

In 1905–1906 the curriculum underwent revision and expanded by four new courses: number 7, physiological chemistry; number 8, histology; number 9, teachers' special laboratory course, which trained prospective high school teachers in the methods of demonstration; and number 10, physiological journal club. Here the staff, graduate students, and interested undergraduates discussed articles in current journals. In 1906–1907 number 10 became a graduate course, and number 103, original research, debuted at the graduate level. In the 1907–1908 spring semester, fifty-seven students enrolled in

146   PART II. ACADEMICS

undergraduate physiology courses and four in the two graduate-level offerings. Of the fifty-seven, forty-one were taking the hygiene-for-teachers course.[6] The department attracted so few students that it did not weigh heavily on the administration's scales. Kemp trained six graduate students in physiology through the master's degree level. Most of them earned medical degrees and practiced medicine. Emory R. Hayhurst earned a doctorate at the University of Chicago and became a professor.

Physiology seemed to be on course when Kemp precipitated a conflict that damaged the department and the University. Kemp was a handsome fellow, said to have money, and he always wore boots. A founding member of the Oratorio Society, he often served as its president. Kemp could be called a "character," and he impressed many undergraduates. Once students locked him out of his classroom, so he mounted a stool and lectured through the transom. He thought nothing of being twenty minutes late to class. His perverse individualism made students love him.[7] Kemp criticized local customs and ignored the unwritten code that in personal habits members of the faculty must be above reproach. His idiosyncrasies led to what David Kinley, dean of the Graduate School, considered justifiable criticisms. Kemp seemed callous, a little flippant in performing operations and wearing blood-stained aprons in his laboratory, in offending young women by sexual allusions in his lectures, and in smoking in his laboratory and office. Some found Kemp's person offensive because of the tobacco odor. He drank beer, and on Sunday, when good people were on their way to church, he could be seen standing outside the Natural History Building with a beaker of potable alcohol. He denied some of these allegations.[8]

These circumstances won Kemp no favor with President James. They probably, in fact, raised prejudices against him. Anyway, Kemp thought so, and complained to James about his salary and about equipment needed for his work.[9] James solicited assessment from Kinley who more or less acquitted Kemp. James told Kemp his research was under par and said he would not recommend for important advances in salary any man whose work was not a marked success. Kemp conceded as much about his scholarship but insisted that it fared well in comparison to other faculty.[10] James and Kemp met in February 1908 and the professor summarized the president's disaffections with his own response in a letter to the president after the meeting. James did not respond. Kemp felt slighted and judged his reputation tarnished. He decided to take his case to the trustees.[11]

The board took up the matter in March and then again in mid-April. At a third meeting, April 23, James testified and called Kemp's charges "so ridiculous as to call for no comment." He described Kemp as "not a first grade man either from a scientific or a pedagogical point of view." He labeled Kemp's scientific work "meager in quantity and on the whole of small significance, though not without some exceptions on the latter point." Nor did his teaching record add anything to his case.[12] But when James asked the board to support him, it revealed that the Kemp affair was solidifying the lines of division in it. Precisely, it brought out those trustees that had had it in for James from the beginning: the women—Carrie T. Alexander-Bahrenberg, Laura B. Evans, and Mary E. Busey, joined now by Frederick Lewis Hatch. A tie vote resulted. Kemp claimed vindication and resigned.[13] In May, with Alexander-Bahrenberg absent, the board accepted Kemp's resignation.[14]

But Kemp had not finished. He now sought to arouse public opinion for his cause. In the October 1908 issue of *Science*, a journal published in New York, he attacked James's monarchical administration and "the abominable state of affairs which exists at some of our universities in America." He interpreted the conflict as one involving academic freedom and described the memorandum James had read to the trustees as full of misleading statements. Kemp used nearly six pages of the journal to unleash a scurrilous attack on James.[15] To this assault the University Senate responded.

On October 15 it passed a resolution stating that Kemp's letters in *Science* unfortunately led the public to think that academic freedom and tenure lacked protection at Illinois. On the contrary, the faculty enjoyed academic freedom, the resolution declared. It also expressed confidence in President James, who, it said, had greatly stimulated the scientific and educational interests of the University. *Dial*, a national magazine, and *Science* both published the Senate's resolution. The Illinois controversy had gained national attention. And the *Independent*, a publication with large readership, also gave its input. "The University of Illinois has been coming to the front in the last few years more rapidly than any of the other State universities," it wrote, and "this rapid progress is to be credited chiefly to the energy and initiative of President Edmund J. James." However, such a radical and rapid transformation might cause some growing pains, the editors remarked. The reason why no definite charges such as would necessitate dismissal were brought against Kemp, the editorial continued, probably owed to there being none to bring. James seemed to have objected to Kemp on the ground that he was not a first-class teacher or administrator, not a distinguished researcher, and was a hard man to get along with, the editorial added. And the *Independent* did support James: "The University of Illinois should have the best physiologist it could find, and it is not clearly demonstrated that Dr. Kemp is that man." Two weeks later *Science* reprinted this editorial.[16]

The Kemp affair demonstrated the damage that a strong-willed but misguided faculty member can bring about. Significantly, the episode reveals James as both patient and courageous in dealing with a troublesome faculty member and a divided board in his effort to create a first-class university. Physiology remained one of the weakest departments in the University throughout the

148   PART II. ACADEMICS

James administration. Apart from prospective medical students, few in number, and two courses in hygiene, the department attracted few students.

Botany and Bacteriology

Beginning in 1904, botany struggled to maintain its place among the strong departments in the College of Science while it became related to bacteriology, a new scientific field that strove to apply its expanding knowledge to courses of study and new state agencies designed to promote health.

The botany department was well established in and beyond the University. Its head, Thomas J. Burrill, had joined the University faculty as an assistant professor of natural history and botany in 1868. In 1870 he became professor of botany and horticulture.[17] He had large stature and influence in every presidential administration and his career was flourishing still when James became president. Burrill and Charles F. Hottes led the botany department from 1904 to 1912. Hottes had earned a BA from the University in 1894, and an MA in 1895. He spent three years in Germany, where he studied vegetable physiology under Julius von Sachs, earning a PhD (1901) at the University of Bonn. Hottes returned to the University and advanced from assistant to instructor, rising in 1903 to assistant professor. He specialized in plant anatomy and physiology.[18]

The botany department offered instruction in four areas: vegetable anatomy and physiology; morphology, taxonomy, and ecology; bacteriology; and vegetable pathology. It emphasized the study of natural objects, not books. In 1904–1905 the department offered eighteen courses. In addition to an introductory course, undergraduates could choose from the following: histology and physiology; morphology; cytology (plant cells) and physiology (a laboratory and lecture course); taxonomy of special groups; plant pathology; three bacteriology courses, including one for sanitation engineers; economic botany; thesis; seminar; German readings; and a teachers' seminar. The department offered graduate courses in biological botany, systematic botany, bacteriology, and evolution of plants.

The curriculum changed little over time. In 1906 the department introduced courses in the taxonomy of special groups and in ecology. Two years later economic botany gave way to bacteriology; advanced cytology and physiology took the place of investigation and thesis; and forestry replaced German readings. In 1910 a course in heredity and the origin of species succeeded the lecture course in cytology and physiology. By that time twenty undergraduate courses, including four in ecology, existed. The curriculum for graduate students remained fixed until 1909–1910, at which time it had seven offerings: cytology, physiology, three courses in bacteriology, vegetable physiology, and ecology and phytogeography.[19]

The University's Herbarium held a collection of the local flora and that of the adjoining countryside that Burrill had assembled, and a few specimens that he had brought back from his expedition to the Colorado Rockies with Major John Wesley Powell in 1869. The compilation included 51,052 specimens in 1904 and 65,000 specimens in 1907, making it the largest assembly of Illinois plants, with great emphasis on the exsiccate of fungi. Orderly arranged in permanent cases, the specimens gave easy access and had convenient reference catalogs.[20] Enrollments in botany from 1905 to 1912 show nearly steady growth. And despite heavy teaching loads, the botanists conducted investigations and on occasion published. Burrill oriented his botanical research toward agricultural problems. Hottes pursued studies in vegetable physiology on an apparatus for recording automatically the flow of sap in trees and transpiration from leaves.

Like Townsend in his domain, Burrill pleaded for a need to understand the new science of bacteriology, to incorporate it into the curriculum, and to apply the new knowledge in the service of society. With the single exception of the doctrine of evolution, Burrill asserted, no other contribution to knowledge had so influenced the life and affairs of mankind in modern times as the discoveries of Pasteur and others concerning bacteria. The revelations made in this scientific field had surpassed all others of the same period in their bearing on human life, he avowed. The new knowledge had rejuvenated medical and surgical practice, transformed agriculture, benefited manufacturing industries, revitalized the study of personal hygiene and public sanitation, and promoted the physical, mental, and moral progress of humanity.[21]

At one time, Burrill declared, the University had a visible leadership among the universities in bacteriology. As he recalled, he had "read the first paper upon bacteria and their work ever presented in America to a scientific association (exclusive of medical societies)." Apart from certain medical colleges, the U of I was the first in the country to introduce instruction in bacteriology, he added. For a time, it enjoyed recognition for having the best provision for bacteriology and doing the most work in it.[22]

From its once proud place, however, the University had fallen behind in this field, Burrill had to concede. The laboratory fitted up for the work in 1892–1893 in the Natural History Building had proved too small; so too had the space made available in 1900 in the new Agricultural Building. Burrill had to refuse many students who wanted to enroll in his bacteriology course. In addition, the University failed to devote resources to the subject. Many universities, including Michigan, Wisconsin, and Ohio, had established a department of bacteriology, Burrill stated. At Wisconsin, a professor, an assistant professor, and an instructor gave their time to the subject. At Illinois, Burrill conducted all of the work in bacteriology, with assistance in the laboratory. So, in early 1906, with a view to improving matters, Burrill proposed leaving

150   **PART II. ACADEMICS**

bacteriology in the botany department under his supervision and enlarging the staff to five. Three new appointments were needed—a professor and two laboratory assistants.[23] Burrill also proposed to relate knowledge about bacteria, "man's indispensable aids" and "his deadliest enemies," to the prevention of disease. Practically all of the transmissible diseases owed to bacterial scourges, he said. As evidence, he observed that every year from seven to eight thousand people in Illinois died from tuberculosis, and pneumonia claimed nearly as many. Actually, in 1907 tuberculosis, the "Great White Plague," accounted for 7,142 deaths in the state, compared to 7,386 for pneumonia.[24]

To deal with the problem, Burrill wanted to introduce a four-year course in sanitary science similar to one at Cornell. It would train students for positions in water works and in sanitary operations. Both the College of Science and the University Senate endorsed the idea. On March 12, 1907, President James presented plans for the course to the trustees along with a recommendation from Dean Townsend for establishment of a department of bacteriology. The trustees postponed "full consideration" of both until after the legislature had made its appropriations for the next biennium.[25]

In July 1907 Burrill's plan had a partial realization with the appointment of Ward J. MacNeal as assistant chief in bacteriology in the Agricultural Laboratory of Physiological Chemistry. MacNeal had an AB (1901), a PhD (1904), and an MD (1905) from the University of Michigan, and had taught for a year at the University of West Virginia. He arrived at Urbana and took charge of the physiological and bacteriological work of the nutrition experiment directed by Harry S. Grindley. In 1908 MacNeal began assisting Burrill in the introductory bacteriology course. Burrill strongly commended MacNeal's services, adding that his publications gave him "clear title to recognition among leading bacteriologists in the country."[26]

In addition to a course in sanitary science, Burrill proposed the establishment of a State Institute of Sanitary Science and Public Health on the model of the Pasteur Institute in Paris. He envisioned one laboratory with various branches. Its purpose: to utilize research discoveries; to aid the State Board of Health, physicians, and existing state agencies whose duties touched on the subject; and to educate health officers and the public on the prevention of disease and the promotion of health. The institute would have a director of high scientific standing, guided by an advisory board, and close connections to the State Board of Health. For reasons of efficiency and economy the institute was to be located at and allied with the University.[27] Dean Townsend had no doubt that such an institute could render important public service. In December he forwarded Burrill's proposal to President James, noting that a College of Science committee had estimated the cost of maintaining the institute at $50,000. James sent a copy of Burrill's proposal to members of the Board of Trustees.[28]

Townsend believed that the State Board of Health was likely to be reorganized in the near future; the time was ripe to obtain University representation on that body. The Board of Health, established in 1877 as the medical department of the state government, was by law charged with supervision of a system of sanitary inspection by municipal and local health authorities, registration of births and deaths, and the licensing of physicians. It regulated the practice of medicine. The Illinois State Medical Society had long wanted to separate the regulatory function from the promotion of public health. Its members characterized the laws under which the board operated as antiquated, inefficient, and essentially worthless. Physicians wanted a law providing for a State Board of Public Health. University people made common cause with them in an effort at reform.[29]

At that time, a movement in the interest of public health was spreading nationally. To promote the cause, Dean Townsend invited William T. Sedgwick to lecture at the University. Sedgwick, a professor of biology, made sanitary science or public health the mainstay of his department's curriculum at MIT. His *Principles of Sanitary Science and the Public Health* (1902) won him renown as a leader in the public health movement. In April 1909 Sedgwick presented five lectures on "Science in the Service of Public Health," treating the subject from the perspective of biology, medicine, chemistry, engineering, statistics, education, and government. To coincide with Sedgwick's visit, Townsend, with the cooperation of President George W. Webster and Secretary James A. Egan of the State Board of Health, invited the municipal health workers of the state to attend a conference at the University. Townsend asked Chicago and downstate newspaper editors to send reporters to cover the proceedings.[30]

The conference took place on April 23, 1909. Webster and Egan spoke on the cooperation of the Board of Trustees and the University in public health service. Burrill outlined his proposed course in sanitary science. William A. Evans, the Chicago Health Commissioner, spoke on the Chicago milk ordinance, Sedgwick on the professional health officer, Dr. John Martin, the health officer of Tolono, Illinois, on the needs of the local health officer, and Professor A. N. Talbot on the engineer and public health. Only five of the state's 5,400 municipal, township, and county health officers attended (four came from Champaign County and one from Chicago).[31] The *Champaign Daily News* ran a story in advance of the event, but the press did not report on the conference.

Nonetheless, Townsend continued to press his larger agenda, and in 1910 he wrote his important major document "Science and Public Service" (see Chapter 7), in which he pleaded for enlisting the new advances in science to improve the quality of life. He sent a copy to Governor Deneen, who read it and said that shortly after the General Assembly met in January, he would

152   PART II. ACADEMICS

take up the matter with the State Board of Health and the advisory board. Deneen did not address the topic in his message to the legislature.[32]

The long-desired reform occurred in 1917 in the Civil Administration Code. The document created the State Department of Public Health and charged it solely with the promotion of health and the prevention of disease. It became one of the nine major departments of the state government. The code also created the Department of Registration and Education. One of its many divisions was the State Board of Health, which retained the power and duty to examine and license physicians, other practitioners, midwives, and embalmers.[33]

While trying to bring science to bear on public service, Townsend dealt with the botany department. Botany might best wait for zoology to develop, but botany would suffer "too severely" if special attention were longer postponed. Burrill did not want to hinder botany's growth. He urged more development in vegetable physiology, which had much in common with animal physiology. He specified more work in the organic evolution of plants, which required a greenhouse. Perhaps the University might construct one on a flat part of the roof over the Natural History Building. An experimental garden with suitable greenhouses for growing plants for instruction and for scientific experimentation he labeled a necessity. In addition, Burrill wished for a botanical museum. These needs involved great expense. Burrill also stressed the importance of bacteriology. During the academic year 1910–1911 the department provided instruction with laboratory practice to 80 out of the 3,400 students. But in May 1911 things worsened when MacNeal left to accept a position in the New York Post-Graduate Medical School at an increase in pay.[34]

A month later Burrill asked President James what place bacteriology had in his plans. Bacteriology, James coolly replied, ranked high in the scientific hierarchy; the sooner it could develop the better. Perhaps something could be done in two years with the next appropriation. His patience exhausted, Burrill declared that the situation needed "a tremendous shaking up." "If it does not come from inside," he predicted, "before long it will from outside." We dare not let slip any opportunity to cultivate so fruitful a field. "To the University rightfully belongs leadership for our part of the country in the stirring and hopefully significant public health propaganda, as well as in the everyday applications of knowledge derived from the study of bacteria—man's unequaled friends and deadliest foes."[35] But rather than showing leadership in bacteriology, the University lagged. For bacteriology and hygiene, Michigan Agricultural College had $35,370; the University of Wisconsin, $24,150; the University of Michigan, $19,470; and the University of Illinois, $7,850. Townsend did hire Otto Rahn from Germany but he stayed only two years.

Meanwhile, word had spread about the practical applications of bacteriology. In June 1911, J. W. McCall, president of the Illinois Canners' Association, asked Burrill if the University would be willing to undertake "certain practical

8. The Life Sciences   153

scientific problems" in the canning industry, for example, how to prevent spoilage in canned corn and other vegetables. The University agreed to conduct the investigations if the canners would provide $1,000 a year for two or three years. The University would use the money to hire an assistant in the Department of Bacteriology and Chemistry. The investigation that began under Burrill continued under Rahn. Little seemed to come out of the research during the first year, but Bronson Barlow, an assistant, struck a promising lead. He and Rahn believed strongly that results of great value would emerge if the canning agreement could continue for two years more. Barlow agreed to give his time to the work for another year at a salary of $1,500; additional expenses were estimated to cost $1,000. So, in 1912 the Illinois Canners' Association agreed to these terms, as did the Board of Trustees and President James.[36]

In June 1912, Burrill announced his retirement, effective September 1. He had been prominent in the University since it opened and had given the botany department great stature. His membership in eight scientific societies and election to the presidency of four of them demonstrated the range of his interest and his prestige. In September the trustees honored Burrill by giving him $3,000 in recognition of the distinguished services he had rendered the University on numerous occasions as vice president and acting president. From 1912 to 1916 Burrill worked on a problem in applied bacteriology—an attempt to induce the formation of nodules on the roots of field crops like corn. Burrill died of pneumonia in 1916, widely recognized for his achievements and for having trained several prominent botanists.

A complicated search to find Burrill's successor led to the appointment of William Trelease in 1913. Trelease came from the East, born 1857 in Mt. Vernon, New York, and educated in public schools there and in Branford, Connecticut. Entering Cornell in 1877, he pursued a course in natural history, emphasizing botany and entomology, and graduated with a BS in 1880. He went on to Harvard, where he studied under a number of eminent scientists, including Asa Gray. Trelease taught botany at the University of Wisconsin from 1881 to 1883. He was promoted to professor and head of the botany department that year. He received a DSc from Harvard in 1884. Trelease left Wisconsin the following year to become Engelmann Professor in the Shaw School of Botany in Washington University in St. Louis. He became director of the Missouri Botanical Garden in 1889. In twenty-three years there, he transformed a great private horticultural garden into a well-regarded scientific institution while increasing its popular appeal. Trelease did almost all of his work on the taxonomy of the flowering plants, but he was always excited by bacteriology and took an interest in all the new approaches to the study of botany. He had published much, had served in many different capacities in a wide variety of scientific organizations, and had received many honors before joining the University faculty.[37] Trelease gave the University of Illinois much

154   PART II. ACADEMICS

distinction in botany, serving as chair of that department from 1913 to 1926, the year of his retirement.

After Trelease's appointment, Townsend arranged for Hottes to be promoted to professor of botany, and James followed through on his stated intention to strengthen the botany department by hiring Frank L. Stevens.

Zoology and Entomology

From the first years of the University, study of zoology, and the other sciences, had a pronounced vocational emphasis. But under Regent Peabody later in the century some "liberation" from this practicality occurred, and Illinois achieved national recognition for its academic work and its connection to the Illinois State Laboratory of Natural History.[38] These departments operated in Natural History Hall in close proximity to the State Laboratory of Natural History and the State Entomologist's office. Stephen A. Forbes, "one of the most brilliant men who has ever graced its faculty,"[39] headed both departments until 1909; then he resigned as professor and head of the zoology department while continuing as professor and head of entomology. He set a high priority on training advanced students to do research and publish.[40]

Forbes had three colleagues in zoology, all with Harvard degrees. In 1904–1905 the zoology department offered thirteen courses to undergraduates. Five were basic: General Zoology, an elementary course in both vertebrate and invertebrate zoology, the only prerequisite for major work in the subject; Teacher's Course, the same as the former with the addition of material on pedagogy; Introductory Zoology, a laboratory and lecture course that prepared students for Vertebrate Zoology and Comparative Anatomy, and included study of the general theory of evolution; and Vertebrate Embryology, the so-called medical course in zoology. The department also offered advanced undergraduate courses: Thesis and Investigation, Statistical Zoology, German Readings, Variation and Heredity, Statistical Data, Experimental and Physiological Zoology, Field Zoology, and Field Ornithology.

In addition to six of the undergraduate courses, graduate students could take four graduate-level courses for credit. According to Forbes, the department had sufficient strengths for students to do graduate work in plankton zoology, ichthyology, zoological physiology, and embryology.[41] Except for embryology, the department did offer such courses.

A noteworthy accomplishment of the biological station came from a book by Forbes and coauthor Robert E. Richardson on *The Fishes of Illinois* (1909), with an atlas showing the distribution of each of 150 different species of fishes in the state.[42] The book took its contents from field observations begun as early as 1876 and continued, at irregular intervals, down to 1903. Richardson (b. 1877) earned an AB (1901) and an AM (1903) at the University. An expert

8. The Life Sciences   155

on fishes, as a staff member at the biological station he helped compile the data for the book. It begins with an account of the topography and hydrography of Illinois prepared by Charles W. Rolfe of the University's geology and geography department. The remainder of the text, including many color illustrations, was devoted to systematic work. Sir Ray Lankester described the volume as "a first-rate specimen of the thoroughness and completeness with which biological work is nowadays carried on in the United States, and of the excellent style in which the results are presented to the public."[43]

The 1907 arrival of John H. McClellan (b. 1876) strengthened the faculty. He had an AB (1897) and an AM (1899) from the University of Michigan, had been on the Illinois faculty from 1899 to 1903 as a zoology instructor, had earned a Harvard PhD (1906), and had then studied in Berlin for a year. Forbes sought to reengage McClellan for the premedical program, but before doing so he wanted assurance of McClellan's commitment to do research. Forbes received it from McClellan's Harvard mentor, who consented to release McClellan from a Harvard appointment he had accepted. So, McClellan returned to Illinois with the rank of an associate. In 1908 he became an assistant professor of histology and embryology, and in 1909 assistant professor of physiology.[44] With McClellan's arrival an undergraduate course in Chemical Zoology replaced Experimental and Physiological Zoology and a course in Microscopic Organisms was introduced. At the graduate level Embryology replaced Plankton Zoology.

In 1908 Charles C. Adams (b. 1873), who had a BS (1895) from Illinois Wesleyan, an MS (1898) from Harvard, and a PhD (1908) from the University of Chicago, joined the faculty as an associate. Previously he had taught biology, entomology, and zoology in several colleges. He specialized in animal ecology.[45] The principal deficiency of the curriculum lay in experimental and ecological zoology. The appointment of a competent teacher and investigator in this field, said Forbes, would enable the department "to take the lead in that line to which we have long been entitled, and to make an important educational advance at a very small expense to the University itself."[46] But Forbes also observed that zoology needed about $9,000 to put the library in an approximate state of parity with its peer institutions. About 20 percent of this sum would be used for books, the remainder for serials old and new, binding, and transportation.[47]

In addition to zoology, Forbes had responsibility for the work in entomology. Noting the existence of an "insatiable demand" for trained entomologists with a capacity for experimental investigation, Forbes said that the main supply for such men came from Cornell and Illinois. Cornell and the agricultural colleges produced many entomologists, those from the former well prepared and the latter poorly prepared, as a rule. Illinois had the equipment, situation, and reputation to train men of the highest caliber, but it had only one faculty

156   PART II. ACADEMICS

member compared to Cornell's five. Forbes wanted to "push into this field much more strongly."[48]

For years the only full-time faculty member in entomology was Justus W. Folsom (b. 1871), a native of Massachusetts with an SB (1895) and an SD (1899) from Harvard. He had spent a year as professor of natural science and physiology at Antioch College in Ohio before joining the faculty in 1900 as an instructor.[49] His preparation and experience focused him on morphological lines rather than on taxonomic or economic lines.[50] Forbes described Folsom as "one of the best prepared and most successful entomological investigators in the United States," "an enthusiastic and indefatigable worker," and "a man whom we may depend upon for the rapid and substantial development of entomology at the University."[51]

Forbes distinguished between purely scientific and economic courses in entomology and insisted that the one thing most needed by students preparing for service in the nation's agricultural experiment stations was technical entomology.[52]

When the budget improved, Forbes considered hiring either O. A. Johannsen of the University of Maine or Alexander D. MacGillivray of Cornell. Dean Townsend urged James to inquire about the two men on a trip east.[53] In April 1911 Forbes opted for MacGillivray. An Ohio native, MacGillivray (b. 1868) entered Cornell in 1889, was an assistant in entomology there from 1890 to 1900, and graduated with a BA degree. An instructor from 1900 to 1906, he earned a PhD in 1904, and became an assistant professor in 1906. He taught systematic entomology and invertebrate zoology and felt overworked because he taught seven hours a day without an assistant.

In mid-June, having agreed to accept an appointment as an assistant professor at $2,500, MacGillivray visited the campus. At the end of the month, he accepted on the terms stated.[54] He said that he cast his lot with Illinois because he saw a fine opportunity to develop systematic entomology at Urbana, with the funds needed for growing the library holdings, and with the great opportunity for advancing graduate work, with sufficient time allowed for research. On July 8 the board appointed MacGillivray as an assistant professor of systematic entomology at $2,500 a year.[55]

MacGillivray enabled Forbes to expand the curriculum. In 1911–1912 Forbes introduced new undergraduate courses. They included Introduction to Research, jointly taught by Forbes, Folsom, and MacGillivray, and Advanced Economic Entomology, which Forbes and Folsom offered. The faculty shared in teaching a seminar. MacGillivray offered four new courses: Elementary Systematic Entomology, Advanced Systematic Entomology, Taxonomy of Immature Insects, and Classification of the Coccidae.

The graduate work also made substantial progress. Students had four research courses available: Morphology and Embryology of Insects (Folsom);

8. The Life Sciences 157

Faunistic and Ecological Entomology (Forbes); Economic Entomology (Forbes); and Systematic Entomology (MacGillivray). In 1912 Forbes realized an old ambition by introducing two specialized courses. Now he taught Medical Entomology, designed primarily for premedical students, a study of insects as related to the transmission of disease, methods of controlling such insects, and preventing the diseases due to them. Advanced Economic Entomology sought to train entomologists for positions with state and federal governments.[56] Entomology attracted students in increasing numbers, from 77 in 1908–1909 to 228 in 1911–1912. By that time, it also had 31 graduate students enrolled.[57]

Meanwhile, Forbes called attention to the things most needed for symmetrical development of the department. He listed first an insectary building. Creation of the old insectary (located east of Wright Street and north of the later Woman's Building) owed to a special legislative appropriation to the State Entomologist in 1889. In 1905, when the Entomology Building was erected (east of the Auditorium on the site of the later Foreign Languages Building), Forbes left the old insectary standing for use in instruction. The University destroyed it in clearing the ground for the Commerce Building (later the David Henry Administration Building) and provided no replacement. So, Forbes wanted a new insectary. It would cost $5,000, together with about an acre of land attached to it for the purpose of rearing insects and their food. Forbes did not know of any entomology department in the country except Illinois that lacked this indispensable accessory.[58]

The program also needed a professor of economic and ecological entomology. Forbes described this field as "an application to human affairs of the principles and data of entomological ecology." Entomology, he said, required special equipment, special methods, and intensive study of organisms that zoologists and botanists usually avoided. Like bacteriology, entomology had bearings on human welfare so varied and important that there existed a special demand for investigation and instruction of a practical character in the interests of the community. The importance of its practical applications gave entomology its strongest claim to full development in higher education, Forbes asserted. MacGillivray was a systematist and morphologist, Folsom a general entomologist. Neither had the qualifications to teach the economic courses. Forbes pleaded for an instructor in economic entomology competent to teach both the scientific principles and practical methods of that division of entomology. He would make this work his own function, he said, if his commitments in the state agencies did not almost wholly dominate his time.[59]

• • •

Forbes's retirement as head of zoology was a defining event. In early January 1909 James named Townsend, Burrill, Forbes, and Kinley as a committee to

President James and the Council of Administration, 1915. David Kinley sits to the left of James and Thomas Arkle Clark to the right. Courtesy of the University of Illinois Archives.

recommend five or six men suitable to a professorship in zoology and headship of the department, arranged, if possible, in order of desirability.[60]

The list included Henry B. Ward. Born in Troy, New York in 1865, where his father was a physician and microscopist of repute, young Ward attended the Troy public schools, graduated from Williams College with an AB (1885), and taught science in the Troy High School for three years. Here he became one of the first to introduce the use of the microscope in secondary schools. In 1888 Ward left for Germany, where he studied with Ernst Heinrich Ehlers at Göttingen for an academic year, later at Freiburg, and then for less than a year at Leipzig with Rudolf Leuckart, an authority on invertebrates and founder of a celebrated laboratory of parasitology. Ward had a particularly strong influence from Leuckart. While in his laboratory he became interested in parasitology and was determined to establish a graduate program in that field in the United States.[61]

In 1890 Ward entered the graduate school of Harvard. He spent one summer at Agassiz's marine laboratory at Newport, Rhode Island, received a PhD from Harvard in 1892, and went to the University of Michigan as an instructor in zoology (animal morphology). In 1893 he left to become an associate professor of zoology at the University of Nebraska, rose to full professor in 1906 and became head of the zoology department. Ward played a major role in developing a two-year premedical course at Nebraska, and in 1902, when it united with the Omaha Medical College to become the College of Medicine of the University of Nebraska, he became its first dean. In 1908 he won election as president of the American Association of Medical Colleges. By 1909 Ward had edited several volumes of zoological studies and published over a hundred articles, mostly on the parasitic diseases of humans.[62]

Ward seemed ideally suited to succeed Forbes. He was "a man of great energy and executive force," wrote Jacob Reighard of the University of Michigan, "a capable administrator, an able teacher, and an eminent investigator." As a researcher, Reighard saw him as "rather a man of detail than of large grasp."[63] Ward had "a somewhat aggressive overbearing manner," wrote Ellery W. Davis of Nebraska, "but he knows his tendency and gets it more and more under control." So, Illinois need not hesitate on the score of Ward's getting along with people, Davis assured. Ward had built up a school of high quality under a united and able faculty and showed himself a good judge of people.[64] A biographer of Ward characterized him as follows: "Aristocratic, autocratic, ambitious, and enthusiastic, he demanded excellence of himself and others."[65]

Ward took up his new duties in Urbana in mid-September. The evening before he departed from Lincoln the speakers at a dinner given by the Pathological Club praised him for the work he had done for the University of Nebraska, especially in the medical school.[66] An anonymous note to "President Illinois State University" followed Ward to Urbana. "If you are as pleased over the acquisition of Ward as Nebr. was to be well rid of him," the author wrote, "it must be like the joy in heaven over a sinner that has been saved. We have peace in the Uni for the first time in years."[67]

Ward would have liked the department to offer a course in anthropology. Students and others had requested it, Ward had great interest in the subject, and several times material had arrived to the department from the Indian burial mounds in Illinois with a request for advice regarding the anthropological questions involved. But anthropology could not be introduced without a new appointment because the faculty could not bear any addition to its already heavy teaching load.[68] More than four decades lapsed before the University appointed an anthropologist.

The available data indicate that the department was growing, but slowly. Student registrations in zoology show a total of 462 students in 1909–1910, 469 in 1910–1911, and 505 in 1911–1912.[69] The increased numbers and the variety and character of the work aggravated the problem of overcrowding.

160   PART II. ACADEMICS

Ward pleaded for more space for classes, experiments, laboratories, offices, and storage. He saw an even more urgent need for a live house, a place where the smaller animals of land and water could be kept under observation in semi-natural conditions for purposes of study. He wanted a vivarium and aquarium constructed after the manner of a greenhouse, with the central area available for small land animals and aquaria on either side, one for fresh water animals, the other for salt water life. In addition, the department needed an area of land with proper conditions for small wildlife. He emphasized the need to preserve Brownfield Woods, the last piece of native woodland in the area. Ward observed that other universities (he cited Indiana, Chicago, and Wisconsin) exceeded Illinois in many of the categories discussed.[70]

During his first or second visit to the University, Ward had discussed the filling of a vacancy in zoology created by the departure of Amos Peters. Ward may have ranked his choices at the time. He listed first Charles Zeleny of Indiana University. Tied for second place were a Dr. Mast of Woman's College, Baltimore, and a Dr. Curtis of the University of Missouri.[71] On June 22, before his own appointment became official, Ward wrote to Zeleny that "a new department of zoology is being organized at the University of Illinois with a view to making it strong in research." Zeleny's special work would fit into the program outlined, he stated. Ward asked if Zeleny had any interest in the position at a salary of $2,500.[72]

Charles Zeleny (b. 1878) had taken a BS (1898) and an MS (1901) at the University of Minnesota. In 1902 he held a fellowship at the Biological Laboratory at Cold Spring Harbor on Long Island and earned a PhD at Columbia. After a year on a Smithsonian Institution appointment at the Naples Zoological Station (1902–1903) he held a fellowship at the University of Chicago (1903–1904) and then went as an instructor to Indiana University, advancing by 1908 to associate professor. He had spent many summers in research at the Marine Biological Laboratory at Woods Hole, Massachusetts.[73] Zeleny had a long and distinguished career at Illinois, lasting to his death in Urbana in 1939. He made contributions to experimental zoology, embryology, genetics, and regeneration. He won election as president of the American Society of Zoologists in 1933.

Ward did secure two new appointments, major additions. Harley J. Van Cleave (b. 1886) joined the faculty as an instructor. Born in Knoxville, Illinois, Van Cleave had a BS (1909) from Knox College, an AM (1910) from Illinois, and from 1911 to 1913 was an assistant in the department. In 1913 he received a PhD and joined the faculty. Van Cleave advanced through the ranks. A steadying influence in the department, he made outstanding contributions as a teacher, a research worker, and a mentor of nearly a score of PhDs.[74]

Also, John S. Kingsley, who filled the vacancy created by Frederick Carpenter's departure for Trinity College, Connecticut, joined the faculty as a full professor. Born in Cincinnatus, New York, in 1856, he attended Brooklyn

Polytechnic and earned an AB in the classical course at Williams College in 1875. He held several government and academic appointments before his arrival at Illinois. From 1884 to 1896 he edited the *American Naturalist*, and since 1910 the *Journal of Morphology*. His many publications dealt with comparative anatomy, embryology, and the morphology of vertebrates.[75] After the board gave him the authority, James offered Kingsley an appointment as professor of zoology at $3,500, adding $1,000 for the purchase of special equipment in zoology for the University, and $1,000 for the purchase of books. He assigned Kingsley a room in the Natural History Building for use as an office, study, and laboratory.[76] Kingsley's appointment occurred on July 21, 1913.

• • •

The zoology and entomology departments developed together and it's difficult to disentangle them. Under Forbes each of them gained distinction. Forbes dedicated himself to research and publication; in these matters he set an example for his colleagues. He took a keen interest in giving undergraduates as well as advanced students a sound scientific education. And through the state agencies he served the people of Illinois by applying science to the solution of practical problems. All of this work went on despite weak financial support, shortage of laboratories and equipment, and lack of space. In sum, the history of these units under Forbes demonstrates strength through adversity. But Ward's appointment significantly helped to lay the foundations for a remarkable advance in zoology at the University of Illinois. To be sure, Ward had little charity for or interest in average or mediocre attainment by members of his staff. Under his leadership the University "became one of the leading centers of the world in parasitology." In that subject, this partisan believed, Illinois led the world.[77]

CHAPTER 9

The Social Sciences

THE LIBERAL ARTS and sciences form the core of a university. In 1904 these studies existed in two units at Illinois: the College of Literature and Arts and the College of Science. James wanted them merged but the science faculty repeatedly voted against the scheme. Not until 1923 did the two colleges unite to become the College of Liberal Arts and Sciences.[1]

• • •

Engineering had long been the colossus on the campus, but President James urgently wanted to create a first-class university, which, he believed, required revitalization of the liberal arts. Evarts B. Greene became the dean of the College of Literature and Arts on February 1, 1906. A Harvard-trained historian in early American history, Greene had served on the faculty since 1894. He was well regarded. He had recently turned down the offer of a Yale professorship because he wanted to develop the liberal arts at Illinois, and in 1910 he declined an offer to head the Johns Hopkins history department because of his faith in securing from President James the changes needed for his college.[2]

Greene and James collaborated in breathing new life into the humanities and social sciences. The work of the College was fundamental to all technical and professional studies, they believed. In 1904 the College included twelve departments.[3]

The College of Literature and Arts provided instruction for students from all the university colleges. People registered in other areas came here for their basic preparation. Greene urged a foundation of general college studies as the basis for specialized work. He hoped to make his college a model for other collegiate institutions by the quality of its instruction and the exacting character of its requirements.[4] He thought it best to strengthen existing departments before adding new ones, but he would have liked to expand into new areas, especially ancient history (including preclassical history and languages), anthropology, American archaeology, and comparative literature. Lack of funds and qualified faculty prevented such new departures.[5]

Knowing that much of the undergraduate work had not moved above an elementary level, Greene outlined several steps essential to developing genuine university work in the liberal arts. First, the College needed several faculty appointments of the highest order as well as more assistants to relieve department heads. Illinois had a disadvantage in competition with older universities, however. In 1907, for example, the maximum salary of a full professor in Literature and Arts at Illinois was $3,000, the same paid to assistant professors at Harvard.[6]

Second, Greene emphasized the need to improve the library. Its holdings in the liberal arts paled in comparison to the nation's leading institutions. Faculty in the liberal arts depended more on the library than others in the University. Illinois would find it difficult to compete with other universities in securing and retaining top scholars unless it could provide the books they needed for instruction and research. In this matter, as detailed earlier, Greene shared a common ambition with President James. Third, Greene highlighted the need for a new building. His college had overcrowded and unattractive quarters in University Hall. The classrooms had constant occupation, poor ventilation, and inadequate sanitary conditions. The situation compared unfavorably with those of the other colleges in the University.[7]

Greene offered several proposals to advance the standards of undergraduate work. He sought to restrict the admission of students who did not meet the entrance requirements and to limit the elective system so that students would devise programs with a clear focus. He wanted more advanced courses; sharper differentiation between freshman courses and those of the junior and senior years, to prevent seniors from counting freshman courses for credit; and careful scrutiny of popular courses that moved along the paths of least resistance. He devised an honors program, induced senior professors to oversee junior faculty, and appointed an assistant dean to supervise undergraduate students in the college.[8]

In November 1910 Greene requested leave of absence for 1911–1912 in order to do research in the United States and England. On returning he wished to devote himself to teaching and scholarship. James wanted Greene to postpone his leave for a year and to continue as dean. In the event, on February 1, 1912, Greene began a leave of absence for a semester and Arthur H. Daniels became acting dean of the College. Greene returned to duty as dean in September, but on February 12, 1913, he resigned as dean to devote his time to teaching and scientific work and Daniels stayed on to serve as acting dean.[9]

Under Greene's leadership the College made a substantial advance. Several excellent scholars came to Illinois, the quality of the departments improved,

164   PART II. ACADEMICS

Table 1. Enrollment by Departments, 1904–1905 to 1912–1913

Year	1904–5	1905–6	1906–7	1907–8	1908–9	1909–10	1910–11	1911–12	1912–13
Art and Design	575	515	417	208	196	172	213	244	235
Economics	981	1057	1141	635	742	736	751	997	1062
Education	130	203	201	79	101	147	168	170	199
English	972	1240	1292	795	866	729	756	826	712
French (It/Sp)	511	545	676	440	524	513	500	490	511
German	1044	1054	1175	707	790	712	747	703	660
Greek	64	83	74	26	19	42	42	37	36
History	507	669	703	357	478	452	386	405	396
Latin	158	177	180	90	132	167	152	143	130
Philosophy	67	124	132	127	110	126	168	224	215
Pol. Science	117	216	216	138	193	252	225	263	310
Psychology	149	192	266	181	226	237	238	172	186
Rhetoric	1666	1672	1950	1061	1134	1069	1224	1346	1286
Sociology	—	—	—	37	58	85	84	115	142

N.B.: The figures for the years to 1906–1907 are total enrollment for the year; those for later years are average enrollment for the year.

and the faculty gained increasing recognition in the nation's literary and scientific associations. Testifying to the gains, in 1907 a Phi Beta Kappa chapter was established at the University.[10]

Total enrollment in Literature and Arts rose from 565 in 1904–1905 to 926 in 1912–1913, an increase of 61 percent. Women outnumbered men, constituting 53 percent of the total enrollment from 1904 to 1913. By 1912–1913, however, the proportions of men and women evened out. Although Greene shifted the emphasis from elementary to advanced work, many freshmen did not complete their college course. From 1906–1907 to 1911–1912 a total of 1,772 freshmen enrolled, but there were only 1,177 sophomores (66 percent of the freshmen) and 764 juniors. The College had 811 seniors. From 1905 to 1913 the number of graduates who earned a BA in Literature and Arts was 1,091, an average of 121 a year. The total included 124 students who had taken the Business Courses and another 28 who had taken Household Science.[11]

Course enrollments, which register student preferences, are illustrated in Table 1.

Economics

In 1904–1905 David Kinley headed the economics department, which had two other professors, one assistant professor, and two instructors. It offered thirty-four undergraduate courses in general economics, economic history, sociology and statistics, finance, commerce and industry, and three graduate courses. The department included a program of Training for Business that offered a miscellany of courses designed to give a university training for general mercantile business, banking, transportation, journalism, insurance, municipal administration, and consular and diplomatic service. The program included a general business course and a course in banking, each with a four-year curriculum. The courses proved attractive; in 1905 they enrolled 140 students.[12]

In February 1906, Kinley remained head of the economics department and director of the business courses when he became dean of the Graduate School. In effect, the Training for Business program was an embryonic school of commerce within the liberal arts college. The course offerings in the economics department expanded primarily with a view to strengthening the business program. In 1907–1908 the mathematics department took over the courses in statistics while those in sociology transferred to the new sociology department. A year later economics introduced seven courses in accountancy and many railway courses. New four-year courses in accountancy, railway traffic and accounting, railway transportation, railway administration, and journalism, plus a course on the consular service, became part of the Training for Business program.[13]

166   PART II. ACADEMICS

Enrollments in economics grew rapidly, partly because some work in the subject was required in civil engineering, and partly because many students registered in the liberal arts wanted the business program. In 1911 about 200 students were taking the four-year business courses, 183 of whom called themselves business students. The others, who were taking the business course but not unwilling to have their diplomas indicate as much, enrolled as general students. Greene deferred to Kinley on economics matters, but he had less interest than Kinley in applied studies. They agreed on the need to develop the work in general economics along with the practical studies that appealed to business students.

The instructional staff grew to keep pace with enrollments. During 1908–1909 it had nine people, including Nathan A. Weston, an assistant professor, described by Kinley as the best teacher in the department, and Simon Litman. Born in Odessa, Russia, Litman had earned an AB at the Odessa Commercial College (1892); had studied and engaged in research in Paris, Munich, and Zurich; and in 1901 had received a doctorate in public law and commerce from the University of Zurich. Since 1903 he had taught business organization and industrial development at the University of California. Despite some disagreeable mannerisms, Litman adapted to local conditions, did well with students, and had a good record in scholarship.

The legislative appropriation for studies in commerce was $25,000 a year. The salaries of economics faculty members other than Kinley came out of the commerce budget. In 1911 Kinley commented on weaknesses in his domain, including insufficient courses in commercial law, the lack of a course in the theory of business organization on the legal and economic sides, the want of a course in shop and factory organization for engineers, and of a similar one in farm management. Kinley regarded his staff as equal to that in any other institution, except for a few leading people elsewhere.

History

In 1904 Evarts B. Greene, described by Kinley as "one of the strongest men in the College,"[14] headed the history department. His own major works included *The Provincial Governor in the English Colonies of North America* (1898) and *Provincial America, 1690–1740* ("American Nation" series, 1905). Greene made excellent appointments and developed the department along the lines of American history and modern European history, adding work in English history, introducing Spanish-American history, and shifting the emphasis from undergraduate to graduate courses. With a faculty of three and growing enrollments, Greene asked for two additional staff members—a scholar-teacher who could attract students and an assistant.[15] James gladly provided funds to build up the department.

9. The Social Sciences   **167**

In 1906 Guy Stanton Ford joined the faculty. A Wisconsin native, Ford had earned a BL at Wisconsin in 1895, had taught school for three years, had taken a year of graduate work at Wisconsin followed by a year at the University of Berlin. In 1903 he had received a PhD from Columbia University. He then joined the Yale faculty, as an assistant professor, and came to Illinois in 1906 as professor of modern European history. Ford's qualities as a scholar, his high standards, and his contributions to the discussion of educational problems made him a valuable faculty member.

In 1907 the department gained two new associates. One was Laurence M. Larson. Born in Bergen, Norway, in 1868, he taught in a Scandinavian academy for five years and then took an AM (1900) and a PhD (1902) at Wisconsin. As a teacher in Milwaukee high schools, he had great success. Shy and scholarly, he published on medieval English and Scandinavian institutions. His book *The King's Household in England before the Norman Conquest* (1904) won high acclaim. In 1907 the University of Wisconsin was ready to appoint Larson in Scandinavian languages and history with the understanding that he would ultimately move to the history department. But Larson accepted an appointment at Illinois as an associate and took charge of English history. He advanced to assistant professor in 1908 and to associate professor in 1912, the year in which he published *Canute the Great, 995 (circa)-1035, and the Rise of Danish Imperialism during the Viking Age*.[16] In 1908 Theodore Calvin Pease, a Chicago PhD (1907), who specialized in both English and American history, joined the faculty. He rose through the ranks and spent his entire career at Illinois, until his death in 1948. A product of Cassopolis, Michigan, he had earned his doctorate at Chicago. His book, *The Leveler Movement: A Study in the History and Political Theory of the English Great Civil War* (1916), became a Herbert Baxter Adams Prize winner. Pease made major contributions to Illinois history, beginning with *The Frontier State* (1918).

In 1909 Greene found William S. Robertson, a historian of Latin America. Born in Glasgow, Scotland, Robertson earned a PhD at Yale (1903) and joined the faculty at Western Reserve University before coming to Illinois. His advanced courses had small enrollments, but he taught the introductory course in American history and developed a strong hold on students. A productive scholar, Robertson became a leading historian of Latin America.

In 1912 Arthur C. Cole, a Pennsylvania PhD (1911), joined the faculty as an assistant. He had just won the Justin Winsor Prize of the American Historical Association for *The Whig Party in the South* (1914). He came highly recommended.[17] In 1913, hearing that Ford might go to Minnesota, Kinley urged James to do anything possible to retain an excellent teacher, fine scholar, and agreeable colleague. Ford did leave for Minnesota, however, to become head of the history department and dean of the graduate school.[18]

168   PART II. ACADEMICS

Albert H. Lybyer replaced Ford in modern European history. Lybyer had a Princeton AB (1896) and AM (1899), and had studied at Princeton Theological Seminary. From 1900 to 1906 he taught at Robert College in Constantinople, and in 1909 he received a Harvard PhD. His 1913 book *The Government of the Ottoman Empire in the Time of Suleiman the Magnificent* won praise as "the most substantial monograph in the field of Continental European history produced in any of our American Universities since the publication of [Guy Stanton] Ford's study in 1903." Lybyer had served on the faculty at Oberlin College (1909 to 1913). James and Greene had inquired at Harvard as to Lybyer's knowledge of the Turkish language. (The point was significant: many Occidental historians who have written on the Mediterranean world and the Ottoman empire, including Fernand Braudel, have not known Turkish.) Lybyer came to Illinois as an associate professor at $2,800. His 1915 article "The Influence of the Rise of the Ottoman Turks on the Routes of Oriental Trade" secured his reputation as an expert on the Near East. This essay led to Lybyer's appointment to the U.S. Peace Delegation in Paris following the world war.[19]

Faculty Portrait #3: Clarence W. Alvord, History

Clarence W. Alvord deserves notice. A native of Massachusetts, born in 1868, he had vintage New England ancestry. Alvord graduated from Williams College in 1891, taught at nearby Milton Academy, and studied at Berlin's Friedrich Wilhelm University, where he imbibed the "scientific" history that reigned there. He finished his studies at the University of Chicago. In 1897 he came to Urbana as an instructor of history and mathematics in the Preparatory School. In 1900–1901, to meet a pressing need, he taught in the history department. In 1901 Greene brought Alvord into the department as an instructor. Alvord helped teach medieval and modern European history and had his own courses in Greek history, Roman history, and the Italian Renaissance, his main interest. Various officials thought that Greene had made a mistake in appointing Alvord. Kinley, hoping to rub out some of Alvord's "angularities" and "personal peculiarities," had a frank talk with him about his "general bearing." Alvord took it "very nicely."[20]

Alvord described himself as having an "essentially radical mind."[21] Students and colleagues remembered a man of slender build with a van Dyke beard, "a brilliant mind, a genial personality, and a childlike conceit." He was alternately dejected and exuberant. He neglected physical exercise and smoked incessantly. "His office looked like an enlarged wastepaper basket," but he could readily find what he wanted.[22] Kinley described Alvord as an excellent teacher who had not won promotion simply because he had not yet

Alvord did historical studies of the Middle West that prompted further investigations of the area by other historians. He also played a major role in establishing the Mississippi Valley Historical Association, later the Organization of American Historians. Courtesy of the University of Illinois Archives.

shown ability in research. But in 1905 Alvord's career took a new turn when the Illinois State Historical Library commissioned him to search in southern Illinois for primary materials relating to the history of the Northwest and the state of Illinois. President James took great interest in this project and gave his full blessing to Alvord in pursuing it. In two summer trips Alvord located the supposedly lost records of two French settlements—the Kaskaskia records in the courthouse at Chester and the Cahokia records in the courthouse at Belleville. Alvord urged a new project for the publication of material on the history of Illinois.[23] He alighted on to this research with grand enthusiasm, and it marked the turning point in his professional career.

James was president of the Illinois State Historical Library and Greene served on its board when it decided to publish on Illinois history. They named Alvord general editor of the *Illinois Historical Collections*. Relieved of part of his teaching duties and paid partly by the State Historical Library, Alvord became an authority on the great basin between the Allegheny and the Rocky

Mountains, most of which had been under French or British sovereignty until after the American Revolution, when portions of it came under the control of Virginia. Alvord transcribed and edited *The Cahokia Records: 1778–1790* (1907) on the Virginia period of Illinois history. Solon J. Buck described the volume as "a work that set a new standard for state historical editing and bookmaking in the West."[24] Alvord's introduction, a monograph on "The County of Illinois" based on the Cahokia manuscripts, printed material, and the Kaskaskia and Menard papers, became his dissertation, for which he received a PhD. Alvord arranged for others to edit volumes on Illinois history, and he directed a wide search for manuscript material pertaining to the Mississippi Valley. Greene and Alvord edited *The Governor's Letter-Books, 1818–1834* (1910); Alvord edited *The Kaskaskia Records, 1778–1790* (1910), fourteen volumes under Alvord's general editorship.

Alvord's course offerings reflected his new research interests. In 1906–1907 he taught a class on the history of Illinois, he and Greene taught a seminar in American history, while Alvord shared with Greene and Ford a graduate course in historical bibliography and criticism. In 1908–1909 Alvord introduced two courses on the history of French colonies and settlements in America through the eighteenth century. A year later he gave these courses at the graduate level. In 1908–1909 Alvord introduced a graduate course in the history of western expansion, 1763–1818.

In 1909 the University established the Illinois Historical Survey in the Graduate School to facilitate research and encourage the production of monographs on Illinois and western history and to lay the foundations for a political history of Illinois in connection with the 1918 centennial of its admission to the Union. When the question of appointing a committee to take charge of the work arose, Kinley noted that neither Greene, Ford, nor Larson would be likely to serve on a committee chaired by Alvord because they knew the difficulties of working with him. Moreover, Greene knew that Alvord had criticized him "both as a scholar and an administrator in no uncertain terms." So, Alvord inherited sole responsibility of planning work on the history of Illinois.[25] In 1913, when the Illinois Centennial Commission was established and charged with preparing a five-volume history of the state, Alvord became editor-in-chief. Solon J. Buck published a preliminary volume, *Illinois in 1818*, the year before the centennial. Alvord assigned the other volumes to faculty members in and beyond the University. The books appeared in 1919 and 1920, including Alvord's *The Illinois Country, 1673–1818* (1919), acknowledged as setting a new standard for state histories. Dixon Ryan Fox of Columbia University described the *Centennial History of Illinois* as "a great work, finely done," and "the latest and best example of success" in writing local history.[26]

Meanwhile, Alvord authored other works, including *The Mississippi Valley in British Politics: A Study of Trade, Land Speculation, and Experiments in*

Imperialism Culminating in the American Revolution (2 vols., 1917), which won the Loubat Prize from the Columbia University trustees for the best work "on the history, geography, archaeology, ethnology, philology, or numismatics of North America . . . published in the English language since January 1, 1913."[27]

Also, Alvord played vital roles in forming important historical enterprises. In 1907 he and six others organized the Mississippi Valley Historical Association (renamed the Organization of American Historians in 1965) for the purpose of promoting western history. In 1909 he served as president of the association. Like other historians in the Midwest Alvord felt alienated from the Eastern-dominated American Historical Association and its perceived neglect of their region of the country. Alvord's own work on the colonial era in the Mississippi Valley had moved the subject beyond the original thirteen colonies and the road they had taken to the American Revolution.[28] In 1912 he proposed a quarterly magazine under its auspices, and a year later he was appointed its managing editor. The first number of the *Mississippi Valley Historical Review* (later, the *Journal of American History*) appeared in January 1914. For nine years Alvord edited the journal, which quickly became the most important scholarly periodical devoted wholly to American history. From 1914 to 1919 the University of Illinois Board of Trustees provided the review a subsidy of $100 a year.[29]

Alvord rose slowly in academic rank. In 1906 he became an associate, in 1907 assistant professor, and in 1909 associate professor. In 1910 he complained about not being recommended for full professor. Ford, acting department head, acknowledged Alvord's merits as a scholar but added that he was neither readily available for the department nor a well-balanced director of the work of advanced students. He was a great stimulus for students well-grounded in American history, but most of the Illinois graduate students needed to be given more breadth and background, said Ford. In 1912 acting dean Daniels said that Alvord's ability as an investigator and his industry did not "so far offset his short-comings as a man and his lack of judgment in University matters as to warrant his promotion to a full professorship at this time."[30] But he did become full professor in 1913. When James retired in 1920, however, Alvord felt like he had lost his principal support at Illinois and he took a position at the University of Minnesota. Nonetheless, Alvord had done more than any historian before his time to win national attention and high regard for the University of Illinois program in history and to gain interest and recognition for it from scholars abroad. And, as a later chapter will record, he trained one of the great American historians of the twentieth century.

Alvord has significance also for the way he entered into discussions on matters that agitated American historians early in the twentieth century. He thus provides us a measure of how the University of Illinois received and reacted to

172   **PART II. ACADEMICS**

new ideas and positioned itself within a large intellectual community. Those historians speaking for change and reform in their profession often embraced the title "the New History." Most of them believed that historical scholarship had too narrow a focus. They wanted to ally it with other social sciences, appropriate their methodologies where useful, and give history a larger foundation, and therefore a better perspective on the historical subjects they investigated. Thus, Frederick Jackson Turner said that "we should enter the borderland between history in its older conception, and economics, politics, psychology, geography, etc." The eclecticists had their manifesto in James Harvey Robinson's book *The New History* (1912), a collection of essays, most of them previously published. Chapter Two had the title "History's New Allies."[31]

The new agenda met "a fierce reaction from traditionalists." They feared in the opening to the social sciences a shift to an imperium of statistical analysis, a recourse to enumeration as the diagnostic tool of historical study. The result would yield the stage to statistically normative actors and the erosion of individual people, players who move history on its always uncertain path. Social science, the traditionalists also feared, would reduce history to overriding "laws," impersonal data-based patterns that disclose the markings of mass behavior. We will have biology, not biography, said one opponent. William M. Sloane of Columbia and George Burton Adams of Yale spoke out in this matter.[32] Alvord, too, had strong views, but not one-sided ones. And he took his case to inform public opinion by making it in two widely read publications—*Popular Science* (a review of Robinson's book) and the *Nation*.

Nearly all the partisans in the history debates appropriated the word "scientific" to the history they defended. Alvord did, too. But for him, a scientific history, one that sought to integrate all its materials into large relationships and progressions over time, did not demand the "scientific method." He feared that too many of the new voices wanted to render history an exact science, in the manner of physicists or biologists. "Within the last generation the cultivation of the science of history has passed virtually into the control of the universities," he testified. But he made a clear distinction: "Whereas in other sciences the facts are open immediately to experiment or observation, the events of history are studied mediately through the reports of them. . . . " Nor is the "evidence" of history at all reliable; it does not have the sound empirical, or observational base of the sciences; the historian learns to mistrust or view skeptically those voices from the past that yield the records, or "evidence," on which we rely. Another differentiation: the historian cannot set up experiments to be repeated and tested for habits and laws, and thereby attain some permanence in our understanding. The historian can always see another turn of events that might have happened. Our data, Alvord elaborated, does not enable induction, the key operational device of the empirical scientist. They

9. The Social Sciences   **173**

cannot lead us to abstractions or generalizations. And furthermore, historians should shun these standards of the scientists because they lead to a serious danger: overdetermination.[33]

Alvord spoke unabashedly for humanist history. He feared that evolutionary theories had led some historians astray. They reduced historical situations and the individuals in the different eras of history to products of their environments. They made evolution a material process, a mechanism of unconscious forces; human beings become the reflective incidents of a blind and purposeless process. We look for universal forces in which human beings become automatons, Alvord charged. Instead of a community of creative human beings we have the "social organism." But reading history so, Alvord urged, misconstrues the meaning of evolution. For the key factor in *human* evolution is mind. And mind underscores human progress and marks the advance of "civilization." Economics, sociology, and political science, Alvord asserted, serve us well in measuring mass behavior; they illustrate "average" or normative patterns. They thus have usefulness in studying the lowest of human societies, where environment and heredity dictate. But Alvord, using the language of the American pragmatic philosophers, celebrated intellect and emphasized the role of "psychic forces" in civilization. "Mind," he wrote, "exercises a control over the material needs and directs the exertions of society." "The mental life of man, which takes the form of religion, science, art, and mechanical invention, creates an environment of a wholly unbiological character," Alvord cautioned the partisans of the New History. "The forces, which are to produce historical movements, are not existent except in the souls of individuals, of which the mass average would make no account." "The higher the civilization," he attested, "the greater the variation from the average," the statistical mass norm. Alvord did not shy from quoting Emerson on the creative, powerful individual as the agent of historical change, and, for the Illinois historian, the imperative focus of the historian.[34]

The New History, as Peter Novick shows, had close affiliation to the social and political reforms of this era. He cited Turner, Charles Beard, and Carl Becker in particular. Alvord wanted to make a balanced assessment, and one feature of the New History that he did admire concerned the role it was playing in bringing the American past into greater scrutiny and raising awareness of our national shortcomings. Too much of our historical writing, Alvord believed, had encouraged complacency, facile celebration of democracy and its progress in this country and around the world. He likened the new writing to the "Muckrakers" that were exposing the wrongs in American society and politics in the Progressive Era. We should all learn to examine our country with honesty and to seek the truth "irrespective of our national pride," he urged.[35]

News of Alvord's enterprising activities at Illinois got around. In July 1918 a reporter from the *New York Times* came to the campus and, amid myriad

174   PART II. ACADEMICS

reports about the events of the war, the paper gave a short account about Alvord. The reporter found his way to the fourth floor of Lincoln Hall to see the professor's office—"or offices," he wrote, "for he has a suite of five large rooms," not counting the storerooms. "You would probably feel that you had strayed by accident into, say, a big insurance office," wrote the journalist. Here you find five typists, a group of "fact checkers," others copy editing, and still others revising manuscripts. Here are documents written in French, German, or Spanish. The main business at hand concerns the five-volume "Centennial History of Illinois" project and the production of the Mississippi Valley historical journal. The inspiration for it all, the *NYT* reported, owes to Clarence Alvord—"the painstaking and thoroughgoing scholar," and withal a kindly man whose humor and personality "vivify and animate" the place.[36] And had the reporter stayed longer he might have observed a man smoking cigars and gulping cups of coffee into the late night hours.[37]

Political Science

Established in 1895, the political science department grew rapidly until 1901, when a dispute as to whether certain courses were to be taught in the department or in the law school ruined it. Enrollments fell from 211 in 1900–1901 to 68 in 1901–1902, and by 1903 the department was extinct. In 1904 James W. Garner was appointed assistant professor and head of the revived department. He had taken his doctorate at Columbia University and had served as an instructor both there and at the University of Pennsylvania before coming to Illinois. A very effective teacher, Garner set high scholarly standards and became a prolific author. He had published *Reconstruction in Mississippi* (1901), and after joining the faculty he produced a steady stream of books and articles on history, government, and international law.[38] In 1910 Garner established a journal in a field where none existed in the English language—the *Journal of Criminal Law and Criminology*. He was its editor-in-chief until he went on sabbatical leave in 1911–1912 to study in Europe, after which he served on its editorial board.

The political science department appealed to young men interested in public service in municipal and state government or as high school teachers of civics, and it attracted students to the study of history and economics. For several years the department had only Garner on its faculty. He taught the nine elective courses, none open to freshmen. When he reduced the number of courses, enrollments increased. His undergraduate offerings included elements of jurisprudence, constitutional and administrative law, colonial government and administration, and political parties. He offered seminars on the police power, citizenship and civil rights, contemporary politics, and political geography.

Greene, who viewed state and municipal administration as a promising field, wanted to appoint a person with academic training who would grasp some practical problems in Illinois local administration.[39] In 1909 John A. Fairlie joined the faculty to fill the need. Born in Glasgow, Scotland, Fairlie had earned a BA (1895) and an MA (1896) at Harvard and a doctorate at Columbia (1898). A lecturer at Columbia during 1899–1900, he went on to teach administrative law at Michigan in 1900. He came highly recommended for his publications and as a leader in state and local government administration. But his classroom teaching did not impress. James agreed to appoint Fairlie as an associate professor at $2,750, with the expectation that Fairlie would make himself a "thoroughly efficient teacher" while continuing his scientific studies. The University wanted an expert on state and municipal administration who would emphasize research and provide advice to legislators as the faculty did at Wisconsin.[40]

In 1910 Walter F. Dodd joined the faculty. He held a Chicago PhD (1905), had worked in the Library of Congress, and had taught constitutional law and government at Johns Hopkins. A former teacher commended his ability as a scholar but doubted his suitability for teaching undergraduates. Dodd took the rank of associate for a two-year term.[41] Garner described Dodd as a scholar and a man of unusual qualities. In 1911 he urged his promotion and a salary increase.[42]

By 1912 standards in political science had risen. With two professors (Garner and Fairlie), one assistant professor (Dodd), and one associate, the department had a larger faculty than any western university except Wisconsin (with ten). But with its large enrollments the department was comparatively understaffed and overworked.[43]

The department, however, did serve state and local government agencies. Garner chaired the Illinois Outdoor Improvement Association and agitated for reform of criminal law. In 1910 the department established a Municipal Reference Bureau and worked on plans to establish a Legislative Reference Bureau similar to the one at Wisconsin. Fairlie developed into an efficient teacher, especially of graduate students. He gave up other duties to work for the Tax Commission and he prepared bills for the governor.[44] The political science department under Garner developed into one of the strongest of its type in the nation.

Sociology

For years the College had offered courses in sociology, but no sociology department existed. In 1904 Julia C. Lathrop, a Chicago reformer active at Hull House, urged the University to introduce training in public service on the campus. Her proposal aimed at enlarging a series of courses for caregivers that she and Graham Taylor had organized a year earlier. In Chicago her work led to the establishment of the Chicago School of Civics and Philanthropy in 1908, the second school of social work in the country.[45]

James and Kinley favored her plan. Kinley envisioned a program for training in public service that would include the establishment of a sociology department with both theoretical and practical work: correspondence work for those unable to attend; summer classes; visits to state institutions by University specialists for lecturing; and opportunities for those who planned to study for the civil service examinations.

When the University finally decided to establish a sociology department, Kinley led the search for a professor. Attention soon focused on Edward C. Hayes. Born in Lewiston, Maine in 1868, he came from old New England stock. His father taught at Bates College and his mother had active memberships in several welfare agencies in the area. Hayes had studied at Cobb Divinity School and then became pastor of a church in Augusta, 1893–1896. But growing discontents with religious service led him to reconfigure his career. He had great interest in philosophy and social science. So, from 1898 to 1900 he was professor of economics and philosophy at Keuka College in Keuka Park, New York. In 1902 Hayes received a PhD under Albion Small at Chicago. He then went to Miami University in Ohio, where he earned high regard as a teacher and scholar. Two influences directed Hayes's career. He had studied in Germany, and at Berlin came under the influence of Schmoller, Wagner, and Paulsen, providing Hayes an orientation toward the primacy of ethics in the social sciences. And at Chicago, along with Small, John Dewey set Hayes in the direction of a new ethics, rooted in experience, as expostulated in Dewey's book *Ethics* (1908), a major document in the movement of philosophical pragmatism.[46]

In 1911 Governor Deneen called the General Assembly's attention to the desirability of establishing a department of sociological research. He prescribed attention to theoretical and practical problems relating to the state work in caring for its dependents and delinquents. He called for a scientific focus and for training of students in these departments. A few weeks later Hayes submitted a plan to promote the social welfare of rural communities in Illinois under the direction of the sociology department, and he urged the appointment of a specialist in criminology and a student of community life. Greene did not believe that these proposals had much merit. Daniels did not favor adding rural sociology, although he admitted the subject might attract students. Such courses would "neither develop mental discipline and systematic power of thinking," wrote Daniels, "nor furnish information that is not accessible in other ways." To admit to the curriculum a subject just because it was one the public needed would likely lead to the depreciation of those subjects.[47]

9. The Social Sciences   177

Enrollment in theoretical sociology increased annually, but the appointment of Arthur J. Todd in 1911 facilitated a move in new directions. A native Californian with a BL from the University of California (1904), Todd had directed boys' clubs and had been chief probation officer in San Francisco. He had studied in Paris and Munich, and had received a Yale PhD in education and sociology when he became an instructor at $1,000 a year.[48] After Todd joined the staff, registrations in sociology increased. But Dean Daniels doubted that the standards of scholarship reached as high in sociology as in the other social science departments. Both Hayes and Todd took an active part in applied sociology, locally and in other parts of the state. In 1913 Todd advanced to associate. When he left the University a year later, Hayes wanted to appoint an instructor in rural sociology. A committee considered the idea, but Daniels opposed it, mainly because it lacked sufficient scientific matter to add to departmental offerings.[49]

Edward Hayes became a major figure in sociology. His *Introduction to the Study of Sociology* (1915) became "one of the principal texts in sociology in this country." Much in demand, Hayes taught during summers at Harvard, Chicago, Penn, and other universities.[50] He served the field actively, most importantly as a founding member of the American Sociological Association (1905) and later as president (1921). He had editorial positions at the *American Journal of Sociology* and the *Journal of Applied Sociology*. He contributed significantly to sociological theory, but he also entered into one of the larger discussions among social scientists, introduced earlier, that concerning ethics. At a time when value neutrality enjoyed an ascendancy, Hayes insisted that sociology must have an ethical base and ethical content. He feared modern "amoralism" in his discipline and in others. So, sociology must not remove itself far from philosophy, he maintained. Every society, Hayes wrote, must have a philosophy, an "ethics," "some generally accepted idea or ideas adapted to give direction and momentum to life." Modern Germany exhibited to him, in 1918, an instance wherein a nation had moved from the large influence of Luther and Kant and lapsed into nihilism, with an inevitable "barbarous unmorality" commandeering its social and political life. But Hayes saw warning signs in America, too—a "ravening individualism," a sanctioning of the power of the strong over the weak—that threatened the sustaining strength of a viable public ethic and its cohesive effects.[51]

Hayes fit very comfortably into the academic ethos of Edmund James's university. He, like James, emphasized the moral factor, and he too, like James, wanted it rooted in "science." We cannot return to a moral guideline founded in theology or metaphysics, Hayes insisted. We need, he said, "a scientific as contrasted with a merely speculative ethics." Nor can we, or ought we, recover a lost Victorian morality. But Hayes strongly opposed all of the modern ideologies that deprived humans of rational control of the "psychic"

178   PART II. ACADEMICS

factor that activated and directed humans in their progressive adaptations to their shifting environment and that advanced their social evolution. He gave little credence to the "social forces" school of thinking in the discipline. One fundamental question in ethics, "what is good?," can be answered, wrote Hayes, "by an inductive study of actual human experience." Another fundamental question, "what is right?," "can be answered only by investigation of the effects of different forms of social conduct on human experience." Philosophies of determinism—whether psychological or social—deprive us of the imperative to investigate these matters. He embraced the humanistic positivism of Auguste Comte and the empiricism of Herbert Spencer. To that extent he stood with the moderns. He wrote: "The thesis of this essay is that sociology as a science, or at least as an attempt to carry on a study of life in a scientific spirit, *cannot escape those very questions which are the problems of ethics*, and furthermore that *the only intellectually satisfying method of seeking the answers to those questions is to be found, not in a priori speculation, which has been the historical method in ethics, but rather in that investigation of the facts of human life which is the work of sociology*."[52]

Hayes provided another voice of Progressivism for the Illinois faculty under James. He expressed his commitments locally, too. Hayes organized the Family Welfare Society of Champaign-Urbana, Illinois and served on the board of directors of that organization and on the advisory committee of the Illinois State Department of Public Welfare (1917–1919). He was president of the Illinois State Conference of Charities and Corrections (1910–1911) as well.[53] Hayes died in 1928. Sociology at Illinois had gone from near nonexistence to national prominence in Hayes's years of service to the University.

CHAPTER 10

The Humanities

PRESIDENT JAMES HAD an inclusive model of the modern university. He welcomed all fields of learning. Although he never lost sight of the Morrill Act's imperative of education in agriculture and engineering, he remained true also to its prescription for classical studies. But in his thinking, one priority above everything pertained to all areas of studies, from the classics to the professions: the scientific way of thinking. He stated in his inaugural address: "There are certain things, then, that must mark this institution in order to make it a true university. The most striking peculiarity is the scientific character of the training it affords." "This feature," he said, "is to my mind, the fundamental and distinguishing quality of the university." And by scientific character James intended no narrow utilitarian training. He wanted all the fields of study undertaken at the University of Illinois to have their foundations in expansive scholarly research; they must grow and develop from the widest investigation that modern learning avails and draw from the fundamental principles appropriate to each discipline. Scientific education did not signify an education grounded in mere "practicality." And, he avowed, its mental discipline will mark the intellect of the university's graduates as they enter into the life of work and citizenship.[1]

Classics

James had immense respect for classical literature and he wanted a prominent school for it at Illinois. Meanwhile, needing classroom instructors, in early 1909 the trustees appointed Arthur S. Pease, then teaching at Harvard and Radcliffe, as an assistant professor beginning on February 1. Pease built a distinguished record at Illinois and gained a large reputation. In 1925 he became president of Amherst College. But when recruiting a top classical scholar reached a dead end, James turned to an assistant professor he had known at Northwestern, William A. Oldfather. Born in Persia in 1880 of Presbyterian missionary parents, Oldfather "emigrated" to America at age ten, graduated from Hanover College with a BA (1899), took another BA (1901) and an MA (1902) at Harvard, and then began teaching at Northwestern in 1903. He earned a PhD *summa cum laude* at Munich (1908) and returned to Northwestern. He did not relish leaving friends and Chicago library facilities, because the library at Urbana would do him little good, he said. It would alter the case, however, if the University would provide $300 to $500 a year for books in his line of work.[2] Oldfather's introduction to the department did not go smoothly. He taught both Greek and Latin courses for advanced undergraduates and graduate students and offered graduate-level courses in both languages. From 1909 to 1911, according to Oldfather, Herbert J. Barton, long-standing member of the department, discriminated against him by keeping his classes small, taking the ablest students for himself, and inviting other faculty members to address the Classical Club before inviting him.[3]

The infusion of young blood invigorated Barton, who did his class work well and participated usefully in other University activities. He had many ideas for promoting classical studies in and beyond the University. In the fall of 1909, a student Classical Club formed. In 1910–1911 a new program of studies leading to a major in classics began. The department gave a Greek play and a Latin play in alternate years. To reach students with no knowledge of the classical languages, Barton wanted courses taught in translation. He also wanted to carry the classics to Illinois high schools, urging that lectures on Rome and Roman life or on Caesar's campaigns would benefit both the department and the high schools. A High School Conference began in 1905, designed to make the University of service to the classics teachers in the state.[4]

Charles M. Moss, department chairman from 1892 to 1918, confined his work almost exclusively to the classroom. He had noticeably small enrollments. Moss should be urged to spend a year in foreign travel and study in the hope that he might return reinvigorated, Dean Arthur H. Daniels wrote in 1912; otherwise, officials should discuss with him his early withdrawal from the department.[5]

Oldfather in turn combined enormous energy with an imperious and combative personality. While at Munich he had learned exact German scholarly and historical method and had become an admirer of German culture. A prolific author and a provocative teacher, he worked best with graduate students. He trained the "Oldfather school" of classicists and helped build a superlative classics library. A champion of liberal causes and academic freedom, he had memberships in national groups that promoted progressive reforms. His life as a committed Presbyterian coexisted well with his politics. Oldfather became widely influential within the University.[6]

English and Rhetoric

In 1904–1905 English and rhetoric existed as separate departments. Daniel K. Dodge headed the English department, which included four regular instructors. Thomas Arkle Clark led the rhetoric and oratory department and served as dean of undergraduates. Rhetoric had the largest enrollment in the University because all students had to take an elementary course in the subject. Also, all liberal arts students had to take an elementary English course taught by assistants and instructors.

In 1907 Greene combined English and rhetoric into one department, of which Dodge and Clark became coadministrators. Because the combined department exercised little influence in the University, Greene wanted to recruit both someone who could administer a large department while maintaining high standards and one or more men of high scholarly achievement. To identify candidates, Greene consulted his brother Jerome, the secretary of the Harvard Corporation, who then consulted President Eliot. Eliot advised getting a promising young man and suggested Chester N. Greenough.

Greenough had taken three degrees at Harvard (AB, 1898; AM, 1899; PhD, 1904) and had an excellent record as an instructor. He had coauthored two books with Barrett Wendell—*A History of Literature in America* (1904) and *Selections from the Writings of Joseph Addison* (1905). In March 1907 James offered Greenough $2,000. He declined. He was earning $2,200 from Harvard and Radcliffe together, with the sure prospect of promotion and a salary of $3,500 in a few years. And he had the offer of another position at $3,000. In April James promised $3,000 and invited Greenough to visit the University. Greenough impressed Greene, Dodge, and Clark, who urged James to make the appointment. Because Greenough was untested as an administrator, James offered him a full professorship on the understanding that Greenough would receive $3,000 for 1907–1908 (the highest salary in the College), and if his first-year work proved satisfactory, he would become head of the English department or chairman of its management committee at $3,500 in 1908. Greenough accepted the offer.[7]

At the same time the trustees made two junior appointments in English. Jacob Zeitlin, born in Moscow, had emigrated at the age of nine when his father was thrown out of business by the exile of the Jews under Czar Alexander III. He attended the Horace Mann and DeWitt Clinton high schools in New York City and earned three degrees from Columbia (AB, 1904; AM, 1905; and PhD, 1908). A philologist who became an authority on the historical development of the English essay, he came as an instructor at $900 a year.[8]

The other appointment went to Stuart Pratt Sherman. Born of New England parents in Anita, Iowa, Sherman had spent five years there, seven years in Los Angeles, and seven months prospecting in a gold-mining camp in

Arizona before returning to New England. He and his family lived in Dorset, Vermont, before settling in Williamstown, Massachusetts. In 1900 Sherman entered Williams College as a sophomore. He made a brilliant scholastic record and decided he wanted to be a teacher of literature. In 1903 Clark wrote to Williams College seeking a promising young man to fill a position in rhetoric at $800. Sherman was attracted by the possibility, but he then received an opportunity for three years of graduate study at Harvard, where he studied English literature, earning an AM (1904) and a PhD (1906), and then became an instructor at Northwestern. A year later Clark renewed his interest in Sherman, then making $1,100. Sherman asked for an assistant professorship and $1,500, but he came as an associate at $1,500.[9]

In 1908 Sherman, who had won praise as a scholar, teacher, and colleague, gained promotion to assistant professor. Meanwhile, he had become a literary journalist, writing for the New York *Evening Post* and the *Nation*. In 1909, after receiving an attractive offer from the *Evening Post*, Sherman was made an associate professor.

In 1908 Greenough became department chairman. He had twenty-six teachers of various grades, six theme readers, and just over two thousand students. The department tried to do too much. A faculty of twenty-six carried thirty-five courses, whereas at Harvard a faculty of thirty-two carried twenty-two and a half courses. At Illinois, the freshman courses in rhetoric and English required the equivalent of fourteen full-time persons. The department needed to add more faculty or reduce the number of courses or do both.

In addition to building up the library, Greenough wanted a more symmetrical program of graduate study in order to grant a more useful degree. At Illinois, the English department focused chiefly on modern literature, whereas at Harvard the department emphasized Old and Middle English and students prepared for the examination in modern literature by cramming textbooks adapted for sophomores. Because Illinois students did not take kindly to Chaucer, the Ballads, and the metrical romances, one might have to prescribe a certain amount of work in linguistics and earlier literature for students focusing on modern literature, Greenough reported.[10]

Greenough's annual report in 1910 noted that the higher standards in the courses offered showed that students with no special aptitude for English no longer found English literature courses a way to get good grades with no labor. However, he said, Rhetoric 1 needed better instruction. (This was Thomas Arkle Clark's domain.) He identified the courses in higher composition as the weakest in the department. In English 1, he noted, some faculty set a stiff pace while others accepted the fact that many students were only of high school grade. Greenough saw a need to raise the standards. The advanced courses did not appeal to undergraduates as they should. Greenough supported women teachers, describing them as very efficient in instructing undergraduates. At

10. The Humanities   183

the graduate level, courses in Middle English had hardly any appeal. Students regarded the teacher, H. S. V. Jones, as dignified to the point of being surly. Greenough saw Jones as an excellent scholar, a man of great dignity and firm manner. He wanted to add courses in comparative literature, but no one on the ground had the competence to give them. He urged the organization of a department of comparative literature as soon as possible.[11]

In spring 1910, after three years in which he had transformed the work in English and rhetoric, Greenough resigned to return to Harvard. He had met the University and found it wanting. Now, with James as president, prospects for a better day brightened.

In the fall, Zeitlin gained promotion to associate primarily on the basis of his dissertation, published as *The Accusative with Infinitive and Some Kindred Constructions in English* (1908). The work, described as an uncommonly learned and acute piece of philological investigation, won praise in America from some of its best scholars.

In November, Sherman described the considerations in the choice of a successor to Greenough. The department needed a productive scholar who would gain public attention and attract and train graduate students as well, he believed. His search committee preferred someone whose interests lay primarily in literature, not philology. Finally, Sherman insisted, the department needed a man with a talent for administration. No single candidate would likely have these qualifications.

Meanwhile, Sherman and others had named Raymond M. Alden of Stanford as their favorite candidate. Alden had an AB (Pennsylvania, 1894), an AM (Harvard, 1896), and a PhD (Pennsylvania, 1899). He had worked at Stanford since 1899, where he taught undergraduate and graduate courses, rising to the rank of associate professor in 1909. A broad and ripe scholar, his books included *The Rise of Formal Satire in England* (1899), *The Art of Debate* (1900), *English Verse* (1904), and *Introduction to Poetry* (1909). His published work, wrote one authority, placed Alden among the first two or three men of his academic generation in the country. Alden had also contributed stories and articles to various popular periodicals. Sherman described Alden as nearly as satisfactory for the position as any the University could find, adding that an interview would be a waste of time. Only one adverse voice surfaced, a warning that at first sight Alden might impress people "as slightly reserved and over-refined." He came by a sort of Puritanism honestly, Earnest W. Ponzer wrote, considering that his father was a Presbyterian minister and his mother the author of the "Pansy Books," but he seemed to have outgrown it. All the recommendations were excellent. The trustees authorized Alden's appointment as professor of English at $4,000 beginning on September 1, 1911.[12]

Alden proved to be an excellent department head, and his influence as a scholar was stimulating. Although committed heavily to English poetry, he showed interest in department activities. He had the capacity for hard work and demonstrated sound judgment in college affairs. But he inherited problems. Rhetoric 1 and English 1 were the feeders for other courses, but Rhetoric 1 was a bad course badly taught. (This again was Thomas Arkle Clark's domain.) It indiscriminately enrolled students, and many of the instructors lacked the ability and the attitude needed to be effective.[13]

The department also put together a program in journalism. In 1907–1908 two Rhetoric courses covered the topics of news gathering, news writing, copy editing, editorial writing, and the history of journalism. Graduate Dean Kinley, several students, and Franklin W. Scott wanted a four-year course in the subject. Scott, a former editor of the *Daily Illini* and a faculty member in English and rhetoric, proposed to add one course in newspaper writing and four courses on the business side of journalism. No one there had the qualifications to offer these subjects, but in fact an embryonic journalism department had come into being.[14]

Faculty Portrait #4: Stuart P. Sherman, English

Stuart Sherman put the University of Illinois on the literary map of the United States. Outspoken and facile of pen, he brought wide attention to the University and plenty of controversy to himself. Sherman had studied with Irving Babbitt at Harvard and Babbitt influenced all of Sherman's subsequent career, however importantly they differed on some matters. Sherman would have many grievances with things in American higher education, and with the study of literature there especially. He would always look to literature as a locus of ideas, and Babbitt, as professor, modeled that approach for Sherman splendidly. He took a course in literary criticism from Babbitt and long remembered the experience: "He deluged you with the wisdom of the world; his thoughts were unpacked and poured out so fast you couldn't keep up with them. He was at you day after day like a battering ram, knocking down your illusions. He was building up a system of ideas."[15] Babbitt introduced Sherman to Paul Elmer More, a friend and colleague in the emerging New Humanism movement, in which Sherman played a critical role. More, editor of the *Nation* (1909–1914) and classics professor at Princeton, opened up the pages of the *Nation* to Sherman for short reviews and commentary. Sherman also contributed to the *Evening Post*. These ventures coincided with Sherman's arrival to Urbana.

Sherman had an abounding love of literature. At Williams he discovered Latin and classical writings. Then came Shakespeare. At Illinois he taught that subject and seventeenth-century drama and held graduate seminars in romanticism. He had married the former Ruth Mears in 1906 and they arrived at the University with their baby boy John, born in November 1907. The family

Sherman engaged prominently and controversially in the "Battle of the Books" that raged in literary criticism. He had popularity and influence as a teacher at Illinois. Courtesy of the University of Illinois Archives.

took up residence at 1016 Nevada Street. For a while the Shermans remained aloof from the formal social events of the faculty but Stuart in time became very active with a cohort that met periodically for discussions of a variety of subjects. Professors Greene, Daniels, Bode, Pease, Ford, and others attended, as did President James. And Sherman enjoyed weekly rehearsals with the University's Choral Society.[16]

Sherman's critical essays and reviews took on the world, and they represent the first of three stages in his academic career, this one going to about 1918.[17] He had by then become virtually a staff contributor for the *Nation* and the *Evening Post*. Novels supplied the largest category of writing he covered, but he wrote also on biography, literary history and criticism, some works of scholarship, medieval legends, Anglo-Saxon texts, new installments of the Oxford

Dictionary, "and sundry other things." He garnered wide attention. It's evident in the collection of Sherman correspondence how many individuals, with no apparent connection to college or university, numbered among those who wrote to him reacting in one way or another to his points of view. He became a national name and he had offers, which he rejected, to become editor of the *Evening Post*, and later, when More retired from the *Nation*, editor of that publication, too. But Sherman gained wide recognition among professors in his field and among academic leaders in general. He turned down invitations from Dartmouth, Williams, and Amherst. President Alexander Meiklejohn of Amherst pressed very hard on Sherman to leave Illinois and come east. "You need to get out of Urbana," he urged. President James for the University gave Sherman promotions and salary increases.[18]

There is more to Sherman's literary journalism than meets the eye. For some time, the subject of teaching literature in the colleges and universities had undergone intense discussion and debate. Coming out of the college era and going into the new university period teachers of literature had set Matthew Arnold as their guidepost. Literature represented culture, its highest form, "the best that has been thought and said," and drew its inspiration from the long reach of history, going back to the Bible and the ancient classics. These traditional humanists did not see literature in any precise or distinct compartments. Nor did they see it as subject matter for "scientific" study. But with the emergence of English departments at American universities in the late nineteenth century, new models of academic culture redefined the study of literature. Philology, represented most prominently by George Lyman Kittredge at Harvard, expressed the scientific turn that arose under the new German standards of scholarship. Its apostles considered themselves "investigators"; they sought "facts," a database that would confirm the discipline in empirical certitude. Quantitative studies came into vogue. How many times a word appeared in a text took on greater significance than its multiple meanings within a large narrative. In fact, these advocates often thought of themselves as scholars not of literature but of language.[19]

But by the turn of the century the revolt against this modernism by those whom Gerald Graff labels "the generalists" had taken off. Harvard had always had a hard core of this group, going back to before the Civil War when it counted Longfellow, Lowell, and Charles Eliot Norton on the faculty. Barrett Wendell of Harvard held high command among these generalists in the early twentieth century, along with William Lyon Phelps at Yale, Brander Matthews at Columbia, John Erskine at Amherst, Robert Morss Lovett at Chicago, and Henry Van Dyke at Princeton. Above all there was Irving Babbitt, "the archgeneralist, whose *Literature and the American College*," Graff wrote, "could be taken as the definitive statement of the generalist philosophy." All in this group shared a sense of the growing vulgarity and materialism of American life in the industrial age; they had a "missionary" view of literature as antidote; and they all faulted the direction of literary studies under the German hegemony. Babbitt issued his book, the opening salvo of the New Humanist movement, in 1908, coinciding with Sherman's arrival to Illinois.[20]

Babbitt had always found inspiration in Matthew Arnold. The "philosophy" that Sherman found so pervasive in Babbitt's writing and classroom pronunciations posited a dualistic view of life: "law for man and law for thing" was the Arnold formula. Culture above all denoted what differentiated the two and gave literature its reason for existence. But Babbitt and the humanists saw too much of social behavior yielding to a mechanistic understanding of life and a corresponding value system that worshiped number, bigness, speed, power, newness, and change. "But unless this bigness is tempered by quality," Babbitt wrote, "we shall sprawl helplessly in the midst of our accumulated wealth and power." The new standards had invaded higher education and corrupted it, the humanists believed. The German pursuit of knowledge—indiscriminate, obsessed with fact, in hot pursuit of anything "new," and thus turning inquiry into investigation—motivated their scholarship. Said Babbitt: "The uncritical adoption of German methods is one of the chief obstacles to a humanistic revival." Babbitt gave voice to this venerable group of generalists, but to a younger group, too, that included Sherman. He often put the matter more forcefully and colorfully than they. But many surely shared Babbitt's sentiments when he wrote: "One can scarcely contemplate the German theses, as they pour by hundreds into a large library, without a sort of intellectual nausea."[21]

At Illinois Sherman wasted no time in making known his feelings in this matter. He went right to the *Nation* in May 1908 and submitted a letter he titled "Graduate Schools and Literature." Why do the best students not pursue advanced study in literature? he asked. And why do the next best, who do, barely last a year at their studies? Typically, he said, we find students finishing up college, fully excited by the study of poetry and novels and longing to expand their acquaintance "with great men and great ideas through further study. But alas, their teachers hold such aspirations in disdain and seek immediately to impose on the student a 'scholarly' discipline, a norm of 'the bare literal fact' . . . unrelieved by humor or feeling." This "student of real literary tastes" soon abandons his project, Sherman lamented. Graduate education had thus moved far away from the spirit of Matthew Arnold. It was adding expansively "to the sum of human knowledge but not to the sum of those acquainted with the immortal works of men's minds in all ages of the world." Those who somehow endure the frigid process come out as "pseudo-scientific specialists." Sherman concluded that what "we need [is] men with an eye for contours and altitudes, a sense of life in its fulness, an eye for the glory of the world."[22]

Sherman's epistle received several replies, in a range of opinion. One offered in his defense came from an unexpected source, a student at the University of

Illinois. His name was Carl Van Doren. The student complimented Sherman for his "fine tilting against the giants of philological method." But he believed he knew why English studies had gone in that direction. The perception reigns, Van Doren said, that the subject, literature, is too easy, "child's play." It needed to be fortified, the moderns were saying, by scientific methodology and empirical temperament, by the regime of fact that would correct the easy indulgence of private experience by doing "accurate scholarship." But Van Doren insisted that the scientific standard is just not the way to study literature, and that history and statistics do not disclose the experience of literature and the creative process that we should expect from our encounter with literary greatness. He called for "careful intuitive study of the critical theories which govern the novel-making of Defoe, Richardson, Sterne, and Goldsmith." We are left otherwise with a materialistic foundation for our pursuits. The philologists have their uses, Van Doren allowed, "but they should not be allowed to think that they are doing literary work."[23]

Carl Van Doren had grown up in rural Illinois, born in 1885 outside of Hope, about halfway between Danville and Urbana. He was the oldest of five boys (with brothers Guy, born 1887; Frank, 1892; Mark, 1894; and Paul, 1899). All attended the University of Illinois. His father, a village doctor, took great care of the farm he owned and on which Carl remembered living for fifteen years "as happy as an animal." But the boy found a greater love in something else. "I can barely remember," he wrote, "when I could not read." And he eagerly took on a wide range of authors: Plutarch, Sir Walter Scott, Dickens, Thackeray, and American writers like Mark Twain and J. Whitcomb Riley. He read typically "hours a day," as farm chores allowed when the family moved to Urbana in 1900. Carl attended the high school there and then entered the University. He had resolved to pursue a career in books but did not know exactly how he could do so. He wrote plays and essays for the collegiate literary magazine and was named class poet, one among other honors that came the way of this very bright student. At the University library, he recounted, Van Doren discovered poet Christopher Marlowe. His passion for the playwright's work had behind it another compelling interest, one that the student now applied to all the literary figures he encountered. Specifically, "My curiosity was about the life stories of the men and women whom I met in history or fiction."[24]

Van Doren had earned his BA degree the year before Sherman came to the University but stayed on for one more year. The Van Dorens lived on the next street from the Shermans and one day the professor and Carl happened to run into each other on the way to campus. Van Doren had heard of Sherman. "He came with his doctor's degree from Harvard and the reputation of having written the best dissertation ever submitted to the English department there. Neither of these things impressed me, since I thought of them as academic and had no academic ambitions." But on this first personal meeting a

10. The Humanities   189

conversation ensued. Van Doren wrote in his autobiography: "I have often wondered what it was he said that made me suddenly see him with new eyes. I cannot remember, though I see him still: broad, strong, a little stooped and sallow, with his habitual smile that was almost a sneer. But I do remember the uprush of my spirit in that moment when it seemed to me that an electric charge of understanding passed between us." Thereafter, Van Doren continues, "I haunted him": constant visits to his home and long talks late into the night, always about books and more books. Two years later in 1910 Sherman and Van Doren traveled abroad together for a summer month, visiting Ireland, Scotland, and England, concluding their tour together in London.[25]

All the while Sherman was taking on another role. He was making himself a spokesman for democracy, the Midwest, and the state university in America. These concerns would also lead Sherman, in his next phase, to his preoccupation with American literature. Here he would seek out the ideological, moral, and spiritual dimensions of the national culture, from the Puritans to the present. These efforts left some of Sherman's eastern friends vexed and puzzled. They could not understand why Sherman repeatedly turned down opportunities to come back east. Sherman could easily cite the stereotypes by which the easterners criticized the western state universities: they did well in producing farmers and engineers, but that's about all; they brought education down to a "popular" level, lowering its standards; they thrived by promising material fulfillment to those who passed through them, but they did not aim higher for richer, deeper meanings of life. Sherman allowed some truth to the stock criticism, but, he insisted, it fails to see the true idealism at work in the state universities. That idealism will thrive within the practical realities of American life and enrich them, he said. Sherman imagined a faculty member of a western university replying to eastern critics: "You have preserved your idealism in glass jars; we have not lost ours by putting it to work in the bread of life."[26] Altogether, as Sherman wrote to editor Maxwell Perkins, "'Out' here, as you Easterners say, we think the line of state universities from Ohio to California is about the most significant hopeful thing that the country has been engaged in for some years."[27]

A democratic idealism, a true and motivating "religion of democracy," Sherman believed, could derive only from an authentic humanism. And humanism must overcome its nemesis, naturalism. Naturalism, along with its evil sibling, romanticism, had spurred Babbitt into his polemics. But the Harvard professor saw in his energetic and combative student some real hope in the fight. And Sherman armed himself for a bigger contest yet when he wrote his first book, *Matthew Arnold: How to Know Him*, in 1916. He had given a lot attention to Arnold since he arrived at the University of Illinois, and the ammunition he now set to discharge against the naturalist evil had its fortifications in the nineteenth-century British humanist.

190   PART II. ACADEMICS

Sherman saw Arnold as a critical resistance to the intellectual and literacy directions of his times. He then followed this book with his blockbuster publication of 1917, *On Contemporary Literature*. Here he turned his attention to books and authors, but naturalism gave him his real target. He wrote in his Introduction: "The great revolutionary task of nineteenth-century thinkers . . . was to put man into nature. The great task of twentieth-century thinkers is to get him out again." "Nature" has been our great deceiver—from "trust your instincts" to "survival of the fittest." But, warned Sherman, "we have trusted our instincts long enough to sound the depths of their treacherousness." "We have followed nature to the last ditch and ditch water." And literary criticism, he attested, "has been an accomplice in the usurpations of the naturalistic philosophy."[28]

This book moved Sherman's name from renown to notoriety. It made him immediately controversial. Dedicated to Paul Elmer More, the volume had essays on H. G. Wells, Arnold Bennett, Anatole France, Henry James, and others. But the piece that really put Sherman in the hot seat had the title "The Barbaric Naturalism of Theodore Dreiser." It would be enlightening to discuss many of these essays, but this review of Sherman will confine itself to this one, as it had wide ramifications. Theodore Dreiser had won recognition as the most forthright exemplar of the naturalist direction in American letters, with novels like *Sister Carrie* (1901), *Jennie Gerhardt* (1911), *The Financier* (1912), *The Titan* (1914), and *The Genius* (1915). Dreiser's literary opus, said Sherman, derives from the naturalistic theory of human nature. "Mr. Dreiser drives home the great truth that man is essentially an animal, impelled by temperament, instinct, physics, chemistry—anything you please that is irrational and uncontrollable." Sherman surveyed Dreiser's language. His characters have "cat-like eyes"; they show "feline grace"; they move with "sinuous strides." Sexual engagement is pure animalism, wherein the rapacious male circles his prey and pounces on her, the female never resisting the urge of the élan vital, succumbing to "the chemistry of her being." And Dreiser and his enthusiasts, Sherman charged, would have us believe that this jungle setting for human life bespeaks a base reality that supplies literature with a meaningful realism. But Sherman saw in this retreat only a convenient rationale for art to divest itself of all moral vision and the suppression of all evidence to this basic reality of our human make-up. A true humanism, as Babbitt said many times over, depends on a "vital check" (a "frein vital") against the élan vital of our expansive natural instincts. Sherman was inscribing that dualism into his humanist critique of Dreiser and many others of "the moderns."[29]

Sherman's attack on Dreiser directly challenged the foremost defender of that writer, the singular H. L. Mencken. Mencken had introduced himself in 1913 with his friendly book on the German philosopher Friedrich Nietzsche. Mencken claimed as well an influence from Darwinism. Those sources sufficed to put him very comfortably in the naturalist view of things, and he made that position clear in an important essay on Dreiser at the same time Sherman was attacking him. The essay appeared in Mencken's *A Book of Prefaces* in 1917. Mencken called Dreiser essentially a tragedian. His novels, he wrote, "aim to show the vast ebb and flow of forces which sway and condition human destiny." No pious nostrums govern Dreiser's cold and hard view of life, no sentimentality. Wrote Mencken of Dreiser: "The struggle of man, as he sees it, is more than impotent; it is gratuitous and purposeless. There is, to his eye, no grand ingenuity, no skillful adaption of means to ends, no moral (or even dramatic) plan in the order of nature."[30]

Mencken and Sherman had words for each other, too, and their quarrels continued into the 1920s. The Illinois professor called Mencken "the Baltimore Arab" and "the man midwife of the naturalistic fiction which makes its bed in the parlor window." Mencken gourmandizes on the raw and rough ingredients of American life, Sherman charged, in recoil from all that is soft and genteel and civilizing. He bears with him all the coarse and rough Teutonism of his Nietzschean superman, of which the world has seen too much.[31] To Mencken, on the other hand, Sherman represented one of the worst American types, "the moralist turned critic." We don't get real art criticism from Sherman, he said; we get "pompous syllogisms" and midwestern piety. "Sherman," wrote Mencken, "tries to save Shakespeare for the right-thinking by proving that he was an Iowa Methodist—a member of his local Chamber of Commerce, a contemner of Reds, an advocate of democracy and the League of Nations." Sherman, Mencken believed, judged Dreiser for his deficiency not as an artist but as a Puritan and an American.[32]

All who followed these disputes knew that they were really just skirmishes in a larger war. The big debate concerned the whole tradition of American literature, going back to the Puritans. That subject took on a special urgency for Sherman, and indeed for other American critics, as they viewed the dangerous world of 1914 and anticipated America's participation in the European war. Sherman watched Europe's march to disaster with great apprehension and fear. It illustrated for him all the marks of a civilization losing itself in the madness of nationalism, militarism, the cult of power, and a cultural direction that could place no restraints on these dangers. But Sherman grew to have increasing admiration for President Woodrow Wilson. Though "I am 'traditionally' a Republican," he told his correspondent, he was supporting Wilson. For somehow the world will have to find a way to reverse its reckless course, with right ideas and the right machinery to make them effective. But Sherman also became convinced, like Wilson, that only one thing could make this outcome possible: an American victory on the battlefield.[33]

So, Sherman entered the verbal war. His statement came first in an address before the National Council of Teachers of English in January 1917. It caught

192   PART II. ACADEMICS

the attention of Guy Stanton Ford, now at Minnesota, who used his connection to the government's Committee on Public Instruction to print it and circulate it widely. Now many outside literary circles who did not know Sherman's name became acquainted with it, and the University of Illinois made this document another component of its support for the war. Sherman commented at the beginning of his piece that the intellectual feels loathe to leave the friendly confines of his study and take up a large cause in the national service. For in doing so, he can easily succumb to "megalomania and national egotism." Sherman warned that one must avoid that temptation but it is not altogether clear that the Illinois professor, in this essay loaded with heavy rhetoric, succeeded in doing so.[34]

We must see this war, Sherman stressed, as a cultural conflict. He rejected as both false and misleading any appeal to race or biological destiny as having anything useful to help us understand what had brought on the disaster the world now confronts. This dismissal coincides, of course, with Sherman's anti-naturalism. No, the roots of the war, he answered, lie in "the prostitution of contemporary German science, philosophy, and scholarship to the service of a barbarous government." Sherman and everyone else by this time had seen the horror of the Belgium invasion, but Sherman had made his case well before August 1914. He admonished his readers to look to Nietzsche, look to Schopenhauer, or Treitschke, or Bernhardi. Their thinking lacks any principles of restraint, no inner check. It well prepares the path to war. We must realize then, wrote Sherman, what we have in our German enemy: a state that "acknowledges no duty but the extension of its own merciless power."[35]

Sherman painted a different picture of the American and Allied ideals. He saw inscribed in them a long history, going back to the Bible and the ancients, that constituted a broad, humanistic foundation, one that underscored the forces arrayed against Teutonic barbarism. Sherman found the distinguishing feature of the good guys in their universalism, and in their ideal of a transcendent common humanity, sufficiently implanted as to make all expressions of national virtue (and all the fighting nations had them) subordinate to that commonality. Crucially, then, among these parties in the war, the Allies had a check on a rampant, tribal nationalism that Germany, previously in lock step with that overriding humanism, now did not. Sherman gave special attention to the United States. Here he cited the Puritans, who gave a high moral flavor to our cultural tradition. He instanced also the Declaration of Independence, rooted in liberal, deistic religion, our great national charter fully invoking the ideals, the basic rights of life, liberty, and the pursuit of happiness that belong properly to all humanity. He saw it also in Abraham Lincoln, who urged Americans in his Second Inaugural to find their purpose "in a humanity so pure and exalted that the humanest citizen may realize his highest ideals in devotion to it." With complete confidence then, Sherman could write, "The cause of America and the Allies is the defense of the common culture of the family of civilized nations."[36]

This superficial outline had a benevolent gloss to it, but that quality did not sustain the entire essay. In fact, Sherman began his entreaty by calling for complete American unity and intellectual conformity as the nation engaged in the war. For, if at stake in the war were the hopes of western civilization, then the victory of America and the Allies had worldly importance. If a lasting peace and the construction of an international organization to sustain it depended on that victory on the battlefield, then we dare not tolerate threats to those ideals at home, Sherman warned. He feared, though, that "assimilation" among all in the country was not proceeding as smoothly as it should, that too many of the recent arrivals to America still clung to their old-world habits, of language especially. But these resisters, he said, "are enemies of the American republic." The United States must register all the military might and all the moral force it can to defeat Germany and ethnic exceptionalism hinders the effort. He certainly didn't mute his language. "The American who has not been thoroughly indoctrinated with American ideals is a menace to the Republic."[37]

Sherman's heavy-handedness in this wartime manifesto has a context larger than the war alone. It falls within the contours of the second phase of his intellectual career. For some time in the United States the whole American literary tradition had come under severe scrutiny, indeed outright attack. From Van Wyck Brooks to H. L. Mencken to Randolph Bourne, the assaults on the literary past came with a fury. All knew that the interrogation of literature was at heart an interrogation of American life itself. Literary warfare signified political warfare, in this, the "battle of the books." So, at issue were the shaping forces of American history; literature (and above all Puritanism), capitalism, and democracy always figured visibly in the debates. Sherman now set out to undo the damaging effects, to take up a rescue mission, and most importantly, to locate a structure of democratic values within the American literary past that could fortify the nation with its historic ideals. "Through the language and literature of America," he wrote, our great writers are "the special custodians of the melting pot," the basis of our unity and national identity.[38] Through his next two books, collections of essays, Sherman would try to demonstrate this vital point. *The Americans* appeared in 1922 and *The Genius of America* in 1923, but with almost all the essays in each published elsewhere before 1920 during the James administration.

Sherman wished to reverse the trends in criticism. In 1917 he reviewed the book in which Mencken had made his clearest assault on Puritanism, a piece Sherman titled "Beautifying American Literature." He clearly had resented Mencken's "tirade against everything respectable in American morals, against everything characteristic of American society, and against everything

194   PART II. ACADEMICS

and everybody distinguished in American scholarship and letters."[39] Sherman wrote to defend just about everybody distinguished in American letters. For *The Americans* and *The Genius of America* he gathered previous essays about American writers. He had done the first, in 1910, on Mark Twain, and, more recently had taken close looks at Franklin, Emerson, Hawthorne, and Whitman. He included an essay on Puritanism in *Genius*, and placed his scathing critique of Mencken in *Americans*.

Much of the writing here comes from within the shadow of the world war and Sherman's intense emotional and intellectual obsession with it. But these essays give much more credit to Sherman as a sensitive critic than did his tract for the Committee on Public Instruction. One critic called Sherman "the most masterly reporter of literature in our time" and described Sherman's essay on Henry James as "the finest study yet written of that fascinating subject."[40] He labeled him "the Illinois Arnold." A reader today could revisit the essays and gain fresh and provocative insights on their subjects. For this brief review of Sherman it will have to suffice to note that collectively the essays amount to Sherman's display of his grand themes of Puritanism and democracy, the great American partnership.[41] Here he agreed with Mencken: the two are the natural complements of each other. But for Sherman that alliance constitutes America's saving grace. The two forces provide the building blocks of a great nation, an exceptional one. What Sherman wrote in 1924 had always been true of him: "I conceive of literature as a partner of politics, religion, and morals." Thus he found much at stake for Americans in knowing their own literary tradition and the national values that thrived in it.[42]

• • •

Meanwhile, Sherman was taking on another project, this one too in the effort to fortify the American tradition in letters. It involved what became the three-part *Cambridge History of America Literature*, published in 1917. It involved Sherman, his friend Carl Van Doren, John Erskine, and William Peterfield Trent, with whom Van Doren had gone on to study at Columbia after his time at Illinois. The collaborators wanted to produce something "on a larger scale than ever before." Essays on a vast variety of subjects would come, they assured, from scholars all over the United States. And this work would not be just another celebration of New England. The editors aimed for expansiveness. Nor would they employ narrowly "aesthetic" standards of inclusion; rather, they looked for varieties of writing, forms of expression that told the story of a nation emerging from its encounter with a new continent, that informed of "the practical activities" of Americans. That history would embrace their moral, religious, and political ideas.[43]

Book I, Colonial and Revolutionary Literature, opens with chapter essays on Travellers [*sic*] and Explorers, Historians, The Puritan Divines (by Vernon

10. The Humanities   **195**

Louis Parrington), and then has the first of others that study particular individuals: Jonathan Edwards, by Paul Elmer More (who also wrote on Emerson), and Franklin, by Sherman.[44] Carl Van Doren wrote chapters on Brown and Cooper, and Fiction Contemporaries of Cooper in Book I and one on The Later Novel: Howells in Book III. Sherman offered Mark Twain in that volume. Erskine took on Hawthorne in Book II, and Trent wrote on Longfellow. Frank W. Scott of Illinois contributed chapters on Newspapers 1775–1860 and Newspapers 1860-Present. Philosophers and theologians fare very well in this big project, with Morris R. Cohen of CCNY giving excellent accounts of the major American standards of the nineteenth and early twentieth centuries, including Scottish Common-Sense Realism, Evolutionary Philosophy, William T. Harris, Josiah Royce, Charles S. Peirce, William James, and John Dewey. Three women contributed, but women writers and thinkers deserved greater attention, as in the appreciative review that Harold Clarke Goddard of Swarthmore College gave of Margaret Fuller in his essay on transcendentalism. As for Black intellectuals, Booker T. Washington, Frederick Douglass, W. E. B. DuBois, and Paul Laurence Dunbar are noted for "merited eminence," but receive no elaboration of their writings. Historians, economists, educators, newspapers and magazines, publicists and orators, political writers and reformers, patriotic songs and hymns, book publishers and publishing, and humorists supply other chapter subjects. There's even one on children's literature. And finally, in its quest for expansiveness, the *Cambridge History* included two substantial chapters on non-English languages. One dealt with German, French, and Yiddish writings. The other explored "Aboriginal" (American Indian) literature in a celebratory piece by Mary Austin. Altogether, and despite limitations, the *History* was quite an accomplishment.

• • •

Stuart Sherman shocked his friends and critical adversaries alike in 1924 when he announced that he was accepting an offer to become the "Books" section editor of the *New York Herald Tribune*. Sherman had so long defended the great democratic tradition of the Middle West and the state universities that many wondered if he no longer found that defense tenable as a mark of regional distinction. Sherman refused to make much of it. He simply thought it might be useful to know some other part of the country. But Sherman had changed, or rather, he had become more expansive, more tolerant in his estimations of the American literary scene. He was seeing much that was good among the young insurgent writers. He saw more true artistry in Dreiser's late work and he spoke kindly of Mencken. Many eagerly awaited what new offerings might come from Sherman in this third state of his intellectual career.[45]

But this phase proved short-lived. On August 21, 1926, the Shermans were entertaining guests at their summer retreat in Dunewood, Michigan. Late in the afternoon Stuart and Ruth took their canoe onto the lake. It capsized. Stuart, a good swimmer, went under and did not resurface—he'd had a powerful heart attack. Funeral services took place in Dorset, Vermont, at the Congregational church where his grandfather had ministered, Carl Van Doren serving as one of the pallbearers. Drowning constituted the formal cause of Sherman's demise. But a life of unrelenting and energetic labor, a record of essays, reviews, and long personal letters to friends and colleagues every year for two decades surely posit another cause. Quite possibly, Sherman had worked himself to death. He died at the age of 44.[46]

Modern Languages

In 1904 the liberal arts college contained the German and the Romance languages departments. A large number of students studied the foreign languages only because it was required. They lowered the standard of work. The German department had a faculty of six and enrolled about a thousand students. In addition to basic courses, it offered many advanced courses.[47] The French department, with three faculty members, offered four years of instruction in French language and literature and one year each in Italian and Spanish to a total of about five hundred students.[48]

In 1906 a major step toward establishing the reputation of the German department occurred with the appointment of Gustaf E. Karsten as professor of German and head of the Department of Modern Languages. Born in West Prussia, Karsten had studied at several German universities before earning a PhD in 1883 at Freiburg. After early research in the Romance languages, he had concentrated on the Germanic languages. He had taught briefly at the universities of Geneva, Tübingen, London, and Paris before joining the Indiana University faculty in 1886. In 1890 he became a professor of Germanic philology, and in 1897 he founded the *Journal of Germanic Philology*. In 1903 it took the name *Journal of English and Germanic Philology*. Karsten then spent three years on the faculties at Cornell and Northwestern.

Learning about Karsten, James interviewed him in Chicago and came away pleased. Believing that Karsten had been discharged at Indiana, James wrote President William Lowe Bryan to learn the inside facts. Bryan replied without addressing the question, but James was satisfied, and on January 30, 1906, the trustees authorized the appointment, with the understanding that the *JEGP* would continue to publish four times a year under Illinois auspices. The trustees assigned $500 to support the journal.[49]

Karsten impressed his scholarly spirit on faculty members, revised the program of courses for graduate students, and fostered a more theoretical approach to advanced study. His seminars emphasized learning how to produce original research. He discontinued the practice of putting graduate fellows in charge of freshman classes and recommended a new system of advising students. Rather than having them supervised by Clark, Karsten wanted students placed under the advising of the department where they expected to do their main work.[50]

In 1907 Otto E. Lessing joined the department as an associate professor. James urged Lessing, in Germany when appointed, to visit the professors of Germanics in the important German universities "to secure in their minds the proper recognition for our department of modern languages. We are going to have, in my opinion, one of the strong departments in this country, . . . one of the strong departments of the world, and I naturally crave for it that recognition . . . which it may deserve."[51] Here James spoke from his Germanic heart.

Karsten died on January 28, 1908, after a brief illness. At great personal sacrifice, James N. Bright of Johns Hopkins wrote, Karsten had done more than any other Germanic scholar to promote his science in America. Paul H. Grumman of Nebraska declared that Karsten "would have made [Illinois] the undisputed head of modern language study in the West."[52]

With Karsten gone the Department of Modern Languages reverted back to German and Romance language departments. In September 1908 Raymond Weeks joined the faculty as professor of Romance languages and head of the department at a salary of $3,500. Weeks had taken an AB (1890) and an AM (1891) at Harvard, had taught at Michigan from 1891 to 1893, and had spent 1893 to 1895 in Europe on a Harvard traveling fellowship, after which he began teaching at the University of Missouri. In 1897 he received a Harvard PhD.[53] After Karsten died, James tried to interest a donor in providing $30,000 to $50,000 to support the *JEGP*. When this effort failed, the trustees appropriated the funds needed. In 1909 Julius Goebel became managing editor of the journal.[54]

Before Karsten died, Goebel had become the prime candidate as professor of German. Born in Germany, he had earned a PhD at Tübingen in 1882 and had taught at Johns Hopkins, Stanford, and Harvard. A journalist and literary scholar, he had published three books on German-American cultural relations. But misgivings attended his candidacy. Neal Brooks reported that the consensus of faculty opinion at Stanford was unfavorable owing to Goebel's personality. Both Brooks and Karsten had advised against hiring him. But, Kinley and President Eliot of Harvard countered, nothing in Goebel's history need prevent his employment. Kuno Francke, head of the Germanic Museum at Harvard, regarded the suspicions about Goebel as wholly unfounded. It would be a mistake, Evarts B. Greene concluded, to discard so strong a scholar. The University hedged its bet, naming Goebel as professor of German and head of the department for a two-year term at $3,000.[55] Both Goebel and Greene recommended adding a professor in this field to round out the instruction in Germanic philology. The leading candidate, George T. Flom, had taught

198   PART II. ACADEMICS

at Vanderbilt before earning a PhD from Columbia in 1900. Since then, he had served on the faculty at Iowa, rising from instructor to professor. He had published monographs on Scandinavians and Norwegians in America. An excellent student of Old Norse, he could not speak any of the modern Scandinavian languages with ease and fluency and had little competence in modern Scandinavian literature. But in his small field no one surpassed him.[56] In 1908 some Scandinavian students petitioned to add Scandinavian languages to the curriculum.

Goebel and Flom enjoyed wide national recognition and shed luster on Illinois Germanic studies. Goebel helpfully cultivated relations with the German-American community, which furthered James's effort to strengthen the University's relations with the nation's diverse ethnic elements. James wrote Goebel about his desire to establish a chair for German *Kultur Geschichte*. Goebel championed German culture and did so with an edge. He assigned to the German intellectual and literary tradition a redemptive role, salvation for the United States to the point that it should adopt and nurture the German tradition. In an address in New York City in 1912, Goebel, in his fourth year at Illinois, set forth these notions forcefully, even linking this high Germanism to "the mother-soil of our folk nature," perhaps a gesture to the democratic ethos of America. More invidiously, he upheld that course against the rival and dangerous "melting pot" notions fostered by the spokesmen for Zionism. Goebel presented too extreme a position for it to win any followers in the United States or Germany—at least for now. The Germanophile Edmund James appears to have given no encouragement to Goebel's chauvinism.[57]

In 1910 Armin H. Koller, a native of Hungary who had prepared in a Budapest gymnasium and had earned an AB (1905) and an AM (1906) at Western Reserve University, joined the German department. A year later he received a PhD from the University of Chicago and won promotion to instructor. Koller, one of the prominent Jewish scholars James appointed, engaged actively in the Jewish social and cultural life of the campus. So also did Leonard Bloomfield reinforce the Jewish presence on the faculty. In 1910 he became an instructor. He had earned a Harvard BA (1906), had studied Germanic philology and Indo-European comparative philology at Wisconsin, and had received a PhD at Chicago (1909). He spent a year as an instructor at the University of Cincinnati before coming to Illinois. In 1913 he was named assistant professor of comparative philology and German. His teaching in Germanic languages was thereafter limited; he offered work mostly in comparative philology. In 1915 he introduced courses in elementary Sanskrit. Bloomfield became one of the great figures in American linguistics.[58]

The Germanic languages faculty had true excellence, but Goebel had an autocratic manner as head of the department and low ability as an administrator. Greene criticized him for not adequately consulting junior faculty and

10. The Humanities 199

for failing to develop a spirit of unity and cooperation among his colleagues. As a remedy, Greene changed the administrative structure from a head to a committee, chaired by the person who had the highest professorial standing.[59]

Although highly regarded by authorities in his field, Lessing chafed at his position in the department. In 1912 he complained that after Karsten's death the promises made to him when he joined the faculty had not been kept and that he had met discrimination in salary and rank. James asked Kinley if Lessing should have a promotion to full professor. Although Lessing was a "modernist," Kinley replied, his philosophical and moral views were such as the University's public constituency might fairly demand, and his promotion would be justifiable. The judgment revealed Kinley's staunch conservatism and sensitivity to political considerations. James advised Lessing not to press matters more rapidly than they would develop naturally.[60]

Poor relations also persisted between Goebel and Lessing. Lessing wrote and spoke freely about Goebel's supposed deficiencies. Both men, Greene declared, had ability and could render high-quality service.[61] When Goebel asked why his appointment had not become permanent and his salary raised, James replied that unqualified endorsement had been withheld because Goebel did not generate loyalty among his subordinates and lacked generosity in his treatment of colleagues. But because of Goebel's reputation as a scholar and teacher the University renewed his appointment.[62]

Arthur R. Seymour taught Spanish and John D. Fitz-Gerald taught French. Seymour also served as adviser to foreign students. Enrollments in Spanish were small. Fitz-Gerald had little success in undergraduate teaching but more in graduate work.[63] The slight demand for Italian was met by Florence N. Jones, who had a PhD from Chicago (1903) and published *Boccaccio and His Imitators in German, English, French, Spanish, and Italian Literature: "The Decameron"* (1910).[64]

Spanish and French language instruction struggled. But the problems in French were more than with merely language instruction. They had to do with one individual—Jean Baptiste Beck—and a "moral scandal" he precipitated. In turn, that matter also became a political battle, one that might have led to James's complete loss of power at Illinois. Instead, it did the opposite.[65]

Beck arrived at Illinois in 1915. A Frenchman, born in 1881, he had several European degrees and had made a mark in French literature, especially in the study of the musical lyrics of the troubadours. Several persons at Illinois set uncomfortably with Beck. They did not like his easy-going French mannerisms and flamboyant dress. And they raised an issue against him when he married the daughter of Goebel. They wanted the board to enforce the "relative rule" that prevented the appointment of more than one family member at the University, and they took the matter to the trustees. James asked the board to give him power to deal with the relative law with some flexibility. But he also told

200   PART II. ACADEMICS

Beck that he would not rehire him. Beck sought out allies on the board and found them in that group of trustees that despised James. That number now included John R. Trevett of Champaign, whose contempt for James knew no bounds. With Mary E. Busey he plotted to turn this incident into a full-scale attack on James.

Trevett proclaimed that James had too much power and sought to reconfigure the University statutes in a way that would put the trustees in control. The anti-James people used the Beck situation to give the matter as much publicity as possible and indeed that effort drew national attention to it. That development in turn charged James's defenders, and they proved to be many. Kinley wrote letters to key individuals, especially businessmen in Chicago. He alerted his correspondents of the insidious plot underway to destroy James "no matter what the cost to the reputation of individuals, or the prosperity of the University." Trevett moved to reappoint Beck by order of the trustees. Meanwhile, David Carnahan, chair of the Romance languages department, was touring Europe and learning some things about Beck's past. A portrait of unsavory behavior emerged. James now began expressing views of Beck that other faculty shared: Beck was a bad fit for American norms and he in turn considered us as "barbarians." He took the case personally and energetically to faculty members and they rallied strongly to his side. James now made "harmony" in the department the governing consideration regarding Beck. Trevett lost the rehiring issue in the board and never again became a threat to James. Beck resigned and left for Bryn Mawr. And, as Solberg concludes: James "emerged from the conflict stronger than ever."[66]

Philosophy

In 1904 philosophy existed as a one-man department headed by Arthur H. Daniels, who had joined the faculty in 1893 upon receiving a PhD from Clark University. An effective teacher, he taught many courses but spread himself too thin. He did not publish much, but he kept in touch with his field. Useful on committees, he played an important role in helping to shape college policy. In 1904, with a course in logic no longer required for graduation and Daniels's courses in anthropology dropped, enrollments in philosophy declined. The time had come for a forward movement in philosophy, said Greene in 1904, who described it as one of the most essential subjects. Daniels wanted to add another instructor and to divide responsibilities. He would teach ethics, the history of philosophy, and the philosophy of religion; the new appointee would teach logic, metaphysics, epistemology, and esthetics.[67]

Queen L. Shepherd had a Northwestern AB (1907), a Wisconsin AM (1910), and was an assistant in Boyd Bode's elementary courses. Upon receiving her doctorate in 1913 she became an instructor in philosophy. Daniels described her as "an exceptionally able woman and thinker."[68] As noted previously, she stood out with only a few other faculty who made known their opposition to the patriotic campaign that swept the campus when the United States went to war in 1917.

The department gained substantial strength in 1909 with the appointment of Boyd H. Bode. He had an AB from Penn College in Oskaloosa, Iowa, in 1896, an AB from Michigan a year later, and a Cornell PhD (1900). He had taught at Wisconsin, rising to the rank of assistant professor. A successful teacher, he had published several articles that received high praise. William James, John Dewey, Frederick Woodbridge, and others described him as an acute and original writer, one of the most promising of the nation's younger philosophers. Having rejected an earlier Illinois offer, Bode accepted an appointment as a full professor at $3,000.[69]

During 1909–1910 Daniels and Bode each offered ten hours of course work throughout the year. A year later they gave forty hours of instruction—twenty hours in elementary courses, twelve in advanced, and eight for graduate students. Bode's elementary courses, logic and introduction to philosophy, were popular. Enrollments in the department rose from 66 in 1906–1907 to 168 in 1910–1911. Bode's course on nineteenth-century philosophic thought as reflected in English literature was open to freshmen. In 1911–1912 it drew nearly forty students. Bode's *Outline of Logic* (1910) attracted favorable attention.[70]

Faculty Portrait #5: Boyd Bode, Philosophy

Boyd Bode, born in Ridott, Illinois, near Rockford, came from a Dutch immigrant family. He knew Dutch and German before the age of eight. The son of a strict Calvinist minister, Boyd alone of eight children gained consent to pursue an education. Even so, he constantly had to assure his father that his interest in philosophy posed no threat to his religious loyalties. Letters to his father would say "Let me again put your mind at ease." He might add, for example, that morality could have no other basis but religion. And indeed, as a student at Cornell, Bode's philosophical studies posed no threat to religion. There he became a devotee of idealist thinking, a longtime ally of theology and friendly companion of Protestant liberalism. But Bode's career has one dominant theme: his slow and often painful transition out of idealism and into pragmatism. His Illinois career brings that story into bold relief.[71]

Philosophical idealism had made slow gains against Scottish realism in American universities going into the late nineteenth century. But Kant and especially Hegel had influenced some American varieties. A small sampling would include Personalism, as articulated by Borden Parker Bowne at Boston University; Speculative or Objective Idealism, advanced by James Edwin Creighton at Cornell (influential for Bode); Dynamic Idealism, by George

202 PART II. ACADEMICS

Sylvester Morris at Johns Hopkins University and at Michigan; Absolute Idealism, powerfully promulgated by Josiah Royce at Harvard. Creighton, elected first president of the American Philosophical Association upon its formation in 1902, secured Bode's affiliation with idealism in this early point of his career. He gave his student a "glowing" recommendation when Bode moved from Wisconsin to Illinois. But by then Bode was moving out of idealism's orbit, becoming increasingly vexed at new inadequacies that he perceived in it, and yielding yearly to the greater appeal of its emerging new rival, pragmatism.[72]

The late nineteenth century recorded an exciting chapter in American philosophy's history, the emergence of a very "American" way of thinking. Pragmatism continued to grow in influence into the next century, when during its first decade Bode began his career, as graduate student and as professor. This "golden age" of American philosophy came from the path-breaking work of Charles Sanders Peirce and William James and, in the twentieth century, of John Dewey, all of whom helped place American philosophy "on the world map." But it involved many others as well.

The pragmatists wanted to break down the dualistic habits of thought long ingrained in Western philosophy—between the natural and supernatural especially. They wanted philosophy to reflect the new understanding of modern science, Darwinian evolution above all. They wanted to secure philosophical thinking in "experience," rendering it less dependent on recourse to occult realities. They celebrated human "intelligence" as the critical agency of the human species' advancement. They employed terms like chance, change, flux, variety, pluralism, and impermanence as the descriptive norms of an "open universe." All expressions of pragmatism, you might say, were more "worldly" than idealism, but that fact did not make them hostile to religion, now understood in refreshingly new ways. Bode cited James and Dewey most frequently among the pragmatists and of the two he had the closer connection, in professional activities and personal correspondence, to Dewey. And both individuals, in terms of their intellectual careers, had at least one very important commonality: they gave their earliest loyalties to idealism and "evolved" into pragmatism.

Bode arrived to Illinois in 1909 a disenchanted idealist. He had come to question any appeal to a transcendent element in reality and sought for meaning in the particulars of sensory experience. That new priority also elevated for Bode the functional versus the speculative character of mind.[73] We get a glimpse of the shift in noting a response Bode made to a piece that Dewey wrote in 1906. In "Experience and Objective Reality" Dewey questioned the curious neo-Kantianism afloat in the country at a time of "declining theology." He found unpersuasive Kant's upholding the forms of intuition as critically functioning to shape our experience of the sensory world. Many facts from our ordinary experience have that role, Dewey asserted. He similarly dismissed

10. The Humanities   203

Kantian Reason as in any way empowered to give us glimpses of an occult or transcendent reality, a realm of spiritual and moral truth; it does not disclose "some super-empirical ego, mind, or consciousness," he wrote. Dewey also bewailed the reactionary character of the forms of intuition (space, time, and causality among them). They thwart novelty, flexibility, freedom, creativity— the essential qualities of experience. They do not assist us in the real work of science, which is discovery. "They are good servants, but harsh and futile masters," he stated.[74]

Bode replied to Dewey's essay. (The editors of John Dewey's works saw fit to include the response as an Appendix to the volume in which his essay appeared.) Bode's response shows him in skeptical mode about pragmatism and, in 1905 and still at Wisconsin, exhibiting some features of the idealism that had nurtured him so far. Bode still gave credence to "objects that are not dependent on consciousness for their existence and nature" and did not want to dismiss from the discussion facts external to our experience. Here Bode supported another philosophical criticism of Dewey, this one made by Frederick J. E. Woodbridge of Columbia, who warned against the pragmatists' demolition of transcendence and its place in cognitive experience. Bode then was willing "to postulate objects which are not dependent upon consciousness for their existence and their nature." "Idealism, whatever its form," Bode wrote, "had difficulties in plenty; yet, to my mind, it indicates the direction in which the solution of our problem is to be sought, if it is to be found at all."[75]

But four years later, when he joined the Illinois department, Bode's grip on idealism was loosening even more. Two essays of his illustrate the slippage. In "Objective Idealism and Its Critics" Bode set forth the contrasting views of the idealist and the pragmatist and looked for some common ground. Dewey's pragmatism, he observed, in looking at experience as an organic whole that merged subject and object in an interdependent relationship, left his system in a kinship affinity with historic idealism. "Immediate empiricism [i.e., Dewey's kind] is idealism so revised as to leave out the transcendental factors," Bode wrote. One can move, then, either into transcendentalism or instrumentalism. But it's time for some sharp clarification, he insisted. "It seems to be true that these two types of interpretation have not always been carefully kept apart. Pragmatists have laid themselves open to the charge of transcendentalism, and idealists have regarded instrumentalism as merely furnishing a psychological setting for idealism." And yet the two interpretations seem entirely incompatible, Bode avowed. "Either we make use of transcendental elements, in order to make our particular experiences cohere, or we do not." Bode was almost ready to declare wholly for pragmatism.[76]

He certainly cleared the way three years later with his essay "The Paradoxes of Pragmatism." But this time he took a defensive position, looking at the alleged paradoxes and effectively dissolving them, giving his own clarification

204   PART II. ACADEMICS

of a viable philosophical program. Bode had overcome his own impediments to embracing fully a philosophy of experience. Citing William James he described experience as a temporal flux, never static, a process, a function. Our notions of truth should reflect these qualities as they open the way to intelligence as the operative agency for engaging the flux of experience. But residuals of the old idealism forestall this critical engagement, Bode was now declaring. We have not sufficiently freed ourselves from the habits of the old idealism, which prevents our looking at experience directly. "As long as a finished and 'absolute' reality or an ideally complete system is our criterion, we are of necessity forced back upon an undefined and undefinable correspondence or 'agreement' as the measure of our success." By "agreement" Bode meant the affirmation of any empirical data by reference to, or enclosure within some hidden, higher mind or intelligence, some Absolute that conjoined this ordinary experience to it. But Bode now had no use for such absolutes and things-in-themselves, which he declared "insidious and dangerous." What he would preserve from idealism is its quest for harmony, unity, cohesion, and integration, but that search must not take us into occult noumena, he warned. It must direct us to the constantly shifting domain of day-to-day realities. Our knowledge will know "success" only in moving from one experience to another. Here he quoted Dewey: "The effective working of an idea and its truth are one and the same thing."[77]

In a brief survey such as this we may go directly to the critical year of 1917. John Dewey had moved gradually but certainly out of the idealism, his neo-Hegelian period, that marked his early career. Five years after George Sylvester Morris's early death Dewey relocated from Michigan to the University of Chicago, in 1894. His idealism remained strong there, supporting also his Christian liberalism and growing commitment to social action. In 1904 Dewey joined the philosophy department of Columbia University and those years, lasting until his retirement in 1930, saw the full maturation of his pragmatic philosophy.[78] But Dewey and the pragmatists never had an easy path. And by 1917 some of them felt the need to make a bold declaration, to take on their critics and make the case for pragmatism on a broad front. Bode partook of this effort and worked with Dewey to prepare a manifesto, in the form of an anthology of essays on behalf of pragmatism. Titled *Creative Intelligence: Essays on the Pragmatic Attitude*, the book appeared in 1917. Contributors, among the eight, included Bode, George Herbert Mead of Chicago, James H. Tufts, also Chicago, and Horace Kallen of Wisconsin. Dewey wrote a very long introductory essay. "The Need for a Recovery of Philosophy" has special significance as a kind of dry run for one of the most important books on philosophy in the twentieth century, Dewey's *Reconstruction in Philosophy*, appearing in 1920.[79]

Dewey's opening salvo postulated philosophy's new possibilities in its various categories (logic, ethics, consciousness, mathematics, psychology) and in

10. The Humanities   205

different social areas (economics, art, religion), subjects to which the various contributors spoke. As much as a "recovery," in fact, Dewey wanted a fresh start. Collectively, the essays would constitute "an attempt to forward the emancipation of philosophy from too intimate and exclusive attachment to traditional problems." Thus, for example, said Dewey, we find empiricism still imprisoned in its restriction to what is given, the "experience" we derive from our sense apparatus and the sense data it furnishes us. The old empiricism had come to represent to Dewey a state of reactionism, delivering to us a fixed world and privileging the condition of a status quo. But in its "vital form," wrote Dewey, experience is anticipatory, forward-looking, and induces the striving to control or manage it as it moves in new directions. Experience so considered requires a living being seeking adjustment to an "environing medium." That interaction looks for "the successful activities of the organism." "Life goes on," Dewey declared, "by means of controlling the environment." This world of shifts, change, and instability summons our thinking and propels the mind into action as an "instrument" of adaptation to these conditions. And this experience constitutes our reality. But, Dewey lamented, we still have the habit of seeing this experience as conjoined to a higher occult existence, an antecedent realm of a universal mind outside or above our world, a "higher" reality that embraces and subsumes our fallen domain of ordinary experience.[80]

In talking about the anticipatory character of consciousness in his *Creative Intelligence* essay Dewey gave a footnote referral to the essay contributed by Bode. Indeed, this subject, consciousness, had been a central concern of the Illinois professor for some time, and Bode titled his essay to the anthology "Consciousness and Psychology."[81] Dewey and Bode considered the idea of consciousness critical to pragmatic philosophy. Bode did not accept behaviorist notions that consciousness did not exist or that, as some philosophers believed, consciousness had no meaning and defied definition. We will get a better understanding of consciousness, Bode insisted, if we do not think of it as some intrinsic entity or substance. Consciousness, our state of awareness, our thinking, said Bode, comes into play responsively. And it is always "tentative or experimental," a gauging or anticipating of possible responses, actions, to a given stimulus. Thus, he could describe the reflex arc not as a given construction, but as something that is constructed, a "progressive organization." This "process of organization and purposive direction" constitutes all that we mean by consciousness. It involves selection, and thus has a "teleological character," marked by careful consideration of means to an end. Bode called the process "the fundamental differentiating trait of conscious behavior." The anticipated outcomes then become stimuli to our thinking and action. "Future results or consequences must be converted into present stimuli: and the accomplishment of this conversion is the miracle of consciousness." Bode reinforced his point:

206 PART II. ACADEMICS

"To be conscious is to have a future possible result of present behavior embodied as a present existence functioning as a stimulus to further behavior."[82]

And finally, insofar as Bode had embraced pragmatism because he wanted philosophy "brought down to earth," he looked for other areas into which he could extend its usefulness. Just at the end of his term at Illinois Bode addressed the subject of law and philosophy in an essay titled "Justice Holmes on Natural Law and the Moral Ideal." Holmes, of course, had gained stature as possibly America's foremost voice in jurisprudence, through his book *The Common Law* (1881) and his service on the Massachusetts Supreme Judicial Court, and, since 1902, as an Associate Justice on the United States Supreme Court. His era also saw the rise of a new school of legal realists in American jurisprudence, Holmes himself moving over the course of his career to a position of "legal pragmatism." Bode shared much in common with Holmes. They disdained identifying the law with absolutes and abstract ideals and dismissed them from any usefulness in the life of the law. Bode, following Holmes, could have said, "all life is an experiment," a viewpoint that would prompt Holmes on many occasions to have a deference toward the legislative branch of government. Law making assists society through law to make the adaptations that any social organism must make for its survival, even when Holmes personally judged the actions foolish or wrong-headed.[83] Both Bode and Holmes saw an intellectual kinship between law and philosophy. Holmes early on, in fact, had an interest in studying law because it "opens a way to philosophy." He joined the Metaphysical Club as an original member.

In this instance Bode responded to an essay on natural law that Holmes wrote for the *Harvard Law Review* in 1918. Bode judged it "a brilliant article." He wholly concurred with Holmes that "it is clearly not the business of philosophy to discover eternal truth or to formulate a system of eternal values" and welcomed deliverance from "the bondage of such prepositions." Law, like philosophy, should not look for the "antecedent nature of things" to find the absolutes or norms that would give moral authority to laws and guide the courts in their work. Both Holmes and Bode brought considerations of Darwinian evolution to this subject. Bode wanted to apply the lessons of philosophical pragmatism to it.[84]

Bode identified himself with many of the social and political reforms of the day and became a voice among the progressive faculty at Urbana. And like Dewey especially among the pragmatists he did not concede that detachment from abstract moral "truths" landed us in amoralism. Both philosophers sought to secure an ethical system derived from experience. But in this matter Bode did stand somewhat apart from Holmes. Bode feared that Holmes had made too great a breach between law and morality and had given too much play to conflict, power, struggle for existence, and survival of the fittest. It was a fatal error. Bode feared that Holmes had too passive a stance toward inherited

10. The Humanities   207

custom and an attitude of resignation toward things as they are because they are. A true pragmatism, Bode believed, in fact gives a larger domain to the ethical life. For ethics, too, is a function of intelligence, and we must "grant to intelligence the same position in morality as elsewhere."[85] Bode, as progressive and reformer, wished especially to invoke a quality of "sympathetic insight" into this process. He, again very much like Dewey, called for an enlarged social ethic against the reigning individualist norm that so dominated American public attitudes and business practices.[86]

Bode brought intellectual excitement to the Illinois campus. Students flocked to his classes. And in the three areas of philosophy, psychology, and law he opened the University to important and invigorating intellectual currents in the nation at large. But by 1920 he had done his major work in philosophy and wanted to expand his vision, to bring the subject "down to earth." He decided that the field of education provided the best outlet. And when Ohio State University sought to go in that direction it made an offer to Bode in 1920 that he accepted. Possibly it mattered, too, that Bode left Illinois the year of James's resignation from the presidency. At any rate, Bode went on to achieve a great reputation in educational studies and to advance his progressive interest in writings about American democracy and its needs.

Psychology

In 1904 Stephen S. Colvin headed the psychology department. Interested in the metaphysical side of the field, he sought close cooperation with philosophy and education. The department attracted undergraduates but showed weakness in advanced undergraduate and elementary graduate work. It could make no great advance, Colvin declared, until it obtained better laboratories, more apparatus, and more equipment. He wanted to develop the graduate work and research along the lines of experimental psychology and child psychology. The department conducted experimental work on the psychology of the learning process in various schools of the state with the cooperation of normal school and secondary school teachers.[87]

In 1912 Colvin resigned to go to Brown University and George Arps left for Ohio State. According to Daniels, much of the writing in academic psychology was not above "newspaper science," and "faddism" was obvious in several branches of the field.[88] Illinois needed someone to put psychology on a sounder basis, but finding that person posed a challenge. The search for the right scholar focused on Isaac Madison Bentley, a Cornell PhD (1898). He had been on the Cornell faculty, rising to the rank of assistant professor. He had a reputation as a conscientious teacher and a scholar with a number of good articles. He leaned toward the comparative and applied sides of psychology. But Bentley had disadvantages: some regarded him as subordinate to the controversial E. B. Titchener. (See Chapter 11.) Most of Titchener's men, according to James Rowland Angell, had "a certain metallic rigidity of outlook with great earnestness and seriousness of purpose." Nevertheless, Bentley was named professor of psychology and director of the Psychological Laboratory at $3,000 starting on September 1, 1912.[89] Enrollments increased considerably that year in the large beginning course.

• • •

By 1913 the College of Literature and Arts had achieved a high level of excellence, with notable scholars in the social sciences and humanities. Greene and James had recruited a remarkable faculty, including Oldfather and Pease in classics; Greenough, Sherman, and Alden in English; Karsten, Weeks, Goebel, Lessing, David Blondheim, and Leonard Bloomfield in the modern languages; Bode in philosophy; Ford, Larson, William Spence Robertson, Lybyer, and Alvord in history; James Wilford Garner and John A. Fairlie in political science; and William Bagley in psychology and education. Moreover, James and Greene had pioneered in appointing Jewish scholars—Zeitlin, Koller, Bloomfield, Blondheim, and Simon Litman (economics)—in humanistic and social science fields of study. Greene had shifted the emphasis from elementary to advanced undergraduate courses, had introduced more graduate-level work, and had raised scholarly standards. He made the University's liberal arts college a model for the state's liberal arts colleges.

The liberal arts faculty generously extended the benefits of its knowledge to the people of Illinois through the various high school conferences and by publishing bulletins, lecturing, serving on commissions, drafting legislative bills, and advising the governor. The College, Greene proudly noted, grew more rapidly during his deanship than its counterpart in any of the comparable universities of the Midwest.[90] And its dramatic upgrading laid a basis for the emergence of the University of Illinois as a leading American university.

10. The Humanities   209

PART III

Educating for the Professions

CHAPTER 11

The School of Education

IN 1887 EDMUND JAMES gave an important address to the Philadelphia Social Science Association. It cast a long shadow over his subsequent career when James presided over the rapid expansion of professional schools at the University of Illinois. In this instance James was speaking about the training of teachers and educators in America, but the principles he defended had application to all of the professions and the education required of those whom the universities were preparing for professional careers. It should come as no surprise then that the College of Education had its formal establishment soon after James began his presidency at Illinois. James's lengthy essay frames this third part of the University's history in these years, Educating for the Professions.

As he surveyed the scene, James saw an unhappy situation. In recent decades many professions—law, medicine, even the ministry—had come into recognition as special areas of learning requiring preparation suitable to the particular nature of each. They had, in other words, James said, entered the era of "scientific" study, the application of laws and norms that marked the educational direction of these fields. And in the new departure of the American university, with its focus on research and the creation of new knowledge, professional education joined the older subjects of the curriculum. But alas, James lamented, the field of education remained outside the new normal. Harvard College, which teaches everything under the sun, James noted, does not offer professional training for teachers. And the record shows the sad results. But herein lies the challenge, he emphasized—to make the "science of education" a critical part of every university worthy of that name. Furthermore, American schools sorely needed such a training for their teachers. And yet: "It is only in the case of those who are to undertake the treatment of the minds of our children of whom we demand absolutely no evidence of skill."[1]

For teaching to become professional, James expanded, those trained for it must have a sense of their belonging to a long tradition, and a large intellectual history that conjoins their current endeavors to a distinct community of thinkers, that is, "consciousness of being a part of a learned professional body." James highly emphasized theory, for it marked the truly "scientific" character of professional status. And any such inquiry will bring us into philosophy, or "the history of speculative thought in this department," which James saw as the essential critical affiliate of education for all the professions. Again, James modeled the German universities as having led in this association. He pointed out that teachers in Prussia, as part of their state certification (for both private and public schools), undergo examination in philosophy and pedagogics. Every member of a profession, James insisted, must have this awareness of a common inheritance, of a unity which that instructor shares with all others, an *esprit de corps*, "the thought and experience of the race in the field in which he is at work." But with some few exceptions, James indicated, our normal schools make little concession to "the science of education."[2]

James's words reflected his ideas about the true nature of the modern university. He resisted at every occasion any notion of it as a utilitarian training school. The field of education spoke to that concern, he believed. Too many in the public, and too many teachers themselves, see their work as "simple, bald, handicraft." They looked to the college to offer "how to" courses. But they serve themselves ill, James attested, and the public holds them in low esteem, indeed often in "common contempt." Such narrow training of our teachers, James added, is "doing the children untold damage." "Scientific training" casts the educated teacher in a new light, however. Characterized by large expanse of learning in the humanities and social sciences, it brings pedagogy into a great intellectual milieu. As it is, James wrote, our teachers "have never been called to look at the relations of their field to other important departments of human science and art." All the more therefore, he added, should future teachers have their training in modern universities, where this interconnection of learning gives substance to the new professional status of educators.[3]

This document, as noted, looks forward to James's career at Illinois. But it looks backward also to his own training in German universities. As such, the document gives an illustration of a unifying soft motif in this book. For although not a philosopher himself James seems to have absorbed and inculcated the intellectual world of the German philosophical idealist. So, it's informative that in an appendix to this essay James twice quoted from J. G. Fichte's "Lectures on Teaching." Teaching, Fichte wrote, "is an art which has its own laws and special philosophy. It is surely fitting that a great University, the bountiful mother whose special office is to care alike for all the bases of human culture and to assign to all arts and sciences their true place and

214   PART III. EDUCATING FOR THE PROFESSIONS

relation, should fill an honored place for the master science, a science which is so closely allied to all else which she teaches—the science of teaching itself."[4]

From Fichte again: "It is not good that this science [i.e., pedagogy] . . . should be mainly pursued per se, in separate training institutions or professional colleges where the horizon is necessarily bounded, and where everything is learned with a special view to the future necessities of the class-room scholar. It is to the Universities that the public should look for [those] influences which will prevent the nobler professions from degenerating into crafts and trades. It is from the University that he [the future teacher] should seek in due time the attestation of his qualifications as a teacher, because that is the authority which can testify that he is not merely a teacher, but a teacher and something else."[5] James may well have stood out, singularly, among his university-president peers, in drawing directly, as here instanced, from German idealist philosophy.

• • •

Little demand existed for the collegiate training of teachers in America. What seemed necessary for that work did not rise to the level of a higher education. And then ironically, in the post–Civil War years, when public schools grew so impressively in the country, schools hired where they could and anyone seeking that work faced few measures of their qualifications. But states did move ahead. The Illinois legislature in 1857 had created the Illinois State Normal University in Normal, where Edmund James would later serve as director, and then two others, in Chicago and in Carbondale. The schools gradually took a greater interest in securing teachers with recognized training. Significantly, it was the State Teachers Association in Illinois that took the initiative, in 1885, of petitioning the University at Urbana to establish a chair in pedagogy. The University thus gained a growing sense of its relevance to the state's schools. Connections expanded through the visitations programs that followed and in discussions among teachers' groups and the University about how best to organize the preparatory school as a training location for teachers. Along with these concerns the question swirled as to what exactly constituted a university program in education. Thomas Burrill said he did not want another normal school at the University, and the petitioners in 1885 also made the University program a higher priority for them than a new normal school.[6]

The School of Education, established in 1906, had as its first dean Edwin Grant Dexter, already on the Illinois faculty when James arrived. Dexter, born in Maine in 1868, had acquired experience teaching high school in Colorado Springs and then college at the Normal School in Greeley. He earned his doctorate at Columbia in 1899 and then began his work at Illinois. So, James did not hire Dexter, but he certainly saw in him one who matched his views about teaching education. For Dexter had made his mark with an impressive

11. The School of Education   215

study, *A History of Education in the United States*, published in 1904. This book took a comprehensive view of the history, with much material on the colonial era, including the colonial colleges, attention to developments in all the different states, and wide coverage of the recent era in American higher education. His twenty-one chapters also included the subjects of professional education (law, medicine, theology, and others); technical and agricultural education; the preparation of teachers; art and manual education; commercial education (i.e., business schools); education of the Negro and the Indian; the education of "defectives" (the blind, the deaf); learned societies and associations; and lyceums, popular lectures, and museums. James wanted all professional education to acquaint students with a sense of their history and tradition. Dexter's book answered the need very nicely.

The school's historians describe Dexter as a man "of the twentieth century." He had an early intention to ground education, as an academic discipline, in philosophy. But Dexter came to judge that foundation insufficiently scientific and now wished to secure pedagogy as the alliance that would make education a scientific province and thus properly placed in university programs. He described education as an empirical study and the classroom as its "laboratory," in the manner of the physical sciences. It acquired knowledge and advanced in scholarship through "experimentation." Study in education should prepare the student for the work of the classroom, Dexter believed. He gained national status through his work, becoming president of the National Society for the Scientific Study of Education in 1905. In turn, Dexter urged creation of more faculty in pedagogy at Illinois, even threatening to resign if the University did not support him. He cited the progress and greater visibility of the work of John Dewey at Chicago, Illinois's main competitor in the state. But Kinley favored philosophy over pedagogy. Dexter left Illinois in 1907 to become commissioner of education in Puerto Rico and chancellor of the University of Puerto Rico.[7]

In the spring Evarts B. Greene traveled to New York City to meet three possible candidates at the Teachers' College to lead the School at Illinois. On March 10, 1908, William Chandler Bagley was named a professor of education at $2,500.[8] Bagley, as noted earlier, had a Cornell PhD (1900) in psychology, neurology, and education. He had been a public school teacher and principal, a professor of psychology and pedagogy, a teachers' institute lecturer, and superintendent of teacher training in normal schools. He spent his summer vacation in 1896 at the University of Chicago where he sought to gain greater knowledge about the "science of the mind" that now seemed so important to him. A few years at the University of Wisconsin earned him an MA. Strong in pedagogy and psychology, he had administrative ability as well. When appointed, Bagley was superintendent of teacher training at the state normal school in Oswego, New York, one of the best of its kind. He

216   PART III. EDUCATING FOR THE PROFESSIONS

had published *The Educative Process* (1905) and *Classroom Management: Its Principles and Techniques* (1907).[9]

Bagley rejuvenated the School. James had, before Bagley's arrival, expressed his dissatisfaction with its progress. It was not keeping pace with other universities, he believed, and not placing the number of teachers it should be placing in the state's public schools.[10] But Bagley introduced courses in the principles of education, the history and theory of industrial education, and school administration and supervision. He placed practice teachers in the University of Illinois Academy. In addition, he won the confidence of teachers and educators in and beyond the University by his excellent teaching, sane ideas, and agreeable personality. He became widely known for his writings. In 1909 Bagley was named director of the School of Education. Later, the Academy converted into a model high school.[11] And Bagley championed the School in a manner that made him at one with James. He wanted education training at the University to instill in students a sense of place within a large and common cause, one that engendered an *esprit de corps* among all teachers, but including as well superintendents, principals, and supervisors on the administrative side, all professionally trained. And he saw the connections of the University to the state school system, which he cultivated carefully and expanded, as part of the great service ideal of the modern university.[12]

The education faculty grew and strengthened. Lewis F. Anderson, a Canadian with a PhD from Clark University (1907), joined the department as an assistant professor and offered a course in the history of vocational and industrial education. Lotus D. Coffman, with a Columbia PhD (1911) and considerable experience as a school principal and superintendent and supervisor of the Training School at the Eastern Illinois Normal School in Charleston, joined the department as a full professor in 1912. He organized extension classes in educational administration. Bagley and his colleagues widely traveled the state and lectured to Illinois teachers' associations. They gave the department a new high standing.[13]

Bagley, too, joined the animated discussion about education as a science, and he forcefully championed that identity. He and his cohorts were basically resorting to psychology, the "science" of the mind, to set pedagogy on a firm intellectual foundation. But they took on a powerful opposition in this matter. Hugo Münsterberg of Harvard had advanced his case against psychology in the classroom through the widely read *Atlantic Monthly*, and colleague William James supported him by stating that psychology does not lend itself to classroom adaptation. Bagley furthermore departed here from his own mentor at Cornell, for Edward Titchener, a noted and controversial behaviorist, spoke as strongly as any against the education-psychology alliance. Bagley had joined with four others in 1908 to establish the *Journal of Educational Psychology* and in his book *The Educative Process* made a major statement on

11. The School of Education   217

behalf of that subject. Bagley wrote in 1909 that educational science would advance by strict empirical studies of classroom instruction, with psychology informing the study of teaching methodologies. The classroom supplied the scientific educators their laboratories. To attain the scholarly level of other professions (medicine, for example) education needs only "a rich and vital infusion of the spirit of experimental science," Bagley insisted.[14]

But Bagley soon underwent a major shift. He conceded that he was not finding that empirical studies yielded the visible results they promised. He was losing confidence in the pretension of empirical science and its claims of useful conclusions and guidance for classroom teaching. Bagley even wrote to President James in 1915 stating that he wanted to rewrite two of the books he had earlier published. Bagley had recently joined in a major project conducted by the Carnegie Foundation. To pursue it he had received a three-year leave with reduced teaching, as James recognized the valuable prominence the project, with Bagley's leadership, brought to the University. When issued in 1920 the commission's report showed Bagley's turn-around. He now declared that education bore comparison not with the applied sciences but with "the fine arts." That affiliation, furthermore, should turn the educator's attention to the subject matter of instruction, that is, course content (literature, history, philosophy, and so on), while not excluding psychology and teaching method. Nonetheless, Bagley now stood clear on one point: "The effective teacher," he wrote, "must be an artist rather than an artisan."[15]

Bagley's career made contacts with other major developments in American intellectual life, as his interests had a wide reach. He had great sympathy for the pragmatist movement in philosophy and the work of John Dewey. Bagley gave much attention to the content of educational and classroom courses as they served to promote social understanding and encourage a social ethic. One could see that emphasis in Bagley after publication of Dewey's book *Democracy and Education* in 1916. That connection, in turn, brought Bagley into affiliation with Illinois colleague Boyd Bode. Bagley introduced Bode to the study of education and, as noted earlier, that subject became Bode's major commitment after he left Illinois and moved to Ohio State. Bagley also invited Bode to teach a course on the philosophical basis of education. And like Bode, Bagley went on to a stellar second career at another institution, leaving Urbana after 1917 to join the faculty of Teachers' College at Columbia. But he left the Illinois School of Education in a condition of respect and wide recognition.[16]

218   PART III. EDUCATING FOR THE PROFESSIONS

CHAPTER 12

Engineering (with Physics and Mathematics)

Engineering

American state universities moved slowly at first and then with high commitment to meet the demands that a growing United States needed for engineers. When Justin Morrill and others created the important legislation of 1862, they had a particular image of the "industrial classes"—mechanics. They ran machine shops and sweated in textile mills; they operated steam engines of various kinds. They constituted the array of skilled workers, with their concentration in the Northeast. But the changing nature of American business called for more. The age of the railroad led the way in huge demands for construction. The age of Edison saw the spreading of electricity, visible from inside the home to the bright city streets outside. And the universities did begin to answer the need. Cornell had a large engineering program in place in 1881. MIT appeared the next year.[1]

James M. White served as the acting dean and then dean of the College of Engineering at Illinois from 1905, the year of its establishment under James, to 1907. White, a University graduate (1890) in architecture, had been the supervising architect for many University buildings. William F. M. Goss became dean of the College of Engineering in 1907. Born in Barnstable, Massachusetts in 1859, he attended the local schools, studied for two years at MIT, and in 1879 went to Purdue, where he taught in a department of practical mechanics until 1883. For the next seven years he advanced from professor of experimental engineering to dean of the school of engineering, and to director of the engineering laboratory at Purdue. Goss then came to Illinois as dean of the College of Engineering. Here too he had different positions: professor of railway engineering; director of the school of railway engineering; and director of the Engineering Experiment Station.

The Civil Engineering department had the largest enrollment in the College of Engineering when Goss arrived. Headed by Ira O. Baker, a University graduate (1874), it enrolled 232 students. Most of the courses dealt with surveying, railroad engineering, masonry construction, bridges, tunneling, and structural design. Baker's writing grew out of his teaching. His *Leveling: Barometric, Trigonometric and Spirit* (1897) had a translation into French. His main interest focused on the principles of road building. Baker's classic work, *Treatise on Roads and Pavements* (1903), went through three editions and sold thousands of copies. Baker became a key figure in establishing the Society for the Promotion of Engineering Education (later the American Society for Engineering Education).

Arthur Newell Talbot of the engineering faculty had a procedure for brick testing that was adopted by the National Brick Manufacturers and used all over the country. In 1910 the Western Society of Engineers awarded Talbot the Chanute medal for the best paper in civil engineering during the preceding year. Titled "Tests of Cast Iron and Reinforced Concrete Culvert Pipe," it described elaborate research at the University. Talbot won awards for his work.

Lester P. Breckenridge headed the Department of Mechanical Engineering, which dealt with the generation and transmission of power and the application of machinery to industry. He had a PhD from Yale's Sheffield Scientific School and had taught at Lehigh and Michigan Agricultural College before arriving at Urbana in 1893. His main interest was railway engineering. George A. Goodenough, a graduate of Michigan Agricultural College who joined the faculty in 1895, became an authority on thermodynamics. Nationally, the number of graduates in mechanical engineering began to exceed those in civil engineering in the late nineteenth century. However, at Illinois in 1903–1904, mechanical engineering with 219 students ran a close second to civil with 232 students. Breckenridge resigned in 1909, and in 1911 President James appointed Charles R. Richards, former dean of the College of Engineering at Nebraska, as professor of mechanical engineering at $4,000 a year. All along, UofI students were flocking to engineering courses. Enrollment (including physics), 252 in 1880, had reached 826 the year before James arrived. That growth had made the University the fourth largest engineering program in the country.[2]

The quest for a big name on the faculty in this important field proceeded. In 1909 Dean Goss recommended the appointment of Ernst Julius Berg. Born in Sweden in 1871, Berg graduated from the Royal Institute of Technology in Stockholm in 1892. He immigrated to the United States, began working as an assistant to the renowned Charles P. Steinmetz at General Electric, and was recommended for the electrical engineering faculty at Union College. Although he had no teaching experience, his intellectual qualities seemed to merit his

220   PART III. EDUCATING FOR THE PROFESSIONS

appointment. However, said President James, a recommendation to appoint in this way would in certain respects mark a departure from University policy. The subject called for most careful consideration. After three trustees examined Berg's papers, he received appointment as professor of electrical engineering.

Berg headed this department from 1909 to 1913. But Berg and his wife did not like Champaign. "There is nothing a man can do in this town on Sundays but smoke," he said, "and I cannot stand to do nothing but smoke." So, Berg left to return to his former positions with General Electric and Union College. Before Berg departed, work to find the magnetic properties of iron had started. Trygve Jensen researched this matter in the Engineering Experiment Station with a view to developing techniques of producing purer iron. By precipitating iron electrolytically, Jensen learned, only pure iron would adhere to the plate. One could then melt it down in an electric furnace, with a vacuum, in order to prevent impurities from entering. Chemists who tested such iron had to learn new methods because this iron was so pure. Jensen published the results of these researches in a periodical of the American Institute of Engineers and in the *Bulletin* of the Engineering Experiment Station. As a result, Westinghouse offered Jensen greatly increased pay to join that corporation. He was to apply for a patent on the new process, for which Westinghouse would pay the costs.[3]

When Ellery Paine, who succeeded Berg and served as department head from 1913 to 1944, learned of this development, he reported it to the University administration. General Electric then proposed to compensate the University for all that it had spent in research on the magnetic properties of iron and an additional sum if the University would assign the patent to General Electric.[4] But as a result of this experience, the University adopted a rule providing that if an idea was developed on the campus under University authorities, the discoverer must patent the results and assign the patent to the University.

• • •

The Engineering Experiment Station of the University of Illinois opened on December 8, 1903, the first of its kind in the nation. The trustees wanted to make the relation between the College and the station as close as possible. On January 23, 1907, the trustees established ten research fellowships in the station, each with a $500 stipend. The trustees also approved a plan to appropriate $150,000 for enlargement and improvement of the College of Engineering and the Experiment Station. In 1915 the board established four additional fellowships in the station. Addressing the Senate on January 4, 1911, Governor Deneen said that the Engineering Experiment Station had had a short life but probably contributed more in experiments and discoveries than the amount of appropriations that had made them possible. In 1913 the governor reported that the station had published sixty bulletins. Its researches

12. Engineering (with Physics and Mathematics)   221

had great value to the industrial interests of Illinois and rivaled those of the Agricultural Station.[5]

In his investigations of major American universities, Edwin Slosson gave high praise to Illinois for taking the lead in establishing experiment stations in engineering. Although universities had created these institutions abundantly in agriculture, they had ignored engineering. But why should the one have priority and not the other? Slosson asked. If one can experiment in cross-breeding cattle, why not experiment with concrete? Educational leaders in engineering and some state politicians thus wanted to do for engineering what the Hatch Act had done for agriculture—use federal money to establish an experimental station in each state. But engineering did not have the political clout that agriculture, with well-situated organizations, did. A bill came before Congress but went nowhere. So, Slosson welcomed Illinois's choice to go it alone and thereby lead the way for other states. On the campus, he observed the testing of concrete. The nation, in this new era of architecture, needed concrete that had proven hardness. With much excitement, then, Slosson reported his observation of the work at Illinois: "That is why they are smashing down concrete columns a foot square and twenty-five feet high in the laboratory of the University of Illinois. Great beams of it are pulled and twisted and bent and broken. Another instrument of torture takes a beam and pushes down on it and then lets up suddenly, 1,500,000 times a day, keeping up this sort of nagging without any rest nights or Sundays until the beam gets all tired out and loses its nerve and goes to pieces. It somehow seemed more cruel to me than the vivisection of dogs and guinea pigs."[6]

In 1915 the Illinois Gas Association established a four-year research fellowship in the station. Other cooperative projects followed: one for stresses in railway track with the American Society of Civil Engineers and the American Railway Engineering Association; another for coking of coal with A. T. Hart of Louisville, Kentucky; still another for chilled car wheels with the Association of Manufacturers of Chilled Car Wheels; and a fourth, with the Railway Fuel Association. In 1917 the American Locomotive Company and the Franklin Railway Company contributed $2,610 to the University for fuel tests.[7] Here we find exemplified in grand scale the model of a service university.

In September 1917 the experimental station published a circular by C. S. Sale: *The Economical Purchase and Use of Coal for Heating Homes with Special Reference to Conditions in Illinois.* It had a very positive reception. Insurance companies publicized it because of its reference to questions connected with the elimination of fire hazards in the use of house-heating equipment.

Railroads had a vital role in the American economy in 1906, when the University decided to establish a Department of Railway Engineering. Goss had a great interest in railways and had taught at Purdue, a major center of railway studies, before coming to Illinois.[8] Graduate School Dean David Kinley

222   PART III. EDUCATING FOR THE PROFESSIONS

believed, however, that the administrative side of engineering should figure largely in the education of engineers. So, in offering instruction in railway construction, operation, and administration the Illinois program would be the only course of its kind in any American university. In 1910 the Chicago and Northwestern Railway Company presented the University a used locomotive testing plant. In 1916 President James, always looking for connections, appointed all Illinois railroad executives to an advisory board for railroad engineering. Goss served on the faculty until 1917, when he became president of the Railway Car Manufacturers' Association and left for New York. He authored several books in his field, and for ten years was contributing editor of the *Railroad Gazette.*

Nature had blessed southern Illinois with immense coal deposits, and with the advent of railroads, boilers, and furnaces the University proposed to lead in exploiting nature's bounty. In February 1907, H. J. C. Beckemeyer, a Democrat of Carlyle, Illinois, introduced in the House a bill to provide for courses in mining education at the University. Favorably reported, the bill went over to the Committee on Appropriations, which reported it unfavorably. Two years later Israel Dudgeon, a Republican of Morris, Illinois, introduced a similar bill in the House. With an amendment that cut the appropriation from $15,000 to $7,500 per annum, the bill passed both the House and the Senate unanimously. In March 1909, 150 mine operators, managers, experts, and inspectors attended an Illinois Fuel Conference called by the College of Engineering. The following July Dean Goss recommended the establishment at the University of a Department of Mining Engineering. The time was ripe and the department soon took shape. In February 1910 five students were receiving special instruction in mining engineering.

A suggestion that the University increase the money available for experiments in coal mining gave James great satisfaction. He perceived the timeliness of the proposal as the Bureau of Mines was considering extending the scope of its work by making Urbana a central testing station for all of the mining industries of the Middle West. We are justified, James added, in saying that Illinois now has a better knowledge of its mining practice than any other state and has laid a sound foundation for a number of other investigations that will probably extend over a number of years. James suggested that the University petition the various associations in Illinois for some financial assistance to support such investigations. The University should not have to carry the whole financial burden, he stated.

By 1910 the University of Illinois had the largest research staff in engineering of any in the country. Its lab "was as well equipped as any university facility in the country."[9] The College of Engineering was a credit to the University when James became president in 1904, and it enlarged its influence in the ways discussed here. Add to the record the role that Illinois engineering played

12. Engineering (with Physics and Mathematics)   223

in the war, especially, as described earlier, that of the new School of Aviation. Though pulled in many directions, it went on from strength to strength until James retired. During these years William F. M. Goss directed the College as dean. A strong and influential presence, he provided good leadership until he was called to a position in New York. The College of Engineering in its outreach created an expansive network of organizations that integrated their work and effected an organic community of university and public, a hallmark of the modern American university.

Physics

When President James took office in 1904 physics had not attained its identity as a distinct academic discipline. From its beginnings at the University of Illinois it existed as a part of Engineering and, despite becoming its own department in 1890 it stayed in place with Engineering. When Draper had become president in 1894 Physics and Electrical Engineering, which came to being within Physics, both occupied the top floors of the new Engineering Hall. But Physics grew steadily and new equipment and more students soon made these quarters practically dysfunctional. A happy day arrived, then, when a $250,000 contribution from the state legislature led to the building of the Physics Laboratory, at Green and Mathews Streets, in 1910. The program granted its first PhD degree that year. Some people, including physics department head Albert P. Carman, seemed quite content with the Physics-Engineering network. Carman, who had three degrees from Princeton and had studied at Berlin, headed the department from then until 1929. His annual reports to his dean almost always express gratitude to Engineering for its support of his program, whose courses filled mostly with engineering students. But Carman stated that the connection did not impair the department's interest in also doing its research "on a sound scientific basis" and not merely as a vocational feeder to Engineering. In fact, Carman noted in one report that among the physics graduate students he saw young men "ambitious to win for themselves a place in science."[10] Carman, however, faced a major deficiency in the physics department. By two candid accounts, the department was missing something. The science of physics was undergoing profound and dramatic intellectual shifts in the early twentieth century. Already people were talking about the age of Albert Einstein, Ernest Rutherford, and Niels Bohr. Relativity theory, quantum mechanics, discovery of the electron, radioactivity—these marvels, so striking and indeed strange to most people—simply did not register at Illinois. Five new hires to the department had occurred between 1901 and 1909, with all these new professors reared in classical, or old-school thinking, the intellectual world of James Clerk Maxwell, Heinrich Hertz,

224   **PART III. EDUCATING FOR THE PROFESSIONS**

Lord Kelvin, Hermann von Helmholtz, and Henri Poincaré. Reportedly, they "ignored or derided" the work of the new theorists, and this was even though Rutherford himself had visited Illinois in 1909 and gave a presentation as part of the valuable and popular lecture programs the department offered. No new additions arrived to the department until 1920 to freshen the intellectual air.[11]

Jakob Kutz, mentioned earlier in his important work with Stebbins in making sensitive alkali hybrid photocells, stood out in his dismissal of the new learning in physics. Kutz, judged by one historian of the department (Almy) as "in many ways the intellectual leader of the department," made clear his objections to quantum theory in the pages of *Physical Review* in 1914.[12] However, only three years later Kutz "made his peace" with the new ideas, offering lesser quarrels with them and enlightening colleagues as to some moderate changes in his views. And indeed, Physics at Illinois did make important contributions in its domain. In 1906 it offered three new courses: mathematical approaches to thermodynamics, mathematical physics, and the theoretical study of light.[13]

The world war caused obstructions to the physics department as it did to many others at Illinois. Enrollments declined; professors took consulting positions with the government. But Carman came out of the year 1918 in an optimistic mood. In his 1919 report to the dean, he addressed the subject he labeled "Physics in the New Era." The American experience in the war, all agreed, exposed many problems. To the careful eye, we had more difficulty than we anticipated. Without giving specifics on the matter, Carman went on to say that the war showed that the United States needs "a more thorough cultivation of the fundamental sciences." Citing a piece by the Johns Hopkins University professor Joseph Ames, and quoting from it, Carman explained that Americans had accustomed themselves to viewing science in terms of the individual genius, the inspired amateur, the Edison, whose brilliance of insight moved science along. But that perspective serves us wrongly, Carman said. Now the demand goes out to "the scientific investigator," whose long and careful laboratory work adds "to our store of knowledge." This "fundamental science" now clams the highest priority at Illinois, he emphasized. We see industries creating large research labs, and private endowment programs, like the Rockefeller Foundation, sponsoring this kind of research, and governments, too. Carman hastened to point out that the work in question constituted "pure research," which now more people than previously believed underscored all applied science. The demand will grow, Carman assured. Even now, he said, the department cannot supply all the employment requests we have for our graduates. And the future, he added, has immense opportunities for women in physics.[14]

12. Engineering (with Physics and Mathematics)   225

Mathematics

Americans had long admitted that Europe had the best mathematicians, but the time had come for the United States to raise its status in the field. The birth of mathematics in America occurred in the 1890s when a number of native sons returned from Germany. There mathematics was undergoing a transition from traditional fields to new ones, the line between pure and applied mathematics was blurring, and Göttingen was strengthening its hold as the center of mathematics in Germany.

Scholars in select universities, including Chicago, Harvard, and Princeton, offered the advanced mathematics they had learned abroad. The Americans conducted independent research, published valuable results, and in 1894 transformed the New York Mathematical Society into the American Mathematical Society. By utilizing the nation's mathematical ability and producing two of the best mathematical journals in the world, the AMS gradually raised the United States to a position of global importance in mathematics.

The Illinois mathematics department, the second largest unit in the College of Science, was headed by Samuel W. Shattuck. He had joined the faculty in 1868 as an assistant professor of mathematics, head of the department, and instructor in military tactics. Edgar Townsend, an associate professor of mathematics, served briefly as Shattuck's subaltern as department head. Returning to Urbana from his leave in Germany, Townsend gained promotion to associate professor. Shattuck remained the titular professor and department head, but Townsend took over the department. He revised its course of study and published a translation of David Hilbert's *Foundations of Geometry* (1902), a highly influential work. In 1904 the mathematics faculty had three assistant professors, all with doctorates, and six instructors. They taught twenty-six courses: two in advanced algebra, two in trigonometry, four in calculus, and one each in several others. Twelve of the courses counted as graduate work. Townsend inherited a department devoted to undergraduate instruction. He hoped, however, to emphasize advanced work and raise the quality of faculty. In President James he had an ally.[15]

In reorganizing the department, Townsend made it his highest priority to fortify the faculty. He wished to offer a balanced array of courses and to upgrade their quality. In recruiting, he looked for PhDs with teaching experience who gave promise of doing research, publishing, and making the University prominent. He thought it best to strengthen the department before widening it. Because the University had strength in both engineering and agriculture, Townsend promoted applied mathematics and engineering problems. With a view to enlarging the course offerings and assembling a faculty that kept in touch with all mathematical interests, he hoped to make

226   PART III. EDUCATING FOR THE PROFESSIONS

appointments in statistics, theory of functions, theory of groups, geometry, and mathematical physics.[16]

To instill in colleagues and students a sense of tradition, Townsend asked President James for a small sum with which to buy portraits of eminent mathematicians.[17] James granted the request, and paintings of giants from Archimedes through the Swiss Leonhard Euler (1707–1783) to the German Carl Friedrich Gauss (1777–1855) and others soon adorned the walls in the mathematics library. More important, Townsend wished to augment the library, to acquire a collection of mathematical calculating devices and models, and to attract able graduate students. His goal: to make the department a mathematical center, worthy of the consideration of the best American mathematicians.[18]

In canvassing for faculty members, Townsend sought the advice of prominent mathematicians and operated with a fairly free hand, although on appointments President James had the final say. In his search, Townsend had to compete with other universities. The salaries of mathematicians at Harvard, Cornell, Columbia, and Chicago ranged from $3,500 to $5,000, and assistant professors received from $2,000 to $2,500.[19] Townsend's salary budget averaged $19,116 a year during the decade starting in 1904, and he had to divide it among many.[20]

In building the faculty, Townsend had a handicap in the University's location and in its weak library. The faculty workload probably approximated that in other universities. Apart from junior instructors who taught only lower-level courses, faculty members at Illinois usually offered a freshman course of five hours, a sophomore course (calculus) of five hours, and a lecture course of three hours in their own specialty. They shared the mathematics seminar.[21] Townsend extolled the value of an Illinois appointment to candidates seeking a position. The University offered career opportunities as good as one could find in any university in the country, he avowed, particularly among the state universities. Moreover, the duties of those who showed an inclination and ability to do research would have arrangements to permit them to pursue their studies. Yet the University made no promises. Faculty members had to make their own way. Townsend pronounced it "survival of the fittest."[22]

While replenishing the junior ranks, Townsend proposed to introduce allied lines—mathematical physics and astronomy. He informed Felix Klein and William Voight at Göttingen of his interest and explained that he proposed to pay from $1,500 to $2,500 to fill such positions. He also arranged with President James for Dean Goss of the College of Engineering to canvass for candidates in mathematical physics on a trip Goss would be making to Cambridge, England and the Continent.[23] In March 1906 Townsend had asked George Miller of Stanford if he would accept a position, conditions proving favorable.

12. Engineering (with Physics and Mathematics)   227

The University, Townsend added, intended to make the math department worthy of consideration of the best American mathematicians. Miller seized the offer. Born in Lynnville, Pennsylvania, he had graduated from Muhlenberg College with a BA (1887), and had served one year as principal of schools in Greeley, Kansas. Some years later he earned a doctorate at Cumberland University (1892). From 1893 to 1895 he was an instructor at the University of Michigan. Then for two years he strengthened his work in group theory at Leipzig and Paris. Miller went to Cornell in 1897 and then to Stanford. Townsend estimated that Miller had published one hundred articles on group theory. He was receiving $2,000 as an associate professor at Stanford and was dissatisfied in being so far away from the mathematical center of things. He could come to Illinois, he said, at no advance in rank or salary. He was perhaps better suited for advanced rather than elementary work, Townsend thought, but the University would make no mistake in appointing him.[24] In June 1906 Miller accepted an appointment as an associate professor at $2,000, his salary at Stanford. A year later he was advanced to full professor with an increase of $500.[25] In Miller, the University had acquired a bright star.

By 1909, Townsend had greatly strengthened the mathematics faculty. It included three professors (Shattuck, Townsend, and Miller), one associate professor (Ernest Julius Wilczynski), four assistant professors, one associate, and five instructors, all with doctorates. All six assistants had bachelor's degrees.[26] In 1911 Townsend added five instructors to the staff, including one female. Women on mathematical faculties were rare in the early twentieth century. Josephine E. Burns, an Illinois native, had an AB (1909) and an AM (1911) from the University, where she also earned her PhD in 1913. She had followed her AB and AM from the University with a year at the University of Wisconsin. At Illinois she wrote her dissertation on group theory with Miller. Townsend appointed her an instructor at a salary of $1,000. Townsend made two junior appointments: James B. Shaw from Millikin University in Decatur and Arnold Emch, from Basel, Switzerland.[27]

The curriculum of the department was designed to meet the needs of students of several types: those who chose math as part of a general education; those who used mathematics in cognate fields, especially engineering; and those who wished to specialize in the subject. Students could major in mathematics in either the College of Science or the College of Literature and Arts. To graduate in mathematics, a student needed to take a number of prescribed courses and an additional twenty hours from a list of major electives that included many mathematics courses.

Over time the 1904–1905 course of study changed gradually but significantly. A course designed for secondary school teachers first became available in 1905–1906. In 1906–1907 George Miller first taught two subjects in his special field: elementary theory of groups and theory of numbers. In 1907–1908 he

228   PART III. EDUCATING FOR THE PROFESSIONS

offered a course in projective differential geometry, and Henry Lewis Rietz introduced three new courses: averages and the mathematics of investment, theory of statistics, and actuarial theory. In 1908–1909 Robert L. Börger taught a course in constructive geometry. Charles H. Haskins replaced a course in spherical harmonics with one on Fourier series. He also introduced a course in theory of Abelian functions and another in vector analysis. John Young taught projective geometry.

The number of undergraduate mathematics majors cannot be determined because data on the subject were apparently not reported and lists of graduates with a bachelor's degree were not categorized by the department. No doubt most of the students who earned degrees in mathematics were male, but several were female.

From 1904 to 1906 the Mathematical Club met biweekly to discuss matters of interest in pure and applied mathematics. The club averaged twenty-seven members a year, with an average of nine faculty and seven or eight female students. In 1904–1905 Nelle W. Reese became president of the club, and Emma B. Connolly succeeded her a year later.[28]

In the early twentieth century American universities awarded relatively few doctorates in mathematics. In the decade ending in 1906–1907, the yearly national average came to 12.7, with most of the degrees awarded by private universities.[29] In 1905 Illinois awarded its first doctorate in mathematics. In 1910 Elizabeth R. Bennett became the first woman and the second person to receive a mathematics PhD from Illinois. She wrote her dissertation on group theory under Miller's direction. In 1912 the University conferred a PhD in mathematics on Ellis B. Stouffer, who had a BS and an MS from Drake University. He wrote his dissertation on invariants of linear differential equations under the direction of Wilczynski. In 1913 Josephine E. Burns had become the second woman to receive a PhD in mathematics from the University. William W. Denton, with an AB from Michigan (1907) and an AM from Illinois (1909), prepared for publication John W. Young's book, *Lectures on Fundamental Concepts of Algebra and Geometry* (1911). In 1914 Denton received a PhD in math with a dissertation on projective differential geometry of developable surfaces. All of these degree recipients later taught mathematics at the college or university level.[30]

In addition to strengthening the faculty and enriching the curriculum, Townsend nurtured the mathematical library located in Natural History Hall. He enjoyed considerable support from James and others in developing a research library there. In 1907 Townsend asked David Kinley, who regularly devoted part of the budget of the newly reorganized Graduate School to aiding departmental libraries, for $2,350 for journals and about $2,000 for books and treatises to put the mathematical library on a competitive basis with other institutions like Harvard and Cornell. At the end of one biennium Kinley gave Townsend $5,000 for the library.[31] Whenever possible, Townsend and University librarian Phineas L. Windsor bought complete sets of the important mathematical journals. Townsend asked Windsor to secure the mathematical theses of students from the leading European universities.[32] In 1910–1911 the math library held only 1,900 volumes. Windsor gave Townsend about $800 a year for books. By 1913–1914 the library had 3,150 volumes.[33]

Townsend also ordered and displayed a mathematical computing machine and built an important collection of mathematical models designed to aid the mind in visualizing mathematical concepts.

Townsend's efforts to build up the faculty matched the labors of Sisyphus. He sought excellent mathematicians but found it difficult to attract and retain them.[34] His appointees, generally of high quality, enriched the curriculum, trained several graduate students to the doctoral level, engaged in research, presented papers at professional meetings, and published books and articles. Some of Townsend's hires ranked among the leading mathematicians of their generation. He rated the department strongest among the state universities.

CHAPTER 13

The Law School

IN THE LATE NINETEENTH CENTURY, many state universities had created a law school: Michigan (1859), Iowa and Wisconsin (1868), Missouri (1872), California and Kansas (1878), Minnesota (1888), Indiana (1889), and Ohio (1891). Without special funds for the purpose, Illinois opened the semblance of a law school in 1894. The legislature had withheld its blessing, and some of the other colleges in the University did not want a law school. Thus, at its inception, the law school struggled as something of an alien element in the academic body.[1]

Before the ascendancy of university law schools, legal education in the United States had consisted of private schools. The one at Litchfield, Connecticut, had won respect. The teaching came from practicing lawyers and, sometimes, retired judges. But in the years after the Civil War, calls came, from lawyers themselves and from university leaders, for improvements in legal education. Indeed, individual states had moved increasingly on their own to require bar examination for entry into the profession. Many reformers wanted to relocate legal education from practitioners and into control of legal scholars, and hence into colleges and universities. The reform that would come to dominate the changes came from Christopher Columbus Langdell, who became dean of the Harvard Law School in 1870. He collaborated closely with President Charles William Eliot in constructing their famous "case method" of instruction. And in James Barr Ames at Harvard a powerful voice for the case method gave it wide attention. Langdell stated repeatedly that the true mark of a law professor meant much more than mere practical experience; it meant learning. And that learning came from study of the great record of appellate rulings, accumulated in a long history. The Anglo-Saxon tradition had high priority. Langdell stated his intentions at Harvard. He wished, as Robert Stevens put it, "to turn the legal profession into a university-educated one." He wanted to admit students to the program only after they had earned undergraduate degrees. Eliot, critical of the professional schools in general, had himself called for such a requirement when he outlined his program for reform in his essay (and Inaugural Address) "The New Education" in 1869.[2]

Langdell, Eliot, and Harvard professors Ames and James B. Thayer believed that the proper study of law affirmed the law as a "science." To that extent, also, Eliot insisted that law move in the direction of the other academic programs in a modern university, and thus fit more appropriately into it. Each of the disciplines had its own database and produced its scholarship from it; likewise must the law, and hence the recourse to the empirical data supplied by the cases in the appellate history. Ultimately, then, the case method educated law students to think like lawyers, a habit acquired by contact with the greatest legal minds that the appellate record contained, one that equipped them to take on legal problems. Ames wrote, "The object arrived by us at Cambridge is the power of legal reasoning, and we think we can best get that by putting before the students the best models to be found in the history of English and American law. . . ."[3]

The case method made quick and steady gains among American law schools. But it also had opposition. The American Bar Association supplied one source. Formed in 1882, the ABA resisted the movement toward scholars, as opposed to practicing attorneys, as the important vehicles of legal education and legal training. Viewing attorneys as a kind of natural aristocracy, the ABA urged a greater emphasis on training a lawyer for "the higher duties of his profession and citizenship." A lawyer should know the literature, science, and philosophy of the law. In reports from its Committee on Legal Education in 1894, the ABA pointed out that Harvard had no place in its program for jurisprudence, political science, or moral philosophy. The case method did not suffice for these imperatives. Furthermore, that method fostered a serious intellectual error, the ABA believed. It implied that judges make the law. But the law, in fact, is a preexisting system of principles that, like laws in physics, are to be discovered. The ABA thus saw the law as embodying permanent, transcendent truths. "The cases are not the original sources of law, and are but the application of principles to the particular facts," said the ABA in an 1891 committee report. These intellectual tensions persisted into the new century. In 1900, thirty-five law schools formed the American Association of Law Schools, purposively separate from the ABA. Not until 1917 did the ABA recognize the academics' claim to primacy in the education of lawyers.[4] Illinois joined the organizational effort and became a charter member of the AALS.[5]

Debates about law education showed some parallels to those in the social sciences. Harvard's case method emphasized the empirical data of the appellate literature. It did not purport to present the law as a moral enterprise or to sanction legal education as an ethical discipline. As William P. LaPiana stated succinctly, at Harvard "all the early teachers [of the case method] were positivists." The strongest resistance came from Yale. There, Simeon Baldwin opposed the case method. "Principles, not cases" were the building stones of the law, he insisted. Yale continued to use the textbook and recitation methodology that had prevailed in the antebellum era. That university had another stalwart of resistance in its Kent Professor of Law Edward J. Phelps. He wrote in 1901: "It is *principles* that the lawyer needs to deal with. *Cases* only illustrate principles; they are not to be neglected or overlooked; they are to be studied and understood; they *illustrate* principles; but they do not *supply* them; they do not *make* them."[6]

• • •

The Law School at Illinois began its life in the old Chemical Laboratory. The faculty included four full professors and one assistant professor. Applicants for admission had to be at least eighteen, of good character, and graduates of an accredited high school or its equivalent. Persons who had studied in another law school or in an attorney's office could gain admission to advanced standing. Members of the Illinois bar could enter as seniors without examination and could graduate in one year. Students over twenty-one, not candidates for a degree, could begin as special students and then these "specials" could become candidates for graduation by meeting the school's requirements.

The course of study lasted three years and consisted mainly of required courses. The faculty emphasized the study of cases,[7] except in common law pleading and equity pleading, which used textbooks, supplemented by selected cases. Seventy-two semester hours of work were needed to graduate. Most of the students came from rural areas or small towns in Illinois, and for years the student body retained a local character.[8]

The law school trained students for admission to the bar, but it did not provide a broad legal education. Students sought to acquire the skills needed to pass the bar examination and practice law. Half of the student body was "eager to learn, the other half immune to learning." Law students also had a reputation for rowdiness. They once launched spitballs and paper airplanes in a faculty member's direction when he turned his back, and a practice of chewing tobacco and spitting on the floor or behind the radiator added to the annoying behavior. But these practices soon died a natural death.[9]

In 1903, President Draper named Oliver A. Harker dean of the law school. An Indiana native, in 1863 he had served in the Civil War with an Illinois volunteer infantry unit. He then entered McKendree College in Lebanon, Illinois; in 1866 he earned a BA. Harker studied law for one year in Indiana. Then he taught school in Vienna, Illinois, while reading law in an attorney's office (1867–1868), and gained admission to the bar. Harker practiced law in Vienna from 1870 to 1878, and then became a circuit court judge. From 1891

Oliver A. Harker, Dean of the Law School. Courtesy of the University of Illinois Archives.

to 1903 he served as a judge on the Illinois Appellate Court. In 1895 Harker held the presidency of the Illinois State Bar Association.[10] In 1897 the law school became the College of Law, formally established that year.

Upon his arrival to Illinois Harker noted that the school had committed its instruction to the case method, even to the extent that it was using Ames's *Cases on Common Law*, an endorsement of Harvard's great champion of that method. Harker described himself as "a firm believer in the case method," but his experience teaching at the University soon persuaded him that the subject assigned to him, Pleadings, "could not be satisfactorily taught by the exclusive use of a textbook." So, he added his own classroom lectures to the course, appropriating the "standard works" of Joseph Chitty (1775–1841; *Precedents of Pleading*) and Henry John Stephen (1787–1864; *A Treatise on the Principles of Pleading in Civil Actions*). Harker had recourse to British common law, because, he said, Illinois, more than any other state, used it.[11]

An adjunct lecturer in the law school, Harker had a keen political sense and many influential friends. But he was not a legal educator. He had no decided views as to the best method of getting young men started. Nevertheless, he thought he would like the work and have greater usefulness as dean than in law practice. In June 1903 Draper appointed him at $2,000 a year to give three days a week to the job and to have $1,000 to add to the law library. In 1904 Harker became a full-time dean and professor at $3,000. "He isn't much of a lawyer," Draper confided to a faculty member, "but I think you'll like him."[12]

President James began to revitalize the law school soon after arriving in Urbana. In January 1905 he circulated a letter to all the lawyers in the state as to how to improve the law school, and he asked Harker to submit the matter to the law faculty.[13] Reorganization depended partly on finances. Since 1897 the trustees had met the school's operating expenses out of general revenue.[14] James did not request an appropriation for the law school for 1905–1907.[15] Perhaps he was not ready to energize a school in which he had limited confidence. For 1907–1909 James requested $25,000 per annum. The General Assembly provided $15,000,[16] the first legislative grant for the law school. The University did derive some revenue from law school fees. Law students paid a $10 matriculation fee and $25 tuition a semester.[17] In 1907 Harker asked that the law school be permitted to retain the tuition fees, confident that he could operate the school with these fees and the $15,000 appropriation. He thought of the law school as an appendage to the University.[18] At the University of Chicago, the total expenditure for the law school in its first year totaled $21,134. In its second year it reached $34,054.[19]

James prodded Harker to relate the law school to a wider constituency. He suggested that Harker prepare a brief address on what the law school ought to be and what it could do for the community. The University would print the statement. James believed in such "indirect advertising."[20] When Dean John Henry Wigmore of the Northwestern Law School sent a circular to the graduates of his law school, James urged Harker to prepare a similar "device for stirring up interest."[21] He exhorted Harker to organize local bar associations,[22] and he asked the law faculty to consider affiliating with some Chicago school that offered night classes. The faculty opposed the idea. In 1906, when Northwestern began to publish the *Illinois Law Review*, James complained that his law faculty ought to have done the same thing.[23]

By 1907 James felt ready to proceed with the reorganization he had in mind. He wanted first to reshape the faculty. His criteria for appointment specified conscientious and effective teaching, contribution to legal scholarship, and cooperation in the work of the law school as an organ of the state government.[24] In other University colleges, James gave the initiative in recruitment to the deans, while he interviewed the top candidate and had the final say. In the law school, James took the lead in recruiting. But he found it difficult to get men who met his requirements; when necessary, he made term appointments. In 1907 two men joined the faculty. Dudley O. McGovney had an Indiana AB (1901), a Harvard AM (1904) in history and political science, and a law degree from Columbia (1907). He came as an instructor at $1,800 a year. This appointment marked the first time since 1902 that the law school had on its

13. The Law School   235

faculty someone below the rank of assistant professor.[25] Barry Gilbert had an AB (1899) and an LLB (1901) from Northwestern, had practiced law in Cedar Rapids, Iowa for two years, and had taught law at the University of Iowa from 1903 to 1907. James hired him as a full professor at $2,000 a year. "You have thoroughly aroused my ambition and . . . enlisted all my sympathies in your plans," Gilbert wrote to James. His acceptance of the Illinois offer, he said, derived almost entirely from James's hopes for the future of the law school, which were "too luminous" to resist.[26]

In 1908 the first book in the new "American Casebook Series" marked the further advance of that method in American law schools. Gilbert became the first of three U of I College of Law professors to contribute to the series. He coauthored (with Floyd Mecham) a work titled *Cases in Damages: Decisions of English and American Courts*, published in 1908. Green introduced his book *Cases on the Law of Carriers Selected from Decisions of English and American Courts* in 1910.

In 1907 the curriculum became a bit more flexible. Although the prescribed work of the first year remained essentially the same as in 1904, in the second year Evidence, Real Property, Agency, Equity, Equity Pleading, Wills, and Moot Court became required courses. Students could then elect seven units of work from Sales, Damages, Carriers, and Quasi-Contracts. In the third year Moot Court and twenty-four units from other third-year courses were required.[27]

Harker strongly wished to stimulate and retain good students, especially in light of the higher entrance requirement and the fact that some state university law schools charged no tuition or gave prizes, whereas Illinois charged tuition and gave no prizes. He also had in mind "a certain rival law school" (presumably Chicago) that offered free tuition and aggressively recruited students. Accordingly, Harker proposed that the law school give four full-tuition ($50) and four half-tuition ($25) awards to the best and second best students in substantive law and adjective law (the law of procedure). The board authorized these awards for 1907–1908; in 1911 it authorized them from year to year.[28]

But the law school unfortunately experienced high faculty turnover. In 1909 Gilbert and George L. Clark went to James and urged setting the salary basis in the law school at $3,000. (Perhaps they knew that a law professor at the University of Chicago received $5,500 when appointed, $6,000 after five years, $6,750 after another five years, and $7,500 after another five years.) The comparable salaries at Harvard were $4,000, $4,500, $5,000, and $5,500.[29] James seized the opening to call the law faculty separately on the carpet and lecture them on their deficiencies. The University law faculty ought to have beaten Northwestern in establishing the *Illinois Law Review*, he said. Regarding the reprimand as "a little presumptuous," Frederick Green in his interview with the president intimated that if James wanted a law review he would have

236   PART III. EDUCATING FOR THE PROFESSIONS

to increase and strengthen the faculty with men that would cost more than $3,000. At this point, Green wrote, James "walked back and forth on his costly rug, clenched his fists, spouted, and got red in the face."[30]

But the aggrieved men had made their point. In June, James raised Harker to $4,000; Green, Clark, and Gilbert, all full professors, to $3,000; Thomas Hughes, also a full professor, to $2,500; and Elliott J. Northrup, an associate professor, to $2,500.[31] But as soon as the increases went through, Clark announced his departure to Michigan and Gilbert returned to Iowa. "James denounced their behavior as outrageous," wrote Green, "but if he had talked to them the way he did to me, I think it was what he might have expected."[32] In a letter to James, Gilbert offered several reasons for resigning, one being that he was not fully convinced of the practicability of developing a law school at Urbana that could compete with its rivals in the state, whereas the Iowa law school had premier status in the state.[33]

American law schools traditionally awarded their graduates the Bachelor of Laws (LLB) degree. This degree fit a time when few students had earned a college degree prior to attending law school. The University of Chicago Law School was envisioned as a graduate law school with admission conditioned on a college degree or, in exceptional cases, three years of college work. When the Chicago law school opened in 1902 it announced that it would award the JD (Juris Doctor), or Doctor of Law. At Chicago the study of law equated to graduate study, but the JD differed from the PhD. In 1908 the University of Michigan Law School received authority to grant the JD.[34]

In 1909, the Illinois Board of Trustees, acting on the recommendation of the faculty of the College of Law and the University Senate, approved the granting of the JD at Illinois. To receive the degree, a student had to have graduated from the College of Law, secured a BA in arts or science at least two academic years prior to obtaining the JD, obtained a minimum average grade of 85 in the College of Law, and presented a thesis on a subject approved by the law faculty. Candidates for the JD in the combined six-year course had to take at least six hours in political and social science during the first year of the law course. According to Harker, Illinois's requirements for the JD posed higher standards than those of any law school in the United States.[35] It is hard to discern a basis for his statement. But James had joined Illinois to the movement that Eliot at Harvard had begun—to raise the professional status of the law degree. He would make the study of law the equivalent of an academic graduate program, built, in all cases, on the required BA degree or its equivalent.

In 1910 Edward S. Thurston and John Norton Pomeroy joined the faculty. Thurston, a native of Massachusetts with three Harvard degrees—AB (1898), AM (1900), and LLB (1901)—graduated first in his law school class. He also served as editor-in-chief of the *Harvard Law Review*. He had practiced law in

13. The Law School   237

New York City until 1906, taught at the Indiana Law School for a year and from 1907 to 1910 at the George Washington University Law School. Letters praised his keen intellect. As a law teacher, one writer said, he had few equals and fewer superiors. William R. Vance, a former dean at George Washington, told James that he thought it inconceivable that Thurston would leave Washington for Champaign. "Surely," he wrote, "you must be mistaken in thinking that he will accept a professorship at the University of Illinois." Nevertheless, on June 29, 1910 Thurston took the position at $3,500 a year.[36]

Pomeroy, the son of John Norton Pomeroy, a prominent American attorney, writer, and law professor, was a law professor and author of legal treatises and had an outstanding record at Yale (AB 1887). He had studied political science there (AM 1889) and at Columbia before taking up law at Columbia and at the University of California, from which he received an LLB in 1891. He had practiced law in San Francisco and filled temporary vacancies on law faculties at Stanford (1895–1896) and Washington and Lee (1900). He wrote for leading law publications and cyclopedias. Pomeroy joined the faculty as an assistant professor at $2,200.[37]

In 1911 the arrival of I. (Isaac) Maurice Wormser and Chester G. Vernier, an outstanding JD graduate of Chicago, strengthened the faculty. Thurston suggested Wormser, from a family of international bankers well known in the nineteenth century. Born in New York in 1887, he graduated from Columbia with an AB (1906) and an LLB (1909). He was practicing law in New York City when James interviewed him in November 1910. Impressed with his evident scholarship and ability, James warned Wormser that his appointment was a "somewhat uncertain undertaking" because his deafness would militate against his success as a teacher, and his appointment would not become permanent until he succeeded in the classroom. On February 1, 1911, Wormser began as an instructor at $1,000 for the semester, the first Jew on the law faculty.[38]

According to Green, Wormser was hard to describe to those who had never seen him. "He was small in stature, hard of hearing, dark and pronouncedly Jewish in looks, emotional, ambitious, self-assured and self-distrustful, audacious and shy, presumptuous and morbidly sensitive, alert, voluble, witty, fiery, and erratic." His colleagues liked him, as did his students after they became used to his peculiarities and until they began to question the sobriety of his judgments. To Wormser there were two classes of beings—angels and devils. He never doubted to which class university deans belonged. His chief course was Corporations, and, said Green, it was a good one.[39]

After his first semester James agreed to promote Wormser to assistant professor at $2,500 for a three-year term. Thus sure of his livelihood, Wormser went back east to be married. When the date had been set and the invitations sent, he received a letter from James saying that Harker had both withdrawn his recommendation for reason of "certain considerations" and insisted that

238   PART III. EDUCATING FOR THE PROFESSIONS

Wormser not be appointed. After considering the matter, James presumed, Wormser would not wish to be considered further for the appointment.[40] "For gods sake help me," Wormser telegraphed James on receiving his letter. "I had considered everything settled and this blow st[r]ikes my little girl and myself on the very eve of our marriage am writing judge Harker and hope he will understand appointment on trial subject to his approval will be all I ask regards."[41]

"Wormser took the first train for Urbana," Green recounts. Missing connections at Indianapolis, he hired a special engine and car to take him to Urbana, where he went straight to Harker, whom he found at his home in the bathtub. Wormser rang the bell, and while Harker was dressing Wormser pounded and then kicked on the door. When Harker opened it, Wormser hugged him with both arms and cried, "My God, what does this mean?" Harker took him to James. The president and dean explained that a charge had been made, after Wormser left town, that he had used improper language in class. The complaint said that an investigation had apparently substantiated the charge. But, Wormser explained, he had used the language after class to a group of inquiring students in reference to a New York judge who had decided a case included in the casebook Wormser used, and the judge had made a ruling in a case that Wormser himself had argued. "The God Damn Son of a Bitch decided against me," Wormser had said. A clergyman's son had heard him. But, "[i]n view of the matrimonial exigency, and Wormser's undertaking to watch his tongue thereafter, the appointment went through and he brought his bride to Urbana in the fall," retained as an assistant professor at $2,200.[42] An idiosyncratic presence in the University, Wormser wrote his way out. His expanding scholarship included another Illinois contribution to the casebook series, his *Cases on Private Corporations*, written with George F. Canfield, in 1913. He left that year to become a professor of law at Fordham with an opportunity for practice. Soon, reportedly, he was earning $30,000 a year.[43]

James had earlier mishandled an attempt to hire Chester G. Vernier in 1907. A graduate of Butler College, Vernier had taken a year of graduate work at Chicago and had just completed a JD *cum laude* with one of the highest scholastic averages in the history of the school. Vernier taught at the Indiana Law School for one year, at Nebraska for one year, and back at Indiana from 1909 to 1911. In 1909 James offered Vernier an assistant professorship at $2,000. But Vernier, by then a full professor at Indiana, declined.[44] In 1911 James renewed the quest, aided by James W. Garner, an Illinois political scientist and the first editor-in-chief of the *Journal of the American Institute of Criminal Law and Criminology*, who wanted Vernier's help with the journal. Letters described Vernier as a man with an exceptional mind and an excellent teacher, though of a retiring disposition. Vernier, who was also negotiating with Wisconsin, wanted to know more about Illinois: he understood that

13. The Law School   239

some unpleasant features had troubled its past. On July 25, 1911, the board approved his appointment as a professor of law at $3,000 and as secretary of the faculty of the College of Law at an additional $500 a year.[45]

The improved quality of the law faculty facilitated the raising of academic standards. In December 1912 members of the Advisory Board of the College of Law, having visited classes and conferred with faculty members, submitted a report that emphasized the need for practical training in the law and declared that they saw no reason why the Michigan law school should constantly have three or four times the enrollment of Illinois. The board recommended increasing entrance requirements to two years of University work, except that a student twenty-one years old or older, having graduated from an accredited high school, should be admitted and should receive a law degree on completing the law course with an average grade of ten above the passing grade.[46] The law faculty and the Faculty Senate both approved the proposal, and on December 13, 1913, the trustees adopted the new entrance requirements, to take effect in the fall of 1915.

• • •

In 1914 William R. Vance, dean of the Minnesota law school, published an article titled "The Function of the State-Supported Law School." He contended that the law school had its primary duty to prepare individuals for the practice of the law, training them in technical matters and emphasizing legal procedures. In addition, a state university law school had an obligation to contribute to knowledge of the law and its operations by conducting research. Hence the need for a graduate department of the law school.[47] James asked the law faculty to respond to the article and to state their views on how to make the law school a more effective agent in the state's legal and judicial system.[48]

The responses rehearsed differences between James on the one hand and Harker and his faculty on the other, differences that had surfaced earlier. Everyone agreed on the need for effective teaching. It constituted the primary function of the law faculty, Harker and Vernier emphatically declared. William G. Hale and Pomeroy affirmed the point. Hale, a native of Hillsboro, Oregon, had a BS (1903) from Pacific University in Forest Grove, Oregon, and an LLB (1906) from Harvard. The law school would make its most substantial contribution to society, said Hale, in turning out better-trained, broader-minded, and higher-principled lawyers. Pomeroy, in turn, emphasized raising the intellectual level of the bar. Warren H. Pillsbury asserted that law school should also give the student a view of the history, ideals, and mode of development of the law, and it should contribute to "the legal knowledge and progress of the state."[49] James had also added Pillsbury and Charles E. Carpenter to the faculty. Pillsbury had a bachelor's degree (1909) and a law degree (1912) from the University of California, had studied for two years at

240 PART III. EDUCATING FOR THE PROFESSIONS

the Harvard Law School, and had been in practice in Oakland. He came as an instructor for the second semester of 1913–1914 at $1,000 a year.

Differences surfaced most visibly with respect to research, writing, and legal reform. Legal research consisted largely of compiling and rearranging adjudicated cases, Harker declared, not in inductively formulating new conclusions, the practice elsewhere in the University. "The lowliest man of science spoke with an authority that the most eminent lawyer could not attain. As understood in scientific circles, there is no such thing as legal research." For Harker, the field for legal research was limited primarily to reform in civil procedure, criminal law, and the treatment of criminal offenders, but the law faculty member might exercise influence in securing legislative reform of the administration of criminal law. Green saw less value than Vance in this kind of legal research. Vernier viewed teaching law and writing on law as distinct. Writing was good for the law school as an advertising feature, but men who were both fine law teachers and fine law writers were rare. The best way to reform and improve law, Vernier believed, was to produce "efficient, moral and progressive lawyers." Hale disliked the idea of a graduate department of legal research and believed it would not appeal to Illinois students. Yet some such work would be of value to the bar.

Whatever their views on teaching and writing, several faculty members did publish. Harker cited books and articles that he, Green, Hale, and Vernier had published, and manuscripts that Pomeroy and Wormser had underway. On occasion, before approving a recommended salary increase, James asked Harker what a faculty member had written.[50]

Some law professors refused James's request that they advise state agencies and promote legal and social reform. Pomeroy, for example, declined an invitation to draft a bill for revision of the law governing the park districts of Chicago. Harker approved his stand. But Harker did make himself the prime mover in establishing the Illinois Society of the American Institute of Criminal Law and Criminology (organized on June 21, 1911). He became its president and Hale its secretary; a year later Vernier became the secretary. Vernier joined the editorial board of the *Journal of Criminal Law and Criminology* and in the work of the Institute at the local and national levels. Harker reminded James that he (Harker) deserved credit for demonstrating the constitutionality of the mill tax law, which had led to a large increase in the legislative appropriation for the University.[51]

The law school had problems. Lack of direction hindered its development. James was particularly "dissatisfied with the administration of Judge Harker," Green wrote, "and in this he felt as the law faculty did." Little shortcomings irritated. Noting that the law school's letterhead printed his name as "Edwin," James wrote, "certainly our official documents ought to have the name of the president straight." He ordered Harker to get new stationery with the name

13. The Law School   241

"Edmund."[52] Harker was often unavailable—he was either in Carbondale, visiting in Los Angeles, or with his rheumatic wife at therapeutic hot springs. In 1906 James inquired by telegram, "When will you be in Urbana?" In 1910 he wrote, "I find it difficult to get track of anybody at the School who is responsible for anything."[53]

George L. Clark, a restless faculty member, "having discovered that Judge Harker was unfitted to be dean," concluded that the school's salvation depended on Clark himself being dean. He tried to rally some students to his cause. When they did not flock to his colors, Clark left for Michigan. People believed that Harker held his position "only because his political influence and his personal friendships were useful to the University, and the antagonism which a request for his resignation would have aroused would be detrimental to it."[54]

Tensions arose within the law school. Thurston and Harker came to lack sympathy for each other. Thurston started the first-year quiz hour and secured a revision of the curriculum and study schedules. He encouraged the four law clubs formed by students to hone their skills by trying hypothetical cases, whereas Harker thought that the clubs detracted from the Moot Court over which he proudly presided. Thurston inspired students more than the rest of the faculty did. He proposed to convert Harker's office into a classroom because its ground floor location provided excellent light. Harker disdained the proposal. After one year Thurston left for Minnesota, but in Green's opinion he accomplished more for the school in one year than anyone else had done in equal time.[55]

Harker thought highly of Northrup, who specialized in Real Property. According to Green, he taught it well, but James would not recommend him for promotion to full professor. The reason, Green explained, lay in Northrup's unwillingness to write a handbook on highway law for the instruction of local highway commissioners. Northrup would not do so because Harker had agreed to write an article for a law encyclopedia but lacked time to do it, so he asked Northrup to write it for him. Northrup slaved over the article for a long time and could not get to the handbook. Northrup did not tell James about the article because, though Harker gave Northrup the money for the article, Harker published it wholly under his own name and without having read it! When Northrup left and Harker had difficulties in getting someone to teach Real Property, Harker lamented, "Oh, I wish we had old Northrup back."[56] In 1916 the faculty experienced a great loss when Vernier left for Stanford. A scholar of the first rank, he attained distinction in criminal law and criminology, commercial law, and family law. He made his greatest contribution in family law.[57]

Illinois trailed other law schools in the effort to give law study a greater appearance of scholarly prestige and professionalism. But in 1913 it did raise admission requirements, specifying one year of college study. It raised that number to two years in 1915. Harker always resisted. And the changes did sharply decrease the enrollment. It had peaked at 193 in 1910.[58] But along with the decline the standard of student scholarship rose. Harker attributed the higher standard to small classes, hard examinations, severe marking, and dropping a large number of students for poor scholarship or advising them not to return. The result, said Harker, placed Illinois "in the front rank as a member of the Association of American Law Schools."[59] Now more of the students had an AB or college training of two years or more, and in 1915–1916 only one special had enrolled. Attendance declined further, however, when America entered the war in 1917.

The law students at Illinois, furthermore, showed a greater maturity and seriousness in forming their own campus organizations or in joining national ones. They created the Lincoln Law Club and the John Marshall Debating Club. They also formed two chapters of Phi Delta Theta national society and a chapter of Theta Kappa Nu, 1902. The Order of the Coit came to the campus in 1910. These groups responded when prominent members of the Illinois bench and bar came to the campus. In 1910–1911, for example, R. W. Olmstead, a judge of the Rock Island County Court, spoke to students on probate practice, and William N. MacChesney of the Chicago bar addressed the subjects of legal ethics and uniform state laws.[60]

Harker continued to build the law library. It usually grew at the rate of a thousand volumes a year, but in 1909–1910 it added two thousand volumes. A year later the library held twelve thousand volumes.[61] In 1913 Harker began asking $5,000 a year for books, apparently the average spent by state university law libraries per year for books and binding.[62] From 1910–1911 to 1917–1918 the Illinois law library grew at about the same rate as the Michigan law library, but Michigan had started from a higher base.

In June 1916 Harker renewed a request to be relieved as dean as soon as the College could find a replacement. The details of the dean's office, he said, plus the demands made on him as legal counsel, had become burdensome. He hoped to remain a professor of law, giving his time to the Moot Court, and at the same salary as he had been receiving.[63] Harker's request led colleagues to evaluate his deanship and James to search for a new dean. Green, the senior member of the faculty, was best qualified to evaluate Harker. Here is what he reported:

> I think it must be said that the Judge did not fully appreciate either the needs or the possibilities of a modern law school, and that his faculty would have preferred policies more vigorous and more advanced. But that tells less than half the story. Judge Harker had a shrewd and practical wisdom, he was aware of rocks in the channel, he preferred to navigate with caution,

13. The Law School   243

and he did bring the law school safely through. He felt himself its godfather. He was the staunchest of its defenders. He gave to it the best of his efforts for many years, and worked for the whole University as well. Judge Harker was unlike anybody else. His humor and his histrionic sense were keen. He was inimitable in anecdote and reminiscence. He never presumed, but his resolute courage always rose to the occasion. His fortitude did not forsake him in adversity. He was continuously loyal to every member of his faculty, even . . . when on rare occasions, he knew the loyalty was not reciprocated. He exerted himself to understand their difficulties and to compose their differences, and was ready at need to take up cudgels in their defense. The unfailing kindness and consideration which he showed the faculty, he also showed to the students. He had a fatherly interest in every one, remembered them when he met them years afterward, watched their careers, and was pleased when they achieved success. It is simple truth to say that his students admired and loved him, and that he deserved their love and admiration.

Harker contributed to scholarship, Green added, but his greatest contribution was in his influence on his students.[64]

Before settling on a particular person for the deanship, Edward H. Decker wrote, some fundamental matters of policy ought to be determined. Decker had graduated from the University of Michigan in 1904, practiced law for a few years, and joined the Illinois staff in 1910. He did not have prior teaching experience. In an important statement to James, he commented, with telling insight, "The time is ripe to make of our school a real university law school, or at least, to adopt that as our aim." The law school had not attained that status yet. "We have failed to measure up to others in all of the important particulars by which a law school should be judged, viz: in faculty, curriculum, and students." Decker thought that a frank discussion of weaknesses might help. As to the faculty: "At the very outset, the school was hampered by considerable opposition both within the university and in the legislature, with the result that funds were inadequate to permit of choosing a faculty of preeminent ability and standing in the field of legal education. The school started in a small way, and has been conducted in a small way ever since." The faculty, Decker went on, had been recruited largely from beginners in the field, and where such was not the case, as with Thurston and Vernier, salaries had been so limited and working conditions so unsatisfactory that good people soon left. Decker intended not to criticize the present faculty, he said, but to note that "such reputation as we have made is a purely local reputation, confined chiefly to our own university community and to the relatively small body of alumni which we have turned out." Decker agreed with James that the faculty should do something in the nature of research and publication in addition to teaching, but he cited his own experience to illustrate that it was impossible for young

244   PART III. EDUCATING FOR THE PROFESSIONS

and inexperienced law teachers to succeed as teachers and also publish. The law school had proceeded in the wrong way. It had not built up a faculty of a real university law school. Most of its personnel worked with the hope of attaining recognition "beyond our own little bailiwick." The school needed some men on the faculty who had already attained that recognition. With the loss of Vernier, wrote Decker, "our most insistent need is for new material at the top and not from the bottom." As for the curriculum:

> A law school which offers no courses in jurisprudence and in Roman law [as James had urged] can hardly be regarded as of university grade. Practitioners can be developed without them, but the aim of a university law school should be higher than the development of mere practitioners. The most crying need of the bar of this country to-day is for men with a broader learning, a deeper insight into the nature and the operation of law and its relations to society and national life. Our school has heretofore offered no systematic instruction in either subject. We have taught exclusively the English common law as developed and applied in this country . . . with the aim of teaching what the law is to-day. Our work lacks the historical background and correlation which could be obtained by the study of the subjects suggested.

The curriculum also needed broadening on the procedural side, Decker asserted. Harker, conceiving of the law school as an Illinois school, had confined the work in procedure to that of Illinois. This restriction might have made sense in the infancy of the school, but not now. Decker thought that most of the faculty agreed. To attract students from other states, the law school needed to extend its instruction to include a form of procedure common throughout the country known to lawyers as "code pleading." The school also needed more practice in drafting legal papers of all kinds and more careful supervision of all such work.

As to the student body, Decker wrote: "We are inferior to the law schools of other universities of our size in both number and quality of our students." In efforts to improve the quality, the school had raised its entrance requirements in accord with the general movement throughout the country, with the result that the numbers had declined to an almost irreducible minimum. But the number of students figured largely in the estimate that the public made of the school's quality. In entrance requirements the law school now stood on a par with the leading law schools of the Middle West, said Decker, but the effect had not brought the student body to a par with such schools as Chicago, Wisconsin, and Michigan, to say nothing of the big eastern schools. "Our students have always been largely drawn from Illinois, and mostly from the central and southern part of the state, and now they are almost entirely men who have obtained their academic training on our own campus. This, I believe, is a distinct source of weakness." Before entering law school, most of the students had joined social fraternities and engaged in student activities bearing no relation to their professional work. "They have also acquired habits of study and ideals of scholarship which . . . do not seem to us to be up to the standard necessary for successful professional work, and in bringing them up to such a standard more friction is caused than if they had come from other institutions." Many of the first-year students were inclined to be critical and to feel rebellious when they had to work harder to earn the same grades to which they considered themselves entitled. The law school needed to attract a majority of its students from other institutions of learning.

In frankly discussing the school's weaknesses, Decker did not want to create the impression of hopelessness. "Of its kind we have had a good school," he wrote, "and we have turned out a large number of competent graduates, and they were making good in their profession. But the law faculty felt a need to grow, and it wished to enlist James's active sympathy and aid to that end." Decker added: "Dean Harker we all love and we recognize the great work he has done for the school, but we feel that his ideas have been somewhat provincial, and that his retirement opens the door to an expansion which was not possible before."[65]

The leading candidates for Harker's successor were Henry W. Ballantine and Eugene A. Gilmore. James made contact with Gilmore and had him genuinely interested in the Illinois opportunity. But salary matters once again upset the apple cart. The College missed a great opportunity to add a legal scholar who went on to great achievement and, later, a Stanford appointment.[66] Ballantine, a Harvard AB (1900) and LLB (1904), thirty-six years of age, had practiced and lectured on law in San Francisco from 1904 to 1911, had been dean of the new University of Montana Law School from 1911 to 1913, and since then had been teaching at the University of Wisconsin. He had written a reasonable amount on personal property and bailment, had become a specialist on martial law, and had published a book on the law of contracts. Reputedly a keen legal scholar and a fine teacher, Ballantine, some believed, had excellent ideas on how to employ the case method of instruction. Ballantine was secretary of the American Institute of Criminal Law and Criminology. Hale described him as more original and with more intellectual initiative than Gilmore.[67]

James, unwilling (or unable) to pay Gilmore's price, invited Ballantine to Urbana. After their discussion he offered him an appointment as dean and professor of law at $5,000. Ballantine accepted and put on paper his understanding of the terms. The law school had arrived at a critical juncture, and James had promised his backing and increased support for it. In order to keep pace with the best state university law schools an annual budget similar to theirs had greatest necessity. James could offer as much as $5,000 to attract qualified faculty, and $5,000 would be made the standard salary to retain them.[68]

246   PART III. EDUCATING FOR THE PROFESSIONS

The law school required "special attention and fostering care," Ballantine insisted, and the faculty needed rapid strengthening. If the next man could be hired at $3,500 or $4,000, $5,000 would be necessary to hold him if he proved successful. "It is not always recognized," Ballantine added, using an argument that was gaining currency among law professors, "that a law school, as a professional school, has to travel on a somewhat different basis from many other departments of a university." The difference was becoming more marked with the competition of such law schools as Chicago, Columbia, Yale, and Iowa. Is it your intention to use the exceptional resources of the University to get the law school up into the front rank? Ballantine asked. "A boy will have an opportunity here to obtain a legal education which is not to be surpassed at present in any other school in the country," James replied; and he expected Ballantine to make the school even better.[69]

Assuming the deanship in September, Ballantine brought a fresh perspective and youthful energy to the office. He corrected deficiencies and initiated new departures while assessing the situation and pondering the school's future. The College of Law, he declared, stood at a turning point. Some parts of the University had achieved a national reputation, but the College of Law had not. What was to be done to build up the law school? Some faculty members, believing it impossible to invigorate the school in its present location, proposed to remove the school to Chicago. Ballantine rejected that notion outright. With sufficient resources and the proper strategy, the school could overcome the handicap of location and attract students from Chicago. Attendance must rise; the public will judge a law school by its enrollment.[70]

In Ballantine, Illinois acquired a law professor committed to the casebook program. But he gave legal instruction careful attention and believed that Langdell's system needed some corrections. Langdell and his Harvard supporters, Ballantine observed, had presented the casebook approach as one grounded in scientific methodology, as noted. Ballantine accepted that notion. But law is an art also, Ballantine insisted, and as such it involves "executing legal operations." And this aspect of the law our universities have badly neglected. Any law librarian, Ballantine stated, will tell you how inept are trained attorneys in accessing all the materials they need to prepare their cases—locating the record of relevant cases, codes, law reviews, and other documents that ground the preparation of briefs and the court activity that follows. The law schools, Ballantine feared, have rested content to have their students master cases given to them. So, we have in fact not improved that much on the old textbook pedagogy. But Ballantine urged: "Permanent scholarly habits cannot be acquired, or the methods of using the mechanism of a great law library inculcated, by a few lectures, moot court cases, or even a course in brief-making and the use of law books." So let us give students their own cases to research and acquire in the process a mastery of the "practitioner's art," or what Ballantine called "the handicraft of practice." They will learn the principles of the law—its

13. The Law School   247

science—but will acquire better powers of reasoning and analyzing, and in a manner much more interesting than underlining preselected casebooks. But above all, this recourse to the art of the law will make for better-prepared lawyers.[71]

To advertise the College of Law and make it useful to the profession, Ballantine proposed to establish the *Illinois Law Bulletin* and publish it three or four times a year with a lead article on some legal topic, notes on recent Illinois cases, and a report on the state and local bar. The trustees appropriated $750 for the purpose, and the first issue appeared in February 1917. Initially the *Bulletin* went out to all practicing lawyers in the state, and later, for a small fee, to those who requested it. Hale, its editor-in-chief, described the *Bulletin* as "the first publication to undertake the scientific study and improvement of the local law of Illinois."[72] It served a useful purpose, became well known, and had a large mailing list. James could not be happier.

Beyond increased attendance, the College of Law faced the great problem of strengthening the faculty. Ballantine wanted to enlarge the number and to pay salaries that matched those at Chicago, Northwestern, Minnesota, and Wisconsin. These moves would permit a broadening of the curriculum and help make the College of Law a center of scholarship and research for the law of the state and the nation, thus enabling the law school to help bring about needed reforms in the law and administration of justice in Illinois.[73]

The law library had developed better than any other part of the College of Law, Ballantine said, but to build it up more, he offered data to show its competitive inadequacy. In 1917, the University's law library had 21,000 volumes, compared to Columbia with 64,000 volumes; Pennsylvania, 58,683; Cornell, 50,000; Northwestern, 43,000; Chicago, 42,000; Michigan, 37,000; Wisconsin, 26,500; and Minnesota, 26,000. Ballantine also recommended appointment of a law librarian.[74]

Late in the summer of 1920 Ballantine resigned as dean. He "rather chafed under administrative work," Harker believed, and when an offer from Minnesota came at an increase in salary, he accepted it.[75] David Kinley, now president of the University, asked Harker to serve as acting dean while he took time to select a replacement and to ponder the future of the law school. Harker served in this capacity until September 1, 1921, when Henry C. Jones became dean at a salary of $7,500.

• • •

President James aspired to develop a first-class law school as part of a first-class university. During his tenure the College of Law made slow progress. Historical circumstances imposed limits to its advance. The legislature gave only minimal support, the location of the University made it difficult to attract students and faculty, and other Illinois law schools competed for students. The story to this point is one of continual gains, but not one of triumph.[76]

248   PART III. EDUCATING FOR THE PROFESSIONS

James bore considerable responsibility for the retarded progress of the law school. He lacked confidence in Harker but considered it impossible to replace him. James worked hard to recruit an excellent faculty, but did not offer competitive salaries, and his appointees seldom achieved excellence. He apparently alienated some of his best faculty members, and the law faculty thought that he had not given the school the support that it had a right to expect.[77]

Harker, on the other hand, failed to give the law school direction. He was content to preside over a narrow-gauged school that emphasized Illinois law and procedure. He showed loyalty to his faculty but did not plead for better faculty salaries. He, too, apparently alienated some of his colleagues and the College suffered from high faculty turnover. When the College raised admission standards enrollment declined. The law school became neither a national nor a state law school. Ballantine gave much energy and imagination to his efforts to revitalize the school, but the onset of war made it impossible for him to realize his plans, and perhaps he expected more than James was able or willing to deliver.

James and Harker collaborated in building the law school, but on another matter, they had strained relations. James tied his progressive political views to his ideals about law schools. He saw reform through law as a crucial corrective for society's ills. He also insisted that law professors be effective teachers and contribute to the legal literature. He wanted "a law faculty that, instead of teaching law as it was, would teach it as it ought to be, shake up the legal profession and make the University famous as a center of legal awakening and reform."[78] Harker had an entirely different view of the law faculty's primary function: to teach the law as a record of Illinois court rulings.[79] As a result of their contrasting views, "James seemed to think of lawyers as of a set of men steeped in tradition, devoted to formula, and blind to the essential forces that were stirring in the world."[80]

But he did not effectively press the matter. Neither through his published essays and public addresses nor through the office available to him did James articulate this vision. By contrast the University of Wisconsin Law School exemplified the model that James embraced. Here, as its historians explain, that law school grew within the larger ambitions of the Wisconsin Idea, with its commitment to social and economic reform. Also, they write: "The faculty believed that it was contributing to the public welfare and exemplifying the Wisconsin ideal of service to the commonwealth in training the majority of the practicing attorneys of the state. Moreover, the growing interest in preparing men for public careers in administrative law was an even more explicit response to the [President Charles R.] Van Hise philosophy."[81] Such ambitions suited James's own social and political progressivism. But with his own College of Law, he essentially abstained from the opportunity to give these ambitions life.

The wider campus took much interest in law school developments. Students who produced the *Siren*, a satirical publication introduced to the campus in

13. The Law School   249

1911, had a strong opinion of the Ballantine appointment. They did not like it. Nothing personal, they insisted, but Ballantine stood in the reactionary mode of the case system. And it produced lawyers who exhibit only "myopia with respect to the law's range." The *Siren* writer called for lawyers trained in the "philosophical aspects of the law, in the relation of the law to government and to social justice." Only as such could the law school get itself "off its skids," locked into obsession with "precedent and procedure." This opinion piece touched off a fury of reaction, including a rebuttal from the student Law Club.[82]

CHAPTER 14

Agriculture (and Home Economics)

THE TRAINING OF FARMERS and mechanics lay at the heart of the Morrill Act of 1862. But whereas engineering fulfilled the great expectations of that legislation, agriculture did not. The story acquired a familiar narrative at many of the new land-grant universities. In Illinois the pattern had a particular poignancy, giving rise to frustration, disappointment, and often anger. Students flocked to courses in engineering and generally ignored the offerings in agriculture. To many Illinoisans the pain felt particularly acute because that state had provided, through the prophecy of Jonathan Baldwin Turner, a special visionary prospect for the great "millennium of labor" that the new education would fulfill. Might there be, however, a turn-around for agriculture at the University in the James era?

Agriculture

Of course, many people, and farmers especially, still believed that formal education had no use in teaching the trade. They especially had suspicions about velvet-gloved professors who knew only abstractions and theories and nothing about raising livestock or growing corn. These prejudices, though overcome eventually, lasted into the twentieth century. At the University itself, debate raged over what to teach the few students who bothered to enroll in the program. Thus, as described by Richard Moores, "Narrow Gaugers" battled "Broad Gaugers." The first wanted to exclude from the curriculum all subjects that did not teach the practical work of farming. The latter group wanted to weave agriculture into the existing curriculum, incorporating it with traditional liberal studies. But it seemed hardly to matter. The College of Agriculture had but a paucity of students. It did, however, have excellent leaders and path-breakers. They included Thomas Burrill, with his pioneering work in plant pathology, and Manly Miles, "the first real professor of agriculture in the country." As "scientific" agriculture made headway in the late nineteenth century, the "Broad Gaugers" gradually succeeded in shaping the curriculum. George E. Morrow had a great vision for the program but stood well ahead of his time and could not advance it. He left a diminished legacy in the familiar "Morrow Experimental Plots" at the University.[1]

However, the College, in the mid-1880s, had better prospects. A breakthrough came with congressional passage of the Hatch Act of 1887. It established extension stations in every state. They had an immediate appeal, finally overcoming some of the prejudices about college professors; the image changed. Some of that change came from the work of Stephen A. Forbes, whose long tenure at Illinois helped to give the College a world renown. He published more than four hundred papers on a wide range of topics—acoustic biology, ornithology, insect pathology—and he did pioneering work in environmental studies (before the term "ecology" had even come into wide use). In this work, too, the University had the great contributions of Cyril George Hopkins. He launched a state-wide program to promote awareness of soil erosion. A vigorous campaigner for this cause also, Forbes used his "Portland Farm" to make visible demonstrations of soil chemistry. People from everywhere took note. (Moores says the Farm became "a Mecca for enterprising farmers.") By the end of the century enrollment in the College had increased noticeably, to 159 students. The new Agricultural Building, an architectural leviathan 248 feet in length, at long last appeared on the campus in 1900. It housed the departments of agronomy, animal husbandry, dairy husbandry, horticulture, and veterinary science, and it accommodated the office of the State Entomologist and the Chemical Laboratory of the Experiment Station. And in 1911 an awakened state legislature provided almost a million dollars for the biennium operations of the College.[2]

In Eugene Davenport the College of Agriculture had its driving force. He served the institution from 1894 to 1922. Davenport, born in Woodland, Michigan in 1856, attended area schools before entering the Michigan Agricultural College (later Michigan State University). He did work on the family farm while also pursuing studies that earned him a master's degree at the College and then an academic appointment there. But Davenport did not sit comfortably with the "trade school" character of the institution. He and his wife did some traveling, returned to Michigan, and then removed to Urbana when Davenport accepted appointment as dean of the College of Agriculture in 1894. He took on the job despite viewing with horror the wretched condition of the university farms and the buildings that housed agricultural instruction. The scarcity of Ag students further testified to the unhappy state of the program. Davenport knew he had his work cut out for him. But he proved equal to the task. And President Draper, despite his stark indifference

252   PART III. EDUCATING FOR THE PROFESSIONS

to the importance of agriculture instruction at the University, worked with the Illinois Farmers Institute to change the old prejudices against "academic farming" and to gain the organization's support in his work with the state legislature. When James succeeded Draper in 1904 a rejuvenated College of Agriculture welcomed him.[3] Growth continued. Under James student enrollment grew noticeably, from 308 to 1,215, and faculty from 37 to 181. James and Davenport worked tirelessly together to make public connections and promote the program.[4]

Davenport championed "scientific agricultural" and thus added his voice to the choir at Illinois that James conducted in its version of that academic theme. As noted in the previous history, Davenport espoused an evolutionary view and hailed how application of that theory underscored the great gains made in modern farming, as exemplified by animal and plant breeding. Science had purged from farmers' work some old superstitions that delayed the more rational practices one sees now, Davenport explained. And, like James, Davenport cast a wide meaning of the word "science." It applied to the economics of farming and to the whole structure of agriculture in the United States. Thus, he asserted, farming has evolved to the point that the old ideal of the individual farm as an autonomous unit no longer described the modern realities. Scientific agriculture, he explained, leads to an organization and mode of conduct "around larger units than that of a single farmer and his family." In an age of modern transportation and manufacturing, the local, individual farm had declining relevance within a large national system. Agriculture, he wrote, is now assuming the form of other capitalized industries. Davenport placed the matter in a larger framework: "This then is the aim and purpose of scientific agriculture: to replace tradition with established facts; to substitute for the irregular and uncertain purposes of the individual a systematic and well organized business of food production by the community at large." Davenport encouraged communal farming. But all the factors cited, he believed, challenge us to find new answers for modern agriculture in "economic science."[5]

Home Economics (Household Science)

In the late nineteenth century, the word "home" resonated large in American cultural, social, and political engagements, both as symbol and template that grounded discussions on a host of subjects agitating Americans in these years and into the next century. In a perceptive chapter titled "Home" in his study of the Gilded Age, Richard White writes: "Home was a concept so pervasive that it is easy to dismiss it as a cliché and to miss its particular resonance in this historical moment." On issues like immigration, Indian relations, women's rights, temperance reform, agriculture, the Chinese, and the free Black population, White shows, "Home" became "the most prized ideological ground,"

14. Agriculture (and Home Economics)   253

the underlying and supportive element of the country's republican future. "It was the political and social ground that could not be ceded."[6]

One may wonder, then, why the study of the home and its extended relationships did not emerge earlier than it did in American higher education. But it did find its place at Illinois early in the institution's history and, after faltering steps in its early years, went on to great successes. Home economics became a subject in which the UofI attained national recognition, and in which it had a leader known the world over for her ideas and practices.

Home economics constituted a social movement. Its leadership came early and most importantly from Ellen Swallow Richards. She grew up in Massachusetts, and when the new Vassar College for women opened in 1867, she entered the school, earning an AB degree in 1870. She had already developed a passion for science and went on next to become the first female to enroll at MIT. The home was her focus and here we see the first significant theme in the home economics movement: it aspired to transfer the home through science. That alliance would vastly improve the way modern people lived, its advocates believed, and it would liberate women from the drudgery of domestic toil. Richards wanted women to cultivate their mental and spiritual natures. So, from Richards and other predecessors of Isabel Bevier at Illinois, home economics, as championed by all of them, had a solid intellectual substance. Catherine Beecher, who launched the movement with her 1841 classic *A Treatise on Domestic Economy*, insisted that management of the home was too complicated an enterprise to be left to amateurs. Richards liked to tell her audiences that science had transformed industry and other aspects of modern life; it had not been applied to the home, however. Home economics would affiliate itself with all the directions of the new learning, with a wide outlook and comprehensive approach to all of them. Hence, its identity with "science."[7]

The home economics movement had ties to social reform and a clear place in the Progressive Era of American history. As Danielle Dreilinger writes, "home economics was about changing the world through the household." And here it also reached across racial barriers. The movement found a major leader in Margaret Murray Washington, a Black woman who had grown up in Macon, Mississippi, a town that had no public schools. But she did attend Fisk College in Nashville, Tennessee. She engaged in the organization activities of Booker T. Washington and became his third wife. Margaret Washington headed the Tuskegee Women's Club and won election as the first president of the new federation of African-American women's clubs.[8] Home economics also allied itself with collateral causes: pure food and drugs, urban social work, schools and curricular reform, temperance, and gender equality. Then at an important conference at Lake Placid, New York in 1899, Ellen Richards urged that American universities more widely embrace home economics. Now a full-scale effort moved ahead—to unite intellect and reform with home economics. The American Home Economics Association formed in 1908.[9]

254   PART III. EDUCATING FOR THE PROFESSIONS

Household Science also registered the quest for professionalization that was aligned with progressivism. What men were doing by way of organization and by creating high standards of their work, women could do as well. What doctors in the AMA and lawyers in the ABA had effected, so could those who moved domestic science on its way. Like the other groups, theirs, too, would embrace the values of science, objectivity, and expertise, which generally registered as cultural ideals of the male sex. These ideals also, of course, followed the new generation of women who were entering universities, and the leaders of the household movement who increasingly located there.[10]

A brief sketch of the program in the years before Isabel Bevier took the leadership will set the background for her career at Illinois.[11] Home Economics (Domestic Science, originally) appeared in the curriculum in the mid-1870s. It attracted hardly any students and under President Peabody languished badly. It had its supporters nonetheless, including trustees Lucy Flower and Mary Turner Carriel, who influenced the establishing of the program in the College of Agriculture. With the arrival of the ambitious Isabel Bevier in 1900 President Draper moved from a general indifference to great encouragement. Both she and the president knew the skepticism that many harbored about the place of home economics in a university curriculum. Draper defined the goal for Bevier: to build "a university department that would be worthy of other university departments." And Bevier needed no persuasion in immersing her program in a broad array of collateral courses in the humanities and social sciences. She did not intend to teach young women to cook and sew. Thus, the new curriculum under Bevier continued the practice from first regent John Gregory: the inscription of other university courses into home economics. "Suggested electives" included French history, literature, psychology, and economics.[12] After 1900 enrollment improved significantly and continued to do so in the James era. But the flourishing of home economics and the signature marks of the program belong to Bevier, both for her administrative work and the intellectual leadership she achieved in shaping the Illinois program as a model for colleges and universities near and far.

Faculty Portrait #6: Isabel Bevier, Home Economics

Bevier came from solid Protestant stock. The arrival of Louis Bevier to New Paltz, New York in 1675 introduced the paternal line to the American colonies, joining the Dutch Huguenot ranks there. Andreas Bevier later moved the family to Ohio, Isabel's birthplace on a farm in 1860. Her mother, in the Brinkerhoff line that came from Amsterdam, bore nine children, Isabel the youngest. She graduated from Presbyterian-affiliated College of Wooster in 1885. She had several teaching experiences at Pennsylvania College in Pittsburgh and at Lake Erie College before joining the Illinois faculty in 1900. But she took advantage of opportunities for individual study as well—most

Isabel Bevier. She led in the national movement to establish home economics as an integral part of American higher education. Courtesy of the University of Illinois Archives.

importantly at MIT where she did work with Ellen Richards, whom Bevier would always consider the true pioneer of home economics in the United States. Two facts have particular significance in this background. One, Bevier did not like teaching at women's colleges and hoped to have her career launched at a coeducational institution. That preference prepared her later to be a champion of the land-grant colleges. Second, and more important, Bevier had her training in science. That subject gave the young student her first intellectual enthusiasm. When she requested to study chemistry at Case School of Applied Sciences in Cleveland, officials there did not know what to say; no woman before had asked to study at Case. But the interest in science preceded her interest in home economics.[13]

Isabel Bevier saw Champaign-Urbana for the first time in spring 1900 when she came as a candidate for the position in household science. "I thought I had never seen so flat and so muddy a place; no trees, no hills, no boundaries of any kind." Her powerful imagination, though, saved her from despair and launched her into optimism. Now she perceived the matter metaphorically.

No boundaries meant opportunities, openness to new ideas, new things. She quickly embraced the land-grant idea, which resonated with ideals of coeducation, science, theory and practice, learning and labor. Hope and expectations soon proved realities for Bevier. She described the campus as "literally buzzing with newness, new courses, new members of the faculty." She described "a spirit of adventure, open-mindedness and experimentation. It opened up a whole new world to me."[14]

Dean Davenport told Bevier that "I believe there will someday be a science of the household. Let's get ready for it and develop it." To the young professor just arriving at Illinois, nothing could have given her more inspiration. For Bevier resolved above anything else to make home economics a scientific subject. And like so many others at Illinois, from James on down, she meant by "science" a large and integrated understanding of life, one characterized by broad learning in areas beyond a narrow focus on mere instruction in household operations. So, Bevier could say that "the wider development, in this case, the truest unfolding of the human spirit was to be accomplished, not by any of the schools but by the correlation of the best elements of each." That prerequisite would signify for Bevier the preferred location of household science instruction in large universities, situating it amid the expansive dimensions of learning that the university sponsored in many different areas. Bevier wanted her program (located in the College of Agriculture) to have connection to the College of Science, "to reveal to the students some of the mysteries of the laws of life," and to the College of Liberal Arts (in which one could in fact take a major in home economics), to acquaint the students with "the history and literature of other people and tongues." It could even offer valuable insights into women's roles in history, in the family, and in public life, she believed. Likewise the social sciences and "those sociological principles which underlie the daily life of the people." Bevier stressed these points whenever the opportunity arose. "The strength of the department," she wrote, "lies in the fact that it has the advantage of the resources afforded by the various departments of the University. Art, architecture, pure science, literature, history, education, and economic courses are open to [our] students." Bevier worked closely with major scholars at Illinois, inviting Davenport, Grindley, A. W. Palmer (a national leader in safe water studies), and James M. White in architecture, to teach in her program.[15]

Her commitment to science led Bevier to ask the critical question, how may it best be useful to women? She saw no need for women to compete with men; she insisted that women overwhelmingly did not seek that competition. They preferred the life of the home. So, the home economics program, in its wide effects, would make women useful supplements to men in their work, and contributors to the civic life of their communities. But that effort must avoid making two major mistakes, Bevier warned. The program must not yield to

14. Agriculture (and Home Economics)   257

utilitarianism. Domestic Science must not become just a series of instructional "how to" courses, Bevier avowed. As noted, Bevier made this point out of her honest convictions, but she made it also because she knew that home economics must struggle to win academic respect. Second, home economics must break from the traditional education of women as practiced in the women's colleges. In their efforts to emulate the prestigious older men's schools, she believed, an undue emphasis on classical languages and literature had given excessive attention to mental development, as in the old faculty psychology. In fact, she urged, we must train the mind and the hand together. Bevier, like contemporary theorists in education, John Dewey especially, wished to break down the dualism of mind and body and to understand humans as organic beings that employ all faculties in coordinated efforts at adaptation to changing environments. Bevier labeled that kind of education as "efficient" education.[16]

Bevier's work in home economics produced an expansive record of scholarship. A few books and many essays added to her wide visibility on the lecture circuit. She served as president of the recently formed American Home Economics Association, 1910–1913, and on the editorial staff of the *Journal of Home Economics*. In 1908 she won election as fellow of the AAAS. Many universities, according to Draper, wanted to lure her away from Illinois.[17]

But Bevier has significance beyond a strict association with the home and the science of its effective operation. She believed that home economics trained its students, females overwhelmingly, for larger roles in their communities. Indeed, Bevier stands as another instance of the Illinois intellect in its contribution to the Progressive Era. "We women," she once wrote, have not contributed to civic affairs as much as we should have. But the opportunity lay before us, because home economics, with its substance in large humanistic and social learning, can move beyond the household sphere to undertake the improvement of the world beyond. Home economics can cultivate "first and foremost an enlargement of vision to see beyond [our] own threshold." "Let us have cleaner streets, more parks and better ones, do away with the unsightly billboard, the ugly bridge, the smoke, and the noise." Dieticians, new products of home economics, will have larger roles to play in the public arena, she explained. "Let us also have better bread, less canned meat and bric-a-brac, more real art and beauty." Early in her career at Illinois, Bevier was contemplating a new stage in the advance of home economics, wherein art would have a significant role as a major agent of improvement in the American household. "The products of home activities," she wrote, "come under the rules of art." And art too, had its beneficial extensions to communal life in the larger society.[18]

Her experiences at Illinois led Bevier to another conviction: that the land-grant colleges of America had taken the lead and now promised the best future for the study of home economics. Bevier thrived at Illinois, found the support

258   **PART III. EDUCATING FOR THE PROFESSIONS**

she needed there, and joined her enthusiasm for her subject to the culture of democratic education as represented by the land-grant institutions. After only a half-dozen years in Urbana she found herself speaking "the vernacular of Illinois." In 1910 she wrote that Illinois and the other land-grant colleges of the West, with their egalitarian spirit, have been "the great agents in the extension of this knowledge of the home. Perhaps no other agency has seen so clearly the need of the scientific basis for the work or been so insistent in the demand for it." Bevier further maintained that the land-grant schools, for this reason, had done more than any other group of colleges to promote the interests of women. For science had a special value for females, she believed. As noted, Bevier wanted to take her love for science in the direction of service to women. Such an effort required breaking female education from the long pattern of training in manners and morals and into useful intellectual directions. To that end also, Bevier wanted to place the educational shift into a large historical framework. She saw the change as part of an extensive record of women's efforts to gain independence and power. In a brief survey she cited the names of Anne Hutchinson, Abigail Adams, Susan B. Anthony, Emma Willard, Mary Lyon, Harriet Beecher Stowe, and Catherine Beecher.[19]

Bevier appropriated land-grant ideals in another way. They inspired a new respect and understanding of work. The home economics program, she said, functioned as a "workshop," where intelligent people prepare food with economy of time, energy, and money. Bevier took heart from the lessons learned in the teaching of agriculture at the land-grant universities. Early skepticism about academic teaching of farming had given way to a new understanding, she observed. So, people now know that the plowing and the sowing "are to be mixed with brains as well as brawn" as this "new farming" draws on the scientific studies of all kinds—from plant breeding to animal feeding. So likewise did Bevier consider home economics an exercise of mind and bodily skill together and one wholly relevant to the great land-grant project. It would, in short, achieve a breakthrough for women as scientific agriculture had done for men.[20] Bevier watched her program grow year by year. It had 20 students when she started in 1900 and more than 150 four years later. Her students shared her ambitions that home economics would become a vehicle of social reform and lead to careers for women outside the home.[21] And it grew to great success around the country, with the land-grant schools registering the largest numbers of students. That pattern also meant that home economics had its largest growth in the Midwest. It troubled and angered Bevier that the old "classical" women's colleges in the East largely resisted home economics. She judged their curriculums anachronistic, still engulfed in the old languages, trying to emulate the elite male colleges. For their part, the women's elite schools often labeled home economics inappropriate for a college. (Indeed, some faculty men at Illinois, and President James at first, did also.) President

14. Agriculture (and Home Economics)   259

Carey Thomas of Bryn Mawr judged the subject too sex-stereotyped and one of insufficient intellect.[22]

But Bevier's work did not go unchallenged at home either. She had faced from the time of her arrival to Illinois the criticism of some influential women who saw home economics as a skills regime with the purpose of training young women to cook and sew, with some additional functions needed to run a household. They objected particularly to the way Bevier had reinforced the tradition at Illinois that had immersed home economics in liberal studies to whose departments home economics sent its students. Bevier described the matter as "the age-old conflict between the cooking and sewing school of adherents and those who believed in the scientific method of approach to the teaching of household science." She added that "these women and I had never spoken the same language."[23]

The demands for a "practical" program came mostly from women who controlled a powerful committee in the Farmers' Institute. That organization had found its cause in the improvement of farm and country life. Women leaders in it wanted home economics to instruct in the techniques of household functions. When one member asked Bevier, where are the courses in cooking, Bevier replied that her students are not studying cooking—they're studying proteins, fats, and carbohydrates. The Institute women wanted a larger number of students, but Bevier would not yield to their demand for lower admission requirements. Nora (Mrs. Henry) Dunlop led in advancing the case against Bevier. Dunlop resented Bevier's "high-handed" independence and her failure to provide instruction in cooking. She threatened to disengage the Institute women from their traditional efforts to lobby the legislature on behalf of the home economics program.[24]

The flare-up occurred in 1909 when Bevier had gone east on a sabbatical. Dean Davenport had long worked with the Farmers Institute and enjoyed its cooperation in securing money from the legislature. He felt himself caught in the middle, even as Bevier's many loyalists rallied to her side. But he buckled and asked Bevier to resign, "in the best interests of all concerned." Bevier asked the advice of her old comrade at Illinois, Andrew Draper. He urged her not to take Davenport's advice.[25]

And she hoped, of course, that President James would support her. When James had become president in 1904 Bevier had her doubts about him. She had heard that James was a dedicated Germanophile, and she feared that his ideas about women reduced to "Kinder, Kuchen, Kirche." But she learned otherwise. She found in James a strong supporter of her work. Dedication of the new Woman's Building, to be Household Science's new home, a beautiful colonial structure, became a prominent feature in the fanfare of events in James's installation. Bevier described James as "businesslike and agreeable," and "so impersonal." He always let you make your point, she said, and "you

260   PART III. EDUCATING FOR THE PROFESSIONS

could do an immense amount of business with him in five minutes." James welcomed Bevier back from her sabbatical. So did Dean Kinley, who actually taught a course in her department. In the event, the legislature gave new money "to advance the art of practical housekeeping in the State," Bevier's program stayed in place, and the controversy passed. Davenport later expressed regret about his action toward Bevier and apologized to her—as well he should have.[26]

Isabel Bevier had ideas, and the administrative skills to give them application. The program had many outreaches to the public. One landmark of her career at Illinois includes the extension program. Here she teamed with Davenport and established a wide-ranging network. She controlled appointments to local units and looked for intellect over skills in the women who assumed authority there. The program had a great boost with congressional passage of the Smith-Lever Act in 1915. The legislation established a system of cooperative extension services tied to the land-grant universities. By 1916 the program at Illinois was reaching fifty thousand people and its famous "Demonstration Car," with its dazzling displays of new washing machines, vacuum cleaners, ice cream freezers, and the like attracted over thirteen thousand visitors in its first year. Equally fascinating, the "Experimental House," near the Woman's Building at the corner of Wright and Daniel, also had modernity on display and often received eighty visitors a day, as well as newspaper reporters, from nearby and from Chicago and St. Louis.[27]

The service ideal came easily to the Home Economics program when the war broke out and the United States entered in 1917. The expanded residence hall for women converted to a barracks for prospective soldiers. Some of the department staff went abroad to assist, and Bevier worked with the federal government to demonstrate and promote food conservation practices. She served also as state director of Herbert Hoover's Food Administration offices. The Smith-Hughes Act of 1917 gave another round of support by financing training of teachers in agriculture, trade and industry, and home economics. And, whereas federal documents now used that reference, at Illinois Household Science changed its name to Home Economics.[28]

Bevier resigned from her professorship in 1921 to become chair of the Department of Home Economics at UCLA. She returned to Illinois in 1928, retiring two years later. She died in 1942, age 81. The University honored her with the change of name from the Woman's Building to Bevier Hall in 1947. Herewith, a portrait of this leader: "Tall and strong, with blue eyes and delicate skin that retained a pink flush, Isabel Bevier had vitality and infectious good humor. She was a devoted Presbyterian. She enjoyed travel, good talk, and people, though some found her brusque in speech and resented the dominant role she played in conversation. Her life work, taken up as a result of circumstances and at the initiative of others, paralleled the first years of the

14. Agriculture (and Home Economics)   261

organized home economics movement. By translating the results of scientific research into the language of the home she helped lay the foundations of modern home-making."[29] In 1933 a chemistry professor at Columbia University wrote that "the scientific esteem in which Home Economics is held in any comparable institution is closely proportional to the fidelity with which it has followed the standards set by Miss Bevier."[30]Altogether, this was perhaps her most important legacy.

PART IV

Students

CHAPTER 15

The Collegiate Revolution

THE DRAMATIC CHANGES that marked the new era of academia in the United States coincided with another profound change. Indeed, the processes inter-related with each other closely. What Roger Geiger describes as "the collegiate revolution" saw a transformation of student life in the late nineteenth and early twentieth centuries. Very quickly campuses everywhere exploded with new activities and organizations, most of them the work of students themselves. Student life became interesting. The long era of dull classrooms and staid cur-ricular fare that had claimed the greater part of students' attention gave way to an extracurriculum—social and intellectual—that offered young men and women choices aplenty. The decades of campus boredom that left a record of riots and rebellion yielded to a campus culture that offered big-time sports for emotional outlet, as well as other things to do for personal enrichment and comradeship. The University of Illinois reflected that pattern as much as any such institution in the United States.[1]

Further, as John R. Thelin denotes, the American college scene became a matter of interest to the American public generally. Articles about campus life abounded in popular newspapers like *The Independent*, and magazines like *Scribner's* and *McClure's* tracked the goings on and placed before the public eye the specter of a new American type, "the collegian." Many sought to define the "collegiate ideal"; clothing styles and fashion kept up the interest. (The Arrow shirt makers knew how to capitalize on the new imagery of the collegian and offered the "Arrow Shirt Man.") And thus while some generic forms emerged from the new culture, so also did particulars reign. These years saw students pick mascots to identify their schools apart from others and to give more pageantry to football games. (Intercollegiate rivalries were national news.) Students also chose school colors to make other marks of institutional differentiation. Hardly any college lacked a special song, an alma mater, that would now link the generations of students to come. Other school songs so proliferated in number as to yield music anthologies (with scores) that constituted a genre of their own.[2] (The third edition of *Illinois Songs* appeared in 1918.) With the collegiate revolution, all history is local. And in the early years of the twentieth century the University of Illinois became a dynamic and interesting place, and a genuine community.

First, a general portrait. When Edmund James assumed the presidency of the University of Illinois in 1904, the institution had 3,734 students, 722 of them, or 19 percent, women. When James retired in 1920, he was overseeing a campus with 9,208 students, 24.55 percent, virtually a quarter of them, females. The College of Liberal Arts and Science (including part of Household Science and Medical Preparatory) enrolled the largest number of students, 2,547, followed by Engineering, 1,768, then Agriculture, 1,215. In 1904, of those who earned degrees at Illinois, 272 came from the state and 44 came from outside Illinois. In 1918, those numbers had risen to 630 and 256. In fact, by that time 26 percent of UofI students came from beyond Illinois, a mark of the University's growing national reputation. One would also find 141 foreign students on the campus. China had sent 37 (all male), Japan 29, India 11, and Canada 10. And finally, indicating even more the growing prestige of the University, of the 188 graduate degrees granted in 1917, 100 went to students who had come from outside Illinois or from abroad. And they had studied in a great variety of programs.[3]

The student body was changing moderately in another way, with campus reconfiguration that reflected the change. Drawing largely from Illinois, and probably mostly outside of Chicago, students had affiliations with mostly Protestant denominations—Methodist heavily, and also Congregational and Presbyterian. At the time of James's arrival, Catholics numbered only 5 percent of the student body. But just at that time they began to establish campus organizations. Two students took the lead in forming the Spalding Guild, whose name honored an important liberal Catholic leader in the nation. In fact, Catholic students had already secured a large place in the leadership positions of students in their various organizations—the literary societies and the student newspaper. They participated widely on the university sports teams, too. In 1908 the Guild acquired its own quarters, Loyola House, at 1202 West Main in Urbana. It sponsored year-round activities—receptions, smokers, dances, picnics. In August 1917 Bishop Edmund M. Dunne of Peoria appointed Fr. John A. O'Brien to lead the effort, supported by the Knights of Columbus in Decatur, to establish a foundation for the religious education of Catholics. The bishop named St. John's Church in Champaign as the "university church." O'Brien took a defensive posture, alert and responsive to any anti-Catholic sentiments. Illinois had 262 Catholic students in 1917 and 14 Catholic professors, mostly of low academic rank.[4]

266　**PART IV. STUDENTS**

The earliest Jewish students at the University came mostly from small towns around the state, second generation in the United States and of German descent, most likely Reform Jews. Champaign and Urbana had a small Jewish population that included the prominent clothier Isaac Kuhn, a product of the Hebrew Union College in Cincinnati. President James encouraged the hiring of Jewish faculty, very much the exception to the prevailing practice at the time. James was broad-minded and ecumenical, and the University of Illinois demonstrated an openness to religious and ethnic diversity quite remarkable in American higher education. As earlier noted, appointments included Jewish professors like Jacob Zeitlin and Armin Koller in the humanities, an academic area considered by many a reserve of Protestant culture. The Menorah Society for Jewish students organized in 1912 and enrolled 75 of the 150 Jewish students on the campus. In the early twentieth century, the American Jewish population drew more heavily from Eastern Europe, representing the impact of the massive migrations from Russia and Poland (the Pale of Settlement) and coming more heavily from American cities, Chicago in this case. The Menorah Society formed a study circle, led by Ray Litman, which met at a local house. It focused on Jewish history and its contemporary relevance, and generally took a greater interest in intellectual and cultural matters than in religion as such.[5]

Ethnic cultures also found expression on the Illinois campus. The Chinese students, whom James, as noted, particularly cultivated, offered various entertainments. Their population had grown to about forty-five by 1912, and now included two women. They had a large clubhouse on East John Street. The students annually celebrated the Chinese New Year and on occasions they would invite the campus to their night of "Oriental games, music, and entertainment," including demonstrations of Oriental boxing or Chinese "magic." Nor did they neglect politics. In October 1917 they celebrated the revolution of 1911 that brought the downfall of the Manchu dynasty. For this occasion, they decorated their clubhouse with Illinois colors and displayed American and Chinese flags.[6]

• • •

The University of Illinois student body, throughout the James years and for a long time thereafter, remained overwhelmingly white in racial identity. African-American enrollment reflected the pattern nationally—a paucity of students attending in the Gilded Age and only slow progress in the Progressive Era. Ten Black students came to the campus in the Draper years, John A. Rogan the first to enroll but attending only one year. William Walter, the first African-American to graduate, earned an AB degree in Literature and Arts in 1900 and then a BS in Civil Engineering in 1907. Among Black women Maudelle Tanner Brown Bousfield led the way. Born in St. Louis in 1895, a

15. The Collegiate Revolution   267

musical prodigy as a teen, and with a will to succeed even as the first woman of her race at the University, she enrolled in 1903. She earned her BA degree in three years and graduated in the third year of James's presidency. She went on to have a distinguished career in education and lived to 1971. In 2013 the University of Illinois opened a new residence facility and named it Bousfield Hall.[7] These students seem to have had a general acceptance by their white colleagues. But racial insensitivity did find expression once in a while. A student writer might use the term "darkies" and the *Illinois Magazine* feature a black-face musician on its cover, with no likelihood of censure or complaint for doing so.[8]

The situation for Black students in American colleges and universities set against a background of historical change. The great promise of the Reconstruction Era, especially in the Thirteenth, Fourteenth, and Fifteenth Amendments to the Constitution, lay painfully unfulfilled. Indeed, they produced a reaction—from "Jim Crow" segregation laws in the southern states (sustained by the United States Supreme Court in 1896), to devices of disenfranchisement, to a horrible record of lynchings—that led historian Rayford Logan famously to label the last decades of the nineteenth century the "nadir of Negro history" in America. The Progressive Era brought little improvement. Indeed, it saw the racial segregation of the federal government under President Woodrow Wilson. All these developments heightened racial consciousness among African-Americans. And they in turn affected American higher education.

Blacks had always employed defensive strategies to confront the realities of their situation in American life. One effort pointed to creating new, separate institutions, parallel to those whites had established. Richard Allen set the pattern when he created the African Methodist Episcopal Church (AME) in Philadelphia in response to whites' action against Blacks in their Philadelphia church in 1816. Also, the Negro colleges grew in number after the Civil War. Fraternal organizations of various kinds materialized, providing social opportunities and outlets for civic and political engagement. In 1906 African-American women created the National Association of Colored Women's Clubs, which, too, reflected "a century-old African-American strategy by creating parallel structures of their own."[9]

Historical circumstances dictated another theme of this era, the commitment to "racial uplift." Especially for educated, professional African-Americans, anxiety about the quality of life among the generality of their race in the United States led them to programs of social, cultural, and intellectual improvement. "For the good of the race" became a by-word of this effort. But this matter also spoke to some social tensions in the Black population. An elite leadership emerged, one that wanted to offer to the nation the image of a particular group, marked by its education and its professional accomplishments. That group felt alienated from the Black masses, often seen as deprived

268 PART IV. STUDENTS

but also depraved. Creation of Sigma Pi Phi by physician Henry McKee Minton in 1904 reflected these concerns. For this Philadelphia organization, which won familiarity as "the Grand Boulé," Minton sought congeniality but also culture, a fraternal group of "accomplished black men."[10] And when the NACWC formed, the northern women who led it offered their own models of education, culture, and refinement to train the Black masses.[11] These ambitions acquired a special emphasis when seen against Black America's leading intellectual, W. E. B. DuBois, above all in his specification of the "Talented Tenth" as the leadership basis for progress and improvement among the people of his race.

In terms of education, this emerging concern often led Black leaders to look beyond the dominant course set by the independent Negro colleges that formed after the Civil War: Fisk in 1866; Howard 1867; Morehouse 1867; Hampton Institute 1867; Tuskegee, 1881. By this time forty-five black colleges and universities existed. Overwhelmingly, with Howard the major exception, these schools placed heavy emphasis on industrial training, reflecting the powerful influence of Booker T. Washington, founder of Tuskegee. Graduation from any of the independent schools, gaining in numbers, especially in the South, supplied a mark of distinction and prestige. Even more so did a degree from the northern schools, open to all races but almost universally white in the student enrollments. The trickle of Black students at these schools through the nineteenth century did yield to increases in the next, yet still at a slow pace. These scholars seldom met outright hostility from the others on their campuses. Rather, they were largely just ignored. They did not receive invitations to take part in the collegiate revolution that so thoroughly redefined student life in the institutions they attended, whether in the social clubs, in the music, literary, and other cultural outlets, or in athletics. The means by which Black male and female students adapted to these conditions gave rise to Black fraternities and sororities and made them central to Black higher education, at Illinois and elsewhere.

When Black men attending Cornell University found themselves excluded from the Greek houses there, they organized their own unit, Alpha Phi Alpha, in 1906. The first Greek-letter society for African-Americans thus appeared at a northern "white" school, and it registered another theme that historians of these groups have perceived as beginning here—that is, the self-help imperative in the segregationist environment against which Black students defined their place on campus. Whereas a racial uniformity existed at the Negro colleges, circumstances there did not compel this defensive recourse and commitment to "the good of the race" that gave a raison d'être to Black Greek life. At Indiana University five years later ten Black students, the only ones on campus, founded Kappa Alpha Psi. Thereafter Howard University led in these organizational efforts. For Black female students Alpha Kappa

15. The Collegiate Revolution   269

Originally Kappa Alpha Nu, pictured here in about 1919, Kappa Alpha Psi fraternity represented the first organization of African-American identity at the UofI. Courtesy of the University of Illinois Archives.

Alpha, founded at Howard in 1908, led in the movement to establish sororities. The service motif stood large in the life of the Black Greek-letter houses, contrasting to the priority of social life among those run by white students. In this way Black campus activity reflected continuity with African-American life outside. From the beginning the Black fraternities and sororities "modeled their core values after the benevolent societies, fraternal orders, churches, and civic associations common to black communities in that era."[12]

The James years saw slow expansion in the numbers of African-American students, of which only about one in seven graduated with earned degrees. One did so in 1906, and two in 1907 and 1908. Five graduated in 1914, and six in 1918, which marked the most of this race during James's presidency.[13] Here and there in the James years, one sees Black students participating in the collegiate revolution. They were most likely to be in athletics, but withal they had a very low representation. Albert Lee (see below) refers to Black prize winners in boxing and tennis. He also confirms that African-American fraternities participated widely in the intramural athletic competition. Hiram R. Wheeler quarterbacked the 1906 football team and others won letters on various university teams.[14]

In scholarly achievement J. Ernest Wilkins won Phi Beta Kappa honors in 1918. He went on to earn a law degree at the University of Chicago and then practiced law, working for the cause of labor. President Eisenhower appointed Wilkins Assistant Secretary of Labor, the first African-American to have a sub-cabinet position in the U.S. government. Wilkins also served prominently on the U.S. Civil Rights Commission, and became the first African-American to head the Judicial Council of the Methodist Church.[15]

The situation for most Black students at Illinois posed critical problems. When they arrived on campus they, like the white students, had no university housing to accommodate them. But they did not, like their white counterparts, have the range of the twin cities to seek housing. The north area of Champaign (the "North Side") had a concentrated African-American population. Many in that community welcomed the new students and arranged for them to reside in their homes. These citizens surely felt a commitment to race improvement as the students themselves did. And, as Vanessa Rouillon writes: "The African-American community made it possible for students to receive their education at one of the premiere universities in the country." But this reality of residential segregation prevailed for a long time.[16]

These circumstances prepared the way for the creation of Black fraternities and sororities at the University. As much as they did elsewhere the societies broke the pattern of detached and isolated students living in separate homes, and furthermore addressed the long-standing problem at Illinois—that of campus housing. Shortly after its beginning at Indiana, Alpha Kappa Nu (changed in 1915 to Alpha Kappa Psi) was founded at Illinois, the first Black fraternity on campus, and offering the only accommodations for African-American students there. Alpha Phi Alpha, following its beginning at Cornell, set up at Illinois in 1917. Kappa Alpha began the same year and then Omega Psi Phi. For Black females, Alpha Kappa Alpha, which had its origins at Howard University in 1908, opened the new directions, chartered at UofI in 1913.[17] J. Ernest Wilkins had membership in Alpha Kappa Psi, to whose national organization he gave years of service. And Maudelle Tanner Brown Bousfield joined Alpha Kappa Alpha.[18] The societies provided pockets of cohesiveness to a small racial component of the Illinois student body. But they did not advance the campus in inclusiveness. One can stroll through the issues of the *Illio* yearbooks in these years and find all-white racial compositions in the several dozens of student literary, social, athletic, and professional groups. The Black students appear almost entirely with their respective fraternities and sororities. The white students generally did not show hostility to their Black classmates, but neither did they reach out to them. Mostly, it seems, they ignored them.

In the James years and well beyond them Black students at Illinois had a very good friend, a man who became a legendary figure on the campus. Albert R. Lee was born on a farm near Champaign in 1874. He attended local schools, including Champaign High School. He attended classes at the University for only a year, in 1897–1898, and then studied on his own, returning later for a few more courses on campus. But Lee became known to President Draper, who appointed him as messenger. President James reappointed him as Assistant

15. The Collegiate Revolution   **271**

Clerk and then two years later made him Clerk. James's successor David Kinley promoted Lee to Chief Clerk. Lee would remember that heretofore the people in the administration generally referred to him as "the boy." Kinley insisted he be called "Mr. Lee." Lee went on to serve six U of I presidents altogether, until his retirement in 1942.[19]

Lee gained the unofficial title "Dean of the Colored Students." He often gave the African-Americans their first experience of the campus, for he played a major role in helping them with the challenge of housing. Lee knew the families of the North Side who made rooms in their homes available to the new arrivals. He himself lived in that area, with his wife Maude and their three children at 605 North Water Street. (His home was designated a historical site in 1976 by the Bicentennial Committee of Champaign County.) In his Clerk's office, Lee kept records of the Black students, especially concerning matriculation and graduation. And for a host of other matters the Black students at Illinois knew that in Lee they had a friend, one readily available for them. Lee fully exemplified the service ideal of Black leadership. He gave years of work to the local Bethel AME Church, where he sang with the choir for thirty-six years. His commitments also extended to the local chapter of the NAACP and to the work of the local Republican Party. In 2019 the University staged a special tribute to Lee.[20]

• • •

All students at the University of Illinois had one thing in common: Thomas Arkle Clark. Himself an Illinois graduate, he had grown up under strict religious controls, orphaned at a young age, and then, on return to Illinois as a rhetoric professor, falling under President Draper's increasing reliance upon him in dealing with students.[21] President James made Clark dean of men, the first designation of its kind in American colleges, in 1909. More than just a large institutional presence, Clark did all in his power to make himself nationally known. He succeeded splendidly, this "dean of deans," as one historian has titled him. Others called him "the Pioneer," for Clark did more than anyone to shape this still new office on the American campus. Clark used public appearances, media outlets, and convention papers (and later the radio) to broadcast wide and far his little sermons and homilies on character and the principles of behavior that would assure that you succeed in life. At Illinois, all knew his Sunday eight o'clock lectures. Then in 1911 he began what became a staple at Illinois, his "Facts for Freshmen" handbook, laying out the rules and regulations of the campus, with admonitions about this and that to guide all students through their new institutional environment. He watched vigilantly to protect the moral health of the students, using Pinkerton detectives to assure that those under his wing did not frequent the bars and whorehouses that flourished on the campus perimeter. Clark, as Robert Schwartz observes, led

272   PART IV. STUDENTS

the institution as dean at a time when, in the new era of research and scholarship, faculty lost connection with the lives of students outside the classroom; they served no longer as their moral watch guards. A new responsibility now emerged, one taken on by the deans of students.[22]

Clark had a favorite campus outlet in the *Illinois Magazine*. In fact, when the journal renewed in 1910 Clark placed a hefty piece in the first issue. Titled "Studies and Other Things," the disquisition showed how astutely Clark read the changing times. He urged students to give highest priority, yes, to their studies, but also to the "other things." By that reference Clark meant all that constituted the collegiate revolution. You must do more than academic work, Clark wrote, because "[t]he college life is as much community life as that which any man will ever live." The college ethic speaks to individual priority in study but to communal priority in the array of organizations and activities that now define the contemporary American university. Clark urged the point: "In a college community no man can live to self alone." Learning, he need not have told the students, prepares the way for your career success; but so also does "social training." Your learning, then, has two components: ideas and principles, the work of the classroom, on the one hand; and work with people, which comes from engagement with the larger campus life, on the other. Clark mentioned literary and debating societies as well as religious groups, on campus and in local churches. As in this essay, there often emerged in Clark's writings the influences of the Social Gospel and its communal ethic, and Progressivism with its models of the organic community in priority to the counter ethic of the autonomous individual.[23]

• • •

In 1908 a young man fresh from the farms in the west central part of the state arrived at the campus of the University of Illinois. His name was Joseph Allan Nevins. He had grown up on the family homestead in Camp Point, born there in 1890. The paternal side of the family had Scottish roots, his father Joseph Nevins a severe Presbyterian who set the tone of family life. His mother, the former Emma Stahl, had German roots. Family history traced a series of moves, after the original immigration to America in the 1840s, that brought the Nevinses ultimately to Camp Point. The father's Calvinist commitments included a serious interest in religious thought, and he established in the home a personal library that swelled with books of that kind. But it had works in Victorian literature, too. Young Allan, as he was called, here found for himself his needed escape from the monotony and drudgery of a hard farm life. He thrilled to the works of Sir Walter Scott and added Victor Hugo as another favorite. He derived from literature as well a cultivation of the emotions that would shape the prolific career in scholarship that was now to begin at his new university. His experience of reading Dickens's *David*

15. The Collegiate Revolution   **273**

Copperfield and *Dombey and Son* remained forever in his memory.[24] Nevins stayed with literature as his academic focus at Illinois. He earned Phi Beta Kappa honors and graduated in 1912. He greatly admired Stuart Sherman and the two maintained a communication in the years ahead. But at Illinois Nevins also made his entry into the study of history, and it became in a few years his lifetime passion. Clarence Alvord and Evarts B. Greene influenced him most, and Greene became his colleague later when Nevins joined the history department at Columbia in 1925. He wrote of Alvord, Greene, and Sherman: "Anyone in my day at the University of Illinois could find at least three examples of what a wise, ripe, exact scholar could be." Nevins stayed a year at Illinois to earn a master's degree, but forsook further university study to launch a career in journalism. Always preoccupied with politics, Nevins had early become attracted to the reforming journalists of the day, individuals like Ida Tarbell. For several years Nevins wrote for various publications—the *Evening Post*, the *Nation*, the New York *World*, and the New York *Herald Tribune*, where he served as book editor.[25]

Nevins's career, for several reasons, informs this story and he will figure largely in the remaining narrative. First, within a few years after finishing his studies at Illinois, and living in New York City, Nevins began a correspondence with President James about writing a history of the University. James wanted Nevins to join the Illinois faculty, but did not make an offer sufficiently enticing to him. But in the end James arranged to send materials to Nevins and the young scholar took up the project at a furious pace. He had recently written his first book, a biography of Robert Rogers, of French and Indian War fame. The history of the University, simply titled *Illinois*, became part of a series of books on major American universities. In this case, Illinois's history had the perspective of a writer who had experienced the institution first hand and much of it within recent memory. Nevins included a lengthy chapter on students. It provides useful material—description, analysis, assessment—for this section.[26]

Second, Nevins served on the staff of the *Daily Illini*, the campus newspaper, and on that of the *Illinois Magazine*, the student literary outlet. These roles gave him campus-wide visibility and, of course, underscored his plans for a career in journalism. The campus paper constituted a major component of the collegiate revolution. It served, like intercollegiate sport, to create a sense of community as American higher education, marked noticeably by the large state universities, rushed headlong into the era of mass education. In his senior year Nevins exercised his influence as director of the DI's editorials.

And third, in a career of prodigious and wide-ranging historical scholarship, Nevins gave recurring attention to the subject of American higher education. The state university and its relationship to democracy provided him a subject worthy of his close interrogation. And within that story Nevins believed that

274   **PART IV. STUDENTS**

his alma mater Illinois had, from the beginning, a special and important place. His DI editorials addressed this topic repeatedly, as did his later literary efforts. In his chapter on students for his *Illinois* book, Nevins described some general characteristics of a group he knew first hand. He saw a practical-minded body of young people, seriously attentive to tasks at hand but lacking in high purpose and a sense of transcendent value about their academic work. "In a word, the Illinois student is industrious and energetic, but a little wanting in imagination," he wrote. Nevins located this habit in the students' social backgrounds: "middle-class homes with little leisure for ideals, dreams, and ambitions." The students still came, he observed, from communities relatively new and unsettled and having a "comparative poverty of cultural and civic institutions." Nevins rendered this judgment: "The atmosphere of the State University is fundamentally rather unfavorable to eager, speculative minds. The earnestness of those who value knowledge as a means of getting on is not encouraging to the disinterested spirits who value it for its own sake." Nevins saw some hope of a correction to this defect, however, in the growing wealth of the state and the derivation of more of the students from urban cultural centers like Chicago and St. Louis.[27]

Nevins did, also, find some welcome, healthy characteristics in the general student body. An effective social egalitarianism prevailed, he asserted. Class distinctions and social backgrounds did not mean much, and Nevins contrasted this generalization with social class distinctions that did weigh heavily at the older eastern colleges. Illinois students, Nevins found, lacked the social sophistication and discrimination that nourished class consciousness. Again, social background figured largely: Coming from "farms, villages, and towns smaller than Peoria," he observed, Illinoisans had not experienced elegant theater or gay restaurants or other "complex facets of our civilization" that foster class differentiation. They had a kind of "unworldly" quality about them, Nevins thought. But this "fresh naïveté" "makes the University a pleasant place for the average impressionable youth," he believed.[28]

Nevins's intellectual life showed remarkable diversity. His early work reflected the influence of his Illinois teacher Clarence Alvord, especially his American Commonwealth series. Nevins wrote *The American States During and After the Revolution, 1775–1789* (1924) and *The Emergence of Modern America, 1865–1878* (1927). Major contributions came in Nevins's two-volume biography of Grover Cleveland, for which Nevins won the 1932 Pulitzer Prize in history. More honors followed with his *Hamilton Fish: The Inner History of the Grant Administration*, which also won the Pulitzer, in 1937. Nevins entered into greater controversy when he undertook a major revision of American business history. He intended to mark the positive contributions of business leaders to American society and to the growth and strength of the United States in the world. Here Nevins set himself against many in the history profession and against sensationalist journalists like Henry Demarest Lloyd, Lincoln Steffens, Ida Tarbell, and Upton Sinclair. Nevins's *Abram S. Hewitt* (1935) started the effort at rehabilitation. Following it came the blockbuster biography of John D. Rockefeller. Nevins worked closely with the Rockefeller family, who, quite frankly, wanted a book that would counteract all that had made the oil titan a hated public figure in America. *John D. Rockefeller: The Heroic Age of American Enterprise*, in two volumes, appeared in 1940. Nevins also coauthored three books on Henry Ford. He wrote often on public affairs, supporting the New Deal, defending the Anglo-American affiliation and the British influence on American history, supporting internationalism in foreign affairs, and taking stances on American presidential politics. He staunchly endorsed fellow Illinoisan Adlai Stevenson for president (three times) and John F. Kennedy in 1960, although Nevins's sympathies lay usually with the Republicans. He was always strongly anti-communist, even in his defense of the war in Vietnam. Just two years before his 1962 return to Illinois Nevins had published the fifth book in his magisterial study of the Civil War, *The Ordeal of the Union*. Three more volumes would follow. In his time Allan Nevins was certainly one of the most widely read historians in the United States.[29]

• • •

Both President James and Nevins cited a proliferation of student groups and activities at Illinois. They fell into categories. The oldest group consisted of the literary societies, the ones for men and the ones for women. Another group, associated with the various academic programs at the University, reflected the changed conditions that marked the new American university. James especially took pride in this group. It included such organizations as the Botanical Club, the Classical Club, the History Club, the English Journal Club, the Political Science Club. The Engineering programs had yielded the Electrical Engineering Society, the Physics Colloquium, and student branches of national organizations and Greek-letter professional societies. The School of Agriculture had the Horticultural Club, the Hoof and Horn Club, the Soils Research Club, the Household Science Club, and others. Some of the student organizations attained large campus visibility. The University Choral and Orchestral Society, the Women's Glee Club, and regimental bands of the Military program put on annual performances for the University public. So did the dramatic groups: the Mask and Bauble Club, the Pierrots, and the Illinois Drama Federation. A Poetry Society formed in 1917. And if none of these academic auxiliaries suited your taste you could join the Rifle Club, the Chess Club, or the Motorcycle Club.[30]

Student demands for an expanded social component in their undergraduate experiences brought a large growth in social fraternities and sororities. This third group significantly changed the campus. When James arrived, these

276   PART IV. STUDENTS

organizations had already posited a long history at the University of Illinois.[31] Between 1900 and 1905, the number of social fraternities tripled. This growth came from various influences. It derived partly from the fact that fraternities and sororities, filling an emotional gap created by absence from home and family, met the psychological and social needs of young people. By about 1910, fraternities assumed a commanding position in campus life. Another reason for this development lay in the continuing need for decent student housing. Enrollment at Urbana increased rapidly in the early twentieth century, making Illinois the fifth largest university in the United States (behind NYU, Columbia, California, and Michigan State). By 1920 the student body was the third largest in the nation. The University lacked dormitories until a late date, and residents of Champaign and Urbana, two oversized villages, could accommodate only a limited number of roomers and boarders. Thus, fraternities arose to meet a desperate need for decent living space.[32]

The attitudes of the administration also aided the prominence of the fraternities. Draper and the two presidents from 1904 to 1930, Edmund J. James and David Kinley, favored fraternities, and Dean Clark, who bore the major responsibility for them, enthusiastically supported the Greek system. Clark endorsed the values they espoused, and he found it easier to control organized groups of young men than a motley collection of independents. He was uncomfortable in dealing with young women, and assigned their supervision to a dean of women.[33] At Illinois, the men's houses grew from twelve to thirty-nine under James and the women's from five to fourteen. As a result, in 1916 Illinois allegedly became the "fraternity capital of the world," toppling Cornell from its supremacy in this area.[34] Twenty-eight men's national social fraternities formed chapters on the campus; of these, Triangle (1907) and Alpha Rho Chi (1914) originated at Illinois and spread to other institutions.

Nevins observed some of this "phenomenal development" and for the most part gave it his blessing. The Greeks, he said, upheld high standards of scholarship; they reflected a social "democracy"; and they influenced a "great public spirit" around the campus. Both he and James highlighted the impressive architectural impact of the new structures built for these young men and women. With their old English, Italian Renaissance, Tudor, and Georgian styles, splendid to behold from the outside, these large houses adorned the expanding campus. The interiors had "luxuries"—libraries and billiard rooms—not available in the dormitories. Both Nevins and James knew that a bad history marked the early years of Greek life. Drinking, gambling, and hazing had plagued administrations along the way. But these sordid practices were now fading. Nevins gave Dean Clark much credit for his "tact and shrewdness" in bringing a new era into existence. President James, resolved from the beginning to bring about change, also worked effectively in the effort, Nevins believed.[35]

• • •

Student life showed great variety. Students from minority religious and ethnic groups, including those from foreign lands, became numerous in the early twentieth century, and naturally they sought to establish their own identities in the dominant white, Anglo-Saxon, Protestant campus culture by banding

Club Latino, ca. 1919. Students often formed organizations that reflected their ethnic, national, or regional identity on the campus. Courtesy of the University of Illinois Archives.

Polonia Club, ca. 1918. Courtesy of the University of Illinois Archives.

together. Thus, there formed the Chinese Students' Club (fifty-five students, all male), and new ones speaking for Japanese, Polish, Hindustani, and other distinctive groups. Ethnic and cultural diversity flourished in such organizations as the Deutsche Verein, the Cercle Français, and the Centro Literario Español. Many students from states outside of Illinois often felt their commonalities with each other and formed groups like the Missouri Club. Southern students had their Dixie Club. And, if any individuals could not exactly match his or her specific ethnic or geographical identity, they could join the Cosmopolitan Club!

In its religious life, the Illinois campus saw its most prominent change in the rise of the YMCA and YWCA as student affiliations. In 1877 the national YMCA, formed five years earlier, moved into campus life, organizing some four hundred chapters around the country. From thence, according to Geiger, they "grew like wildfire" and by century's end forty-two thousand students had joined over five hundred chapters. They had visible strength at the growing state universities especially. A 1908 survey at these schools found that 60 percent of students there reported having church memberships and that on these campuses the YMCA could expect to enlist a quarter of men students and a half of the women in Bible studies. The YMCA represented the evangelical wing of the campuses, an ecumenical Protestantism, sponsoring Bible readings and revivals, and working for the moral straight path of the students in its midst. At Illinois, the Y had secured a foothold at the time of James's arrival. Under James YMCA and YWCA growth accelerated. Both organizations erected new buildings that housed dormitories, parlors, game rooms, libraries, cafeteria and dining rooms, and spaces for meetings. In 1913–1914 Illinois had the largest YMCA collegiate membership in the nation, with nearly three thousand students before the war. The YWCA had 516 members that year. At Illinois and on American campuses generally the Ys effectively integrated religion into the official secular culture and the modern curriculum of the new public university.[36]

At Illinois and elsewhere, entertainments of all kinds flourished on the new campus, and off campus, too. In town the pleasure seekers could enjoy two movie and play theaters, too. As for dances, student groups sponsored them all the time. (In March 1912 alone Illinoisans could attend the Chemistry Dance, the Law Dance, the Glee Club Easter Dance, and the Annual Irish Banquet.) On the rest of the calendar, you wouldn't want to miss the Ag Dance, the Law Dance, the Chem Dance, or the Engineering Dance. At the UofI, the students danced, and they danced, and they danced. Formal events like the Sophomore Cotilion, the Junior Prom, and the Military Ball also attracted them. There were other outlets: the Orange and Blue Dancing Club; the Varsity Dancing Club; the College Dancing Club; the Crystal Dancing Club; the Onyx Dancing Club; and the Gridiron Dancing Club.

15. The Collegiate Revolution   279

THE TANGO TEA

"Mamma, may I go to the Tango Tea?"
Asked the maiden in manner prairful.
"Yes, dear, but tho you can't be good,
For the love of Mike, be careful."

A *Siren* cover page. Courtesy of the University of Illinois Archives.

Women offered two big annual events: the Maypole Dance and the Girls' Annual Stunt Show. "Smokers"—informal social gatherings for men—were also big-time. Within a two-week span in October 1919 five different campus organizations sponsored one.

All these new entertainments contributed to the decline of student rioting and campus pranks. None, however, seemed quite to have that effect so much as sports. Especially in two towns with few big-city amusements available, sports answered the social needs of many Illinois students.[37] University officials encouraged greater physical activity among students and inter-campus competitions among them proved to be one way of doing it. James was constantly encouraging students to be less spectators and more participants. Intramural athletics took place as organized games between Greek houses, between the classes, and between different student societies. Nevins counted

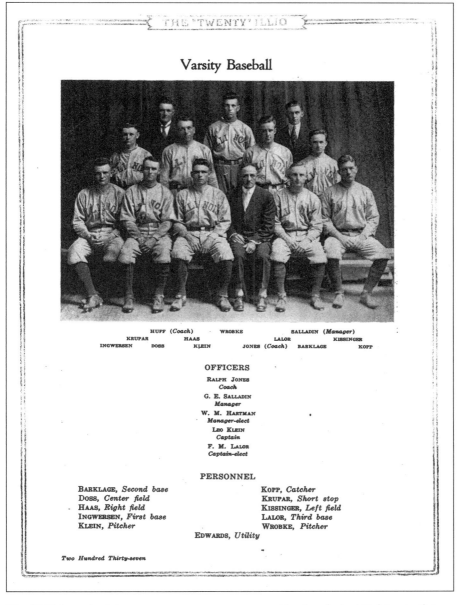

The 1919 baseball team won seven games and lost only to Michigan, the conference champion. This picture shows legendary coach George Huff (top row, far left). Courtesy of the University of Illinois Archives.

this phenomenon among the marks of an improving university environment and gave much credit to the organizing role of George Huff, "not merely as an efficient director of athletics, but as a man whose influence upon the moral standards of members of University teams had been of the highest sort." On a nice spring day one could see Illinois Field and the wide south campus swelled with tennis players, lacrosse teams, baseball players, and others.[38]

Of course, nothing entertained like big-time sports. Intercollegiate competition in the United States dated back to 1869 and for a few decades baseball ignited the most public interest. It evolved into mass entertainment and captured the attention of newspaper readers all over the country. By the end of the century football could claim greatest interest among competitive colleges and universities. James welcomed football and other intercollegiate sports, as they encouraged a wider participation from students. But football created a mass of spectators. Nevins reported fifteen thousand people, students and public, attending a Saturday afternoon game in Champaign as Illinois increasingly established intense rivalries with other universities. (And only three years after James left the University the campus introduced the massive Memorial Stadium, able to hold some seventy-five thousand people.) Events moved quickly along the lines of this competition and eventuated in creation of the Big Ten athletic conference, another hallmark of the James years at Illinois. And the president rather rejoiced in the success of the Fighting Illini: in baseball, a record of 161 wins and 55 losses during his administration; in football, 82 wins, 26 losses, and 8 ties.[39]

• • •

Student journalism became another enterprise of the new American university. The campus newspaper, the *Illini*, debuted in 1874. It grew steadily in frequency of appearance and in 1903 became the *Daily Illini*. An aspiring journalist, Allan Nevins joined the paper's staff as a reporter and became manager of its editorials during his senior year. He had an interest in the paper's history as well as in the directions it might now pursue, and in 1912 he wrote for the new alumni quarterly a forty-year history of the paper, which, he then observed, had won a ranking as one of the top five student newspapers in the country. Along the way it had established a large base of advertisers that enabled the increased frequency of printing. For head staff members the DI was a money opportunity and "a prize worth fighting for," said Nevins. Whereas it had early on heavily featured literary entrees it now gave its attention overwhelmingly to news, mostly from the campus. The DI, located in the Law Building and then moved in 1911 to the basement of the University Building, had made itself "the vital center of student life," Nevins remarked, a medium for discussion of campus matters "unifying the student body and uniting them with the faculty and with the spirit of the institution." Reinforcing that role, the University

282   PART IV. STUDENTS

also had another student publication, the *Illinois Magazine* (sometimes titled *The Illinois*), debuting in 1904 and also a financial success, with leadership roles by Carl Van Doren and Avery Brundage.[40] A humorous publication, the *Siren*, arrived in 1911. The yearbook had the title *The Illio*. More specialized outlets included the *Agriculturalist* and the *Technograph*.

Student experience with the *Illinois Magazine* launched another literary career. Mark Van Doren, one of Carl's younger brothers, wrote extensively for the publication and became its editor his senior year. Mark, Class of 1914, had the same recollections of growing up on the family farm in Hope and then in Urbana as those of his brother Carl. "We were a reading family," he wrote, and Mark became a reader at age four. Like all the boys he did farm chores. (But Mark and a friend also earned a little cash for themselves when they arranged to take the laundry of two women neighbors to have it cleaned and then returned by the boys. One of the women in this scheme was Isabel Bevier, head of the home economics department!) But reading governed Mark's early life also: Scott, Dickens, Thackeray, Twain, and many others. Mark's University of Illinois education resembled brother Carl's in another way—in the immense influence of Stuart Sherman. Mark took Sherman's course on Shakespeare. He saw in the classroom a teacher whose words barely outran his thoughts, his mind "a critical and a creative element." But you would find Sherman most of the time at his typewriter, Mark wrote later. He found great joy in writing. Mark Van Doren said of Sherman: "If there is such a thing as a born writer he was one." And of Sherman's private letters: they "are among the best, I think, ever written in America."[41]

Literature had now become Mark's great love and he stayed another year to secure a master's degree.[42] He served in an army office during the war, took a tour of Europe, and then enrolled for doctoral work at Columbia, joining his brother. Mark, also like Carl, pursued journalism and became literary editor of the *Nation*, 1924–1928. When it came to the world of letters Mark Van Doren was a man for all seasons. He did literary criticism and literary biography. He edited anthologies, and wrote a novel and books of poetry. When he graduated from Illinois his mother gave him the collected works of Nathaniel Hawthorne, and in 1949 he published a biography of Hawthorne. In 1939 Mark Van Doren won the Pulitzer Prize for his *Collected Poems, 1922–1938*, the year after his brother won the Pulitzer for his biography of Franklin.

• • •

From here this chapter will take a closer look at student life by way of the *Daily Illini*. The academic year 1911–1912 will provide much of the perspectives. It represented the halfway point of James's presidency. More importantly, Allan Nevins became editor of the *Summer Illini* for 1911, then, in his senior year, served as chief news manager and then editorial page manager. We have thus

15. The Collegiate Revolution   283

an overview of student affairs and a glimpse at the early intellectual career of one of the University's most famous alumni.

On any given day (but no publication on Monday) a reader of the DI would find a rather standard format. Page one had five long columns: sports teams results; reports of a new play by a student group; plans for a new campus building; what's up at the YMCA. Pages two and three gave their space almost entirely to ads: clothes cleaners; a florist; a sports equipment store; the Beardsley Hotel; the Urbana Banking Company; this evening's play at the Orpheum or the Illinois theaters. "Exchange News" (sometimes "News of the Colleges") reported on matters involving other universities (interesting items posted here). On page four was a list of the DI staff and then the day's editorials. This page also had the "Local and Personal" postings: "H. J. Smith '14 of Lincoln, Illinois has withdrawn from the University." "George Nutt, '13, has returned from a week-end visit to his home at Kankakee." The page also had a large ad by J. M. Kaufman, "Champaign's Largest Store": "Follow the Path of the Best Dressed Men." Classified ads ("For Sale"; "To Rent") followed on pages five, seven, or eight. Found there also was the University Calendar with the week's events. And you could not miss the half-page ad by F. K. Robeson Drug Store on Church Street. Here you can buy Pond's vanishing cream for 15 cents and Sanitol tooth paste for 19 cents.

The YMCA sponsored one of the big campus events of 1911–1912. By then it had become a large, ecumenical religious organization. Anyone could obtain a "General" membership, although "Full" membership went to those who could show involvement with an evangelical church. The *Student Handbook* for this year listed six main purposes of the Y, including: "To unite all of the men of the University who are either followers of Jesus Christ or in sympathy with Him and His program," and "To counteract and overcome the forces or influences which tend to disintegrate character, faith and influence." And just a few years before, in 1908, the Y had made itself a large physical presence on the Illinois campus with the construction of its "enormous" new building, on the corner of Wright and John Streets. Named Association Hall, this edifice had forty-two dormitory rooms, the University's first housing arrangement for students. In the basement one found a barber shop, cafeteria, lunchroom, "smoking" room, and bowling alley. On the first floor, the new Y had an auditorium that could seat 450 people, and a reading room and library that made available "hometown" newspapers from around the state. The second floor had offices and guest rooms.[43]

The big event for the Y in 1911, the campus visit of John Raleigh Mott, has a larger religious and intellectual context. The YMCA, at the national and local levels, reflected and sponsored the liberal Protestantism that marked the major trend in Protestant thinking in the United States during the half-century following the end of the Civil War.[44] It incorporated modern science, especially

284   PART IV. STUDENTS

evolution, into its theology at the same time that it turned its attention to the social problems incidental to the industrial and urban age emerging in these years. The Y had always embraced a nurturing and protective posture toward its member students, from welcoming them to campus upon their arrival to helping them find employment while students. The Illinois Y now also turned its attention to its own social milieu. It moved out into Urbana and Champaign, where it worked to establish boys' clubs. It also made an outreach to industrial workers, and offered assistance to "foreigners" by helping them learn English. Dwight Lyman Moody's urban revivalism had inspired this new priority. Altogether it gave the Y a certain cast, a progressive character that fell short of the reformist bent of the larger Social Gospel program led by Washington Gladden, Walter Rauschenbusch, Richard T. Ely, and others. The Y did not threaten business; in fact, it had great support from businesses; it did not promote "socialism"; it was "safe."[45]

John R. Mott was the biggest name in the national YMCA. He had made a successful visit to the campus in 1901, so, much advanced notice attended his return in December 1911. Nevins and his staff covered the event in detail, and the paper distributed a special supplement for the various programs prepared by the University Christian Association. Mott, born in 1865, had grown up in Iowa and attended a small Methodist college before enrolling at Cornell University in New York. He became active in the YMCA there and embraced the work of Moody, though at first Mott and his friends committed themselves to missionary work. He earned Phi Beta Kappa honors, majoring in philosophy and history. In 1888 he began a service of twenty-seven years as national secretary of the Intercollegiate YMCA. Here Mott worked to orient the organization toward addressing the social ills of the commercial system. A prolific writer, he authored sixteen books and received recognitions for his work from nations around the world—Finland, Greece, Hungary, Japan, and Siam among them, and honorary degrees from six universities. In 1946 Mott shared the Nobel Prize for Peace. He championed the Social Gospel.[46]

The "Mott Campaign" began on December 16. It led off with a "Women's Meeting" and followed with other specialized audiences: athletes, men, Bible groups, and young people's societies in Champaign and Urbana. The DI called the first meeting "perhaps the largest number of women ever gathered together at the University." Special visitors also spoke and the YWCA Quartet furnished the music. The men had five separate meetings with Mott, attendants numbering about 1,500 in average. Mott also appeared at various local churches. The large program embraced by the campaign also included nine classes under faculty leadership.[47]

The campaign reveals much about the religious culture at the University of Illinois. And so does the reaction to it, as made by Nevins and the DI staff. First, they judged it a "huge success," then they gave it their endorsement.

15. The Collegiate Revolution   285

"The *Illini*," said its editorial page, "is fully in sympathy with the effort which the associations are making." "That Mr. Mott made an impression on the student consciousness is an entirely obvious fact. He made his appeal even to the most hypercritical student, to whom the ordinary evangelical methods are so much poppycock." Mott, the editors added, "won approval by his very liberal-mindedness, which placed essentials above creeds and dogmas."[48] From President James on down at Illinois many at the University welcomed religion "broad-minded" in its outlook. It expressed liberal Protestantism and looked beyond denominational markings to a common Christian sociology that gave the faith a proper contemporary relevance. Allan Nevins knew that he spoke for a good-sized part of the student body, with social and religious backgrounds such as his, when he offered an editorial titled "Church Going." "Of all the great advances in liberalism which the world has made since 1795," he wrote, "few have been greater and few more salutary than that in religious thought. Those of us who came up to the University from the confined surroundings of the little towns of the state, where dogmatism in creed has survived with that Puritanism in conduct which has been worthy of preservation at any cost, know with what a shock the infinitely richer and freer atmosphere of the churches here struck us; for the pulpits surrounding the institution are at once inspiring and wholesomely open to modern thought." Nevins judged this new condition part of "the invigorating independence" that described these students' university experiences.[49]

So, the YMCA and the YWCA helped to give Illinois student life something of a common culture but never so strongly as to prevent varieties within it. At the national level, denominational leaders were beginning now to look more closely at the fast-growing state universities around the country. They observed that often a state university might have more students of their own particular denominations attending it than an area college long under the auspices of that denomination.[50] Thus also, as noted, the Ys led in meeting a critical problem for the students—the housing situation. The new YMCA made a big step in addressing it, but it didn't dominate for long. Now the denominational houses began to enter the campus scene.

During this year of 1911–1912 the Presbyterians gave full example of the emerging trend. They built a new dormitory for women and they built a new church on the campus. The DI announced that "a project which will assist materially in fulfilling a long-felt want at the University is the new Presbyterian Hall at 805 South Fifth Street, a dormitory for young women," twenty-three to be precise. The project involved moving and reconfiguring the older Presbyterian House, and it cost $30,000. Several individuals and parties collaborated to see the work through: Dean Clark; the pastor of the University Presbyterian Church; the pastor of the First Presbyterian Church of Urbana; the Presbyterian Synod of Illinois; and the Young Women's Society

286 PART IV. STUDENTS

of the First Presbyterian Church of Champaign. The dormitory welcomed women students on a nonsectarian basis. The DI noted that "[t]he work was started largely at the request of President James, who realizes the need of such institutions."[51]

As this development proceeded Presbyterians moved on another front and announced plans for a new campus church. Located at the former site of Presbyterian House, the corner of Fifth and John Streets, and also costing $30,000, this enterprise came from the contribution of Republican Congressman William B. McKinley, a graduate of the University, long-standing friend, and a former trustee. He had gained his wealth in banking and in the building and operating of public utilities and bridges. The new church would have the McKinley name in honor of the congressman's father, the late George McKinley, former pastor of the First Presbyterian Church of Champaign. Dean Clark had a membership in the church. McKinley Memorial Presbyterian Church belonged to the Presbyterian Synod of Illinois, which would run its operations. Church officials announced their intention "to make a special effort to contribute to the social life of the students."[52]

Although President James envisioned a pluralistic religious community at the University he did have a partiality for the Methodists. His family history led him that way and he had membership in the First Methodist Church, Urbana. Parks Chapel stood at the corner of Mathews and Springfield streets and had an active leadership in Willard Nathan Tobie. A growing number of Methodist students from the University, representing the largest denomination among the student body, attended Parks. Tobie saw the need to provide for them, and he furthermore insisted that the Methodists all over the state had a responsibility for their children attending the state university. He wrote articles and spoke widely about this charge and went to regional conferences to promote it. From the beginning he had the cooperation of Thomas J. Burrill and some other Methodists on the faculty. The next step occurred in making Parks into a new church, at first called the Second Methodist Church of Urbana and then renamed Trinity Church in 1905. James and other faculty immediately joined it.[53]

But James wanted to do more. Fully aware of the collegiate revolution taking place around the country, he now talked to local people about creating a social place for Methodist students. It would stand apart from the church but have a clear connection to it. Hence there emerged the idea of a foundation and the beginnings of the Wesley Foundation at the University of Illinois. The idea did not have an easy time of it. Many Methodists from around the state saw the University as a secular institution unfriendly to religion. But the local people engaged the important support of Illinois Bishop William Fraser McDowell. The Wesley Foundation gained its charter in October 1913. Soon a new building appeared, on the corner of Wright and Goodwin streets, an appealing structure with late sixteenth-century effects grafted onto a medieval English frame. The building and its program served two purposes. It registered another social outpost for Illinois students, offering Friday night "socials" and sponsoring such events as an annual banquet (yet another) on the campus. It arranged to greet and assist newly arriving students and attend to those who had become sick. And it had an academic function along the lines that James had endorsed. It offered courses, taught in university classrooms. In 1919 the University Senate approved up to ten credits of such courses that students could apply toward graduation, when taught by qualified instructors. For decades this pattern of instruction in religion prevailed at the University of Illinois, where local religious bodies taught the courses. Not until the early 1970s did the UofI establish a Religious Studies program and then finally an autonomous Department of Religion in 2008.[54]

In contrast to earlier years, when personal friendships often led to organization of a fraternity, many groups established during this period represented religious, ethnic, or professional affiliations. Local social fraternities in particular reflected this trend, indicative of the growing diversity of the student body. The social societies established by religious groups like Presbyterian House included Bethany Circle (Disciples of Christ), Congregational House, and Seymour Guild House (later Osborne Hall, Episcopal). Congregational students formed the Bushnell Guild, the name honoring an important liberal Protestant theologian.

The first Roman Catholic fraternity at Illinois evolved from the Spalding Guild, founded by Catholic students in 1905, and from Loyola House, a center for Catholic students established in Urbana in 1908, which apparently housed some Catholic men. In 1912 a chapter of the national Catholic fraternity Phi Kappa was established, and in 1923 a second, Theta Kappa Phi. Jewish fraternities originated in the East when anti-Semitism became common in the early twentieth century, and they spread to Illinois when the increasing number of Jewish students gave rise to religious discrimination in Urbana. Local chapters of national Jewish fraternities included Zeta Beta Tau (1912), Alpha Epsilon Pi (1920), and Phi Epsilon Pi (1920). Local chapters of national Jewish sororities included Alpha Epsilon Phi (1920); local Jewish sororities were Delta Alpha Omega (1918) and Rho Beta Iota (1920). The Jewish sorority Delta Alpha Omega formed in 1918. Jewish students numbered about one hundred at that time. They acted in a self-conscious way when, during the war, they joined the fund-raising campaigns, but as a separate group. They sent money to national Jewish organizations led by Henry Morgenthau and Jacob Schiff.[55]

In all these developments President James took a keen interest and a supportive role. James highlighted the significance of religion in American higher education by including a five-day conference on religion in state universities,

288   PART IV. STUDENTS

involving more than twenty speakers, in his installation week in 1905. Shailer Mathews of the University of Chicago Divinity School, a rising influence in Protestant liberal theology, led the program. The conference received much attention.

James, always sensitive to the criticism that state universities fostered a secular culture and diminished religion by their very nature as nonsectarian, public institutions, contested those charges. He avowed that students at Illinois had as much commitment to Bible study and to church attendance as any segment of young people in the country, and he acknowledged the "extremely valuable work" being done by the YMCA and the YWCA on the Illinois campus. James wished, moreover, to have religion acquire a larger academic place in state universities. He urged that the various denominations cooperate in hiring instructors who would teach religion courses in which students could earn credit. We should give as much dedication and care to the study of religion, and especially religious history, as we do to the study of science, he said. Because religion, as much as engineering or agriculture, demands intellectual power and pedagogical skill. The different sectarian groups should also cooperate to build up on the campus the needed facilities to enhance the academic presence of religion, the president believed.[56]

• • •

When senior Allan Nevins took the editorial reins of the *Summer Illini* in 1911, he came out fighting. Recent criticism of the University had come from some state legislators and from the *Chicago Tribune*, rarely friendly to it. They had questioned some of the University's expenditures. President James had responded and, the student paper believed, convincingly. It discounted the mean assaults of these "reactionaries" and their "sensationalist" accusations. But it could see real damage at hand, and Nevins took the editorial page into high idealism and reminded readers of what was at stake. "There is nothing more practically wise and nothing more honorable to a state than the upholding and maintenance of a great university, a radiating center of knowledge to be its intellectual capital." The University, he urged, must stay its course and continue to advance the cause of "democratic intelligence."[57]

Nevins soon had to contend with another enemy of the University, one Richard Teller Crane, a "millionaire ironmaster and foe of college education." The previous year he had published a scathing invective. He seemed to have it in for all state universities, and he included Michigan along with Illinois in the pamphlet he issued in October 1911. Crane had been heard from before and now he went after the technical programs at each school, accusing that they had no public respect and had failed to place their students into useful employment. And furthermore, no one really wanted their agricultural graduates. Only "practical" farmers had any use, Crane proclaimed. The universities thus constituted gigantic frauds that steal the public's money. Crane renewed his assault in January. He said the University should be burned down and its money spent where it could do some good. Burt C. Powell, James's secretary, replied for the University, with statistical evidence against Crane's case. The DI reviewed the issue and then went into editorial mode. Crane, it said, offered only one-sided, selective reporting, only "such facts as served his purpose," thus yielding only "a distorted picture of actual conditions." Moreover, Crane, it added, had persuaded no one. But the January 10, 1912 issue of the paper decided to go easy on Crane. He had died just four days before.[58]

• • •

Amid all the new variety of student activities politics had a place. It's difficult to gauge how much the normal student took the measure of the national scene. Some students clearly did, and with commitment. The national Democratic and Republican Parties each had a local student "Club" that worked for its respective causes on the campus, and also maintained contacts with the party beyond campus. Illinois students had also formed a Lincoln League that aspired to expand political awareness and engagement among the students. Allan Nevins, the editor-in-chief, and his *Illinois Magazine* staff wanted it to overcome "our apathy" with respect to state and national politics. From its work should come a body of students who would strengthen their civic society in the years after their graduation. The League made Senator Robert La Follette of Wisconsin an "honorary member." It held annual elections for its eight officers, and in 1911 had a membership of 160 students, and growing. It also sent members to the Student Senate. Nevins joined this organization. He also ran for one of its offices, but lost.[59] The La Follette designation showed the progressive/reformist bent of the League.

All these groups' activities occurred as the United States anticipated a historic presidential election in 1912. A straw poll of student preferences gave overwhelming endorsement to Theodore Roosevelt of the break-away Bull Moose Party. He had 519 first-place votes. Independent "Fighting Bob" La Follette came in second with 197 first-place votes, and Democrat Woodrow Wilson third with 180. Incumbent Republican Howard Taft had only 111 first-place votes and Socialist Eugene Debs only 9. But when counted along with second- and third-place preferences the tally placed La Follette in a closer second place.[60] Notwithstanding the abysmal showing of the Socialists, Vice President Kinley called the students into the Assembly the next week and lectured them on the dangers of socialism. He used Milwaukee as an American example of socialism at work and judged its record a failure. He got this subject all wrong.[61]

But perhaps something else had led Kinley to express his fears. At the beginning of the year the *Illini* had brought up the subject of socialism. It noted

290   PART IV. STUDENTS

the recent forming of the Intercollegiate Socialist Society of America and the convention it had held in New York City. It attracted student supporters from thirty-four different universities. An Illinois branch also formed. The *Illini* editors gave no endorsement to the movement but did convey the sense that Illinois ought to be in discussion with other universities about the subject. So, they called for some organizing for the study of socialism. "Societies formed for the study of such a great and fundamental human movement as socialism really is," they wrote, " . . . can hardly do any harm."[62] Sometime thereafter such an organization did form, and in fact called itself the Socialist Study Club. It is noted that it did not convene on the campus, but had its earliest sessions at the Unitarian Church of Urbana. Otto Beyer from the Department of Railway Engineering won election as the group's president and H. Amsterdam, an assistant in the library, as vice president. Lucile Bradley from the Class of 1918 gained the secretary-treasurer position, and Carl Haessler, lead faculty dissenter, played an important role, too. The newspaper estimated that about seventy-five students and faculty attended this meeting. It took as its subject "Socialism for the Student."[63]

But one issue on the national marquee dominated campus politics and received constant attention from Nevins and his DI staff: prohibition. That's because it had immediate local consequences, and the paper promoted the cause with greater urging than it gave to any other political issue. The effort to undo Champaign's "dry" status would be coming up in the April 1912 local election, but the DI got onto it as early as November the year before. It urged students to enroll to vote and "use their power to oust the barrooms from the vicinity of the institution," as they had done in 1907. The paper noted that local churches were on board in the campaign, and admonished that "[t]here is no excuse for public apathy." Then in March it took up the editorials with renewed passion. The election constitutes a matter "whose issue is momentous to the institution," said the DI editorial board. "The saloon question is the one topic in Twin City politics that is of grave importance to the University." The editors warned: "The return of the old liquor regimes would be the most serious moral blight, as well as the greatest moral disgrace that the University could suffer." The approximately one thousand university voters must flock to the polls; they hold the balance in the election, the DI exhorted.[64]

Other university groups marched in lock step with the DI on prohibition. The Council of Administration called saloons a great menace to the University. The Pan-Hellenic Council pledged its support, as did the Lincoln League and the boards of the Student Union. The YMCA organized its student members to work on the anti-liquor cause, providing automobiles to take students to the polls. And the DI took great pleasure in posting an open letter by President James, who on this subject, a long-standing priority with him,[65] wrote with unaccustomed hyperbole. Too many students, he said, cannot resist the

15. The Collegiate Revolution **291**

temptation to drink, and a local situation like ours, "where every street [had] an open grogery," compounds the matter. He believed the change in 1907 had made things better and that we ought not to revert to an open city that brings moral ruin to many students. He warned: "Gambling, and whore-mongering and loafing . . . are inevitable accompaniments of the type of saloon which would again flourish in this community, if the bars are again let down." The pro-liquor factions came out in force, too, and tensions in the area mounted. An Illinois student, one L. W. Ramsey, walking home with a friend from the Orpheum Theatre one night, had just crossed the tracks. He wore a "Vote Yes" tag on his coat. A hostile group of eight "wets" encountered the student and gave him a blow to the head that knocked him unconscious. But the party of good prevailed and prohibition carried the day in a vote of 1,962 to 1,483.[66]

The DI's pitch for local prohibition set within a larger profile of the paper's goals and purposes on the campus. It wanted to do more than report news. It saw itself as defender of the University, its work, and its reputation. It kept vigilance of those persons, inside and outside (and especially students) who would damage its standing and erode its image in the public eye. In executing this charge, the DI looked widely across the campus scene, and its record in journalism enriched the history of the institution it sought to protect and preserve.

Fostering school spirit had a lot to do with this effort, *Illini* personnel believed. Loyalty meant much and the paper's staff encouraged large participation at events that involved the whole campus community. Thus, in October of 1911, a short editorial had the headline "Attend the Convocation." Here's its reasoning: "The University, with its diversity of colleges and schools, has indeed very little outside its athletics to draw it into a unified whole; and our rare convocations should be a fuller expression of oneness of spirit and of interest in the institution than they have been in the past." The editorial wished that the University could have events that convened everyone in the Auditorium at least once a semester, if not more frequently.[67]

Left mostly, then, to champion athletics, the DI went all out. Anticipating the big football game against arch rival Chicago the paper urged students to travel north in massive numbers, making an "invasion." "The feeling of unity, of pride in a great institution," it editorialized, " . . . is as stimulating to the collegiate body as some rejuvenation to the individual." So, "let us overflow the Midway with a crusading abandon, as if to take its Gothic towers by storm," and all this to demonstrate "the spirit of student unity." And if that spirit seemed to lag, as amid a losing season, the *Illini* renewed the charge. In "When Loyalty Flags" Nevins and the editors asked, "Where is the boasted loyalty to the teams which represents us? Where is that never-give-up spirit which we so proudly sing?"[68]

Campus image did not mean only a matter of good or bad; it also involved identity. What was the University of Illinois? What did it mean to be a large

292 PART IV. STUDENTS

state institution? And what did it mean to be a midwestern university? Reading the DI in 1911–1912 one notices recurring references to the older, eastern colleges of the nation and commentary on how "we" differ, usually in a good way, but not always, from "them." Thus, in November 1911 the paper took note of a recent article that compared eastern college students with "western" students. The latter, said the author, a University of Minnesota professor, had a spirit of "ultraearnest dogged study," in contrast with the former's "lighter, more debonair" method of learning. The one group looked like sweating laborers, the other like sophisticated savants. The difference had its roots, said the author, in the social origins of the two groups. The westerner came out of homes, many immigrant, of little money and little of the atmosphere of true culture. Hence the westerner's "zeal for unremitting labor," his bent for informational knowledge and technical know-how.[69]

The *Illini* folk found the piece "stimulating," but feared it would mislead people. Our students, it said, actually come largely from the same middle classes as those in the eastern schools. Furthermore, "the imputation of the writer that the universities of Minnesota, Wisconsin, Chicago, and Illinois are composed of men largely from immigrant families who have settled upon small farms or in urban factory districts . . . is to be heartily resented." The DI responded that the differences in question owed not to social backgrounds but to educational priorities in the two regions. Liberal studies and social sciences dominate in the East; technical studies in the West. But the author, the DI editors conceded, had some sound advice to the students in both sections. It summarized that opinion: Western students "have much to learn from the East. They must learn that loitering over a wise old book is not necessarily idleness; that information is not knowledge; that many things are worth knowing even if they will never add a penny to one's income." That judgment was pure Nevins.[70]

So was much of the commentary that he offered on student life at Illinois. A good portion of it concerned the larger subject of democracy and the state universities, a matter, as noted, that preoccupied Nevins through his long intellectual career. Nevins's DI editorial essays often considered the student social life of the campus. Sometimes observations and opinion from around the country captured his attention and he followed them up in the paper. On two occasions these outside sources raised the matter of social distinctions and indeed, "snobbery," as found at the eastern schools and the western. The argument went that in the eastern schools no class distinctions affected the intellectual competition among students, where a kind of egalitarianism existed. But, according to this notion, in the extracurricular life, the student organizations and clubs, social snobbery reigned and social class affiliation determined the allocation of powerful and influential roles in student life. Nevins, in response, allowed that Illinois student life had its instances of "snobbery": that of the Greeks (men and women, against non-Greeks, or "the Barbarians"), of the

15. The Collegiate Revolution   293

athlete, of the guy with the largest date list, the highbrow, the fancy dresser. But with respect to attribution of campus influence a real equality of opportunity maintains, and Nevins defended "the fundamental democracy of our western student life." The Greek organizations, which dominated the campus clubs and cultural organizations, offered access without attention to a student's social class. "We have no moneyed influence with regard to student leadership." "The poor man," said the editorial, in contrasting Illinois with Yale and Princeton, "has as equal a chance with the rich to win extra-curricular honors as he has to win honors in scholarship." Nevins would go even further: "In fact, we have often gone to the opposite extreme from that of the East, and filled our offices with men of the roughest class, whose uncouth directness of method and democratic control of the general student vote has given them their power." But nevertheless here at Illinois, and quite properly for a state university, "[t]he only aristocracy is an intellectual one."[71]

The DI in this academic year gave much attention to other aspects of manners and morals in the Illinois student body. As Illinois partook of the collegiate revolution of the early twentieth century campus organizations formed and flourished; social activities proliferated. So, the *Illini* made itself a kind of *in loco parentis* overseer of the collegiate culture, judge of its rights and wrongs and seeking to effect a portrait of the model Illinois student. Here are some instances from this year:

- Two downtown theaters were presenting plays. One of them the paper judged rather trashy, the other of high quality and craftsmanship. However, the Illinois students were attending the first in far greater numbers than the other. But if we support only "cheap farces" and do not back creative works, the paper warned, "no reputable company will visit the Twin Cities." (Editorial, "Our Dramatic Taste," *Daily Illini*, October 20, 1911, 4.)
- We need to watch our dress. Students are not too bad; the faculty are. "Some of our best-paid professors are the most loosely Bohemian in appearance, and some of our poorest students are the most fastidious." Go figure. But at least our students don't show an affection for "lumber-jack's dress—heavy shoes, coarse baggy trousers"—like those at Wisconsin and Minnesota do. (Editorial, "College Dress," *Daily Illini*, November 11, 1911, 4.)
- We need a proper sense of the place for athletics in the University. For too many it means going to the big-time intercollegiate events. Here prevails a "feverish emphasis upon the mere winning of games." But at Illinois and across the country too few students engage in exercise for themselves and for the love of sport. We need to get outside more. (Editorial, "Athletics For Its Own Sake," *Daily Illini*, November 10, 1911, 4.)

294 **PART IV. STUDENTS**

- Our traditional "smokers" have become "a perversion of sociability." We have moved away from our good roots in the English ideals of Tom Brown and the more recent German university example. Here at Illinois these smokers used to offer honest and inspiring speeches. Now we have boxing matches and cheap vaudeville, "loose and unclean talk," and general "rowdyism," "worthy only of a variety house." In this matter we could learn from the long-standing practices of the eastern schools and the "dignified manner" of their smokers. The "disgraceful features" we display create a resentment against us in the public view. (Editorials, "A Perversion of Sociability," *Daily Illini*, January 7, 1912, 4; "Smokers," February 18, 1912, 4.)
- The "Wild Irishmen" are preparing to celebrate St. Patrick's Day and plan to make this year's event a "blowout." They have scheduled speakers, a singer, piano player, and quartet, all versed in the great Irish tunes. Hosts will distribute Irish tobacco and clay pipes and bless their guests with a seven-course dinner served at the Columbian Hotel in Urbana. Unfortunately, the annual affair has grown so large that the Hibernian Club must now demand proof of Irish identity to partake and no "hybrid Swedes or Mongolians" will enter to "spoil the species." ("A Regrettable Turn," *Daily Illini*, March 9, 1912, 1, and March 15, 1912, 1.)
- The next "L. and A." party approaches. The work of Literature and Arts students, this event has grown quickly into a campus-wide affair because it has become "too generally attractive." The paper, however, judged that development as one "not to be regretted." The University needs these all-inclusive socials because they counteract an unwelcome tendency of the contemporary large university. "Our students," said the editorial, "are already too much inclined to associate only with those whom they meet in their classes or professional clubs." Few feel the need to "place themselves with ease upon a common intellectual footing with others whose everyday work and ambitions are not their own." Let us hope that the eight societies in charge of L. and A. hospitality keep the participation open to all students. (Editorial, "L. and A. Hospitality," *Daily Illini*, January 19, 1912, 4.)
- The fraternities need to stock their chapter house libraries with more magazines and books. Many of the shelves stand empty. We should consider books as "ornaments of the home" and "indispensable" as furniture. Such an esthetic improvement will also help us better to impress visitors from the East. (Editorial, "Greeks and Their Books," *Daily Illini*, October 22, 1911, 4.)
- The Council of Administration has punished a student for drunkenness. Good! News of this kind of bad behavior finds its way into the

Chicago newspapers and into the hands of those who wish to blacken the University's reputation. (Editorial, "A Salutary Punishment," *Daily Illini*, November 3, 1911, 4.)

- Some seniors are petitioning for discontinuance of second-semester final exams. We say no. "The final examinations are one of the salutary restraints upon the natural feeling of the senior that he is growing above the petty tapebound rules of daily University procedure." Abolish them and his studying would fall to pieces. The existing standards give substance to the worth and prestige of our diplomas. (Editorial, "Senior Examinations," *Daily Illini*, May 7, 1912, 4.)

This role of campus overseer that the DI assigned itself applied also to the academic life of the University. By this avenue the newspaper entered into the discussions about the modern university and the changes it had undergone in recent decades. And in Nevins the DI had a student journalist with a keen interest in the subject and very pronounced opinions on it. He and his staff championed the University's march into high academic prestige. It reported on faculty hires and promotions and gave wide coverage to distinguished scholars who visited the campus, encouraging attendance at their presentations. The newspaper addressed from time to time the curriculum and course requirements as well as the intellectual culture of the students and took up the ever-challenging question of what constitutes an educated person.

Nevins had left his farm home to come to the University, bringing with him a motivating love of literature. That much at least he had acquired from the library built by his Calvinist father. But Nevins observed that too many of like students came from homes destitute of books and magazines. They thus did not take literature and language courses when they arrived on campus. Herein lies a severe deficiency, Nevins believed. For literature, he insisted, marks the central focus of a useful, university education. That education, he often wrote, builds the whole person, and mere information cannot furnish those qualities of feeling, taste, and imagination that mark that individual. "Education in literature," he wrote, "is the paramount problem of all education," of essential importance to "the mental and spiritual stature of the modern man." Thus, speaking to a particular matter concerning course requirements for commerce students, Nevins sided with those in the program who wanted business students also to study foreign languages. He judged such requirements entirely consistent with the "cosmopolitan" ideals of contemporary higher education.[72]

Nevins and the DI staff wished a large public relation for their school. We must do more, he editorialized, by way of "breaking down the barriers which separate the life from within the college from the life without." He acknowledged that "one great state university—Wisconsin—has already pressed far in such work." Nevins made that recommendation in early 1912, the year when

296 PART IV. STUDENTS

Charles McCarthy at Wisconsin published his influential book *The Wisconsin Idea*. But Nevins did believe that Illinois was making gains in this direction. He cited the proposal to house in Lincoln Hall new bureaus "for civic, social, and economic research in the public interest." Hereby Illinois would create "new vistas of opportunities for service." Indeed, the DI believed, these programs should model the platform for all state universities to emulate.[73]

Here are a few more instances of the watchdog role of the *Daily Illini*:

- The student literary societies have long ceased to be the props of a viable program for the study of literature. They are now "moribund." And they have become more like debating clubs addressing mundane subjects, like tariffs or political parties. We see now only "the dullness, torpid temper" of these organizations. They should return to the poem or the essay—creative literature—as their main concern. (Editorial, "Debating Clubs or Literary Societies?," *Daily Illini*, May 17, 1912, 4; Editorial, "The Literary Interests at Illinois," March 24, 1912, 4.)[74]
- The academic honorary societies are a joke. "Most of them are absolutely and utterly inane." Anybody majoring in the appropriate subject can get a membership in that discipline's honorary society. They cast a spurious glamour and prestige over extracurricular activities, and feed the students' mania for attaching Greek letters to their names. "We already have men among us, of no especial distinction of mind or character, who can write as many Greek characters after their names as the most eminent Englishman can write of Roman initials." Proliferation of these fraudulent entities cheapens the worth of the few "really dignified ones," like Sigma Xi (Science) and Tau Beta Pi (Engineering). (Editorial, "Empty Honors," *Daily Illini*, February 15, 1912, 4.)
- The DI kept a sharp vigilance on the campus environs. In December 1911 the University celebrated the completion of the new Lincoln Hall, to be a great boost to its academic life. The newspaper praised the building's nice features—exterior bas-reliefs, a marble and gilt entrance that housed the bust of Abraham Lincoln, all worthy of a great hero. But the editorial expressed disdain for the placing of the one hundred words of the Gettysburg Address, arranged as a tablet, on the floor of the entrance. The editorialists judged it a terrible indignity to have the noble words there inscribed, under the feet of moving crowds of people, such that it "must momentarily shock any newcomer." Let us spend the money and properly relocate these inspiring words to the side wall. (Editorial, "The Gettysburg Address," *Daily Illini*, December 13, 1911, 4.) And there it stands today.
- The Greek houses. They swarm with social interactions, "endless purposeless visitors" in and out of the rooms constantly. Many of these

15. The Collegiate Revolution   297

rooms already have too many inhabitants. This situation does not conduce to good study habits or the "arduous concentration" necessary for them. And it's one reason why the frats have lower scholastic averages than other residences. (Editorial, "The Crowded Home," *Daily Illini*, March 5, 1912, 4.)

- Philosophical idealism paid a visit to the University in November 1911 in the person of Harvard professor Josiah Royce. The DI made the most of the occasion, welcoming a person "of international reputation," a just description. Nevins and the editors reminded readers that Royce had previously visited the campus, in 1897. There he gave lectures that led to his book *The Philosophy of Loyalty*. The newspaper had a follow-up report after Royce's visit, providing a review and appraisal of his statements about religion, faith, and science. And those, too, it applauded. (*Daily Illini*, November 19, 1911, 1; Editorial, "Royce Lecture," November 22, 1911, 4.)

Allan Nevins wrote his last editorial for the DI in late May 1912 as he and his senior class looked to their imminent graduation. We in this group, he wrote, naturally think back on our four years here and reflect on the changes we have seen. Most will likely mark the visible material growth of the institution, above all the new buildings, and the thousands more students now here. Nevins also detailed the signs of an improving student culture—campus athletics, drama, clubs, journalism, discipline in the fraternities, and more. The library books and the number of graduate students have tripled and quadrupled in size, he observed. But one should note something else, he said, specifically, the "new and impressive names on the faculty rolls," one reason why "the prestige of the university has made great forward strides." And that fact really mattered, he said.[75]

Also, when Nevins wrote his history of the University in 1917 he sounded another positive note. He could see the real promise of the institution coming into place in a new, important way—in the service of its students to the state. For the state, he wrote, will be paid back in full for all the thousands of dollars it has invested in each student. Graduates go forth from the University "to all corners of the State, and to every trade and profession—the farm, the shop, the railway, the architect's studio, the newspaper, the high school and college classroom, the counting office, the lawyer's study." And they bring more than skills, Nevins avowed. They bring "new mental and moral equipment," a "sense of obligation to every office, their sense of an obligation to serve," and above all "a public idealism" put in place for the good of the commonwealth.[76]

CHAPTER 16

Women

THE YOUNG WOMEN who attended the University of Illinois in the James years represented the second generation of their cohort in American higher education. Society and gender culture were changing. The long-standing "separate spheres" standard of the Victorian era was dissolving. The new pattern stood between that era and modern America. The earlier generation of women graduates generally forsook marriage. Now more women anticipated both family and career, a pattern more visible after 1910. They embraced and reflected Progressive-Era values of professionalism and sought active lives in business and the public sphere. Campus life reflected the shifts. Women, slowly at first, joined in the proliferation of new student organizations, honorary societies, and campus sports, and they participated in the collegiate revolution described in the previous chapter. The transition did not always move smoothly. Some saw it as so profound as to make the campus an "effeminate" place. Many male students did not like it. Indeed, some campuses sought to moderate the change by establishing separate classes for men and women. Stanford and Michigan adopted quotas for admitting women. Tufts, Rochester, and Western Reserve set up coordinate colleges for their female students. And old prejudices persisted. Even at as progressive a campus as the University of California, its president, Benjamin Ide Wheeler, said to the women, in 1904: "You are not here with the ambition to be school teachers or old maids; but you are here for the preparation of marriage and motherhood. This education should tend to make you more serviceable as wives and mothers." Nonetheless, by 1920 47 percent of American college students were female, a rate much higher than at Illinois.[1]

Although coeducation no longer raged in controversy, neither had it become a settled matter. Charles W. Eliot at Harvard remained to the end of his long presidency, 1869 to 1909, an opponent. So did Woodrow Wilson at Princeton.

Edmund James, on the other hand, had made clear his views before his arrival to Illinois. He wanted women and men educated together on equal terms, and he resisted any ideas about separating the sexes for academic purposes. James believed that the higher education of women marked one of the distinctions and one of the achievements of the United States, in contrast to other nations around the world.[2]

On the Illinois campus the Woman's Building made its debut in 1905. (It later became the English Building.) James welcomed it and did much to highlight it. The new structure became right away a scene of campus social events that transformed the building "into such a festive sight that graduates remembered it for years." It would now house the Household Science Department and the Office of the Dean of Women, and it had a gymnasium for the female students.[3] But the new edifice did nothing to resolve a long-standing problem, one that plagued many other campuses, too: housing. For years arriving students faced the immediate challenge of finding a place to live. Women had a harder time than men because people in Champaign and Urbana simply preferred to rent out rooms to male students. The administration tried to keep some oversight of women's living conditions in the towns; the dean of women maintained a list of approved places, setting minimum standards of health and cleanliness for them.[4] The situation partly explains the growth and appeal of sororities. By 1912 two hundred women lived in a dozen and a half houses, with four hundred still in boarding houses. For Black female students the situation hardly improved. They faced discrimination in the towns and also on campus. Even after Alpha Kappa Alpha appeared in 1914 local residents resisted its locating in their vicinity. The *Daily Illini* decried what it saw as another "shameful disparity" between the two groups of women—Greek and non-Greek. The Greek set enjoyed huge advantage in social opportunities, it editorialized. Greeks also dominated the student campus organizations. The non-Greeks (i.e., "the Barbarians") "are lonely, unadvised, and in their isolation often conscious of a certain social stigma." It's like the condition of "rich and poor in a large city." The newspaper urged an energetic campaign for women's dormitories on campus and a heavy lobbying effort with the legislature to secure them. The Women's Residence Hall finally materialized in 1918.[5]

• • •

How did women make their mark on university life—socially, academically, and culturally? One change in the demographics of the student body became readily evident: the rush of females into dominancy in the liberal arts programs of the curriculum. In his 1917 history of the University Allan Nevins marked the change and noted that often in other universities that influx caused resentment among male students—it was the "effeminacy" issue.[6] But Nevins

300   PART IV. STUDENTS

Completed at the time of James's arrival to Illinois in 1904, the Woman's Building later became the English Building. Courtesy of the University of Illinois Archives.

asserted that Illinois did not reflect that reaction. And he stated outright that "the best students are the women." Dean Clark reported from time to time on the pattern of grades among the students. Non-sorority women did best; fraternity men did the worst. But he noted that the last group had the clear domination of the campus student organizations. Nevins offered a reason for women's better academic record: the women had a more purposeful approach to their college experience. They came to college out of their desire to learn and not because of parental pressures. Nevins extolled their presence. Coming more than the men from the wealthier parts of the state and from the cities—Chicago and St. Louis—they had a "liberalizing influence" on the student body, he thought. And they deflated a bit the "businesslike" tone that generally prevailed.[7]

In campus social activities, the situation for women, Nevins believed, had improved enormously. For years, he said, there just wasn't much for them to do. But inequities and imbalances remained. The *Illio* yearbook of 1913 (for the year 1911–1912) gives a good view of the matter. Of the senior class offices for the first and then the second semester women held two of the ten. On the prestigious *Illio* staff in 1913 men held the offices of editor-in-chief and business manager; women held two of the ten positions on the editorial staff. The newspaper had long been a male preserve, but now one woman, Fay Armstrong, served on the reporters' staff, designated as "Woman's Reporter." *The Illinois*, the popular campus literary magazine, had, yes, Allan Nevins also as its editor-in-chief, but more females on its staff than any of the campus journals, three of the fifteen. Throughout the James years no woman served as editor-in-chief of the DI and men overwhelmingly dominated its staff. The discrepancy of the sexes appeared most glaringly in intercollegiate sports. Baseball, football, and basketball captured the attention of the student body, faculty, and public. The *Daily Illini*, as noted, gave detailed coverage of the home games and sent its reporters with the teams when they traveled. Women had no inter-campus games.

The Uof I community enjoyed on-campus events throughout the academic year. Debate and oratory contests against rival universities dealt with topical subjects, but men monopolized the debates. Theater had gained much in popularity in these years and the campus saw productions aplenty. When the Mask and Bauble Society presented Sheridan's "School for Scandal" eight women had places in the cast, and nine played in the production "The Lion Rampant." Some social and cultural groups were all their own. They had the Woman's League, the Young Women's Christian Association, and the Girls Athletic Association. The four classes each had its own basketball team, for local competition. They had their own literary societies: the Alethenai, the Illiola, and the Athenean. Their Household Science Club had forty-eight members. In 1912 the Pan-Hellenic Society served all seventeen sororities. Women had some shared memberships with men in other organizations, like the Mask and Bauble, the Landscape Garden's Club (one woman out of twelve), and the Scribblers' Club (eight of nineteen), the Centro Literario Español (four of seventeen), and the Cercle Français (several). Three women had joined the newly formed Railway Club, which had twenty-three members. And in the Student Volunteer Band for Foreign Missions six women joined nine men.

Three students who contributed abundantly to the campus literary activity also wrote fictional memoirs of their student experiences. And they offer a treasure trove of reporting on students—the social life of the sororities especially, but intellectual activities as well, and with references to familiar professors, deans, and campus buildings. The three authors all graduated from Illinois and spent all their times there in the James era. Their stories focus particularly on a type of female student at Illinois that became very visible in the authors' years. This student threw herself into campus activities, all kinds of them. She may have joined a sorority, and if so made it a base of her advancement into many of the collegiate groups where she found her interests. But the literary outlets predominated as the vehicle of expression for these women. They participated, often prominently, in the prestigious Scribblers' Club. They wrote short stories

302 PART IV. STUDENTS

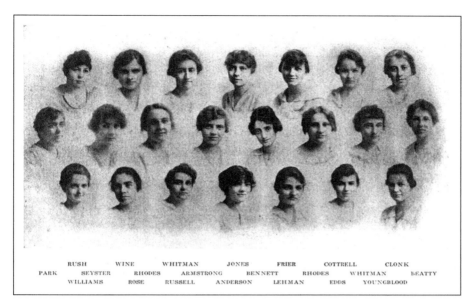

Many student organizations at the University had exclusive male or female memberships, religious organization included. Thus, men formed the Bushnell Club (Congregationalist denomination), and women formed the Bethany Circle (Christian denomination). As noted here, Lois Seyster, who later wrote short stories about UofI campus life, had a membership in Bethany Circle. Courtesy of the University of Illinois Archives.

and poetry for the *Illinois Magazine* and the *Siren*. Lois Seyster was one of these. Born in Kempton, Illinois in 1897, she belonged to the Class of 1919, graduating with Honors and writing her BA thesis on "Walt Whitman and the Modern Movement in American Poetry." She had a sorority membership in Alpha Xi Delta. Her eclectic cultural interests involved her with the Scribblers' Club, the Athenian Literary Society, Glee Club, and in writing contributions to the campus publications. She also served as editor of the *Illinois Magazine*. Wider interests in women students took her into Mortarboard, the Woman's League, and Student Council. She became Permanent Class Secretary.

At Illinois Seyster met Lynn Montross. He had attended the University of Nebraska for three years and then transferred to Illinois. They married in 1921 and formed a writing partnership. In 1923 they published their collection of short stories *Town and Gown*. Each wrote separate entries, all about campus life at Illinois (although Lynn Montross's entrees may include his Nebraska experience). This book enjoyed great popularity, going into three editions. But the stories do not give a very favorable picture of Illinois, and Dean Kinley especially detested the book (it had student sex in it). The couple went on to offer more collaborative works. But they divorced in 1933. Seyster wrote ten novels in the 1930s. Montross became "one of the foremost post–World War II Western military historians," with works such as *War Through the Ages* (1960), and served as the official historian of the U.S. Marine Corps. Both died in 1961.

Olive Deane Hormel was born in Chicago in 1892. She lived in Austin, Texas from 1894 to 1899, where her father served as pastor of a Presbyterian church. She also lived in Iowa and Missouri, and earned a degree at Lindonwood College in St. Charles. She entered UofI with the Class of 1916. Her Illinois activities include Kappa Kappa Gamma sorority, the Alethenai Literary Society, Scribblers' Club, and the editorial staff of the *Magazine* (*The Illinois*). She earned Phi Beta Kappa honors. Her novel, the first of many from this prolific writer, had the title *Co-Ed*, published in 1926. It tells the story of Lucia Leigh and her sojourn through "Gamma" sorority. But it relates also her transformation from compulsive social butterfly to committed academic and the personal self-discovery that comes from the change. (See below.) This book gives a much richer and rounded portrait of the University than does *Town and Gown*. And the Illinois administration liked it a lot more. Hormel, among her other work, served as literary editor of the *Christian Science Monitor*. She died in 1961.

• • •

As female students became more numerous and more important to campus life, the prominence of one administrator was raised: the dean of women. The University of Wisconsin established this office in 1892 as did Chicago shortly thereafter. California's came in 1898 and Indiana's in 1901. The Illinois Board of Trustees took action and created the position in 1898. In 1896 the board had created the Woman's Department, which would consist of all female faculty. It was intended to help attract more women to the campus and then look after their well-being. President Draper appointed Violet D. Jayne, who also won a promotion to associate professor in the English department. The board carefully specified the office's functions: to endeavor to become "the representative, guide, and friend" of the women students and to advise them in their academic work and social life, with the ultimate end that they might attain "the highest attributes of independent but truly womanly character." Jayne right away took on a matter that confronted her and every one of her successors—the housing problem. She began the system of approved off-campus (and therefore all) residences for women. Jayne served in the new office until 1904 when she resigned to marry Edward C. Schmidt, a faculty member.[8]

James arrived at this point. He sincerely wished to improve the situation for women at Illinois, and he greatly wanted the deanship for women to have high prestige, equal in status with the faculty in general, as that dean would

304   PART IV. STUDENTS

hold an academic department position. To that extent he judged it imperative that the dean of women hold a doctorate degree. But those two concerns too often worked at cross-purposes to each other, which resulted in a series of three-year tenures more or less and a frustrating history that pleased few.[9]

James often worked with the women trustees in his search for a dean of women. Thus, in 1907 he sent Mary Busey and Carrie Alexander-Bahrenberg to Minneapolis to interview Lily G. Kollock, who had visited Illinois earlier. She had a doctorate in science from Penn and served on the faculty at Minnesota. She joined the University in 1907, but for whatever reason, James soon lost confidence in Kollock and another search ensued. Again James discussed the matter with the women trustees and in 1910 the board appointed Mary E. Fawcett. Fawcett made high academic demands on the female students and had low tolerance for slackness, especially when it came to attending classes. One year she issued three hundred summonses warning individual students about their delinquency. Through her office forty-two students were dropped from the University.[10]

Fawcett had some "Suggested Ideals," a title she gave to an op-ed piece she wrote for the *Illinois* in 1912. It has some significance as Fawcett pondered the meaning of a university education to women of the modern era. She quoted Ruskin and Aristotle in an effort to relate relevant, contemporary ideals to a larger tradition. Although she addressed the subject of women, she inscribed little gender specificity in her reflections. But she did quote Evelyn Wright, by then a legendary dean of women at Stanford, citing her "liberty of thought and action" as the imperative objective of women's education. And although Fawcett spoke of "service to humanity" she intended no ideal of self-sacrifice or self-denial as modeled by the fading cult of true womanhood. "Completeness of womanhood," that end to which education leads, Fawcett asserted, entails high ideals of "power, service and culture." For that education, she explained (and quoting again) now signifies "less embroidery, more physics, chemistry, biology"; it means "less sordello [*sic*!], more economics and sociology"; less playing cards and "more biography and history." "True womanliness," Fawcett believed, embraces all those forces that endow a woman with "a self-determining power in the world."[11] But James did not retain Fawcett. She did not have a doctorate degree.

Neither did Martha Kyle, whom James appointed as interim dean in 1913, renewing her for the next two years. Kyle had clear reservations about the way Illinois women were conducting themselves. She really did not like the sororities, although she acknowledged that they helpfully eased the housing problem. Social life, she believed, had become too much the ascendant ideal of the women students and their scholarship had suffered. She wanted to reverse priorities. Now the subject of dancing became quite topical. Not only did the seemingly endless dancing events take too much of the students' time,

16. Women   305

Kyle believed, but the kind of dances now popular made the matter worse. The Council of Administration also took note. It and Kyle found no offense in the waltz and the two-step, but they drew the line at the tango and rumba. So, they expressed their wish that the instructors in physical training teach all their students ballroom dancing.[12]

James moved on to Fanny Gates in 1916. Here was a woman with a superb record in science, with publications on radioactivity and a letter of recommendation from Ernest Rutherford, with whom she had worked in England. She tackled the job energetically, also giving much time to the housing situation. Her relentless work took a toll on her and she asked James to appoint an assistant to help her out. Other deans here had much greater staffs and, she showed James, so did other deans of women at other institutions. The death of her father in 1917 induced a physical and emotional breakdown, and Gates entered a sanitarium at Hinsdale. She resigned the next year. Her departure deprived the University of a potential valuable contribution from her. In December 1917 she prepared a course, a series of lectures from her, under the auspices of the sociology department. Gates wished to give subjects pertaining to women a larger presence in the curriculum. Her selected topics for this course included "The Female Temperament"; "The Professional Woman"; Women and Health"; "Women and the Home"; and "Women and the Larger Public Citizenship." And finally, James made his last appointment to this office in 1918. Ruby E. C. Mason did not have a doctorate, but had previous experience as dean of women at Indiana University. She remained at the University until 1923. Mason, a moral tyrant, plagued James and his successor David Kinley.[13]

This side of Edmund James's record as Illinois president does not reflect well on him. His negotiations with candidates, always complicated, show him as often patronizing and disingenuous. In one instance he missed a prime opportunity in discussions with Mina Kerr, a Smith College graduate with a PhD in English literature from Penn, and solid experience in administration, who had provided James an impressive outline of her intentions with respect to the deanship. At one point, as James dallied, she wrote in her letter that she had heard repeatedly that "Illinois does not care for her women." The accusation applied to presidents, trustees, and faculty. "One dean after another," she reminded James in 1916, "had not made good at Illinois."[14] There are several reasons for this problem. First, James never resolved in his own mind just what the job should look like. It was relatively new and did not fit into the model of the German university that James brought to his presidency at Illinois. Second, "he could not and did not apply his standard consistently." Third, James always felt overwhelmed by the burdens of his office, but too often failed to delegate responsibilities to others. The women's deanship competed for other big-ticket items in his playbook and did not receive the time and care it merited. Fourth, "James obviously needed to have the upper hand in

306   PART IV. STUDENTS

dealing with a difficult woman." And withal, much here "remains a mystery" that does not square with James's record of superb hiring that marked the great growth in stature of the university he headed.[15]

• • •

Women made their largest contribution to the collegiate revolution at the University in the literary publication, the *Illinois*. The first issue had appeared in 1904, a work of one of the new academic societies in the collegiate revolution, the English Club. It had that arrangement into 1907. In this last year Carl Van Doren served as editor and the publication had a staff of four, two of them women. Van Doren, exemplifying his growing passion for American literature, placed a lengthy, highly informed essay titled "Studies in American Literature: Whitman and His Future" in the issue.[16] In 1909 *The Illinois* reappeared. It announced itself as the *Illinois Magazine*.[17] It had A. W. Eisenmayer, Jr. as editor-in-chief and a staff of four editors, including Allan Nevins and three women—Miriam Gerlach, Bertha Bourdette, and Margaret H. Hallett—who would have large roles in the publication. Hallett became editor-in-chief at the next issue, which included her short story, "The Decisive Moment."[18] The April 1910 issue also introduced another important player for the journal, Margaret Dupuy, who contributed several stories. For the next volume of the *Illinois* in October 1910 Gerlach had the title editor-in-chief.

Miriam Gerlach had an exceptional career. Born in Chester, Illinois in 1886 she attended local schools and then entered the University. She joined the Alethenai Literary Society and the Scribblers' Club. She was a campus phenomenon, with roles in all the major journalistic efforts of the students—*The Illinois*, the *Daily Illini*, and the *Illio* yearbook. She was Class Poet and her outstanding academic work won her a Phi Beta Kappa membership. Gerlach remained at Illinois after her senior year and earned a master's degree. People knew her as a woman of iron will and unwavering resolve. Practical-minded and an excellent manager, she tackled what she knew she could do and no more. She played a major role in the establishment of the Phi Beta chapter of Gamma Phi Beta sorority, giving her time and imagination to the project. Gerlach served as business manager of the national order. After Illinois she had a series of academic appointments that allowed her to pursue her love of literature but also her interest in university women. This work took her to Northwestern and then North Dakota State University, where she served as dean of women. She had this title also at Washington State and at the University of Oklahoma. Her crowning achievement came with her becoming chair of the English department at the University of Nebraska. That position marked a rarity for a woman in American higher education in these years.[19]

The ascendancy of Gerlach and these other women at *The Illinois* gave them a far larger representation on that publication than they ever attained on the

16. Women   307

Daily Illini in the James years. Although their presence could vary from few to several they always had a voice in this literary journal. Usually, an even balance of men and women maintained. And the position titles changed from time to time. Thus, in March 1913 the *Illinois* listed a Short Story Department, headed by Nellie Roberts; a Verse Department, all three women; and an Essay Department, two members female, joined by Mark Van Doren. For the new volume in September the journal posted Van Doren as editor, supported by a staff, all of whom were women. The October 1916 issue introduced a new position titled Woman's Editor, occupied by Florence Lindahl. The position reappeared in ensuing issues, but not consistently. In December 1913 began the tradition of the "Woman's Number" of the *Illinois*, in which female students took over all offices (except business manager) of the publication. Katherine Chase had a staff of four. In the next Woman's Number, with Lucile Needham as editor, the women expressed "our thanks and gratitude" to the men of the *Illinois* for the "privilege" (their quotation marks) of publishing the special issue, "whether the privilege be granted by way of a compliment, a courtesy, or a sop to our vanity."[20]

• • •

Whereas the Illinois student body had a pair of remarkable brothers—Carl and Mark Van Doren—it had also a highly talented pair of sisters—Lucile and Catherine Needham. Like the Van Dorens, the Needhams came to the University from Urbana. Their parents, William Alexander Needham and Alice Rosella Brown Needham, had moved from Kentucky and then Nebraska, where all their seven children were born. Catherine had a twin, Marguerite. Another daughter, Grace Alice, also graduated from U of I and later married a controversial, if not notorious Illinois professor, Revilo P. Oliver, a classicist, and a founding member of the John Birch Society. She ran a local publishing and printing business. Carrie Isabel, the oldest of the six children, earned an AB degree in Household Science in the Class of 1912. Brother William also graduated from the University.

Lucile Needham was born in 1892. After the family relocation to Urbana, she attended Thornburn High School on the North Side near the Boneyard Creek. Mark Van Doren also attended the school at that time and he remembered Lucile as "a brilliant girl whom I admired." Carl was student editor of the school magazine, the *Thornburn Thistle*, and he knew Needham through her contributions to the publication. In terms of literary merit, Van Doren conceded, "I could not compete with Lucile," and added that by all right she, not he, should have been editor of the magazine.[21] In addition to the *Illinois* Lucile Needham had memberships in the Scribblers' Club and the Household Science Club, and won election as president of the Alethenai Literary Society. She also secured a rare female position with the *Daily Illini* staff. Phi Beta

308   PART IV. STUDENTS

The Illinois Magazine

          Tietje   Bourdette   Cartwright
Gerlach   Hight   Hallett   Nevins

ILLINOIS MAGAZINE BOARD

MARGARET H. HALLETT, '10 . . . . . Editor-in-Chief
E. S. HIGHT, '10 . . . . Business Manager

EDITORS

BERTHA E. BOURDETTE, '11
C. F. CARTWRIGHT, '11
MIRIAM GERLACH, '11
J. A. NEVIN, '12
RALPH E. TIETJE, '12

"To flunk is to make a gloomy fizzle. It is the bluffer's signal of distress, and sometimes the finish of a star that once shone brilliantly."

226

The Illinois Magazine (sometimes titled *The Illinois*) supplied literary outlets to a large number of students, who wrote short stories, poems, and essays. The publication offers major documentation about the American student mind in the early twentieth century. Pictured here are Miriam Gerlach (first row, far left), Bertha Bourdette (top row, middle), Margaret Hope Hallett (bottom row, second from right), and Allan Nevins, who became one of the most distinguished American historians in the twentieth century. Courtesy of the University of Illinois Archives.

Kappa honors confirmed her outstanding academic record. And even before she graduated from the University of Illinois she had placed an essay in the prestigious literary journal *Sewanee Review*, as did Olive Dean Hormel.[22] Immediately upon her graduation in 1916 Lucile Needham married James Vail Stevenson, UofI Class of 1912. They engaged in progressive farming in La Salle County and raised four children there. For some thirty-seven years Needham wrote a daily household column for the *Cornbelt Farm Daily*.

Catherine Needham, a year younger than Lucile, exemplified the kind of student resolved to take advantage of every college opportunity available to her; she modeled the collegiate revolution on the feminine side possibly even more than did her talented sister. Catherine joined the same activities as Lucile, including Scribblers' (vice president). Catherine added the Woman's Hockey team, the Banquet Committee, the Women's Athletic Association, Student Council, Class Secretary, and the Cercle Français. She finished her first year with the highest academic average in the University and two years later made Phi Beta Kappa, one of only three juniors to do so.[23]

But Catherine had a special love for the pen and made herself one of the most frequent contributors to the short story and poetry work of the *Illinois Magazine*. The *Illini* Board of Trustees, consisting of faculty and students, had general oversight of the various campus publications. In 1917 the board offered a prize of $25 for the best short story submitted to the magazine. Twenty-two entries emerged, many of them judged of high quality. In giving the prize to Catherine Needham for her piece "When Windy was the Weather," the board commented that she had contributed frequently, but this story "surpasses even the best of her previous efforts."[24] When the contest took place again the next year Catherine once more gained the award with her offering, "A Perfect Understanding." The magazine editors wrote: "This is a blue ribbon story by a blue ribbon writer."[25] In 1916 when the University broke ground for the new women's residence hall, Laura B. Evans from the trustees took the shovel; President James gave an address, as did Dean of Women Fanny Gates. Catherine Needham spoke for the women students. After Illinois Needham taught for a while in the English Extension program at Columbia University. She married Lyle Elwood Severance of the Class of 1916 and they lived for years in Michigan. He ran a small business there and the couple had six children. In 1953 she published her novel *The Last Day of Ikhnaton*, a thriller set in ancient Egypt.

But the extraordinary Needham sisters did have the company of many talented female writers on the campus. They expressed themselves mainly through the short story, less through formal serious essays, and often in poetry. Some names one saw frequently as writers and as the personnel of the *Illinois Magazine*'s staff offices included especially Ruth Llwellyn, Marie Goebel, Gertrude Fleming, Katherine Chase, Eleanor Jewett, Lois Seyster, Elizabeth Leitzbach,

310 PART IV. STUDENTS

and Zelomia Ainsworth. What did they write about? Variety thrived, yet withal one subject occupied the women's attention above all others: romance and courtship, or in short, the dynamics of the sexes in their social interactions, with the Illinois campus the favorite venue for the playing out of these interconnections. One could perceive a slight feminist edge in the stories, but that slant carried little ideological weight. It did, however, work its way through plots laced with deception, staged confusions, and altogether a kind of friendly war of wits in the ongoing battle of the sexes. A moral ambiguity marks the stories, as lies and falsehoods often work their way into happy outcomes. They could be sentimental stories but never maudlin ones.[26] Some may judge them insufficiently "serious," but one can read them with enjoyment. They offer cleverness of plot, and the writers have a command of the language that gives liveliness and engagement to their works.[27] In many ways they reflect the American middle-brow culture. Certainly, they give us a feel for the campus life in the James era.

In 1914 the editors of the *Illinois Magazine* published a piece by a Harvard man who had carefully compared the literary and dramatic products of the students at Illinois and Harvard. He wrote: "I have read stories in the Illinois Magazine that from a purist standpoint would have made the Harvard pedagogue's hair stand on end; but I have yet to read anything in a Harvard publication of similar nature that will have half the glow of creative impulse in the Illinois Magazine's work. The same is true of drama."[28]

• • •

One may wonder how large a presence did feminist thinking have in the student culture of UofI's women. Certainly, all on campus knew that gender roles in America were changing and higher education reflected them. Catherine Needham, in one of her stories in the *Illinois*, has her character Stephen say: "It's the modern women who have put the quietus on romance. I don't believe there are any Juliets or Rosalinds now-a-days. Oh, I admit the modern woman's superiority over the simpering, fainting female of 'ye olden tymes'; but the fact remains that women don't fall in love the way they used to. They are simply too intelligent to see anything wonderful or awe-inspiring about ordinary men." His friend Hilda responds: "You are wrong, all wrong!," and she accuses men of ignoring the many women who would take an interest in them if they would take their romantic bent away from the fictional Juliets and Marianas and engage the real women all about them.[29] Exchanges such as this one often surfaced in the essays as well, but they did not command a lot of space in the magazine.[30] Women students had platforms on which to register their disaffections or advance a program of feminism. The recurring "Woman's Number" of the *Illinois Magazine* provided one of them. In the December 1913 issue Bernice Powell pondered why so few females sought high

16. Women 311

A *Siren* Magazine cover. Gentle feminism. Courtesy of the University of Illinois Archives.

positions in the various student activities. Many, she said, stated that they did not have time to learn all the "mysterious methods of student politics." Powell noted that the editor of the *Daily Illini* had reported that of approximately nine hundred women students on campus only one had tried out for a place on the staff.[31] But Katherine Chase believed that women could do more. They should constitute themselves a mass voting bloc. Such an advantage, however, required that they know each other better and more widely. They should attend the Woman's League parties held every week. (They are always announced in the DI.) But few do.[32] The next Woman's Number of the magazine argued for greater control of the election process by the campus females. But "the men resist."[33] Perhaps, but not all of them did. Nevins and the *Daily Illini* called

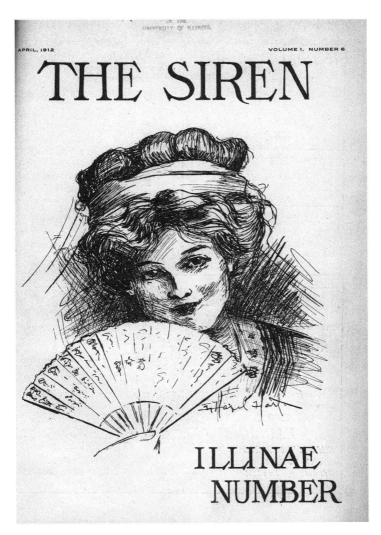

A *Siren* Magazine cover. It got attention. Courtesy of the University of Illinois Archives.

for a larger presence of women in campus politics and social organizations. He suggested formation of a student club for such a purpose.[34]

Another opportunity for women to vent their cause, or their grievances, came with the new publication, the *Siren*, which made its debut in 1911 and announced itself as dedicated wholly to satire and humor. It would appear seven times a year. Nevins and the *Daily Illini* staff welcomed its debut, noting that many other universities had such an offering. They flourished mostly in the East; Harvard's *Lampoon* and the *Cornell Widow* had the most prominence. But Wisconsin, Michigan, and Minnesota also had these publications and Illinois "should have had one long ago." Nonetheless, wrote Nevins, the new *Siren* "will be a big boost for the University."[35]

The next year the *Siren* journal gave over the April issue to women, who produced the "Illinae Number." Eva Mitchell served as editor for this issue of the *Siren* and on behalf of her colleagues welcomed the opportunity to express themselves, free of interference from male overseers as at the DI and without having to importune more space in any given issue of the *Illinois Magazine*.[36] The cover of this issue featured a striking portrait sketch of a female face— fashionable, sophisticated, flirtatious, visible behind a fan below the chin. The woman projects a "come hither" look. The *Daily Illini* reviewer called the picture "bewitching." The issue flourishes with wit and clever humor, much of it short quips. Poetry abounds, as do cartoons. Some pieces are smart plays on popular or classical verse, familiar to most readers. The issue also took a few jabs at the boys. There was loads of advertising, including a full-page ad for Fatima "Turkish Blend" cigarettes.[37] Perhaps the whole issue was meant to be light-hearted. But what's missing is any recourse to hard complaint respecting the female situation on campus—no intonation of feminist ideology, no pleas for egalitarianism, no inventories of resentment. But Allan Nevins, always ready to act as supreme judge of literature on campus, gave high praise to the "Illinae Number." He rejoiced in its gentle satire of student politics, its artful cartoon sketches, and the often "inspired genius" it brought into soft maligning by the "girl-humorists" of vulnerable targets in the classroom experience of Illinois students. (The DI almost always referred to the female students as "girls" and the male students as "men"; but so also did the women writers.) Wrote the reviewer: "There is a femininity about the issue that an office-full of males could not scare up in a long time." The commentary headline read: "Masculine Efforts Put to Shame by Co-Ed Siren."[38]

• • •

One might have expected to find some considerable attention given by the women writers of the *Illinois*, and perhaps of the *Siren*, also, to the subject of women's suffrage. It never became a major issue, although the *Daily Illini* reported on campus activities that addressed equal rights for women. The events occurred from time to time in different organizational efforts, campus visitations, and oratorical offerings. In these years leading up to the passage of the Nineteenth Amendment to the Constitution in 1920, the battle took place state by state—in legislation respecting women's suffrage and in the ratification process. Illinois had allowed the vote to females only in qualified school elections. But in 1913 it became the first state east of the Mississippi River to permit women to vote for presidential electors.[39] The movement

314 PART IV. STUDENTS

long had ties to Prohibition, which, too, revolved around state action until, the year before the suffrage amendment, Prohibition also found its way into the U.S. Constitution.

Illinois had a state Women's Equal Suffrage Association, and it sponsored an oratory competition that invited each campus to send its best to the state finals. The contest at Urbana had entrants making their most convincing cases for the right of women to vote. In 1908 six finalists spoke before a panel of three judges that included Stuart Sherman and Dean of Women Martha Kyle. Five of the speakers were men and the winner was one of them, V. Halliday, a student in chemical engineering.[40]

The next year efforts continued. Caroline Lerow, national secretary of the College Equal Suffrage League, spoke on the campus. That organization had formed in 1900 and now had chapters at fifteen universities, including Northwestern, Iowa, and Nebraska. Some students at Illinois wanted the University's participation in the national organization. Miriam Gerlach, with two others, formed a committee to make it a reality. The effort did not go well. There was another event two years later when Harriet Grim came to Urbana and gave an address, open to the campus and to the community public, but forbidding male attendants. Grim, whom the *Daily Illini* called "the first out and out suffragette to visit this University," had made a name for herself. Born in Fulton, Illinois, 1885, she had attended the University of Chicago and served as president of the Equal Suffrage League of that institution. She graduated in 1908 and embarked on extensive lecture tours, championing women's suffrage to women's clubs, labor organizations, and other groups, mostly in Wisconsin and Illinois. This "comely, attractive woman," as the campus paper described her, gave her talk in May 1911. The restrictions assured a small crowd but Grim aroused much enthusiasm, "especially among the younger girls who were present." It was expected that the excitement would re-ignite the effort to organize on campus, with "the more militant of the co-eds" taking the lead.[41] Three years later, however, the main group that existed to promote women's suffrage, the WESA, consisted of women in Champaign and Urbana, with some members of the faculty and some students from the University. But it held its meetings, as in the case of May 1912, off campus at the home of one of the members, in this instance Trustee Mary Busey.[42] A campus organization for suffrage had not formed, a dozen years after the founding of the CESL.

The suffrage question bore directly on a related matter of long-standing discussion on the campus: the apolitical indifference of women to both national and institutional politics. *The Illinois*, through Editor-in-Chief Margaret H. Hallett, had something to say about it. The recent visit of Helen L. Grenfell of Colorado to the campus occasioned a brief opinion. Grenfell spoke to the women students on the subject of the suffrage and of equal rights generally. "The theme is trite," said the editorial. During campus elections girls sell their votes to any boy who will buy them or who delivers up a fine car for a ride. And yet naive men, especially those who tie the women's vote to the triumph of Prohibition, think females will purify our political system. This "fetish" should die hard, Hallett urged. It "passeth all understanding."[43]

In 1915 Dean Kyle was saying something similar. She gave a talk to some women students and stated firmly that they must not lead isolated lives, even if that choice seems to be an easier one than any alternative. She urged her audience to join organizations—social and political. "We want public-spirited women as types of college women," she said. By no other means can women have a large service role, on the campus now and in the world later, the dean urged.[44] A year earlier the DI editors voiced their vexation with what they denounced as pervasive indifference on the part of the women students to politics—on campus and at the national level. They disdained such attitudes as, "I don't believe in voting. Let the men do something by themselves for once"—words they quoted from a female asked about why women were so "dormant" on political questions. The editors described other reasons they had heard and showed no patience with them.[45]

But matters seemed to be changing somewhat just as the daily paper advanced these criticisms. In March 1914 the campus witnessed the "hardest fought senior election ever held." Joseph J. Pitts and Mark Van Doren contested for class president and campaigners for each candidate paid particular attention to the female vote. Indeed, it registered unprecedented high numbers and this "girl vote," the DI concluded, went overwhelmingly for Van Doren and delivered the Class of 1914 presidency to him.[46] The election had taken place under some new circumstances wherein women, after much pleading to do so, voted separately, in the Woman's Building. They assured that in this way they would not face the intimidating presence of male watch guards.[47]

• • •

In 1914 three extraordinary personalities came to the University of Illinois to begin their student careers. They arrived on the same train. Two were engaged to be married. The third would, a short while later, join them in a great friendship that governed much of what distinguished each individual in their time together.

Dorothy Day was born in Brooklyn, New York, in 1897. Her family never had much money, and her father's work as a newspaper reporter covering horse races underwent frequent shifts. Dorothy grew up also in Oakland, California, and in Chicago. Despite having brothers and sisters, including a little brother whom she took care of, she felt lonely. But she also experienced a certain joy in being alone. She learned little about tolerance from her father, who disdained all "foreigners" and political "agitators." As a girl, Dorothy did

316   PART IV. STUDENTS

not care much for most of the literary works in the home library and found a way to smuggle in romances and dime novels. She often visited an Episcopal church and found emotional comfort in the beauty of the Psalms. In Chicago Dorothy attended the local high school, with no intention and no means to continue her education thereafter. But she won a writing contest sponsored by the Hearst newspapers and with $300 now at her disposal, she opted for college and prepared to move downstate to Champaign-Urbana.[48]

Dorothy Day came to the University of Illinois thoroughly self-educated in radicalism. She had rested ill at ease with her social surroundings in Oakland and Chicago, with so much poverty, so much exploitation of workers, and "so much ugliness of life in a world that professed to be Christian." The plight of women especially troubled her. They had moved from the slavery of the sweatshops to the slavery of marriage, she lamented. Day had learned about the Haymarket rebellion in Chicago three decades before. She was taking now an interest in Eugene Debs and socialism. She paired these economic and political matters with intellectual ones also. She read the novels of Frank Harris, Jack London, and Upton Sinclair and opened up to the Russians with Peter Prokoptkin. With a rebellious mind already in place, reinforced by her habits of smoking and swearing, Day did not set well with the people who ran the YWCA, where she first lodged at the University. Her courses, except for those in literature, did not excite her, but her self-education proceeded apace. "I was greedy for books," she recalled. Living with a faculty family and doing work for the household earned her a little money. It all went to buy books. She plunged further into the Russians—Gorky, Dostoevsky, Tolstoy. For a while she had no friendships and felt "completely alone in the world." But her politics supplied the want and sustained her. "I was in love now with the masses." And then she met a new love.[49]

Her name was Rayna Simons. She also came from Chicago, born there in 1894. But *her* family had money. Her Jewish father served on the Chicago Board of Trade, and she grew up with six other children (two of them cousins) in the household. From her local high school she went on to the University of Chicago and then changed to Illinois where she took up residence in a Jewish boarding house. She met Dorothy Day in the Scribblers' Club. People who knew Rayna Simons rarely forgot her. Day didn't. "She had bright red curly hair. It was loose enough about her face to form an aureole, a flaming aureole, with sun and brightness in it." With Rayna, wrote Day, "a new love came into my life." Simons invited Day to move in with her. Rayna paid for Dorothy's food and room, and even loaned her some of her clothes to replace the threadbare ones her friend was wearing. Both women had a passion for writing and for leftist politics. But Rayna also showed Dorothy a great love of life, enthusiasm, and withal a brilliant mind. Simons made Phi Beta Kappa.

However, Day lamented, "In spite of brilliant scholarship and an outstanding personality, good looks and wealth, she was not invited to join any sorority. It was my first contact with anti-Semitism."[50]

Simons was engaged to Samson Raphaelson. He came from a Jewish family in New York City where he was born in 1896. He lived with his grandparents for some of that time and then rejoined his mother and father, who had relocated to Chicago. At McKinley High School he met Rayna Simons and there began a long, turbulent relationship.[51] They made the decision to go together to Illinois when she finished her first year at Chicago. They joined the Scribblers' Club and, with Day, the Socialists. He and Rayna took a course on socialism, taught by Paul Douglas, future senator from Illinois. At the time, Samson, too, had an ambition to write. He studied with Stuart Sherman and formed a lasting friendship with him, as Illinois students often did. "I fell in love with him," Raphaelson said. "He was my first father image." The Socialists provided other interests as they often invited speakers to the campus. So, the three students heard John Masefield, Edgar Lee Masters, Vachel Lindsay, and, more politically charged, Scott Nearing and Rose Pastor Stokes. The last, a firebrand for the cause who had gained notoriety on national speaking tours, also identified with Margaret Sanger's campaign for birth control. Vassar and Wellesley had barred her from their campuses—thus the comment from Day's biographers that Stokes's appearance at Illinois "says something about the liberalism of the James administration." Simons became the women's editor of the *Daily Illini* (with Catherine Needham) and editor of the *Siren*, with Raphaelson its co-business manager. Above all, the three enjoyed each other's company. Dorothy remembered her sophomore year as "idyllic."[52]

Day left the University after only two years. Her father had taken another position, this one in New York City, and she decided to relocate there with her family. Of course, for Day, there lie ahead the profound personal experiences she had in New York, Chicago, and other places that engaged her further in reformist politics. But there occurred also her powerful religious transformation, her role in founding the Catholic Workers' movement, and the journalism that made Dorothy Day a name familiar to all students of American religious history and a legendary person in the Catholic Church in the United States.

Samson Raphaelson moved from writing to music as his greater interest. One night at Illinois he attended an off-campus performance by the singer Al Jolson, in black face. He went "out of my mind" in enthusiasm. Raphaelson wrote a short story, "The Day of Atonement," about a Jewish cantor and his son. His story became a play, "The Jazz Singer," and then was adapted as a motion picture in 1927. As the historic first of the "talkies," it marked the beginning of Raphaelson's prominent Hollywood career as script writer and partner with Ernst Lubitsch in such movie classics as "The Merry Widow,"

318   **PART IV. STUDENTS**

A *Siren* Magazine cover in 1915. It appears to have elicited no critical reaction or commentary.

with Maurice Chevalier and Jeanette MacDonald.[53] After Illinois, Simons joined Day in New York for a while before she and Raphaelson married in early 1918. They continued to work for the old causes and even met up with Carl Haessler, now in Alcatraz prison for refusing induction into the military. The couple divorced in 1922. But Simons (now Rayna Prohme), too, became a legend. She worked for the Communist cause in China and then went to Moscow to study at the Lenin Institute and commit to the revolution. Simons died in that city in 1927, buried there with honors, a martyr to the Left.

• • •

So, Illinois did have its radical moment. But, to many, as noticed, and regrettably to them, the student body remained rather apolitical. One may look at this matter another way, however. Florence Yoch came to the University of Illinois after attending the University of California at Berkeley and Cornell. She was born in Santa Ana, California in 1890 to Joseph and Catherine Yoch, the youngest of six girls. The parents owned the popular Laguna Beach Hotel and the family lived in a large Italian-Revival home nearby. When she graduated from Illinois in the Class of 1915, Yoch returned to her home state and set up a landscape gardening practice in Pasadena. In 1921 she met Lucile Council and their partnership thrived personally and commercially. Yoch had a passion for travel and she studied historical and contemporary sites in Europe and Africa. Her work began to catch the attention of Hollywood moguls in the movie industry. She did the exterior designs for the new palatial estate of David O. Selznick and Irene Mayer. When Selznick turned his attention to producing the great and historic film *Gone with the Wind* (1939), he called on Yoch to create the grounds of Tara. In an energetic, innovative, and creative effort she set the plantation house of the famous movie in lush, romantic grandeur but with intimations of a decaying family establishment. Millions of people around the world would come to know the work of Florence Yoch, though few would know her name.[54]

As a student, in a 1914 issue of the *Illinois Magazine*, Florence Yoch contributed a piece titled "New Professions for Women." She gave descriptive accounts about the work of magazine illustrating, landscape architecture, scientific agriculture, interior and landscape design, the social survey (frequently with endowed foundations), and other new possibilities. The essay anticipated her own post-graduate career, but certainly would have attracted interest as it gave women readers a raison d'être they would have welcomed. And Nevins, in his history of the University, again leaves a clue. When he said that women students had a more serious approach to their academic work than did the men, he in fact spoke to a reality of this second generation of higher education females in the United States. Attention to their studies went right along with the career goals that described this new generation. These goals further

320 **PART IV. STUDENTS**

claimed a priority over political concerns in the minds of what appears to be a large representation in the female student body. For, Yoch wrote of the new professions, "all of them require brains, imagination, and serious study." And "the college woman" has these necessary skills.[55] One may believe that Yoch claimed the attention of her readers among the women students of the University more than did those who had been asking for their political commitment all these years.

And finally, one may notice another model of the female student, one who made her university experience a personal, intellectual awakening. Olive Deane Hormel provides a fully illustrated example in her autobiographical narrative of Lucia Leigh, the protagonist of her novel *Co-Ed*. Lucia experiences her first year at the University as little else than a social whirlwind. A member of "Gamma" sorority (Hormel belonged to Kappa Kappa Gamma), the affairs of that society claimed her full devotion; studies meant nothing to her.[56] And on it went into her second year. Her father, wise to the way his daughter lives on campus, admonishes her, and tells her that she's missing out on the real business there, and her prime responsibility—academics. Time to stop being just a "dance major," he exhorts.[57] But her father's words come just when Lucia herself is tiring of the relentless socializing, and she agrees that better opportunities await her at the University. She vows now to commit to academics. "For the first time in her life, she worked only for grades."[58]

What began as an effort to get a better GPA, however, quickly became something more. Lucia discovers in her courses things of intrinsic worth, indeed exciting things. "It was her courses that semester which gave Lucia her first keen consciousness of the thrill attendant upon an earnest venture in constructive thought." Particular faculty helped bring about the transformation in this student. She takes a course in Shakespeare with "Tudor B. Sheridan" (Stuart P. Sherman). He "unlocked a magic realm peopled with dramatis personae vividly real." With Professor "Ziegler" (Jacob Zeitlin) the English romantic poets, heretofore for her "only minstrels of surpassing charm," became serious propagandists and philosophers with large visions and suggestions of a different reality. Her courses in sociology give her close looks at poverty, immigration, and other issues heretofore obscured from her awareness. And her "case studies" in the seminar bring the social pathologies of the twin city population directly to her attention.[59]

But Lucia found the course that above all others brought her intellectual self-discovery in Professor "Gode's" (Boyd Bode) philosophy class. Whereas she expected from it a "leisurely excursion" through Aristotle and Plato, she received instead "a kind of breathless sortie in the history and development of thought, with all its diverse and conflicting theories as to what it means to be a 'living soul.'" Bode made his jam-packed class an unrelenting assault on dogmas. He presented his students "with a vision of a world in flux." But

	DREW		FULLER	
REESE	HARWOOD	SHELDON	JEWETT	
VAN DOREN	STOUTZENBERG	NEEDHAM	HORMEL	IRWIN

The Scribblers' Club attracted students interested in writing, and it had special value for women students, who had a consistently higher representation in it than they usually did in campus organizations not exclusively female. Here, in 1915, we see Lucile Needham, president of the club, in the middle, first row. Olive Dean Hormel, future author of the UofI Illinois novel *Co-Ed*, sits to Needham's left. Mark Van Doren is front row, far left. Courtesy of the University of Illinois Archives.

therein, he urged, lay not the grounds for despair, but the hope for progress and improvement. "With humor and insight, he aroused [his students] to fatal distrust of the fetishes and formulae men had invented as an escape from the arduous labor of thinking—all of which brought them to poignant realization that a 'liberal education' may involve quite literally the building for oneself a new heaven and a new earth." And, thus inspired, Lucia joins the Philosophy Club.[60] She realizes, too, that all these intellectual excursions together had changed her. "She had glimpsed something high and splendid and infinitely remote from the petty concerns of [her friends'] undergraduate world."[61]

As the novel comes to its conclusion Lucia is preparing for graduation and contemplating her future. She faces a momentous decision, one that will determine her course for the rest of her life. How to resolve the dilemma before her? She contemplates a line from Walt Whitman and other words, from her recent studies, by Ralph Waldo Emerson. All then becomes clear to her; she makes her decision and then feels very happy. Her liberal education at the University has come to her rescue. No wonder the administration loved this book.

The 1916 membership of Scribblers' included Lucile Needham again, middle of the first row, and sister Catherine, at the far right, first row. Dorothy Day is in the middle of the top row, with Samson Raphaelson on her left. Courtesy of the University of Illinois Archives.

The 1917 Scribblers' has Catherine Needham, far right first row, and Samson Raphaelson, far left first row. Rayna Simons sits next to him. Lois Seyster, future coauthor of the UofI short stories collection *Town and Gown*, is third from right in second row. Courtesy of the University of Illinois Archives.

Afterword

An Illinois Promise

THE CONCLUDING SECTION of any book of this type usually looks for a convenient summary or overriding thematic statement that will place all its material into sharp focus and clarification. It's always a temptation, but one should proceed cautiously. In this instance, a narrative of the events, personalities, and academic developments at the University of Illinois in the years of Edmund Janes James's presidency, 1904 to 1920, has yielded a record of institutional transformation. In all aspects of its intellectual life especially, research and scholarship produced new learning marked by an expanse of exploration and inquiry. No orthodoxies or ideological platforms could give this information explosion any easy generalization. Indeed, one could say that if any "essence" describes the modern university, then surely intellectual diversity and openness, the drama of the new, and the persistent rethinking and revision of inherited ideas describe its governing principles. To that end, an institution given to the defense of a particular truth or code of higher principles would set uncomfortably with these intrinsic characteristics of the modern university.

Nonetheless, something was occurring at Illinois that helps to frame the material in this book. Going into the second decade of the century a new institutional self-awareness emerged. Key individuals looked back to rediscover landmarks of its history and sought by this means to provide the University with its own special identity and mission. The effort did not overwhelm or dictate the University's life in these years; but it did inspire in some of its leaders a purpose, or a promise, special to this particular body of students, teachers, administrators, and the citizens of Illinois. Their views set this book in a wider intellectual parameter.

• • •

In February 1912, the *Daily Illini*, with Allan Nevins as chief news editor, ran an editorial lamenting the fact that the University had no book describing its history. "With each passing year," said the piece, "the pity must grow that no adequate written history of the University has ever been prepared." Yet all was in place for it to happen—the records of this paper, professors with long memories, department and college files and documents. Such a chronicle would capture also local history, color, tradition; it would describe student life, student manners, and collegiate ideals; it "would be more than entertaining and informational; it would be inspiring."[1] Discussion seems to have driven the matter further because in May the Board of Trustees authorized Burt E. Powell in the College of Agriculture and secretary to the president to gather materials for this purpose. The *Daily Illini* welcomed the new initiative.[2]

Many others on the campus also knew the significance of the year 1912. They took note of the fiftieth anniversary of the Morrill Act. The *Daily Illini* proclaimed the land-grant legislation of 1862 as "the greatest endowment of higher education ever made at one time by the act of any legislature." The editors clearly knew the long history surrounding the act and some of the disputes about it. They knew that Illinoisans had always championed the name of Jonathan Baldwin Turner as the true inspiration of the legislation and hence its true author. The paper did acknowledge that the question remained open. But no matter, at all events the half-century anniversary "deserves commemoration of some sort." What matters to us, however, said the DI, is the fact that Turner "was a resident of Illinois."[3] Now, in this time of institutional self-reflection and quest for identity, Jonathan B. Turner became the center of the universe for Illinoisans resolved to define for their school its special place in the panoply of American colleges and universities.

Readers of Winton Solberg's first volume of the University's history know the name of Jonathan B. Turner. Others will gain by an introduction. To date, the biography written by Turner's daughter Mary Turner Carriel, which appeared amid the semicentennial commemorations, remains the most comprehensive study of the man. The *Daily Illini* took due note of it and reasserted, "to him the University of Illinois owes its being," and the journal expressed regret that his memory had diminished among people in the state.[4]

Turner came from New England, born outside Worcester, Massachusetts in 1805. Family history included a grandfather who fought at the Battle of Saratoga in the Revolutionary War, and his father, one of the insurgents who marched in rebellion with Daniel Shays against the state in 1786. Turner entered Yale at age 22 and then joined the famous Yale Band in evangelizing the West, with the intention also to start new colleges in their great design for a Protestant America. Turner himself took a position at Illinois College in

326   **AFTERWORD**

Jacksonville where he also started a Bible class at the nearby Congregational church. The Presbyterian denomination had jurisdiction of the College and Turner's views, clearly non-Calvinist, raised skepticism about him. So also did Turner's vehement abolitionist stance on the slavery question. He resigned his post in 1848. By this time the creative Turner was teaming with new ideas, and he sought new platforms to advance some bold proposals.[5]

Turner's attention had turned to the working classes—farmers and mechanics—often referenced as the "industrial classes." As he took up this subject he joined his thoughts to an agrarian literature then flourishing in Illinois and elsewhere. It focused not merely on the low economic status of workers but on their lives, too—the drudgery of their work, the deprivation of culture and intellect that beset them. So, education played a large part in the essays and editorials that one could find in such journals as the *Prairie Farmer*.[6] At Granville in 1851 Turner gave his first major address. He reviewed a long history that depicted the division of human society into the industrial classes and the "professional" classes. One factor alone, asserted Turner, explained the disparities between them: intellect. Turner described a system of elite rule in which power derived from the mastery of language and word culture. From the church and the theologians, to the aristocracy, to the institutions of law, medicine, business, and the arts the power of language secured the ruling professionals in social dominance and status. In a speech titled "Industrial Universities" Turner called for an education appropriate to the industrial classes. And he meant much more than the three "r's." What the laborers need, he asserted, was intellectual power—power appropriate to the work they do, the skills they have. They need the knowledge that underscores these skills, the ruling laws of nature, "the living waters of knowledge within their own domain." They need, in short, just what the professional classes have—knowledge relevant to them. But, asked Turner, "Where are the universities, the apparatus, the professors, and the literature, specifically adapted to any one of the industrial classes?" So, Turner proposed a new set of universities in each state—public universities. Congress should provide the money, by land grants or other means, with the objective of producing "thinking laborers."[7] Turner had formed the Industrial League in Illinois to promote the cause nationally. But President Pierce and the Democrats had no taste for the idea. Turner then succeeded in having his home state take the lead.

Turner secured much of his enduring fame in an address two years later that he titled "The Millenium of Labor." (Turner always spelled it this way.) He again decried the situation in higher learning and the still dominant place of the ancient languages and of dead philosophy. But he saw a great new age emerging, evidenced by the signs of technological progress and innovation everywhere. And herein lie the means of liberation for the industrial classes, Turner believed, if they could be brought within the great learning, the sciences, that enabled these marvels. But we have old habits that defy that possibility, old stereotypes, he lamented. Thus, Turner wrote: "It is our miserably low idea of agricultural and industrial art that is dwarfing and crippling and ruining us—and not the nature of these pursuits." Thus, we need a new start in education. But the farmers and mechanics must see themselves differently. We are not oppressed by our brethren professionals, he said. Turner saw no necessity of class warfare in his scheme. He looked rather to a harmony of all society's different components and an effective democracy that would emerge from it. No, we are oppressed, Turner insisted, because we have neglected to do for ourselves what the professional classes have done for themselves. Thus, we must move away from our prejudices against book learning—what we need are the right books. Satan, Turner avowed, has done no worse than to deprive workers of mental power. Labor's millennium lies within reach, and university reform can secure it. Turner's prescription: learning and labor.[8]

Turner called for his program of state universities because none other would suffice to meet the crisis at hand. The old curriculum still showed its staying power, "the old prejudice of caste and creed." Turner also resisted, vehemently, calls from the older religious colleges to share in any new land grants, seeing in them the narrow denominational habits of dogmas and confessions. Indeed, they represented the very "old prejudices" that have so long plagued the course of learning. These old-time colleges could never generate the grand intellectual outreach of science and the fullest expansion of mind that the times demanded. Turner looked to state universities established on a grand scale: "No species of knowledge should be excluded, practical or theoretical," he urged. To that extent as well, "professors should conduct, each in his own department, a continued series of annual experiments."[9] Turner called his educational reform "Liberal Industrial Education" and gave it his time and energy. He traveled the crossroads speaking for the state university program and later welcomed the legislative act of 1862 that created it.[10]

• • •

President James did not miss a step in the march of recovery for Jonathan Baldwin Turner's legacy. He arranged to give his thoughts on the matter in a forceful and visible way: the commencement events of 1912. The University planned a special day by inviting to the campus all living graduates from the University's first class. About 125, a third of the invitees, expressed their intentions to attend.[11] James spoke entirely on Turner and his great importance, and later revised his address for publication in the *Journal of the Illinois State Historical Society*, which organization he had helped to establish.

First, James affirmed the great significance of the Morrill Act. To be sure, James had written about these subjects earlier. Just four years into his

328 **AFTERWORD**

presidency he brought the matter of the land-grant movement to the attention of a national readership. His letter in the *Nation* proclaimed "the growing prominence" of the land-grant universities generally, but took pains also to note the role of the Illinois state legislature and Jonathan B. Turner, who "deserves credit" for initiating what became the Morrill Act.[12]

At the commencement, James took a long view of history. He noted the creation of the University of Leyden in the midst of famine in sixteenth-century Holland; the organization of the University of Berlin ("the greatest university of this or any other time") amid the national humiliation of the Napoleonic occupation; and the inauguration of the land-grant system of public state universities while the Union fought for its survival amid civil war. James had unstinting praise for Justin Morrill, the Vermont senator, and "the services of this great man to American education." But, he went on, "great as is the honor due to Mr. Morrill, the real credit for originating the plan incorporated in the Land Grant Act, belongs to an Illinois farmer and professor, Jonathan B. Turner."[13] James feared that many in his audience, and especially the students, did not know this name. He intended to correct the oversight.[14]

James carefully constructed his presentation of Turner, integrating his ideas in a way that confirmed principles that James had advanced and defended in his presidency to date. Indeed, the occasion enables a summary view of James's presidency as he carefully appropriated Turner in a way that articulated James's vision of his own academic leadership. Thus, he upheld Turner as "Prophet of democracy" and his system as the very expression of that great American ideal, and one affiliated especially with the West. Turner, James said, made his cause the education of the common man and saw the state university system as the critical vehicle of that goal. Furthermore, James went on, Turner spoke for "scientific" education in all branches of learning. And he did so in the manner that James himself had upheld "science" as the standard of knowledge—science as the broadest expanse of intellectual outreach. James reminded his listeners that Turner was, after all, not just a farmer but a "philosopher," and one in quest of the "true philosophy" that underscored the science and art of every vocation. Turner, James emphasized, "realized as no man of equal education of his own time, the fundamental necessity of higher scientific education for the farmer and the mechanic if our democracy was to be developed." James quoted Turner on the imperative of securing this basis of knowledge as much for the industrial classes as for the professional classes. To that end Turner would look to the new state universities to do advanced research in all fields and bring the heretofore excluded classes into it. Our university today, James avowed, can do no better than to follow this ideal and "to lay broad and deep the foundations of an ever advancing social and industrial improvement."[15]

An Illinois Promise   329

• • •

Dean of the College of Agriculture Eugene Davenport also contributed to the Turner revival. He had long written on matters of higher education and now in 1914, revising and expanding an offering from 1909, he published *Education for Efficiency* (which surely deserved a better title), a booklet of nearly two hundred pages. It represented a systematic effort to revisit the ideas of Turner and give them a restatement and renewal. Davenport herein provided one of the most valuable documents of the University of Illinois in the James era.

Davenport began with a look at the social scheme that had given Turner his consistent perspectives on education and democracy. He quoted from the reformer's "Plan for an Industrial University": "All civilized society is, necessarily, divided into two distinct, cooperative, not antagonistic, classes." He restated Turner's positing of the industrial classes and the professional classes, and then quoted Turner's big question: "where are the universities, the apparatus, the professors, and the literature adapted to any one of the industrial classes?" Davenport considered Turner the great visionary behind the Morrill Act and judged that act "the most far-reaching bit of federal legislation ever enacted." The Morrill Act, he asserted, had significance precisely in the way Turner saw. It "marked a new epoch in the life of industrial people," Davenport wrote, because hitherto the policy of the world had been to keep working folk ignorant, "so that they remained content with the hard lot that Providence had presumably assigned them." Davenport wished to use his lengthened essay to show why Turner's outlook had continued relevance.[16]

Several points stand out in Davenport's essay that mark a continuity between Turner and the Illinois dean. Some quotations from the essay will show these connections and show Davenport's powerful voice in this important document about American democracy and the role of the nation's universities in perfecting it.

- Universal higher education breaks down those historical barriers that conspire against harmonious democracy. So, we "must see to it that [in addition to technical education] every individual has a fair share of the liberal as well, for the chief distinction of the educated man is, after all, his ability to view the world from a standpoint broader than his own surroundings." (P. 20)
- Davenport called for the education of farmers' and mechanics' sons and daughters in a common educational program with all others and together in the same institution. It would mark a major step in overcoming the invidious distinctions that persisted because of the separate life patterns imposed on the two classes. "I would have it so that the

330   AFTERWORD

occupation of an American citizen shall not be known by his dress, his manner, his speech, or his prejudices." (P. 33)

- "Unless we can do this, [that is, provide 'universal education'] democracy will, in the end, fail. We cannot go on with one half of the people educated and the other half ignorant, any more than we could live with one half free and the other half slave." (P. 16)
- "The aristocracy of education, like the aristocracy of religion, whereby a few were saved while the many groaned, is over, and education, like religion, must help the common man to meet and solve the common issues of life better than they have ever been met and solved before— hence industrial education, hence vocational education, hence universal education." (P. 70)
- College education has a critical role to play in breaking down the static social norms that have overly determined what each individual might become. Thus, he stated, "Because a girl is born in the country is no sign in America that she should be a farmer's wife." (P. 107)
- Davenport joined Turner in calling for the broadest kind of education for the industrial classes. Both individuals rejected agricultural education and mechanical education as mere "training," mere utilitarian application to a specific kind of work. Davenport included a chapter titled "The Culture Aim in Education." Thus, "[every man] is something more than a farmer or a doctor or a lawyer or else he is something less than a man. His education is not to be limited by the demands of his vocation."(P. 62)
- "Every man is, or ought to be, bigger than his business." (P. 171)
- "The American farmer is not a peasant." (P. 106)
- Turner's conviction that true university education underscored American democracy had Davenport's full endorsement. Thus, the new policy "is working successfully in our great state universities where men of all classes, aims, and prospects are educated together from the standpoint not of private interest but of the public good." (P. 115)

• • •

In 1912 student Allan Nevins, through the offices of the *Daily Illini*, campaigned for celebration of the Morrill Act on its semicentennial, and for renewed recognition of Jonathan Baldwin Turner, its inspiration. In 1962 Nevins returned to Champaign-Urbana to give a series of four lectures commemorating the centennial of the Morrill Act. Those lectures constituted Nevins's book of that year, *The State Universities and Democracy*, a history of the land-grant institutions and a look to their future. Clearly, Nevins intended to champion their cause, and the book fit appropriately with the career of historian that Nevins had pursued since he finished at Illinois and the great record of achievements he had recorded. As noted earlier, he first published the biography of Robert Rogers and then in 1917 wrote the first history of the University of Illinois. Even in his years as journalist Nevins kept up his interest in higher education. In a 1916 piece for the New York *Evening Post*, for example, Nevins, now a New Yorker, observed how the state universities of the Middle West had become the vital intellectual centers of their states and had joined their academic research with a resolve to promote the common good. He believed that the East would gain by the example.[17]

In his lectures for the centennial and in the ensuing book on the state universities, Nevins offered this observation: these relatively new institutions face the difficult challenges of creating "an atmosphere, a tradition, a sense of the past." These elements, he said, can come from beautiful campus architecture and landscape, and they can come from the memory of "inspiring personalities." The school song "Old Nassau" at Princeton evokes this mystique, as does Daniel Webster's famous plea for Dartmouth College before the United States Supreme Court in 1819.[18] Nevins, though, had already done work in making such an effort for his own school, and Jonathan B. Turner was giving him just the occasion he needed. So, in writing the University of Illinois's first history, and still fresh from his studies there, Nevins made the case for Turner. The movement for a federal program to support new state universities, he wrote, "originated not with Vermont, as is commonly believed, but with Illinois, and was headed not by Justin Morrill but by Jonathan B. Turner." Further, "in the definite form assumed in Illinois [the movement] was clearly responsible for the ultimate passage of the Land Grant Act."[19] In his later writing on the state universities Nevins had high praise for Morrill and gave him much credit. But he saw to it that Turner got his due. He cited Turner, along with the Marquis de Condorcet, Thomas Jefferson, John Stuart Mill, and H. G. Wells, among writers who looked to universities for liberating the mind, for undoing the corruption in church and state, and for empowering new classes of people.[20] The Morrill Act itself caused some states to move ahead more ambitiously, and they achieved much as a result, Nevins attested, a major example being the University of Illinois, which has "since become one of the greatest universities in the country."[21]

The movement of institutional self-consciousness took another turn the year after Nevins published his history of the University. Burt E. Powell, James's secretary, introduced his own history, *Semi-Centennial History of the University of Illinois, Volume I: The Movement for Industrial Education and the Establishment of the University, 1840–1870* (Urbana: University of Illinois, 1918). James wrote an introduction for it. Powell accumulated an immense amount of documents on which to base his study. In it he proclaimed the dominant and crucial role, not only of Jonathan Baldwin Turner, but of a

332 AFTERWORD

host of Illinoisans, as individuals and groups, who defined and promoted the land-grant idea. Because up to now "it had never been proposed," it was "entirely new." He rehearsed Turner's demand, throughout the campaign, that industrial education must include liberal studies. By no other means will the industrial classes rise to the place in human society "for which God intended them (Turner)." Powell wished especially to show that Turner's ideas moved beyond local dispersion into national attention, and luminous figures like Horace Greeley endorsed and encouraged them. So did other agriculture societies in other states. Successive conventions, in Illinois and beyond, moved to ratify the land-grant idea. Turner and colleagues established an educational journal, the *Illinois Teacher*, to give more intellectual force to the movement. And finally, Powell argued, the Morrill Act itself incorporates language directly borrowed from Turner. The congressional land-grant legislation of 1862 so much reflected the long work of Illinoisans that Powell could label its features "the Illinois idea," so nominated just seven years after the term the "Wisconsin Idea" had its coinage.[22]

• • •

Finally, Turner has another significance for this book. He provides a connection that links the philosophical idealism of the Germans to the James generation of thinkers at the University of Illinois who sought to give the school an institutional identity and historical location. Turner's social ideas about higher education, just observed, flourished within a large metaphysical, theological, and cosmological framework. That outlook Turner rooted in his notions of mental and physical reality. Turner had, like the German thinkers, confidence in the power of mind, in its expansive outreach, to connect these two realms. The effort placed Turner squarely in the romantic movement in Europe and in the United States. And that location helped the Illinoisans of the James era to articulate their own ideals about education and the curricular needs of the modern American university, their own especially.

A glimpse at some of Turner's writings will clarify his identity with the romantic movement. It is everywhere. Sometimes he affirms the idealists' ontology. "Mind," Turner wrote, is "the great motive power of the universe." In its unrelenting quest it seeks to link and connect things, to see through nature to God, and to grasp the underlying divine laws of all reality. It provides us "intimate knowledge of all the hidden processes of nature." This knowledge we call "science."[23] But they have a critical interdependency, these two realms of spiritual and material being, Turner insisted. No complete knowledge comes to us apart from these links. In application, this conviction prompted Turner's decrying of empty metaphysics and all disconnections from practical action and applied knowledge in the college curriculums—hence his strenuous attacks on the old-time colleges. But mere labor, mere training in skills, immersion

An Illinois Promise   333

in material reality alone, has deadening effects, Turner also emphasized. Work must have connections to the mind and its powers. Turner, like some others of the romantics, postulated a dualism that radically differentiated mind and matter. "Mind," he wrote, "is the only freeman and matter the only slave God ever made. Its powers and resources are infinite and eternal." But the industrial classes, long trapped in an education only in material things and trained only in technique, thus had lived like slaves. Turner prescribed the joining of these two realities as the only hope for these classes and as the only liberating education for them or any other group of people. "The most natural and effectual mental discipline possible for any man," Turner urged, "arises from setting him to earnest and constant thought about the things he daily does, sees, and handles, and all their connected relations and interests." Salvation comes to any or all only when we can see nature as God made it, that is, "with the true poet's and philosopher's eye." Otherwise, we have only the tyranny of material fact.[24] Turner said in an 1853 address at Springfield: "Each son and daughter of Adam's race should learn through the handicraft of their daily toil, to look through nature up to nature's God, trace his deep designs, and derive their daily mental and moral culture, as well as their daily food, from that toil."[25]

Importantly, also, Turner has an intellectual kinship with the American romantics, the Transcendentalists in particular.[26] And that relation provides the key point of interconnection and symmetry in this book. Drawing on roots in German philosophical idealism as modified by English thinkers Samuel Taylor Coleridge and Thomas Carlyle, Ralph Waldo Emerson and the Americans speculated about the powers of the human mind and the nature of the reality it confronted. They validated the truth that derived from sense data as processed through the Understanding, but they looked beyond this empirical base to a higher, invisible, or "transcendent" realm of being, as accessed by the Reason (or intuition).[27] But these thinkers did not lose themselves in mystical ascent. Rather they sought to derive a truth from ordinary experience as informed or enlightened by the intuitive insight. "We reason from our hands to our heads," Henry David Thoreau wrote in *Walden*. We seek to know "the near, the low, the common," said Emerson. And in these words resound echoes of the earlier German philosophers, for they had among their hopes, to "poetize" even the most ordinary life. Thus, rather than disdaining the mundane, the practical, and the quotidian, the Transcendentalists made them the springboard to a higher vision, of Nature, or God, or the Oversoul. Emerson put the point most memorably in his provocative essay "The American Scholar."

> What would we really know the meaning of? The meal in the firkin; the milk in the pan; the ballad in the street; the news of the boat; the glance of the eye; the form and the gait of the body;—show me the ultimate reason

of these matters; show me the sublime presence of the highest spiritual cause lurking, as always it does lurk, in these suburbs and extremities of nature; let me see every trifle bristling with the polarity that ranges it instantly on an eternal law; and the shop, the plow, and the ledger referred to the like cause by which light undulates and poets sing;—and the world lies no longer a dull miscellany and lumber-room, but has form and order: there is no trifle, there is no puzzle, but one design unites and animates the farthest pinnacle and the lowest trench.

Emerson here "justified the preoccupation with familiar everyday things which early characterized schools founded on the Morrill Act." From these notions the earlier German philosophical idealists do not seem very far. Historian Peter Neumann describes their views on artistic creativity: "Poeticization occur[s] by investing lowly matters with a higher meaning, lending the commonplace a transcendental touch, and giving the finite the sheen of infinity."[28]

But Illinoisans could, and did, derive such notions from the man in their midst, Jonathan B. Turner. At his Springfield address in 1853 Turner urged his listeners to consider how the two realms of matter and spirit communicate with each other, and that we do indeed learn from the hand to the head. Turner excoriated that view that could see "no foundation for the development and culture of a high order of science and literature, and the noblest capacities of mind, heart, and soul," in connection with "the daily employments of the industrial classes!" Some others, Turner lamented, would discount his educational scheme because they judged the ordinary thing, the practical, as too sensuous, too gross for any elevation, any access to the great truths of nature and God. "How came such a heathenish and apostate idea ever to get abroad in the world?" Turner asked.[29]

As Dean Eugene Davenport celebrated Turner's role in the land-grant movement, he also appropriated Turner's ideas about life and about education. He made the burden of his little book *Education for Efficiency* the necessity of liberal learning (what he called "universal education") for all classes. The working classes, Turner insisted, have fully the capability for "the loftiest intellectual achievements." (Consider the Jews: "shepherds of the Judean hills.") As Turner had condemned strictly manual training as "mere servile imitation," so did Davenport. Some people "are always careful to speak of industrial education as 'training,' using a term whose meaning is understood from its frequent application to horses and dogs." We may think of the old-time college as an institution given to liberal education and the schools for farmers and mechanics as given to practical training, Davenport said. But we make a fatal mistake in radically differentiating the types of learning. Davenport looked for a "golden mean" between them to break down the harsh dualism in our thinking and in our educational arrangements.[30]

An Illinois Promise   335

Davenport located the way out by making the point so emphasized by Emerson and Turner. "One of the things that is needed now," he wrote, "is to put more of idealism into common things and more of culture into the common man." For if we see the world the right way, we will recognize that immersion in common things prepares the way to an opening to higher things, if we so allow it to. Davenport desired "especially" to emphasize this point: "And that is the intellectual development that comes to the individual as the direct result of doing extremely well whatever is undertaken, even though it be the most common things of everyday life."[31] Nor should we fall into the deception of idealizing our meditation on "lofty thoughts" that project us out of our alleged deficient commonplace world. We should give them no certification "*unless that meditation leads to action.*" Davenport employed the Turnerian and Emersonian language of the interrelatedness and harmony of all things and warned against any pedagogy that broke down that reality. The intellectual and the practical have a common bond, he assured. "All branches of learning are both useful" and an education in one enhances the education in another, he urged. "Every man needs two educations," Davenport specified, "one that is vocational and one that is not."[32]

We have yet another measure of these intellectual connections from Allan Nevins. In writing about the state universities Nevins gave attention to the historic ideas that motivated the American reformers in the land-grant movement. He gave a prominent place to the romantic movement. He pointed to its roots in Germany and its powerful thinkers—Fichte, Schelling, and Hegel among them—and the creation of the University of Berlin. They all helped instill "a sense of the illimitable possibilities of science," Nevins reported. And as the movement made its way to England and then to America it took on new emphases. In Thomas Carlyle, Nevins saw "the gospel of the innate goodness of Work," and the recourse to nature and ordinary things as an aspect of spirituality. "All true Work is religion," Carlyle wrote in *Past and Present*. "All true Work is sacred; in all true Work, were it but true hand-labor, there is something of divineness. Labor, wide as the earth, has its summit in Heaven." Emerson, greatly influenced by Carlyle, testified, in Nevins's account, to romanticism's invocation of science and the great extension of human intellect generated in pursuit of it. He cites Emerson's "Education" (a collection of pieces assembled by later editors) and notes his modeling of Newton and Humboldt in their bringing all the universe under "relation and law." We will find like qualities in the American romantics—Thoreau, Poe, Melville, Holmes—all devotees of "science," Nevins asserted.[33]

Nevins had a particular urgency in tracing these roots of the state universities, because ultimately, they are about democracy. And Nevins, like Turner, considered democracy greatly a matter of the social classes. On this matter, Germany, for all its intellectual achievement, had failed, Nevins attested. It

336   AFTERWORD

perpetuated a class-based system of education that kept the working classes in an inferior position. Nevins saw that problem early on, but now, like Turner, he made democracy a matter of intellectual liberation, the breaking of the industrial classes from the deprivation of true learning. For, wrote Nevins, not only does democracy imply "intellectual liberty with full freedom to think, write, and speak. It implies an open society, without caste lines, giving its members full freedom to move from calling to calling, rank to rank."[34]

But still the question raged, Nevins said, "education for what?" One hundred years after creation of the Morrill program that question provoked strong and often bitter feelings, as it does today, a hundred years after Edmund James finished his work at the University of Illinois. Nevins considered the matter in his book on the state universities. One might expect these institutions, he said, to promote education for utility, for practical outcomes that justified themselves to a tax-paying public. On the other side, we still have spokesmen for education as mental discipline, promoting, as Harvard President A. Lawrence Lowell put it, "study that challenges and embraces the mind." Nevins would have neither. Almost as though he were resorting to the philosophical models he had discussed earlier in the book, wherein reality blends the spiritual and material, the speculative and the practical, Nevins asked, are we going to have an education for doing, or an education for being? (Or, as Davenport put it, Man needs one education "that will fit him to work and one that will fit him to live.") But our best philosophy has taught us that "the two ideals are by no means mutually exclusive, and account should be taken of both." And our best state university presidents today insist as much on education for being as they do on education for doing.[35]

Dean Davenport also wanted to undo the entrenched dualism that hindered the progress of college education and that had conspired against the social democracy he envisioned through Turner's eyes. "I care everything," he wrote, "for the principle and the practice of uniting by the closest possible educational bonds, day by day and every day, the vocational and non-vocational." Davenport would not diminish the differences between learning and labor, but instead would create educational programs that assure the advantages of both by requiring both. Or, as he put it, every graduate "will have some education of the head with some initiative of the body." In short, "I must earnestly urge the closest possible joining of the two."[36] Thus the motto "Learning and Labor."

The Illinoisans who made this effort to define the true character of the modern university and its relation to democracy included President James. He had offered his views in a national forum just before coming to the University, and he reinforced them on occasions thereafter. Happily, he observed, events like the Morrill Act and the academic revolution inspired by Germany had enabled the United States to move beyond the irrelevant disputes about

An Illinois Promise   **337**

liberal education and practical education. He celebrated "the peculiar way in which we have combined the work of technical instruction with that of the humanities and the professions in one institution." And both branches of the university have gained from it. On the one hand, "the technical school has made university work more practical, compelled it to measure itself by new and healthful standards and brought a new spirit into much of its activity." On the other hand, the university has humanized the technical work. James, long a friend of the ancient classics, even urged that those engaged in critical technical studies as well as those pursuing "pure science" yet acquire some depth in this ancient literature and "interpret for our day and generation the imperishable experiences of Greece and Rome." The national interest will gain from it.[37]

At Illinois, James's views seem to have elaborated this model of the true university under the influence of Turner. They now took a progressive turn as James spoke to the matter of social classes and the democratic ideals of the research university. He recognized in Turner the truth that true change and effective advancement to social equality among the classes in America required an intellectual liberation for those heretofore denied it. But mere technical training could not secure that liberation, he insisted. It could emerge only from the expansive "scientific" education that informs and underscores the work of the industrial classes and raises them to large awareness of higher realities. James quoted with approval Turner's statement: "Our industrial classes want, and they ought to have, the same facilities for understanding the true philosophy, the science and the art of their several pursuits . . . applying existing knowledge thereto and widening its domain" as the professional classes had always enjoyed.[38] "Learning and Labor."

Finally, the celebration of Turner seems not to have been the work of only faculty and administration at Illinois. It had a place even in the common population. Thus, at the beginning of Olive Dean Hormel's novel, we see Lucia's father, talking to her and her friends, giving his daughter all the reasons he can summon for her attending the University. (He seeks to dissuade her from her choice of Vassar.) It's not just that the Chemistry Building is "the largest biggest college building in the world," he says. No, it goes back to the very ur-moment of the land-grant university movement, to Jonathan B. Turner. Mr. Leigh knows all about the meeting in Granville in 1851 when Turner unraveled his design. Horace Greeley recognized Turner's great significance, the father proclaimed, and so did Justin Morrill, who brought Turner's proposal to Congress "after much correspondence with Turner."[39]

• • •

"Learning and Labor." This motto reached back to the very beginning of the University of Illinois, formally adopted by the Board of Trustees in 1868.

Regent John Milton Gregory welcomed it and related it to the educational needs of the industrial classes in a manner that underscored the views of Turner.[40] Generations of Illinois students have known this expression, inscribed in the University's seal. The words greet visitors and all others at the entrance to the campus, at the base of the "Alma Mater" statute of Lorado Taft. "Learning and Labor" spoke to the controversial issues of the day that led to the Morrill Act of 1862, and the pairing animated debates about how to implement the path-breaking legislation.[41] But the two words have yet a greater significance, appropriate only to the University of Illinois.

This book earlier described the intellectual world of Edmund James. It reviewed the formative role of German philosophy as the originating ideas of the modern research university. A remarkable continuity becomes apparent in the life and trajectory of this idealistic philosophy, through English romantics, American Transcendentalists, Jonathan Baldwin Turner, and some University of Illinois leaders in the James era. They sealed a long quest to bring "learning" and "labor" into cohabitation and harmony. They knew the invidious class distinctions that had long kept them separate and exclusive. They sought to undo the isolation of learning from the broad society and public, and they sought to remove labor from its confinement to toil and drudgery. They brought learning and labor into components of a healthy humanism that looked to the spiritual and moral growth of the individual, the *Bildung* project of modern university education. In inspired thinkers like James, Davenport, and Nevins this new alliance had above all an importance for democracy. "Learning and Labor" thus gave the University of Illinois its special place within a long and rich intellectual history.

Notes

Chapter 1. A New Leader at Illinois

1. The proceedings of these conferences were edited and published separately and in the *Installation of Edmund Janes James* (Urbana, 1906). Inclusion of all texts of the addresses given at the events yielded a volume of 547 pages.

2. Edmund Janes James, "Rev. Colin Dew James: A Pioneer Methodist Preacher of Early Illinois," *Journal of the Illinois State Historical Society*, 9 (January 1917), 451–52, 453–54, 456, 460–61. See also the *Daily Illini*, student newspaper, "Dr. James, President," which has more genealogical information about James on both his parents' sides. November 14, 1904, 1.

3. James, "Colin Dew James," 451, 454, 457–58, 465, 467.

4. James, "Colin Dew James," 463–65.

5. James, "Colin Dew James," 468–69.

6. Though he did not graduate from Harvard, James was considered part of the class of 1878—in Harvard terms, the "social class of 1878."

7. Dorothy Ross, *The Origins of American Social Science* (New York: Cambridge University Press, 1991), 111–12; see E. J. James, "The State as an Economic Factor," in *Science Economics Discussion* (New York: The Science Company, 1886), 24–25. Chapter 5 considers James's intellectual career in greater depth.

8. James B. Childs, "A Bibliography of the Published Writings and Addresses of Edmund Janes James," University of Illinois (1920), 1–81. An earlier "List of Published Papers" contains two parts. Part A, "Monographs and Longer Papers," lists fifty titles dating from 1877 to 1895. Part B, "Briefer Papers and Reviews," lists forty-eight titles dating from 1877 to 1895. *Annals of the American Academy of Political and Social Science*, 7 (January 1896), 81–86.

9. Ernest Minor Patterson, "The Career of Edmund Janes James," *Annals of the American Academy of Political and Social Science*, 301 (September 1955), 97–100; Richard A. Swanson, "Edmund J. James, 1855–1925: A Conservative Progressive in American Higher Education" (doctoral dissertation, University of Illinois, 1966),

a comprehensive study; Joshua L. Chamberlain, ed., *University of Pennsylvania: Its History, Influence, Equipment and Characteristics*, 2 vols. (Boston: R. Herndon Co., 1902), 1:388–90.

10. Steven A. Sass, *The Pragmatic Imagination: A History of the Wharton School, 1881–1981* (Philadelphia: University of Pennsylvania Press, 1982), on which this account of James at the Wharton School draws.

11. Edward P. Cheyney, *History of the University of Pennsylvania, 1740–1940* (Philadelphia: University of Pennsylvania Press, 1940), 289; Steven A. Sass, "An Uneasy Relationship: The Business Community and the Academic Economists at the University of Pennsylvania," in *Breaking the Academic Mould: Economists and American Higher Learning in the Nineteenth Century*, ed. William J. Barber (Middletown, CT: Wesleyan University Press, 1988), 230.

12. Edmund J. James, "The Relation of the Modern Municipality to the Gas Supply," *Publications of the American Economic Association*, 1 (May-July, 1886), 7–76; Sass, *Pragmatic Imagination*, 74–77; Sidney Fine, *Laissez Faire and the General-Welfare State: A Study of Conflict in American Thought, 1865–1901* (Ann Arbor: University of Michigan Press, 1956), 225.

13. Edmund J. James, "Schools of Finance and Economy," *Proceedings of the Eighteenth Annual Convention of the American Bankers' Association* (New York, 1892), 10–11.

14. Edmund J. James, *Education of Businessmen* (New York: William H. Greene, 1891), 14–15.

15. James, *Education of Businessmen*, 20–21.

16. *Proceedings of the American Bankers Association*, 36–39.

17. Edmund J. James, "Education of Business Men, II," (New York: American Bankers Association, 1892), 1–16.

18. James, "Education II," 24–26.

19. University of Illinois Archives, RS 2/5/7, James's Diaries, January 1, 1895. See also Cheyney, *University of Pennsylvania*, 293–94.

20. Sass, *Pragmatic Imagination*, 85.

21. Harper to James, February 29, 1904, February 15, 1905, RS 2/5/1, B:4, F:Correspondence, 1901–4; Harry Pratt Judson to James, January 11, 1906, RS 2/5/1, B:6, F:August 1904-June 1906.

22. Arthur H. Wilde, *Northwestern University: A History, 1855–1905*, 4 vols. (New York: Universal Publishing Society, 1905), 1:363–66; Estelle F. Ward, *The Story of Northwestern University* (New York: Dodd, Mead and Co., 1924), 237–44; Harold F. Williamson and Payson S. Wild, *Northwestern University: A History, 1850–1975* ([Evanston]: Northwestern University, 1976), 71–105 (quotation); Horace Butterworth to James, December 15, 1904, RS 2/5/1, B:6, F:B (second quotation).

23. Kinley to Frederic Hatch, March 15 and 16, 1904, University of Illinois Archives, RS 15/1/4.

24. Kinley to R. N. Talbot, March 21, 1904, University of Illinois Archives, RS 15/1/4.

25. BT, 22nd *Report* (1904), 335.

26. Draper to Augustus F. Nightingale, May 14, 1904, University of Illinois

Archives, RS 2/5/1, B:6, F:Nightingale; Bullard to Draper, May 28, 1904, RS 2/4/1, B:1, F:Bullard; [Draper] to William B. McKinley, May 31, 1904, RS 2/5/3, B:10, F:McKinley.

27. Clark to D. H. Carnahan, July 15, 1904; Clark to Evarts B. Greene, July 27, 1904, RS 41/2/20, Thomas A. Clark Papers, B:5, F:Personal Letterbooks, No. 3.

28. BT, 22nd *Report* (1904), 334. Notes on August 16 Meeting, RS 1/1/6, Board of Trustees Secretary's File, B:5.

29. Patten to James, August 16, 1904; Harris to James, August 23, 1904, RS 2/5/1, B:4, F:Correspondence 1901–4.

30. BT, 22nd *Report* (1904), 335.

31. James, "The Function of the State University," in *Installation of Edmund Janes James*, 441–42.

32. James, "State University," 442–43, 445–46.

33. James, "State University," 448.

34. James, "State University," 456–61, 464.

35. Edmund Janes James, "The Function of the State University," *Science*, n.s. 22 (November 17, 1905), 609–28.

Chapter 2. Money and Politics

1. For a full account of this history, see Edwin D. Duryea, *The Academic Corporation: A History of College and University Governing Boards* (New York: Falmer Press, 2000), passim.

2. F. B. Garver, "Some Phases of Tax Reform in Illinois," *Journal of Political Economy*, 19 (July 1911), 574–90; John A. Fairlie, "Taxation in Illinois," *American Economic Review*, 1 (September 1911), 519–34.

3. BT, 23rd *Report* (1906), 26. The board also submitted a separate bill for funds for agricultural operations.

4. Robert P. Howard, *The Illinois Governors: Mostly Good and Competent*, revised and updated by Taylor Pensonaeu and Peggy Boyer Long (Springfield, IL: Center Publications/Illini Issues), 185–90; Howard, *Illinois: A History of the Prairie State* (Grand Rapids, MI: William B. Eerdmans, 1972), 421–24.

5. BT, 25th *Report* (1911), 158.

6. BT, 25th *Report* (1911), 89–91.

7. *Journal of the Senate of the 46th General Assembly* (Springfield, 1909), 231–32, 242, 243–44, 511–12; BT, 25th *Report* (1911), 122–23. For statistical details of the budgetary record in the James years, see James, *Sixteen Years*, 30.

8. Edmund J. James, "What the University Needs," AQ, 3 (April 1909), 65–67.

9. https://en.wikipedia.org/wiki/Carrie_Thomas_Alexander-Bahrenberg; https://amp.en.google-info.org/57582588/1/carrie-thomas-alexander-bahrenberg.html. Clippings from several newspapers in Chicago and around the state that describe the conflict are in RS 2/5/3, B:18, F:Bahrenberg; *Chicago Tribune*, April 28, 1909; and *Chicago Record-Herald*, May 5, 1909.

10. BT, 25th *Report* (1911), 135; unidentified news clipping, April 30, 1909, in RS 2/5/3, B:18, F:Bahrenberg.

11. *Chicago Inter Ocean*, May 5, 1909, in RS 2/5/3, B:18, F:Bahrenberg.

12. Newspaper clipping in RS 2/5/3, B:18, F:Bahrenberg.

13. *Chicago Inter Ocean*, May 5, 1909 (the quotation); *Journal of the Senate of the 46th General Assembly* (Springfield, 1909), 958–59, 1034.

14. Roger L. Geiger, *To Advance Knowledge: The Growth of American Research Universities, 1900–1940* (New York: Oxford University Press, 1986), 11–12.

15. *Journal of the House of Representatives of the 47th General Assembly of the State of Illinois* (Springfield, 1911), 18–22.

16. See Merle Curti and Vernon Carstensen, *The University of Wisconsin: A History, 1848–1925*, 2 vols. (Madison: University of Wisconsin Press, 1949), II: 363, 437, 553, 589–90.

17. Edmund J. James, "Means and Effects," AQ, 5 (January 1911), 17–22 (quotation at 17).

18. James, "Means and Effects," 18–21.

19. Jerome Leon Rodnitzky, "President James and His Campaign for University of Illinois Funds," *Journal of the Illinois State Historical Society*, 63 (Spring 1970), 75–76, 85n.

20. Rodnitzky, "President James," 74, 78–80, 85–86; Allan Nevins, *Illinois* (New York: Oxford University Press, 1917), 247–48. Edwin E. Slosson, in his famous study of American universities in 1910, found James an exceptional president in the eagerness and openness of his approach to the state legislature: "President James has adopted the opposite policy from most State university presidents. He seeks rather than avoids legislative attention, and takes the people into his confidence when he does not have to. He is trying to educate the public to the expressed approval of his ideal of a university." Slosson, *Great American Universities* (1910; Delhi, India: Facsimile Publishers, 2019), 286–87.

21. James to Edwin E. Slosson, June 13, 1911, RS 2/5/3, B:21, F:Independent; James to Walter H[ines] Page, July 12, 1911, RS 2/5/3, B:25, F:World's Work.

22. https://en.wikipedia.org/wiki/William_L. Abbott; N. Clifford Ricker to President A. S. Draper, June 4, 1904, RS 2/5/6, B:1, F:E.J. James Faculty Correspondence, 6/1/04–4/1/05.

23. "Mary E. Busey," Local History and Genealogy Digital Exhibits, Urbana Free Library. https://urbanafree.omeka.net/exhibits/show/maryebusey/mebusey.

24. Kinley to President James, July 1908, RS 2/5/6, B:9, F:Kinley.

25. Howard, *Illinois Governors*, 179–82.

26. https://en.wikipedia.org/wiki/Ellen_Martin_Henrotin.

27. J. Van Fenstermaker, "A Century of Service: History of the Trevett-Mattis Banking Company," [1965?], mimeographed, 19 pp., copy in author's [Solberg's] possession.

28. Obituary notices from the *Champaign-Urbana Courier*, August 16, 1968 and the *Champaign News Gazette*, August 19, 1968, in 26/4/1, Florence [Watson] Burrell Morgue File.

29. BT, 20th *Report* (1901), 20.

30. *Official Vote of the State of Illinois Cast at the General Election Held on November 3, 1914* (Springfield, 1915), 18–19.

31. BT, 28th *Report* (1916), 926.

32. Professor L. S. Rowe of Penn, in 1912 President of the American Academy of Political and Social Science, began the movement. James, perhaps for reasons of health, gave it no encouragement. "President James and the Other Presidency," AQFN 1 (February 1915), 202.

Chapter 3. The Graduate School

1. For general histories of these subjects see, among other studies, Richard J. Storr, *The Beginnings of Graduate Education in America* (Chicago: University of Chicago Press, 1953); Roger L. Geiger, *To Advance Knowledge: The Growth of American Research Universities, 1900–1940* (New York: Oxford University Press, 1986).

2. Geiger, *To Advance Knowledge*, 1. The universities that Geiger places in this group include five founded in the colonial era (Harvard, Yale, Princeton, Columbia, and Penn), five private foundations formed in the late nineteenth century (Johns Hopkins, Cornell, Chicago, Stanford, and MIT), and five state universities (Michigan, Wisconsin, Minnesota, California, and Illinois), 3.

3. Frederick C. Dietz, "History of the Graduate College [of the University of Illinois]," [1957], 2–3, and Daniel E. Worthington, "Advanced Training on the Prairie: The University of Illinois Graduate College, 1867–1980," [1990], both in University of Illinois Archives, RS 7/1/5.

4. On the early history of the Graduate School, see Solberg 2, 216–20.

5. Geiger, *To Advance Knowledge*, 18–19.

6. Senate Minutes, RS 4/2/1, October 14, 1901; February 9, 1903; March 28, 1904; April 4 and 11, 1904; "Report of the Senate Committee on Graduate Work," March 28, 1904, RS 5/1/20, Burrill Papers, B:1, 273–79.

7. James to Deneen, December 19, 1904; James to George P. Brown, December 19, 1904; James to J. E. Armstrong, January 4, 1905, RS 2/5/4, B:1, Ltrbk. 36.

8. *Journal of Proceedings of the 51st Annual Meeting of the Illinois State Teachers' Association* (Springfield, 1905), 21.

9. James to J. E. Armstrong, January 4 and 26, 1905; James to C. W. Groves, January 19, 1905; James to George W. Hinman, January 23, 1905; James to Alice A. Abbott, January 31, 1905; J. W. Wilson (James's secretary) to J. E. Armstrong, February 9, 1905, RS 2/5/4, B:1, Ltrbks. 36, 37.

10. James to George P. Brown, January 4, 1905; James to D. A. Campbell, February 25, 1905; James to C. F. Coleman, March 17, 1905 [Committee of the State Teachers Association], draft of a letter to high school principals, c. February 1, 1905, RS 2/5/4, B:1, Ltrbks. 36, 37.

11. James to William E. Trautman, April 8, 1905; James to Walter Reeves, April 20, 1905; James to A. R. Van Skiver, April 20, 1905; James to J. E. Armstrong, May 16, 1905, RS 2/5/4, B:1, Ltrbks. 37, 38.

12. Burrill to James, June 1, 1905, RS 2/5/6, B:2, F:A–D 4/1/05–8/1/05.

13. James to Kinley, January 11, 1905, RS 2/5/4, B:2, Ltrbk. 41.

14. Kinley to James, June 20 and 22, 1905, RS 2/5/6, B:2, F:David Kinley.

15. Ely to Kinley, June 26, 1905, Richard T. Ely Correspondence, Reel 31, Wisconsin Historical Society, Madison, Wisconsin.

16. University of Illinois Archives, RS 4/2/1, December 5, 1905, January 6, 1906; BT, 23rd *Report* (1906), 311.

17. Kinley to James, December 12 and 13, 1905, RS 2/5/6, B:2, F:David Kinley.

18. Kinley to Ely, January 8, 1906, RS 15/1/4, B:4.

19. Kinley to Ely, January 20, 1906, RS 15/1/4, B:4; Ely to Kinley, January 22, 1906, Richard T. Ely Correspondence, Reel 33, Wisconsin Historical Society. The letters from James to Kinley that Kinley sent to Ely cannot be located either in the University of Illinois Archives or in the Ely Correspondence.

20. Kinley to James, January 24, 1906, RS 15/1/4, B:4; BT, 23rd *Report* (1906), 311–12, 313.

21. The minutes of the Graduate School Faculty (GSF) are in bound books kept in the office of the dean of the Graduate College. The first book, paginated, covers 1906 to 1912. The second, unpaginated, covers 1912 to 1916. Hereafter, the minutes are cited by initials, volume number, page or date, and where helpful, by both—e.g., GSF, 1:1 or GSF 2:24 (November 1913). On this paragraph, see also Kinley to James, February 22, 1906, RS 7/1/2, B:1, F:Establishment of Graduate College 1906–1909; BT, 24th *Report* (1908), 389.

22. From 1904 to 1917 at Illinois one hundred research appointments were made, an average of over seven a year, with most of them in the sciences, especially chemistry. "Research Appointments," RS 2/5/3, B:84, F:Filbey, E.J.

23. GSF, 1:2–51 passim; Kinley to Burrill and members of the Executive Faculty, October 8, 1908, RS 2/5/5, B:13, F:Graduate College 1908–1909 Dean Kinley; see also Association of American Universities, *Journal of the Proceedings and Addresses*, 1906 to 1908.

24. Kinley to James, May 4, 1906, RS 2/5/6, B:4, F:L-Z 5/1/06–9/30/06.

25. *Journal of the House of Representatives of the 45th General Assembly of the State of Illinois* (1908), 30–31.

26. Blanchard to James, October 6, 1906, Leavitt to James, October 20, 1906, and other correspondence between James and the college presidents are in RS 2/5/5, B:13, F:Graduate School, 1906–1907.

27. David Kinley, "Graduate Study at Illinois," AQ, 2 (April 1908), 61–62.

28. Kinley to James, June 1, 1907, a "Confidential Report," RS 7/1/2, B:1, F:Establishment of Graduate College, 1906–1909.

29. BT, 24th *Report* (1908), 133–34. The difference between Kinley's sixteen and James's twelve fields is not as great as the figures suggest. Kinley listed agronomy and animal husbandry; James substituted agriculture. Kinley listed Greek and Latin; James substituted ancient languages. The difference concerned engineering: Kinley did not list it; James did.

30. BT, 24th *Report* (1908), 158, 441.

31. Kinley to James, February 22, 1907, RS 2/5/5, B:13, F:Graduate School 1906–1907; Greene to James, March 4, 1907, RS 2/5/6, B:6, F:Evarts B. Greene; Association of American Universities, *Journal of Proceedings and Addresses of the Ninth Annual Conference* (1905), 10–11; (1908), 10–11.

32. Kinley to James, January 17, 1908, RS 2/5/5, B:13, F:Graduate School 1905–1908.

33. Harker to James, April 18, 1908; "Report of Dean David Kinley on the Conference of College Presidents of Illinois," RS 2/5/5, B:13, F:Graduate College 1908–1909: Conference of College Presidents.

34. *Journal of the House of Representatives of the 46th General Assembly of the State of Illinois* (1909), 56.

35. BT, 25th *Report* (1911), 89, 164.

36. James D. Nowlan, comp., *Illinois Major Party Platforms: 1900–1964* (University of Illinois, Urbana, Illinois: Institute of Government and Public Affairs, 1966), 63–64 (quoting the *Illinois State Journal*, 24 (September 1910)); Burrill to Kinley, September 26, 1910, RS 7/1/2, B:1; F:Establishment of Graduate College, 1906–1909.

37. Kinley was required to submit an annual report on the Graduate School. The reports for 1906–1907, 1908–1909, and 1911–1912 cannot be located. For this paragraph, see *Annual Report*, 1909–1910, 10.

38. GD, *Annual Report*, 1914–1915, 13–14.

39. GSF, 2:15 (January 1915). For specific degrees and their requirements, see University of Illinois, *Register 1907–1908*, 128–34.

40. GD, *Annual Report*, 1914–1915, 12–13.

41. GSF, 2:15 (October 1915) (see letters to various committees of September 29, October 11, 15, 1915); GSF, 1:12 (November 1, 1906).

42. GSF, 1:161, 164–66, 177, 179, 184 (November 22, 1911 with committee report dated October 23, 1911), April 5 and 24 (June 14, 1912).

43. GSF, 2:5 (December 1913), January 20, February 23 and 26, March 11 and 30, 1914; BT, 28th *Report* (1916), 191.

44. GSF, 2:18 (February 1916).

45. GD, *Annual Report*, 1907–1908, 2; BT, 24th *Report* (1908), 439.

46. Kinley to James, January 18, 1919, RS 2/5/3, B:182; F:Kinley, Dean David 1918–1919.

47. Howard J. Brownson to Edmund J. James, November 23, 1908; Ernest S. Reynolds to James, April 12, 1909, RS 2/5/5, B:13; F:Graduate College General Correspondence 1908–1909.

48. GSF, 2:24 (November 9, 1912), May 8, 1914, January 29, 1915; "Report of Graduate Faculty Committee on 'Student Contact,'" November 30, 1914, RS 7/1/2, B:1, F:1912–14 Reports.

49. GSF, 1:156, 178 (May 30, 1911, April 5, 1912); GSF, 2:25 (October 1912, January 31, 1913).

50. Kinley to James, February 11, 1910, RS 2/5/5, B:13, F:Graduate College, 1909–1910; Kinley to James, March 28, 1912, RS 2/5/6, B:20, F:David Kinley.

51. James to Kinley, Kinley to James, June 5 to July 1, 1912; RS 2/5/6, B:20, F:David Kinley—Grad School.

52. Kinley to James, December 16, 1908; James to S. W. Shattuck, January 30, 1909, RS 2/5/5, B:13, F:Graduate College General Correspondence, 1908–09.

53. Geiger, *To Advance Knowledge*, 30–33, which has the subject titles of these publications.

54. GD, *Annual Report*, 1912–1913; GD, *Annual Report*, 1909–1910, 14.

55. BT, 27th *Report* (1914), 193. For the dramatic full account of this adventure, see Winton U. Solberg, *Arctic Mirage: The 1913–1920 Expedition in Search of Crocker Land* (Jefferson, NC: McFarland, 2019).

56. Savage to Kinley, October 3, 1916, GD, *Annual Report*, 1916–1917, Appendix II.

57. Kinley to James, November 29, 1916; James to Kinley, December 2, 1916, RS 2/5/3, B:123, F:Kinley, David Sep.-Dec. 1916. A copy of the constitution is in ibid., F:Kinley, David Jly., Aug. '17; *Transactions of the Board of Trustees, 1916–1918* [1920], 502. See also *Annual Report, 1916–1917*, 6; *Annual Report, 1917–1918*, 11.

58. James, *Sixteen Years*, 161, 200.

59. James, *Sixteen Years*, 154–72. See the large statistical database for these and other items here.

60. David Kinley, "Democracy and Scholarship," *Science*, n.s. 28 (October 16, 1908), 497–500.

61. Kinley, "Democracy and Scholarship," 501–3 (the quotation).

62. Kinley, "Democracy and Scholarship," 499–500, 506 (quotation).

63. Kinley, "Democracy and Scholarship," 506–7.

64. Kinley, "Democracy and Scholarship," 509.

Chapter 4. Infrastructure for a Research University

1. Paul H. Mattingly, *American Academic Cultures: A History of Higher Education* (Chicago: University of Chicago Press, 2017), 194.

2. For a list of the buildings and equipment on the Illinois campus at the time of James's arrival, and for a list of those items that appeared during his presidency, see James, *Sixteen Years*, 77–84.

3. W. N. C. Carlton, "Universities and Librarians," Public Libraries, 20 (December 1915), 451.

4. "Final Report: Council Committee on Distribution of Library Funds," May 29, 1905, RS 15/1/3, B:10, F:Library Funds; Library Committee Minutes, October 9, 1905, RS 2/5/6, B:2, F:L-Z.

5. On Sharp's early career and the establishment of the University of Illinois Library School, see Solberg 2, 40–41, 189–201. See also Laurel A. Grotzinger, "The Power and the Dignity: Librarianship and Katharine L. Sharp" (PhD dissertation, University of Illinois, 1964), published under the same title (New York: Scarecrow Press, 1966). Later references are to the dissertation. See also Donald Krummel, "Katherine L. Sharp and the Creation of the University Library," in *No Boundaries: University of Illinois Vignettes*, ed. Lillian Hoddeson (Urbana: University of Illinois Press, 2004), 13–28.

6. This account of Sharp as librarian from 1904 to 1907 draws on her annual reports for these years, RS 35/1/801, B:2, 3. Thomas E. Ratcliffe, "Development of the Buildings, Policy and Collections of the University of Illinois Library in Urbana, 1897–1940" (MA thesis, University of Illinois, 1949), and Wayne S. Yenawine, "The Influence of Scholars on Research Library Development at the University of Illinois" (PhD dissertation, University of Illinois, 1955), are both useful.

7. BT, 24th *Report* (1908), 101; Sharp, Annual Report for 1906–1907, RS 35/1/801, B:2.

8. RS 2/5/15, F:Drury, Francis K. W. The records of the Board of Trustees for 1905 do not list Drury as a graduate of the Library School, but the commencement program does. See also Edwin S. Greaves, "Drury, Francis Keese Wynkoop (1878–1954)," in *Dictionary of American Library Biography*, 143–45.

9. Greaves, "Drury," 144.

10. Library Journal, 34 (January 1909), 35; 35 (November 1910), 509.

11. James to Drury, December 2, 1907, RS 2/5/6, B:7, F:F. K. W. Drury.

12. BT, 24th *Report* (1908), 366.

13. Drury to James, December 3, 1907, RS 2/5/6, B:7, F:F. K. W. Drury.

14. James I. Wyer, Jr. to Drury, December 18, 1907, RS 2/5/6, B:7, F:F.K. W. Drury; RS 2/5/15, F:Denio, H. W.

15. Goebel to James, April 17, 1909, RS 2/5/6, B:12, F:C-G.

16. BT, 24th *Report* (1908), 48, 50.

17. Drury, Annual Report for 1908–1909, RS 35/1/801, B:2.

18. RS 2/5/15, F:Windsor, Phineas L. See also Robert B. Downs, "Windsor, Phineas Lawrence (1871–1965)," in *Dictionary of American Library Biography*, 561–64.

19. James to Windsor, October 15, 1908, 13; January 16, 1909; Windsor to James, January 15 and 19, 1909, RS 2/5/15, F:Windsor, Phineas L.; BT, 25th *Report* (1910), 98.

20. This material comes mostly from the James-Windsor correspondence, RS 2/5/6, F:Windsor, Phineas L. See also Philip S. Goulding [Catalog Librarian], "The Classification of Literatures in the University of Illinois Library," *Library Journal*, 39 (April 1914), 266–73 and *Library Journal*, 37 (December 1912), 687; 43 (June 1918), 434; 34 (August 1909), 373, and 44 (August 1919), 517.

21. Senate Committee on the Library, Report for 1914–1915, RS 4/2/817, B:1.

22. Windsor to James, March 25, 1915, RS 2/5/6, B:57, F:Windsor, Phineas Jan.-Mch 1915; James to Windsor, January 25, 1913; Windsor to James, January 27, 1913, RS 35/1/4, B:1, F:Jan. 1913-Dec. 1914; Windsor to James, September 21, 1915, RS 35/1/4, B:1, F:Jan. 1915/Dec. 1916.

23. Windsor, "Certification of Librarians," *Library Journal*, 42 (February 1917), 121.

24. Windsor to James, May 30, 1913, RS 2/5/6, B:30, F:P. L. Windsor.

25. Ward to Townsend, November 12, 1912; Windsor to James, November 2, 1912; James to Windsor, December 14, 1912, and other letters relating to the matter in RS 2/5/6, B:29, F:E.J. Townsend 9/1/12–3/31/13.

26. Kinley to James, September 23 and 26, 1912, RS 2/5/6, B:27, F:Kinley, Dean David.

27. Windsor to James, April 22, 1918, RS 2/5/3, B:168, F:Windsor, P. L. March-August 1918. See also Kathleen M. Ruckman, "Gifts and Exchanges in the University of Illinois Library" (MA thesis, University of Illinois, 1936).

28. Windsor to James, October 25, 1913, RS 15/1/4, B:1, F:Jan. 1913/Dec. 1914. Copies of the form letters are in RS 2/5/3, B:140, F:Windsor, P. L. and RS 2/5/6, B:30, F:P. L. Windsor (with a note dated March 13, 1913).

29. James to Windsor, March 8, 1912; Vergil V. Phelps (James's secretary) to Windsor, March 14, 1914; James to Windsor, October 27, 1913, RS 35/1/4, B:1, F:July 1911/Dec. 1912; Jan. 1913/Dec. 1914.

30. Windsor to James, July 13, 1915, RS 35/1/4, B:1, F:Jan. 1915/Dec. 1916.

31. Windsor to James, October 16, 1914; James to Windsor, October 17, 1914, RS 2/5/6, B:57, F:Windsor, Phineas Aug.-Dec. 1914.

32. Windsor to James, May 25, 1915, RS 2/5/6, B:57, F:Windsor, Phineas L. Apr-May 1915; F. K. W. Drury, "The University Library at a Quarter Million Volumes," AQ, 9 (April 1915), 72.

33. Ruckman, "Gifts and Exchanges," 9, 48–49; Windsor, "Building the University Collection," tape recording of a talk given on April 7, 1949, RS 35/1/20, Phineas L. Windsor Papers, and published, with prefatory note by Robert B. Downs, as "Librariendipity," Non Solus: A Publication of the University of Illinois Library Friends at Urbana-Champaign, no. 2 (1975), 35–44; BT, 25th *Report* (1911), 89, 134–35, 161–62, 163; 26th *Report* (1912), 76–77, 139.

34. Windsor to James, January 19, 1916, RS 35/1/4, B:1, F:Jan.1915/Dec. 1916; Windsor, "Building the University Collection."

35. James's correspondence with Blondheim, Kuhn, and IOBB members from October 27, 1911 to May 21, 1912 is in RS 2/5/3, B:26, F:B'nai B'rith. James reported receiving the $500 check to the board on June 12, 1912: BT, 26th *Report* (1912), 598.

36. BT, 27th *Report* (1914), 735–36.

37. On the commissions' objectives, see "Commission for German-American History and Culture," RS 2/5/3, B:32, F:German-American Culture University of Illinois Commission.

38. James to Kinley, November 6, 1912, RS 2/5/6, B:26, F:Kinley, Dean David; Hexamer to James, November 12, 1912, RS 2/5/3, B:32, F:German-American Culture University of Illinois Commission; James to Otto L. Schmidt, February 27, 1914, RS 2/5/3, B:47, F:Illinois Centennial.

39. James to Carnegie, March 17, 1914; J. A. Poynton to James, March 24, 1914, RS 2/5/3, B:41, F:Carnegie, Andrew; James to Otto L. Schmidt, February 27, 1914, RS 2/5/3, B:47, F:Illinois Centennial; James to Dunne, March 14, 1914, Dunne to James, March 20, 1914, RS 2/5/3, B:43, F:Dunne, Edward F.

40. David H. Carnahan to Kinley, December 14, 1911; Kinley to James, December 14, 1911; James to Elisabet Gröber, June 27, 1912, RS 2/5/6, B:20, F:David Kinley Graduate School; correspondence relating to the Gröber collection is in RS 2/5/3, B:27, F:Libraries.

41. James to Townsend, January 17, 1912, RS 15/1/3, B:6, F:1911–1913 I-J.

42. BT, 26th *Report* (1912), 594–97. James reproduced the report in full in his *Sixteen Years*. See Chapter IV for this report and many more statistics about the Illinois libraries.

43. RS 4/2/1, 3:60, 64.

44. *Journal of the House of Representatives of the 48th General Assembly of the State of Illinois* (Springfield, 1914), 129.

45. *Daily Illini*, October 31, 1914, 2.

46. J. T. Gerould, Statistics of University Libraries (n.d., n.p.), copy in the University of Illinois Library.

47. BT, 28th *Report* (1916), 776–77; see also Collections File, Rare Book and Special Collections Library.

48. BT, 28th *Report* (1916), 773; Transactions of the Board of Trustees, 1916 to 1918 (1918), 105–6; Collections File.

49. Windsor to James, October 29, 1915, with appended note by Pease dated October 28; Pease to Windsor, April 24, 1916; James to Windsor, May 2 and 20, 1916; Windsor to James, May 23, 1916, RS 35/1/4, B:1, F:Jan. 1915/Dec. 1916; BT, 28th *Report* (1916), 942.

50. BT, 28th *Report* (1916), 941; Collections File.

51. James to Windsor, June 27, 1916, RS 35/1/4, B:1, F:Jan. 1915/Dec. 1916; Collections File.

52. James to Windsor, March 2, 1916, RS 35/1/4, B:1, F:Jan. 1915/Dec. 1916.

53. Windsor to James, April 2, 1917; James to Windsor, April 30, 1917, RS 35/1/4, B:1, F:Jan. 1917/Dec. 1918.

54. "Library School and Library," AQFN, 3 (June 1919), 169.

55. Guido Bruno, "The Romance of a Chicago Bookseller," in *Adventures in American Bookshops, Antique Stores and Auction Rooms* (Detroit: The Douglas Book Shop, 1922), 87–91; Collections File.

56. Downs, "Windsor," 564.

57. Gerould, Statistics of University Libraries.

58. One may find many more details of these efforts on James's part in Winton U. Solberg, "Edmund Janes James Builds a Library: The University of Illinois Library, 1904–1920," *Libraries & Culture*, 39 (2004), 36–75. The growth of the library had a parallel development in the Library School. Begun in 1893, it came under Sharp's leadership in 1898, with Windsor succeeding her and seeing it into significant expansion. James at first slighted the School in favor of the library, his larger commitment. See Laurel Grotzinger, "Remarkable Beginnings: The First Half Century of the Graduate School of Library and Information Science," in *Ideals and Standards: The History of the University of Illinois Graduate School of Library and Information Science, 1893–1993*, ed. Leigh Estabrook (n.p., 1893), 1–19.

59. BT, 23rd *Report* (1906), 47–48.

60. Frank Scott to James, BT, 24th *Report* (1908), 21.

61. BT, 27th *Report* (1914), 242–43.

62. BT, 28th *Report* (1916), 225.

63. BT, 28th *Report* (1916), 941.

64. BT, 28th *Report* (1916), 941.

65. BT, 29th *Report* (1918), 333.

66. Kinley to James, June 27, 1917, James General Correspondence, RS 2/5/3, B:123.

67. BT, 29th *Report* (1918), 747.

68. "The University Press," University of Illinois, Annual Register, 1919–1920, 411–12.

69. James to Cunningham, March 23, 1920, RS 38/1/20–1, Cunningham Papers, B:1.

70. Cunningham to W. F. M. Goss, June 12, 1920, RS 38/1/20, Harrison E. Cunningham Papers, F:1920.

Notes to Chapter 4   351

71. "He's Been at It Twenty-five Years," *Illinois Alumni News*, 17 (May 1939), 9; "The University of Illinois Press," *The Nightmare*, 18 (January 1940), 1, 3.

Chapter 5. The Intellectual World of Edmund J. James

1. Claude Welch, *Protestant Thought in the Nineteenth Century, Volume I, 1799–1870* (New Haven: Yale University Press, 1972), 22–26.

2. Thomas Albert Howard, *Protestant Theology and the Making of the Modern German University* (Oxford: Oxford University Press, 2006), 81, 88–89, 93.

3. Peter Watson, *The German Genius: Europe's Third Renaissance, the Second Scientific Revolution, and the Twentieth Century* (New York: HarperCollins, 2010), 52; Howard, *Protestant Theology*, 139–40.

4. Friedrich Paulsen, *The German Universities: Their Character and Historical Development* (New York: Macmillan & Co., 1895), 59–61 (quotation), 68; see, for examples, James, *Municipal Administration in Germany: As Seen in the Government of a Typical Prussian City, Halle A/S* (Chicago: University of Chicago Press, 1901); James, "Street Railway Franchises in the City of Berlin," *Journal of Political Economy*, 2 (March 1901), 260–71; James, "City Administration in Germany," *American Journal of Sociology*, 7 (July 1901), 29–52; James, "The City Council of Berlin," *American Journal of Sociology*, 6 (November 1900), 407–15; James, "Municipal Economy in Prussia," *Nation*, October 23, 1881.

5. Watson, *German Genius*, 226, 228; Wilhelm von Humboldt, "On Germany's Educational System," in *The Rise of the Research University: A Sourcebook*, ed. Louis Menand, Paul Reitter, and Chad Wellmon (Chicago: University of Chicago Press, 2017), 110; Jurgen Herbst, *The German Historical School in American Scholarship: A Study in the Transfer of Culture* (Ithaca: Cornell University Press, 1965), 9–10, 157.

6. A. C. Grayling, *The History of Philosophy* (New York: Penguin Press, 2019), 259–63.

7. Howard, *Protestant Theology*, 126–27.

8. They also included a major literary figure. Friedrich Schiller gave his popular lecture on universal history at Jena in 1790. It inspired many reformers and added new ones to the ranks. Schiller made his major distinction between the "career scholar"—timid and defensive, attached to systems—and the "philosophical mind"—restless to join his domain of knowledge to other domains, always in pursuit of integration and comprehensiveness. He thrives to create a "coherent totality." That is what Schiller meant by "scientific thinking." F. W. J. Schiller, "What is Universal History?," in *Rise of the Research University*, 33–34, 42–43.

9. As the focus here is on educational thinking, interested readers may find a useful summary of Schleiermacher's religious ideas in Gary Dorrien, *Kantian Reason and Hegelian Spirit: The Idealistic Logic of Modern Theology* (Chichester, England: Wiley-Blackwell, 2012), 84–108.

10. Friedrich Schleiermacher, "Occasional Thoughts on German Universities in the German Sense," in *Research University*, 48–49, 53–54, 56, 60–61; Howard, *Protestant Theology*, 28, 156–57, 169. Schleiermacher carried the intellectual case of

352   Notes to Chapters 4 and 5

the German idealists against philosophical empiricism into their effort to capture the universities. "How empty the works of the academy would be if they dealt in sheer empiricism and had no faith in any principles of systematic knowledge," he wrote. *Research University*, 59.

11. Dorrien, *Kantian Reason*, 105. One will find helpful accounts of all the principal idealists in this book.

12. See Dorrien, *Kantian Reason*, 63–74.

13. J. G. Fichte, "A Plan Deduced" in *Research University*, 70, 73–74, 77, 79 (quotation), 83 (quotation).

14. Editors, "Introduction to Schelling's Lectures," in *Research University*, 85. For an excellent account of Schelling's thought, again see Dorrien, *Kantian Reason*, 16–18, 159–60, 169–73, and elsewhere.

15. F. W. J. Schelling, "Lectures on the Method of Academic Study," in *Research University*, 85, 88–90, 92–93.

16. Schelling, "Lectures," 90, 99, 100–101, 102–3; Howard, *Protestant Theology*, 158.

17. Howard, *Protestant Theology*, 139–40; Editors, "Introduction to Humboldt's Texts," in *Research University*, 107; Watson, *German Genius*, 229.

18. Wilhelm von Humboldt, "On Germany's Educational System," in *Research University*, 111–13; Watson, *German Genius*, 262–63.

19. Herbst, *German Historical School*, 16, 39–40, 56–57; Watson, *German Genius*, 228, 231 (quotation), 16; Howard, *Protestant Theology*, 29, 31, 273–74. John B. Parrish provides a helpful list of Americans who studied in Germany, with their institutions and dates of attendance. See his "Rise of Economics as an Academic Discipline: The Formative Years to 1900," *Southern Economic Journal*, 34 (July 1967), 18.

20. Joseph Dorfman, "The Role of the German Historical School in American Economic Thought," *American Economic Review*, 45 (May 1955), 22 (Walker quotation), 19, 28; Herbst, *German Historical School*, 124, 131, 135, 151–52.

21. Thomas W. Goodspeed, "Albion Woodward Small," *American Journal of Sociology*, 31 (July 1926), 1–14.

22. Albion W. Small, "The Restoration of Ethics in Economic Theory. The Professorial Socialists. The Verein fur Sozilialpolitik," *American Journal of Sociology*, 29 (May 1924), 707–25. Quotation on p. 710.

23. Sidney Fine, *Laissez Faire and the General-Welfare State: A Study of Conflict in American Thought* (Ann Arbor: University of Michigan Press, 1956), 199; Herbst, *German Historical School*, 144–45 (quotation).

24. Frank A. Fetter, "The Economists and the American Public," *American Economic Review*, 15 (March 1925), 14. And another assessment: "More striking new departures occurred in American economics than in any other comparable period." A. W. Coats, "The Political Economy Club: A Neglected Episode in American Economic Thought," *American Economic Review*, 51 (September 1961), 624.

25. Daniel M. Fox, *The Discovery of Abundance: Simon N. Patten and the Transformation of Social Theory* (Ithaca: Cornell University Press, 1967), 13–17, 18–19, 23.

26. Fox, *Patten*, 35–36; Daniel T. Rodgers, *Atlantic Crossings: Social Politics in a Progressive Age* (Cambridge, MA: Harvard University Press, 1998), 97 (quotation).

27. James quoted by Ely in Richard T. Ely, *Ground Under Our Feet: An Autobiography* (New York: Macmillan, 1938), 134. See in this book Appendix III for "The Constitution of the Society for the Study of National Economy," 296–99.

28. James quoted by Ely in Richard T. Ely, "The American Economic Association 1885–1909," *American Economic Association Quarterly*, 11 (1910), 57–58; also, Ely, *Ground Under Our Feet: An Autobiography* (New York: Macmillan, 1938). See in Ely's book Appendix III for "The Constitution of the Society for the Study of National Economy," 296–99; see also Fine, *Laissez Faire*, 213–16.

29. Quoted by Herbst, *German Historical School*, 19.

30. Benjamin G. Rader, *The Academic Mind and Reform: The Influence of Richard T. Ely in American Life* (Lexington: University of Kentucky Press, 1966), 11–12.

31. Rodgers, *Atlantic Crossings*, 78–79.

32. Fine, *Laissez Faire*, 29.

33. E. J. James, "Newcomb's Political Economy," *Science*, 27 (November 1885), 470–71. James relished this kind of debate and, it seems, personal confrontations as well. Apparently, when Francis A. Walker prepared to host a party at his house he was careful to tell Simon Newcomb that James would not be there. Hence, there was no danger of a riot! Coats, "Political Economic Club," 632–33.

34. A. W. Coats, "The First Two Decades of the American Economic Association," *American Economic Review*, 50 (September 1960), 557.

35. Coats, "AEA," 562–63, 566; Parrish, "Rise of Economics," 4. For more on this significant shift, see Mary O. Furner, *Advocacy and Objectivity: A Crisis in the Professionalization of American Social Science, 1865–1905* (Lexington: University Press of Kentucky, 1975), 76–79, 262–64.

36. Taussig, Hadley, J. Laurence Laughlin of Chicago, and Henry W. Farnam of Yale were four voices of orthodoxy and all sons of successful businessmen or professionals. They effectively contrast with the evangelical backgrounds of James, Ely, Patten, and Simon. Dorothy Ross, *The Origins of American Social Science* (Cambridge: Cambridge University Press, 1991), 103.

37. E. J. James, "The State as an Economic Factor," in *Science Economic Discussion*, ed. Richard T. Ely (1886; Delhi, India, 2019), 24 (quotation)–30, 32–34, 43. James wrote: "Government should interfere in all instances where its interference will tell for better health, better education, better morals, greater comfort of the community," and "assist to the extent of its power in bettering the conditions under which the great mass of the people have to earn their living." James, "State Interference," *The Chautauquan*, 8 (June 1888), 535–36.

38. [Edmund J. James], "Proceedings," *Annals of the American Academy of Political and Social Science*, 1 (July 1890), 132–37.

39. Upon James's retirement from the AAPSS the journal published a statement of appreciation to him. "It has been peculiarly his own creation, and only those who in recent years have assumed the active conduct of its work, know how completely the spirit which rules in all its branches is that of Dr. James. That without his presence they have been able to carry on the work of the organization so successfully,

is ample evidence of the skill with which Dr. James planned and builded." Roland P. Falkner, "Editorial," *Annals*, 17 (March 1901), 108.

40. Edmund Janes James, "What is a German University?," *Illinois School Journal*, 1 (September 1881), 1.

41. Edmund Janes James, "The Lecture versus the Recitation System: A Comparison Between the Methods of Instruction in German and American Universities," *Illinois School Journal*, 1 (March 1882), 13–14. James had helped to establish this journal.

42. James, "Comparison," 14; Edmund Janes James, "German Student Life," *Illinois School Journal*, 1 (January 1882), 13; "Personal Notes," *Annals of the American Academy of Political and Social Science*, 7 (January 1896), 79.

43. James, "German Student Life," 14–15; James, "Political Economy in German Universities," *Nation*, September 28, 1882, 261–62.

44. Edmund J. James, "The Degree of Ph.D. in Germany," *Andover Review*, 9 (June 1888), 611–16; James, "Political Economy," 262.

45. Edmund J. James, *The Place of the Political and Social Sciences in Modern Education, and Their Bearing on the Training for Citizenship in a Free State* (1897; Delhi, India: Facsimile Publisher, 2019), 47–48.

46. James, *Political and Social Sciences*, 54.

47. James, *Political and Social Sciences*, 57–60.

48. James, *Political and Social Sciences*, 63–65.

49. A vast literature, far too large to detail here, drove the case for the traditionalists. To grasp the rich variety of it all, see Laurence R. Veysey, *The Emergence of the American University* (Chicago: University of Chicago Press, 1965), 180–251.

50. See W. Bruce Leslie, *Gentlemen and Scholars: Colleges and Communities in the Age of the University* (1986; New Brunswick: Transaction, 2005).

51. Julie A. Reuben, *The Making of the Modern University: Intellectual Transformation and the Marginalization of Morality* (Chicago: University of Chicago Press, 1996), 5–6.

52. These philosophical rivalries persisted into the years of James's early career. President James McCosh of Princeton defended the Scottish system against German idealism. See his "The Scottish Philosophy as Contrasted with the German," *Princeton Review*, 10 (1882), 326–44. McCosh, to be sure, thoroughly grounded his system in the reality of the supernatural.

53. Reuben, *Modern University*, 30, 35–36, 49–51, Chapter Five, "Scientific Substitutes for Religion," 176 (quotation), 179, 180–81, 189–91.

54. James Axtell, *Wisdom's Workshop: The Rise of the Modern University* (Princeton: Princeton University Press, 2016), 271–72. However plausible as a generalization one may find Axtell's account, this study of Edmund James tells the story of one academic leader who does not fit that pattern, and in whom the original German inspiration persisted, revitalized now not in philosophy but in the social sciences.

55. Veysey, *Emergence of the American University*, 126–27.

56. Andrew Jewett, *Science, Democracy and the American University: From the Civil War to the Cold War* (New York: Cambridge University Press, 2012).

57. Sylvia D. Fries, "Staatstheorie and the New American Science of Politics," *Journal of the History of Ideas*, 34 (September 1973), 391–92.

58. Edmund J. James, "State Interference," 534–36.

59. Edmund J. James, Review of *Grundlegung der Theortischen Staatswirthschaft*, by Emil Sax, *Political Science Quarterly*, 5 (March 1890), 166–69.

60. Edmund J. James, "The Farmer and Taxation," [Part 1], *Annals*, 18 (September 4, 1891), 128–32.

61. Edmund J. James, "The Farmer and Taxation," [Part 2], *Annals*, 18 (September 11, 1891), 146–49 (quotation).

62. Edmund J. James, "The Agitation for the Federal Regulation of Railways," in *The Railway Question: The Report of the Committee on Transportation of the American Economic Association* (n.p.: American Economic Association, 1887), 246–55.

63. John A. Garraty, *The New Commonwealth: 1877–1890* (New York: Harper & Row, 1968), 128, 135.

64. Front page of *Our Day*, 1 (February 1888).

65. Edmund J. James, "Socialists and Anarchists in the United States," *Our Day*, 1 (February 1888), 83–84.

66. James, "Socialists and Anarchists," 86.

67. James, "Socialists and Anarchists," 88–92.

68. Page Smith, *The Rise of Industrial America: A People's History of the Post-Reconstruction Era* (New York: McGraw-Hill, 1984), 700 (quotation); John L. Thomas, *Alternative America: Henry George, Edward Bellamy, Henry Demarest Lloyd, and the Adversary Tradition* (Cambridge, MA: Harvard University Press, 1983), 216–17.

69. Edmund J. James, Review of *A Strike of Millionaires Against Miners, or, the Story of Spring Valley*, by Henry D. Lloyd, in *International Journal of Ethics*, 1 (January 1891), 259–60.

70. George E. McNeil, "Preface," *The Labor Movement: The Problem of To-Day*, ed. George E. McNeil (New York: M. W. Hazen, 1892), iii-iv; James, "The Rise of the Modern Laborer," in McNeil, *Labor Movement*, 1.

Chapter 6. A University at War

1. Gary Marotta, "The Academic Mind and the Rise of U.S. Imperialism: Historians and Economists as Publicists for Ideas of Colonial Expansion," *American Journal of Economics and Sociology*, 42 (April 1983), 217–25.

2. Edmund J. James, "The East and the West," in *The Foreign Policy of the United States: Political and Commercial Addresses and Discussion at the Annual Meeting of the American Academy of Political and Social Science, April 7–8, 1899* (1899; Philadelphia: American Academy of Political and Social Science, 1899), 215–16.

3. Page Smith, *America Enters the World: A People's History of the Progressive Era and World War I* (New York: Viking Penguin, 1985), 127, 133–34.

4. Paul F. Boller, Jr., *American Thought in Transition: The Impact of Evolutionary Naturalism, 1865–1900* (Chicago: Rand-McNally Press, 1969), 212–13.

5. Boller, *American Thought in Transition*, 214 (on Adams); Raymond J. Cunningham, "The German Historical World of Herbert Baxter Adams: 1874–1876," *Journal of American History*, 68 (September 1981), 261–71.

356   Notes to Chapters 5 and 6

6. Jurgen Herbst, *The German Historical School in American Scholarship: A Study in the Transfer of Culture* (Ithaca: Cornell University Press, 1965), 67, 113, 121–23, 126, 127; Boller, *American Thought in Transition*, 214–15; Robert A. McCaughey, *Stand, Columbia: A History of Columbia in the City of New York, 1754–2004* (New York: Columbia University Press, 2003), 160–64.

7. Edmund J. James, Review of *Political Science and Comparative Constitutional Law*, by John W. Burgess, in *Annals of the American Academy of Political and Social Science* 1 (April 1891), 681–85.

8. Thomas C. Leonard, *Illiberal Reformers: Race, Eugenics & American Economics in the Progressive Era* (Princeton: Princeton University Press, 2016), 50, 102. Ross hurled his rhetorical invective on this group, describing in crude language the physical ugliness of these immigrants and referencing "the slime at the bottom of our foreignized cities." Pp. 121, 148.

9. John R. Commons, *Race and Immigrants in America* (New York: Macmillan, 1907), 7.

10. Leonard, *Illiberal Reformers*, 110, 117–18. The individuals (in addition to those cited) whom Leonard enrolls to support his thesis about race and progressivism include Woodrow Wilson, Hebert Baxter Adams, John W. Burgess, W. E. B. DuBois, Walter Rauschensbusch, Jane Addams, Frances Willard, Eugene Debs, John Bates Clark, and Simon Patten. Edmund James makes no appearance in the book.

11. Edmund J. James, Review of *Fallacies of Race Theories as Applied to National Characteristics: Essays by William Dalton Babington*, *Annals of the American Academy of Political and Social Science*, 8 (July 1896), 167–69.

12. Theodore Marburg, "The Backward Nation," *Independent*, June 20, 1912, 1365–70.

13. Edmund J. James, "The Backward Nation," *Independent*, November 7, 1912, 1062–63.

14. Rivka Shpak Lissak, "The National Liberal Immigration League, 1906–1917," *American Jewish Archives*, 47 (Fall/Winter 1994), 197–205, 223.

15. Lissak, "National Immigration League," 200–201.

16. Edmund J. James, "Preface," in *The Immigrant Jew in America*, ed. Edmund J. James (New York: B. F. Buck & Co, 1906), 3–6. "Issued by the National Liberal Immigration League."

17. Richard White, *The Republic for Which It Stands: The United States During Reconstruction and the Gilded Age, 1865–1896* (New York: Oxford University Press, 2017), 380; Rosanne Currarino, *The Labor Question in America: Economic Democracy in the Gilded Age* (Urbana: University of Illinois Press, 2011), 43–46.

18. E. J. James, "The Chinese Question," *Nation*, April 20, 1882, 337–38.

19. James, "The Chinese Question," 337–38.

20. Edmund J. James, "An Educational Commission to China," *Journal of Education*, 63 (April 5, 1906), 369–70.

21. Poshek Fu, "Across the Pacific: The University of Illinois and China," in *Engine of Innovation: The University of Illinois*, ed. Frederick E. Hoxie (Urbana: University of Illinois Press, 2017), 189. See also Poshek Fu, "Trans-Pacific Cultural Connections: The University of Illinois and China," *Journal of American-East Asian Relations*, 24 (2017), 27–40, a revised article of the first.

Notes to Chapter 6   **357**

22. Arthur Henderson Smith, *China and America Today: A Study of Conditions and Relations* (New York: F. H. Revel Co., 1907), 213–18. These pages have all of James's letter to President Roosevelt. Wikipedia, "Boxer Indemnity Scholarship"; Madeline Y. Hsu, "Chinese and American Collaborations through Educational Exchange during the Era of Exclusion, 1872–1955," *Pacific Historical Review*, 83 (2014): 321–22.

23. Poshek Fu, "Across the Pacific," 190–91; Poshek Fu, "Trans-Pacific Cultural Connections," 34.

24. James, *Sixteen Years*, 170–71; Mary Timmins, "Enter the Dragon," University of Illinois *Alumni Magazine*, December 15, 2011.

25. Edmund J. James, "The Men of 1848 and Their Influence on America," in *Carl Schurz Memorial Services at the Auditorium, Chicago* (1906; India: Pranava Books, n.d.), 21–27.

26. Anon., "Mrs. Anna Margaret Lange James. Death of the Wife of the President of the University of Illinois," *Journal of the Illinois State Historical Society*, 7 (January 1915), 408–16.

27. Hugo Munsterberg Collection, 1860–1916, Boston Public Library (and Digital Commonwealth, Massachusetts Collections Online).

28. *Daily Illini*, October 28, 1915, 1; "The President on Preparedness," AQFN, 1 (December 1, 1915), 112; "Military and Other Preparedness," AQFN, 2 (March 15, 1916), 256; "More to Our Military," AQFN, 2 (January 1, 1917), 156.

29. Edmund J. James, "Colleges as Training Centers for an Adequate Staff of Officers," *Proceedings of the American Academy of Political Science in the City of New York*, 6 (July 1916), 221–28; James, "University Soldiers," *Journal of Education*, 83 (February 24, 1916), 202–3.

30. James to Frau Maria Kiukenberg, July 8, 1915.

31. "The Fortnight," AQFN, 2 (April 15, 1917), 275.

32. *Daily Illini*, January 10, 1918, 2; January 9, 1918, 1; April 18, 1917, 4; "The University and the War," AQFN, 2 (May 15, 1917), 310, 328. A year after American entry the Uof I had lost almost one-third of its student body to enlistments. *Daily Illini*, April 18, 1918, 1.

33. AQFN (October 1, 1917), 4. David Kinley, *The Autobiography of David Kinley* (Urbana: University of Illinois Press, 1949), 85–86, 88–90.

34. "Our Knitters," AQFN, 3 (February 1, 1918), 185; "The Woman's Part," AQFN, 3 (May 1, 1917), 311; *Daily Illini*, October 12, 1917, 1; February 9, 1918, 1; November 16, 1917, 7.

35. "The University and the War," AQFN, 2 (May 1917), 313.

36. *Daily Illini*, March 21, 1917, 1; March 31, 1917, 1; April 11, 1917, 1.

37. *Daily Illini*, November 22, 1917, 1; October 21, 1918, 3.

38. *Daily Illini*, October 19, 2015, 4; October 1, 1917, 1; April 18, 1917, 1; April 26, 1017, 1; April 27, 1918, 1; October 3, 1917, 1.

39. *Daily Illini*, November 17, 1917, 5. This report provides a full list of the faculty and the various organizations participating.

40. *Daily Illini*, November 10, 1917, 1; November 3, 1917, 1.

41. *Daily Illini*, December 5, 1917, 1.

42. *Daily Illini*, February 15, 1918, 5; February 19, 1918, 5. See Carol S. Gruber, *Mars and Minerva: World War I and the Uses of the Higher Learning in America* (Baton Rouge: Louisiana State University Press, 1975), 238–42.

43. "The Ultimate Philosophy," *Illinois Magazine*, 8 (March 1917), 176–77.

44. "The War," *Illinois Magazine*, 8 (April 1917), 229.

45. *Daily Illini*, April 11, 1917, 4.

46. "With Chemistry to Victory," AQFN, 4 (January 1, 1919), 123–24.

47. Roger Adams, "The Manufacture of Organic Chemicals at the University of Illinois," *Science*, n.s., 47 (March 8, 1918), 225–28.

48. "The University and the War," AQFN, 3 (January 15, 1918), 165–66; *Daily Illini*, May 17, 1918, 1.

49. Windsor to James, August 20 and September 25, 1917; James to Windsor, August 21, 1917, RS 35/1/4, B:1, F:Jan. 1917/Dec. 1918. See also "Library School and Library," AQFN, 3 (1918), 169.

50. Windsor to James, November 9, 1917; James to Herbert Putnam, November 14, 1917; Putnam to James, November 16, 1917, RS 2/5/3, B:168, F:Windsor, P. L. March-August 1918; August 2 and 8, 1918, B:1, F:Jan. 1917/Dec. 1918.

51. Windsor to James, August 2, 8, 1918, RS 35/1/4, B:1, F:Jan. 1917/Dec. 1918.

52. James to Windsor, March 18, 1918, RS 35/1/4, B:1, F:Jan. 1917/Dec. 1918.

53. Benjamin F. Shearer, "An Experiment in Military and Civilian Education: The Students' Army Training Corps at the University of Illinois," *Journal of the Illinois State Historical Society*, 72 (August 1979), 213–16, 218.

54. Shearer, "An Experiment," 215–16, 218; James, *Sixteen Years*, 56, 248–50; "A New Wondrous Story," AQFN, 3 (October 1, 1918), 2. For the national setting and operation of the SATC, see Gruber, *Mars and Minerva*, 213–19.

55. A memorandum from the federal government's Committee on Education and Special Training did not mince words in stating the expectations of the participating colleges and universities: "Academic instruction must necessarily be modified along lines of direct military value. The War Department will prescribe or suggest such modifications. The colleges are asked to devote the whole energy and educational power of the institution to the phases and lines of training desired by the Government." All SATC students took the War Aims course that had originated in the army and gave eleven hours a week to drill. Professors changed the contents of their courses. The academic calendar was rearranged. The government of the United States had essentially commandeered American higher education. Gruber, *Mars and Minerva*, 213–19 (quotation).

56. Shearer, "Experiment," 216–22; Kinley, *Autobiography*, 97–98. James sometimes showed his frustration with the SATC program. At a panel discussion he made this comment: "We have all had the experience of S. A. T. C. Uncle Sam is an awfully wise old gentleman, but he talks like a driveling idiot sometimes through the mouth of the second lieutenant. (Laughter and applause.)" Edmund J. James, "The Colleges and Our National Ideals," *Bulletin of the Association of American Colleges*, 5 (April 1919), 1–6 [panel discussion], 5.

57. "THE DAY—for Illinois," AQFN, 4 (November 15, 1918), 81; *Daily Illini*, November 12, 1918, 1; Kinley, *Autobiography*, 98.

Notes to Chapter 6   359

58. The *Daily Illini* reported on the progression of the influenza and the responses to it throughout October 1918.

59. European intellectuals displayed these traits also, although the issues they addressed differed from the ones that concerned American thinkers. For a comparison, see Roland N. Stromberg, *Redemption by War: The Intellectuals and 1914* (Lawrence: The Regents Press of Kansas, 1982). The great philosophers, poets and novelists, scientists, Socialists and other varied species of "the Left," sociologists, and "modernists" of all kinds, Stromberg shows, did not merely go along with the patriotic sentiments around them, they positively thrilled to the prospects of war and they looked to a "redemption" by war.

60. Gruber, *Mars and Minerva*, 20; Daniel T. Rodgers, *Atlantic Crossings: Social Politics in a Progressive Age* (Cambridge, MA: Harvard University Press, 1998), 274.

61. Gruber, *Mars and Minerva*, 70, 74 (Hadley), 72–73 (Farnam), 56 (Small); Daniel M. Fox, *The Discovery of Abundance: Simon N. Patten and the Transformation of Social Theory* (Ithaca: Cornell University Press, 1967), 122–26.

62. Peter Novick, *That Noble Dream: The "Objectivity Question" and the American Historical Profession* (Cambridge: Cambridge University Press, 1988), 116.

63. Edmund J. James, "America and France," AQFN, 3 (April 15, 1918), 248–51.

64. Edmund Janes James, *What the United States Has Achieved in War Activities and Moral Leadership* [an address] (published by the University Under the Direction of the War Committee, Urbana, May 6, 1918), 2–5 (quotation on p. 4).

65. James, *What the United States Has Achieved*, 5–7.

66. These views joined James to a large and ongoing discussion, especially sharp among American liberal and progressive intellectuals, about the relation of reform at home to the war abroad. He has an affinity with a group that Charles Hirschfield called "neo-liberals," most of them associated with the *New Republic*. But that group had in mind mostly economic reforms—nationalization of the railroads, labor and the union movement, taxation—and, but much less than James, racial equality. See "Nationalist Progressivism and World War I," *Mid-America*, 45 (July 1963), 139–56.

67. Edmund Janes James, "The College and the War" [Commencement Address], AQFN, 3 (July 15, 1918), 331.

68. Laurence R. Veysey, *The Emergence of the American University* (Chicago: University of Chicago Press, 1965), 57–120.

69. Gruber, *Mars and Minerva*, 28–30, 116–17.

70. James, "Commencement Address," 333–34, 336–37.

71. James, "Commencement Address," 337.

72. Gruber, *Mars and Minerva*, 114.

73. "The University and the War," AQFN, 3 (May 15, 1918), 288.

74. "The President's Address," AQFN, 4 (October 15, 1918), 18–20. James made a summary of the University's contribution to the war for the public record. In addition to the material above he detailed that altogether 5,379 men and 108 women (not counting the students in the SATC program) had enlisted in the American armed services. "The State University and the War," *Illinois Office of Secretary of State, Illinois Blue Book, 1919-1920*, 121. One hundred thirty-two people gave their lives. *Daily Illini*, March 18, 1919, 8. This source says 8,438 served.

360   Notes to Chapter 6

75. Smith, *America Enters the World*, 566.

76. Gruber, *Mars and Minerva*, 132–38, 146–47; Novick, *Noble Dream*, 121–24.

77. Gruber, *Mars and Minerva*, 176–206.

78. Howard H. Peckham, *The Making of the University of Michigan, 1817–1992*, edited and updated by Margaret L. Steneck and Nicholas H. Steneck (1967; University of Michigan: Bentley Historical Library, 1994), 145–46.

79. Gruber, *Mars and Minerva*, 256.

80. Robert P. Howard, *The Illinois Governors: Mostly Good and Competent*, revised and updated by Taylor Pensoneau and Peggy Boyer Long (Springfield, IL: Center Publications/*Illini Issues*), 185–90; Howard, *Illinois: A History of the Prairie State* (Grand Rapids, MI: William B. Eerdmans, 1972), 438, 442–43; Roger Biles, *Illinois: A History of the Land and Its People* (DeKalb: Northern Illinois University Press, 2005), 185, 186 (first Lowden quotation), 188–89, 192, 193 (second Lowden quotation).

81. This section of this chapter owes mostly to Bruce Tap, author of an essay titled "Suppression of Dissent: Academic Freedom at the University of Illinois during the World War I Era," *Illinois Historical Journal*, 85 (Spring 1992), 2–22. Tap, as he explains, had help from Winton Solberg in preparing the piece. Solberg's raw manuscript follows this essay quite closely, but has scant documentation. This author has supplied the needed documentation by using Tap's references. Interested readers will find more details of this story in Tap's excellent essay.

82. "University of Illinois Faculty Disloyalty Investigation, Special Committee, Board of Trustees, November 27, 1917" (hereafter "Disloyalty Investigation"), TS, RS 2/5/3, B:152, General Correspondence 1904–1919; Edmund James Papers.

83. *Daily Illini*, November 3, 1917, 1.

84. *Daily Illini*, April 4, 1918, 1.

85. "Disloyalty Investigation," 3–10; Robert A. Feer, "Academic Freedom at the University of Illinois, 1867–1950: A Case Study." Honors thesis, Harvard University, 1950, 60–61, 64–65; M. C. Otto, "An Experiment in Conscience," *Socialist Review*, 8 (1919), 51–55; *Daily Illini*, November 3, 1917, 1.

86. "Disloyalty Investigation," 11–12, 13–15, 73–74.

87. "Disloyalty Investigation," 75–79.

88. *Champaign Daily News*, November 1, 1917, 1, 8; *Champaign Daily Gazette*, November 2, 1917, 10; *Urbana Courier*, November 2, 1917, 1; President James Clipping File, RS 2/5/12, B:12, James Papers.

89. "The Fortnight," AQFN, 3 (November 15, 1917), 66.

90. "A Letter on Loyalty," AQFN, 3 (January 15, 1918), 165.

91. Kinley, *Autobiography*, 95.

92. "Directory of Illini in War Service," "Introduction by President James," AQFN, 3 (December 1 and 15, 1917), 87–88.

93. *Daily Illini*, November 8, 1917, 1.

94. David Grisso, "David Kinley, 1861–1944: The Career of the Fifth President of the University of Illinois," PhD dissertation, University of Illinois, 1980, 339; James to Cole, November 14, 1917, Box 142, James General Correspondence.

95. *Daily Illini*, November 28, 1917, 1; *Champaign Daily News*, December 2, 13; *Board Transactions* (1917), 625. Alice Abbott, president of the board, went one

Notes to Chapter 6   361

step further. Despite the acquittal of those charged, she avowed that "nothing but perfect loyalty will be tolerated on the University staff." "The Fortnight," AQFN, 3 (January 1, 1918), 130; Tap, "Suppression of Dissent," 19.

96. Tap, "Suppression of Dissent," 19–22.

97. Roger L. Geiger, *The History of American Higher Education: Learning and Culture from the Founding to World War II* (Princeton: Princeton University Press, 2015), 425.

Chapter 7. The Physical Sciences

1. E. J. Townsend, "Ready for Duty," September 10, 1904, College of Science Letterbook, RS 15/1/2, 107.

2. E. J. Townsend, "Science and Public Service," *Science*, n.s., 32 (November 4, 1910), 610–11.

3. Townsend, "Science and Public Service," 611.

4. Townsend, "Science and Public Service," 614.

5. See Daniel J. Kevles, *The Physicists: The History of a Scientific Community in Modern America* (1971; Cambridge, MA: Harvard University Press, 1995), 45, 47, 50 and all of Chapter IV, "Pure Science and Practical Politics."

6. Townsend, "Science and Public Service," 615–20.

7. Townsend, "Science and Public Service," 620.

8. Townsend, "Science and Public Service," 619–21. In discussing this theme of science and progressive reform Daniel Kevles singled out for citation David Kinley's address at the University of Illinois's Graduate School opening, "Democracy and Scholarship," noted earlier in Chapter 3 of this book. Kevles, *The Physicists*, 74. See his Chapter V, "Research and Reform."

9. Forbes to Draper, February 23, 1904, RS 15/1/2, B:1.

10. Nominal recognition of two departments came into use years earlier to forestall friction in administration between Palmer and Parr, both full professors, said Parr, but the division had little foundation in fact or practice. Parr to Townsend, May 4, 1907, RS 15/1/3, B:8, F:Chemistry (1) 1904–1907.

11. Forbes to Burrill, June 27, and August 13, 1904, RS 15/1/2, B:2; BT, 22nd *Report* (1904), 328, 329.

12. Parr, Grindley, et al., to Townsend, January 5, 1906, RS 15/1/3, B:2, F:1905–1907-P.

13. James to Noyes, January 20 and 25, 1906, RS 2/5/4, B:3, Ltrbk. 42.

14. RS 2/5/15, William A. Noyes Folder; Roger Adams, "William Albert Noyes," National Academy of Sciences, *Biographical Memoirs*, 27 (1952), 179–208; Elizabeth Noble Shur, "Noyes, William Albert," *American National Biography*, 16:551–52; George B. Kauffman, "Noyes, W. Albert, Jr.," *American National Biography*, 16:549–51.

15. *Science*, n.s. (November 22, 1907), 689–714.

16. Noyes to Townsend, March 15, 1909, RS 15/1/3, B:8, F:Chemistry (2).

17. Townsend to James, May 4, 1909, RS 15/1/2, B:3.

18. Grindley, "Brief Sketch of the Life of H. S. Grindley," attached to Grindley

to Robert S. Woodward, June 14, 1905, RS 2/5/6, James Faculty Correspondence, B:2, F:E-L 4–8/1905.

19. Grindley to A. W. Palmer, September 5, 1900; Palmer to Stephen A. Forbes, June 18, 1898, 2/4/2 (Andrew Sloan Draper Faculty Correspondence), B:7, 4; F:Palmer; H. S. Grindley and J. L. Sammis, "Dietary Studies at the University of Illinois," in *Nutrition Investigations at the University of Illinois, North Dakota Agricultural College, and Lake Erie College, Ohio, 1896 to 1900*. U.S. Department of Agriculture, Office of Experiment Stations, Bulletin 91 (Washington: GPO, 1900), 7–20.

20. Jane Addams and H. S. Grindley, *A Study of the Milk Supply of Chicago*. University of Illinois, Agricultural Experiment Station, Circular 13 (December 1898).

21. BT, 20th *Report*, (1901), 27.

22. H. S. Grindley and A. D. Emmett, *Studies on the Influence of Cooking upon the Nutritive Value of Meats at the University of Illinois, 1903–04*. U.S. Department of Agriculture, Office of Experiment Stations, Bulletin 162 (Washington: GPO, 1905), 7; Grindley to President Edmund J. James, May 7, 1906, 2/5/6, B:4, F:G-K.

23. H. S. Grindley and Timothy Mojonnier, *Experiments on Losses in Cooking Meat, 1900–1903*. U.S. Department of Agriculture, Office of Experiment Stations, Bulletin 141 (Washington: GPO, 1904), 8.

24. Colin W. Whittaker and Frank O. Lundstrom, *A Review of the Patents and Literature on the Manufacture of Potassium Nitrate with Notes on Its Occurrence and Uses*. U.S. Department of Agriculture, Miscellaneous Publication 192 (Washington, D.C., July 1934); Merle D. Pierson and Leslie A. Smoot, "Nitrite, Nitrite Alternatives, and the Control of *Clostridium Botulinum* in Cured Meats," *Critical Reviews in Food Science and Nutrition*, 17 (1982), 141–42.

25. Oscar E. Anderson, Jr., *The Health of a Nation: Harvey W. Wiley and the Fight for Pure Food* (published for the University of Cincinnati by the University of Chicago Press, 1958); Wallace F. Janssen, "The Squad that Ate Poison," *FDA Consumer*, 15 (December 1981-January 1982), 6–11; James Harvey Young, *Pure Food: Securing the Federal Food and Drugs Act of 1906* (Princeton: Princeton University Press, 1989); Young, "Wiley, Harvey Washington," *American National Biography*, 23:391–92; Lorine Swainston Goodwin, *The Pure Food, Drink, and Drug Crusaders, 1879–1914* (Jefferson, NC: McFarland & Co., 1999).

26. James to R. H. Chittenden, December 1, 1906, 2/5/3, James General Correspondence, B:28, F:Nutrition Experiment (Exhibit A, attached to "Minutes of the . . . Advisory Board . . . November 25, 1911"). Contemporary documents describe this body as both the Nutrition Commission and the Advisory Panel.

27. BT, 24th *Report*, (1908), 100–101.

28. Winton U. Solberg, "The Quest for a College and Research Laboratory of Veterinary Medicine at the University of Illinois, 1896–1921," *Journal of Illinois History*, 3 (Winter 2000), 246–66.

29. Tilden to James, September 8, 1911, 2/5/3, B:28, F:Nutrition Experiment.

30. BT, 24th *Report* (1908), 106–7, 151–52.

31. BT, 24th *Report* (1908), 106–7, 362–63, 386–87, 394; Harry S. Grindley and

Notes to Chapter 7   363

Harold H. Mitchell, *Studies in Nutrition*, volume 1, *Discussion and Interpretation of the Biochemical Data* ([Urbana]: From the Laboratory of Physiological Chemistry, Department of Animal Husbandry, University of Illinois, 1917), 1–6.

32. BT, 25th *Report* (1910), 580–81.

33. Solberg 2, 108–9.

34. Rolfe to Townsend, April 25, 1907 and February 14, 1908, RS 15/1/3, B:8, F:Geology 1905–1913.

35. For Rolfe's publications, see RS 26/20/12, Charles W. Rolfe Papers, B:1, F:Articles by Charles W. Rolfe.

36. Townsend to James, March 10, 1906, RS 15/1/2, B:2.

37. RS 2/5/15, William S. Bayley Folder; James to Bayley, May 8, 1906, RS 2/5/4, B:4, Ltrbk. 45.

38. RS 2/5/15, Thomas L. Savage Folder.

39. Rolfe to Townsend, April 25, 1907, RS 15/1/3, B:8, F:Geology 1905–1913; RS 2/5/15, Rufus M. Bagg Folder.

40. Townsend to James, June 1, 1910, RS 2/5/5, B:9, F:Deans' Reports 1910; "Registrations in Geology 1910–1911," RS 15/1/3, B:8, F:Geology 1905–1913.

41. Rolfe to Draper, August 24, 1894, RS 2/4/2, B:1, F:Rolfe, Charles W.; C. W. Rolfe, "Plea for the Establishment of a Laboratory of Economic Geology," and [C. W. Rolfe], "Some Things for Young Men to Think About," printed brochures, RS 26/20/12, Rolfe Family Papers, B:1, F:Charles W. Rolfe, Ceramic Engineering.

42. BT, 23rd *Report* (1906), 25. University documents refer to both the Illinois Clay Manufacturers' Association and the Illinois Clayworkers' Association. They are one and the same. This text uses the former throughout.

43. *Journal of the House of Representatives of the 44th General Assembly of . . . Illinois* (1905), 71–72, 100.

44. James to Editor, *Prairie Farmer*, March 29, 1905, RS 25/5/4, B:1, Ltrbk. 37.

45. James wrote more than thirty letters between January 19, and May 3, 1905 regarding the bill for a geological survey.

46. *Journal of the House of Representatives of the 44th General Assembly of . . . Illinois* (1905), 684, 971–72, 993–95, 1076, 1279.

47. BT, 23rd *Report* (1906), 74.

48. James to Bain, April 6, 1906, RS 2/5/4, B:3, Ltrbk. 44; Bain to Townsend, March 19, 1909, RS 15/1/3, B:3, F:1908–1909-B.

49. BT, 23rd *Report* (1906), 284.

50. Townsend to Joseph N. Ivy, October 12, 1906, pottery, RS 15/1/2, B:2.

51. Ray Thomas Stull, "Growth of the Department of Ceramics," December 2, 1912, RS 15/1/3, B:8, F:Geology, 1905–1913.

52. "Report on the Work of the Department of Ceramics from July 1, 1907 to September 1908, Made at the Request of Governor C. S. Deneen," RS 15/1/3, B:8, F:Ceramics, 1907–1913; Cullen W. Parmelee, "History of Ceramic Education at the University of Illinois," *Journal of the American Ceramic Society*, 6 (January 1923), 101. The research papers noted here were published in the *University of Illinois Bulletin*, from volume 4, no. 12 (February 15, 1907), through volume 11, no. 47 (July 30, 1914).

364   Notes to Chapter 7

53. Stull to Townsend, December 4, 1912, a covering letter to a report dated December 2, 1912 and titled "Growth of the Department of Ceramics," RS 15/1/3, B:8, F:Ceramics 1907–1913. Stull includes a list of the bulletins published by ceramics faculty along with a list of the more important discoveries of research work.

54. Stull, "Growth of the Department of Ceramics," December 2, 1912, RS 15/1/3, B:8, F:Ceramics 1907–1913.

55. BT, 28th *Report* (1916), 866, 918; James to Blackwelder, December 17, 1915, Blackwelder to James, January 27, 1916, RS 2/5/15, Eliot Blackwelder Folder.

56. Solberg 2, 97–99; Michael T. Svec, "The Astronomical Observatory of the University of Illinois" (1986, rev. 1987), RS 15/3/12, Astronomy Department Observatory History, is helpful. In 1989, the University of Illinois Observatory was placed on the National Register of Historic Places.

57. Stebbins, "Early Photometry at Illinois," *Publications of the Astronomical Society of the Pacific*, 69 (December 1957), 506–10; RS 2/5/15, Staff Appointment Files, Stebbins Folder, and 15/1/3, B:7, F:Astronomy, 1902–1913, contain the Stebbins-Draper correspondence and Stebbins's Application Form. See also BT, 22nd *Report* (1904), 42. For biographical accounts, see Donald E. Osterbrock, "Stebbins, Joel," *American National Biography*, 20:600–602, and A. E. Whitford, "Joel Stebbins," National Academy of Sciences, *Biographical Memoirs*, 49 (1978), 293–316, with a list (which is neither complete nor scrupulously accurate) of Stebbins's scientific publications.

58. Michael T. Svec, "The Birth of Electronic Astronomy," *Sky & Telescope*, 83 (May 1992), 496–99, a brief account of this aspect of Stebbins's achievement.

59. Joel Stebbins, "The Electrical Photometry of Stars," *Science*, n.s. 41 (June 4, 1915), 809–12, 810.

60. Stebbins, "The Electrical Photometry of Stars," in "Symposium on the Photoelectric Cell in Astrophysical Research," *Publications of the Astronomical Society of the Pacific*, 52 (1940), 235 (quotation)–43. This article is not the same as the one cited previously. Hereafter each of these citations will be followed by either *Science* or PASP and the page(s). Brown's MA thesis (1906) was "Investigation in the Behavior of Selenium Cell with Special Reference to the Effect of Pressure on the Electrical Resistance."

61. Stebbins, "Early Photometry," 507 (the quotation); Stebbins, "The Electrical Photometry of Stars," PASP, 236.

62. Stebbins to Townsend, April 16, 1907, RS 15/1/3, B:7, F:Astronomy 1902–1913.

63. Stebbins, "Electrical Photometry," PASP, 236.

64. Stebbins, "Electrical Photometry," *Science*, 810; Stebbins, "Early Photometry at Illinois," 508.

65. Stebbins, "Electrical Photometry," *Science*, 810; Stebbins, "Early Photometry," PASP, 508.

66. Stebbins to Townsend, May 22, 1908 and February 23, 1910, RS 15/1/3, B:7, F:Astronomy 1902–1913; *Proceedings of the American Academy of Arts and Sciences*, 43 (1908), 528; 44 (1909), 738.

67. A complete listing of Stebbins's publication may be found in Whitford, "Stebbins," 310–16.

Notes to Chapter 7   365

68. Stebbins to Townsend, May 22, 1908, RS 15/1/3, B:7, F:Astronomy 1902–1913.

69. Stebbins, "Early Photometry," *Science*, 506–10; Stebbins, "Electrical Photometry," PASP, 236; Osterbrock, "Stebbins, Joel," 600–601.

70. Stebbins to Townsend, April 21, 1909, RS 15/1/3, B:7, F:Astronomy 1902–1913.

71. Pickering to Stebbins, September 27, 1910, RS 2/5/6, B:17, F:1909–11 S.

72. Kinley to James, October 13 and 30, 1911, RS 2/5/6, B:22, F:Joel Stebbins.

73. Stebbins to Townsend, December 8, 1912, RS 15/1/3, B:7, F:Astronomy 1902–1913.

74. The two men forged a collaboration that lasted for a quarter of a century, writes J. B. Hearnshaw, *The Measurement of Starlight: Two Centuries of Astronomical Photometry* (Cambridge: Cambridge University Press, 1996), 206.

75. Stebbins," Electrical Photometry," *Science*, 810.

76. Stebbins, "Photo-Electric Photometry of Stars," 5; Osterbrock, "Stebbins, Joel," 601.

77. Osterbrock, "Stebbins, Joel," 601–2.

78. Kron, "Joel Stebbins," 215, 216.

79. C. T. Elvey and A. E. Whitford in Jesse L. Greenstein, "The Seventieth Anniversary of Professor Joel Stebbins and the Washburn Observatory," *Popular Astronomy*, 56 (June 1948), 281–99. Readers might derive an enriched image of the singing astronomer if they viewed the movie *Naughty Marietta* (1935), where at the dramatic conclusion Jeanette MacDonald and Nelson Eddy sing the Victor Herbert classic "Ah, Sweet Mystery of Life."

80. Kron, "Joel Stebbins," 217.

81. *Proceedings of the American Academy of Arts and Sciences*, 50 (1915), 355–56; 49 (1914), 713–14 (on the Rumford Premium).

82. Stebbins, "Electrical Photometry," *Science*, 809–12; *Report of the National Academy of Sciences for the Year 1915* (Washington: GPO, 1916), 23–24.

83. Stebbins to Kinley, October 26, 1921, RS 2/6/1, David Kinley Correspondence, B:66, F:Ste 1921–22.

84. Whitford, "American Pioneer," 269.

Chapter 8. The Life Sciences

1. BT, 21st *Report* (1902), 3.

2. Thomas Arkle Clark to Kemp, March 20 and 22, 1903; March 22, 1904, RS 41/2/20.

3. For the Chicago institute, see Winton U. Solberg, *Reforming Medical Education: The University of Illinois College of Medicine, 1880–1920* (Urbana: University of Illinois Press, 2009).

4. Forbes to James, June 7, 1906; Kemp to Edgar Townsend, November 20, 1906, along with Kemp, "Reasons for Department of Anatomy Here," RS 15/1/3, B:9, F:Physiology (1).

5. University of Illinois, *Register for 1904–1905*, 121–23; James to William H. Brown, September 14, 1905, RS 15/1/4, B:2; James to Forbes, February 14, 1906, RS

366   Notes to Chapters 7 and 8

15/1/4, B:3; Townsend to William E. Quine, August 16, September 7, and October 27 and 30, 1905; Townsend to W. L. Pillsbury, January 11, 1906; University of Illinois, *Register for 1905–1906*, 33, 39, 109–11.

6. Townsend to W. L. Pillsbury, May 22, 1908, RS 15/1/2, B:3.

7. Charles W. Hottes, Oral History Interview (1964), RS 15/4/21, Reel 1; Mrs. W. E. Burge, cited in Walter P. Elhardt, "History of the Physiology Department," RS 5/17/10, 71 (Burge arrived on the campus in 1912. What she reports is hearsay, but with the ring of truth); Archie J. Graham, "Lobbying Days," 28, RS 52/38/20; Archie J. Graham Papers, B:1.

8. Kinley to James, July 17, 1907, RS 2/5/5, B:13, F:Graduate School 1906–1907.

9. Kemp to James, April 20 and September 7, 1906, RS 15/1/3, B:9, F:Physiology (1); Townsend to James, April 24, 1907, RS 15/1/2, B:2; Kemp to Townsend, November 19, 1907, RS 15/1/3, B:9, F:Physiology (1).

10. Kinley to James, July 17, 1907, RS 2/5/5, B:13, F:Graduate School 1906–1907.

11. Kemp to James, February 14, 1908, RS 15/1/3, B:9, F:Psychology (1).

12. In 1897 Kemp's salary was $2,000. From 1901–1902 through 1904–1905 it was $2,200, and in 1907–1908, $2,500.

13. BT, 24th *Report* (1908), 449.

14. Kemp to the Honorable Board of Trustees, May 1, 1908, RS 1/1/3, B:10, F:23 April 1908-May 2, 1908; James, Diaries, RS 2/5/7, April 25, 1908; BT, 24th *Report* (1908), 460.

15. George T. Kemp, "The Administration at the University of Illinois," *Science*, 28 (October 9, 1908), 483–88.

16. "The Administration at the University of Illinois," *Independent*, 65, December 31, 1908, 1629–30; "The Administration at the University of Illinois," *Science*, 29 (January 15, 1909), 108–9.

17. For Burrill's early years in the University, see relevant sections of Solberg 1 and Solberg 2. Vassiliki Betty Smocovitis, "Burrill, Thomas Jonathan," *Dictionary of National Biography*, 4:43–44. Burrill was described as "the world's senior plant bacteriologist." His discovery of the bacterial origin of pear-blight gave a vital start to work in plant pathology. His achievement earned him high standing in the scientific community, and in the University wide appreciation.

18. RS 2/5/15, Charles F. Hottes Folder.

19. These details come from the annual catalogs for the years 1904–1905 to 1911–1912.

20. Charles F. Hottes, "Personal Recollections of Thomas J. Burrill and His Work," *Illinois Alumni News* (February 1940), 6–7; Andrew D. Rodgers III, *Erwin Frank Smith: A Story of North American Plant Pathology* (Philadelphia: American Philosophical Society, 1952), 43.

21. Burrill to Townsend, April 21 and 29, 1904 and April 29, 1907, RS 15/1/3, B:8, F:Botany (1).

22. Burrill's plea for emphasis on bacteriology began in 1906 and became increasingly strong. See Burrill to Townsend, November 16, 1906 and February 23, 1907, RS 15/1/3, F:Bacteriology; Burrill to Townsend, April 29, 1907, and May 4, 1909, and November 14, 1910, RS 15/1/3, B:8, F:Botany (1).

Notes to Chapter 8   367

23. Burrill to Townsend, February 23, 1906 and November 16, 1906, RS 15/1/3, B:7, F:Bacteriology.

24. Burrill to Townsend, February 3, 1908, RS 15/1/3, B:8, F:Botany (1); *Bulletin of the Illinois State Board of Health*, 4 (February 1908), 69.

25. RS 4/2/1, 1:169–71 [December 21, 1906]; Townsend to James, 4, 7 March (two letters) 1907, RS 15/1/2, B:2; BT 24th *Report* (1908), 77.

26. Burrill to Townsend, May 4, 1909, RS 15/1/3, B:8, F:Botany 1903–1910. Official and unofficial documents spell the name both "MacNeal" and "Mac Neal." For consistency, MacNeal is used here.

27. Burrill, "A State Institute of Sanitary Science and Public Health," [November 1908], RS 15/4/1, B:2 (in bound volume 17, pp. 147–53). The document is between one dated October 26, 1908 and another dated December 17, 1908.

28. Townsend to James, December 16, 1908, RS 2/5/5, B:9, F:Deans's Reports 1908; James to Townsend, December 17, 1908, RS 15/1/3, B:4, F:1908–1909 I-J.

29. Isaac D. Rawlings, *The Rise and Fall of Disease in Illinois*, 2 vols. (Springfield: The State Department of Public Health, 1927), 1:405; *Bulletin of the Illinois State Board of Health*, 4 (October 1908), 587–92, 639; (December 1908), 727, 744.

30. James to Townsend, December 3, 1908; Sedgwick to Townsend, January 15, 1909, RS 15/1/3, B:4, F:1908–1909 I-J and S; Barbara Guttmann Rosenkrantz, "Sedgwick, William T.," *Dictionary of National Biography*, 19:586–87.

31. *Daily Illini*, April 18, 21, 23, 24, 1909. The paper did not report all of the lectures.

32. Townsend, "Science in the Public Service," *Science*, n.s. 32 (November 4, 1910), 609–21; Deneen to Townsend, August 20, 1910 and December 28, 1910, RS 15/1/3, B:5, F:C-D 1910–1911; *Journal of the House of Representatives of the 47th General Assembly of the State of Illinois* (Springfield, 1911), 29–30.

33. *Blue Book of the State of Illinois, 1917–1918*, 312–13; St. Clair Drake, "Public Health Activities Under the Civil Administrative Code," *Blue Book of the State of Illinois, 1919–1920*, 22–23.

34. Townsend to James, June 1, 1910, RS 2/5/5, B:9, F:Deans' Reports 1910.

35. Burrill to Kinley, July 10, 1907, RS 15/4/20, B:1 (in a volume numbered 12); Burrill to Townsend, April 8, 1910, RS 15/1/3, B:8, F:Botany (1); Townsend to James, June 1, 1910, RS 2/5/5, B:9, F:Deans' Reports 1910.

36. BT, 27th *Report* (1914), 121.

37. L. H. Pammel, *Prominent Men I Have Met: Dr. William Trelease* (Ames, Iowa, n.p., 1927); L. H. Bailey, "William Trelease (1857–1945)," American Philosophical Society, *Year Book 1945* (Philadelphia: The American Philosophical Society, 1946), 420–25; Louis O. Kunkel, "William Trelease, February 22, 1857-January 1, 1945," National Academy of Sciences, *Biographical Memoirs*, vol. 35 (Columbia University Press for The National Academy of Sciences: New York, 1961), 307–16 (followed by a bibliography of Trelease's writings).

38. Harley J. Van Cleave, "A History of the Department of Zoology at the University of Illinois," *Bios*, 18 (May 1947), 80–82.

39. Van Cleave, "Department of Zoology," 81.

40. And Forbes clearly shared James's ideas about the modern university. Forbes

368   **Notes to Chapter 8**

stood committed to the scientific method and placed his faith in it even to the point of making it a prescriptive answer for all society's challenges and defects. See S. A. Forbes, "The Teaching of the Scientific Method," *Addresses and Journal of Proceedings of the National Education Association of the United States* (June-July 1904), 879–88.

41. Forbes to Kinley, May 14, 1906, 15/24/1, B:1.

42. *The Fishes of Illinois* was issued in 1909 by the Natural History Survey of Illinois of the State Laboratory of Natural History, second edition, 1920. Stephen A. Forbes and Robert E. Richardson, *Maps Showing Distribution of Illinois Fishes to Accompany a Report on the Fishes of Illinois* was published in 1908 by authority of the state legislature.

43. [Sir] R[ay] L[ankester], "Three Fish-Faunas," *Nature*, 81 (August 19, 1909), 216–18; Forbes to James, April 19, 1911, identified the author, 43/1/5, B:29, F:Correspondence E. J. James 1909–1912.

44. 2/5/15, John H. McClellan Folder, Forbes to McClellan, March 11, 1907, 15/24/1; Forbes to James, July 22, 1907, 2/5/6, B:6, F:C-F.

45. 2/5/15, Charles C. Adams Folder.

46. Forbes to Townsend, May 23, 1908, 15/1/3, B:9, F:Zoology 1907–1913.

47. Forbes to Townsend, November 20, 1906.

48. Forbes to James, July 23, 1907, 2/5/6, B:6; F:C-F. See also Forbes to Townsend, January 31, 1908, 15/1/3, B:9, F:Zoology 1907–1913.

49. 2/5/15, Justus W. Folsom Folder.

50. Forbes to James, July 23, 1907, 2/5/6, B:6, F:C-F.

51. Forbes to Townsend, April 27, 1907 (not the annual report of this date), 15/1/3, B:9, F:Zoology 1907–1913.

52. Forbes to James, January 20, 1910, 15/1/3, B:8, F:Entomology 1910–1913.

53. Townsend to James, November 8, 1910, 15/1/2, B:3.

54. BT, 26th *Report* (1912), 458.

55. MacGillivray to Forbes, July 9, 1911, 43/1/5, B:29; F:Alexander D. MacGillivray.

56. "New Courses Proposed in Entomology," a document in 43/1/5, B:29, F:Entomology Department of Appropriations 1909–1911.

57. Forbes to Townsend, April 14, 1911; April 18, 1912; and December 4, 1912, 15/1/3, B:8, F:Entomology 1910–1913.

58. Forbes to Townsend, February 22 and December 4, 1912; May 5, 1913, 15/1/3, B:8, F:Entomology 1910–1913.

59. Forbes to Townsend, December 4, 1912; May 5, 1913, 15/1/3, F:Entomology 1910–1913.

60. James to Townsend, January 5, 1909, 2/5/6, B:11, F:E. J. Townsend. For more on Forbes, see the several sections of Solberg 2 and p. 115n2 especially.

61. "Ward, Henry Baldwin," *National Cyclopaedia of American Biography*, 35 (1949), 174–75; Horace W. Stunkard, "Ward, Henry Baldwin," *Dictionary of American Biography*, Suppl. III (1973), 802–3; Elizabeth Noble Shor, "Ward, Henry Baldwin," *American National Biography*, 22:628–29.

62. 2/5/15, Henry B. Ward Folder.

63. Reighard to Townsend, February 1, 1909, 2/5/15, Henry W. Baldwin Folder.

64. Davis to Townsend, May 11, 1909, 2/5/15, Henry W. Baldwin Folder.

65. Stunkard, "Ward, Henry B.," 803.

66. Clipping from an unidentified newspaper in 15/24/21, Henry B. Ward Papers, B:4, F:1908–1910.

67. "An ex officio" to President Illinois State University, n.d., 2/5/6, B:18, F:H. B. Ward.

68. Ward to Townsend, April 15 and December 4, 1912; May 12, 1913, 15/1/3, B:9, F:Zoology 1907–1913.

69. Townsend to James, June 1, 1910; 2/5/5, B:9, F:Deans' Reports 1910; Ward to Townsend, April 15, 1912, 15/1/3, B:9, F:Zoology 1907–1913.

70. Ward to Townsend, November 15 and April 28, 1911; April 15 and December 4, 1912; May 14, 1913; July 1, 1913, 15/1/3, B:9, F:Zoology 1907–1913.

71. Townsend to James, July 1, 1909, 15/1/2, B:3. This letter is the first evidence as to Ward's choices.

72. Ward to Zeleny, June 22, 1915, 2/5/15, Henry B. Ward Folder.

73. 2/5/15, Charles Zeleny Folder.

74. 2/5/15, Harley J. Van Cleave Folder; John D. Mizelle, "A Memorial to Harley Jones Van Cleave," *American Midland Naturalist* 49 no. 3 (1953), 685–95.

75. 2/5/15, John S. Kingsley Folder.

76. BT, 27th *Report* (1914), 599, 613, 630; James to Kingsley, July 3, 1913, 2/5/15, James S. Kingsley Folder.

77. Van Cleave, "Department of Zoology," 84–85, 87. Note: A department of biology did not yet exist at Illinois.

Chapter 9. The Social Sciences

1. RS 15/1/6, College of Science Record Book, November 3, 1905 to June 10, 1913, 8; Edgar F. Townsend to James, January 26, 1906, RS 2/5/6, B:3, F:1/1/06–4/1/06 L-Z; James Diary, RS 2/5/7, December 24, 1906; January 8, 1907; James to Townsend, April 3, 1912, RS 2/5/6, B:22, F:E. J. Townsend.

2. Greene to James, May 26, 1906; April 20, 1910, RS 2/5/6, B:4, F:E-K; B:15, F:Evarts B. Greene Sept. 1909-Aug. 1910. See also Jack R. Kirby, "Evarts Boutell Greene: The Career of a Professional Historian" (PhD dissertation, University of Illinois, 1969). For background on Greene, see Solberg 2, 81–83.

3. Greene to James, April 27 and May 14, 1908, RS 2/5/6, B:9, F:Evarts B. Greene.

4. Greene to James, May 28, 1909, RS 15/1/11, B:2, F:Annual Report 1908–09.

5. Greene to James, April 4, 1907, RS 2/5/6, B:6, F:Evarts B. Greene.

6. Greene to James, April 4 and May 1, 1907, RS 2/5/6, B:6, F:Evarts B. Greene, and RS 15/1/11, B:2, F:Annual Report 1906–1907.

7. Greene to James, September 11, 1907 and March 6, 1908, RS 2/5/6, B:8, F:Evarts B. Greene; Greene to James, May 1, 1908, RS 15/1/11, B:2.

8. Greene to James, May 1, 1908, RS 15/1/11, B:2.

9. Greene to James, October 24 and November 15, 1910; James to Greene, November 8, 1910; Greene to James, May 26, 1911, RS 2/5/6, B:15, F:Evarts B.

370   Notes to Chapters 8 and 9

Greene, Sept. 1910-Jan. 1911; BT, 26th *Report* (1912), 520; BT, 27th *Report* (1914), 72, 175.

10. See the portrait of Greene by a long-standing colleague: Theodore C. Pease, Evarts Boutell Greene, 1870–1947, *Journal of the Illinois State Historical Society* (1908–1984) 41 (1948): 7–15.

11. [David Kinley], "Statistics," February 9, 1905, RS 15/1/11, B:1, F:Liberal Arts Annual Reports 1904–1905.

12. [Kinley], "Statistics," February 9, 1905, RS 15/1/11, B:1, F:Liberal Arts Annual Reports 1904–1905.

13. A separate College of Commerce and Business Administration, however, did not emerge until 1915. The fact seems strange considering James's early career at Wharton and his reformist publications on training for careers in business.

14. Kinley, Annual Report for 1904–1905, RS 5/1/11, B:1.

15. Greene to James, March 3, 1906, RS 2/5/6, B:3, F:E-K.

16. RS 2/5/15, F:Larson, Laurence M; Julius E. Olson to David Kinley, May 13, 1907, on the Wisconsin offer, in Larson's folder.

17. RS 2/5/15, F:Cole, Arthur C.

18. Kinley to James, March 12 and 26, 1913, RS 2/5/6, B:27, F:David Kinley.

19. RS 2/5/15, F:Lybyer, Alfred H. The quotation is from an anonymous typewritten document in this folder.

20. Kinley to Greene, October 9 and November 26, 1901, RS 15/1/4, B:1.

21. As quoted in Peter Novick, *That Noble Dream: The "Objectivity Question" and the American Historical Profession* (New York: Cambridge University Press, 1988), 94n.

22. Marion Dargan Jr., "Clarence Walworth Alvord," in *The Marcus W. Jernegan Essays in American Historiography*, ed. William T. Hutchinson (Chicago: University of Chicago Press, 1937), 326–27, 333. See also Dominic F. Abram, "Alvord, Clarence Walworth," *American National Biography*, 1:398–99.

23. Kinley to The Albert Teachers' Agency, July 22, 1905, RS 15/1/4, B:3.

24. Greene to James, March 22, 1907, RS 2/5/6, B:6, F:Evarts B. Greene; Solon J. Buck, "Clarence Walworth Alvord, Historian," *Mississippi Valley Historical Review*, 15 (December 1928), 310, 317.

25. Kinley to James, November 21 and December 3, 1912 (the quotation), RS 2/5/6, B:27, F:Kinley, David.

26. Buck, "Alvord," 312; Dixon Ryan Fox, "State History. II," *Political Science Quarterly*, 37 (March 1922), 99–118 (quotations at 118, 99).

27. Buck, "Alvord," 312–13. For Alvord's literary output, see Solon J. Buck, comp., "Bibliography of the Published Works of Clarence W. Alvord," *Mississippi Valley Historical Review*, 15 (1928–1929), 385–90.

28. Robert Michael Morrissey, "Clarence W. Alvord: The Illinois Historical Survey and the Invention of Local History," in *Engine of Innovation: The University of Illinois*, ed. Frederick E. Hoxie (Urbana: University of Illinois Press, 2017), 107.

29. Buck, "Alvord," 314–15. Alvord increasingly championed the Midwest and its superiority to other regions of the country. When historian Frederick Jackson Turner departed the University of Wisconsin to join the Harvard faculty in 1910,

Alvord conveyed his great regret to Turner. His going to the "effete East," he said, registered a great blow to "us western historians." David S. Brown, *Beyond the Frontier: The Midwestern Voice in American Historical Writing* (Chicago: University of Chicago Press, 2009), 8, 42.

30. Daniels, "Statement Supplementary to the Annual Report," s.v. Alvord, RS 15/1/11, B:2, F:Annual Report for 1911–12.

31. Novick, *Noble Dream*, 90 (Turner quotation). See James Harvey Robinson, "The New History," in *The New History: Essays Illustrating the Modern Historical Outlook* (1912; Bibliolife, n.d.), and Robinson, "The New Allies of History," in *The New History*, 70–100.

32. Novick, *Noble Dream*, 90–91.

33. Clarence Alvord, "The New History," *Nation*, May 9, 1912, 457 (first quotation); Alvord, "The Science of History," *Popular Science Monthly*, 84 (January to June 1914), 490 (second quotation)-96.

34. Alvord, "New History," 459; idem, 493. Emerson wrote: "An institution is the lengthened shadow of one man. All history resolves itself very easily into the biography of a few stout and earnest persons."

35. Alvord, "New History," 459.

36. Anon., "Up-to-Date Methods of Illinois Centennial Historian," *New York Times* (July 14, 1918), 53; Morrissey, "Alvord," 103.

37. Morrissey, "Alvord," 108.

38. James W. Garner, *Publications*, in the University of Illinois Library, contains offprints of many of his articles.

39. Greene to James, April 4, 1907, RS 2/5/6, B:7, F:Evarts B. Greene.

40. RS 2/5/15, F:Fairlie, John A. (see especially James to Fairlie, June 28, 1909); BT, 25th *Report* (1911), 169; BT, 26th *Report* (1912), 440.

41. RS 2/5/15, F:Dodd, Walter F.; BT, 25th *Report* (1911), 598; BT, 26th *Report* (1912), 440.

42. Garner to Greene, March 23, 1911, Annual Report (n.d.), RS 15/1/11, B:2, F:Deptl. Annual Reports 1910–11.

43. Garner to Daniels, [March 1913], RS 15/1/5, B:12, F:10.12 Annual Reports Departmental.

44. Garner to Greene, February 14, 1910, [March 1911], RS 15/1/11, B:2, F:Deptl. Annual Reports 1909–10, 1910–11.

45. James to Kinley, December 12, 1904, RS 2/5/4, B:1. See also Sandra Opdycke, "Lathrop, Julia Clifford," *American National Biography*, 13:231–33, and Louise C. Wade, "Taylor, Graham," *American National Biography*, 21:376–77.

46. RS 2/5/15, F:Hayes, Edward C.; BT, 24th *Report* (1908), 163; E. H. Sutherland, "Edward Cary Hayes, 1868–1928," *American Journal of Sociology*, 35 (July 1929), 93–94.

47. *Journal of the Senate of the 47th General Assembly of the State of Illinois* (1911), 27; Hayes to James, February 10, 1911, Greene to James, February 1911, RS 2/5/6, B:15, F:Evarts B. Greene Sept. 1910-Jan. 1911; Daniels to James, June 17, 1913 (quotation), RS 2/5/6, B:25, F:Daniels, A. H. May-Sept. 1913.

48. Hayes to Greene, February 20, 1911, RS 15/1/11, B:2, F:Deptl. Annual Reports 1910–11; RS 2/5/15, F:Todd, Arthur J.

49. Daniels, Annual Report for 1912–13, RS 15/1/11, B:2.

50. E. H. Sutherland, "Edward Cary Hayes, 1868–1928," *American Journal of Sociology*, 35 (July 1929), 93–94, 94, 96, 97.

51. Edward Cary Hayes, "Sociology as Ethics," *American Journal of Sociology* 24 (November 1918), 289–90. This essay constituted the first two chapters of Hayes's book of 1921, *Sociology and Ethics*.

52. Hayes, "Sociology and Ethics," 296–97, 298–99 (long quotation).

53. Sutherland, 97–98; *Daily Illini*, November 22, 1917, 6.

Chapter 10. The Humanities

1. Edmund J. James, [Inaugural Address], "The Function of a State University," in *University of Illinois: Installation of Edmund Janes James, Ph.D., LL.D, as President of the University* (Urbana: n.p., n.d.), 137–38.

2. Oldfather to James, June 10, 1909, RS 2/5/15, F:William A. Oldfather.

3. Greene to James, May 1, 1907, RS 15/1/11, B:2, F:Annual Report 1906–7.

4. Barton to Greene, March 2, 1908, and February 28, 1911, RS 15/1/11, B:2, F:Deptl. Annual Reports 1907–1908, 1910–1911.

5. Daniels, Annual Report for 1911–1912; Annual Report for 1912–1913, p. 24, RS 15/1/11, B:2.

6. For more details on Oldfather, see Winton U. Solberg, "William Abbott Old-father: Making the Classics Relevant to Modern Life," *Classical World*, 97 (Winter 2004), 158–77.

7. Correspondence from May 17, 1906 to June 8, 1907 relating to Greenough's appointment is in RS 2/5/15, F:Greenough, Chester N. Jerome D.

8. RS 2/5/15, F:Jacob Zeitlin.

9. Greenough to Greene, n.d. [ca. January 23, 1908], RS 15/1/11, B:2, F:Deptl. Annual Reports 1907–1908; BT, 24th *Report* (1908), 452; Jacob Zeitlin and Homer Woodbridge, *Life and Letters of Stuart P. Sherman*, 2 vols. (New York: Farrar & Rinehart, 1929), 1:174–84; BT, 25th *Report* (1911), 134.

10. Greenough to Greene, n.d. [ca. January 23, 1908], RS 15/1/11, B:2, F:Deptl. Annual Reports 1907–1908; BT, 24th *Report* (1908), 452; Zeitlin and Woodbridge, *Stuart P. Sherman*, 1:174–84; BT, 25th *Report* (1910), 134.

11. Greenough to Greene, June 9, 1910, RS 15/1/11, B:2, F:Deptl. Annual Reports 1909–1910; Greenough to James, February 8, 1909, RS 2/5/6, B:11, F:E. B. Greene; BT, 25th *Report* (1910), 530.

12. See the letters regarding Alden, especially Ponzer to Kinley, November 27, 1910, and Sherman to Greene, December 29, 1910, in RS 2/5/15, F:Alden, Raymond M.; BT, 26th *Report* (1912), 85.

13. Scott to Sherman, February 21, 1911, RS 15/1/11, B:2, F:Deptl. Annual Reports 1910–11.

14. Scott to Kinley, November 10, 1908, RS 15/1/11, B:2, F:Deptl. Annual Reports 1907–1908.

15. Zeitlin and Woodbridge, *Stuart P. Sherman*, 1:117.

16. Zeitlin and Woodbridge, *Stuart P. Sherman*, 1:72, 161, 163–64.

17. Frederick F. W. McDowell, "Stuart P. Sherman: The Evolution of His Critical Philosophy and Method," *Studies in Philology*, 50 (July 1953), 540.

18. Zeitlin and Woodbridge, *Stuart P. Sherman*, 1:178–79, 203–4, 250–51.

19. Gerald Graff, *Professing Literature: An Institutional History* (Chicago: University of Chicago Press, 1987), 3–4, 55, 66, 68.

20. Graff, *Professing Literature*, 66, 81, 83, 88–89.

21. Irving Babbitt, *Literature and the American College: Essays in Defense of the Humanities* (Boston: Houghton Mifflin, 1908), 106, 134, 136.

22. Stuart P. Sherman, "Graduate Schools and Literature," [correspondence], *Nation*, May 14, 1908, 442.

23. Carl Van Doren, "Another View of the Graduate School," *Nation*, July 9, 1908, 31.

24. Carl Van Doren, *Three Worlds* (New York: Harper & Brothers, 1936), 1 (first quotation), 28, 49–50, 76, 79 (second quotation); Robin K. Foster, *Carl Van Doren: A Man of Ideas* (Arlington, VA: Armillary Press, 2018), 23, 25–26.

25. Van Doren, *Three Worlds*, 81–82, 98–102 (trip); Foster, *Carl Van Doren*, 45–46.

26. Stuart P. Sherman, *The Genius of America: Studies in Behalf of the Younger Generation* (New York: Charles Scribner's Sons, 1924), 149–53 (quotation) (first published as "Education by the People," *Nation*, May 8, 1913), 461–64.

27. Zeitlin and Woodbridge, *Stuart P. Sherman*, I: 385.

28. Stuart P. Sherman, *On Contemporary Literature* (New York: Henry Holt and Company, 1917), 9–11.

29. Sherman, *On Contemporary Literature*, 93–94, 101.

30. H. L. Mencken, *A Book of Prefaces* (New York: Alfred A. Knopf, 1917), 97, 98.

31. Sherman, *Americans* (New York: Charles Scribner's Sons, 1922), 5, 9.

32. Mencken, *Prejudices: Second Series* (London: Jonathan Cape, 1921), 12, 14, 17.

33. Zeitlin and Woodbridge, *Stuart P. Sherman*, I: 252–53, 302, 355.

34. Stuart P. Sherman, *American and Allied Ideals: An Appeal to Those Who are Neither Hot Nor Cold* [War Information Series, no. 12, February 1918]. Issued by the Committee on Public Information, Washington, D.C., 4.

35. Sherman, *American and Allied Ideals*, 5 (first quotation), 12, 15, 22 (second quotation).

36. Sherman, *American and Allied Ideals*, 13–14, 17–23 (quotation).

37. Sherman, *American and Allied Ideals*, 7–10 (quotation).

38. Sherman, *American and Allied Ideals*, 6.

39. Stuart P. Sherman, "Beautifying American Literature," *Nation*, November 29, 1917, 593.

40. George E. DeMille, "Stuart P. Sherman: The Illinois Arnold," *Sewanee Review*, 35 (January 1927), 80, 81.

41. Fuller readings of these essays can be found in J. David Hoeveler, Jr., *The New*

374   Notes to Chapter 10

Humanism: A Critique of Modern America, 1900–1940 (Charlottesville: University Press of Virginia, 1977).

42. Zeitlin and Woodbridge, *Stuart P. Sherman*, II: 680.

43. *The Cambridge History of American Literature*, ed. William Peterfield Trent, John Erskine, Stuart P. Sherman, and Carl Van Doren, 3 vols. Volume I: *Early National Literature* (New York: Macmillan, 1917), I: x; Van Doren, *Three Worlds*, 108.

44. This last may seem a bit unusual because it was Carl Van Doren who later wrote the classic biography of Franklin, a Pulitzer Prize winner in 1936.

45. McDowell, "Sherman," 553–57.

46. Zeitlin and Woodbridge, *Stuart P. Sherman*, II: 799–800. For a helpful review of Sherman's career and for much more information about him after he left Illinois, see Joan Shelley Rubin, *The Making of Middlebrow Culture* (Chapel Hill: University of North Carolina Press, 1992).

47. On the German department, see James M. McGlathery, *Germanic Languages and Literatures at the University of Illinois at Urbana-Champaign, 1867 to the Present: A History* (Urbana: Department of Germanic Languages and Literatures, 1988), 16–50.

48. Brooks to James, June 12, 1905, RS 2/5/6, B:2, F:A-D.

49. RS 2/5/15, F:Gustaf E. Karsten; James's fourteen letters to Bryan, Curme, and others seeking information about Karsten from January 3 to January 25, 1906 are in RS 2/5/4, B:3; BT, 23rd *Report* (1906), 316.

50. Karsten to Greene, March 2, 1907, RS 15/1/11, B:2, F:Deptl. Annual Reports 1906–1907.

51. BT, 24th *Report* (1908), 110; James to Lessing, July 8, 1908, RS 2/5/15, F:Lessing, Otto E.

52. Bright to James, February 24, 1908; Grumman to James, January 31, 1908, RS 2/5/15, F:Gustaf E. Karsten.

53. BT, 24th *Report* (1908), 452.

54. James to Greene, December 24, 1908, RS 2/5/6, B:11, F:E. B. Greene; James to Otto L. Schmidt, April 15, 1908, RS 2/5/15, F:Gustaf E. Karsten; BT, 26th *Report* (1912), 456.

55. Brooks to James, May 13, 1907, RS 2/5/6, B:6, F:Faculty A-B; Greene to James, April 18, 1908; April 24, 1908, RS 2/5/6, B:9, F:Evarts B. Greene; Kinley to James, April 14, 1908; Francke to James, March 2, 1908, RS 2/5/15, F:Gustaf F. Karsten; BT, 24th *Report* (1908), 452.

56. Thomas E. Oliver to Greene, April 15, 1908, along with an undated petition "To the Committee on Modern Languages," RS 2/5/6, B:9, F:Evarts B. Greene; letters of recommendation in RS 2/5/15, F:George T. Flom.

57. Hinrich C. Seeba, "Cultural History: An American Refuge for a German Idea," in *German Culture in Nineteenth-Century America: Reception, Adaptation, Transformation*, ed. Lynne Tatlock and Matt Erlin (Rochester, NY: Woodbridge, Suffolk, UK, 2005), 11.

58. RS 2/5/15, F:Leonard Bloomfield; BT, 26th *Report* (1912), 23; Bernard Bloch, "Leonard Bloomfield," *Language*, 25 (April-June 1940), 87–98.

59. Greene to Kinley, April 14, 1910; Greene to Goebel, July 7, 1910; Greene to James, July 7, 1910, RS 2/5/6, B:15, F:Evarts B. Greene Sept 1909-Aug 1910.

60. Lessing to James, March 29, 1912, RS 2/5/15, F:Otto E. Lessing; Kinley to James, May 24, 1912, RS 2/5/6, B:20, F:David Kinley Graduate School; Lessing to James, July 15, 1912; James to Lessing, July 18, 1912, RS 2/5/6, B:21, F:O. E. Lessing (which contains other letters that evaluate Lessing).

61. Greene to Lessing, July 11, 1910, RS 2/5/6, B:15, F:Evarts B. Greene Sept. 1909-Aug 1910.

62. Goebel to James, July 28, 1912; James to Goebel, August 12, 1912, RS 2/5/6, B:20, F:Julius Goebel.

63. David Carnahan to Daniels, April 15, 1913, RS 15/1/5, B:12, F:10.12 Annual Reports Departmental.

64. Weeks to Greene, February 18, 1909, RS 15/1/11, B:2, F:Deptl. Annual Reports 1908–1909.

65. The following represents a summary of the detailed analysis of the Beck case as presented in Winton U. Solberg, "A Struggle for Control and a Moral Scandal: President Edmund J. James and the Powers of the President at the University of Illinois, 1911–1914," *History of Education Quarterly*, 49 (February 2009), 39–67.

66. Solberg, "Struggle for Control," 67.

67. Daniels to Greene, March 22, 1906, RS 15/1/11, B:2, F:Deptl. Annual Reports 1905–1906.

68. RS 2/5/15, F:Shepherd, Queen L.; Daniels, Annual Report for 1912–13 (the quotation), RS 15/1/11, B:2, F:Annual Report for 1912–1913.

69. On Bode's personal history and the letters about him, see RS 2/5/15, F:Boyd H. Bode.

70. RS 2/5/15, F:Bode, Boyd H.; Bode to Greene, February 22, 1910, RS 15/1/11, B:2, F:Deptl. Annual Report 1909–1910; Daniels to Greene, March 4, 1911, RS 15/1/11, B:2, F:Deptl. Annual Report 1909–1910.

71. Robert V. Bullough, Jr., "Boyd H. Bode and the Social Aims of Education," *Vitae Scholasticae*, 22 (Spring 2005), Gale Academic OneFile, accessed June 28, 2020.

72. Herbert W. Schneider, *A History of American Philosophy* (New York: Columbia University Press, 1963), 402, 405–7; Bullough, "Bode"; Joseph James Chambliss, *Boyd H. Bode's Philosophy of Education* (Columbus: Ohio State University Press, 1963), 3–4.

73. Chambliss, *Bode's Philosophy*, 3–5.

74. John Dewey, "Experience and Objective Idealism," in *John Dewey: The Middle Works, 1899–1924, Volume 3: Essays on the New Empiricism, 1903–1906*, ed. Jo Ann Boydston (1905; Carbondale: Southern Illinois University Press, 1977), 130, 135–37.

75. B. H. Bode, "Cognitive Experience and Its Object," *John Dewey: The Middle Works*, 398–404 (quotation). First published in the *Journal of Philosophy, Psychology, and Scientific Methods*, 2 (1905), 653–63. The next year Bode continued this discussion with his essay "Realism and Pragmatism," *Journal of Philosophy, Psychology, and Scientific Methods*, 3 (July 19, 1906), 393–401.

76. B. H. Bode, "Objective Idealism and Its Critics," *Philosophical Review*, 19 (November 1910), 597–602 (quotation).

376   Notes to Chapter 10

77. B. H. Bode, "The Paradoxes of Pragmatism," *The Monist*, 23 (January 1913), 112–22. Quotations on 117, 118.

78. Of the many excellent Dewey biographies, the one that most emphasizes the religious and humanistic content in his thinking is Steven C. Rockefeller, *John Dewey: Religious Faith and Democratic Humanism* (New York: Columbia University Press, 1991).

79. Alan Ryan, *John Dewey and the High Tide of American Liberalism* (New York: W. W. Norton, 1995), 187.

80. John Dewey, "The Need for a Recovery of Philosophy" (1917) in *John Dewey: Middle Works, 1889–1924, Volume 10, Essays on Philosophy and Education, 1916–1917*, 3–24. (First published in *Creative Intelligence: Essays in the Pragmatic Attitude* (New York: Henry Holt & Company), 3–69.)

81. See, for example, Bode, "Realistic Conceptions of Consciousness," *Philosophical Review*, 20 (May 1911), 265–79; Bode, "The Method of Introspection," *Journal of Philosophy, Psychology, and Scientific Methods*, 10 (February 13, 1913), 85–91.

82. Boyd H. Bode, "Consciousness and Psychology," in *Creative Intelligence*, 228–40. Quotations on 240.

83. Thomas C. Grey, "Holmes and Legal Pragmatism," *Stanford Law Review*, 41 (April 1989), 787–870; Liva Baker, *Justice from Beacon Hill: The Life and Times of Oliver Wendell Holmes* (New York: HarperCollins, 1991), 11, 840.

84. Boyd H. Bode, "Justice Holmes on Natural Law and the Moral Ideal," *International Journal of Ethics*, 29 (July 1919), 397–99.

85. Bode, "Holmes," 401–4.

86. Bode, "Holmes," 402–4.

87. Colvin to Greene, March 14, 1906; February 7, 1907; July 17, 1907; February 19, 1908, RS 15/1/11, B:1, 2, F:Deptl. Annual Reports 1905–1906, 1906–1907, 1907–1908.

88. Daniels, Annual Report for 1911–1912, RS 15/1/11, B:2, F:Annual Report 1911–1912.

89. RS 2/5/15, F:Bentley, Madison (includes Angell to James, August 14, 1912, the quotation); BT, 27th *Report* (1914), 103. Bentley used the given name of Madison.

90. Greene, Annual Report for 1910–1911, RS 15/1/11, B:2, which compares the University of Illinois with the universities of Michigan, Wisconsin, Minnesota, Ohio, Indiana, Iowa, Kansas, and Nebraska.

Chapter 11. The School of Education

1. Edmund J. James, *Chairs of Pedagogics in Our Universities: A Discussion of the Science and Art of Education as University Disciplines* (1887; Delhi, India: Facsimile Publisher, 2019), 1–7, 10–12 (quotation).

2. James, *Pedagogics*, 9, 10, 15–16, 19–20, 26.

3. James, *Pedagogics*, 16–17.

4. James, *Pedagogics* (quoting Fichte), 33.

5. James, *Pedagogics* (quoting Fichte), 37–38.

6. Henry C. Johnson, Jr. and Erwin V. Johanningmeier, *Teachers for the Prairie: The University of Illinois and the Schools, 1868–1945* (Urbana: University of Illinois

Notes to Chapters 10 and 11   377

Press, 1972), 22, 42–43, 47–49, 58–59, 95. See this work for a full, detailed discussion of the study of education at the University of Illinois in the years before James and afterward.

7. Johnson and Johanningmeier, *Teachers for the Prairie*, 121, 126, 129, 142–44. Dexter to Kinley, October 27, 1904, along with Dexter, "Plan for a School of Education at the University of Illinois"; Dexter to James, November 24, 1905; Dexter to James, November 2 and April 8, 1907, RS 2/5/6, B:1, F:A-F, B:2, F:A-D; B:5, F:D-G; B:6, F:Edwin G. Dexter.

8. [Greene], "Education," a memo of his interview at Teachers College, RS 2/5/6, B:9, F:Evarts B. Greene.

9. RS 2/5/15, F:Bagley; Johnson and Johanningmeier, *Teachers for the Prairie*, 160–63.

10. A committee report for the Board of Trustees shared these criticisms. Johnson and Johanningmeier, *Teachers for the Prairie*, 141, 152–53; James to Greene, January 3, 1909; Stephen Colvin to Bagley, January 19, 1909, with an attachment [by Bagley], "A Plan for the Trial of Practice Teachers in the Academy in 1909–10," RS 2/5/6, B:11, F:E. B. Greene.

11. Bagley to Greene, January 6 and 22, 1910, RS 2/5/6, B:15, F:Evarts B. Greene Sept. 1909-Aug. 1910.

12. Johnson and Johanningmeier, *Teachers for the Prairie*, 178, 180.

13. Johnson and Johanningmeier, *Teachers for the Prairie*, 196, 207.

14. Erwin V. Johanningmeier, "William Chandler Bagley's Changing Views on the Relationship between Psychology and Education," *History of Education Quarterly*, 9 (Spring 1969), 4–6, 9, 12.

15. Johanningmeier, "Bagley," 15–19. James, even while encouraging the "scientific" study of education, had long insisted that it must be considered an art as well. See Edmund J. James and Charles de Garno, "Is Teaching a Learned Profession?," *Illinois School Journal*, 1 (August 1882), 18ff.

16. Joseph Watras, "Developing a Democratic View of Academic Subject Matters: John Dewey, William Chandler Bagley, and Boyd Henry Bode," *Philosophical Studies in Education*, 43 (2012), 164–69. In the late 1930s Bagley gained controversy for his leadership in the "Essentialist" movement among educators.

Chapter 12. Engineering (with Physics and Mathematics)

1. Roger L. Geiger, *The History of American Higher Education: Learning and Culture from the Founding to World War II* (Princeton: Princeton University Press, 2015), 290, 306–7, 312.

2. Bruce E. Seely, "Engineering and the Land-Grant Tradition at the University of Illinois, 1868–1950," in *Science as Service: Establishing and Reformulating Land-Grant Universities, 1865–1930*, ed. Alan I. Marcus (Tuscaloosa: University of Alabama Press, 2015), 269–96.

3. Solberg interview with Ellery Paine, November 21, 1963.

4. Interview with Paine.

5. BT, 23rd *Report* (1906).

6. Edwin E. Slosson, *Great American Universities* (New York: Macmillan Company, 1910), 290; Seely, "Engineering at the University of Illinois," 272, 277; Alan I. Marcus, "Introduction," *Science as Service*, 5, 7.

7. James General Correspondence, B:132.

8. BT, 23rd *Report* (1906), 214–15.

9. Seely, "Engineering at the University of Illinois," 277, 278.

10. Lisa Warne, "Vignettes from A Century of Service to the University, the State, and the Nation, 1890–1990" (n.p., n.d.), 9–13; https://www.ideals.illinois .edu/handle/2142/48719; G. M. Almy, "A Century of Physics at the University of Illinois, 1869–1968" (talk given before the History of Science Society in December 1967 during the Centennial Year at the University of Illinois); https://www.ideals .illinois.edu/handle/2142/48722; A. P. Carman, "Report of the Department of Physics to the Dean of the College of Engineering, May 1, 1913," 12–13; https://archives .library.illinois.edu/erec/University%20Archives/1110804/Physics_Department_ Annual_Reports/physics_annual_reports_1912_1913_opt.pdf.

11. Warne, "Vignettes," 10–11; Almy, "A Century of Physics," 8, 10–11.

12. Jakob Kutz, "An Attempt at an Electromagnetic Emission Theory of Light," *Physical Review*, 3 (June 1914), 464–75.

13. Warne, "Vignettes," 11.

14. Carman, "Report," [1918], 2–3; "Report," [1919], 3–4.

15. See Chapter 7 for Townsend's publications.

16. Townsend to Kinley, March 21, 1907, RS 15/1/2, B:2; Townsend to James, April 26, 1910, RS 15/1/2, B:3.

17. Townsend to James, February 14, 1906, RS 15/1/2, B:2.

18. Townsend to James, February 14, 1906; Townsend to G. A. Miller, March 21, 1906, RS 15/1/2, B:2.

19. Townsend to Kinley, March 21, 1907, RS 15/1/2, B:2.

20. RS 15/14/5, F:Budgeted Salaries.

21. Townsend to G. A. Bliss, March 13, 1906, RS 15/1/2, B:2.

22. Townsend to E. B. Marrow, May 25, 1906; Townsend to E. L. Dodd, July 13 and August 1, 1906; Townsend to G. A. Bliss, March 13, 1906, RS 15/1/2, B:2.

23. Townsend to Klein, June 15, 1906; Townsend to Voight, June 15, 1906; Townsend to Goss, July 9 and 19, 1907, RS 15/1/2, B:2.

24. Townsend to Miller, March 4, 13, and 21, and April 30, 1906; Townsend to James, April 25, 1906, RS 15/1/2, B:2; RS 2/5/15, George A. Miller Folder; Della D. Fenster, "Miller, George Abram," *Dictionary of Scientific Biography*, 15:487–88.

25. Townsend to Virgil Snyder, April 28, 1906, RS 15/1/2, B:2; BT, 23rd *Report* (1906), 390; BT, 24th *Report* (1908), 144.

26. University of Illinois, Register 1909–1910, 70, RS 2/5/15, Thomas Buck Folder.

27. Townsend to A. E. Young, May 5, 1912, RS 15/1/2, B:5.

28. Illio 1906, 227; Illio 1908, 299.

29. "Notes," Bulletin of the American Mathematical Society, 10 (November 1903), 93; 14 (October 1907), 40–41.

30. BT, 25th *Report* (1911), 592; BT, 26th *Report* (1912), 132; BT, 27th *Report* (1914), 51, 237; Franklin M. Scott, ed., Semi-Centennial Alumni Record.

31. Townsend to Kinley, March 21, 1907, RS 15/1/2, B:2; Townsend (autobiography).

32. Townsend to Windsor, April 5, 1910, RS 15/1/2, B:3.

33. Edna Cleo Sanford, "The History of the Department of Mathematics, at the University of Illinois" (thesis), at Reference Desk, Mathematics Library, Altgeld Hall, 30–31.

34. This pattern proved especially frustrating in the case of Ernest Julius Wilczynski and Henry Lewis Rietz.

Chapter 13. The Law School

1. Frederick Green, "Law School Recollections" [unpublished manuscript, 1937], 15–16, 2/1, B:11, F:Law School Reminiscences. Green had come to Illinois the same year as James. He had earned three degrees at Harvard, including the LLB in 1893. Thereafter he practiced law in New York City. Green married Queen Lois Shepherd in 1920.

2. William P. LaPiana, *Logic and Experience: The Origin of Modern American Legal Education* (New York: Oxford University Press, 1994) 16, 150–51; John Henry Schlegel, "Between the Harvard Founders and the American Legal Realists: The Professionalization of the American Law School Professor," *Digital Commons @ University of Buffalo School of Law* (1985), 325 (quotation).

3. Robert Stevens, *Law School: Legal Education in America from the 1850s to the 1980s* (Chapel Hill: University of North Carolina Press, 1983), 3–5, 25, 36–37, 52, 56; LaPiana, *Logic and Experience*, 16, 150–51; Schlegel, "Between the Harvard Founders," 7, 10.

4. LaPiana, *Logic and Experience*, 133, 136, 137–38; Schlegel, "Between the Harvard Founders," 317.

5. [Wayne D. Smart], *Law in the Grand Manner: Law, 1897–1967: A Popular History of the College of Law at the University of Illinois* (n.p., 1967), 11.

6. LaPiana, *Logic and Experience*, 133 (quotation), 142–43, 145.

7. Green, "Law School Recollections," 15–16, 26.

8. The home residence of the students is given in the *Register for 1904–1905*, 404–7, and in registers for other years.

9. Green, "Law School Recollections," 19–20, 25.

10. Frederic B. Crossley, *Courts and Lawyers of Illinois*, 3 vols. (Chicago: The American Historical Society, 1916), 1:396, 397, 407; 3:895–96; Oliver A. Harker, "Fifty Years with Bench and Bar in Southern Illinois," *Transactions of the Illinois State Historical Society for the Year 1920*, 27 (1921), 41–53; Harker, "Annual Address delivered before the Illinois State Bar Association," *Proceedings of the Illinois State Bar Association* (Springfield, 1896), 3–14.

11. *Cases on Common Law Pleadings*, ed. Oliver A. Harker (Chicago: Burdette J. Smith & Company, 1924), iii-iv. Professor George Enos Gardner employed casebook practice at the beginning of the law school. "Now nobody seriously doubts that this is the better way," he said. Not exactly. [Smart], *Law in the Grand Manner*, 5.

12. Green, "Law School Recollections," 7.

13. James, "Draft of a Letter to the Lawyers of the State," January 23, 1905, along with "Question Sheet"; John G. Wilson (James's clerk) to Harker, January 23, 1905; James to Harker, February 2, 1905; James, "Questions to Law School Faculty," February 2, 1905, 2/5/4, B:1, Ltrbks. 36, 37.

14. The state legislature did provide funds to furnish and equip the Law Building—in 1903, $2,500, and in 1906, $10,000.

15. BT, 23rd *Report* (1906), 26, 53, 123.

16. BT, 24th *Report* (1908), 48, 49, 132. The legislature also granted $50,000 to fireproof the stacks of the law library.

17. *Register for 1904–1905*, 331, 332.

18. Green, "Law School Recollections," 27; Harker to James, July 2, 1907, 2/5/6, B:6, F:G-J. The trustees of the University of Chicago had specified that the total expense of the law school for the first year, excluding the cost of the library, was not to exceed $18,000. Frank L. Ellsworth, *Law on the Midway: The Founding of the University of Chicago Law School* (Chicago: University of Chicago Press, 1977), 60.

19. Ellsworth, *Law on the Midway*, 134.

20. James to Harker, February 21, 1905, 2/5/4, B:1, Ltrbk. 37.

21. James to Harker, March 30, 1905, 2/5/4, B:1, Ltrbk. 37.

22. James to Harker, February 21, 1907, 2/5/6, B:6, F:G-J.

23. James to J. J. Tobias, March 24, 1905, 2/5/4, B:1, Ltrbk. 37; James to Harker, B:4, Ltrbk. 45.

24. James to Edward S. Thurston, July 2, 1910, 2/5/15, Edward S. Thurston Folder, for his views on appointments.

25. 2/5/15, Dudley O. McGovney Folder; BT, 24th *Report* (1908), 110; Green, "Law School Recollections," 22.

26. Gilbert to James, June 3 and 10, 1907, 2/5/15, Barry Gilbert Folder; BT, 24th *Report* (1908), 134.

27. *Register 1907–1908*, 170–71.

28. BT, 23rd *Report* (1906), 380; see also Harker to James, December 8, 1910, 2/5/6, B:16, F:Oliver A. Harker; BT, 26th *Report* (1912), 67.

29. Ellsworth, *Law on the Midway*, 89.

30. Green, "Law School Recollections," 22–23.

31. BT, 25th *Report* (1911), 183.

32. Green, "Law School Recollections," 22–23.

33. Gilbert to James, August 12, 1909, 2/5/6, B:12, F:C-G.

34. Ellsworth, *Law on the Midway*, 118–24; Elizabeth G. Brown, *Legal Education at Michigan, 1859–1959* (University of Michigan Law School, 1959), ix.

35. BT, 25th *Report* (1911), 193. The requirements for the degree are included in *Annual Registers* starting in 1910–1911; see *Annual Register 1913–1914*, 172. Harker to James, *Annual Report, 1914–1915*, 4; *Annual Report, 1915–1916*, 5. As dean, Harker should have submitted twelve annual reports from 1904–1905 to 1915–1916. Six of these cannot be located (if submitted); three of the others were brief and perfunctory. The reports for 1909–1910 and 1910–1911 are in 2/5/5, B:9; those for 1911–1912, 1912–1913, and 1914–1915 are in 2/5/6, B:20, 26, and 49. The one for 1915–1916 is in 2/5/3, B:87.

Notes to Chapter 13   **381**

36. 2/5/15, Edward S. Thurston Folder (which contains Vance to James, June 22, 1910); BT, 25th *Report* (1911), 578.

37. 2/5/15, John N. Pomeroy Folder; BT, 25th *Report* (1911), 578.

38. 2/5/15, I. Maurice Wormser Folder; BT, 26th *Report* (1912), 46, 443, 585.

39. Green, "Law School Recollections," 31–32.

40. Wormser to James, June 1, 1911; James to Wormser, June 28, 1911, 2/5/6, B:18, F:T-Z; James to Harker, June 28, 1911, ibid., B:16, F:Oliver A. Harker.

41. Wormser to James, n.d., 2/5/6, B:18, F:T-Z.

42. Green, "Law School Recollections," 3.

43. Green, "Law School Recollections," 34.

44. BT, 24th *Report* (1908), 136; Vernier to James, September 17, 1909, 2/5/6, B:6, F:G-J.

45. 2/5/15, Chester G. Vernier Folder (Vernier's letter to Garner expressing his concern is dated April 1, 1911) BT, 26th *Report* (1912), 463.

46. George T. Page (president) and Peter P. Shaefer of the Advisory Board to President James, n.d., 2/5/6, B:26, F:O. A. Harker.

47. William R. Vance, "The Function of the State-Supported Law School," *American Law School Review*, 3 (Winter 1914), 409–16.

48. James to each member of the law faculty, February 24, 1914, 2/5/6, B:42, F:T-V.

49. Except for Harker to James, June 23, 1913 (*Annual Report*), 3–5, 2/5/6, B:26, F:O. A. Harker, all of the responses to James discussed here are in 2/5/6, B:42, F:T-V.

50. Harker to James, May 31, 1911, 2/5/5, B:9, F:Deans' Reports 1911; Harker to James, July 1, 1915, 2/5/6, B:49, F:Harker, Dean O. A., Harker to James, May 26, 1916, 2/5/3, B:87, F:Harker, O. A.

51. Harker to James, March 17, 1913, 2/5/6, B:26, F:O. A. Harker; *Journal of the American Institute of Criminal Law and Criminology*, 2 (September 1911), 330; 3 (July 1912), 249–55; 4 (May 1913-March 1914), 196–203. In 1931 the publication was renamed the *Journal of Criminal Law and Criminology*.

52. James to Harker, April 24, 1906, 2/5/4, B:3, Ltrbk. 44.

53. James to Harker, July 21, 1910, 2/5/6, B:16, F:Harker, Oliver A.

54. Green, "Law School Recollections," 45.

55. Green, "Law School Recollections," 29–30.

56. Green, "Law School Recollections," 28–29.

57. "Chester Garfield Vernier," *Proceedings of the Association of American Law Schools*, 49 (1949), 124–26.

58. [Smart], *Law in the Grand Manner*, 16, 19.

59. Harker to James, *Annual Report, 1914–1915*, 4.

60. *Annual Register 1910–1911*, 258; *Annual Register 1911–1912*, 253; Green, "Law School Recollections," 24; [Smart], *Law in the Grand Manner*, 11.

61. These statements are based on Harker's annual reports and University catalogs for the years noted.

62. H. W. Ballantine to James, May 21, 1918, 2/5/3, B:145, F:Ballantine, H. W.

63. Harker to James, June 13, 1916, 2/5/3, B:87, F:Harker, O.A. In addition

to his duties in the law school, in January 1907 Harker had begun acting as legal counsel for the University.

64. Green, "Law School Recollections," 49–50. Harker died on December 3, 1936. Green did not date his Recollections, but an unknown hand on his manuscript gives a date of 1937. Henry W. Ballantine was a member of the committee that wrote the Memorial to Harker published in the *Proceedings of the Association of American Law Schools*, 35 (1937), 265–67. It repeats verbatim some of Green's evaluation.

65. Decker to James, July 3, 1916, 2/5/3, B:91, F:Law Deanship.

66. Garner to James, June 24, 1916; James to Garner, June 27, 1916; Garner to James, June 28, 1916; Gilmore to Garner, July 1, 1916 (the quotations); Garner to James, July 3, 1916, 2/5/3, B:91, F:Law Deanship. Gilmore served as dean of the University of Iowa Law School from 1930 to 1934 and as president of the University of Iowa from 1934 to 1940.

67. Green to James, June 23, 1916; Carpenter to James, June 27, 1916; Hale to James, June 29, 1916; Decker to James, July 3, 1916; Pomeroy to James, July 5, 1916, 2/5/3, B:91, F:Law Deanship.

68. James to Ballantine, July 17, 1916, 2/5/15, H. W. Ballantine Folder.

69. Ballantine to James, July 18, 1916, 2/5/15, H. W. Ballantine Folder; James to Ballantine, July 24, 1916, 14/1/1, B:2, F:Deans' Office 1920 K.

70. Ballantine to James, June 6, 1917 (*Annual Report for 1916–17*), 2/5/3, B:107, F:Ballantine, H. W.

71. Henry Winthrop Ballantine, "Adapting the Case-Book to the Needs of Professional Training," *American Law School Review*, 2, no. 4 (1908), 135–40.

72. Ballantine to James, September, 23, 1916; James to Ballantine, September 29 and October 21, 1916, 2/5/3, B:107, F:Ballantine, H. W.; *Transactions of the Board of Trustees 1916–1918*, 122; Ballantine to James, "The Case of Ballantine, Dean H. W."

73. Ballantine to James, June 6, 1917, 2/5/3, B:107, F:Ballantine, H. W.

74. Ballantine to James, May 21, 1918, 2/5/3, B:145, F:Ballantine, Dean H. W.

75. Harker to Albert M. Kales, December 18, 1920, 14/1/1, B:2, F:Dean's Office Files.

76. Schlegel says that among writers and commentators in the law journals a kind of hierarchy of prestige, or "pecking order," had emerged, as follows: "Montana and North Dakota were the pits; Kansas and Missouri a step up; then Illinois, Wisconsin, and Minnesota, with Iowa and perhaps Nebraska after [Roscoe] Pound, a half-step in between; and finally the big time, Chicago, Michigan, Columbia, and Harvard." Schlegel, "Between the Harvard Founders," 319.

77. Green, "Law School Recollections," 46.

78. Green, "Law School Recollections," 45.

79. Harker to James, April 7, 1905, 2/5/6, B:2, F:4–8/1905; E-L; Harker, "Discussion," *Proceedings of the Tenth Annual Meeting of the Association of American Law Schools* (1910), 9; *Annual Register, 1910–1911*, 258.

80. Green, "Law School Recollections," 45.

81. Merle Curti and Vernon Carstensen, *University of Wisconsin: A History, 1848–1925*, 2 vols. (Madison: University of Wisconsin Press), I: 441–43. As the

Notes to Chapter 13 383

Progressive movement gained ascendancy in the United States in the early twentieth century, many in the legal field sought changes that would join their work to the reform efforts. Advocates who so hoped saw another obstacle in the case method, now almost wholly dominant in the law schools. They perceived the law as effectively integrated with the social milieu in which it grew and developed and hence a vehicle, if so understood, of change in the social and political structures in which it operated. But the case method, they complained, confined the law to a hermetic and self-contained locus, preoccupied with "pure law" with its own intellectual domain. It thus removed law study from any affiliation with political reform. The main and most formidable challenge to this conception of law came from University of Nebraska professor Roscoe Pound, who advanced the alternative model of "sociological jurisprudence." With its understanding of the law as an organic presence in a large social system, Pound and the other progressives emphasized the greater value of a social ethic over the priority of the individual that had long prevailed in American thinking and in the legal system. In Louis Brandeis the reformers saw their major champion. In his famous brief in the U.S. Supreme Court case of *Muller v. Oregon* in 1908 attorney Brandeis employed a wealth of statistical data to show the effects of industrial labor on the health of workers. Overall, however, sociological jurisprudence made few gains among the programs of American law schools. (LaPiana, *Logic and Experience*, 153–56.) Bruce A. Kimball, "The Proliferation of Case Method Teaching in American Law Schools: Mr. Langdell's Emblematic 'Abomination,' 1890–1915," *History of Education Quarterly*, 46 (Summer 2006), 191–247.

82. *Siren*, 6 (November 1, 1916), 8; (November 16, 1916), 13; (January 19, 1917), 16.

Chapter 14. Agriculture (and Home Economics)

1. This background review summarizes the history recorded by Richard Gordon Moores in his *Fields of Rich Toil: The Development of the University of Illinois College of Agriculture* (Urbana: University of Illinois Press, 1970), Chapters One through Four.

2. Moores, *Fields of Rich Toil*, Chapters Five through Seven.

3. Solberg 2, 120–33; Moores, *Field of Rich Toil*, 105, 108, 112–13, 115–16, 122 and elsewhere.

4. For these and other activities, see Jerome L. Rodnitzky, "Farm and Gown: The University of Illinois and the Farmer, 1904–1918," *Journal of the Illinois State Historical Society*, 72 (February 1979), 13–20.

5. Eugene Davenport, "Scientific Farming," *Annals of the American Academy of Political and Social Science*, 40 (March 1912), 45–50. Larger quotation on p. 49.

6. Richard White, *The Republic For Which It Stands: The United States during Reconstruction and the Gilded Age, 1865–1896* (New York: Oxford University Press, 2017), Chapter 4. Quotations, pp. 137, 171.

7. Danielle Dreilinger, *The Secret History of Home Economics: How Trailblazing Women Harnessed the Power of Home and Changed the Way We Live* (New York: W. W. Norton, 2021), iv, 7–8, 20–21, 29–30; Sarah Stage, "Ellen Richards and

the Social Significance of the Home Economics Movement," in *Rethinking Home Economics*, 17–33.

8. Dreilinger, *Secret History*, x (quotation), 9, 14, 19.

9. Dreilinger, *Secret History*, 28, 40; Stage, "Richards," 27.

10. Stage, "Richards," 3–4.

11. Drawn from Solberg 2.

12. Lita Bane, *The Story of Isabel Bevier* (1955; Facsimile Publisher, 2019), 31, 32, 37. Lita Bane was a student of Bevier and combined in this book biographical material, reflections by Bevier, and selections from Bevier's major publications. Moores rightly says of the book: "Although unabashedly worshipful, her book (the only published biography of Miss Bevier) contains useful information not available elsewhere." *Fields of Rich Toil*, 178n.7.

13. Winton U. Solberg, "Bevier, Isabel," in *Notable American Women: A Biographical Dictionary*, 3 vols., ed. Edward T. James, *Volume I A-F* (Cambridge, MA: Belknap Press of Harvard University Press, 1971), 141–42; Bane, *Bevier*, 14–15, 17, 21, 23. See also Isabel Bevier, "Home Economics: Its Opportunities and Obligations," *School and Society*, 3 (1916), 738.

14. Paula A. Treichler, "Isabel Bevier and Home Economics," in *No Boundaries: University of Illinois Vignettes*, ed. Lillian Hoddeson (Urbana: University of Illinois Press, 2004), 31, 34; Elisa Miller, "Isabel Bevier: Bringing Science into the Home," in *Engine of Innovation: The University of Illinois*, ed. Frederick E. Hoxie (Urbana: University of Illinois Press, 2017), 11.

15. Bane, *Bevier*, 35 (Davenport), 45, 72–73, 124, 127; Treichler, "Bevier," 37.

16. Bane, *Bevier*, 44, 108–9, 111, 122.

17. Bane, *Bevier*, 12–13, 27.

18. Bane, *Bevier*, 114, 158, 162 (long quotation). Isabel Bevier, "The Development of Home Economics," *Journal of Home Economics*, 9 (January 1917), 3, 5, 7; Isabel Bevier and Susannah Usher, *The Home Economics Movement, Part I* (Boston: Whitcomb and Barrows, 1906), 14. [There was no Part II.]

19. Beverly Bartow, "Isabel Bevier at the University of Illinois and the Home Economics Movement," *Journal of the Illinois State Historical Society*, 72 (February 1979), 29; Bane, *Bevier*, 29, 128, 132–33, 135–37, 161–62. Bevier presented these views in two addresses: "Home Economics in a College Course," at the 1907 meeting of the Association of American Agricultural Colleges Experiment Stations and "The Land-Grant Colleges and the Education of Women," at Ohio State University in 1920.

20. Bane, *Bevier*, 127, 148; Bevier and Usher, *Home Economics Movement*, 13–14; Miller, "Bevier," 16. Bevier wrote: "Now, what had been done for the boy in agriculture and engineering needs to be done for the girl in domestic art and science." Bevier and Usher, *Home Economics Movement*, 39.

21. Mills, "Bevier," 14, 33–34; Stage, "Richards," 23.

22. Treichler, "Bevier," 33; Dreilinger, *Secret History*, 14, 33, 35; Miller, "Bevier," 14; Stage, "Richards," 7, 23.

23. Bane, *Bevier*, 53 (Bevier quotations), 175, 186; Moores, *Fields of Rich Toil*, 186–88.

Notes to Chapter 14   385

24. Bartow, "Isabel Bevier," 36; Treichler, "Bevier," 37, 41; Miller, "Bevier," 28.

25. Miller, "Bevier," 28. Davenport wholly supported Bevier in her emphatic description of home economics, as he put it, "a part of a liberal education." Eugene Davenport, "Home Economics at Illinois," *Journal of Home Economics*, 13 (August 1921), 339.

26. Moores, *Fields of Rich Toil*, 189–91; Bane, *Bevier*, 53–55.

27. Moores, *Fields of Rich Toil*, 197–98; Bane, *Bevier*, 52–53, 59–60, 172, 196.

28. Bane, *Bevier*, 1, 58; Bartow, "Isabel Bevier," 36–37.

29. Solberg, "Bevier," 142.

30. In Treichler, "Bevier," 32.

Chapter 15. The Collegiate Revolution

1. See Chapter 9 of Roger Geiger, "The Collegiate Revolution," in *The History of American Higher Education: Learning and Culture from the Founding to World War II* (Princeton: Princeton University Press, 2015). Readers will find here parallel material to the developments described in the rest of the chapter.

2. John R. Thelin, *A History of American Higher Education*, Third Edition (Baltimore: Johns Hopkins University Press, 2019), 156–57, 159, 166.

3. James, *Sixteen Years*, 155–57, 168–71.

4. Winton U. Solberg, "The Catholic Presence at the University of Illinois," *Catholic Historical Review*, 76 (October 1990), 765–70.

5. Winton U. Solberg, "The Early Years of the Jewish Presence at the University of Illinois," *Religion and American Culture: A Journal of Interpretation*, 2 (Summer 1992), 215–21. For the larger issue of Jewish admissions into American colleges and universities (and especially the elite eastern schools), see Harold S. Wechsler, *The Qualified Student: A History of Selective College Admission in America* (New York: John Wiley & Sons, 1977), especially 133–85.

6. *Daily Illini*, January 11, 1917, 1; September 25, 1912, 4; October 31, 1917, 2.

7. University of Illinois Archives, "Guide to African-American Research Resources," https://archives.library.illinois.edu/guides/afamer.php; Abigail Paeth and Dave Evensen, "The Legacy of a Pioneer," *LAS News, College of Liberal Arts and Sciences* (Spring 2019), 26–27.

8. Allan Nevins, "A College Springtime, A 'Now," [*sic*] *Illinois Magazine*, 2 (May 1911), 410; *Illinois Magazine*, Post Exam Jubilee [February 1915], cover.

9. Gloria Harper Dickinson, "Pledged to Remember": Africa in the Life and Lore of Black Greek-Letter Organizations," in *African American Fraternities and Sororities: The Legacy and the Vision*, Second Edition, ed. Tamara Brown et al., (Lexington: University of Kentucky Press, 2012), 9–32. For some of the major organizations that illustrate this pattern, see Anne S. Butler, "Black Fraternal and Benevolent Societies in Nineteenth-Century America," in *African American Fraternities and Sororities*, 75–97.

10. See the essay by Michael H. Washington and Cheryl L. Nuñez, "Education, Racial Uplift, and the Rise of the Greek-Letter Tradition: The African American Quest for Status in the Early Twentieth Century," in *African American Fraternities and Sororities*, 141–45, 151–53.

11. Washington and Nuñez, "Racial Uplift," 43.

12. Craig L. Torbenson, "The Origin and Evolution of College Fraternities and Sororities," in *African American Fraternities and Sororities*, 56, 60; Dickinson, "Pledged to Remember," 12 (quotation). See also Lawrence C. Ross Jr., *The Divine Nine: The History of African American Fraternities and Sororities* (New York: Dafina Books, 2000), 5–7.

13. Albert R. Lee, "The University of Illinois Negro Students: Data Concerning Negro Students at the State University," unpublished typescript dated June 29, 1940, University of Illinois Archives, 2–8.

14. Lee, "Negro Students," 3–4.

15. https://www.atomicheritage.org/profile/j-ernest-wilkins- jr/en.wikipedia .org/wiki/J. Ernest_Wilkins_Sr. Wilkins married Lucille Robinson, also an attorney, and they had three sons. J. Ernest Wilkins Jr., a prodigy, entered the University of Chicago at age thirteen and had a PhD in mathematics from there at age nineteen. He did work at Chicago with the team of scientists led by Enrico Fermi—the Manhattan Project to build an atomic bomb. He later collaborated with Eugene Wigner, studying neutron absorption and yielding the Wilkins-Wigner methodology. Anon., "Wilkins: Portrait of a Mathematician," *Nuclear News*, 17 (July 1974), 79–85; Atomic Heritage Foundation: https://www.atomicheritage.org/profile/j-ernest -wilkins-jr k.

16. [Vanessa Rouillon], "African-American Student Housing at the University of Illinois" [Champaign County Historic Museum], https://www.champaign countyhistory.org/single-post/2018/02/24/african-american-student-housing-at -the-university-of-illinois (February 28, 2018).

17. Ross, *Divine Nine*, 165–66.

18. Dara Stack, "Making a Home: Black Greek Life on Campus," *Daily Illini*, January 19, 2022, 1.

19. https://localwiki:org/cu/Albert_R. Lee.

20. Debra Pressey, "UI's 'Unofficial Dean' of Black Students, Getting Well Overdue Honors," *News-Gazette*, June 25, 2019.

21. For more on Clark's background, see Solberg 2, 289–90 ff.

22. Robert Schwartz, *Deans of Men and the Shaping of Modern College Culture* (New York: Palgrave Macmillan, 2010), 5, 21, 28, 37–38, 44.

23. Thomas Arkle Clark, "Studies and Other Things," *The Illinois*, 2 (October 1910), 27–31.

24. Gerald L. Fetner, *Immersed in Great Affairs: Allan Nevins and the Heroic Age of American History* (Albany: State University of New York Press, 2004), 2–4; Ray Allen Billington, "Allan Nevins, Historian: A Personal Reminiscence," in *Allan Nevins on History*, compiled and introduced by Ray Allen Billington (New York: Charles Scribner's Sons, 1975), x; Allan Nevins, "The Essence of Biography," in Billington, *Nevins*, 218.

25. Fetner, *Nevins*, 12, 16–18; Billington, *Nevins*, x-xi; Nevins, "The Newspaperman and the Scholar," in Billington, *Nevins*, 40.

26. Fetner, *Nevins*, 19–20.

27. Allan Nevins, *Illinois* (New York: Oxford University Press, 1917), 295–96, 314.

Notes to Chapter 15   **387**

28. Nevins, *Illinois*, 316.

29. Gerald L. Fetner, *Immersed in Great Affairs: Allan Nevins and the Heroic Age of American History* (Albany: State University of New York Press, 2004), 136, 137, 149, 154. For a thoughtful assessment of Nevins's scholarship, see Robert Middlekauff, "Telling the Story of the Civil War: Allan Nevins as a Narrative Historian," *Huntington Library Quarterly*, 56 (Winter 1993), 67–81.

30. James, *Sixteen Years*, 179–81, 185–87.

31. See the appropriate sections of Solberg 1 and Solberg 2.

32. For a listing of U of I fraternities and sororities, see James, *Sixteen Years*, 185.

33. See Chapter 16 of this book.

34. Many claims are made as to which university had the largest number of fraternities, and the problem of determining the result is admittedly difficult. Based on data in *Baird's Manual*, it appears that by 1916 the University of Illinois had a larger number of social fraternities and sororities than Cornell, and probably also more than Berkeley.

35. Nevins, *Illinois*, 305–12; James, *Sixteen Years*, 184–85. For a fuller account, see Winton U. Solberg, "Harmless Pranks or Brutal Practices? Hazing at the University of Illinois, 1868–1913," *Journal of the Illinois State Historical Society*, 91 (Winter 1898), 233–59.

36. Geiger, *History*, 369–70; James, *Sixteen Years*, 180–81; George M. Marsden, *The Soul of the American University: From Protestant Establishment to Established Nonbelief* (New York: Oxford University Press, 1994), 269, 334.

37. Nevins, *Illinois*, 297, 301.

38. Nevins, *Illinois*, 294, 299; James, *Sixteen Years*, 182.

39. Nevins, *Illinois*, 318; James, *Sixteen Years*, 182. For a comprehensive history of this long road to creation of the conference, see Winton U. Solberg, *Creating the Big Ten: Courage, Corruption, and Commercialization* (Urbana: University of Illinois Press, 2018).

40. J. Allan Nevins, "Forty Years of *The Illini*," UIAQ, 6 (July 1912), 202, 204–5. Avery Brundage graduated with a degree in civil engineering. A fine athlete, he later became the fifth president of the International Olympic Committee, 1952 to 1972, the only American to attain that position.

41. Mark Van Doren, *The Autobiography of Mark Van Doren* (1939; New York: Harcourt, Brace and Company, 1958), 5–6, 52–53, 65–66; Katherine Woods, "The Van Doren Brothers," *English Journal*, 29 (October 1940), 609–20; Mark Van Doren, "Stuart Sherman," *Nation*, December 4, 1929, 675.

42. For another example of brilliant undergraduate writing, see Mark Van Doren's informed piece, "Province of Modern Poetry," in *Illinois Magazine*, 5 (April 1914), 482 ff.

43. Scott J. Peters, *The Promise of Association: A History of the Mission and Work of the YMCA at the University of Illinois, 1873–1997* (Champaign: University YMCA, 1997), 30, 31.

44. Gary Dorrien, *The Making of American Liberal Theology: Imagining Progressive Religion, 1805–1900* (Louisville: Westminster John Knox Press, 2001).

45. Peters, *Promise of Association*, 33, 39, 43. The DI quoted one student: "I came here an entire stranger. The Young Men's Christian Association found me a room and a good job." September 20, 1911, 1.

46. Mott wrote: "There are not two gospels, one social and one individual. There is but one Christ who lived, died, and rose again, and relates Himself to the lives of men. The Association is summoned imperatively to give itself more fully than heretofore to discharge its social responsibility." Quoted in Peters, *Promise of Association*, 48.

47. *Daily Illini*, December 10, 1911, 4; December 16, 1911, 3; December 17, 1911, 1; December 19, 1911, 1–2.

48. Editorial, "The Mott Campaign," *Daily Illini*, December 12, 1911, 4; Editorial, "Mott is Gone," December 19, 1911, 1.

49. Editorial, "Mott Campaign," *Daily Illini*, December 10, 2011, 4; Editorial, "Mott is Gone," December 19, 2011, 4; Editorial, "Church Going," February 25, 1912, 4 (Nevins quotation.) The Illinois campus heard another prominent voice of liberal Protestantism and the Social Gospel when Washington Gladden visited in 1913. He spoke on "The Basis of the New Social Order" in 1913. The University had offered Gladden the presidency in 1892. *Daily Illini*, April 30, 1913, 1; May 1, 1913, 1; Solberg 2, 5. On the other hand, when William Bell Riley, the self-styled "grand old man of old-time religion," spoke at the Orpheum Theatre in 1919, matters did not go well for him. He blasted the "heathenish" University of Illinois and the teachings of modern science. A bunch of fraternity members walked out on the events halfway through them. *Daily Illini*, October 18, 1919, 1.

50. Marsden, *Soul of the American University*, 334.

51. *Daily Illini*, September 21, 1911, 1.

52. *Daily Illini*, September 22, 1911, 1.

53. W. G. Piersel, "The Wesley Foundation in Urbana: The Origin of an Idea," *Journal of the State Historical Society (1908–1984)*, 38 (September 1945), 321–26, 331.

54. Piersel, "Wesley Foundation," 328–29, 332, 335, 341, 343.

55. *Daily Illini*, January 12, 1918, 5.

56. Edmund Janes James, "Religious Work at State Universities," *Journal of Gospel Liberty*, 105 (December 4, 1913), 1312–13.

57. Editorial, "The University Defended," *Summer Illini*, July 6, 1911, 2.

58. *Daily Illini*, October 24, 1911, 1; Editorial, "The Last Attack," January 10, 1912, 1, 4.

59. *Daily Illini*, November 22, 1911, 1; November 23, 1911, 4; Arthur Ray Warnock, "National Politics and College Undergraduates," *The Illinois* (October 1911), 165–68; Editorial, "The Lincoln League," *The Illinois* (October 1911), 177.

60. *Daily Illini*, February 10, 1912, 1.

61. *Daily Illini*, February 16, 1912, 3. On Milwaukee, see Judith Walzer Leavitt, *The Healthiest City: Milwaukee and the Politics of Health Reform* (Princeton: Princeton University Press, 1982).

62. *Daily Illini*, January 4, 1912, 1; November 7, 1915, 4.

Notes to Chapter 15   389

63. *Daily Illini*, October 10, 1916, 5.

64. *Daily Illini* Editorials: "Twin City Bootlegging," November 24, 1911, 4; "The Coming Campaign," March 24, 1912, 4; "Wet vs. Dry City," March 31, 1912, 4.

65. See Edmund J. James, "Economic Effects of the Saloon," *Chautauquan*, February 8, 1883, 297.

66. *Daily Illini* Editorials: "Wet vs. Dry City," March 21, 1931, 1; "Pan-Hellenic Council in Favor of Dry Vote," March 31, 1912, 4; "Vote Yes Today," April 2, 1912, 4; Also, "President James Believes Saloons are Detrimental," March 28, 1912, 1; "Student Assailed by Wets," April 4, 1912, 4.

67. *Daily Illini*, October 13, 1911, 4.

68. *Daily Illini*, November 11, 1911, 4.

69. Editorial, "East and West in Education," *Daily Illini*, November 9, 1911, 4.

70. Editorial, "East and West," *Daily Illini*, November 9, 1911, 4.

71. *Daily Illini* Editorials: "Circles within Circles," January 6, 1912, 4; "Democracy in Student Affairs," January 20, 1912, 4. Nevins liked to salt his essays with literary references, and he begins the first item here with Thackeray's listing of the snobbish types in the England of his day. See also "The Growth of Fraternities," *Daily Illini*, May 19, 1912, 4.

72. Editorial, "The English Courses," *Daily Illini*, December 10, 1911, 4; Editorial, "Language Study in the Commercial Courses," May 21, 1912, 4. Nevins had already gained a wide acquaintance with American literature, most impressively for a college undergraduate. He measured the needs of contemporary American letters in a masterly essay he wrote for the student literary magazine. See his "An Essay on Materials," *Illinois Magazine*, 2 (February 1911), 282–89.

73. *Daily Illini*, January 18, 1912, 4.

74. For background on the rise and decline of the literary societies, see Solberg 2, 309–11.

75. Editorial, "The World Does Move," *Daily Illini*, May 26, 1912, 4.

76. Nevins, *Illinois*, 322.

Chapter 16. Women

1. Lynn D. Gordon, *Gender and Higher Education in the Progressive Era* (New Haven: Yale University Press, 1990), 1–8, 33–34, 41, 43–44, 70–71 (Wheeler quotation), 73.

2. Hugh Hawkins, *Between Harvard and America: The Educational Leadership of Charles William Eliot* (New York: Oxford University Press, 1972), 194–96; James Axtell, *The Making of Princeton University: From Woodrow Wilson to the Present* (Princeton: Princeton University Press, 200), 10–11; Edmund J. James, "Some Features of American Higher Education," *Science*, New Series, 16 (October 31, 1902), 687.

3. Paula A. Treichler, "Alma Mater's Sorority: Women and the University of Illinois, 1890–1925," in *For Alma Mater: Theory and Practice in Feminist Scholarship*, ed. Paula A. Treichler et al. (Urbana: University of Illinois Press, 1985), 22.

4. Winton U. Solberg, "The Hardscrabble Quest for a Dean of Women at the University of Illinois, 1896–1923," *Journal of Illinois History*, 18 (Spring 2013), 5.

5. Editorial, "The Girls' Housing Problem," *Daily Illini*, March 14, 1912, 4; Treichler, "Alma Mater's Sorority," 22, 23, 27.

6. Allan Nevins, *Illinois* (New York: Oxford University Press, 1917), 313; *Daily Illini*, December 11, 1911, 4. This matter seemed to be universal. Frederick Rudolph writes: "Coeducation helped to divide the subjects of the curriculum . . . into those which were useful, full-blooded and manly, and those which were ornamental, dilettantish, and feminine." The latter embraced "all the older liberal studies." Women on campus thus became the bearers of a noble intellectual and cultural inheritance. *The American College and University: A History* (New York: Alfred A. Knopf, 1962), 324. At the University of Michigan in 1900 women represented 47 percent of the literature department and outnumbered men in the graduating class. Ruth Bordin, *Women at Michigan: The "Dangerous Experiment," 1870s to the Present* (Ann Arbor: University of Michigan Press, 1999), 19.

7. Nevins, *Illinois*, 313; *Daily Illini*, December 11, 1911, 4.

8. Solberg, "Hardscrabble Quest," 2–6. This lengthy article has immense detail about this subject, with listing of primary sources. What follows highlights the main points of the essay.

9. Solberg, "Hardscrabble Quest," 9.

10. Solberg, "Hardscrabble Quest," 9–16.

11. Mary E. Fawcett, "Suggested Ideals," *The Illinois*, 3 (March 1912), 301–3.

12. Solberg, "Hardscrabble Quest," 19. Against the rise of this "progressive dancing" sometimes the men also decried the shift in styles. See Gordon, *Gender and Higher Education*, 83. Lyle Montross's short story in *Town and Gown* depicts Dean of Women "Agnes Watson" (Martha Kyle) as "a model of propriety." And as such she wages a determined warfare against student immorality, from the two vaudeville theaters in town to the festivities on campus. She decries "their vulgarity, their frankness, their cigarettes, their dancing, the shows they saw." All this yields from the dean a mammoth edict for reform of student behavior. It was completely ignored. Lynn Montross, "Brass Drums," in Lynn Montross and Lois Seyster Montross, *Town and Gown* (New York: George H. Doran Company, 1923), 18, 190, 193.

13. Solberg, "Hardscrabble Quest," 23–39; *Daily Illini*, December 12, 1917, 1.

14. Solberg, "Hardscrabble Quest," 23.

15. Solberg, "Hardscrabble Quest," 39.

16. *The Illinois*, 4 (June 1907), 122–25.

17. Each separate volume of this publication had this title, but the individual issues all had the heading "*The Illinois*," remaining thus, with but a brief exception, until September 1914 when "*Illinois Magazine*" became the permanent title (but again with a brief shift back in April 1916).

18. *Illinois Magazine*, 1 (December 1909), 61–67.

19. AQFN, 6 (February 1, 1921), 124.

20. *The Illinois*, 6 (December 1914), 3245 [*sic*].

21. Mark Van Doren, *The Autobiography of Mark Van Doren* (1939; New York: Harcourt, Brace and Company, 1958), 64.

22. Lucile Needham, "Quips and Cranks of the American Irish," *Sewanee Review*, 24 (July 1916), 313–30; *Daily Illini*, November 16, 1915, 3.

23. *Daily Illini*, March 28, 1915, 3.

24. Catherine Needham, "When Windy was the Weather," *Illinois Magazine*, 8 (March 1917), 149–53.

25. Catherine Needham, "A Perfect Understanding," *Illinois Magazine*, 9 (New Year's Number) [January 1917], 155–60.

26. The genre of campus literature in the collegiate revolution, touched on lightly here, would seem to deserve more scholarly attention.

27. To cite just one instance, in "The Last Laugh," Miriam Gerlach tells the story of an Illinois student, Charles Lumford, who is visited by his cousin, the spitting image of him, Jack Graham. Charles, however, has a severe cold and dares not keep a date he has with Gertrude Neville for the big "Chicago game." So, they conspire to have Jack take Charles's place and go with Gertrude as "Charlie Lumford" to the event. The clever, tense discourse that ensues between them at the game shows that Jack has successfully represented himself as the cousin. Then, as the smitten Jack prepares to ask Gertrude out for the evening, he fesses up. She agrees to go, but, "her eyes full of mischief," she has something to tell him: "I'm not Gertrude. I'm her sister Peggy. Bob Levery [Gertrude's friend] came down at the last minute so we thought we'd fool Charlie." Peggy whisks into the house. *The Illinois*, 2 (December 1910), 131–37.

28. Calvin White, "Dramatics at Harvard," *The Illinois*, 5 (April 1914), 339–47.

29. Catherine Needham, "Between Dances," *The Illinois*, 8 (November 1916), 73–74.

30. But see, for example, K. H., "Other Girls' Beaux," *The Illinois* (Spring Number) [March 1915], 260–62; J. M. K., "Other Fellows' Girls," *The Illinois*, 6 (May 1915), 2012–14 [*sic*]; Editorial, "Consider the Co-Ed," *The Illinois*, 7 (May 1915), 164–66; Anon., "The Man I Want," *The Illinois* (Christmas Number) [December 1916], 132–33. This piece won a contest "opened to University Women," sponsored by the *Illini* board for the best essay on this subject. It was "written by a prominent University woman."

31. Bernice Powell, "University Women in Student Activities," *Illinois Magazine* (Woman's Number) [December 1913], 187–88.

32. Editorial, "The Woman's League Teas," *The Illinois* (Woman's Number) [December 1913], 204–5.

33. Editorial, "Class Elections," *The Illinois* (Woman's Number) [December 1914], 153.

34. Editorial, "The College Woman's Ballot," *Daily Illini*, February 13, 1912, 4.

35. *Daily Illini*, November 24, 1911, 1, 4.

36. *The Siren*, 1 (April 1912), 136.

37. Both the campus novels referred to portray men and women students as habitual smokers.

38. *Daily Illini*, April 25, 1912, 1. Some histories describe an intense male-female rivalry among students, marked by resentment and struggle for power and influence. The U of I situation does not reflect anything so extreme. See Helen Lefkowitz Horowitz, *Campus Life: Undergraduate Cultures From the End of the Eighteenth Century to the Present* (Chicago: University of Chicago Press, 1988): at coeducational

392 Notes to Chapter 16

schools "organized male students moved to exclude women completely from their organizations," that is, the extracurriculum. She considers that situation a "dress rehearsal" for the world they would enter after college. P. 42. On the other hand, Ruth Bordin found that in the early years at the University of Michigan women had prominence in the professional organizations and that "there were no hard and fast barriers between the sexes for students at Michigan." Women felt "empowered"; they were "unafraid and uncowed." But in the later decades and into the twentieth century the situation changed. "Two communities" came into being on the campus, a separation marked by the academic curriculum and the extracurriculum. "It was a sad time for women at the University of Michigan." Bordin, *Women at Michigan*, 16, 18, 20–22, 35.

39. Adade Mitchell Wheeler, "Conflicts in the Illinois Woman Suffrage Movement of 1913," *Journal of the Illinois State Historical Society* (1908–1984), 76 (Summer 1983), 95.

40. *Daily Illini*, February 28, 1908, 1 (no results found for other annual contests).

41. *Daily Illini*, January 21, 1909, 1; May 25, 1911, 1.

42. *Daily Illini*, May 24, 1912, 5.

43. Editorial, "The Fall of Women," *The Illinois*, 1 (March 1908), 189–90.

44. *Daily Illini*, October 19, 1915, 3.

45. Editorial, "University Suffragists?," *Daily Illini*, October 14, 1914, 4.

46. *Daily Illini*, March 14, 1914, 1.

47. *Daily Illini*, October 17, 1913, 4.

48. Dorothy Day, *The Long Loneliness* (New York: Harper, 1952), 19, 25–26, 28–29, 40.

49. Day, *Long Loneliness*, 42–43, 45–46.

50. Day, *Long Loneliness*, 47–49; John Loughery and Blythe Randolph, *Dorothy Day: Dissenting Voice of the Twentieth Century* (New York: Simon and Schuster, 2020), 31–34.

51. Robert D. Sampson, "Red Illini: Dorothy Day, Samson Raphaelson, and Rayna Simons at the University of Illinois, 1914–1916," *Journal of Illinois History*, 5 (November 2002), 172. This section borrows much from this informative essay about this intriguing triumvirate.

52. Sampson, "Red Illini," 180–82; Day, *Long Loneliness*, 50; Loughery and Randolph, *Dorothy Day*, 32. These three Illinois students would seem to fit the classification of "rebel" that Helen Lefkowitz Horowitz identifies as one of the campus "types" at the early modern university. They took ideas very seriously. They challenged the standing order in their efforts to have influence in the campus organizations, the literary ones and the newspaper. They had a leftist and reformist political perspective and for most of them membership in the Intercollegiate Socialist Society confirmed the "rebel" status. Horowitz briefly reviews the campus careers of Walter Lippmann (Harvard), Max Eastman (Williams), Randolph Bourne (Columbia), and Margaret Mead (Barnard) as illustrations. Horowitz, *Campus Life*, 84–96.

53. Sampson, "Red Illini," 186, 188–89, 193.

54. See James J. Yoch (cousin), *Landscaping the American Dream: The Garden and*

Film Sets of Florence Yoch, 1890–1972 (New York: Henry M. Abrams and Sagapress, 1989). Florence Yoch appears in *Co-Ed* as Maria Marks, a student friend for whom Lucia has great admiration.

55. Florence Yoch, "New Professions for Women," *Illinois Magazine*, 6 (December 1914), 177–78, 182.

56. "Her real attention was elsewhere—thrillingly preempted by the multitudinous life about her with its increasingly varied and instant appeals." She thrives on "the giddy round of dates and dances." Olive Deane Hormel, *Co-Ed* (New York: Charles Scribner's Sons, 1926), 60, 69.

57. Hormel, *Co-Ed*, 175.

58. Hormel, *Co-Ed*, 128.

59. Hormel, *Co-Ed*, 208, 268, 269. See more on Sherman, pp. 294–95. As one can see, Hormel barely disguised the names of real people at Illinois. Thus, she also references "President Johns," "Professor Oldman," "Dean Davenant," "Leonardo Craft," "Miss Bovard" (Bevier), "Miss Simmons" (Catherine Sharp).

60. Hormel, *Co-Ed*, 270–72.

61. Hormel, *Co-Ed*, 274.

Afterword

1. *Daily Illini*, Editorial, "A History of the University," February 20, 1912, 4.

2. *Daily Illini*, May 23, 1912, 1.

3. *Daily Illini*, February 17, 1912, 1.

4. Editorial, "Jonathan B. Turner," *Daily Illini*, December 12, 1912, 4.

5. Mary Turner Carriel, *The Life of Jonathan Baldwin Turner* (1911; Urbana: University of Illinois Press, 1961), 2–6, 55–56.

6. For larger description of this reform movement, see Jon Francis McKenna, "Disputed Destiny: The Political and Intellectual Origins of Public-Supported Higher Education in Illinois," PhD thesis, University of Illinois, 1973, 9, 17–22.

7. J. B. Turner, *A Plan for an Industrial University for the State of Illinois* [address presented to the Farmers' Convention at Granville, November 18, 1851] (n., 1851), 7–9, 13; Carriel, *Turner*, 114.

8. J. B. Turner, "The Millenium of Labor" [annual address], *Transactions of the Illinois State Agricultural Society . . . ,* 1 (1853–54), 52–53, 56–59; see also J. B. Turner, "Education—The State and the Church" (continued), *Prairie Farmer* (June 21, 1873), 196.

9. Turner, "Industrial University," 9. On the matter of creeds in Christendom and their affiliation with political corruption as Turner warned of them, see his *Universal Law and Its Opposites* (Chicago: Open Court Publishing Company, 1892).

10. Brett H. Smith, *Labor's Millennium: Christianity, Industrial Education, and the Founding of the University of Illinois*. Princeton Theological Monograph Series. (Eugene, OR: Pickwick Publication, 2010), 20–28; McKenna, "Disputed Destiny," 69.

11. *Daily Illini*, May 21, 1912, 2.

12. Edmund J. James, "The Origin of the Land Grant Bill" (correspondence)

Nation (December 31, 1908), 649. See also James, *The Origins of the Land-Grant Act of 1862 . . . and Some Account of Its Author, Jonathan B. Turner, University of Illinois Studies*, 4, no. 1 (Urbana-Champaign, November 1910).

13. And James does have support among some scholars in this affirmation. Donald R. Brown wrote in 1962: "In the land-grant movement Jonathan Baldwin Turner had no peers; he was the significant promoter of ideas underlying the movement." He added that "it is highly likely that Morrill borrowed directly from Turner's plan." "Jonathan Baldwin Turner and the Land-Grant Idea," *Journal of the Illinois State Historical Society* (1908–1984), 55 (Winter 1962), 373, 381.

14. Edmund J. James, "The Life and Labors of Jonathan B. Turner," *Journal of the Illinois State Historical Society*, 8 (April 1915), 1–16 [his 1912 speech].

15. James, "Turner," 15–20. Quotations on p. 18 and p. 20.

16. E. Davenport, *Education for Efficiency: A Discussion of Certain Phases of the Problem of Universal Education with Special Reference to Academic Ideals and Methods*, rev. ed. (Boston: D. C. Heath, 1914), 1–4, 63, 159.

17. Nevins, "A People's University," New York *Evening Post*, September 9, 1916, 6.

18. Allan Nevins, *The State Universities and Democracy* (Urbana: University of Illinois Press, 1962), 104.

19. Allan Nevins, *Illinois* (New York: Oxford University Press, 1917), 12–13.

20. Nevins, *State Universities*, v-vi.

21. Allan Nevins, *The Origins of the Land-Grant Colleges and State Universities: A Brief Account of the Morrill Act of 1862 and Its Results* (Washington DC: Civil War Centennial Commission, 1962), 28. This essay repeated some material from the book of the same year, but added important new information, too.

22. Burt E. Powell, *Semi-Centennial History of the University of Illinois, Volume I: The Movement for Industrial Education and the Establishment of the University, 1840–1870* (Urbana: University of Illinois, 1918), 3, 19–20, 32, 38–39, 54, 55, 57, 75, 94.

23. Turner, *Millenium of Labor*, 55, 58, 59.

24. Turner, *Millenium of Labor*, 55; McKenna, "Disputed Destiny," 72, 74; Smith, *Labor's Millennium*, 22–23, 25; Turner, *A Plan for an Industrial University*, 13 (longer quotation).

25. Turner, "Industrial Education," 13.

26. This insight is owed to Winton Solberg, whose account, alone of all those this author has read about Turner, directly makes this critical connection to the romantic movement and Emerson in particular. In showing the links that this concluding section draws this author has tried to build on this connection.

27. Philip R. Gura, *American Transcendentalism: A History* (New York: Hill and Wang, 2007), 91–92. For more on these interconnections, see Patrick J. Keane, *Emerson, Romanticism, and Intuitive Reason: The Transatlantic "Light of All Our Day"* (Columbia: University of Missouri Press, 2005), 113–15, 211, 260–62. Two essays that give effective summaries of the Transcendentalists' epistemology are Emerson's "The Transcendentalist," and Theodore Parker's "Transcendentalism."

28. *The Complete Works of Ralph Waldo Emerson*. 12 vols. (New York, 1883–1906),

I, 110–11; Solberg 1, 29. On the Germans, see Peter Neumann, *Jena 1800: The Republic of Free Spirits*, trans. Shelley Frisch (New York: Farrar, Straus and Giroux, 2022), 194. The author here was referring to Friedrich Schlegel, August Wilhelm Schlegel, and Friedrich von Hardenburg ("Novalis"). P. 195.

29. Turner, "Industrial Education," 13.

30. Davenport, *Education for Efficiency*, 6–7, 69, 91–92.

31. Davenport, *Education for Efficiency*, 34, 95–96.

32. Davenport, *Education for Efficiency*, 35, 61.

33. Nevins, *Origins*, 8–9, 12–13, 17–18.

34. Fetner, *Immersed in Great Affairs*, 29; Nevins, *Origins*, 21–22.

35. Nevins, *State Universities*, 131–32; Davenport, *Education for Efficiency*, 61.

36. Davenport, *Education for Efficiency*, 85, 88.

37. Edmund J. James, "Some Features of American Higher Education," *Science*, New Series 16 (October 31, 1902), 687–88.

38. James, "Turner," 19.

39. Olive Deane Hormel, *Co-Ed* (New York: Charles Scribner's Sons, 1926), 7, 8.

40. Solberg 1, 100–101.

41. As a graduate student in the late 1960s this author found it amusing that the university officials, in promoting the forthcoming program of summer studies, changed the university motto to "Learning and Leisure"!

Index

Alumni Directory: EJJ forms, 18

Alumni Quarterly, 18

Alumni Record, 52

Alvord, Clarence W., 209; career, 169–70; commissioned to study early Illinois, 170; courses taught, 171; education, 169; helps establish *Mississippi Valley Historical Review*, 172; and James, 30; Nevins and, 274, 275; and the "New History," 172–75; *New York Times* reporter visits office, 174–75; publications, 170, 172; retires, 172; and the war, 113

American Academy of Social and Political Science (AAPPS): *Annals*, 71; EJJ address at, 3–74; EJJ president, 71, 354–55n39

American Association of Law Schools, 232

American Association of University Professors, 119

American Bankers Association: and EJJ, 8

American Bar Association, 232

American Defense Society, 114

American Economic Association (AEA): formed, 69–70; and imperialism, 86; and railroads, 81

American Federation of Labor, 91

American Historical Association: Alvord and, 172; and imperialism, 85

Abbott, William: attacks Alexander-Bahrenberg,16; career, 20, 23

Abercrombie, William R., 105–6

Adams, Abigail, 259

Adams, Charles C., 156

Adams, Henry Carter, 70

Adams, Herbert Baxter, 88, 90, 356n10

Addams, Jane, 35n10; and Grindley, 130

Agriculture Building, 252

Ainsworth, Zelomia, 311

Alden, Raymond M.: career, 184; heads department, 184; successes, 184–85

Alethenai, 302; and Gerlach, 307; and Hormel, 304; and L. Needham, 308

Alexander-Barhenberg, Carrie: feuds with EJJ, 15–18; and Kemp affair, 148; in search for dean of women, 30; trustees denounce, 16

Allen, Richard, 268

Alpha Kappa Alpha sorority, 269–70, 300; Bousfield member, 272

Alpha Kappa Nu fraternity, 271

Alpha Phi Alpha fraternity, 269

Alpha Rho fraternity, 277

Alpha Zi Delta, 303

alumni (UofI): EJJ cultivates to support University political interests, new associations, 18

Alumni Association: Scott appeals to, 118; and trustees, 20

American Home Economics Association, 254
American Locomotive Association: gives to UofI, 222
American Meatpackers Association, 133
American Philosophical Society, 4
American Railway Engineers, 222
American Society for Engineering Education, 220
American Society of Civil Engineers, 222
American Sociological Association, 178
Amsterdam, H.: and socialism, 291
Andrews, Charles M., 86
Angell, James B., 3
Anglo-Saxonism, 86, 87, 90–91, 95–99, 109; Babington and, 90; EJJ and, 91; Fiske and, 87
Anthony, Susan B., 259
Architecture, School of, library, 43
Arnold, Matthew: Babbitt and, 188; Sherman and, 187; Sherman book on, 190
Association Hall (YWCA), 284
Association of Manufacturers, 222
Association of Manufactures of Chilled Car Wheels, 222
Athenian, 302; Seyster and, 303
athletics. *See* sports
Austin, Mary, 196
Axtell, James, 76, 355n54

Babbitt, Irving, 75; and New Humanism, 185; and Sherman, 185, 187
Babington, William Dalton, 90
bacteriology: Burrill urges importance of, 150–51, 153; EJJ and, 153
Bagg, Rufus, 135
Bagley, William Chandler: becomes Director of the School of Education, 217; and Dewey, 218; on education as an empirical discipline, 216; on education as "art," 218; for education as a science, 217–18; invigorates program in education, 217; shift in views, 218; on teaching psychology, 217–18
Baker, Ira O.: writings, 220
Baldwin, Simeon, 233
Ballantine, Henry W., 383n64; assessment, 249; career, 346; and casebook

method, 248; EJJ appoints dean, 246; establishes *Illinois Law Bulletin*, 248; and law library, 248; resigns, 248
Banquet Committee, 310
Barlow, Benson, 154
Barr, James, 231
Barton, Herbert J.: plans for department, 181
Bastiat, Frédéric, 79
Bayley, William S., 135
Bayliss, Alfred, 11
Beard, Charles, 115, 176
Beck, Jean-Baptiste: career, 200; resigns, 201; scandalous behavior, 200; and the trustees, 201
Beckemeyer, H. T. C., 223
Becker, Carl, 115, 176
Beecher, Catherine, 254, 259
Belgian Relief, 102
Bell, Alexander Graham: opposes pure science, 125
Bennett, Arnold, 191
Bennett, Elizabeth R.: first PhD in mathematics, 229
Bentley, Isaac Madison, 208–9
Berg, Ernst Julius: career, 220–21; heads Physics department, 220–21
Berkeley, George, 76
Berlin Institute of Hygiene, 125
Bethany Circle, 288, 303; Seyster member, 303
Bevier, Isabel: battle with traditionalists, 260–61; criticism of women's colleges, 258, 259; and Davenport, 260–61; and Draper, 255, 258, 260, 261; early career, 255–56; and EJJ, 260–61; and extension program, 261; first visit to UofI, 255–56; genealogy, 255; and Grindley, 257; on home economics and land-grant universities, 258–59; and Kinley, 262; opposition to utility, 258; and Palmer, 257; Presbyterian, 261; and Progressive Era, 258; on science and home economics, 257; on value of science for women, 259; views of curriculum, 255, 257; and the war, 262; on women in civic life, 258; works with Richards, 255

398   Index

Beyer, Otto: and socialism, 291

Big Ten, 282

Bildung: and German philosophers, 62–63, 67, 77; and UofI, 339

Bismarck, Otto Von, 6

Blacks, 93; and black face comedy, 289, 318; and race words, 288; at Uof I, 267–72

Blackwelder, Eliot, 139

Blanchard, Charles A., 29

Bleininger, Albert V., 138

Bloomfield, Leonard: Jewish scholar, 199

Bluntschli, Johann K.: and Burgess, 88; and H. K. Adams, 88; social scientist, 77

Board of Trustees (University of Illinois): Alexander-Bahrenberg on, opposes James, 15-17; appoints committee to replace Draper, 11; approves course in ceramics, 137; authorized history of the University (Powell), 326; and the Beck case, 200–201; and Dean of Women, 304, 305; Democrats win 1912 election to, 21; dominated by Republicans, 20; elects James as new president, 11–13; and the Engineering Experiment Station, 221; functions of, 20; and Illinois Canners' Association, 154; and Illinois Clay Manufactures Association, 136, 137; James and appeal to state legislature, 14–15; and Kemp case, 147–48; Kinley concerned about business representation on, 20–21; and the Law School, 235, 237, 240, 248; negotiates with James regarding Graduate School deanship, 28; and 1907–1909 biennium, 29; 1913 meeting, 23; power struggle with James, 23; and public health services, 152; and salary policy, 15; sets up Graduate School with James, 30; supports Grindley's program, 132; supports publication of *JEGP*, 197, 198; supports publication of *Mississippi Valley Historical Review*, 172; and University Press, 54–55; and the war, 115–18

Bode, Boyd: career, 212; *Creative Intelligence* project, 205; critique of dualism, 205; ethical character of law, 207; on Holmes, 207–8; leaves for Ohio, 208; moves toward pragmatism, 203; new philosophy of mind, 204–5; and philosophical idealism, 202–3; questions ideas of transcendent reality, 204–5; work with Dewey, 204–7

Bohr, Niels, 224

Bolles, Albert S., 6, 7

Bordin, Ruth, 393n38

Börger, Robert, 229

Boston University, 5

Botanical Club, 276

botany department curriculum, 149

Bourdette, Bertha: and *Illinois Magazine*, 307

Bourne, Randolph, 194

Bousfield, Mandella Tanner Brown: Bousfield Hall, 268; career, 268; student, 267–68

Bowen, Borden Parker, 202

Bradley, Lucile: and socialism, 291

Brandeis, Louis, 383-84n81

Braudel, Fernand, 169

Breckenridge, Lester C.: career, 220

Brooks, Van Wyck, 194

Brown, Donald R, 395n13

Brown, Faye C., 140–41

Brundage, Avery: and *Illinois Magazine*, 283; later career, 388n40

Bryan, William Lowe, 197

Buck, Solon, 171

Burgess, John W., 90, 357n10; and EJJ, 88; race theory, 88–89; study in Germany, 88

Burns, Josephine, 228

Burrill, Thomas, 149, 367n17; brings in new faculty, 151; career, 149; and College of Agriculture, 251; cooperation with Illinois Canners' Association, 153–54; course in sanitary science, 152; death, 154; directs botany program, 10; and education of teachers, 215; established Graduate School, 26; Methodist, 287; pleads for development of bacteriology, 150–51, 152–53; praise for achievement, 26, 251; programs in public healthy, 151–52; retirement, 154

Index   399

Busey, Mary Elizabeth Bowen: assists in search for dean of women, 305; and Beck case, 201; career, 20; dislike for EJJ, 201; and "loyalty" cases, 117; and women's suffrage, 315
Busey, Samuel, 20
Bushnell Guild, 288
Butler, Nicholas Murray, 11

Calvinism, 4, 67
Cambridge History of America Literature, 195–96
Carlyle, Thomas, 334; on work, 336
Carman, Albert P.: heads Physics department, 223; on the war and modern science, 225
Carnahan, David: and the Beck case, 201
Carnegie, Andrew, 48, 68; anti-imperialism, 8
Carpenter, Charles E., 240
Casad, Anthony Wayne, 5
case method (in law education): Ballantine and, 246; at Harvard, 231–32; Langdell and, 231; resistance to, at Yale, 232–33; student reaction, 384; and UofI, 234
Catholics, 87, 310; and Day, 318; fraternities, 288; Gov. Dunne as, 21; Loyola House, 266, 288; St. John's Church, 266; in student body, 266
Cattell, James McKeen, 115
Centro Literario Espano, 279, 302
Cercle Franççais, 279
Chase, Katherine: and *Illinois Magazine*, 308, 310; on women students as a voting bloc, 313
Chess Club, 276
Chicago, 11, 16, 18, 20, 21, 233
Chicago and Northwestern Railroad, 223
Chicago School of Civics and Philanthropy, 177
Chicago Tribune: hostility to UofI, 289
Chinese: Boxer Rebellion, 92; immigration, 92; James on, 92–93; James's plan to increase students, 92–93; students at UofI, 267
Chinese Students' Club, 279
Church, Chester W.: bill to establish state geology survey, 136

Clark, George L., 236, 237
Clark, John Bates, 86, 356n1
Clark, Thomas Arkle, 181; advice to student columns in *Illinois Magazine*, 273; as Dean of Men, 272–73; on patterns of student grades, 277; Presbyterian, 286; and Sherman, 183, 182; supports fraternities, 277; teaches Rhetoric, 183, 185
Clark University, 3, 25
Classical Club, 181, 276
Cohen, Morris, 196
Cole, Arthur C., 168; and "loyalty" controversy, 116
Coleridge, Samuel Taylor, 334
College Dancing Club, 279
College Equal Suffrage League, 315
College of Literature and Arts: enrollments by department, 165–66
College of Physicians and Surgeons, 145–46
Collins, James, 50–51
Columbia University, 3, 18; and academic journals, 35; and astronomy, 142; Burgess at, 88; Carl Van Doren studies at, 195; Cattell at, 115; Dewey at, 205; Ely attends, 68; enrollment, 277; graduate school, 345n2; law library, 248; law school, 242; library, 44, 50, 51; Nevins joins history department, 274; opposes University of Illinois, 30; salaries at, 227; School of Political and Social Sciences, 25; university press, 56; and the war, 104
Colvin, Stephen S.: on needs of department, 208
Committee on Public Information, 115, 116
Commons, John R., 71; eugenics, 89; on immigration, 89; and the war, 115
Comstock, George C., 140, 143–44
Comte, Auguste, 63
Congregational House, 288
Cook, Joseph, 82
Cornell University, 209, 219, 272, 277; Alpha Phil Alpha formed, 269; and graduate studies, 345n2
Cornell Widow, 314
Corwin, Edward S., 115

400 Index

Cosmopolitan Club, 279; and the war, 102

Crane, Richard Teller: campaign against UofI, 289–90; Nevins rebukes, 289–90

Creighton, James Edwin, 202

Crocker Land Expedition, 35

Crystal Dancing Club, 279

Cunningham, Harrison, E.: and University Press, 52, 53, 55, 56

Cyclopaedia of Political Science, Political Economy, and the Political History of the United States: EJJ writes for, 6

Daily Illini: calls for history of the University, 326; as campus watchdog and cheer leader, 292–96; history, 282, 312; standard format, 284; student competition for offices, 282; on women in campus life, 316; women students on staff, 302

dances, variety, and frequency, 279; Council of Administration prefers waltz to tango, 306; Kyle opposes excess of, 306

Daniels, Arthur H.: appointed, 164; on Alvord, 172; campus activity, 18; on Moss 181; and philosophy department, 201–2; on scholarship in psychology, 208

Davenport, Eugene, 11; and Bevier, 257, 259–60; and development of the College, 253; on higher education, 331–32, 335–39; on J. B. Turner, 329; and "scientific" farming, 253

Day, Dorothy: family, 316; goes to UofI, 317; high school award, 316; later career, 318; radicalization, socialism, 317; and Simons, 317–18; at YWCA, 317

Dean of Women: EJJ search for, 304–7

Debs, Eugene: and race, 357n10; and student straw poll, 290

Decker, Edward H.: on needs of the Law School, 244–46

Declaration of Independence: EJJ on, 111

democracy, 57, 74, 110–11, 192; Alvord on, 174; Bode and, 208; Davenport on, 330, 331, 337, 339; EJJ and social studies, 74; EJJ on reform and modern democracy, 66; as intellectual liberation, 337; J. B. Turner and, 328, 329; Jewett on science and, 77; Kinley related to graduate studies, 36–40; Mencken on, 192; and the Middle West, 196; Nevins, state universities and, 274–75, 293–94, 331, 339; "New Economics" and, 78–81; Sherman and, 190, 195; Teutonic theory of, 87–88; and the war and military, 95–96, 110–11, 113, 338; Wilson, relates to the war, 89, 99

Democratic Club, 290

Deneen, Charles S., 3; career, 14; and Engineering Experiment Station, 221; and Geological Survey, 135; Methodism and, 14; priorities for the University, 17; supports state money for the graduate school, 29, 31; and Townsend, 152–53; and University budget, 14, 15

Denio, Herbert W., 43

Department of Public Health, 153

Department of Railway Engineering, 222

Deutsche Verein, 279

Dewey, John, 196, 258; Bagley supports, 218; and Bode, 202, 204–7; *Creative Intelligence*, 205–6; Dexter praises, 216; *Ethics*, 177; and pragmatism, 203, 206; *Reconstruction in Philosophy*, 205; as "scientific democrat," 77

Dewey, Melvill, 42, 45

Dexter, Edwin Grant: *A History of Education in the United States*, 215–16

Dittenberger, Karl Friedrich Wilhelm, 43

Dixie Club, 279

Dodd, Walter E., 176

Dodge, Daniel K., 182

Doerner, Julius, 51

Dorrien, Gary, 3352n9

Dostoevsky, Fyodor, 317

Douglas, Paul, 318

Draper, Andrew S., 3; appoints Jayne dean of women, 304; and Bevier, 255, 258; favors fraternities, 277; on Kemp, 145; and Lea, 271; names Harker dean of law school, 223,

Index   401

Draper, Andrew S. (*continued*) 234–35; on potential for ceramics, 13; resigns as president, 11; and Rolfe, 134; on search for successor, 4

Dreilinger, Danielle, 254

Dreiser, Theodore: Mencken defends, 192; Sherman criticizes, 191–92

Droysen, Gustav, 77; and H. K. Adams, 88

Drury, Francis K. W., 42; decentralization plan, 43

DuBois, W. E. B., 196, 269, 35n10

Dudgeon, Israel, 223

Dunlop, Henry, 15

Dunlop, Nora, 260

Dunne, Bishop Edmund M., 266

Dunne, Edward F.: career, 23; and Irish-American Commission, 48; and library, 49; and Trevett, 21

DuPuy, Margaret C.: and *Illinois Magazine*, 307

Dziatzko, Karl, 42

Einstein, Albert, 224

Ekblaw, Elmer: Crocker expedition, 35

Elliot, Charles W., 30, 182, 184, 198; and Law School, 231–32; and NLI, 91; opposes women students at Harvard, 299–30; service ideal, 112–13

Ely, Richard T.: career, 67–68; and Social Gospel, 68; studies at German universities, 68

Emerson, Ralph Waldo, 174, 195, 322, 334–35, 395n27; *Nature*, 334–35, 336

empiricism: and American scientists, 77; Bode, 204–6; British, 59, 61, 63; Dewey, 204–6; Hayes and, 179

Engineering, College of: and the war, 100

Engineering Experiment Station, 126, 137, 219; Deneen and, 221–22; fellowship program, 221

Engineering Society, 276

English Journal Club, 276

enrollments, 266

entomology: Forbes urges expansion of courses and instructors for, 156–57

Entomology Building, 158

Erlangen, University of, 73

Erskine, John, 187

eugenics, 89

Evans, Laura, B., 23; dislike for EJJ, 148; and groundbreaking for Women's Dormitory, 310; and Kemp controversy, 148; on "loyalty" investigation committee, 118

Evans, William, 152

Evanston (Illinois) High School: EJJ attends, 6

Fairlie, John A., 209; career, 176; and Deneen, 21; supports women's suffrage, 21; teacher, 176

Falkner, Roland P.: and foreign policy, 85

Farnam, Henry W.: and Germany, 109

Fawcett, Mary E.: and EJJ, 305; prescriptions for model woman, 305

Fichte, Johann Gottlieb, 60–61; and *Bildung*, 62; EJJ quotes, 214–15; Nevins references, 336; and the state, 78

Fine, Sidney, 69

First Methodist Church of Urbana, 287

Fish, Carl Russell, 115

Fisk University, 269

Fitz-Gerald, John D., 200

Fleming, Gertrude, 310

Flom, George T., 198–99; and Scandinavian literature, 199

Flower, Lucy, 255

Folsom, Justus W., 157

Forbes, Stephen A., 11, 122, 127; achievements, 252; on needs of zoology department, 155, 156; retirement, 158; and State Laboratory of Natural History, 123; teaching, 157

Ford, Guy Stanton, 115, 168, 171–72

Fox, Dixon Ryan, 171

France, Anatole, 191

Francke, August Hermann, 57, 58

Franklin, Benjamin, 195

Franklin Railway Co., 222

fraternities and sororities, 277

Frederick III (Emperor of Prussia), 57

French Revolution, 111

Fuller, Margaret, 196

402 Index

Garner, James W.: career, 177; courses taught, 177

Garrison, Lindley, 98

Gates, Fanny: and EJJ, 306; and groundbreaking for Women's Residence Hall, 310; proposes program of women's studies, 306

Geiger, Roger, 17, 25, 26, 119, 265; on collegiate revolution, 266; YMCA, 279

General Electric Co.: ties to Physics department, 221

General Federation of Women's Clubs, 21

Gerlach, Miriam: career, 307; and College Equal Suffrage League, 315; and *Illinois Magazine*, 307; "The Last Laugh," 392n27; student activities, 307

German University League, 109

Giessen, University of, 73

Gilbert, Barry: writings, 236

Girls Athletic Association, 302

Gladden, Washington, 285, 389n49

Godkin, William, 69, 93; and anti-imperialism, 86

Goebel, Julius: advocate of German cultural superiority, 199; autocratic manner, 199–200; Beck and, 200; and Flom, 199; and Henry Moritz Heyne library, 43; and Kinley, 34; and Lessing, 200; manger of *JEGP*, 198; opinions about, 199

Goebel, Mabel, 310

Gompers, Samuel, 71, 86; and anti-imperialism, 86

Gone with the Wind (movie), 320

Gorky, Maxim, 317

Goss, William F. M., 58, 220, 223; made dean of the College, 1907; and railways, 222–23, search for new faculty, 227

Graduate School: enrollment patterns, 3; establishes rules of admission, 33; finances special research projects, 35; financial awards to departments, 33; foreign students in, 37; Graduate Club formed, 33; Kinley oversees budget, 34; opening ceremonies, 31; scholarships, 33. *See also* Kinley, David S.; James, Edmund J.

Graff, Gerald, 187

Grayling, A. C., 59

Great American Universities (Slosson): on EJJ, 255, 344n20; engineering observed, 222; UofI included, 38

Greeley, Horace, 338

Greene, Evarts P., 101, 115, 203; and Alvord, 169, 171; becomes dean of College of Literature and Arts, 1906, 183; and EJJ, 164–66; and Goebel, 198, 200; and Jewish scholars, 209; and Kinley, 167; and Lessing, 299; on library; 50; and National Board for Historical Services, 104; Nevins on, 274; and philosophy department, 201; and political science department, 176; reservations about sociology, 177

Greenough, Chester N., 182, 184; designs for department, 183; made department chair, 182; resigns, 184; on women teachers, 183–84

Gregory, John Milton, 5; and home economics, 255; on "learning and Labor," 339

Gridiron Dancing Club, 279

Grim, Harriet: address at UofI, 315; career, 315

Grindley, Harry S., 52; and American Meat Packers, 132–33; education, 52; nutrition studies, 129–30; publishes results of studies, 133–34; studies of Chicago milk with Jane Addams, 130–31; studies of saltpeter, 131

Gröber, Gustav, 48

Grout, A. P., 20

Gruber, Carol S., 108–9, 115

Hadley, Arthur T., 70, 109n3; and foreign policy, 85; and Germany, 109

Haessler, Carl H.: in federal prison, 169, 320; and "loyalty" controversy, 117; promotion of socialism, 291

Hale, William C.: on Ballantine, 246; on goals of the Law School, 240; professional activities, 241, 248

Hallett, Margaret H.: and *Illinois Magazine*, 307; on women students and voting, 315

Halliday, V., 315

Index   403

Hampton Institute, 269

Harker, Joseph R., 31

Harker, Oliver A.: assessments of, 243–44, 246; becomes dean, 1904, 234; and British common law, 234; career, 233–334; and case method, 234; death, 383n64; and Decker, 245; and EJJ make plans for the Law School, 235, 249; and Illinois Society of the American Institute of Criminal Law and Criminology, 241; and programs for law students, 236–37; relations with law faculty, 242; resigns as dean, 243; salary, 237; and Wormser, 238–39

Harper, William Rainey: and EJJ, 19

Harris, Frank, 317

Harris, N. W., 11

Harris, William Tory, 96

Harrison, Charles C.: dismisses EJJ from Wharton, 9

Hart, Albert Bushnell, 86

Harvard University, 4, 18; academic journals, 35; admits no women students, 300; EJJ on education program, 213; EJJ studies, 5; F. J. Turner joins history department, 371n29; "generalists" (literature) at, 187; Grindley studies at, 130; Kittredge at, 187; Law School, 231–33, 237, 247, 383n76; library, 4–50, 229, 236; mathematics, 226; professors at, 163; salaries at, 15; Sherman, student at, 185; student writing compared to Illinois, 311, 314; telescopic mirror loaned to Illinois, 142–43; university press, 50

Haskins, Charles H., 229

Hatch, Frederic, 11

Hatch, Frederick Lewis: opposes EJJ, 148

Hatch Act, 149, 222, 252

Hawthorne, Nathaniel, 195, 196, 283

Hay, John, 93

Hayes, Edward C.: accomplishments in sociology, 178; career, 177; and Dewey, 177; local work, 179; on modern Germany, 178; and progressivism, 179; and rural communities in Illinois, 177; on scientific sociology, 178–79; and Small, 177; on sociology and ethics, 178

Haym, Rudolph, 72

Hegel, Georg Wilhelm Friedrich: Nevins references, 336

Henrotin, Ellen, M.: career, 21

Herbst, Jurgen, 64

Herder, Johann Gottfried, 72

Hexamer, Charles T., 48

Heyne, Moritz, 47, 52

Hibernian Club, 295

Hindustani Club, 279

Hirschfield, Charles, 360n66

History Club, 276

Hohenzollerns, 58

Holmes, Oliver Wendell, 336

Holmes, Oliver Wendell, Jr.: Bode on, 207–9

Hopkins, Cyril George, 252

Hormel, Olive Dean: background, 304; *Co-Ed*, 304, 320–22; and *Sewanee Review*, 310; student activities, 304

Horowitz, Helen Lefkowitz, 392n38

Horticultural Society, 302

Hottes, Charles F., 149–50, 155

Household Science Club, 276

Howard University, 269

Howells, William Dean, 196; and anti-imperialism, 86

Huff, George, 281; Nevins on, 282

Humboldt, Wilhelm von, 59, 72; on German universities, 190; Nevins cites, 336; and University of Berlin, 62

Hume, David, 76

Hutchinson, Anne, 259

Illinois: funding of the University, 14–15; mill tax, 19; taxation system, 13–14

Illinois, the. See *Illinois Magazine*

Illinois Canners Association: UofI contract with, 153–54

Illinois Centennial Commission, 171

Illinois Clay Manufacturers, 136, 137

Illinois College, 326

Illinois Drama Federation, 276

Illinois Gas Association: fellowships in engineering, 222

Illinois Historical Collections: Alvord editor, 171–72

404   Index

Illinois Historical Society, 171
Illinois Industrial University, 5
Illinois Law Bulletin, 248
Illinois Law Review, 235
Illinois Magazine, 283; appearance, 307; and C. Needham, 310; and C. Van Doren, 283; and Dean Clark, 273; and feminism, 311–12; and Lincoln League, 290; and Nevins, 274; and racial expression, 268; and Seyster, 303; and women contributors, officers, 307–8. *See also* the *Illinois*
Illinois Outdoor Improvement Association, 176
Illinois Society of the American Institute of Criminal Law and Criminology, 241
Illinois State Council of Defense, 116
Illinois State Journal: EJJ writes for, 6
Illinois State Medical Society, 152
Illinois State Normal School: assessed by UofI Graduate School, 32; created, 215; EJJ attends, 5; EJJ directs Model High School at, 5
Illio, The, 272, 283; women students on staff, 301, 307
Illiola, 302
Immigration Restriction League, 91
Indiana University, 26, 56, 161, 231, 306; and Black fraternities, 269, 271
Industrial League, 327
Influenza (Spanish flu), 107–8
Institute for the Investigation of Infectious Diseases, 125–26
Insul, Samuel, 116
Intercollegiate Socialist Society of America, 291
Ireland: Windsor seeks books from, 50
Isham, Helen, 129

Jackson, Andrew, 69
Jacksonville, Illinois: birthplace of James, 4
James, Amanda K. Casad (mother of EJJ): influence on EJJ, 5; and library collection in her name, 58
James, Anna Margaret Lange (wife of EJJ), 96–98
James, Anthony John (son), 98

James, Colin Drew (father of EJJ): influence on EJJ, 54; intellectual interests, 4; as Methodist circuit rider, 57
James, Edmund J.: AAPPS celebrates leadership of, 354n39; and Albert R. Lee, 271–72; and alumni, 15, 18–19; and Alvord, 10; and Anna Margaret Lange James, 96–97; appointed president of University of Illinois, 11–12; appoints Fairlie in political science department, 176; appoints Jewish professors, 199, 209; and Bevier, 20–61, 259; and Board of Trustees, 23; builds geology department, 134–35; challenges Philadelphia "Gas Ring," 7; and Chicago Meat Packers, 133; and Clark, 272–73; compares German and American professors, 71–72; dealing with state legislature, 13–14, 16, 17–19, 23, 24, 235; death, 24; desires large presence of religion in curriculum, 288–89; does not encourage German chauvinism of Goebel, 199; early education, 5–6; encourages building of Wesley Foundation, 287; encourages student athletics, 280; and Evarts B. Greene, 163, 164–65, 167, 169; forms advisory committee for ceramics program, 133; founder of AAPSS, 71, 73; and fraternities, 277; gains State Geological Society for the University, 13–37; genealogy, 4–5; German intellectual influence on, 214; gives address an groundbreaking of new dormitory for women, 310; gives large place to religion in installation events, 288–89; and Governor Deneen, 136; growth of students in College of Agriculture under, 252; and Hayes, 177; hesitates to promote Goebel, 200; hires Blackwelder in Geology, 139; hires Greenough, 182; hires Karsten, 197–98; hires Kingsley, 161–62; hires Noyes, 31, 127; hires Oldfather, 181; his search for dean of women, 304–7; and Hugo Münsterberg, 98; and Illinois Canners Association, 154; influence of father, 4–5; influence of mother, 5;

James, Edmund J. (*continued*)
installation of, 3; installation speech, 12; and Jews, 4, 91–92; joins Second Methodist Church of Urbana, 287; and Julia C. Lathrop, 176; and Kemp, 145–49; on the legacy of Jonathan Baldwin Turner, 328–29; and Lessing, 198, 200; and liberal education, 75; on liberal education and the classics, 337–38; on the library school, 351n58; and MacGillivray, 157; member, First Methodist Church of Urbana, 287; and Methodism, 4–5, 57–58, 287–88; and the mill tax, 19–20; and Nevins, 274–75, 276, 277; and Newcomb, 69, 70, 354n33; and the "New Economics," 68–70, 79; opposes separate education of men and women, 300; and philosophical idealism, 74; plans for department of bacteriology, 151–53; pleads for the lectures system, 72; pleads for seminars, 72; president of the Illinois State Historical Library, 170, 172; president of Northwestern University, 10–11; problems with Alexander-Bahrenberg, 15–17; on program of studies in German universities, 73; promotes studies in human nutrition, 132; quoted on roll of government, 364n43; quotes Fichte, 214; and reform of business education, 8–9; and religious houses for students, 286–87; scandal concerning Beck, 200–201; on scientific education as an art, 378n15; on "scientific study," 76, 180, 212; seeks to strengthen ties with diverse ethnic groups, 198; sees opportunities in developing ceramics industry, 136; shares views of "Scientific agriculture" with Dean Davenport, 251; and Sherman, 186, 187; and Simon Patten, 65–67, 69–70; Slosson credits for political skills, 344n20; on the social sciences, 74–75, 77; student at University of Halle, 18, 66–67; suggested for United States president, 23; summarized University's contribution to the war, 30n74; supports Begley in

his Carnegie Foundation project, 218; supports history program, 167; supports the JEGP, 198; supports liberal religion, 286, 287; supports temperance, 291; on training of teachers, 214; and Trevett, 201; at University of Chicago, 10; views of teacher education similar to those of Edwin Grant Dexter, 216; wants mapping plan of state mineral resources, 137–38; welcomes construction of Woman's Building, 1905, 300; welcomes intercollegiate athletics, 282; and Wharton School of Finance, 6-10; and women students, 300; writes introduction to Powell's history of the University, 332; and YMCA, 279

—and College of Engineering: appoints Richards, as professor of mechanical engineering, 220; creates advisory board of railroad executives, 223; established under James, 219; favors expansion of training in coal mining, 223; hires Berg, 220–21; and James M. White, 219; works with Townsend in mathematics, 222–27, 229

—and the Graduate School: and Alvord, 35; appeals to Graduate School to support Crocker Land Expedition, 35; appeals to presidents of colleges in state for support of, 29; appeal to Governor Deneen, 29; dealings with Kinley to become dean, 27–28; disagreements with Kinley, 34; opening ceremonies, 31; recognized in Slosson's *Great American Universities*, 344n20; trustees support his design for, 29, 30; works with Kinley on, 32; works with state legislature, 2–3

—and the law school: appoints Ballantine as dean, 246–47; and Dean Harker, 235, 241–42, 243, 249; and Decker, 244–45; and Gilmore, 246; hires Carpenter, 240–41; hires Gilbert 23; hires McGovney, 23; hires Pillsbury, 240; hires Pomeroy, 237–38; hires Thurston, 237–38; and *Illinois Law Bulletin*, 248; and Northrup, 24; and salary issues in, 23–37; seeks

406   Index

money from legislature, 235; solicits opinions of law faculty about direction of the College, 240–41; urges University of Illinois law reviews, 235, 23; wants law school to support political and social reform, 24–47; wants to make law program more solidly academic, prestigious, 237; and Wormser, 238–39

—and the library: and acting head librarian Drury, 42–43, 44; expands collections, 4–48, 50–51, 52; German universities offer models for, 41, 48; gets money from state legislature for, 43; and head librarian Sharp, 42; and head librarian Windsor, 44, 45; his goals for, 49; personal donation to, 50; purchases other libraries for, 48; rearranges library during war, 104

—and progressivism, 12, 17, 76–77, 78, 255, 249; contributes to *Our Day*, 82–83; on the labor movement, 82–84, 24; in law, 246–47; and race, 367n10; on rural America, railroads, and reform, 79–81; on the "social question," 82, 83; views of government, 79; and the war, 85, 360n66

—on race and immigration: on Chinese, 92–95; creates Office of Advisor to Foreign Students, 94; on German immigrants, 96; on Jews, 90–91; on the modern age, optimism, 8; opposes imperialism, 93–94; plans for Chinese students to attend American universities, 93–94; on race, 86, 90–91; rejects Anglo-Saxonism, 88–91

—and the University Press: arranges for first publication, *Sixteen Years at the University of Illinois*, 55; earlier efforts, *Alumni Record*, 52; favors publication of academic journals, 54; forms Committee on University Press, 54; hires Harrison E. Cunningham, 54; trustees favor his request to organize, 18, 55

—and World War I: blames Germany for the war, 113; calls for total victory over Germany, 114, 118; celebrates France, 110–11; forms University War Committee, 101; intolerance of

wartime dissent, 108, 118; offers university facilities to War Department, 100; ordeal of loyalty to Germany, 99–100, 106; organizes patriotic rallies, 102; pride in UofI service to American cause, 116; and SATC, 104, 114; speaks for preparedness, 98; suspends his loyalty to Germany, 110; and "trials" of faculty dissenters, 119; universities to train officers for army, 98–99; on the war and racial justice at home, 111–12; on the war and "social science," 112–13; works with War Department on curriculum changes, 105

James, Eliza Ana Plaster, 5
James, Harman Gerlach (son), 88
James, Helen Dixon (daughter), 98
James, Henry, 191, 195
James, William, 196; and anti-imperialism, 86; and Bagley, 207; on Bode, 202; Bode appropriates, 205; and pragmatism, 203
James, William B. (paternal grandfather of EJJ), and antislavery, 5
Jameson, J. Franklin, 114–15
Janes, Edmund, 5
Jayne, Violet: and EJJ, 304–5
Jefferson, Thomas, 69
Jensen, Trygve: studies in iron purification, 221
Jewett, Andrew, 77
Jewett, Eleanor, 310
Jews, 88; and Burgess, 88; and faculty, 199, 209, 238, 267; fraternities and sonorities, 288; James and, 47, 48, 91–92; and Jewish materials in library, 47–48; and students, 267, 288, 317, 312, 3866n5
John Marshall Debating Club, 243
Johns Hopkins University, 3, 4, 25; and academic journals, 35; Adams at, 88; and graduate school, 345n2; Newcomb at, 69; university press, 5; and the war, 164
Jones, Florence N., 200
Jones, H. S. V., 184
Jordan, David Starr: and anti-imperialism, 86

Index   407

journalism: in English department, 185
Journalism, School of, curriculum, 54
Journal of English and German Philology (JEGP), 46, 52, 198
Journal of the Illinois State Historical Society, 328

Kallen, Horace, 206
Kant, Immanuel, 59; American influence, 202–4; in German universities, 60–62; Hayes on, 118; influence, 58–59; philosophical idealism, 59; on science, 60
Kappa Alpha Psi, 269
Karsten, Gustaf E.: career, 187; teaching, 197–98
Kemp, George Theophilus: antagonizes EJJ, 147–48; case in the national media, 148; character and perverse behavior, 147; faulted by Kinley, 147; Senate retaliates against, 148
Kerrick, Leonidas H., 11
Kerrick, William H.: and "loyalty" investigation, 117–18
Kevles, Daniel J., 125, 362n8
Kingsley, John S.: career, 161–62
King's Mirror, The (Levine, trans.), 52
Kinley, David S., 346n29; and Alvord, 35, 169, 171; assessment of role as graduate dean, 38; and Bevier, 261; and Cole, 168; considers accepting of offer to be dean of the graduate school, 26–28; contributes to journal of the AAPSS, 71; control of graduate school, 31–30; for course on journalism, 185; defends James against Trevett, 201; denounces socialism, 290; and departmental libraries, 229; describes wartime campus, 100; disdains novel *Town and Gown*, 303; and economics department, 16–17; and education of engineers, 222–23; and establishment of sociology department, 177; favors fraternities, 277; forms committee to study graduate education at other universities, 32; forms graduate school executive committee, 28; and Goebel, 34, 198; and Greene, 165–68; and the Illini

Publication Company, 55; and Kemp, 147; and Lee, 272; and Lessing, 200; and "loyalty" issue, 118–20; major address (and publication) of graduate education and democracy, 39–40; on the meaning of graduate education, 32; priorities for School of Education, 21; proposes University of Illinois Institute of Research, 36; and publication of faculty research, 34–35, 52; solicits faculty preferences regarding new president, 19–20; solicits support of private colleges on behalf of graduate school, 28–29; and Stebbins, 143–44; temperament, 30; wants greater selectivity of departments in graduate school, 29, 346n31; wartime activities, 101–2, 105–6; on weaknesses of library, 45–46; worries about business interests in the University, 19–20; and zoology department, 166–67
Kittredge, George Lyman, 187
Knies, Karl, 64
Knights of Labor, 84
Koller, Armin H.: Jewish scholar, 199
Kollock, Lily G.: and EJJ, 305–6
Königsberg, University of, 73
Kuhn, Isaac, 267
Kyle, Martha: on excesses of social life among women students, 305–6; judge of suffrage speech context, 315; on wider campus activity for women students, 316

Ladd, George T., 75
LaFollette, Robert, 290
laissez-faire economics: EJJ opposes, 81; German social scientists oppose, 63–64; large influence in American higher education, 68; New Economics opposes, 6, 68, 79
Lalor, John J., 6
Lampoon, 314
Landscape Garden Club, 302; and Yoch, 320
Langdell, Christopher Columbus: Ballantine on, 247; develops case system, 232; law as a "science," 232
La Piano, 232–33

408 Index

Larson, Lawrence M., 52, 104; career, 166

Lathrop, Julia C.: recommends sociology department at UofI, 176–77

law library, 248

law school: early program of studies, 233; expansion of program, 236; JD degree, 237

"Learning and Labor," 4, 337; Davenport on, 337; Gregory on, 339; J. B. Turner references, 238–39

Lee, Albert R., 270; and Bethel AME Church, 272; "Dean of Colored Students" and NAACP, 272; and Draper, 272; and EJJ, 272; and Kinley, 272; youth and education, 272

Legislative Reference Library, 17

Leitzbach, Elizabeth, 310

Leonard, Thomas C., 89, 357n10

Lerow, Caroline, 315

Lessing, Otto E., 198; complaints, 200

liberal education: EJJ on, 75

liberal Protestantism: Jewett on, 77; Mott and 286; Schleiermacher influences, 60; and YMCA, 284–85

Liberty Loan campaign, 116–17

library: and civil service system, 45; compared to other university libraries, 43, 49, 51–52; gifts to, 46; Kinley complaints, 45–46

library school, 42, 44, 45, 258, 351, 351n58

Lick Observatory: Stebbins at, 140, 143–44

Lincoln, Jeanette Carpenter, 146

Lincoln Law Club, 243

Lincoln League: Nevins and, 290; supports LaFollette, 291; supports prohibition, 291

Lindahl, Florence: and *Illinois Magazine*, 308

List, Friedrich, 79

Litchfield (CT): law school, 231

literary societies, 302

Litman, Ray, 267

Litman, Simon, 167

Lloyd, Henry Demarest, 83

Llwellyn, Ruth, 310

Logan, Rayford, 268

London Times, 42

Longfellow, Henry Wadsworth, 187

Lowden, Frank O., 19, 115–16

Lowell, Abbott Lawrence, 3, 337

Lowell, James Russell, 187

Loyola House, 266, 288

Lybyer, Albert H., 58, 169

Lyon, Mary, 259

MacGillivray, Alexander D.: introduces new courses, 157–58

Mack, Julian, 48

MacNeal, Ward J., 134; and Burrill, help to establish Department of Bacteriology, 151

Marburg, Theodore, 96

Marlowe, Christopher, 189–90

Mask and Bauble Club, 276, 302

Mason, Ruby, 306

Mathematical Club: women presidents, 229

mathematics department: graduate program, 229

mathematics library: growth, 229

Mathews, Shailer, 289

Matthews, Brander, 187

Mattis, Ross, R., 21

Mayo-Smith, Richmond, 70

McAdoo, William G., 116

McCall, J. W., 153–54

McCarthy, Charles, 17, 29

McClellan, John H., 15; career, 15; teaching program, 156

McCosh, James, 355n52

McDowell, Bishop Francis William Fraser, 287

McGovney, Dudley O., 236

McKinley, William B., 287

McKinley Memorial Presbyterian Church, 287

McLaughlin, Andrew, 115

McMaster, John Bach: and imperialism, 82

Mead, George Herbert, 206

Meeker, Arthur, 20, 23

Meiklejohn, Alexander, 187

Melancthon, Philip, 58

Melville, Herman, 336

Menorah Society, 267

Index   409

Methodism: influence on EJJ, 4; and Northwestern University, 10; and Wesley Foundation, 287
Meyer, Irene, 320
Michigan Agricultural College, 153, 220, 252
Middle High School (Illinois State Normal University): James attends, 6
Miles, Manley, 252
Mill, John Stuart, 6, 63
Miller, George R.: career, 228; instruction, 228–29
Minton, Henry McKee, 269
Missouri Club, 279
Moot Court, 242, 243
More, Paul Elmer, 185
Morehouse University, 269
Morrill, Justin, 215, 329, 332, 338. *See also* Morrill Act
Morrill Act, 12; EJJ on, 329, 330, 334; Emerson related to, 335; 50th anniversary, 326; Illinois uses, 4; and military instruction, 99; Nevins on, 331–32; Powell on, 333; provisions, 3, 180, 210, 259
Morris, George Sylvester, 203
Morrow, George E., 252
Mortarboard, 303
Motorcycle Club, 276
Mott, John Raleigh: career, 285; impact on students, 286; and liberal Protestantism, 285; "Mott Campaign," 285–86; Nevins on, 285–86
Muller v. Oregon, 384n81
Myers, George W., 139

Nation, the: Alvord writes in, 174; EJJ writes to, 92–93, 329; and Godkin, 68; Mark Van Doren, 283; Nevins writes in, 274; and P. E. More, 185; Sherman writes for, 183, 186, 188
National Association of Colored Women's Clubs, 268
National Board for Historical Service, 115
National Liberal Immigration League (NLIL), 91
National Security League, 114
National Society for the Scientific Study of Education, 21

Natural History Building, 150
Naturphilosophie, 59
Needham, Catherine, 318; campus activities, 310; family, 308; at groundbreaking for Women's Residence Hall, 310; on modern women, 311; after UofI, 310; wins literary prizes, 310
Needham, Lucile: campus memberships and activities, 308–9; family, 308; high school in Urbana, 308; and Mark Van Doren, 308; *Sewanee Review* essay, 309; after UofI, 310
Needham, Marguerite, 308
Neumann, Peter, 335
Nevins, Joseph Allan: books on American history, 275–76; and the *Daily Illini*, 274, 282, 283, 296; defends University against criticism, 289; on the educational purposes of the state university, 337; and *Illinois Magazine*, 274, 290, 307; on Illinois students, 275, 276, 280–81, 292, 339; and liberal religion of the students, 286; on literature, 296; on the Morrill Act, 331, 332; parental influences, 274; and prohibition, 291; rights and wrongs of the University, 296–98; on the romantic movement and the state universities, 336–37; on service to the state, 288; and the *Siren*, 314–15; on the state universities and democracy, 274, 275, 293–94; *The State Universities and Democracy*, 332–32; student at UofI, 274; on the University of Wisconsin, 296–97; and visit of Mott, 285–86; on women students, 296–97; writes first history of the UofI, 274; youth, 273
Newcomb, Simon, 69, 354n33
"New Economics": EJJ and, 60–70; Ely and 70; influence from German thinkers, 64, 66
"New History," the, 175–76
New Humanism: and Babbitt, 185; and More, 185
"New Immigration," 87, 91
Northrup, Elliott, J.: and Harker, 242
Northwestern University, 5, 56, 136, 248; EJJ as president, 10–11; EJJ as

student there, 5; and law review, 235, 236; Methodism, 10; and Oldfather, 181; and Patten, 7

Norton, Charles Eliot, 75, 187

Novick, Peter, 110, 174

Noyes, William Abbott: career, 127; inauguration address, 128; research, 128

O'Brien, Fr, John A., 266

Oldfather, William A.: career, 181; in "loyalty" hearings, 117–19; and "Old-father school" of classics, 181

Oliver, Revilo P., 308

Omega Psi Phi: Wilkins member, 271

Onyx Dancing Club, 279

Orange and Blue Dance Club, 279

Osgood, Herbert Levi, 86

Oxford University, 4

Paine, Ellery, 221

Palmer, Arthur W., 128–27, 257

Parr, Samuel W., 126–27; research, 129

Parrington, Vernon Louis, 195–96

Parrish, John, 352n8

Patten, James, 11

Patten, Simon: and Conrad, 67; career, 66–67; and EJJ, 67; ideas, 70–74; and study of national economy, 67; and the war, 109–10

Paulsen, Friedrich, 58

Pease, Arthur, 181, 183, 209; gift to library, 50

Pease, Theodore Calvin, 168; books, 168

Peirce, Charles Sanders, 196, 203

Pepper, William: resigns, 9; and Wharton School, 6; works with James at, 7

Perkin, Sir William Henry, 125

Perry, Arthur Lapham, 68

Phelps, Edward J., 233

philology: and Kittredge, 187

philosophical idealism, 58–59, 75, 77, 214; and American Transcendentalists, 234; Bode and, 202–3; challenged by Scottish realism, 202; and J. B. B. Turner, 333–34; Royce and, 298. *See also individual philosophers*

Philosophy Club, 322

Phipps Institute for the Study of Tuberculosis, 125

physics: study in lags in appropriating new theories, 224

physiology, curriculum in, 146–47

Pierce, Franklin, 327

Pierrots, 276

pietism, 57

Pillsbury, Warren H.: career, 240

Pi Phi Rho: and war effort, 102

Political Science Club, 276

Polonia Club, 279

Pomeroy, John Norton: career, 237–38; on needs of Law School, 240; and state agencies, 241

Populist (People's) Party, 79–80

Powderly, Terrence V., 84

Presbyterianism, 66; Bevier and, 255; buildings on campus, 286–88; Busey and, 20; Clark and, 287; Dean Clark as, 287; First Presbyterian Church, Urbana, 286; and Illinois College, 327; Nevins' father as, 273; Oldfather and, 187; Presbyterian House dormitory for women, 286; Presbyterian Synod of Illinois, 286; in student body, 266

Progressive Era. *See* progressivism

prohibition, 5, 73, 314, 316; and campus politics, 291–92; EJJ supports, 291–92

Pulitzer Prize: C. Van Doren, 283, 375n44; M. Van Doren, 283, 375n44; Nevins, 275

Pure Food and Drug Act, 132

Puritans: Mencken on, 194; Sherman on, 193

race: Babington, 90; Burgess, 88; Commons, 88; Fiske, 87; Kinley, 40; Marburg, 90–91. *See also* James, Edmund J.

Railroad Gazette, 223

railroads, study of at UofI, 223

Railway Club, 302

Railway Fuel Association, 222

Ratterman Collection, 52

Rauschenbusch, Walter, 285, 35n10

Red Cross: and women students in war effort, 101–2

Index   411

Reid, Thomas, 76. *See also* Scottish philosophy
Reighard, Jacob, 160; speaks for program in anthropology, 160
Remsen, Ira, 128
Republican Club, 290
Reuben, Julie, 75
Ricardo, David, 79
Richards, Charles R., 220
Richards, Ellen Swallow: career, 254; on home economics and science, 254, 255
Richardson, Robert E.: *The Fishes of Illinois*, 155–56
Rietz, Henry Lewis, 229
Rifle Club, 262
Riley, William Bell, 389n49
Roberts, Nellie: and *Illinois Magazine*, 308
Robertson, William S., 168
Robinson, James Harvey: and the "New History," 173
Rockefeller Foundation, 225
Rockefeller Institute for Medical Research, 125
Rodgers, Daniel, 69
Rogan, John A., 267
Rolfe, Charles W., 156; chair of department, 134–35, 139; development of ceramics program, 136–37, 138–39; and Townsend, 136, 137, 138
Roman Catholics. *See* Catholics
Roosevelt, Theodore, 14; and immigration, 86; and James on Chinese students, 94, 358n22; and 1912 election, 21; in straw poll of students, 290
Roscher, Wilhelm, 64
Rosenwald, Julius, 48
Ross, Edward A.: racial views, 89
Rouillon, Vanessa, 271
Rowland, Henry: and pure science, 125
Royce, Josiah, 196, 203; speech at UofI, 298
Rutherford, Ernst, 224; visit to UofI, 225

salaries of faculty: EJ's new policy, 16
Sanger, Margaret, 318
Sass, Steven, 10

Savage, Thomas, 35–36
Sax, Emil, 79
Schaper, William A., 115
Schelling, Friedrich, 60, 61–62; Nevins references, 33; opposes utilitarian education, 61
Schiller, Friedrich, 352n8
Schleiermacher, Friedrich, 62; and Kant, 60; organic ideal of knowledge, 60; philosophy of, 60
Schmoller, Gustav, 62, 66, 109; Hayes and, 177
Schoepperle, Gertrude, 51
Schopenhauer, Arthur, 194
Schurz, Carl, 96
Schwartz, Robert, 272
Science magazine, 69
scientific thinking: Alvord, 173; and home economics, 255; Humboldt and, 663; Schiller, 302n8. *See also* Edmund James and
Scott, Franklin W., 154, 196; for course in journalism, 185; defends University against attacks, 118
Scottish philosophy, 59, 62, 76, 196; and McCosh, 355n52; and philosophical idealism, 202
Scribblers' Club, 302; and C. Needham, 310; and Day, 317; and Gerlach, 307; and Hormel; 304; and L. Needham, 308; and Seyster, 303; and Simons, 317, 318; and Raphaelson, 318
Sedgwick, William T., 152
Seligman, Edwin R. A., 70
Selznick, David O., 320
seminar: at German universities, 58
Seymour, Arthur R., 200
Seymour, James, 95
Seymour Guild House, 288
Seyster, Lois, 310; literary career and novel, *Town and Gown*, 303, 304, 391n12
Sharp, Katherine L., 42, 51
Shattuck, Samuel, 226, 228
Shaw, James H., 228
Sheffield Scientific School, 129
Shepherd, Lois: career, 201–2; "loyalty" trial, 117–18; not retained, 201–2; opposes war, 116

412   Index

Sherman, Stuart P., 205, 315; on American ethics and loyalty, 194; on American Writers, 194–95; attacks Dreiser, 191–92; attacks Mencken, 181–92; book on Matthew Arnold, 190–91; and *Cambridge History of American Literature*, 192–94; and Carl Van Doren, 88–89; death in Michigan, 197; defense of United States in war, 115; on democracy and the Midwest, 190; early life and education, 183; as faculty member, 18; on graduate education in literary studies, 188; influence of Babbitt on, 185, 188; literary reviews and essays, 188; and Mark Van Doren, 283; on needs of English department, 184; and Nevins, 274; in novel *Co-Ed*, 321; offers from other universities, 187; and Raphaelson, 283; and the war, Wilson, and the Allies, 192–94

Sigma Pi Phi, 269

Sinclair, Upton, 132

Sixteen Years at the University of Illinois: A Statistical Study of the Administration of President Edmund J. James (James), 55

Sloane, William M., 171

Slosson, Edwin F.: on EJJ, 344n20; *Great American Universities*, 38; observes testing of cement, 222; praises UofI, 38

Small, Albion: career, 64; at Chicago, 177; and the war, 102–3, 109

Smith, Adam, 70

Smith-Hughes Act, 261

Smith-Lever Act, 261

social gospel, 81, 285

socialism, 81, 285; Day and, 317; EJJ on, 82; and Haessler, 291; Kinley denounces, 290; Raphaelson and, 88, 318; Simons and, 318; student poll, 290; students discuss, 291

"social question," the, 81, 87

Sociology, Department of: established in 1908, 166, 177

Solberg, Winton U., 395n26

Spalding Guild, 266, 288

Spencer, Herbert, 8

sports: intercollegiate, 280–81; intramural, 280–81

Spring Valley: 1888 strike in, 83

Stahl, Friedrich, 78

Standard Oil Company, 80

Stanford University, 3, 4; Evelyn White at, 305; faculty assessment of Goebel, 198; graduate school, 345n2; quotas for women students, 299

State Board of Health, 151–53

State Laboratory of Natural History, 155

State Teachers Association (Illinois), 215

State Universities and Democracy, The (Nevins), 337

Stebbins, Joel, 131; awards from AAAS, 141–42; begins electrical measure of starlight, 140; character, 143–44; education, 140; honors and recognitions, 144; measures eclipse, 142; publications, 142; resigns, 144; and telescopic mirror, 142–143; uses selenium cell, 141

St. Louis, 18, 261, 275, 301

Stowe, Harriet Beecher, 259

Stromberg, Roland S., 360n59

Strong, Josiah: and Anglo-Saxonism, 87

Stuart, James C.: and "loyalty" controversy, 117

Students' Army Training Corps, 104–6, 113

Sumner, William Graham, 8; and anti-imperialism, 86

Swain, Joseph, 11

Talbot, Arthur Newell: awards, 52, 220

Tanquary, Maurice, 35–36, 135

Tap, Bruce, 119, 361n81

Tau Beta, 297

Taussig, Frank W., 70

temperance, 82, 252, 254. *See also* prohibition

Thelin, John R., 265

Tilden, Edward, 133

Titchener, F. B., 209, 217–18

Tobie, William Nathan, 287

Todd, Arthur C.: career, 178

Tolman, Richard C.: and "loyalty" controversy, 117–18

Tolstoy, Leo, 317

Townsend, Edgar B.: and bacteriology, 151; and botany, 153; career, 123–24; and ceramics, 138; as chair of Mathematics Department, 226–30; and entomology, 157; and medical education, 146; priority of public health, 151–53; pure science, 125; on Rolfe, 135; on science and service ideal, 124–25; and scientific thinking, 124–25; and on women in faculty, 129

Training for Business program, 16

Treitschke, Hermann von, 193

Trelease, William: career, 154

Trevett, John R.: conflict with EJJ, 201

Triangle Club, 277; and war effort, 102

Tsinghu University, 94

Tufts, James H., 205

Tufts College, 209

Turner, Frederick Jackson, 115, 371n29; endorses the "new history," 175

Turner, Jonathan Baldwin, 251; abolitionist, 327; Davenport on, 330–31; early career, 326–27; 1851 speech at Granville, 327; forms Industrial League, 327; genealogy, 326; and Gregory, 338; Illinois College, 326–27; James on, 329; on knowledge and social class divisions, 327, 328; "Liberal Industrial Education," 328; "Millenium [sic] of Labor," 327–28; on needs of the industrial classes, 327; Nevins on, 332; as philosophical idealist, 333; plan for "industrial universities," 327–28; Powell on, 332–33; and romanticism, 333–34

Tuskegee Institute, 269

Twain, Mark, 195

Unitarian Church of Urbana, 291

University Choral and Orchestral Club, 276

University Herbarium, 150

University of Berlin, 52, 58, 64; Carman, student at, 224; EJJ attends lectures, 5, 66; EJJ praises, 329; EJJ writes about, 352n64; Fichte at, 60–61; Hayes at, 177; library, 48; Nevins on, 336; Schleiermacher at,

60; Wagner at, 64; young Americans attend, 63

University of California, 23, 35, 49, 149, 240, 320; enrollments, 277; graduate school, 345n2; law school, 231; Sherman reference, 190; Stebbins at, 140; Wheeler on women at, 299; Yoch attends, 320

University of Chicago: and academic publications, 35; Alvord at, 164; Dewey at, 295; EJJ at, 19; Harper and, 41; law school, 235, 236, 237; Mathews and, 289; Raphaelson at, 318; Simons at, 317; Small and, 64

University of Erlangen, 73

University of Frankfort, 58

University of Freiburg, 73

University of Giesen, 73

University of Halle: Anna Margaret Lange James at, 96; Conrad at, 66; EJJ at, 5–6, 58, 66, 68; Ely at 68; Francke influence, 57–58; Gerlach at, 96; Haym, 72; and Napoleonic wars, 62; Patten at, 67; PhD program at, 73; Schleiermacher at, 60; Schmoller at, 66; significance to modern university, 58; Wolff at, 58

University of Heidelberg, 58, 88

University of Illinois Academy, 217

University of Illinois Institute of Research: later becomes University of Illinois Research Park, 3

University of Illinois Press: 1913 plan, 54. See also Cunningham and; Kinley and; James and

University of Illinois Studies in the Social Sciences, 35

University of Jena, 58; and EJJ, 73; Ely at, 66; Schelling at, 61; Schilling lecture at, 352n8

University of Königsberg, 58, 73

University of Leipzig, 58, 73, 96; EJJ at, 5; Ely at, 6; Small at, 64; Townsend at, 228

University of Marburg, 58

University of Michigan, 377n90; and bacteriology, 150, 153; and graduate school, 345n2; graduate students, 26; law school, 231, 240, 243, 245,

414 Index

248; library, 49–51; Morris at, 202–3; quotas for women students, 29; Slosson on, 38; state support, 18; student publications, 314; university press, 56; and the war, 104, 115
University of Minnesota, 30, 115, 128, 172, 293
University of Munich, 73, 128
University of Nebraska, 315
University of Pennsylvania, 4, 6, 8; enrollments, 51; law library, 248; and library, 49; and Patten, 110. *See also* Wharton School of Business
University of Rochester, 209
University of Rome, 315
University of Tübingen, 58, 197, 198; James and, 73
University of Wisconsin: academic journals, 35; and bacteriology, 153; Ely at, 27; law school, 249; and library, 51; and racial thinking, 89; and Wisconsin Idea, 17, 249
University of Wittenberg, 57
University Studies, 28, 34, 52; and university press, 41, 54

Vahlen, Johannes, 51–52
Vance, William R., 236–37
Van Cleave, Harley J., 161
Vanderbilt, Cornelius, 70
Van Doren, Carl: *Cambridge History of America Literature*, 195–96; and creating of *Illinois Magazine*, 307; criticism of graduate studies, 189; and Sherman, 189–90, 197; youth and education, at UofI, 189
Van Doren, Mark: at Columbia, 283; editor of *Illinois Magazine*, 307; elected class president, 316; family, 283; and the *Illinois Magazines*, 283, 307; and L. Needham, 308; and the *Nation*, 283; Pulitzer Prize, 283; and Sherman, 283
Van Dyke, Henry, 187
Van Hise, Charles, 3; and education for public service, 249; endorses Wisconsin sterilization law, 39
Van Tuyl, Francis M., 35–36
Varsity Dance Club, 279

Verein für Sozialpolitik, 5; model for Americans, 65–67, 69, 71
Vernier, Chester G., 244, 245; career, 239–40; on function of Law School, 240; leaves for Stanford, 242; professional work, 241
Veysey, Laurence, 77, 112

Wagner, Adolph, 64, 66; and Hayes, 177
Waitz, Georg, 77, 100
war aims courses, 103, 359n53
Ward, Henry B.: career, 159–60; demeanor, 160, 162; significance, 162
Ward, Richard B., 23
Washington, Booker T., 196, 254, 269
Washington, Margaret Murray, 254
Watson, Florence. E., 21–22
Watson, Peter, 59, 62
Wayland, Francis, 68
Weeks, Raymond: career, 198
Weiss, Camillo: and "loyalty" controversy, 117
Welch, Claude, 57
Wells, H. G., 191
Wendell, Barrett, 75, 182
Wesley, John, 4–5, 57
Wesleyan University, 5
Wesley Foundation: activities, 288; EJJ encouragers creating, 287
West, Andrew F., 11, 31, 75
Western Reserve University, 209
Weston, Nathan, 167
Wharton, Joseph, 6
Wheaton College, 2, 31; rated by UofI Graduate School, 5
Wheeler, Benjamin Ide, 209
Wheeler, Hiram R., 270
White, James M.: dean of the College, 219
White, Richard, 92, 253–54
Whitman, Walt, 195, 322
Wilczynski, Ernest Julius, 228, 380n3
Wiley, Harvey W.: food studies, 132
Wilhelm II, 48
Wilkes, J. Ernest: career, 270–71; student, 270
Willard, Emma, 259
Willard, Frances, 82, 357n10
Williams, Walter, 267

Wilson, Woodrow: AAPSS *Annals* contributor, 71; and National Immigration League, 91; and 1912 election, 21; opposes women students at Princeton, 300; and race, 208, 357n10; on service ideal, 112–13; and Sherman, 192; student of H. B. Adams, 88; in student straw poll, 290; and the war, 85, 99, 110, 111, 114

Windsor, Phineas L.: collaboration with EJJ, 52, 58; exchanges and gifts, 4; expands acquisitions, 45–46, 47–48; hiring difficulties at library, 45; honors and recognitions, 44; and money issues at library, 46, 47; problems with EJJ; and Senate Library Committee, 44–45; and the war, 104

Wisconsin Idea, 17, 249

Wissenschaft, 58, 59, 62, 63; and social sciences, 64

Wolff, Christian, 58

Woman's Building: female students vote there, 316; holds Household Science department, 260; during war, 100

women, as employees in library, 45

Women's Equal Suffrage Association, 315

Women's Glee Club, 276

Women's League, 100–101, 303, 312

women's residence hall, 300, 310

women's suffrage: Dunne supports, 21; in Illinois, 314–15; and the *Siren*, 314; and the WEIA, 315; Women's Equal Suffrage Society (Illinois chapter), 15

women students: service to war, efforts, 100–101

Wood, Leonard, 98

Woodbridge, Frederick, 202, 204

Woodbury, George L., 75

Wormser, I. (Isaac) Maurice (Law): career, 238; embroilment about promotion, 238–39; publications, 239

Wright, Evelyn, 305

Yale Band, 326

Yale Report, 75

YMCA, 279; Association Hall, 284; program and membership, 284

Yoch, Florence: career, 320; family background, 320; and Lucile Council, 320; "New Professions for Women," 320–21

YWCA Quartet, 285, 302

Zeitlin, Jacob: advancing career, 184; exemplifies EJJ's appointment of Jewish faculty, 209, 267; expertise in philology, 182; in novel *Co-Ed*, 321

Zeleny, Charles: career, 161

WINTON U. SOLBERG (1922-2019) was a professor of American intellectual and cultural history and served at the University of Illinois Urbana-Champaign from 1961 until his death. His books include *The University of Illinois, 1867–1894: An Intellectual and Cultural History*; *The University of Illinois, 1894–1904: The Shaping of the University*; and *Creating the Big Ten: Courage, Corruption, and Commercialism.*

J. DAVID HOEVELER is a Distinguished Professor Emeritus of history at the University of Wisconsin Milwaukee. His books include *John Bascom and the Origins of the Wisconsin Idea* and *Creating the American Mind: Intellect and Politics in the Colonial Colleges.*

With profound gratitude Gail, Andrew, and Kristin Solberg are pleased to acknowledge David Hoeveler's sustained dedication to a thorough revision and substantial enhancement of the manuscript their father left unfinished in 2018.

The University of Illinois Press
is a founding member of the
Association of University Presses.

———————————————

Composed in 11.5/13 Adobe Garamond
with Gotham display
by Jim Proefrock
at the University of Illinois Press
Manufactured by Sheridan Books, Inc.

University of Illinois Press
1325 South Oak Street
Champaign, IL 61820-6903
www.press.uillinois.edu